Introduction to Sociology

Introduction to Sociology

James B. McKee
Michigan State University

Holt,
Rinehart
and
Winston,
Inc.

NEW YORK
CHICAGO
SAN FRANCISCO
ATLANTA
DALLAS
MONTREAL
TORONTO
LONDON
SYDNEY

Preface

The teaching of the elementary course in sociology is not an elementary task; to convey to beginning students an appropriate sense of the range and scope of the discipline and its distinctive problematic setting within the social sciences, in the limitations of a term or semester, is a challenging and often frustrating undertaking. In that task the introductory textbook plays an important part, for its discussions of the nature and substance of sociology can be read and reread, studied and underlined, by the student. Whether it reads well and interests him, and whether it conveys in any systematic way some organized sense of the discipline of sociology, has a great deal to do with what the teacher accomplishes in the course.

There seem to be two different and even somewhat conflicting strains today in sociology that bear significantly upon the teaching of the discipline, particularly to undergraduates. One is to demonstrate the *scientific* worth and commitment of the discipline, the other is to show its *relevance* for the vexing social issues that beset modern American society. I have sought a judicious balance between these two, on the simple assumption that neither one alone properly reflects the temper or concerns of working sociologists.

In writing this book it has been my intent to convey to the reader the scope and concern of the discipline, a conception of what sociology is all about. This, I believe, is best done, not by one specific thing, but by the general framework utilized for organizing the book and by the tone and milieu created by the writing. I have sought to impart to the student the knowledge that sociology has grown, particularly over the past century, as an intellectual enterprise focused on the concerns of modern urban man and has emerged from an exploration and inquiry into a number of problems about the organization of social life that can be subsumed under the generic term, *social order*. Specifically, the second chapter gives a moderately historical approach—a sociology of sociology perspective—of the emergence and development of sociology over the past century, viewing it in terms of its origins in intellectual concerns and ideas of the nineteenth century, of the social reform impulses of the late-nineteenth and early-twentieth century urban middle class, and of the concern of sociologists since the 1930s about the scientific status of their discipline. But this chapter is not merely or even primarily an historical review. I have tried to tie in the historical material with both the idea of the problematic and a sense of sociology's concern with the problems of social organization and social order. Furthermore, I have followed it with a brief chapter that attempts to discuss what sociologists have come to mean by scientific sociology.

In seeking to determine what is appropriate coverage for an introductory text, I have been guided by the principle that the choice of topics to be included or excluded in a given course is the option of the teacher; consequently, I have not sought to restrict coverage by any formula of my own and have stayed with a more conventional range of topics. Instead, I have sought to enlarge the coverage in two areas, stratification and collective behavior, because these are areas in which the contemporary relevance of sociology warrants such an expansion. Thus, besides one chapter on stratification, I have added one on minority status and one on the lower class. I have treated collective behavior in two chapters, one on crowds and publics and one on social movements.

An elementary textbook, being an intellectual effort to set forth the basic outlines and orientations of the discipline, implies for me scholarly obligations incurred over a quarter century of teaching and studying, and one is never sure that he is properly conscious of the due weight of his intellectual debts. Nevertheless, I know I owe a great deal to Hans Gerth and John Useem. It was Hans Gerth who first introduced me to the immense scope as well as the humanistic commitment of European sociological scholarship and to Max Weber, who has since cast a giant shadow over my personal intellectual landscape. I first knew John Useem as teacher and advisor, but he has long since become friend and colleague. To him I owe an appreciation of being committed to but undogmatic about sociology, and of the value of eschewing a too early theoretical closure in order to avoid sterile orthodoxy. I have learned from him to appreciate whatever sociological work seeks wider relevance and sets off to explore fresh paths for research by a constant interplay between a sensitivity to what is going on in society and an effort to be scientific in studying that society. It is, I hope, readily apparent that neither of them bears any responsibility for this modest product of my thinking. I merely hope that it does not embarrass them to have some influence thereon attributed to them.

A number of anonymous critics have read earlier drafts of the manuscript, and I am indebted to them for their careful reading and critical comments. I was guided by much of what they said; that they were not always consistent with one another and sometimes even contradictory still served me well by pointing up matters that I was forced to think through more carefully. Then, too, I am grateful to the people at Holt, Rinehart and Winston whose long patience and courteous prodding have finally brought this book to completion; in particular, I am indebted to Brian Heald and Caleb Smith. Also, I would be remiss if I did not acknowledge the expert typing of Mrs. Grace Rutherford, who made a difficult schedule attainable. Lastly, I remain immeasurably indebted to my wife, Alice, for her patience and encouragement and her assistance in more ways than she probably realizes.

Finally, I am humbly aware of how much this book reflects the many students who patiently listened to me in my classrooms over two decades. What I owe to them is the decency of their response as I sought diligently to make sociology understandable as a scientific enterprise and relevant to their lives. Some of what I learned in that hard but rewarding task is hopefully reflected in the pages that follow.

J. B. McKEE

East Lansing, Michigan
February 1969

Contents

Introduction to Sociology

THE ISSUE OF MOB VIOLENCE AND ITS RELATION TO OUR EDUCATION SYSTEM HAS RAISED A NUMBER OF INTERESTING QUESTIONS.

WE ALL AGREE THAT THE ROLE OF THE EDUCATOR IS NOT ONLY TO TEACH HIS SUBJECT BUT TO IMPART AN UNDERSTANDING OF MORAL VALUES.

BUT ONE CAN NOT PUSH A STUDENT BEYOND THE POINT HE IS WILLING TO GO. ONE MUST WORK WITHIN THE SPIRIT OF HIS CULTURE. THE SPIRIT OF OUR CULTURE IS LATENT VIOLENCE.

THOUGH ACHIEVING TEMPORARY RELEASE THROUGH TELEVISION PROGRAMS AND NEWSPAPER HEADLINES, THIS SPIRIT MUST OCCASIONALLY FIND A DIRECT OUTLET: MURDER WON'T DO. IT LOSES ONE THE RESPECT OF HIS NEIGHBORS.

HOWEVER, MOB VIOLENCE WILL DO PERFECTLY. HOW CAN ONE LOSE THE RESPECT OF HIS NEIGHBORS IF THEY TOO ARE BURNING AUTOMOBILES?

OUR PROBLEM THEN IS THAT, WHILE IT MAY BE ALL TO THE GOOD TO LECTURE AGAINST THE SPIRIT OF LATENT VIOLENCE, IS IT DESIRABLE TO LECTURE THAT SPIRIT INTO EXTINCTION?

CAN ONE BLANKETLY CONDEMN A SPIRIT WHICH IN ITS MORE ORGANIZED FORM IS DEPENDED ON TO DEFEND THE FREE WORLD?

SO OUR BASIC QUESTION REMAINS: IF WE ROB MEN OF THEIR DESIRE TO TAKE THE UNIVERSITY OF MISSISSIPPI, DO WE ALSO ROB THEM OF THEIR DESIRE TO TAKE CUBA?

IT IS NOT EASY TO TEACH IN THE TWENTIETH CENTURY.

Jules Feiffer

PART 1 THE STUDY OF SOCIAL LIFE

1 2

3

1. A Haight-Ashbury "hippie house" group.
2. Schoolchildren saluting the flag at a rural schoolhouse.
3. Middle-class suburbia.
4. Flower children.
5. The age of automation: a computer room.

4 5

THE STUDY
OF SOCIOLOGY

1

From the beginning of time, men have known that they do not live as isolated creatures. "No man is an island, entire of itself," John Donne observed long ago, and each of us is "involved in mankind." But if all men have observed that social life is a universal condition of mankind, not all have attached the same significance to this observation, nor sought to trace out its logical implications. Although it is quite commonplace to quote Aristotle's famous remark, "Man is a political (i.e., social) animal," it is not necessarily obvious just what this implies.

This book will be concerned with what it means to say that men are involved in a social life, and thus what it means to be both social and human. Not that we intend, or possibly could, say everything there is to say about the social and human aspects of man. Instead, our concern will be limited to that part of the social and human that involves social relationships.

Man: Human and Social   To say that man is social is to say that he is constantly involved in association with other men. Much of what can be observed about man's conduct can be explained by these associations. How men act under some circumstances is largely a consequence of the demands and expectations created by human association. Men are not free to follow every personal whim, or otherwise to act exactly as they might wish, unless they live alone. But few men ever crave the freedom of individual action that would be possible if they lived alone on a desert island. To explain the action of men, then, this fact of association must be emphasized.

Yet it is not association with one's own kind that sets man apart from all other living organisms. Most other creatures in the animal kingdom do that. Ants, as we know, live in complex ant societies. Many of the larger animals live in packs or herds. In short, types of association can be found among most forms of organic life other than the human. What distinguishes human association from the association found among other organisms is that human association is *cultural,* whereas the social life of animals is not. Man is born without innate tendencies to act in specific ways toward other humans. He *learns* to act toward others in ways that humans themselves have created from the common experiences of a shared life. Nor is this learned behavior always the same everywhere. What is considered right or sensible at one time or in one society may be thought wrong or stupid at another time or in another society. Learned behavior—what will hereafter be called action or conduct—is subject to repeated change in a way that inborn or instinctive behavior cannot be.

To assert the significance of a social life that is cultural and thus distinctively human, let us emphasize how men differ from animals. To be sure, man is a part of the great world of nature, and this is never to be forgotten. The biologist and the physiologist, for example, place man in a great system of living organisms; biological theory can clearly indicate how the physical nature of man is comparable to that of other organisms. But this approach is *nonsocial*, for it has to do with those aspects of man that are not learned and, therefore, not cultural. Where it concerns man's behavior, it deals either with behavior that is organic, not learned, or else it deals with biological influences upon human conduct and with the way that the organism sets limits upon the development of culture.

The study of man as human, rather than organic, is probably as old as mankind itself. Certainly, as far back as man was literate, he has penned commentaries on the nature of man and society. The prophets of the Old Testament, the Greek philosophers, the creative minds of the Renaissance, all made significant comments on the meaning of man and his culture. Ever since the Renaissance, some five centuries ago, the term *humanities* has been used to refer not only to a point of view about man, but also to a range of creative efforts—art, poetry, drama—and to those scholarly studies, such as theology, philosophy, and history, which, until recently, contained all the wisdom and knowledge there was about man and his cultural life. A great deal of this knowledge was incorporated into a program in the universities that is still called the *humanities:* language and literature, philosophy, art, and so on, which the present-day college student studies (selectively, and usually inadequately) as his introduction to the great heritage of ideas about man and his culture.

The present-day social sciences, including sociology, are a somewhat newer development in the study of man, the sources of which, however, lie deeply embedded in the humanities. History, for example, is one of the oldest humanistic studies, and many historians regard themselves as both humanists and social scientists. What is now called political science still contains political philosophy, a branch of thought with an illustrious tradition that goes back at least to ancient Greece. Sociology, along with anthropology and psychology, are somewhat newer fields; they have been separate areas of study for only a century or so. Yet they too carry on the humanistic tradition of exploring and analyzing man and society, and they are deeply indebted to this tradition for many of their ideas and concepts. Still, the social sciences have separated from the older humanities by virtue of a somewhat different approach to the study of man, one that seeks to be scientific. They emerged when social thinkers attempted to link together the *subject matter* of the humanities (man) with the *method* of science.

Here are two issues clearly deserving further exploration for anyone beginning to study sociology: the emergence of sociology as a separate discipline with a conceptual focus of its own, and the construction of a scientific approach to the study of man. These will be the concern of Chapters 2 and 3, respectively.

THE FIELD OF SOCIOLOGY

Sociology emerged about a century ago as a separate and special field concerned with the study of human society. The study of society itself has a long, brilliant intellectual tradition of social thought, going back hundreds of years, and containing much sound knowledge about human life. But this social thought, while frequently resting upon careful observation of human conduct, was not supported by systematic empirical investigation. Earlier social thinkers lacked the research methods that enable today's social scientists to make many precise observations and measurements of social action. Sociology, then, has primary emphasis upon building a sound and reliable body of knowledge about social life, based upon facts gathered by systematic empirical investigation. It owes its development to a profound intellectual concern for understanding what human society is like, as well as a recognition that there is a great deal to learn, despite "the wisdom of the ages."

Sociology is concerned with phenomena to which terms like *society, group* and *community* are applied, terms about which everyone has some common-sense conception. Later we shall be concerned with more precise definitions, but for now we can proceed on the assumption that these terms communicate to each of us a roughly similar idea. To begin with, it is clear that we are not talking directly about individual persons. Obviously, there are no groups without persons, but *group* is not a term that refers only to an aggregate of persons; mere numbers do not make a group.

As a simple example, take a college. It is made up of a number of people, sometimes a large number. Each person in the college can be observed doing definite things at definite times and places, not always because he wants to, but because he is expected to. Each day many of these people show up at a given time in classrooms or laboratories, take appointed places, and proceed with a given task. From their action, they can be recognized as students and teachers. In short, the college is not a mere aggregate of persons; instead, *it is people organized in some particular way.* There are specific ways for people to act, and there are standards and rules of conduct. Those who participate know what is expected of them and know what to expect of others in specific situations.

It would seem to follow from this that one cannot know about the college by knowing only the persons who make it up. One also needs to describe the ways of behaving that are recognized by the words *student* and *teacher,* the standards and rules that govern individual conduct, and many other things. None of these words are *personal* characteristics of the individuals involved; rather, they only exist when individuals are interacting in some organized or patterned way, that is, when they are participating in *social relationships.*

For the sociologist, this idea of a social relationship means that interaction between persons proceeds according to a shared understanding of what is expected of each in that interaction. The interaction then becomes regulated by these expectations. When a young person becomes a student in a college, for example, he learns a social role, a set of existing expectations of conduct. In turn, he learns to expect certain action from his teachers. These reciprocal expectations then function to pattern the social interaction between people who are students and teachers. It is these social relationships and the patterns of social organization built upon them that is the central focus of sociology. Sociology is not primarily concerned with the nature of the individual person, but rather with the structure of social relationships in which individuals participate. There would, of course, be no social structure, no society, without persons, but also, as we shall see, there would be no socialized persons without a society.

To define sociology in terms of *social relationships* is far from restrictive, for it leaves open to the sociologist more than one angle of vision. He can, in the first place, focus on the simple and immediate *social relations* to be found in myriad form among interacting human beings: male-female relationships; relations among kin or among friends; between brothers; between business partners; and so on. Or, he can focus on the set of several relationships which, taken together, constitute a *social structure*, as, for example, that of the family, or indeed, of any social group. So, too, he can utilize an older sociological focus that defines sociology as the study of *social institutions;* familial, political, educational, economic, religious. It is possible to enlarge even further the frame of reference and view sociology as the study of *society,* when society is defined as the largest and most encompassing of social structures, whose diverse groups and institutions are organized with a reasonable coherence into a single entity.

What should be evident by now is the idea that man, while always an individual who lives his own personal life, is at the same time a participant in a social life shared with others; he lives *collectively* as well as individually. He enters into relations with others, and from these he constructs relatively enduring social forms: groups, institutions, associations, communities, societies, and the like. This is social order, a regularity, and a patterning that invites scientific study.

However, this regularity and patterning of social relations exhibits a stability that is only relative; *change* is endemic to social life. From its beginning to now, sociology has been defined as the study of both organization and change in social life. Auguste Comte (1798–1857), who coined the term "sociology," spoke of *statics* and *dynamics* to convey this idea of a complementary emphasis in examining social order.

THE SOCIOLOGICAL PERSPECTIVE

It should be evident by now that sociology has a point of view that places social interaction in the foreground of perception. The sociologist is trained to see interaction among human beings, and to see it in specific form. He pays close attention to such things as the relatively stable network of relations that emerge from persistent social interaction, the growth and change within social groups, and the processes by which individuals are inducted as members into social groups. He is trained to look for differences in social behavior, as well as differences in beliefs and values, which are a consequence of differences in social relations.

This is not all. To view the world so as to perceive social interaction and to hold it up for critical inspection is but one dimension of the sociological perspective. To develop such a perspective—a sociological way of looking at the world and interpreting it—also requires the sociologist to ask sociological questions and thereby pose sociological problems. Unless the sociologist's perspective generates questions that other perspectives do not, there is no scholarly or scientific justification for the independent status of the discipline. Therefore, the sociologist does not merely observe social interaction in all the forms it takes. He asks questions about the consequences of social interaction and about the many relatively stable forms that social interaction takes. For example, sociologists ask questions about interaction between people of different races. They may ask what social factors sustain segregation in some schools and what ones induce integration in others; also, what aids or impedes the change from a segregated to an integrated urban school system in American society. They may ask how the particular features of the urban middle-class family in America distinguish it from lower middle and working-class families. Or, they may ask about the political beliefs and partisan voting behavior of industrial workers.

Questions like these are about the contemporary period and they are about American society. But they could just as easily be questions about earlier periods in history or about other societies than American. All such questions, in short, are *historical,* for they ask something about a particular society or about a limited segment of a society at some particular point in time. Sociologists usually regard such questions as particular and historical versions of more general and abstract ones.

Because sociologists intend the sociological perspective to be scientific, they feel compelled to draw some generalizations from the data of their studies, for these data are not in themselves necessarily of great interest to them. They are interested in the data only so long as they provide a means for testing some more general observations about social life. The specific questions that sociologists ask, then, are particular versions of necessarily more abstract ones. If the sociologist studies segregation and integration in today's urban schools, he is interested (probably) in both the chances of integration in America's urban schools and in more abstract questions of theoretical import, such as what social factors are necessary to maintain segregation in a social structure. Or, he may be interested in discovering whether the industrialization and urbanization of society are compatible with racial segregation. When a sociologist seeks to provide a fairly detailed description of the urban middle-class family in America in order to differentiate it from lower-middle and working-class families, he may be trying to answer a quite general sociological question, such as what is the relation of family structure to the class structure of the society? And a sociologist who asks a sample of industrial workers in Detroit or Chicago what their political beliefs are, and what party they generally vote for, is not likely to be interested in merely documenting the well-known fact that most workers vote for the Democratic party. Instead, he is interested in exploring the connection between the class structure and constituencies of political parties. This, in turn, is but one aspect of an even larger theoretical issue, the relation between stratification and the political institution.

The Comparative Perspective   The specific questions raised by sociologists have in most cases been about America. American sociologists have studied their own society extensively and other societies but little, and many of their generalizations are based almost exclusively upon American data. The warranted criticism of parochialism has been one that sociologists themselves have expressed frequently in recent years, but a new interest in comparative study has emerged since World War II.

There are a number of factors responsible for this new interest in a comparative perspective, but perhaps two are most readily evident. One is certainly the postwar emergence of sustained American involvement in areas beyond our borders and even outside this hemisphere. The newly independent nations in Africa and Asia, with their recently defined status as *developing* nations, provide a new intellectual context in which social scientists have been forced to reexamine those theories and assumptions derived from more parochial studies. Secondly, the commitment to build a scientific sociology has pressed sociologists to take their empirical research beyond the boundaries of American society, else the level of generalization remain too parochial to construct a genuinely abstract theory of society. For American sociologists, then, the sociological perspective now looks to a wider and more culturally varied world of developing social structures.

Sociological Consciousness   We have been talking about *perspective* as a way of looking at the world that is sensitive to some things and not to others. The *sociological* perspective is sensitive to, and carefully perceives interaction among people and the social groups that emerge from this interaction; thus, it concentrates on the formative structures of man's collective life, not the psychological organization of his individual life. All people have a perspective, and from their perspective they selectively view the social world, but most people probably give little thought to the fact that they view the world from a particular set of colored lens. They take their own viewpoint so much for granted that they are unaware that it constitutes a distinctive outlook on life, different in significant ways from other outlooks. Thus, not only are most people *ethnocentric*—looking at the world from the viewpoint of their own particular group or society—but also they are so often innocently unaware that their perspective is only one among many and that it takes for granted as real what others may believe to be myth. Even scholars and scientists are not immune to being unaware of their own taken-for-granted assumptions about reality and how those assumptions then shape their perceptions.

Sociologists have always been quite aware of their own perspective. This is so in part because they have had to defend and validate a sociological perspective in a culture that finds a psychological perspective more congenial, and, indeed, has frequently responded more favorably to biological and psychological explanations of human behavior than to sociological ones. Still, this consciousness of its own perspective has served sociology well. It has made many sociologists acutely aware that their discipline presented a point of view that was increasingly useful, even necessary, in a world moving rapidly from small-scale to large-scale organization. Thus, the sociological perspective becomes a unique and invaluable intellectual outlook for the modern world, and some of the most able and perceptive of sociologists, such as Peter Berger and C. Wright Mills, have elaborated upon its significance and its contribution.

In his fascinating book, *Invitation to Sociology: A Humanistic Perspective,* Peter Berger has argued convincingly that sociology as a form of *social consciousness* includes a skepticism about the official claims or common-sense explanation of human behavior.[1] The sociological perspective becomes a process of "seeing through" the facades of social structure. Behind the visible political or bureaucratic organization of social life is a social reality that may be more enduring than official structures. The sociologist goes off in pursuit of it, seeking the motives and actions and complex patternings of human relationships that may go unnoticed or even be denied by official explanations. Sociology, therefore, often undertakes, even if unintentionally, a *debunking* function.

Sociologists have also long been fascinated by the underside of society, the unrespectable phases of life, where again the official explanations are dis-

---

[1] Peter Berger, *Invitation to Sociology: A Humanistic Perspective* (Garden City, N.Y.: Anchor Books, 1963).

believed, and where quite different and sometimes quite contradictory versions of social reality prevail. In the ghetto and in the slums, in the underworld and in the deviant communities, and in the subworlds of those of marginal status in American society, one finds another language, other norms and values, other life-styles; and these, says Berger, have always exercised a powerful attraction for sociologists. The consciousness of sociology has always included a sensitivity to these worlds neither inhabited by nor even well-known to the broad stratum of the respectable and established.

Then, too, sociology manifests a modern consciousness "of a world in which values have been radically relativized." Modern society is characterized by such social mobility and geographical movement that large segments of the population cannot help but be exposed to other ways of life, other moral outlooks and social values. The mass media only further contribute to this cultural exposure. It is difficult to be totally insulated within a single, traditional perspective in modern society. Although for many this broader exposure remains a rather superficial experience, nonetheless, there are few indeed who can escape the awareness that the values of one's own culture are quite relative to time and place.

What Peter Berger analyzed so well in one manner, the late C. Wright Mills did in another. In one of sociology's most provocative and stimulating books, *The Sociological Imagination,*[2] Mills in effect criticized, by implication, many of his contemporaries and yet stimulated and inspired others by his conception of a consciousness peculiar to the sociological mind:

> For that imagination is the capacity to shift from one perspective to another—from the political to the psychological; from examination of a single family to comparative assessment of the national budgets of the world; from the theological school to the military establishment; from considerations of an oil industry to studies of contemporary poetry. It is the capacity to range from the most impersonal and remote transformations to the most intimate features of the human self —and to see the relations between the two. Back of its use there is always the urge to know the historical and social meaning of the individual in the society and in the period in which he has his quality and his being.
>
> That, in brief, is why it is by means of the sociological imagination that men now hope to grasp what is going on in the world and to understand what is happening in themselves as minute points of the intersections of biography and history within society. In large part, contemporary man's self-conscious view of himself as at least an outsider, if not a permanent stranger, rests upon an absorbed realization of social relativity and of the transformative power of history. The sociological imagination is the most fruitful form of this self-consciousness. . . .[3]

[2] C. Wright Mills, *The Sociological Imagination* (New York: Oxford, 1959; paperback edition, Grove, 1961).

[3] Mills, pp. 7–8 (paperback ed.).

At the same time, it must not be overlooked that the sociological perspective requires a *disciplined* consciousness and a disciplined use of the sociologist's imagination—disciplined by the use of the scientific method. There is no escaping a careful search for data relevant to a problem, and a cautious and thorough analysis of these data in order to construct valid propositions about social reality. Furthermore, this is to be done with as much precision of research technique and as much logical rigor as is consistent with the demands of the problem under investigation and the methodological state of the discipline. Without such a disciplining of the mind, the most ambitious sociological effort would yield only an array of sociological insights that accumulated to no sustained propositions and led to no theory; or that, in turn, produced generalizations too broad and unqualified to be sustained by the data brought into support of it.

This commitment to scientific analysis is also part of the sociological perspective. It places a disciplined control upon the consciousness of the sociologist by keeping his probing within the bounds of logic and evidence. So important is this to an understanding of the procedures of the sociologist and of his claims to the existence of sociological knowledge that Chapter 3 examines in detail what it means to develop a scientific sociology.

HEREDITY AND ENVIRONMENT

One of the necessary functions of social science has been not only to provide some better understanding of what causes social action, but also to demonstrate that many of the things that people believe about humans and their actions are simply not so. Social science strives to replace outmoded ideas with more valid ones. The terms *heredity* and *environment* cover a multitude of the erroneous ideas which men have about social life. It is easy and superficially plausible to blame heredity or environment for many human problems, or to see either of these factors as the cause of wars, depressions, personal success, great leadership, talent, social conflict, bad tempers, and almost everything else in the human sphere that people want to account for. It is easy—but it has led to much intellectual confusion. Historically, the heart of the issue is in the once dominant argument that contrasted heredity and environment in such a way as to assert that either one or the other was the sole cause of some social event. This is the well-known "nature vs. nurture" argument, in which the human being is defined either as having inherited through biological process his aptitudes and characteristics, indeed his whole personality, or as having been shaped and determined by the social life into which he was born. Scientists now agree that the "nature/nurture" argument is false, because it presents a false dichotomy; that is, a false choice between one or the other, when in fact both have a part in the final process.

Modern social science does, however, give a less prominent role to heredity in the determination of human action than men have done in the past. Certainly, it is no longer regarded as scientifically acceptable to believe that one inherits one's personality. Also, most of the assertions about the inherited differences among the races of man are, from a scientific point of view, nonsense. However, this does not warrant any conclusion that heredity is of no importance. The problem, instead, is to determine more specifically what heredity contributes to human personality and to the observable differences among various races.

The term *environment* presents us with somewhat different problems. In the first place, the term is rarely used with a precise meaning. Perhaps this is partly because the term is so all-inclusive; the tendency to think of it as including everything produces a certain vagueness, a lack of specificity and preciseness. As the term is ordinarily used, environment refers to the conditions, circumstances, and influences surrounding and affecting the organism. Evidently, then, environment is everything outside the organism that influences it in some way. If we say that environment causes behavior, we are saying that everything surrounding the organism causes its behavior. But what the social scientist wants to do is to be able to pick out of the total environment those specific elements or factors that caused some specific event or form of behavior. The concept of environment doesn't help much here; indeed, it becomes something of a meaningless idea.

When environment is posed against heredity in the nature versus nurture argument, what seems to be meant by environment is really the social—and particularly the cultural—surroundings of the individual. Probably most statements on the role of environment in causing social action really refer to the *cultural* environment. What is left out by implication is the *physical* environment: the world of natural objects, of climate and terrain that surrounds and influences us.

Yet, there have also been many who have tried to demonstrate that the physical environment is the major cause of action. Climate and terrain, it has frequently been asserted, largely determine man's social life. The idea is not new; over two thousand years ago Aristotle tried to explain the superiority of the Greeks to the people both south and north of them by reference to their fortunate geographical location. Many other writers have tried to show that the cold climate of northern Europe produced a vigorous people and civilization, whereas the tropical climates reduced human energy, severely limiting man's capacity to build a great civilization.

Plausible as these ideas may seem, they do not stand up under careful scrutiny. Although a vigorous culture arose in northern Europe, it is no less true that some of the great civilizations of the past have arisen in hot climates. If one takes a long enough historical span, it is not possible to relate climate to human society in such a way as to prove that reference to climate provides the best explanation for different types of social life. Rather, an examination of the relationship between geography and culture shows that vigorous cultures develop in quite different geographical environments and that quite different cultures develop at different times in the same geographical environment.

Where geography provides a rich and generous environment, man has an opportunity to exploit it for the building of a great civilization. But how he will make use of geography depends upon his already existing culture, particularly his technical knowledge and skills; for example, the North American Indian lived for centuries on a continent rich with great stores of coal and oil beneath his feet. Yet this did not produce an industrial society; the American Indian remained a primitive, quite unaware of the opportunities for economic development that were so close at hand. By the same token, men cannot utilize the physical environment as a means for creating a flourishing culture when geography offers them extremely harsh and unrewarding conditions. The Eskimo must adapt to the extremes of Arctic conditions, for example, and nomadic herdsmen must eke out a living in arid and barren deserts or tundras. Here the limitations of the environment reward men with little in return for their ingenuity and labor, and may so tax their energy in merely surviving that they are unable to develop one of the literate cultures that have emerged from time to time in man's long history.

Here, then, is the relation of physical environment to social action. It provides limiting conditions, on the one hand, and creates opportunities for man, on the other, but opportunities that can only be utilized if man's already existing culture enables him to recognize and utilize them. Certainly, what men now do to their physical environment suggests that they influence it as much as it influences them. They can mine the earth for coal and minerals, extract oil and gas from deep within the ground, change the course of rivers, create great bodies of water by dams, change arid land into fertile soil by irrigation, drain swamps, tunnel through mountains, domesticate the wild life, and in many other ways turn the natural environment to their own use. Our attempts to explain man's social life, then, must take proper account of his biological heredity and of the physical environment, which he must adapt for his survival and utilize in creating his social life. Nevertheless these nonsocial factors are not to explain social action. Instead, after taking due account of their influence, social conditions and situations are sought as the causes of social action.

THE STUDY OF SOCIOLOGY

The study of man and his social life is not the prerogative or monopoly of any one field of study. The biological sciences, the social sciences, and the humanities are all concerned with man, and all contribute to the understanding of human conduct. All are committed, furthermore, to adding to this as yet quite limited understanding. Sociology, as one of these disciplines, focuses upon man's unique capacity to create and recreate, in manifold ways, a structure of social relationships that enables men to live in a social order, and not in a human jungle where life would be a war of all against all.

We shall start our study by developing in some greater detail an understanding of the approach the sociologist takes to social life; that is, his particular way of thinking about and analyzing social structures, and the terms he finds most useful to express his approach. After our base and our point of view have been established, we can proceed to look at society in the manner of the sociologist, and to discover why human society has been viewed as problematic. To do this, we shall examine the traditional sociological effort to give precise conceptual form to such perceived contrasting patterns in social relations as primary and secondary groups, formal and informal organization, folk and urban society, and others. Sociologists have classified these patterns as a means of getting some fruitful starting point in analyzing social reality. But sociology is not always concerned with the "big picture." Most sociologists are busy exploring smaller and more manageable segments of social life. They examine the way in which society is stratified, how group effort is organized into bureaucracies, how the community changes from rural to urban, how social elites exercise social power, how organizational forms effect human personality, and a myriad of other problems about how man behaves in society.

At this point, one word of caution to the student is necessary. As noted before, sociology is a specialized field that has existed for only a hundred years or so, though it has built upon much of the wisdom and insights contributed by the great thinkers of the past centuries. In particular, however, it emerged as a specialized approach to the study of society when that society, at least in the Western world, was undergoing such radical changes that the ideas of the past were of less and less use in understanding it. Modern society, created by the Industrial Revolution, clearly needs a modern approach with newer insights and ideas about its structure and organization. What this implies, it seems clear, is that sociology has not been studying society long enough to have built up the impressive body of theory that is found in such natural sciences as physics or chemistry, and perhaps even biology. There is much that is still problematic, that is still a problem for which answers are being sought. As a consequence, there are many points at which sociologists are not in full agreement. It is not our intent to claim for sociology wisdom and knowledge it does not possess or to give the student the impression that certain concepts or theories in sociology are *the* answer to the problem, when in fact sociologists are not in themselves agreed. To do so would not only be dogmatic and pretentious, but it would cause the student to miss all the fun. For the fun in sociology is the same to be found in any intellectual discipline, that of exploring ideas and facts to try to solve intriguing problems, in this case problems about the why's of social action.

1

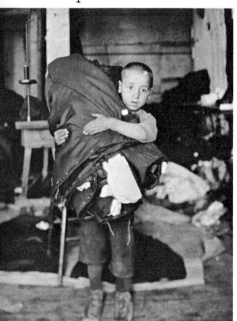

2

3

4

1. Greek, Yiddish, and Italian posters demand an eight-hour work day.
2. A boy from a New York City tenement carrying home piecework for his family (1910).
3. Stacking hay in Nebraska (1903).
4. Chicago (1911): a tenement visit by an Infant Welfare Society worker.
5. Hester Street on New York's Lower East Side at the turn of the century.

5

THE ORIGINS OF SOCIOLOGY

2

Any scholarly discipline is a human enterprise, and its growth and development is affected by the historical experiences of those who carry it on. Scholars cannot avoid being involved in the events of their time, and this involvement always leaves its indelible mark on the discipline. Each discipline, however, also grows by the dedicated attention of its scholars to internal issues and problems. By such attention, scholars create a mode of inquiry, a set of disciplined procedures for gathering evidence and developing theory. A discipline, in fact, is a discipline because of this.

As one discipline among the social sciences, sociology reveals an unmistakable pattern of historical influence, as well as development and growth by close attention to its own intellectual problems. Some consideration of these major influences is necessary to an understanding of why sociology is what it is. A history of sociology is beyond the compass of this book and is probably not the best way to introduce anyone to the discipline. But what may very well be warranted is a brief examination of some major factors in the historical shaping and forming of sociology as a discipline, factors relevant not only for understanding the development of sociology but also for understanding what sociology is now. Though it requires a great deal of simplifying and telescoping of an involved historical process, the history of sociology can be understood primarily in terms of the following major influences:

1. Its nineteenth century European origin in a context of deep intellectual concern about historical change, which concern led to a conception of the nature of the discipline and its legitimate problems.

2. At the beginning of the twentieth century, an involvement of sociology with social reform and social problems in American life.

3. In more recent decades, a conscious dedication of sociologists to making their discipline a science.

The first two of these will be the concern of this chapter, while the third will be the concern of the chapter that follows.

THE NINETEENTH CENTURY ORIGINS OF SOCIOLOGY

Though it is undeniably true that the intellectual sources of sociology go far back in human thought, sociology took on its name and identity only during the nineteenth century. It grew during a time of new and creative social thought that transformed and modernized all of the social sciences. One consequence of this was an increasing specialization among the disciplines. The study of economic phenomena, for example, did not produce the field of *economics* until, under laissez-faire capitalism, the economic system of a society was thought of as separate and apart from the political process, especially the state. Only then did men study economics instead of political economy and history.

Later on, the newer social sciences of anthropology and sociology were defined, not as studying a limited institutional area of society (such as the political or economic) but as new perspectives for looking at and understanding social life. Anthropology received its impetus from the interest that Europeans developed in the non-Western peoples of the world. For three centuries, Europeans had explored and colonized the vast world beyond the European continent. European traders sought to do business with these non-Western peoples and to profit on the untapped natural resources to be found in their lands. Missionaries, in turn, sought converts to Christianity, while soldiers and politicians transformed these lands into European colonies. After them came the anthropologist. His concern with the native peoples was less immediately practical but was nonetheless a European interest. He represented the intellectual and scholarly interest that educated Europeans had in learning about people all over the world. Thus, the anthropologist became the specialist on non-Western peoples, very often the people called primitive or preliterate.

Although this specialization has in practice often distinguished the working anthropologist from the sociologist and psychologist, few anthropologists would probably admit such a distinction was a legitimate basis for defining their field. Instead, we have come to think of the anthropologist as the student of human culture. When the anthropologist went to study a non-Western people, he usually tried to describe their way of life as a coherent whole; thus, he was the first specialist in social science who tried to compare and contrast Western and non-Western cultures. The anthropologist led the way in taking modern social science beyond the cultural limits of Western (European and American) social life.

Sociology, in contrast, emerged out of problems and issues vital to nineteenth century Europe. In part, it took on the study of those aspects of social life that had not already been claimed by other specialized disciplines. Thus, there was economics, but no social science concerned with family life; and there was political science, but no social science concerned with religion and the church. Neither had there developed a social science concerned with the community. Sociology, then, assumed the task of studying what had been left over, and what was often by implication less important. Certainly, under the impact of industrialism, capitalism, and nationalism, the community and such institutions as the family and the church came to be regarded as less important in determining human behavior than were political and economic processes.

But this was not to be the really crucial factor in the emergence of sociology; instead, it developed in response to a much deeper crisis in modern society—the gradually cumulative effect of the Industrial Revolution that radically changed the structure of human society. The Industrial Revolution moved rural people into urban centers, changed peasants into workers, and produced cities where villages once stood. Two significant consequences followed from this: (1) the individual's daily range of personal experiences became too limited in scope to provide him with sufficient familiarity with his own social world, for that world had grown to be vast and complex; (2) his world changed before his eyes even as he learned about it. It became apparent that no one could assume that the world of his time was to be the same as the world of his father, or that the world of his son would be like his own. It now seemed not only that the world was changing, but that change was ceaseless, rather than a temporary disruption of an ordered and stable way of life. Men found themselves living in a social world too large and complex to be understood by any individual's experiences in it, and changing too rapidly and too persistently to learn about it from the older generations.

Yet, one should not assume that the people of the nineteenth century resisted or even resented the great changes that swept away the old forms of life. Undoubtedly millions of Europeans, especially those of more humble social status, welcomed the break with an oppressive and burdensome past and responded eagerly to the opportunity for a life better at both the material and social levels. But others, especially those of a more privileged status, feared the loss of their privileges and the new power of the common man. To the educated classes, and to many social thinkers, the great industrial transformation that had been going on for over a century produced both hope and anxiety. Those educated men of Europe who drew their ideals from the Enlightenment found much to be hopeful about in the changing patterns of society. Yet, they also felt a deep anxiety over the future of human society. Did all this great change suggest the breakup of society itself? If men no longer had a familiar and relatively fixed social position, how would they behave? If men no longer accepted at face value the moral standards of their ancestors, what did this loss of traditional morality mean for human behavior?

These questions and others served to emphasize, not only the significance of the revolutionary changes in human society, but also the realization that human life was necessarily organized into a society and was not merely an aggregate of independent individuals, each acting in his own interest or as he saw fit. There was evidently more to social life than the state and the economy, important as these were. For one of the few times in history, men no longer took the existence of human society for granted, but wondered and worried about how and under what conditions people could live together in a relatively peaceful and stable social life.

Sociology emerged out of this effort to provide some intellectual understanding of the revolutionary forces that had so radically transformed the structure of human society. Men could no longer take the organization of social life and the beliefs and values necessary to that organization for granted.

Old assumptions about man and society were called into question by the very alteration of society and of man himself as a consequence of living a new kind of life. Society, in short, was no longer a "given" in the lives of men— it was a *problem*.

The Nature of the Problematic   What does it mean to say that society was no longer a *given*, but was a *problem*? The terms, as used here, are from the vocabulary of science. From the scientific perspective, a problem is whatever needs to be explained; anything is problematic if we do not understand it sufficiently, if we are puzzled by it.

Human beings live in a social world that they know and understand by virtue of a relatively coherent set of explanations and assumptions. These explanations and assumptions, commonly shared among a given people, makes the social universe of man's existence intelligible and meaningful. They are woven together into some relatively coherent whole, into a *Weltanschauung*, (a view of the world), made up of empirical observations, common-sense understandings, myths, superstitions, magic, and, at a higher intellectual level, explanations that are philosophical and theological and only sometimes (and then partially) scientific. Nor is everything necessarily understood and therefore explainable. Most prescientific world-views accepted much as essentially mysterious and beyond the understanding of mere mortals. The world then contained an aura of mystery and sacredness and was full of secrets that men could not, and perhaps thought they should not, understand. But even the sphere of the mysterious and sacred, while creating attitudes of reverence and awe, fitted into some overall conception of the universe that "made sense." Men could live comfortably with the idea that they knew and understood the world of which they were a part.

When men can live with a comfortable set of assumptions and explanations, then little is problematic. But for the last hundred years or more, wider circles of men in the Western world have been able to hold comfortably to fewer and fewer assumptions about their world. The historic transformations of the Western world by industrialization and urbanization, by technology and science, had rendered the world no longer understandable by traditional modes of scholarly thought. But a problem demands answers, and this means seeking knowledge, for only knowledge changes the problematic to the known. For a century now, the dominant if not the only accepted way of seeking answers has been provided by science. Science is a mode of inquiry into the empirical world, both social and physical, a way of asking questions and seeking answers that produces a greater degree of certitude and validity for modern man than any other mode of inquiry.

To think of science as a mode of inquiry is to give emphasis to science as *method*. There are those who assert that this is really all that science is, whereas others would insist upon including more in the definition of science, such as *theory*, the body of generalized statements developed from scientific inquiry. Whether it be defined only as method or not, science is a mode of rigorous, empirical inquiry. It is a problem-solving activity when *problem* is here understood as a statement of what is not known or understood about the empirical world.

Each one of the sciences is a mode of disciplined inquiry into a problem, or more likely, a set of related problems. The subject matter of a science merely defines the kind of problematic phenomena, which men explore by whatever means meet the canons of scientific method and yield effective results. The physical sciences apply the scientific method to the problems posed in explaining and understanding the physical world. Similarly, the biological sciences apply the scientific method to problems about living organisms. The social sciences, in turn, are concerned with what men want to know about themselves and their social world—about man and society. Sociology, as one of the social sciences, can be defined in terms of one set of problems, for which its practitioners seek answers by scientific study.

Human Society as Problematic   Any time when social changes so alter the familiar social world that it is no longer adequately understandable or explainable by the usual categories of thought common to a society, it is then that men become conscious of their social world. They examine it with a new level of social awareness and ask questions about it that never occurred to them before. The modern world has provoked a sustained and intense level of social consciousness for over a century; it has created social ideologies and social sciences that have one thing in common: they attempt to provide answers to the questions men ask about modern society.

The source of this sustained social consciousness is rooted in the crisis of thought to which we have been referring—the vastly impressive reordering of European social life under the impact of industrialization and urbanization. For many, their very conception of human society was jarred by this revolutionary change. They wondered if society was dissolving when the familiar social forms of village and kinship seemed to break up before the impact of industrialism. Did these vast changes signify the onset of a great disorder? Were new and hitherto unknown types of society emerging?

Such questions as these, while inevitably rooted in the observations men made about a particular transition, nonetheless led logically to more general questions. How was it possible for men to create and maintain human societies? How were men able to sustain social order and avoid chaos and disorder? What were the basic elements necessary to the existence of society? What were the social bonds that united men in a common life? And what were the sources of social change? There were other questions, too. How did society control individual conduct? What was the necessary relationship of the individual to the group? And what was the importance of the small social groups in society —family and community, for example—both for the individual and his relation to society, and for the organization of society?

Sociology in the nineteenth century took shape and substance from the great philosophical debates that ranged over these questions. Indeed, the content of sociology was greatly influenced by critical perspectives, both conservative and radical, that challenged the dominant, liberal view-point. But the influence was less from the ideological polemics, more from the searching critiques of fundamental assumptions about the nature of man and society.

Classic liberalism (rather than what is called liberalism in contemporary American politics) was a view of society giving abstract expression to the needs and interests of the new industrial middle class. It postulated an image of the good society as one in which the several basic institutions (familial, political, economic, religious) were independent and separate from one another, thus limited in social power, in which government was limited in its functions and authority, and in which the individual was free to pursue his interests as he saw fit, limited only by the rights of others. It was a view of society in which the major values were *liberty* and *individualism* (and liberty was specifically the liberty of the individual, his freedom being freedom from the coercive restraint of social organization, whether in the form of guild, church, or state). And its view of history was one of increasing improvement in the lot of man— the idea of *progress*.

A consistent intellectual opposition to this emphasis on the free and unencumbered, thus, implicitly, unorganized individual was presented by classical conservative thought, its fundamental perspective standing in opposition to the new social world coming into being. Such thinkers as Louis DeBonald and Joseph DeMaistre in France and Edmund Burke in England challenged the basic assumptions of liberal thought. They pointed out what they took to be its fundamental weakness: its lack of a coherent conception of society. Instead, they advanced a set of interrelated ideas that came in time to influence greatly the new discipline of sociology. The major ideas were the following:[1]

1. *The nature of society* is not that of a mere aggregate or collection of individuals but an organic entity with a tradition and a history, whose very existence is independent of that of its individual members.

2. *The primacy of society* to the individual is evident in the fact that society goes on though men die. Society precedes the individual, who is in fact born into an ongoing society. Man becomes human only through his participation in an existing society.

---

[1] The argument that follows borrows generously from Robert Nisbet, but the particular formulation here does not make use of all the points that he developed in his article, "Conservatism and Sociology," *American Journal of Sociology,* LVIII (September, 1952), 167–175.

3. *Society cannot be reduced to individuals.* As a distinct social entity, and not a mere aggregate of individuals, its irreducible unit is not the individual but something social, that is, a relationship.

4. *Interdependence of all social phenomena* characterizes social life, for society is a great "seamless web," complex and intricate, and a disruption at one point will ramify along the lines of relationships.

These several common assumptions of conservative thought became cornerstones of the new discipline of sociology. On the basis of them, the founders of the discipline were able to argue that sociology existed independently of psychology because there was an entity, society, to be studied.

Durkheim: The Reality of Society   One of the great names in the founding of the discipline, Emile Durkheim (1858–1916), argued, forcefully and polemically, for this independent existence of sociology and also for the notion that explanations of social phenomena had to be made by reference to "social facts," not to the attributes of individuals. Explanations about society were not to be sought by reduction to the psychological level of individual characteristics.[2]

Sociologists recognize Durkheim as one of the giants who defined and delineated the new field of sociology. He could not be called a conservative; a Jew and religious skeptic in a Catholic country (France) and a political liberal, he nonetheless shared the conservative concern about the capacity of man in modern society to maintain the cohesion and solidarity deemed necessary for the existence of society. For this reason, he can be regarded as the intellectual link between nineteenth century conservative thought and modern sociology. This basic problem of human solidarity he pursued in such great monographs as *Suicide, On the Division of Labor,* and *The Elementary Forms of Religious Life.*

One of Durkheim's central concepts was *anomie,* a term that defies literal translation but means a state of normlessness, a social condition of disorganization when the accepted rules and moral standards of group or society no longer effectively govern individual conduct. Durkheim thus introduced into sociology one of its most salient issues, no less relevant today than it was a half century ago. In its concern about anomie, sociology reflects the conservative worry about the disorganizing impact of industrialization and urbanization, and the decline of the small and cohesive communities that presumably were the more natural habitat of man. Indeed, we can add to the set of influential ideas derived from conservative thought the following idea:

[2] Durkheim developed this argument most consistently in his *The Rules of Sociological Method,* trans. Sarah A. Soloway and John H. Mueller; ed. George E. G. Catlin (New York: Free Press, 1950).

5. *The reality of social disorganization* evident in urbanism, commerce, class mobility, and religious individualism. Not progress, but disorganization, was declared to be the consequence of the great social changes altering society. Here sociology drew from some of the great minds of Europe, like Jacob Burckhardt, the cultural historian, who foresaw the emergence of a mass society, the loss of human liberty and individualism in the emergence of totalitarian forms that were to become so real in the twentieth century. Sociology was substantively enriched by these somber concerns of nineteenth century intellectuals who sought to peer toward the oncoming twentieth century, and to suggest boldly that the future of man in industrial society might have to be interpreted in terms other than that of progress.

Toennies: Gemeinschaft und Gesellschaft   A number of sociologists sought to define the nature of the change wrought by industrialization by delineating two contrasting types: society before and after industrialization. Ferdinand Toennies (1855–1936) introduced this influential mode of analysis into the main stream of sociology, though he was not the first to construct contrasting types for modern and pre-industrial society. In 1887, Toennies published *Gemeinschaft und Gesellschaft (Community and Society)*.[3] He defined *Gemeinschaft* as the kind of society that was essentially communal, one in which shared values and a respected tradition characterized a way of life. It was a rural way of life, where the small village is the organized social unit. In the *Gemeinschaft* world, there is solidarity stemming from homogeneous values, there is a strong "we-feeling," a common identity, and kinship is a most significant social group. In contrast, industrialization marks a transition to a *Gesellschaft* world of commerce and contracts, of swift change and social mobility, where differences weaken solidarity and where culture is no longer as homogeneous. Individualism becomes a strong value, and the ties of kinship, less binding.

This effort at a typological contrast between the small and cohesive agrarian society and the large and differentiated industrial society gave emphasis to the importance of the small social group in the life of man. We can therefore say that the following significant idea for sociology derives from the critical social thinking of the nineteenth century:

6. *The small groups of society* are essential for man and for society, for they are the microcosms of society and the true source of morality and of society itself.

The idea that society is generated out of small social groups—community, kinship, and family—and that in the "primary" relations of such groups originates the humanness of man, the sense of morality, the feelings of loy-

---

[3] Ferdinand Toennies, *Community and Society,* trans. and ed. by Charles P. Loomis (East Lansing: Michigan State University Press, 1957).

alty, respect, and consideration, places both moral value and social importance upon such small groups. It makes them seem highly preferable to the large and impersonal groups more characteristic of industrial society. Here sociology absorbs a significant idea that is also a major value. Sociological analysis can be biased toward a moral preference for the old and small over the new and large unless conscious effort is made not to do so. That sociologists were not always successful in avoiding such bias is now a part of the history of sociology. You shall see at points throughout this book just where the value preference for *Gemeinschaft* has made a difference in the sociological effort to provide an assessment of modern society.

Max Weber: Bureaucracy and Rationalization   The typological tradition was based upon the creation of two distinctive types that sought to state the essential characteristics of human society before and after industrialization and thus to give some comparative understanding of what the future held. A comparable effort was undertaken by Max Weber (1864–1920), who, in his concepts of *bureaucracy* and *rationalization,* gives significant meaning to the transition through which the Western world was passing.

Weber was the first sociologist to explore the nature of bureaucracy as the typical social unit of modern society. He depicted bureaucracy as a mode of social organization that is large and impersonal and is organized in terms of rules and formal procedures, with all necessary action and procedures systematized. It constitutes the development of rational administration, which is but one instance of the rationalization of the world. By rationalization, in turn, Weber meant the increasingly rational quality to Western life, which he took to be its most salient feature and its one most significant historical trend. A world more rational is a world less magical; it is a world more organized and routinized, less spontaneous; a world proceeding by calculation and predictability, by law and rule, by plan and stable procedure. It produces that "disenchantment of the world" that for Weber was the central character of Western culture.

Max Weber, along with Durkheim and Toennies, although deeply involved in the world of their day, sketched in large outline the new discipline of sociology as they sought for more general and abstract terms in which to assess their changing world. The problematic nature of this world led them into significant and imaginative intellectual efforts that created the theoretical foundations of sociology.

Ideology and Sociology   Following Robert Nisbet, we have suggested that conservative ideas were one major intellectual source of the early ideas of the fledgling discipline of sociology. This conservatism refers more to the source of the ideas and problems, however, than it does to the ideological orientation of the major thinkers. Durkheim, as we noted, was a political liberal and so was Max Weber, but other liberal thinkers also contributed to sociology's origins. Among them was one of the foremost liberal protagonists of laissez-faire capitalism, Herbert Spencer (1820–1903). His three-volume *Principles of Sociology,* published in 1877, was the first major effort to provide a systematic outline of sociology as an independent discipline. Greatly impressed by Darwin's concepts of biological evolution, Spencer was the best intellectual talent among those who sought to apply these ideas to the analysis of human society. Although his conception of social evolution was eventually severely criticized and practically discarded by social scientists, what remains as his enduring contribution is his conception of society as an organized entity, the parts of which (groups and institutions) stand in "constant relation" to one another. His was the first explicit development of the concepts of *structure* and *function* as tools for the analysis of human societies. Thus, though liberal thought was frequently accused of recognizing a reality only of separate individuals, Herbert Spencer offered a conception of society as an interrelated structure, each part of which was a functioning unit within the integrated entity.

Radical perspectives, however, such as Karl Marx's, also contributed to the development of sociology. Although Marx is probably not usually thought of as a sociologist, the fact remains that he was concerned with the same things that concern the sociologist: how society is organized and how it changes. His ideas about social class were a major contribution to the sociology of stratification, and his concepts of revolutionary change suggested to many others a conception of society as containing inherent cleavages of class and property. These were the source of internal social conflict in society, and through that conflict, of revolutionary social change. Radically new social structures were seen as emerging from the internal discord generated within changing social structures.

Marx, and indeed all nineteenth century European socialists, were as convinced as were conservatives that a major crisis was developing in Western societies, though their interpretation of that crisis was quite different than the conservative one. Yet, it was this conviction of societal crisis that gave to sociology its fundamental concern with society rather than with the individual, with social relationships among men rather than with individual behavior, and so with the dual issues of how society was organized and how it changed —Comte's famous statics and dynamics. Before the end of the century, sociology was the intellectual concern of a diverse set of adherents who represented, ideologically, the then viable range of perspectives to be found in Europe and the United States: conservative, liberal, and radical.

Sociology and the Problem of Order   Whatever their divergent perspectives, these first sociologists were acutely conscious of a revolution underway: the transformation of society from old and traditional forms to new structures neither experienced nor understood. The asserted decline of common faith and values in previously homogeneous populations and the emergence of conflicting social differences within the newly industrialized populations posed crucial questions about how men can move from an old order to a new order (not from order to disorder), about the sources of solidarity, and about the consequences of a complex division of labor.

It should be evident that all these questions center around one issue: that some common modes of believing and behaving unite a collection of otherwise distinct individuals into a society. Man lives in a *social order*. The ability of men to maintain enduring social relations with one another and so to avoid disorder—that war of each man against the other that Thomas Hobbes spoke about in the seventeenth century—is the *problem of social order*. It is this problem that defines sociology as a discipline.

If social order is the problem of sociology, what, then, about the definition of sociology presented in the first chapter: *social relationships and the patterns of social organization built upon them, which is the central focus of sociology?* Questions about the continuity of social order that the founders of sociology were asking a century ago were expressed in an older style and vocabulary. The contemporary sociological vocabulary tells us that modern sociologists have tried to find a more precise language for the various aspects of social order. Thus, the sociological language has developed over time, the conception of the sociological enterprise has remained. To speak of human beings constructing complex patterns of social relationships from their interactions, and these then constituting a social structure, is to express the idea of social order in contemporary sociological language.

The questions posed by the founders of sociology and those that sociologists pose today, also tell us of other changes that have taken place. Questions of the order, how is society possible are global and all-encompassing questions posed at the highest level of generality. Contemporary sociologists are likely to ask more modest questions and to insist that the questions be asked in such a way as to be empirically answerable. The more modest and lower-range questions of today's sociology, such as, what is the relationship between social class and educational aspiration? are directed to finding relationships that are part of the larger social order. Most sociologists undoubtedly take for granted that there is a larger and encompassing social order, an organized society, so that they direct their inquiries to questions about how it is organized. They look for the networks of social relationships that make up an organized social life.

The problem of sociology, then, is social order. Social relations and social structure, the patterns that make an organized social life, are the phenomena the sociologist studies in order to understand the social order.

SOCIOLOGY AND SOCIAL REFORM

It would be an error to assume that sociology as it is today can be understood entirely in terms of the nineteenth century intellectual concerns about social order and potential social disintegration. These concerns were salient in defining the problems of sociology but were less influential in determining the directions taken by sociologists to develop the discipline. No understanding of contemporary sociology is possible without recognizing the role played by the involvement of earlier sociologists in social reform.

The period from 1880 to 1920 was one of intense involvement of middle class citizens (particularly in Britain and the United States) in humane efforts both to understand and to change the life of the underprivileged and disadvantaged groups and classes in industrial society. This concern for the lower classes, whose daily lot in an industrialized and urbanized world was largely unknown to the comfortable and affluent middle classes, generated intense activities to describe and explain "how the other half lives," as well as organized reform efforts to alleviate the condition of the poor and disadvantaged in one way or another. A generation of intelligent and reform-minded citizens pioneered in new forms of social welfare and in developing what came in time to be social work. Beatrice Webb in England, a brilliant woman born of high social status, teamed up with her husband, Sidney Webb, to provide intellectual leadership for the critical and reforming Fabian Society, out of which evolved the British Labor Party. Like others of her time, Beatrice Webb took it upon herself to explore at first hand the hitherto strange and distant social world of London's working classes.

Perhaps the most significant influence on sociology in this period was a major research project undertaken in the 1880s and 1890s by a wealthy British industrialist, Charles Booth. This detailed, factual study of the living conditions of the poor in London, entitled *Life and Labour of the People of London,* was published in several volumes from 1891 to 1903. It was significant for several reasons: (1) it was a major document in encouraging significant reforms in Britain; (2) it clearly set a pattern for basing public policy upon carefully gathered facts; and (3) it pioneered the empirical social study of the ordinary lives of urban people, particularly people of the lower classes.

In the United States, the remarkable Jane Addams pioneered in urban social work, particularly the establishment of settlement houses deliberately located among the poor and the immigrants in the great working class sections of burgeoning industrial cities. Hull House in Chicago, which she directed, was a model for the development of other settlement houses and social work. She and her staff, stimulated by Booth's work in London, produced *Hull House Maps and Papers* in 1895. The differently colored maps marked out the areas characterized by degrees of poverty, just as had Booth's, but in addition (for this was Chicago) they differentiated the ethnic areas created by the immigrant settlements. Similarly generated from Booth's work was W. E. DuBois' pioneering study *The Philadelphia Negro* in 1899. Such works stimulated much other quite practical research intended to promote social reform.

This close relationship between social reform and social research had the effect of encouraging empirical research. Booth's work, for example, stimulated a vast amount of research on the social conditions of both rural and urban life. Sociologists learned how to gather facts in a systematic and quantitative way and how to use statistics to analyze large bodies of data. More importantly, these efforts got sociologists out of the study and into the community, and developed their skills in observing and recording facts about human behavior.

This early involvement of sociologists in social problems also had another important consequence: it led the educated public as well as policy makers to turn to sociology for an understanding of poverty, of urban social disorders, of race and ethnic conflict, indeed, for a vast array of social problems besetting modern society. The sociologist became society's expert on many such problems, and his research often took on an applied purpose.

But if sociology has had a continuous influence on public thinking about social problems, it has also been influenced, in turn, by its involvement in these problems. The teaching of sociology in the United States began in the 1880s but spread rapidly after the founding of the first department at the University of Chicago in 1895. (The first scholarly periodical in sociology in the United States, the *American Journal of Sociology*, was established at Chicago that same year.) These first decades of American sociology—from the 1890s to World War I—was a time of intense social concern and intellectual unrest in America, reflecting immense changes that had been under way since the Civil War. During that quarter century, the United States became industrialized and urbanized. A nation of farmers and pioneers became a nation of blue- and white-collar urbanites. Generations of youths headed for the cities, as did millions of European immigrants, particularly the rural, peasant people from Eastern and Southern Europe. American sociology emerged from this ferment of change organized around some very particular concerns: (1) urban and rural life; (2) immigration and the assimilation of immigrants into American life; and (3) those urban-located problems presumed to be associated with urban migration—poverty, delinquency and crime, and so on.

By 1920, sociology had become a well-established academic discipline in the United States, characterized in the public mind primarily by its concern for social problems. Though as yet only crudely aware of what was required to be scientific, sociologists had established an American version of their discipline that placed considerable value upon being relevant to the issues and problems that bothered men in a rapidly urbanizing society. This impetus to be relevant was to remain a major value for sociology, even when a soon-to-emerge demand to become scientific led to the criticism that sociologists were too closely involved in social reform and social policy.

THE DISCIPLINE OF SOCIOLOGY

Probably no sociologist would regard his discipline as being fully mature. Its short and recent history testifies to its youthfulness, and the enthusiasm and optimism that sociologists express about their discipline is in itself youthful. Nonetheless, the century or so of its growth and development has given sociology the elements of a scholarly and scientific discipline: a perspective and the problems generated by a perspective.

A perspective is a way of looking at the world, a point of view that selectively places some things in the foreground and gives them salience and places other things in the background. The sociological perspective sees, and puts in the foreground, society, in its largeness and its smallness, in its sense of being social order, in its sense of being social worlds constructed by men out of their social interaction. It sees the intricate connections among the facts of social life, the linkage of behavior and belief, which suggests that man lives a collective existence and that each man only discovers his individual, private existence within the social worlds significant to him.

It is only from the sociological perspective that there can be postulated sociological problems. How a sharing of religious or political beliefs contributes significantly to the organization of a group becomes a sociological problem only when one's perspective focuses on the fact that there are sources of unity and cohesion that bind men together in a social order. The way the sociologist looks at human life, focusing on it as a collective enterprise, generates the problems that become the object of his scientific inquiry.

To read through this book will be to share in the sociological perspective, to see the defining of sociological problems, and to learn the kinds of scientific inquiry developed to explore these problems, as well as to discover what sociologists have found out about these problems. Perhaps, then, when the last pages have been read, the reader will have developed, by his immersion in the sociological enterprise, some sense of the sociological perspective and some appreciation of the problems the sociologist finds challenging. Perhaps also, by then, his consciousness of himself and his place in his social world will have been broadened and deepened. The ancient dictum, know thyself takes on new and particular meaning from the sociological perspective. Man can only know himself if he knows the social world that is the mutable context within which he shares with others the conditions of a human existence.

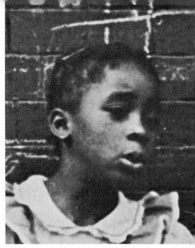
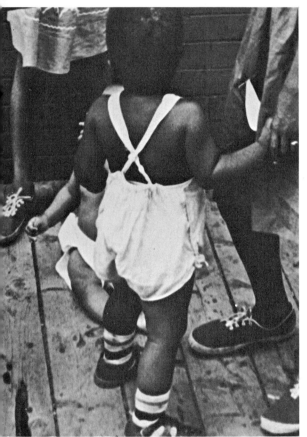

A kaleidoscopic view of playing slum children.

SCIENTIFIC
SOCIOLOGY

3

Ever since its origins in the nineteenth century, sociology had been regarded by its practitioners as a science. But for a long time there was no systematic effort to make explicit just what this meant or to build into sociology the specific elements of a science. In particular there had been only a small amount of genuinely empirical research. Most of the major contributors to sociology were men engaged in writing their own sociological opus of great encompassing scope—"grand theory," as it was to be called later. However, the reformist concerns of American sociologists, as we have seen, did lead many of them out of the study and into the community, where they practiced the arduous task of observing human behavior and of gathering data from which some reasonable generalizations could be made.

The development of a scientific sociology has been almost entirely an American process, though the first significant empirical study in sociology was Emile Durkheim's *Suicide,* published in 1897. During that same period, as we saw in Chapter 2, Booth's pioneering work in studying the London poor provided further empirical experience for the developing new science of sociology. Durkheim's study was an imaginative and innovative use of empirical data, largely from official sources, to test propositions about the social factors that caused rates of suicides in varying types of integrated populations, religious and national. A major empirical research work in the United States did not come until 1919, when William I. Thomas and Florian Znaniecki published *The Polish Peasant in Europe and America.*[1] This work ushered in a creative and fertile period of research at the University of Chicago, during which a new generation of sociologists undertook the direct observation of the varied and colorful aspects of the burgeoning urban milieu, with Chicago serving as the laboratory. They experimented with a wide variety of forms for gathering data, including official and unofficial records, personal documents, interviews, and participant observation. During that same decade Robert and Helen Lynd also utilized a variety of techniques in undertaking the first major community study in American sociology, *Middletown.* During this pioneering decade self-taught researchers established a thoroughgoing empirical tradition in American sociology. If much of that research seems imprecise by present standards, it nonetheless cultivated the ground from which a more scientific sociology was to grow.[2]

During the 1930s, a demand by a new generation of sociologists that the discipline become *scientific* as well as (and for some, instead of) socially *relevant* led to significant changes. A new era of a scientific sociology was underway. Sociologists developed a heightened sense of the necessity for objectivity in

[1] William I. Thomas and Florian Znaniecki, *The Polish Peasant in Europe and America* (1st ed., Boston: Gorham Press, 1918–20; 2nd ed., New York: Knopf, 1927).

[2] For an excellent description and analysis of the development of an empirical sociology, see John Madge, *The Origins of Scientific Sociology* (New York: Free Press, 1962).

social research. They widened their experience in empirical research and extended the array of research techniques available to them. They refined the technique of the questionnaire, the interview, and the random survey, as well as the statistical techniques related to these. They also became more sophisticated about the nature of scientific method. Increasingly, research projects were designed, which carefully stated the problem under inquiry, thus more rigorously defining and delimiting the behavior to be explained. Also, the research design stated hypotheses, statements of relationships expected to be found in the data; these relationships, if found, would provide explanations of the observed behavior. The stating of hypotheses improved the rigor of research by specifying the data to be sought in order to test hypotheses. By the growth of a sociological methodology, then, the discipline of sociology moved from being simply empirical, in the sense of gathering facts, to being scientific, in the sense of testing hypotheses, developing propositions, and thus creating verified knowledge.

These two decades, then, marked a growth in the methodological sophistication of sociologists and marked also their commitment to develop a science of sociology. Such a commitment has changed sociology considerably from what it was in the 1930s. Most contemporary sociologists are likely to design their studies more for their potential scientific yield than for their social or cultural relevance. They are also likely to attempt to study a small and easily manageable aspect of the observable world, consistent with the limits of their research techniques. Nonetheless, such a commitment has not forced sociology into a single pattern of scientific research. Although most sociology involves quantified data and statistical procedures, a more qualitative form of fieldwork is still much evident among sociologists. Nor has all research become large-scale survey research conducted by research teams. Despite the fact that some research now is so large in scope and so complex that the aid of computers is essential, other research is still that of the lone investigator going out into the field by himself, listening and observing, recording his own notes, and examining in detail and in depth some small range of human action in a limited and individually manageable context.

SOCIOLOGICAL ANALYSIS

The effort to develop a scientific sociology has been primarily an effort to make sociological work consistent with the canons of scientific method. It is no longer sufficient simply to gather facts; rather, hypotheses are formulated to establish relations between *independent* and *dependent variables,* the latter being the phenomenon whose variation is explained as variation in the former. Thus, if income increases with education, variation in education (independent variable) accounts for variation in income (dependent variable). The stating of sociological problems is often an effort to provide quite precise hypotheses about relations between variables.

For most sociological research, the specifying of a single independent variable is inadequate; the social order is of sufficient complexity so that a multiplicity of variables need to be invoked in order to account in some reasonable fashion for the variation in the dependent variable. As a consequence most sociological research is *multivariate analysis,* and the modern statistical techniques for multivariate analysis have become conventional tools for many sociologists. The sample survey has become the most typical means for gathering data, for such a technique lends itself well to multivariate analysis. It permits the gathering of a wide range of items about a representative sample of persons in the universe of study, in sufficient numbers to make statistically valid generalizations. It should be evident from this that part of the sustained effort to develop a scientific sociology has emphasized the *quantification* of data and statistical *measurement,* for, as most sociologists read the philosophy of science and use physics as a model, such a movement from a more qualitative to a more quantitative analysis is regarded as necessary to achieve rigor.

Yet if it is true that the major trend in the development of the discipline has been toward increasing quantification, a qualitative research tradition, as noted above, has remained viable and creative. Such studies as *Tally's Corner,*[3] an intimate portrait of Negro street-corner men, and *Justice Without Trial,*[4] an analysis of how law is actually enforced by policemen, both winners of the C. Wright Mills Award, are recent examples of the kind of qualitative study that seeks to explore the "inner" world of its subjects from close observation and participation. Studies such as these and others have often provided their own methodological prescriptions, though the qualitative study of social life still lacks the highly developed rationale that methodological positivists have provided for quantitative analysis.

Research and Theory For a long time in sociology, and even now to some extent, *research* and *theory* have been somewhat separate and distinct operations, with research so often barren of theoretical relevance and theory so often unrelated to ongoing empirical research, and furthermore, largely untested and unconfirmed. The "grand theory" of the past has often been criticized as not being theory in any scientific sense, for it does not constitute a set of logically interrelated propositions about determinate relations among

[3] Elliot Liebow, *Tally's Corner* (Boston: Little, Brown, 1967).
[4] Jerome H. Skolnick, *Justice Without Trial: Law Enforcement in Democratic Society* (New York: Wiley, 1966).

phenomena. Furthermore, it has not been empirically tested, and a scientific theory not validated is not a theory but a hypothesis. From these criticisms, then, has come a new conception of research and theory being closely inter-related, indeed, as aspects of the same process of scientific inquiry. Research draws from theory the concepts and hypotheses from which problems are defined, and theory in turn is constantly refined and modified by research. As a framework, theory guides research, and its central concepts select the data needed to test hypotheses.

How to relate theory and research in sociology has long been an issue fraught with a number of problems, but perhaps the major one has been that of the *level of abstraction*. The rich and suggestive grand theory of the past has often been an encompassing theory of social order, its concepts so abstract and general that sociologists undertaking empirical observations about limited aspects of the social world could not easily relate their empirical data to them. Consequently, sociologists have opted for what they have come to call *middle-range theory,* an idea that owes its inspiration to Robert Merton. The stated hope was that success in constructing a number of middle-range theories would eventually lead to a general and encompassing sociological theory. So, too, the more recent formal sociologists seek to "construct" theory as a logical outcome of their rigorously controlled empirical inquiry. In both these instances, the intent is the same: to treat research and theory as closely related processes, each necessary to the other in what is essentially a mutually reciprocal process.

When Robert Merton suggested some two decades ago that sociology abandon theory "in the large" and seek instead to develop special theories "adequate to limited ranges of phenomena"[5]—what soon came to be called *theories of the middle range*—he quickly established an orthodoxy for a discipline concerned with the apparent gap between theory and research. Certainly one factor in the quick acceptance of his idea was that it argued for a close relation of theory to ongoing research, and so for a modest level of theoretical abstraction that could remain close to the empirical operations of the research. Merton mildly denigrated the heritage of social thought that was the theory of the past and present; he spoke of it as consisting "of general orientations toward data . . . rather than clear, verifiable statements of relationships between specified variables"; he rejected the "scientific sterility" of "master conceptual schemes," and he argued for the disutility of most of the theory of the past as being "the false starts, the archaic doctrines and the plain errors of the past."[6] That the long history of social thought, and the shorter history

---

[5] Merton presented his ideas as a comment on a paper by Talcott Parsons. See "Discussion," *American Sociological Review,* 13 (April, 1948), 164–168.

[6] Merton, pp. 165–166.

of sociological thought, are filled with errors, blind alleys, and archaic doctrines is undoubtedly the case. That it is also an intellectual reservoir of ideas about social life, of concepts and propositions about social relations, and that it contains the classic questions about man in society that still inform and guide the theoretical efforts of contemporary sociologists, is no less true—and a great deal more important. This is why sociology does not outgrow its intellectual past in the same way that natural science does. Perhaps it never can. It depends on what one perceives theory to be. Merton is consistent with the dominant position in contemporary sociology when he speaks of theory as "verifiable statements of relationships between specified variables." Such a position does indeed imply the abandoning of much of the inclusive, encompassing theories of the past, at least in the major outlines of their logical structure. But even the most empirical of sociologists can read them profitably for insights and ideas. Nor is all the sociology before 1950 outdated; Max Weber and Emile Durkheim, whose major creative works appeared more than a half century ago, are still the contemporaries of present-day sociologists.

The conception of theory that Merton and probably most other sociologists use is the one explicated from physical theory by the philosophers of science. Scientific theory is viewed as a cumulative outcome of progressively improved and refined generalizations at ever higher levels of abstraction. Since theory develops and progresses, it outgrows, outmodes, and discards older theory. But some sociologists retain a conception of sociological theory that is different, at least to some extent. Dennis Wrong has articulated one such view by explicitly arguing against a cumulative conception of theory for sociology. He asserted that "social theory must be seen primarily as a set of answers to questions we ask of social reality."[7] He views theory as posing a set of "classical" questions that are timeless, such as: "How are men capable of uniting to form enduring societies in the first place?"[8] This, of course, is the fundamental question of how is social order possible? Another classic question is: "Why and to what degree is change inherent in human societies, and what are the sources of change?"[9] Questions such as these, Wrong maintains, "are not questions which lend themselves to successively more precise answers as the result of cumulative empirical research, for they remain eternally problematic."[10] What sociological theory should be, then, is by no means a settled issue. But what is probably not in dispute is the effort to put theory into a mutually supporting relation to empirical inquiry.

[7] Dennis H. Wrong, "The Oversocialized Conception of Man in Modern Sociology," *American Sociological Review,* 26 (April, 1961), 183.
[8] Wrong, p. 184.
[9] Wrong, p. 184.
[10] Wrong, p. 184.

On Concepts   Perhaps theory and research are nowhere more closely linked than through *concepts*. So significant are concepts that much of the history of sociology is a history of the creation, development, and modification of concepts. A new concept is often a means of expressing radically new insights into human action. It is often the creative contribution of a great intellectual innovator, such as a Freud or a Marx, that he provides us with a new set of interrelated concepts, a new conceptual framework by which we can see and think in radical new ways about the social world.

In contrast to the names of *particular* things, a concept is a *general* term that names a class of objects, persons, relationships, processes, or events. Every language of course is filled with concepts, for without them we could not speak except in the most concrete and particular terms. The concepts of science differ from the concepts of ordinary language only in the scientific effort to be more precise and abstract. For sociology this presents problems that disciplines such as physics do not have, for most of the concepts of sociology have come from the ordinary language; therefore, they retain some of the imprecision and ambiguity of ordinary words. Sociologists seek to provide a more precise definition, of course, but this often proves not to be easy; a concept such as *status* or *role* or *community* or *group* not only reflects the varying and imprecise meaning of ordinary language, but it also comes to be defined in somewhat different ways by sociologists, too.

The concepts of a science specify the classes of objects and events about which the science is concerned, for a science analyses classes of phenomena, not particular events. If a particular event is studied, or a small number of them, it is only because such study explains something about all members of that class. Thus, in the development of a science, concepts are constructed deliberately by scientists in order to render in a clear and unambiguous fashion the meaning of their observations.

Though constructed by men, concepts are not simply arbitrary creations; like all men, scientists are simply trying to impose order upon the flux of the universe and to render meaningful and stable the observational experiences of scientists. But in doing so concepts are necessarily *selective,* for they choose what to observe from the infinite aspects of reality. They put boundaries around the observable world of the discipline. Concepts indicate what the scientist is to look *at* in observing social phenomenon, and they also tell him what to look *for* in pursuing empirical questions.

For the sociologist his fundamental concepts are concepts of social order (which is itself a concept): *group, community, relation, institution, organization, culture, interaction,* and the like. These are the kind of concepts that specify the universe of discourse about which the sociologist seeks to make empirical generalizations as a basis for constructing a scientific sociology.

Concepts and Jargon   Sociology has frequently been criticized for using "jargon," and often this criticism is justified. However, this criticism frequently overlooks the more basic point that, since communication requires language, the communication of a distinctive perspective necessitates the development of a vocabulary adequate to the task. Sociology may be legitimately asked to speak "plain English" when speaking to others, and when what it has to say can be said in that "plain English." But "plain English" as our everyday, commonsense speech is notoriously ambiguous and imprecise. The compulsion that sociologists feel to speak unambiguously and precisely leads them to struggle to improve their sociological language and to develop something of a specialized vocabulary. Sometimes this consists of nothing more than giving new and more precise definitions to old and established terms, like group and society. Sometimes it means inventing concepts by adopting words from other contexts and using them sociologically—for example, social role, a term from drama. Less frequently, it means inventing a word or phrase that simply never existed before, to convey an idea that is not even imprecisely captured by any common-sense word.

Sociology like psychology, has an additional problem that is less bothersome to the natural sciences. The concepts of sociology and psychology, being about human beings, capture the interest and attention of those same human beings, who after all are the very objects of study the concepts were intended to help analyze. As a consequence, these concepts, often with remarkable swiftness, come to be incorporated into the working vocabulary of the everyday speech of at least the more educated segments of the population. Note how the Freudian vocabulary diffused so widely, and how such psychological terms as neurotic, tension, ego, IQ, self, and so forth, have become parts of our speech, although not always used with the same precision as the psychologist. So, too, in sociology, the concept of *role* is now in such general use that few realize how basic a term it is for sociology. Indeed, the basic terms of *culture* and *society* have been common to our speech only for about a hundred years; *status* has become a particularly fashionable term in recent decades.

There is no simple answer to the vexing problem of vocabulary for sociologists, who undoubtedly will go on creating new terms to convey more precisely the theoretical import of their sociological research. When their terms are pretentious and dress up the obvious, the criticism of "jargon" will probably signify that the terms will not last. Those that do last will do so because they say something not as precisely said in "plain English." The sociological vocabulary in this book will be that which has won its place by acceptance over time.

The Sociological Problem   The origin of sociology was rooted in the nineteenth century crisis of thought that rendered society as *problematic.* Society could no longer be understood by familiar modes of thought; what was required was a new pattern of explanation. A problem in a scientific sense is whatever needs to be explained, and science grows and develops by the stating and resolving of problems; science is a problem-solving activity, but one in which the resolution of the problem is valid knowledge. It is for this reason that science is regarded by many as basically *method*, a mode of rigorous empirical inquiry. The various sciences, then, are each a mode of disciplined inquiry into a set of related problems. Sociology, we saw, is organized around a set of problems about social order.

The development of scientific problems in any discipline is not, as Robert Merton has cogently pointed out, a simple matter.[11] One can, of course, ask *why?* about anything, but a science has to decide what questions are worth asking, as well as how they are best asked. It has long been evident that one of the greatest difficulties in science is in asking the right question. There are many examples in the history of science of asking the wrong question, but in social science perhaps none is more relevant than the famous nature-nurture question, which we discussed in Chapter One. To ask whether it is heredity *or* environment that determines behavior, we said there, is a false dichotomy; it is an either/or question when the issue is not either/or. Only when social scientists stopped asking the question in either/or terms could any scientific progress be made. Reformulating the question, then, a task that took several decades, was a major step in creating a genuine scientific problem. As Robert Merton notes:

> . . . in science, the questions that matter are of a particular kind. They are questions so formulated that the answers to them will confirm, amplify, or variously revise some part of what is currently taken as knowledge in the field. In short, although every problem in science involves a question, or series of questions, not every question qualifies as a scientific problem.[12]

The progressive development of a problem, according to Merton, then involves three components: (1) the *originating* question or observation; (2) the *rationale* for the question; and (3) the *specifying* questions that point to possible answers to the originating question in terms that satisfy the rationale. The relevance of a rationale is that it states why it is scientifically worthwhile to pursue this particular question instead of others. It distinguishes between the scientifically trivial and the scientifically consequential. What Merton calls the specifying question is the recasting of the originating question "to indicate the observations that will provide a provisional answer to it. Only then

[11] Robert K. Merton, "Notes on Problem-Finding in Sociology," in Robert K. Merton, Leonard Broom, and Leonard S. Cottrell, Jr., *Sociology Today: Problems and Prospects* (New York: Basic Books, 1959), ix–xxxiv.
[12] Merton, p. x.

has the problem been definitely posed."[13] This latter process often involves the *operationalizing* of the problem, the specification of what observations are to be made in order to obtain data about concepts stated in the question. Thus, if a sociologist wants to study the *morale* of a group, he must specify what concrete observations, and the operations for making those observations, will indicate morale. He needs *indicators,* and these he may construct by developing a scale that will serve as an index of degree of morale. A more common example is intelligence being measured by scores on an intelligence test.

Science is always a *rational* process of rigorously logical reasoning, but it is also an *empirical* process, in that it reasons with and from *facts.* The most abstract of generalizations that a sociologist can legitimately make can always be grounded in some observable facts. Fact gathering, then, in sociology as in any science is a fundamental process, and the task of accurately observing the world of social facts is always central to sociological method. Whether it is by interviews or questionnaires, by direct or indirect observations, or by laboratory experimentation, sociologists have always given considerable attention to the process of gathering data and to separating fact from opinion and from value. In doing so the whole issue of objectivity becomes a central preoccupation.

On Objectivity   One way in which sociology differs from the social thought of the past is in its primary intent to make an *objective* study of social life. Most sociologists today insist that their function is not to moralize about social life but rather to build up a reliable body of knowledge about it. To do so they seek to separate sharply the moral, philosophical, ideological, and religious views of life from the sociological. Their ultimate goal is a scientific explanation of social life. Such a goal, admittedly, incurs several difficult issues, not the least of which is a methodological issue: how to apply the scientific method to the study of man. There are also knotty philosophical and ethical issues having to do with the place of social science in human life and the responsibilities and functions of social scientists in society. But whatever the difficulties that the goal of scientific explanation incurs, there is, nonetheless, a point of view generally shared by most sociologists. It begins with the idea that sociology deals with observations of behavior, with facts about social life. Furthermore, sociology seeks to interpret these facts in such a way as to build up reliable statements about how men behave under specified social and cultural conditions.

Such an approach requires objectivity. Objectivity is social thought sufficiently disciplined to reduce the possible distortions in observation and analysis produced by one's more personal attitudes, emotions, values, and dislikes. In

---

[13] Merton, p. xxvi.

being objective, one seeks to be relatively unbiased in looking at social facts; one tries not to confuse social facts with one's feelings about them.

There is no guarantee, of course, that because one wishes to be objective, one will be. Objectivity does not come automatically because it is desired. Sociologists have become familiar, however, with certain typical ways in which bias and prejudice can characterize thinking about social life, and they have learned to guard against a great deal of it. Experimental psychology has taught us, for example, that if we are emotionally involved in something, or intensely prejudiced about it, or if our own interests are at stake, our social perceptions are likely to be strongly influenced. In short, we do not see the situation as others do; our emotions and our attitudes stand between us and their more dispassionate definitions of reality.

Objective thinking then, is not easily acquired; it requires training and experience. Few of us are taught to be very objective in the normal course of our everyday lives. Rather, we learn to respond *subjectively* to the behavior of others, to judge morally and to evaluate, to like and dislike, in terms of our own standards and those of our social groups. Yet objective thinking is not entirely strange to us, and probably more is required daily of the members of an urban, industrial society than we realize. There are situations in which we must be guided, for our own self-interest if nothing else, by an objective assessment of what is likely to happen, whether we like that or not. A businessman, for example, must do a good deal of objective thinking. To the best of his ability, he must objectively assess market conditions, the state of his own industry and his own firm, the abilities of his competitors, the likely demands of labor unions, and a host of other factors, in order to work out successful policies of business operation. He must be guided primarily by his objective understanding of what others are going to do, not what he would like them to do. Similarly, the very political survival of a politician and his party depends on his objective ability to ascertain the thinking of the voters and of other politicians. How people respond to certain symbols and slogans, how they interpret issues, is necessary knowledge for the politician. For businessmen, for politicians, and for all of us to some degree, it is essential to be able to think and analyze objectively.

Clearly enough, objectivity is not an all-or-nothing matter. Rather, one person is more objective than another, or less so. It is a matter of degree, always viewed relative to a standard of objectivity. Sociologists strive to be as objective as possible and to eliminate all factors reducing objectivity. In this they have achieved a modest measure of success, and contemporary sociological research is carried out by research techniques that enable sociologists to make relatively objective observations of social behavior.

Objectivity, it must be recognized, is a value of contemporary social science and, thus, is part of a value system. It is associated with such other values as truth and reason. The sociologist seeks to study social life objectively because he believes there is a truth to be discovered, a truth not contained in any of the existing beliefs that men now share. If objectivity is thus held as a value, it is because it is an aid in the search for knowledge. And this is clearly a value-judgment, the judgment that it is better to know than to be ignorant.

Such a point of view would seem to suggest that many, perhaps most men are not content with what existing beliefs can tell them about their physical and social world. Certainly, the consequence of the Industrial Revolution has been to create a *value-plural* society; that is, a society in which more than one system of beliefs and values exists. No one way of valuing or believing has a monopoly on the minds of men. As a result men are more willing to test beliefs against experience and to pursue knowledge by the methods of science. Conflicts and confusions of belief and value motivate men to extend their horizons of knowledge and by so doing to change their perspectives and values on man and his social life.

This search for objective knowledge proceeds on the assumption that we do not know all there is to know and undoubtedly never will. The state of knowledge is never complete and is always changing. But as our knowledge changes, so do our values. For knowledge always influences our moral outlooks, and new knowledge brings new moral attitudes. In turn new moral perspectives make us more aware of gaps in knowledge that we are anxious to fill in, and this motivates us to persist in our search for greater knowledge. In this fashion knowledge and moral values maintain a mutual influence on one another. Neither is ever final; rather, both knowing and valuing are a continuous process, ever subject to change and development.

PHILOSOPHY, EPISTEMOLOGY, AND SCIENTIFIC SOCIOLOGY

There are a number of significant issues in the development of a scientific sociology that go beyond the matter of objectivity in research procedures but touch instead upon issues of philosophy, particularly epistemology, that branch of philosophy that concerns itself with the study of the origin, nature, methods, and limits of knowledge—in short, how we know what we know. Of these several issues, there are perhaps two central ones. One has to do with how sociology becomes defined as an objective science, rather than an ideology. The other has to do with whether or not sociology is a natural science, like physics, or a human study, like history and philosophy. Though any exhaustive exploration of these issues is far beyond the scope of this book, an awareness of their origin and development will give a better appreciation of what has been intellectually at stake in the effort to develop a scientific sociology.

Bias as Ideological Perspective The success of sociologists in attaining objectivity is largely confined to those sources of bias, such as "loaded" questions and unrepresentative samples, which can be handled by careful techniques and which are common to most research projects. It is about these that sociologists have learned a great deal by experience. But subjectivity comes into social research largely through the unquestioned premises and unconscious assumptions about social reality that sociologists posit in their concepts and their statements of the problem. Thus, contemporary American sociologists are Western, urban, professional, educated, middle-class people, and not all of the assumptions inherent in the world-view of such people can be consciously guarded against as an influence on research. In Chapter 9, for example, we discuss how the study of the community in American sociology proceeded on the largely unconscious utilization of rural values, inducing an anti-urban bias in American sociology that lasted for fifty years. It should be noted that the kind of bias that sociologists have been most successful in countering is individualistic, that is, the bias of the individual researcher. However, the subjectivity that is due to unquestioned premises and unconscious assumptions is collective, not individual, in that it is shared by the discipline as a whole just by virtue of the sociologist being Western, urban, educated, and so on. It is subjectivity due to shared premises and perspectives, not to individual likes and prejudices.

This concern with the distorting effect of bias and the search for an objective stance for the sociologist must be understood as being based upon a very important assumption, namely, that there exists an objective reality "out there" that is to be discovered and described and understood by our techniques of research, a reality that is independent of our assumptions and values. The social perspective derived from our social milieu of social class, profession, and organizations, as well as the values and beliefs generated out of our particular life-style, are then viewed as hindrances to perceiving that reality; so they become biases. Biases we try to shed or overcome in order to achieve objective knowledge.

Perceiving values and belief and emotional responses as biases standing between us and objective knowledge is one common but by no means universal perspective on the scientific process. It is, in fact, one answer to the complex issues that emerge once it is recognized that science is as much a human creation as is anything else. Science is a distinctly social process, as is all thinking, for thinking proceeds through that most basic human creation, language. If that is so, then even science is an historical and cultural product of man.

Despite this recognition of the social character of all scientific research, for over a century now natural science has been generally conceded the status of objective knowledge independent of the particular perspectives of social groups, but the social sciences have not. Instead, they have often been defined as *ideology,* when that term is used to mean nonscientific, nonobjective idea-systems emanating from the particular perspectives and interests of social groups and classes. Much of the effort to create a scientific sociology has been an effort to move sociology from the status of an ideology to that of a science. A brief look at the origins of this issue in nineteenth century intellectual concerns may clarify some of the problems about a scientific sociology.

Sociology: Science or Ideology?   Like so many of the ideas current in modern social science, the recognition of the social determination of thinking is not a new idea, but it has only become a critical one within the last century. Robert Merton has asserted that this is so because modern society is so characterized by group differences in values, attitudes, and modes of thought that there occurs a fundamental distrust between groups; consequently, inquiry shifts from a concern with the validity of another group's beliefs to the question as to why they believe what is so manifestly untrue.[14] Thought, then says Merton, becomes "functionalized; it is interpreted in terms of its psychological or economic or social or racial sources and functions."[15] People are imputed to believe what they do because of their class interests, their collective insecurity, or their psychic needs. Yet, Merton insists, the sociology of knowledge (the study of the relation of ideas to society) could not emerge as long as analysis was restricted to the exposure of lies, myths, ideologies, and distortions of truth in the service of interest groups. No one doubted that unscientific beliefs and illusory opinion had to be explained by finding some reason for people believing what they did. But the sociology of knowledge came into being with the emergence of the "signal hypothesis that even truths were to be held socially accountable, were to be related to the historical society in which they emerged."[16] Ideas, true or not, had social roots and were always socially located.

The Marxian Origins   Karl Marx first set forth the issues that have been central to the modern sociology of knowledge as an outcome of his efforts to establish some connection between the German philosophy of his day and German society. In his struggle against Hegel's dominant influence on philosophy, particularly against prevailing conceptions that ideas are eternal laws or absolutes, he ruthlessly relativized all ideas as expressions of dominant social interests. Marx was thus led to treat ideas as functions of the social interests of social groups, and particularly social classes. Ideas, he argued,

---

[14] Robert K. Merton, "The Sociology of Knowledge," in his *Social Theory and Social Structure,* revised and enlarged edition (New York: Free Press, 1957), p. 457.

[15] Merton, p. 457.

[16] Merton, p. 460.

originated in the concerns of social classes about the terms of their social life and their relation to other classes. Marx then made his famous distinction between structure and superstructure: the mode of production was the basic structure that determined the superstructure of a family, a religion, a political structure, art and intellect, philosophy and theology. The entire range of intellectual production was a product of the economic organization of society and its division into social classes. "It is not the consciousness of men that determine their existence," said Marx, "but on the contrary their social existence determines their consciousness."[17]

While much of Marx's analysis was focused on the ideology of the bourgeoisie, the class that dominated capitalist society, he did not in principal restrict his analysis to such a class. There could not be, he asserted, revolutionary ideas without the existence of a revolutionary class. Such a revolutionary class had its own social perspective, a radical one that gave it an insight into historical truth not apparent to the bourgeois theorists.

Much of this argument was part of Marx's polemical attack upon the illusions of the scholarly community that their enterprise was somehow independent of the "real" social life of their society and autonomous in respect to its economic structure. Marx's skilled analysis served as a brilliant unmasking of the ideological pretensions of the middle classes. But it also became a radical challenge of singular power, which immensely influenced an entire generation of European scholars who could not escape the confrontation with Marx's ideas, even if only to try to find reasons for disproving them.

Marx had posited the mode of production as the existential basis—the location in the social structure—for thought, but it remained for subsequent contributors to the sociology of knowledge to broaden this basis. One of the most influential of these was Karl Mannheim (1893–1947), a German sociologist who fled Nazi Germany in the 1930s and lived in England until his death. Though not a Marxian, Mannheim was deeply influenced by Marxian thought and sought to provide a broader conception of the existential basis for ideas, as well as to remove so much of the polemical character of the Marxian argument. To Mannheim all ideas were located within the social process, but this location was not restricted to social class. Rather, Mannheim suggested the need to explore a variety of formations for the source of ideas: status groups, sects, generational groups, integrated groups, and socially uprooted, unintegrated ones.

However, an even more important modification of the original Marxian interpretation of thought was Frederich Engels' earlier distinction between scientific and nonscientific thought. Engels conceded to natural science a pre-

---

[17] Karl Marx, *A Contribution to the Critique of Political Economy* (Chicago: Charles H. Kerr and Co., 1904), p. 12.

cision of thought and a status quite different from that of ideological thought. From this came a Marxian position that viewed science as having its focus of attention (*what* it studies) determined socially, but not its concepts or its scientific findings. However, social science was not regarded as a natural science but as an ideology. Mannheim, though modifying the Marxian position in other ways, accepted this distinction and thus exempted the "exact sciences," but not the social sciences, from existential determination. This persistent distinction between science and ideology has been persuasively influential in effecting a general definition of natural science as independent of social influence, and thus valid, but of social science as still suffering from ideological taint. The influence of this, in turn, on sociologists has been the following: (1) they have sought to develop sociology philosophically and methodologically along the lines of natural science; (2) they have struggled to free sociology from involvement with social work and reform activities; and (3) they have adopted a position, which asserts that the influence of such existential factors as values and interests is limited to the selection of the problem and does not affect the method of study or the scientific results. The result is a definition of sociology as a science that has become an orthodox viewpoint within the discipline.

Mannheim did not claim that relating ideas to social structure replaced an intrinsic analysis of these ideas, and he once said: "It is, of course, true that in the social sciences, as elsewhere, the ultimate criterion of truth and falsity is to be found in the investigation of the object, and the sociology of knowledge is no substitute for this."[18] Sociologists seized upon this comment and made of it a fundamental position by which they can acknowledge the relevancy of the sociology of knowledge, while yet avoiding its full implications. The widely accepted *genesis-validity* position permits this; it says that the genesis of an idea is not a test of its validity. This permits the sociologist not only to grant that ideas in fact originate in the social perspective of particular groups, but also to assert that this does not say anything about whether they are true or not—that, so goes the position, is a matter of validation by scientific testing.

Such a position does not resolve the issue of the social origins of ideas and, in the process, does sociology an injustice. Taken literally, one would think that sociology did nothing more than determine the validity of ideas that originated in other social groups and classes, and that sociological thinking was incapable of developing any ideas of its own. It has done so, of course, though not without making use of a rich heritage of intellectual thought. The issue then becomes something else: whether its location in modern society and its relation to other groups induces in sociology a social perspective that influences its pursuit of knowledge.

[18] Karl Mannheim, *Ideology and Utopia* (New York: Harcourt, 1936), p. 67.

Philosophy and Social Research   Though sociologists are persistent students of almost all forms of social life, they have given little attention to social research as a social process.[19] Few textbooks of social research seem to recognize the human element in the role of the researcher, the normative character of social research, or the structural and ideological constraints that make ongoing research something less than textbook pure. Indeed, good research rarely follows the prescriptions of the textbook, in which one forms a hypothesis and then gathers data to test it; many good studies reflect the development of a sustained interest by a sociologist in a particular problem or even simply in a single concept. Recently Phillip Hammond brought together in a single volume a series of essays by a group of sociologists, detailing their actual experiences and problems in conducting some of the better known and respected research studies.[20] It constitutes one of the few sources about how research actually goes on in good studies.

That actual research would not conform to any cookbook formula is hardly surprising in sociology, but in fact this is true in all the sciences. What is more important in sociology is that there are significant differences in research that relate to two different traditions in sociology. The *positivists* would apply the methods of natural science to the study of social processes. Positivism has a long and involved philosophical history that cannot be reviewed here, but in sociology the positivist tradition has been significant since Auguste Comte developed his *positive philosophie* in the 1830s. Under the leadership of George Lundberg in the 1930s a new and resurgent positivism associated with an emphasis upon quantification brought a natural science emphasis into contemporary sociology. Although those who call themselves positivists are only loosely united with one another, they have probably shared consensus on the idea of the unity of scientific method; positivists insist that the natural and social sciences are basically alike because they share the logical structure of the scientific method. Any difference among any of the sciences is regarded simply as a substantive problem having to do with the individual character of the particular phenomena the science studies.

This emphasis upon the unity of method in science, and the confident belief in the possibility of objective knowledge in the social as well as the natural order, is a strong point of positivism, but perhaps its major weakness is its failure to perceive the fact that the nature of the data under study clearly affects the very process of research. In sociology as in all the social sciences there is a complex and often subtle interaction between the researcher and the social order, or the portion of it he would study.

In contrast to the positivists, the *neo-idealists* draw from a philosophical tra-

---

[19] For a thorough analysis of social research as a social process, see Gideon Sjoberg and Roger Nett, *A Methodology for Social Research* (New York: Harper & Row, 1968).

[20] Phillip E. Hammond, ed., *Sociologists at Work: Essays on the Craft of Social Research* (New York: Basic Books, 1964).

dition developed by a group of German thinkers in the late nineteenth and early twentieth century, particularly Wilhelm Dilthey;[21] the most creative sociologist influenced by them was Max Weber. There is also an American tradition, *symbolic interaction,* which shares some premises with the neo-idealists. The fundamental premise of this outlook is that the social and natural sciences differ because man is a conscious, intending, valuing phenomenon, and also because the social scientist is inescapably a part of what he studies. There is a radical difference between nature and society that requires different modes of inquiry. First, nature is observed only from the outside, not from within, and the observed relations among natural phenomena are mechanical relations of causality. But society can be understood and studied from the inside, and we only understand it because we ourselves belong to that world and can comprehend its relations as those of value and intent, not simply mechanical relations of causation.

The position that the data of the natural and social sciences are radically different has been reflected in many ways, including research procedures. Social data are seen as differing from natural data in several ways: first, the social scientist is part of the reality he studies, and the natural scientist is not. Indeed, to interpret and understand human action by taking the role of the other is basic to this perspective, for it requires that any adequate explanation be developed in categories that incorporate the subjective meaning of the action held by the actors. An empathic participation by the researcher is often an effort to grasp that meaning. Max Weber has been the foremost sociologist emphasizing the necessity of this approach, and this was the basis for his *verstehende* (understanding) *sociologie.* He insisted that sociological explanation must be both adequate at the level of meaning—being understandable from the perspective of those involved—and adequate at the level of causation, that is, logically explained according to accepted scientific procedures.[22] Such noted sociologists as Robert MacIver and Florian Znaniecki have emphasized the significance of categories that incorporate the meaning of the action for the actors.[23]

There is also a difference between positivists and neo-idealists (and sym-

[21] Little of the work of Dilthey has been translated into English. For an enlightening exposition of his views and some translated excerpts, see H. A. Hodges, *Wilhelm Dilthey: An Introduction* (London: Routledge and Kegan Paul, Ltd., 1944), and Wilhelm Dilthey, *Meaning in History,* H. P. Rickman (London: G. Allen, 1961). This is now in a Harper Torchbook edition under the title, *Pattern and Meaning in History.*

[22] See Max Weber, *The Theory of Economic and Social Organization,* trans. by A. M. Henderson and Talcott Parsons and edited with an introduction by Talcott Parsons (New York: Oxford 1947), pp. 8–29 and 89–112.

[23] See Robert MacIver, *Social Causation* (Boston: Ginn, 1942); Florian Znaniecki, *The Method of Sociology* (New York: Holt, Rinehart and Winston, 1934), and *Cultural Sciences: Their Origin and Development* (Urbana: University of Illinois Press, 1952; paperback edition, 1963).

bolic interactionists) in the emphasis the latter gives to the fact that man has a history. What man is today is largely a consequence of what he has been and what he has done in the past. The social order from this perspective is often seen as in a state of becoming. As a consequence there is a much greater emphasis upon human culture and upon the radical differences in cultures (and subcultures) in developing distinctive meanings about the human experience. There is, however, the danger that such an analysis will lapse into *historicism,* the idea that each society has its own unique laws and development, and that social analysis can do no more than understand the essence of a given culture. Such a position denies the possibility of objective knowledge. From Max Weber on, however, sociologists of whatever philosophical perspective have been concerned with developing the basis for objective knowledge and for developing sociology as a *generalizing* science.

Then, lastly, the neo-idealists recognize what the positivists have largely ignored: that the scientist interacts with the world he studies, and in the case of social science this has profound impact upon the research process. For one thing the actions of the scientist clearly affect those studied, and in turn the responses of the subjects have implications for the social scientist and his research procedures. Though in fact they have as yet done little about it, sociologists who draw from the neo-idealist tradition recognize that the social scientist himself is a variable in the research design.

Philosophy and Research Style   One of the differences between positivists and *verstehen* sociologists is reflected in research styles. Positivists of course emphasize rigor, and they have gone from the development of a quantitative sociology to one that proceeds according to a logical model, of which a mathematical model is regarded as ideal. Perhaps their strong point has been in the rigorous analysis of data and the development of modes of analysis to fit varying types and sources of data. They are innovators in the use of the computer. But such an emphasis has often led them to be weak on just that point that is so often the strength of their critics: the careful gathering of valid data. Sustained observation over time as well as participant observation—the forte of the fieldworker—remains the creative skill of those sociologists who believe in close and detailed observation *in vivo* of their human subjects. Such classics as William F. Whyte's *Street Corner Society*[24] have been crucial in the growth of the discipline; it has remained alive and relevant long after other research of its period has been forgotten and has served as a model for generations of sociologists to emulate. Herbert Gans' *The Urban Villagers*[25] is a model of the

[24] William F. Whyte, *Street Corner Society,* enlarged edition (Chicago: University of Chicago Press, 1955).
[25] Herbert Gans, *The Urban Villagers* (New York: Free Press, 1962).

contemporary genre. Thus, if positivists lean toward sample surveys dependent upon the responses of varied subjects to a questionnaire, or under the best circumstances to a carefully designed and rigorously controlled experiment, neo-idealists are likely to be less rigorous but also less mechanical, more saturated in the context of the subject under study. Positivists are less likely to undertake a sustained study over a period of time, but *verstehen* sociologists have a developmental perspective that encourages longitudinal studies as well as a still embryonic *historical sociology.* Positivists are more likely to be team researchers and analyzers of large bodies of data; *verstehen* sociologists are more likely to be fieldworkers, many of whom are still *qualitative* sociologists. Note here, however, that we are but pointing out probabilities, not in any sense hard and fast differences.

It would be a serious error to present these two positions as warring camps within sociology. Different as may be their assumptions about a scientific sociology, probably most sociologists make no clear-cut identification with either philosophical orientation. Indeed, over time many of the differences have been blurred. Gone is that natural science position that once led George Lundberg to observe that a man running before a crowd was, scientifically, the same as a leaf blown before the wind; in short, both were processes to be observed from the outside and explained by some law. Lundberg soon retreated from that rather extreme position, and contemporary positivists in sociology do not hesitate to include the intentions and values of men in the data they analyze.

Society and Social Research   There are a number of problems that emerge from the effort to do social research, some of which are reflected in the philosophical differences between positivists and others. Sociologists do not dispute the necessity for objectivity, but an extension of this, *value-neutrality,* is another matter. To be value-free goes beyond the objective attitude in research and asserts a particular political stance, namely, that the social scientist's commitment to the search for knowledge does not allow him, *as a scientist,* to make value-judgments or to advocate any moral or political position. He is ethically neutral. The rationale of this argument is that science is a process for discovering knowledge but is neutral about the uses to which that knowledge might be put. Thus, the atomic physics that can create destructive bombs can also be put to peaceful and constructive purposes. What is done with this knowledge, so goes the argument, is an ethical and political issue outside of science itself.

In a gradual development of a more scientific sociology in the United States in the last thirty years, this perspective became increasingly dominant. As a position it furthered the increasing professionalization of sociology and aided its relations to a society and to various elites in that society that increasingly saw a social usefulness in the research skills and scientific knowledge of sociologists. Though most American sociologists have probably been moderately liberal in their social and political stances, they have made a distinction between the role of the *scientist* who is neutral on political issues, and the role of the *citizen* who might espouse ideological and political positions. But in fact sociologists have not always been as neutral as they have proclaimed. In the field of race relations, for example, few American sociologists have been ethically neutral. With the rise of the civil rights movement in the 1960s and the conflict over poverty, a renewed critical stance toward such a value-neutral role has been widely apparent. The minority of sociologists who have not shared the wider sociological consensus on neutrality found their ranks joined by many younger sociologists. Furthermore, Alvin Gouldner's penetrating and influential essay made it abundantly clear to many sociologists that value-neutrality was simply a myth, once functionally useful in the building of a strong discipline, but perhaps now a no longer useful illusion for sociologists.[26] All this has made sociologists fully conscious of the larger implications of value-neutrality and has restored it to a major issue within the discipline.

Nonetheless, a scientific sociology pursuing objective knowledge, and however pristinely value-free, depends upon the climate and receptivity of the society for the success of its activity. Sociologists always experience constraint imposed, deliberately or informally, consciously or unconsciously, upon them by the society. Only now have sociologists begun to explore the full implications of social science as a social process. The first effect is to recognize the role of nonscientific norms, values, and ideologies in limiting and constraining social science. But that does not mean any abandonment of the objective of a generalizing sociology, a science of society. Instead, sociologists are becoming increasingly conscious of the need to analyze the human conditions that are the necessary context for sociological work and that have an unavoidable effect upon the outcome of sociological research.

---

[26] Alvin Gouldner, "Anti-Minotaur: The Myth of a Value-Free Sociology," *Social Problems,* 9 (Winter, 1962), 199–213.

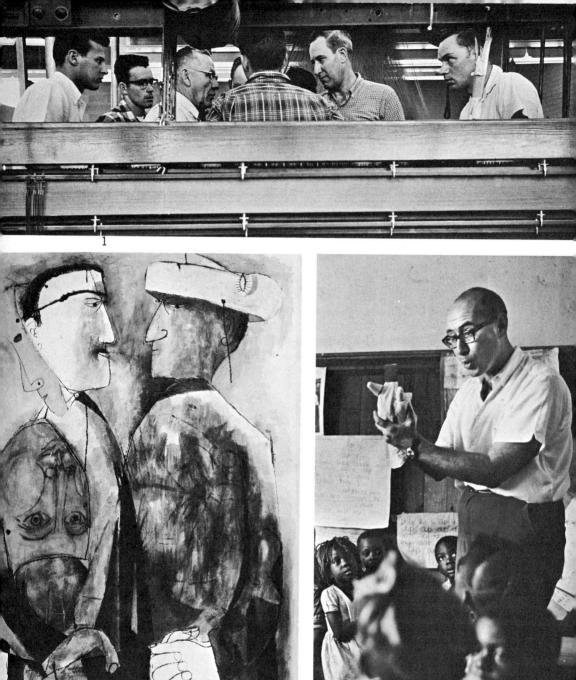

1. A retraining program in weaving.
2. Ben Shahn's painting, *Conversations*.
3. Peace Corps teacher in Jamaica, B.W.I.
4. Father and son (disguised as "Batman").
5. India: mother washing her child's hair.
6. Leapfrog on the beach.

4 6

5

SOCIAL
INTERACTION

4

The distinctive social perspective of sociology developed out of a century of intellectual experiment and creation, during which old assumptions about man and society had to be challenged, changed, and sometimes destroyed. As is so frequently the case, to learn new ideas, men had to unlearn old ones. Perhaps most basic to this learning and unlearning was the necessity to free the conception of man from older models, including older scientific ones, particularly those that postulated the determination of human behavior by instincts or by such external factors as geography, climate, and race. The modern social sciences came into being around the simple but fundamental idea that neither individual conduct nor the organization of group life is to be explained as instinctual responses to external stimuli. Rather, human life is created by men out of their collective experiences.

A fundamental starting point for the sociological analysis that flows from such perspective is conveyed by two basic concepts: *interaction* and *culture*. Interaction refers to the processes of men acting toward one another, of being involved with one another. Culture refers to the beliefs and meanings, ideas and values, cognitively shared by men in interaction. It is a creation of their interaction, on the one hand, and it influences the pattern of their interaction, on the other. In this chapter we shall focus upon interaction and its patterning. Culture will be the concern of the next chapter. In sociological analysis the two concepts are inseparable, but in learning about them it is useful to take each one in turn.

INTERACTION: SOCIAL AND SYMBOLIC

When Pavlov, the great pioneering Russian psychologist, demonstrated that dogs could be conditioned to salivate upon the ringing of a bell, he was helping to create a mode of explanation for behavior, including human behavior, that we have come to call *stimulus-response*. The organism learns to (or is conditioned to) respond to stimuli that originate outside the organism itself, whether the stimuli take the form of sounds heard or gestures seen. The stimulus gets the otherwise passive organism to respond in some predictable way. This approach has been developed in psychology to explore a considerable range of problems, particularly those of learning behavior. It possesses, however, some obvious limitations, the most significant of which is its view of man. By implication, man seems to be a passive organism who only behaves in response to a stimulus. *Man reacts.* But the sociological image of man attributes more to him than the capacity to react. He can also *act;* he can initiate and direct action toward other objects (including persons) in the world around him. His action is not merely that of responding to stimulus outside of himself.

Sociology began with the concept of *interaction*. As the prefix "inter" suggests, we have reference to action among several persons, namely, the situation in which two or more persons are both acting toward, and responding to one another at the same time. A conversation between two persons is a simple example. Each person directs his verbal behavior at the other and simultaneously responds to the verbal behavior of the other. Furthermore, the action of each person is determined by his taking account of the other person. To "take account" means to be aware of the other person, to define him as a social object of particular meaning (he is friend, teacher, salesman; he is friendly, cold, impersonal; he is important, prestigious, lowly), and to include that definition of the other in deciding how to act toward him. Thus, the action of persons in social interaction is *meaningful* action, that is, the acting persons are acting *intentionally;* they are not merely responding unconsciously to various stimuli directed toward them from some external source.

To say that a conversation is the meaningful action of persons in social interaction is to say: (1) that to converse is not just to emit sounds but to express some cultural meaning through words—verbal symbols; and (2) that the meaning of these words must be *shared,* that is, held in common by both the actor who conveys a meaning by his action and by the person to whom the action is directed and who must interpret it. The latter person must understand the meaning intended by the actor's conduct; for this to occur, there must be *communication.* Man communicates through *language,* a complex system of verbal and written *symbols* (spoken and written words) that are "conventional," socially created and adopted by men to convey meaning.

The recognition that man is a creature who lives with and through symbols, and that language is his most basic symbolic process, is not a new idea. René Descartes and John Locke said this centuries ago. But it has only been within the last century, and particularly within the first quarter of this century, that the importance of man's symbolic capacities has become a firm pillar of our assumptions about man. The anthropologist, Leslie A. White, in his book, *The Science of Culture,* offers a vigorous argument for the idea that the symbol is basic to making man human and to building civilization.[1] Acknowledging that there are impressive similarities between the behavior of man and animals, White insists that there is nonetheless a basic difference in behavior that stems from the fact that animals do not enter into the world of man—the symbolic world. Animals, it is true enough, says White, can be taught to re-

---

[1] Leslie A. White, *The Science of Culture* (New York: Farrar, Straus, 1949). See particularly Chapter 2, "The Symbol: The Origin and Basis of Human Behavior."

spond to a vocal command, and any kind of vocal sound can be used for such a purpose. Here we are dealing with a *sign,* not a symbol. A sign, White says, is "a physical thing or event whose function is to indicate some other thing or event."[2] Some signs occur in nature, such as dark clouds and wind signifying a coming storm, but many are man-made, such as the traffic signal on a busy street. Animals can learn signs, even very complex sign-systems, and the stimulus-response process is one of conditioning animals (including man) to respond in set ways to contrived signs. White, however, makes the significant point that although a dog can learn appropriate signs, it is only man that "can and does play an active role in determining what value the vocal stimulus is to have. . . ."

But if animals can respond to signs, only men can respond to symbols, and even then only when they have learned what particular set of meanings and values are represented by the symbol. Thus, the "sign" of the cross is not a form, the meaning of which is to signify any particular event or action. Rather, the cross represents the complex set of *meanings* and *values* of the Christian faith. Symbols, then, come into being only when men make objects (including words), representative of meanings and values. One of the major philosophers of this century, Ernst Cassirer (1874–1945), seeing in man's symbol-creating character the distinctiveness of what is human, credited man alone with having "the *symbolic system.*"[3] "This new acquisition," he said, "transforms the whole of human life. As compared with the other animals, man lives not merely in a broader reality; he lives, so to speak, in a new *dimension* of reality."[4] On this basis Cassirer asserts that man should be defined as an *animal symbolicum.*[5]

The Social Nature of Language   Language emerges from social interaction—and thus is socially created—but it is at the same time a major determinant of social life. It is a humanly constructed symbolic system that permits the expression of human meanings and allows men to communicate. Though the capacity to speak is universal, men do not inherit language as a dimension of their biological organism but must create it. They do so out of the particularities of common human experience and among those who share a common existence within a human community. It is within a common life that a language emerges. Like culture, of which it is a basic dimension, language is a relative thing—a particular language emerges from a particular social context.

[2] White, p. 27 (Grove Press paperback edition).

[3] Ernst Cassirer, *An Essay on Man: An Introduction to a Philosophy of Human Culture* (New Haven, Conn.: Yale University Press, 1944; Doubleday, 1953).

[4] Cassirer.

[5] Cassirer.

Because they possess a language, men are able to do more than make reflexive and instinctive responses to what is going on around them. Men *experience* the world by being conscious of its attributes and qualities and of the consequences this has for themselves. Furthermore, they assess and interpret this experience, and compare it to experiences of their own or of others; thus, they assign *meanings* to their experience and so give to it a specific significance. But the meanings that become assigned to experiences and thus to all experienced objects encountered in the physical and social environment is not the product of the single individual but rather is based, as John Dewey noted, on *consensus*.[6] It is the outcome of a social act of communication and agreement; thus, for experience to have any specific significance, that is, to have meaning, it must be shared and communicated.

But to confer meanings on experience and to communicate them requires that they be given cognitive form. The blurring, buzzing confusion of sensations that the encounter with the world gives to us requires an act of conceptualization in order to produce a stable order of experience and meanings. The array of discrete perceptions must be integrated into concepts that specify qualities or relations; thus, concepts are necessary for there to be "facts." Such a simple perception that rain follows hard wind and dark clouds would not be mentally possible except through the utilization of cognitive forms that name and categorize "wind," "clouds," and "rain," and that also enable the specification of the sequence in which they are perceived. Such a simple "fact," then, is a conceptual construction that requires language to name and categorize events and to specify the order in which they appear.

This conceptualization of experience by creating cognitive forms that name, identify, and categorize is only possible because of man's unique capacity for representing experience by verbal (and also written) symbols. It is through the symbolic representation of the environment that we define and understand *reality*, for reality is not the rush of impressions and perceptions, the array of sensations that happen to man the sensing creature, but rather the symbolic organization of these into a system of meanings that define what is and can be for man the knower. And language is the basic symbol system of man; all other symbol systems can be created and understood only through language. In the classic *Mind, Self, and Society*, George Herbert Mead (1863–1931), the foremost social thinker in the development of the symbolic interactionist perspective, put it this way:

> Symbolization constitutes objects not constituted before, objects which would not exist except for the context of social relationships wherein symbolization occurs.

---

[6] John Dewey, *Experience and Nature* (New York: Open Court, 1925), p. 179.

> Language does not simply symbolize a situation or object which is already there in advance; it makes possible the existence or the appearance of that situation or object, for it is part of the mechanism whereby that situation or object is created.[7]

Here, then, is what is fundamental about language and mind. Man is a reasoning and thinking creature by virtue of language, for language is the socially constructed instrumentality that makes mind possible. Through language, man constructs a symbolic environment, and it is this he inhabits; reality is not something that lies outside of man, an objective environment independent of his existence, but rather reality for man is what is defined by his symbols. Even the difference between *objective* and *subjective* is a construction of the human mind. Reality is not objective existence but rather all those sense impressions and perceptions that have been sifted through a symbolic screen and then given a recognizable form and set of relations by man-made symbols. It is a human construct, a product of the mind.

What Language Does   Language, we have been noting, names and so identifies some experienced quality or object or event. Only then can it be remembered and communicated and only then does it become *known.* Language also enables us to categorize these perceived events and experiences, therefore, to make distinctions among named objects and to differentiate in ways that have both practical utility in controlling and mastering the environment and value in constructing a rich and complex symbolic system of knowledge about the universe we inhabit. But beyond that, once language is established, what we even perceive depends upon the naming and identifying words available to us in our language. They become the spectacles by which we "see" the world. Walter Lippmann's famous aphorism is apropos: "First we look, then we name, and only then do we see." In short, language *organizes* our perceiving process; it identifies, selects, and also omits. Significantly, what language cannot identify may go unperceived; perception is always highly selective, and words are the instruments of selection.

However, we do more than perceive by the aid of language, we *think* with language. To think is to speak, and there is neither thinking without speaking nor speaking without thinking. Without the grammatical ordering of words, thought is vague and inchoate. One is reminded of the well-known remark that Plato had Socrates say: "When the mind is thinking, it is talking to itself." Yet, this ancient recognition of the dependence of thought on language by no means became commonplace. When Max Muller, a pioneering student of language, in his *Three Lectures* in 1887, delivered his famous dictum: "No thought without words," it became a source of controversy just because the idea was not obvious. Today, it is accepted without serious dispute.

[7] (Chicago: The University of Chicago Press, 1934), p. 78.

Symbolic Interaction   To the extent that social interaction proceeds through the communication of meanings by language or other symbol-using processes, it is *symbolic interaction*. Persons in social interaction communicate meanings and intentions by their verbal behavior, as well as by conventionally defined (thus symbolic) gestures, such as winking or thumbing one's nose. These gestures, according to George Herbert Mead, become *significant symbols,* not merely physical actions, because they are *conscious* gestures and also convey a conventional and shared meaning.

The use of symbols in social interaction makes it possible for interacting persons to define the social situations in which interaction occurs. The human actors are never interacting in a social vacuum; there is always a larger context in which interaction takes place. For example, people conversing over dinner may be guests in the home of a host, or they may be businessmen carrying out a business transaction in an expensive restaurant, with one of them paying the bill and putting it on his expense account, or yet again, the host may be entertaining his employer at dinner in his home. The interaction that is "conversation over dinner" takes place in different social situations, and this has consequences for the conduct of the participants. Friends at dinner may engage in serious discussions, feel free to express themselves freely and even dare to disagree, while remaining friends. Businessmen intent on a transaction are likely to avoid serious subjects (besides the business deal) and stick to sports or shoptalk. The host entertaining his employer, and his wife-hostess, are likely to behave in such a way as to maximize a good impression, which is likely to limit the kind of conversation carried on. In each of these instances, the social interaction has occurred in a particular kind of social situation. And it was the kind of situation it was because it was *defined* that way by the actors in the situation. What each situation "really" was, was a matter of definition by those involved in the interaction. Because the actors in each situation defined it as a particular kind of social reality, they conducted themselves accordingly. They acted, in short, in terms of how they defined the situation.

To recognize that human beings proceed to interact with others in terms of how they define the situation, is to recognize two fundamental points. One is that "if men define a situation as real, it is real in its consequences," which is what W. I. Thomas (1863–1947) meant by *the definition of the situation.* Thus, if actors define a situation as hostile and threatening, they will act accordingly, for that is their definition of the reality. To assert that objectively they were incorrect may be true but irrelevant for the purpose of understanding their action. It requires that we understand what the situation meant to them. Two, it would seem clear by now that when the sociologist says that action is "situational," he means the conduct of interacting persons, not the stimulated responses of organisms nor even the attitudinally-based behavior of unique persons. And all such conduct occurs in a situation that has been symbolically defined. One type of situation, such as a social party, permits one kind of interaction, whereas a work situation requires another. Consequently, the interaction of several persons on the job is quite different than when these same persons relax at a friendly bar. The persons are the same, but their interaction is shaped by the situation in which it occurs.

PATTERNS OF INTERACTION: ROLE AND STRUCTURE

The concept of interaction is not unique to sociology, but is basic to all the social sciences. Even the individual person can be understood only with reference to the social interactions that have been significant in his life-experience. That being so, the concept of interaction becomes fundamental to the sociological perspective and to the effort to develop a mode of sociological inquiry. The concepts by which sociologists seek to express their inquiry into human conduct are but extensions of the concept of social interaction. In the study of social order, then, we begin with *men in interaction*. From this starting point we can speak of a *patterning* of social interaction: *roles, relations,* and *social structure.*

Roles and Relations   Social interaction is eternal and pervasive among men, but the sociologist is particularly interested in those interactions that occur with some regularity and occur in defined situations. Not all interactions happen this way, for some are transitory and ephemeral. An interaction that is not passing and ephemeral relates us to other persons; that is, involves us in a somewhat more stable and persisting pattern of interaction. A situation of relatedness exists, or, in our vocabulary, is a *social relation.* Marriage is a social relation, so is friendship. There is an almost endless list: the relation of foreman to worker, of father to son, of doctor to patient, of student to teacher. These social relations can, in turn, be analyzed into constituent parts: *positions* and *roles.* (*Status* is frequently used in place of position, but this confuses its meaning with that of social rank. We shall use *position* here and employ *status* as a concept of stratification.) A social position is a socially defined location or place in a system of social interaction, as, for example, the position of professor in a university. Social role, which is the more important concept, gets its meaning from the fact that the occupants of social positions always share some mutual *expectations* about how each will act toward the other. A social role, then, is an expectation of behavior shared among actors in social relations. It emerges from and gives some stability to interaction, and it does not exist outside of the interactional process from which the expectation emerges.

These expectations are never spelled out precisely, as if they were lines in a play. A role in life is not the same as a role in the theater, where the actor carefully learns his lines and then, on cue, acts out his part as the author wrote it or as someone else directs it. It is a conceptual error to conceive of social roles in such a way or of role playing as a process of conformity by the actor to a prescribed routine. Roles are simply not like that. The expectation of role does not prescribe actual behavior but, instead, suggests an orientation to a particular other. A role only exists when there are relevant other-roles to which it is oriented. The sociologist, Ralph Turner, has argued cogently against a view of role that sees it as *conformity* to prescribed behavior and for a view of role as *consistency* in orientation to others.[8] Such a consistency specifies no particular conduct; rather, it implies the sharing of a perspective among those actors involved in the relation, a perspective that involves some common norms and some common basis for interaction. A role, in short, constitutes an agreed upon basis for social interaction, which then makes possible some consistency in the modes of action that occur.

"Expected behavior" then is potentially misleading because it might suggest rather specifically prescribed behavior, nevertheless we need not abandon *expectation* as central to the concept of role. In the first place, expectations are grounded in *understandings* of the meaning and salience of the actions we are carrying out when we "act" in a role. By our projected action, we are proposing to interact with another as an "actor," that is, in a definable way. To be an actor, we select a relevant mode of action for developing a consistent set of interactions with another. The symbolically expressed meanings that we learn as members of an organized society are incorporated into these interactions. So, too, are the understandings of specific social situations, and the meanings which these situations have for those involved in them. Those understandings then lead us to *expect* from the actor some *type* of action. Therefore, if the expectations that define role do not prescribe specific behavior, they do lead us to expect that the actor will act to accomplish some purpose or end or to symbolize some meaning, and that he will *not* do certain other things.

Let us take an example. A female in any society learns to act like a woman, to act toward others consistent with a shared expectation of what womanly behavior is. When she marries, she must act like a wife, an expectation that may not prescribe conduct but will certainly limit it, and will always require her to act in such a way as to validate her claim to being a woman and a

---

[8] Ralph Turner, "Role Taking: Process Versus Conformity," in Arnold M. Rose, ed., *Human Behavior and Social Processes* (Boston: Houghton Mifflin, 1962), pp. 20–40.

wife. So, too, when she becomes a mother, another generalized set of expectations defines an orientation, to both her husband and her child and to others, in which her actions must validate her claims to being a mother. She must, in short, act as a mother is supposed to act. And how is that? The blueprint does not exist, so that each woman must construct a role of mother for herself. But what behavioral pattern she constructs is oriented to the expectation that she *ought* to care for her child—nurture and comfort it, tend to its material and physical needs, train it, and, when necessary, punish it. We expect that a woman will have the sentiments of "motherhood" that will combine caring and devotion and gentleness. From this, we can and do construct some expectations of how a mother will act, even though this does not necessarily come down to any minute specifics of behavior.

Role playing, then, *organizes* behavior. It serves to define a mode of interaction that enables people to share certain common expectations of what they are to one another (wife, friend, teacher, and so forth) and thus to define what can legitimately and validly be expected from each other. What can be expected, and thus what becomes defined as legitimate role-playing, is consistency in an actor's orientation to others. Indeed, roles are validated each day that people give understandable symbolic expression in their behavior to shared expectations. Because people meet these expectations, society remains organized. But since roles are never precisely defined and are always somewhat ambiguous, role playing is subject to redefinition and remaking. Ralph Turner speaks in this context of role-making.

The concept of role is the basic analytical step by social science beyond the psychological level of the person. It conceptualizes the process of the person's action as consistently fitting into expectations held of others, thus making an organized social life possible. Role is, consequently, a fundamental and basic unit for the analysis of social order. It permits us to move toward sociological analysis because we can think analytically, not of total and unique persons, but of types of actors (mother, teacher, judge, friend, leader) responding to expectations based upon shared understandings. We can begin to explicate the pattern of organization by which we live. Furthermore, what the sociologist does here is only an analytical refinement of what goes on in the mind of people as members of society. Our commonsense vocabulary is filled with terms that denote role: voter, citizen, politician, prostitute, policeman, criminal, soldier, father, brother, worker, foreman, teacher, administrator, delinquent, and thousands of others. These terms are used in ordinary life to characterize each other as actors from whom certain ways of acting are expected. Such an enumeration of roles also leads to the realization that many different persons can take the same role. Yet, despite the undeniable fact of the uniqueness of each person, there can be observed an identifiable pattern that is the role, not the person.

Role-Set.   The occupant of any given social position soon finds that no one set of expectations can define his role and appropriately orient his action toward the occupants of complementary positions. To this point, then, we have spoken as if there were but one role associated with a position. But the patterning of social interaction is hardly that simple. The man who is a professor, for example, finds that the expectations of the professorial role are one thing when interacting with students, something else when interacting with his fellow professors, and something else again when interacting with deans and other administrators. In short, there is no one definition of his role that tells him how he is expected to interact with all those other actors whose relationships with him make up the university. As we suggested before, the expectation of role suggests an orientation to a *particular* other; thus, one set of expectations orients the professor to undergraduate students, another to graduate assistants, and yet another to his colleagues. For the position of professor, then, there is not one role but a *role-set,* a concept that tells us to anticipate a somewhat differentiated set of role-expectations to orient the occupant of a social position toward the other actors in the interactional system.[9]

Social Structure   In its general dictionary sense, *structure* means the arrangement or interrelation of the parts of a whole. It says that the basic parts that make up the whole are put together in some particular way. A pile of bricks and boards does not constitute a building until it is put together in some manner. In the same way, when a composer writes a song, he takes the notes of the musical scale and arranges them in some created order that gives music. A pile of bricks and boards is not a building; the notes of the scale do not constitute a song. They must be put together by some design.

The concept of structure in these examples is not difficult to grasp, for the structure materializes before our eyes. Bricks and boards become a building when construction takes place; a song appears in a recognizable melody that we hear when it is sung or played. But social structure is not a material thing; rather, it is a concept utilized by the sociologist to convey the idea that men interact in roles that are related to one another in some systematic way. It becomes useful for the sociologist to think of a role as a constituent part of some larger organized or constructed entity. So, also, is a social relation; for example, the family includes such roles as father, mother, son, and daughter. There are, therefore, a number of social relations, that is, the interaction among the family members in their roles. But these different relations must exemplify some coherence with one another to make a family an organized

---

[9] We owe the concept of *role-set* to Robert K. Merton. See his "The Role-Set: Problems in Sociological Theory," *The British Journal of Sociology,* 8 (June, 1957), 110–111.

entity. Social structure, then, is the integration of social roles into a relatively coherent pattern of interaction. Such an entity *has* a structure—let us not confuse the structure *of* a group with the group itself. (The existence of a structure is necessary but not sufficient to define a group, as will be seen in Chapter 7.)

By the same token, let us not assume that a social structure is ever a perfect integration of roles. No social structure is perfectly coherent; there is always some strain and tension present and thus, some internal sources of conflict and pressure for social change. Nonetheless, the idea of social structure connotes the sociologist's search for the more stable and "fixed" elements in social life, and the term gives analytical reality to this idea.

From another perspective, one might ask, what does a lack of structure mean? Sociologists speak of "unstructured" situations where there is no set of expectations to orient people to interact in any given way, when, in short, people do not know what they are supposed to do or how they are expected to act. They do not have a role to take, and so they do not know what kind of an actor to be. People are uneasy and tense in such circumstances. Consequently, they proceed, tentatively and haltingly, to find some common bases on which to interact, some common expectations to orient them and provide roles. They construct modes of acting; they put structure into the situation.

Social Structure, Social System, and Social Organization   Before we move on to consider the concept of social process, let us note in passing that what some sociologists call a social structure others call a social system. Both terms are intended to convey the idea that social interaction builds up into complex patterns that are relatively stable and persistent. Another related term is social organization. Sometimes social organization becomes a broadly encompassing term, simply to state that men live together, not in isolation, as noted at the very outset of this book. Accordingly, human behavior can only be understood by reference to the organization always found in social life. There is also a more special meaning for social organization (sometimes merely the one word, organization), referring to the large and rational social groups that we call *bureaucracies* or *formal* organizations (see Chapter 8).

Social Process and Social Change   When sociologists speak of social process they are saying that there are *forms* or *modes of social interaction*. Process, then, designates human beings acting, doing things, and in this sense the term has seemed to be "dynamic," in contrast to the "static" idea of structure. This is probably an over-simplified distinction, but nevertheless process does refer to ongoing activity, and structure in turn has primary reference to the "fixed" elements that give coherence to the social relations of any group.

The concept of social process was once a dominant concern of American sociologists, and much of their sociological analysis was a delineation of the varied social processes to be found in social life. One of the pioneering and most influential textbooks in American sociology, *An Introduction to the Science of Sociology,* by Robert Park and Ernest Burgess, gave a major emphasis to the place of the social processes in society.[10] After the publication of the Park and Burgess volume, generations of sociology students learned that the basic social processes were the following: *cooperation, competition, accommodation, assimilation,* and *conflict.* Indeed, some decline in sociological interest in the concept can perhaps be attributed to a tendency to limit consideration to only these five processes, about which little more could be said than the truism that all societies exemplified these processes. Other sociologists listed processes endlessly, much as psychologists once kept adding to their list of instincts.

What was important, however, was that this concern with ongoing activity by an earlier generation of sociologists meant that the study of social process was the study of sequences of social development, namely, the bringing about of change in human affairs. In short, social life is not only organized, it is continually reorganized. These "interactionists" assumed social life to be ever in flux, to be in process, rather than set into static structural patterns. Charles Horton Cooley (1864–1929), one of the great American pioneers in sociology, wrote a treatise *Social Process* (1918) after reading Charles Darwin, in which he attempted to translate natural selection and adaptation into sociological terms and to invoke a perspective that viewed social process as continual change and development. The concept of social process, then, connotes a fundamental aspect of the sociological perspective. Valuable as is the viewpoint that abstracts structural patterning in social interaction, it is equally valuable to see interaction as change and flux. It is necessary to counter the useful emphasis that the concept of structure puts upon the search for stability in the patterning of interaction by never allowing the concept of process, with its connotations of flux and change, to slip from a central place in our sociological perspective.

Social Change   The social processes designate various modes of social interaction that lead to social change, and *social change* has become for many sociologists the concept that complements social structure. Once sociologists spoke of statics and dynamics, then of structure and process (and many still do), but now usually of structure and change.

Social change is pervasive and cumulative in social life, and it is theoretically an error to assume a social stability that is unchanging. Thus, the concept of social order is not to be juxtaposed to a concept of change. To do so would

---

[10] Robert Park and Ernest Burgess, *An Introduction to the Science of Sociology* (Chicago: University of Chicago Press, 1921).

be to make two errors: (1) to assume that order implied an unchanging pattern of social relationship; and (2) to identify change with disturbance, instability, and disruption. To confuse social order with stability and to identify change with disruption is a heritage from an earlier generation of sociologists who were deeply concerned about the radical impact of industrialization on social life. They gave to sociology an intellectual tradition of concern for the conditions that sustain a society in some stable pattern. *Integration* is the concept that refers to the effective structural patterning of a society whereby the various segments or parts, such as roles and subgroups, fit together into a relatively well-functioning structure with a minimum of friction and tension. *Consensus,* in turn, means the sharing of values and norms, of a common cultural set of expectations and meanings. *Solidarity* and *social cohesion* refer to the capacity of a group to exhibit unity and common action toward outsiders and to maintain a bond of unity.

This integrative focus has frequently viewed social change as lessening the integration of the society; its resultant loss of consensus leads to *social disorganization.* Emile Durkheim used the term, *anomie,* to identify a final endpoint where the social bonds had so disintegrated that social norms no longer regulated human behavior. Here, indeed, is a perspective that interprets change as constituting a threat to social order. Yet, sociologists readily enough recognize that social order does not disintegrate into nothing, that a disorganizing process is the prelude to the emergence of new social relationships, for reorganization follows disorganization. Although the disruption of a long existing social pattern is certainly evidence of social change, so too is the rebuilding of a disrupted relationship, the creation of a new relationship, the further integration of a poorly organized group, the acceptance of new beliefs and attitudes, and in general, the process of reorganization that follows the disorganization of older patterns.

But the direction of social change is not interpreted always as being from integration to anomie. What Durkheim also clearly recognized and described in *The Division of Labor in Society* as a major trend in the modern world—so did Herbert Spencer—was a change from a smaller, simpler, and more integrated society to a larger and more complex one. The term, *division of labor,* identifies a differentiating process whereby the specialization of occupational and other social roles—*role differentiation*—leads to a more complex social structure. Complexity in social organization, in turn, leads to *segmentalization,* the emergence of differentiated subgroups where before there was but a single structure.

Social Conflict Whether the analytical emphasis is on disorganizing or differentiating change, it nonetheless means the altering of patterns of integration and consensus. When that happens, strains and tensions become apparent, and sociological analysis focuses on the *social conflict* that such conditions generate in social groups. Sociologists use the concept of conflict in two different ways. When they speak of *role-conflict*, they refer to the incompatibility of role expectations in the group and to the consequence for the individual of being unable to satisfy two such incompatible expectations at the same time or in the same situation. A second conception of conflict is that of struggle or contest over values or over scarce resources, in which two contesting groups are each seeking to impose their definition on the situation and so to maintain or change the social order in terms of their values. This latter conception of conflict has often been treated by sociologists as *dysfunctional* for social order; that is, as destructive of established patterns and resulting in the disorganization of social life. Conflict has then been viewed as the antithesis of order. But the sociologist, Lewis Coser, has made the contemporary generation of sociologists sensitive to the idea that conflict has positive functions as well and is not to be interpreted only as disorganization. His book, *The Functions of Social Conflict,* is a brilliant rendering into contemporary thoughtways of the earlier work of a gifted and seminal European sociologist, Georg Simmel.[11]

As part of the vocabulary of sociology, the concepts of change and conflict focus our attention on the processes of disorganization and differentiation that mark a transformation from one pattern of social relationships to another. In turn, the structure of social relationships speaks to the stable patterning of social interactions. Both modes of interpreting social order are necessary, for neither alone provides us with a full sociological perspective; rather, each is complementary to the other.

THE MEANING OF SOCIAL ORDER

If the idea of social order expresses our conception of the sociological concern, perhaps it would be useful to clarify further its meaning in the sociological context, now that the interactional context for human behavior has been established. The very idea of order, of course, is basic to science. That there is order in phenomena is the fundamental assumption of science; if there is not, then science is not possible. The predictability of phenomena that science seeks assumes discoverable regularities. The concept of *social* order assumes the scientific idea of orderliness, but the modifier, *social,* gives it a distinctive meaning. The order that the natural scientist states in his laws are regularities in the behavior and relations of physical and organic phenom-

---

[11] Lewis Coser, *The Functions of Social Conflict* (New York: Free Press, 1956).

ena that are observed and understood, not by the phenomena but by the scientist. Thus, the conception of order is external to the phenomena that is ordered. Physical and biological phenomena may function in orderly relations, but they have no consciousness of such an order. If their behavior follows "laws," these are unknown to them.

But man is conscious of the order in which he lives. He has a sense, even though at times but dimly, of a pattern of orderly expectations that make possible the commonsense world of his everyday experience; most of it he usually takes for granted—until it is disrupted. Then, a consciousness of his world and its ordering of human relationships that he has taken for granted and assumed to be right and natural comes to the fore. This potentiality by man for intense consciousness of his own social order can be viewed as necessary for one basic reason: the social order in which men live is their own creation. Here, again, is where the physical order differs from the social: physical phenomena do not construct their own pattern of relations, but men construct the social worlds that they also come to take for granted as natural and right. There is a necessary extension of this: if men construct their social order, they construct very different social orders under different conditions and circumstances. What is universal for man is that he lives in a persisting though always changing social order. But the internal organization of that social order has no preordained pattern, given in the genetic nature of man. At different times in the long span of history, and at different places over man's still only inhabitable planet, men have constructed very different societies.

Social order also implies *stability*, but it would be an error to assume that this is all that social order means. It is an ideological bias to invoke the necessity for "law and order" as a reason for insisting on maintaining a particular social pattern. Many times in history men have viewed the historical challenges to their way of life as a choice between order and disorder, as though their particular way of life was synonymous with order, and any threat to it meant disorder. In fact, the perceived threat to an old order is always a response to the emergence of a new order.

Yet, the change to new forms of social order is not easy. People have built their own individual existences into meaningful patterns within the context of some existing social order. Their attachment to it is likely to be understandably deep and abiding and not easily given up. It is at this point that it can be obvious to us that social order is not merely some nonrandom patterning of human behavior. If human behavior were explainable as instincts, or merely as the conditioned responses of learning organisms, then a conception of social order as primarily stability and regularity would be sufficient. But if social order is constructed by men out of their social interactions, then (because social interaction is also symbolic interaction), *a social order is a symbolic order.* A social order is patterned around the symbolic meanings that men have created. This is what social order is sociologically: the ordering of the behavior of conscious actors into patterns meaningful to those actors.

To conceive of social order as the constructed patterns of meaning and behavior by which men can *live* in a human society, not merely exist as organisms, gives direction to the manner in which sociology pursues its inquiry into human behavior. It makes clearer Max Weber's injunction to us to pursue a mode of inquiry that is *verstehen:* to understand social behavior in terms of the intentional meanings of the social actors as well as our external observations of regularities in behavior and the correlation of these with other phenomena.

1

1. Heads of state at President Kennedy's funeral.
2. Watching a parade in Chinatown, N.Y.
3. New York City policemen and their admirers.
4. Santa Claus in Nigeria.

2 4

3

CULTURE

5

The existence of language through which men communicate, the use of symbols that find expression in language, and the act of defining the situation, are all indicative of the fact that man creates something we call *culture*. No other creature does. The concept of culture refers to something that is understandable when we first grasp this about the biological nature of man: that he is a flexible and learning creature who devises ways to come to terms with his environment and to develop some limited mastery and control over it. It is the nature of man that requires that there be culture.

The word "culture" has long suggested—and still does for some—a condition of refinement and manners, a meaning quite alien to its present usage by social scientists. But this first meaning shares historical links with the mid-nineteenth century anthropological meaning, when *culture* and *civilization* were used to characterize one kind of society, and *savage* and *barbaric* were used to characterize another. The concept of culture began, then, in a context of invidious distinctions about the quality of social life among the earth's peoples. However, when Edward B. Tylor published his classic work, *Primitive Culture,* in 1871, the anthropological meaning of culture applied to even the most primitive of people.[1] All men had culture, it was agreed, and indeed, all men had to have culture. Before this point of intellectual development was reached, however, culture gradually evolved from a prenineteenth century meaning of "tending of natural growth" and then human training, to a more particular nineteenth century use that only gradually came to signify a way of life. The British scholar, Raymond Williams, has followed the development of the word in his *Culture and Society 1780–1950.*[2] By tracing its changing use by the major English thinkers from the latter part of the eighteenth century on—from Edmund Burke to George Orwell—Williams demonstrated that *culture* came to be used in its present meaning only with the onset of industrial society and the revolutionary changes in social life that industrialization brought about. Furthermore, he argued that it was one of five key words that became significant in giving meaning to the experience of these vast changes; the others were *industry, democracy, class,* and *art.*[3]

The long effort in the social sciences, particularly in anthropology, to define the concept of culture has yielded a vast literature without producing any precise consensus on what culture is. Yet, in the last hundred years, there has been a steady development of the accepted meaning of this central concept, reflecting the changing context of social-scientific problems and an altered relevance of the concept of culture for the intellectual concerns of the sociologist. The problems of the emerging social sciences of sociology and anthropology in the 1860s and 1870s, particularly in the face of the exciting new

[1] Edward Tylor, *Primitive Culture: Researches into the Development of Mythology, Philosophy, Religion, Language, Art and Custom* (London: J. Murray, 1871).
[2] Raymond Williams, *Culture and Society 1780–1950* (New York: Anchor Books, 1959).
[3] Williams, pp. xi–xiv.

biology set in motion by Charles Darwin, which was the context for the first development of the concept of culture among social scientists, were quite different from those of a century later. Over time, several different emphases about culture have come to the fore in sociological writings. If we examine what was said about the concept of culture in its order of development, we can grasp its meaning and significance as a concept in the vocabulary of modern social scientists and, indeed, of all educated people.

Culture as the Social Heritage   One thing is readily apparent from reading about the concept of culture in the sociological and anthropological literature since Tylor defined it as ". . . that complex whole which includes knowledge, belief, art, morals, law, custom, and any other capabilities and habits acquired by man as a member of society"[4]: that culture, for social scientists, has been an *inclusive* term. Indeed, it easily borders on the idea that "everything is culture," for it has been defined to include all that man receives from previous generations as his social heritage. This particular emphasis upon the meaning of culture has its origin in the nineteenth century concern of social scientists to distinguish man's *cultural* world from the *biological,* and to delineate those aspects of behavior not biologically determined. Historically, it was part of the very struggle of social science to get established. During the latter decades of the last century, spurred by Charles Darwin's discoveries, biology was the new and exciting discipline, the one that seemed to be able to tell man most about himself. There was a strong tendency, therefore, to extend biological explanation into the area of social life—witness our long experience with ideas of inherited traits and of social instincts. Therefore, to view as culture all that is not genetically inherited helped enormously at one time to set the limits of biology and to establish the legitimate boundaries of the social sciences. It was one significant conceptual orientation in an emerging new view of man.

To define culture as man's social heritage, the sum total of what he receives from previous generations, emphasizes the fact that culture is *learned.* Tylor's definition does this in speaking of culture as "acquired by man as a member of society." It also speaks of the content of culture: "that complex whole which includes knowledge, belief, art, morals, law, custom, and any other capabilities and habits. . . ." But as a definition, it does not suggest why man needs culture.

Culture as a Social Adjustment   A concern with what culture was for was prominent in discussions among anthropologists from the late 1800s until recently. The answer was clear and unequivocal: culture was the means by which man adjusted to his environment; it was his means of survival. His

---

[4] Tylor, I, p. 1.

capacity to develop skills and knowledge testified to man's remarkable ability to adapt to a wide variety of physical environments. In their influential book, *The Science of Society* (1927), one of the outstanding names in the first generation of American sociologists, William Graham Sumner (1840–1910), and his student and associate, Charles Keller, discussed culture (which they spoke of as custom, folkways and mores) as men's "adjustments" to their "life-conditions."[5] This emphasis upon culture as adjustment is clearly rooted in nineteenth century social science. Specifically, it emerges from the intellectual context of social evolution, in which man's necessary adaptation to changing conditions had to be made culturally. Biological evolution is a slow process over eons of time, and biologically, man does not make rapid changes for purposes of adjustment. Furthermore, biological evolution has apparently left him without an instinctive apparatus that *biologically* adjusts him to specific physical environments. What man does possess is a human capacity to learn from experience and thus to adapt to varying circumstances by modes of learned behavior. Man devises ways of adjusting to the necessary demands of the physical environment in order to ensure his own survival. Over long periods of time, as men accumulate learning from experience, and as they are increasingly able to shape their own social world within the world of nature, there is a slow evolving of more complex cultures. This is social evolution.

Social evolution was one of the major ideas of social science in the 1800s. As a concept, it was clearly borrowed and adapted from the concept of evolution in biology, where the work of Darwin and others had revolutionized the conception of life on earth. The sweeping intellectual power of the idea made it an attractive analogy for social scientists. Herbert Spencer (1820–1903) was the best known and most intellectually gifted of those earlier sociologists who used an organic analogy and a social evolutionary approach in studying society. But social evolution has ceased to be an acceptable model for the analysis of human society, and comparing society to an organism has long since come to be regarded as a fruitless scientific analogy. Tylor's definition of culture—and remember that his definition was written in 1871—fitted in with the social evolutionary approach. It sought to emphasize what was *not* biological at a time when biological evolution was a scientific theory to which was attributed a capacity to explain much about human behavior. Culture was a powerful concept that clearly stated what it was that man created for himself.

Culture is Shared   Social scientists have always defined culture as *shared* and as common to some group of people; it is never a personal phenomenon. This

---

[5] William Graham Sumner and Charles Keller, *The Science of Society* (New Haven, Conn.: Yale University Press, 1927), I. See especially Part I, pp. 3–92.

emphasis upon the shared and common quality of culture leads to a concern to identify the human population within which there is such a sharing. Herein lies a problem, rooted in the historic differences in analytic interests of anthropologists and sociologists. The anthropologists have studied culture among primitive and peasant peoples. As a consequence, they have often sought to delineate, not culture, but *a* culture, the way of life of such a people. They have viewed culture as an entity, as having organization and coherence, so that the various components of culture that Tylor enumerated somehow fit together into a consistent scheme. But for sociologists, the sharing of culture was a different problem. Their researches have not usually been directed to an analysis of an entire people, particularly since sociologists have concentrated on modern, industrial societies. Though most sociologists seem to have accepted the anthropological conception of a culture as a whole, few sociologists ever studied it that way. Instead, most sociological studies were interested in some cultural elements—norms, values, or political beliefs—shared in some segment —ethnic group or social class—of a large society. For the sociologist, to identify who did and who did not share, say, a social value helped to explain why some people acted in a particular way and others did not.

If anthropologists could speak of Navaho culture or of Hopi culture—as they did—by implication there was also American culture or French culture. But practically all American sociologists were involved in studying segments of American life. The nearest they came to studying culture as a whole was in examining the central and decisive values and beliefs of some social group, such as a delinquent gang, or even of some large interacting segment of the population, such as the working class or adolescents. For this purpose, sociologists came to speak of a *subculture*, to identify the distinctive set of beliefs and values that were consistent with and helped make intelligible the particular social conduct of these people. In particular, sociologists have invoked the concept of subculture when the beliefs and values were seen as inconsistent or even in conflict with the values taken to be dominant within the society. The sociologist, J. Milton Yinger, has suggested that here we might more accurately speak of *contraculture*.[6]

Culture as a Whole   Let us return now to the issue of culture viewed as a whole. The experience of anthropologists in studying small preliterate and peasant societies understandably generated in them an interest in specifying the whole fabric of life of such a people: the total network of social interaction that was their society and the complete set of cultural elements that could be called their culture. If there were among such elements some (even

[6] J. Milton Yinger, "Contraculture and Subculture," *American Sociological Review*, 25 (October, 1960), 625–635.

many) that were to be found elsewhere, there were also many that were unique. What was crucial for the anthropologist was not simply an enumeration of those cultural elements unique to a people, but a concern for testing the idea that the culture shared by a people is more than a mere collection or aggregate of such elements. What the anthropologist looked for was some internal consistency among the cultural elements, a relationship of one to another that revealed an internal logic. A culture was seen as an organized entity, with coherence and pattern, just what the linguist had taught us to be true about the organization of any language.

But for the American sociologist the existence of an integrated culture among the people of a great, industrial national society was something else again. At the least, it was not obvious to casual observation. The sheer magnitude of a large, modern society made evident an almost uncountable number of cultural elements, and defied any effort at detailed ethnographic description. But the scientific concern of the sociologist had not focused primarily upon delineating the outlines of a total culture. That was hardly his problem. Sociology had come into existence when the consciousness of modern man manifested a persistent anxiety about the possibly destructive impact of industrialization on human society. Intimations of change, disruption, and disorganization were frequent in the observations of sociologists. The integration of society (and thus, inferentially, of culture) was problematic, a question to be answered, not a premise about contemporary reality to be taken for granted. There can be little mystery, then, that sociologists did not undertake the task of demonstrating the existence of *an* American culture. Whether there was some integrated pattern of cultural elements that could be called American culture was, at best, an hypothesis viewed favorably by some (probably most) sociologists, unfavorably by others, and simply a matter of indifference to still others concerned with quite other kinds of problems.

The conception of culture as an integrated whole has perhaps been most significant to those sociologists who made use of the concept of subculture, for they were often trying to find an integrated pattern of beliefs and values made evident in the behavior of some social group, but not in the whole society. Sociologists studying prisons, military organizations, or high schools, or observing street-corner gangs, dope addicts, hippies, or professional thieves have often looked for some integrating pattern of values and beliefs that constitute a distinctive interpretation of human experience. Other sociologists, particularly in studying less deviant subcultures, have done the same thing in speaking of *life-style*, a term that seems to serve in many cases as a synonym for subculture. Thus, "the suburban life-style" invokes a conception of a somewhat consistent way of living among middle-class Americans who reside in highly homogeneous suburbs, and who generally commute to the central city for employment. It suggests that a pattern of shared values and beliefs are revealed in common behavioral patterns, and thus there is some reasonable consistency between belief and conduct.

Yet, many sociologists have treated culture as an integrated whole when they borrowed the terminology of the anthropologist Clyde Kluckhohn, who (with W. H. Kelly) spoke of culture as a "design for living." Kluckhohn said: "A culture is an historically created system of explicit and implicit designs for living, which tends to be shared by all or specially designated members of a group at a specified point in time."[7] Such a perspective seems to view culture as an historically derived pattern that guides and directs the behavior of those who share it. It is not equated with actual behavior but is thought of as a model of idealized behavior, a prescribed structure of expectancies.

Culture as Material and Nonmaterial If by culture we mean all that men manage to create and then transmit as a social heritage, what about technology and the material artifacts that men construct? Are these, too, not culture? Almost all discussions of culture among social scientists makes some reference to material objects. For many decades social scientists did indeed use the term material culture to refer to tools, buildings, boats and wagons, decorative objects, and the like, and the term nonmaterial culture to refer to values and beliefs, knowledge, and ideas. But the more recent position is that these objects are not, in themselves included in the concept of culture. However, the *definition* of these objects—the knowledge of how to make them, how to use them, and what value to place upon them—is included. A wedding ring, for example, is a small artifact. This physical object becomes a wedding ring only because an object of such dimensions and physical characteristics is *defined* as a wedding ring by people for whom this is its meaning and use. Such an object, if found by, perhaps, a South American Indian tribe, might be a curiosity of no known meaning, or it might be converted to quite different functions, perhaps to symbolize something other than marriage. In short, a ring is a wedding ring because we define it to be so, because the artifact carries for us this meaning. It is a *symbol,* embodied in a concrete form, of a particular human relationship. "Culture" lies in the symbolic meaning of the object, not in the object itself.

The Concept of Culture: Varied and Changing Over the past century the concept of culture has not remained static. It is to be expected in any scientific field that basic concepts are refined and redefined as changing usage and scientific developments alter their meaning and significance. But for the sociologist, certain basic ideas about culture have persisted amid a welter of

---

[7] Clyde Kluckhohn and W. H. Kelly, "The Concept of Culture," in Ralph Linton, ed., *The Science of Man in the World Crisis* (New York: Columbia University Press, 1945), pp. 78–107.

changing definitions. Talcott Parsons has noted *three* such ideas: "First, that culture is *transmitted,* it constitutes a heritage or a social tradition; secondly, that it is *learned,* it is not a manifestation, in particular content, of man's genetic constitution; and third, that it is *shared.*"[8] It is probably quite safe to say that most sociologists still stress these as basic to a conception of culture.

Yet, two critical observations about conceptualizing culture in this established fashion are warranted. First of all, an emphasis upon culture as social heredity may fail to make the equally valid point that no social heritage is transmitted unchanged and intact from generation to generation. For the sociologist today, and indeed for all social scientists engaged in studying the modern world, social and cultural change is the dominant issue. Old structures and old traditions are being replaced by new ones, albeit not always without conflict or resistance. To say, accurately enough, that man learns his culture and transmits it to the next generation fails, however, to build into the conception of culture the necessary recognition that culture changes. We must remember that culture is generated by men out of their interaction with one another; men *create* culture. Each generation takes its social heritage, uses it, and recreates it by adding new cultural elements before transmitting it to the next generation. The recognition that culture *persists* over time is necessary to our conception of it, but this persistance must not be emphasized at the expense of the equally necessary conception that culture *changes,* that men can and do discard cultural elements and create new ones. Culture is created by men out of their experiences in interaction, and so culture changes as do human experiences.

By the same token, one of the difficulties with "design for living" as a definition of culture is that it implies the idea of a behavioral blueprint, a pattern already laid out in advance, to which men will normally conform. Although some people's behavior does conform to almost blueprinted prescriptions for behavior, this occurs only in a highly stable world in which the prescriptions and expectations derived from the past still adequately fit the present. But social change means that people face new situations, and the "designs" must be redesigned.

Secondly, culture is not merely a process of adapting to an environment for survival. Not all culture enhances biological survival. Medicine, for example, improves the chances for human survival. But when some people refuse medicine for religious reasons, culture has inhibited biological survival. Culture, however, is also concerned with much that goes beyond survival. This concern for survival is a heritage of the nineteenth century perspective that stressed the adaptation and evolution of organic species in the physical environment, in which the capacity of man to survive had to be viewed in more than biological terms. Such successful adaptation to the physical environment hardly

[8] Talcott Parsons, *The Social System* (New York: Free Press, 1951), p. 15.

seems to be the issue of theoretical import that it was a century ago. It is not that culture does not have a survival meaning for man, for it only too obviously does. But this concern for survival is no longer either a theoretical or a practical one for modern man (except for the obvious issue about his capacity to destroy himself with nuclear power). Modern men are changing their world drastically by building new societies from old and traditional ones. Nor is the physical environment the source of danger it once was to preliterate and peasant peoples; modern man has constructed a technological civilization that impressively extends his control and mastery of nature. Whatever threat now exists for mankind is not in nature but in culture itself, in the scientific capacity for both good and evil, but is even more in the meanings and definitions that men apply to one another, making possible both race genocide and a cold war that can escalate into nuclear holocaust.

The necessary context for understanding culture in our time is not merely the fact of rapid and often revolutionary change, but the growing awareness that man can deliberately change his culture and create it anew. The impressive power of science and technology has bred a new generation of social thinkers who proclaim confidently that we can create the future, deliberately and rationally. They are committed to designing the future state of affairs through the innovation of new cultural forms and new social structures. These "futurists" seek to alter our settled perceptions of reality, our received wisdom, and to create new perceptions and outlooks, new meanings about the potentialities of human existence. In such a context, culture is better seen analytically in terms of the meanings and understandings that men share with one another in constructing their social world. Perhaps this recognition first emerges when social scientists began to leave the artifact out of the definition of culture and to assert that what was cultural was the meaning of the artifact in social interaction, not the artifact itself. From there, it was but a short step to the idea that what man transmits is *meaning*, conveyed by symbols.

Culture as Symbolic The felt need of the contemporary generation of social scientists to redefine the concept of culture is not by any means restricted to sociologists; anthropologists, too, have shared in this redefining process. Almost 30 years ago, Robert Redfield hinted at what was to come when he said, "Culture is an organization of conventional understandings manifest in act and artifact."[9] Perhaps the most influential outcome of this has been a definition of culture offered jointly by two of this generation's most distinguished social scientists, the sociologist, Talcott Parsons, and the anthropologist, A. L. Kroeber. They defined culture as: "transmitted and created content and patterns of values, ideas, and other symbolic-meaningful systems as factors in

[9] Robert Redfield, *The Folk Culture of Yucatan* (Chicago: The University of Chicago Press, 1941), p. 133.

the shaping of human behavior and the artifacts produced through behavior."[10] Take particular note of this definition; observe the balance struck by deliberately referring to both "transmitted and created." Observe also that artifacts are *not* included in the definition of culture; instead, culture shapes the artifacts that are "produced through behavior." A definition similar in intent is somewhat differently worded is the recent one by Philip and Gertrude Selznick: "Culture consists of everything that is produced by, and is capable of sustaining, shared symbolic experience."[11] The central idea is that man has the creative capacity to give meaning to behavior, to events, and even to nonsocial phenomena; to confer or bestow a meaning that is not found in the object itself but is created by man out of those experiences in which the objects become meaningful to him. Perhaps no better expression of this newer view has been given than the conception of culture offered by Max Weber: " 'Culture' is a finite segment of the meaningless infinity of the world process, a segment on which *human beings* confer meaning and significance."[12]

All of the above definitions emphasize the *symbol* as basic to a conception of culture. The meaning that men bestow upon a segment of the world process is expressed through symbols, whether these be words, actions, or material objects. The cross and the flag are objects that serve as significant symbols, evoking a rich pattern of ideas, values, and emotions. Similarly, the donkey and the elephant are symbols for two American political parties. Music can be symbolic—think of the type of music appropriate for church, for funerals, for patriotic occasions, for military marches, and for dances. But language is the basic symbolic process; all other symbols depend upon man using language to enter into symbolic interaction with others.

So What Is Culture? We have been trying to show that what the social scientist means by the concept of culture has consistently undergone a change of meaning, though sometimes this is but a shift of emphasis. This is to be expected, for concepts do not remain static when there is scientific development. To this point in the chapter, we have presented the briefest of excursions into the history of the changing meaning of the concept of culture, intended only to highlight those changes, significant for the sociologist's use of the concept.

Culture, then, has two divergent though related meanings. A still useful conception conceives of culture as encompassing the vast range of nonbiological phenomena that men themselves *create* and then *transmit* from one generation to another. It constitutes a *social heritage,* albeit an ever changing

[10] Talcott Parsons and A. L. Kroeber, "The Concepts of Culture and of Social System," *American Sociological Review,* 23 (October 1958), 582–583.

[11] Gertrude Jaeger [Selznick] and Philip Selznick, "A Normative Theory of Culture," *American Sociological Review,* 29 (October, 1964), 653–669.

[12] Max Weber, *The Methodology of the Social Sciences* (New York: Free Press, 1949), p. 81.

one. Another conception of culture places emphasis upon the fact that man organizes his life and gives meaning and significance to it by means of symbols. It clearly implies that human beings desire to do more than organically survive. Through symbols people confer meaning upon their lives and construct styles of life. The values that they create are then used to interpret and organize their lives within the limits of objective contingencies and human power. Human beings, in essence, do not merely biologically *exist*, they *live* by values and meanings expressed in symbols. This more recent conception of culture, then, views it as a symbolic pattern of values and ideas, a relatively coherent set of meanings and understandings.

THE SOCIAL NORM

The social order that a people share and maintain is at the same time a moral order. Social life is not possible without some agreement upon and relative adherence to moral rules and standards that define what people "ought" to do in given situations. Only a man alone on a desert island might be free of moral restraints on his behavior. But as long as men live a collective existence, their social lives are governed by a moral consensus, however relative and less than complete that consensus may be. All social behavior is normatively oriented; that is, given direction and definition by *norms,* rules of conduct that specify the "should" and "ought" of behavior in social situations. Such norms are significant elements of culture.

Norms can obviously vary in their importance to the group in which they are held, and in the intensity by which they are believed in. William Graham Sumner made a famous distinction between *folkways* and *mores* that has long since become a basic part of the sociological vocabulary.[13] Folkways are those customary ways of doing things that are usually accepted as the right way, such as manners, ways of greeting people, correctness of attire. Violation of folkways does not necessarily bring punishment, though it may result in ridicule or gossip; such violations suggest that the person is somewhat incompetent in the customs of the group, and he may consequently suffer in the eyes of others. His very desire for good standing serves to exact conformity to the folkways, but those who deliberately persist in violating some folkways are not likely to suffer too severely. Indeed, they may even profit by a reputation for being different or interesting, independent, or nonconformist.

Mores, however, are those standards that people regard as crucial for the welfare of the group. In this case, a violation is a serious matter and generally means that some kind of group-enforced punishment will be invoked. It is

[13] William Graham Sumner, *Folkways* (Boston: Ginn, 1907).

one thing not to wear a necktie in a situation that usually prescribes one, but it is quite another thing to violate group standards about the rights of persons to their lives, property, and social opportunities. Similarly, it is a serious matter to abrogate one's obligations to a wife and children, to a business partner, or to anyone with whom one has entered into a contractual relationship.

Group life is built around conceptions of rights and privileges, obligations, and duties, all of which are morally significant to the groups' members. No sociological analysis of group life can, therefore, ignore the normative element in human behavior. Norms are regulative and controlling standards that exist as shared moral expectations of behavior. Social order is necessarily moral order. When the moral standards are put into a written code, with specified punishment for violation, and social agencies are created to enforce them, these written rules constitute *law*. Law, in effect, is a body of *institutionalized norms*. (We shall examine the meaning of *institution* in a later chapter.)

Social norms emerge out of the social interaction that creates a social order and are an integral part of that order. Like the very behavior they serve to regulate, however, they are subject to change as new situations and problems develop for the group. Thus, however sacred and revered some norms may be for a social group, they are not immutable and eternal; they change, as does all life. Folkways, of course, are more easily subject to change than are mores. Moral standards intensely held and defining the behavior taken by its members as most crucial for the very cultural meaning of the group, will change less easily, and efforts at change are likely to produce conflict within the group. Laws are particularly susceptible to this, for they are backed by agencies that have the obligation to enforce them, even when changes have made them no longer popular or even morally acceptable. Although laws can and frequently are repealed, they nonetheless clearly present greater difficulties in the problems of normative change than do those that are not so institutionalized.

INTERACTION AND CULTURE

If social interaction is symbolic, then men interact in a cultural context, for the symbols that mediate their interaction are cultural elements. Symbols express values and meanings that are collectively held and give orientation to the processes of interaction. Social interaction thus occurs in a context of cultural meanings: men communicate in interaction through language; they define each other as well as the situation in which they interact; they express values and beliefs; and they act in terms of what they take to be the common understandings they share with others. Social interaction, therefore, cannot be conceived of sociologically without culture; it cannot be sociologically described if denuded of the meanings and norms that the actors share in the very process of interaction. From another angle, we would stress the idea that when men interact, they do so in situations that are culturally defined and they do so on the basis of meaning, values, and norms that they carry with them into the interaction situations. Interaction always proceeds so as to manifest the cultural elements. Culture *precedes* any given interaction, just as society exists prior to any given individual.

But that same culture is the *product* of historically past interactions and, thus, is subject to the influence of new interactions. If culture shapes social interaction, interaction has consequences for culture. Every interaction is common *experience* for its participants; they derive from the interaction some meaning that remains after the interaction is over. Such experience can and frequently does reinforce the values and meanings that were there when the interaction began. But experience does not always validate existing culture; it may modify it or even bring a new cultural element, a new attitude or value or meaning, into being. Thus, interaction can produce a change in culture as well as serve to sustain culture.

Interaction and *culture,* then, are two basic concepts central to the sociological perspective. They convey a conception of man that stresses that he creates his social life by his interactions with others and that he orients himself to his world, to his very human existence, by a set of shared meanings and values, itself a creation of past human interactions. If social life is constructed out of past experience in interaction with others, it is also continually modified through the continuing experience provided by social interaction. Such a perspective tells us that social life is in constant flux and that social order is relative, not absolute. Nor is social order the antithesis of change. If the sociologist's task is the search for order in social life, if he looks for the more stable patterns of interaction, he is assuming that there are some persistent structural features, some recurring processes in social interaction; he is assuming that a discoverable order lies beneath the confusing change and variation that appears before our eyes. This is a scientifically legitimate assumption, an intellectually reasonable one, and practically, a necessary one—necessary, if men are to orient themselves to the world around them in such a way as to act and to confer a viable meaning on their lives.

While it is necessary and reasonable to make this assumption of order, it is equally necessary to remember that this is a construct of the human mind, a cognitive mode of orientation to observable phenomena, an intellectual abstraction intended to foster analysis. It should not be *reified,* that is, treated as if it named a real thing. If this is done, then perhaps we can avoid that common error implicit in so much sociological analysis, namely, to talk of order separate from change and to overemphasize the stability to be found in social life.

1. A gathering of young adults.
2. A drum majorette and marching companion.
3. Watching Daddy shave.
4. Ben Shahn's painting, *Everyman*.
5. California girl, alone among the motorcycles.
6. Playing "grown-up."

4

5

6

THE PERSON
IN SOCIETY

6

There has been no end in Western thought—and none apparently in sight—to discussion of the ancient issue of the relation of the individual to society. In our time, when to "drop out" for many young people means to drop out of society, not merely out of school, there is a strong sense of strain in this unavoidable relation. Some of the most important writing in our century has explored the idea that there is an inevitable conflict between the person and the collectivity in which he is a member. The contemporary versions of this ancient issue then suggest once more what intellectual confusion there always seems to be about such things as *individual* and *society*.

For the student of society, the study of human personality is a closely related yet quite distinct enterprise; it belongs to the discipline of psychology. But despite the understandable efforts of sociologists to build a theory of society without reference to psychological theories of any kind, some conception of human nature and of the relation of the individual to society is necessarily built into sociological work, albeit often only in unstated and unconscious assumptions. Emile Durkheim is the foremost name among those sociologists intent on creating a discipline of sociology, the propositions and generalizations of which could not be reduced to psychological principles. For Durkheim, there was a need to validate sociology, to fight off a possible psychological monopoly on explaining man's action, and to make men aware of the necessity of giving due credence to the place of social factors in social-scientific explanations. Since Durkheim, sociologists have properly resisted a "psychologizing" of social structure, but they need, nonetheless, to explicate the psychological assumptions underlying the concept of society and of social interaction, assumptions about the nature of human nature and of the person.

John Locke, Jean-Jacques Rousseau and Thomas Hobbes are among those who wrestled with this issue, and their answers have become intellectual perspectives that have by no means disappeared from modern thought. All three were exponents of the *social contract* theory of society, an interpretation that views men as having consciously imposed upon a "state of nature" a deliberately constructed phenomenon: society. They argued that men were born free and unencumbered but had assumed the trappings and limitations of society for the sake of their common welfare. Men preceded society, their human nature thus being independent of it. Rousseau saw this nature of man as noble but chained and corrupted by society, whereas Hobbes viewed it as brutal and selfish.

But the origin of human society was not the primary interest of the social contract theorists. What did concern them was the source of the social bonds that tied men together into a society—an issue, we saw previously, that also concerned the sociologists of the nineteenth century. Hobbes is usually recognized as having stated the problem—what Talcott Parsons called "the Hobbesian problem of order"—by his assertion that men's actions stem from their "passions," and their passions are different and independent, not common.[1] Thus, any one man can be an obstacle to another man's successful pursuit of the goals set by his passions. If each man sought vigorously to satisfy his personal passions, the resulting conflict could not avoid being what Hobbes, in a famous phrase, called "the war of every man against every man."[2] Human society, then, comes to be necessary, something men have to invent in order to submerge their individual interests in a common welfare that will avoid destructive conflict. For Hobbes, then, society is a necessary mechanism for regulating and restraining the naturally brutal and selfish behavior of men.

But for many contemporary social scientists, the Hobbesian problem is not a problem at all. There is no separation between the individual and society for them, and certainly they accept no "state of nature." That human nature is shaped and developed within and through society, not prior to or outside of it, is a fundamental proposition of modern social science. Man becomes human and social only through his participation in society. The anthropologist, Ruth Benedict, argued that there "is no proper antagonism between the role of society and that of the individual."[3] "Most people," she said, "are shaped to the form of their culture because of the enormous malleability of their original endowment. They are plastic to the moulding force of the society into which they are born."[4] Man lives in, not outside of, society—and so, in fact, do most primates—and thus there is no "state of nature." The persistent myth that there is flourished in Europe from the seventeenth century on, stimulated in part apparently by the discovery of preliterate peoples, and a romantic interpretation of them as being more free and uninhibited than man in literate society. But subsequent anthropological study has made it clear that such people are less free in an individualistic sense; they are much more bound to custom and ritual, and that the individualism valued by modern men emerges in a complex society, not a simple one.

But if today's social scientists reject the position of Hobbes, Locke, and Rousseau about a human nature independent of society, and thus find the Hobbesian problem no problem at all, there are still strong proponents of the position that there are some human attributes that are not derived from society, though they may be influenced by social experience. Sigmund Freud is probably the most significant name in our century to argue for an image of man that imputed to him "instinctual endowments," among which was a "powerful share of aggressiveness."[5] Freud spoke glumly of the rapacity and

---

[1] Talcott Parsons, *The Structure of Social Action* (New York: McGraw-Hill, 1937), pp. 89–94.

[2] Thomas Hobbes, *Leviathan* (Oxford, England: James Thornton, 1881), p. 95.

[3] Ruth Benedict, *Patterns of Culture* (Baltimore: Penguin, 1946), p. 232.

[4] Benedict, p. 235.

[5] Sigmund Freud, *Civilization and Its Discontents* (New York: Norton, 1961), p. 58.

exploitation of man by other men: "Homo homini lupus" (man is a wolf to man), he said.[6] Within recent years, let it be noted, there has been a re-emergence of literature asserting the "natural" aggressiveness of man. Among sociologists, Dennis Wrong asserts that modern sociology presents an *over-socialized* view of man and an *overintegrated* view of society.[7] What Wrong objects to is the view of man that sees him as nothing but the *role-player,* so thoroughly socialized by society that there is a complete internalization of the norms of society producing a consistency between person and society. Such a society, where role-expectations mesh into a smoothly working social system without friction or conflict, is what Wrong means by overintegrated.

This integrated view of man was apparent in most anthropological literature about primitive societies, particularly in the first half of this century. In time, it became an unspoken and possibly unconscious assumption about man in much of the sociological literature. According to Wrong, sociologists answered the Hobbesian question by stressing *internalization* of the social norms and *motivation* "to achieve a positive image of self by winning acceptance or status in the eyes of others."[8] Thus, the social constraints of society are viewed almost entirely as *self-controls,* producing a high degree of self-induced *conformity.* As he notes, "The degree to which conformity is frequently the result of coercion rather than conviction is minimized."[9] Indeed, if the oversocialized view of man is the scientifically correct one, how is it, "that violence, conflict, revo-lution, and the individual's sense of coercion by society manage to exist at all . . .?"[10] Wrong readily grants the major shaping influence of internaliza-tion and the motivation for acceptance, but he balks at regarding this as a theory of human nature. "All men are socialized in the latter sense, but this does not mean that they have been completely molded by the particular norms and values of their culture."[11] He turns to Freud's view of man as "a *social* animal without being entirely a *socialized* animal,"[12] and then asserts: "His very social nature is the source of conflicts that create resistance to socializa-tion by the norms of any of the societies which have existed in the course of human history."[13]

Sociologists overreacted to previous conceptions of human nature stated largely in biological terms, says Wrong, by establishing an image of man as

[6] Freud, p. 58.
[7] Dennis Wrong, "The Oversocialized Conception of Man in Modern Sociology," *American Sociological Review,* 26 (April, 1961), 183–193.
[8] Wrong, p. 185.
[9] Wrong, p. 188.
[10] Wrong, p. 186.
[11] Wrong, p. 192.
[12] Wrong, p. 192.
[13] Wrong, p. 192.

completely socialized. He feels that they have leaned too far and have ignored the *body,* as well as sex and power drives, and material interests. Neither biological determinism nor psychologism need be assumed while working with an adequate conception of human nature. Wrong warns the sociologist that if his "sociological theory over-stresses the stability and integration of society we will end up imagining that man is the disembodied, conscience-driven, status-seeking phantom of current theory."[14]

This attack upon a sociologically inadequate conception of man has prompted sociologists to reexamine their assumptions about human nature and to meet these objections. Wrong, in turn, has been criticized for falling back upon drives and instincts and, thus, for assuming some universal biological nature of man that resists socialization. Many sociologists have argued that there is and must always be norm-violating (*contra-normative*) action just because the norms of any society are always inconsistent and contradictory, and this is particularly true in a large, complex society. The process of socialization, then, cannot help but yield inconsistencies and conflicts rather than any easy fit in the relation of the individual to society. Of course, there is always some sense in which there is agreement between individual and society—there has to be— yet there is also always conflict. Judith Blake and Kingsley Davis have reviewed a vast amount of sociological literature to make the case that the sources of *contra-normative* action lie, not in man's biological drives, but in the complex relation of the individual to society and its norms.[15] They point out that norms do not merely motivate desired behavior, but that they also can legitimate cruelty, horror, and violence. That there is no perfect fit between individual and society, then, and that man is not the perfectly compliant creature who wants only to conform to norms and live up to social expectations, in no way denies that he is social and only becomes so by his interaction with others in a society. Some such conception of the nature of man is implicit in all sociological analysis.

SOCIALIZATION

The existence of any society depends upon the existence of people who share in the culture, and who know how to play the roles and otherwise manifest the action that makes of the society an ongoing process. In one very important sense, society only exists in the minds of its members, those who

[14] Wrong, p. 193.

[15] Judith Blake and Kingsley Davis, "Norms, Values, and Sanctions," in Robert E. L. Faris, ed., *Handbook of Modern Sociology* (Skokie, Ill.: Rand-McNally, 1964).

know what people are supposed to do, who can do it, and who believe in the importance of doing it. But man is a most mortal creature, and the life of a society always exceeds the life of a person or of a generation. To be continuous, a society must engage in the constant process of inducting new members into it. It must turn the human raw material of newborn infants into successfully functioning members of society. No human is born a fully developed person; indeed, he is not a person at all, but a human organism who knows nothing and can do practically nothing. At birth he is totally helpless and dependent on others, and has, relative to other organisms, a longer period of learning and developing in which he remains dependent. Everything he eventually will know and be able to do, he must learn.

If a society, then, continually needs to acquire new members, individuals need the organized society as a milieu within which their dependency is recognized and provided for, in order that they may have the time and the kinds of experience that will enable them to develop into functioning persons. The social and human characteristics of persons are not there at birth; they develop over time only when and if the individual is involved with others in the experiences of living in a society.

Since a child is always cared for by others and would die if not, there is little contrary evidence against which to test the proposition that one becomes human only by being in society. How do we know how much man gets from his interaction with others and how much is inborn and native to him, if all men exist from birth in a society? What evidence there is comes from a very few cases of children who survived physically even though in virtual isolation from human contact—*feral* children—and who were thus denied the humanizing influence of the socialization process. Two actual cases observed by the sociologist, Kingsley Davis, were girls who had missed the first six years of normal socialization.[16] Both were unable to speak, and one could not walk or in fact make any move for herself. They had no "mind" as we know it; one was completely apathetic and apparently without emotion, whereas the other manifested fear and hostility toward others. Both were believed to be feebleminded at first, but in fact they made considerable progress toward recovering the pattern of learning and cultural meaning they had failed to acquire earlier. But the condition Davis observed in both when they were six-year-old organisms presents us with an impressive argument that the development of the human organism requires interaction and communication with others to become human. As further evidence, studies by René Spitz and William Goldfarb[16a] have compared impersonal if physically adequate infant care to the normal mothering a child receives. The infants without mothering

[16] Kingsley Davis, *Human Society* (New York: Macmillan, 1949), pp. 204–208.
[16a] For a review of evidence and sources, see Blake and Davis, p. 471.

displayed apathy and little emotional response and their death rate, despite good physical conditions, was much higher than for those cared for by their mothers.

Such evidence as this does seem to provide reason to say that the individual *acquires* his social nature. The process by which he does so is called *socialization.* Individual and society, then, are not two different things, but exist within the same social process. One of the foremost names in American sociology, Charles Horton Cooley (1864–1929), put it this way: "A separate individual is an abstraction unknown to experience, and so likewise is society when regarded as something apart from individuals."[17] Human society is nothing more than the system of interactions that occur among individuals, but the person is equally a product of those same interactions. Thus, the individual is no more (and, of course, no less) "real" than is society. Indeed, the concepts of *person* and *character* are conceptual abstractions, just as are *society* and *group.* None of these words denote physical entities; the physical substance that is the body or organism is essential to being a person but is not to be confused with the person.

How a human being becomes socialized is a complex process as yet only partially understood. The psychological dynamics of the process are of primary interest to the psychologist, but the sociologist needs to know not only that it does occur but also something about the basic process of interaction by which it occurs. No matter how devoid of personality the newborn infant may be, he is loved and nurtured as a person by loving parents—at least, most infants are, and those who are not fail to develop and mature in the same manner as others. From the outset, other persons treat him as a valued person, care for him, respond to his cries, and engage him in interaction from the first early moment when he responds to others. Gradually, the new human learns. He acquires skills, learns the common meaning of objects in his environment and their ordinary use, learns to identify persons, to respond to them, and to communicate with them. This act of *communication* is crucial for the socialization process, for now the new human begins to enter the complex symbolic world of man, and to learn and to share in the culture.

Communication is possible because of *language,* and the early acquisition of language by the new human enables him to participate in more complex social interaction and to acquire distinctly social characteristics. George Herbert Mead (1864–1931), a contemporary of Cooley's and a philosopher who contributed significantly to the development of the idea of *symbolic interaction,* stressed this crucial role of language in learning and socialization. The acquisition of language not only permits more subtle and influential interaction by the new

---

[17] Charles Horton Cooley, *Human Nature and the Social Order* (New York: Scribner, 1902), p. 236.

human, it is also a major factor in the development of the organism into a person, which occurs when a *self* begins to emerge. Prior to this, society as experienced by the new human is an *external* process, something "out there" that constrains and controls him, which compels him to do some things and does not let him do others. In the processing of learning this, he discovers that it is *others* who will not allow him to do something; but this constraint on his behavior, this control over his actions, is still something outside of himself. The notable Swiss psychologist, Jean Piaget, has made the point that morality is external to the very young child and exists only by virtue of the authority of the parent.

Although the *externality* of a moral sense is characteristic of the child in his early years, perhaps his first step toward the development of a self occurs very early, when he is first able to discriminate among objects in his experience. At some quite early point, the new human knows that the world around him is made up of separate and distinct objects, and he learns to tell one from another; he can tell mother from father long before he knows the words or understands the relationships. This capacity to perceive the world as a congeries of discrete objects permits him to engage in differential interaction with those other selves who are objects to him. But while other persons are objects to him, that is, are distinct and identifiable units in a surrounding milieu, he is not as yet an object to himself. He is conscious of others, but he is not yet self-conscious.

The concept of *self* has its meaning in this process of being aware of and responding to oneself, even as one responds to other persons. But to be able to respond to oneself, to evaluate oneself, to approve or disapprove of oneself, requires that one be able to look at oneself from the outside—to be an object to oneself. This capacity to get outside ourselves develops only through social interaction and the development of that empathic quality that enables us to see from the perspective of another. Cooley suggested that we all undergo a process of imagining how we appear in the eyes of others, depending on what judgments or responses those others make, and of then feeling mortified or pleased or whatever about this. This process of a self-image as we see it reflected in others, Cooley called the "looking glass self."[18] This concept, formulated in 1902, was one of the first efforts to understand the development of the self as a consequence of social interaction. George Herbert Mead carried this approach even further. His remarkable set of ideas about language, mind, and the development of the self has profoundly influenced our understanding of the relation of the person to society.[19]

---

[18] Cooley, pp. 183–184.

[19] See George Herbert Mead, *Mind, Self, and Society* (Chicago: University of Chicago Press, 1934), especially Chapters II and III.

The Meadian Perspective   Mead started from the fact that interaction and communication could and indeed do exist for animals without language. Each newborn human also engages in interaction before he learns any language, and through such interaction he learns the meaning of *natural signs,* such as facial expressions and voice tones, so that he knows when another is pleased or angry. The learning of *gestures* forms the basis for learning language; the child already knows the meaning of many objects and events before he learns the words for them. Once language is a part of the socialization process, however, it makes possible ideas about behavior; now the child can engage in that mental process we call thinking. Thus, to learn language is to acquire a mind. The child can now reflect upon others' actions toward him and also about the meaning of his own actions.

The interaction between the child and a significant other such as his mother now involves his learning the attitudes that are expressed in words, which convey emotional responses of liking and disliking, approving and disapproving. When language opens up the complex world of symbolic communication, he not only learns to speak like others, he also learns to use language to convey the same ideas and feelings as they do toward the familiar objects in the environment: he learns to respond in similar fashion.

Like Cooley, Mead noticed how children imitate adults in their actions and how significant this is in their learning. For Mead, this meant that, *by taking the roles of others,* the child learns how they respond to objects around them; thus, he is able to internalize these responses as his own. By taking their roles, he learns to feel and think as they do. At first, this process is one of taking the role of a *particular* other, such as mother or father, but later it becomes taking the role of what Mead called the *generalized other.* Mead saw this aspect as best evident in children playing games, in which there are rules and general expectations of the group about the behavior of each participant. This generalized attitude of the group becomes evident to the individual child through his own participation, and through his sharing in the rules of the game. When he has general expectations of performance for every participant, including himself, he has invoked the generalized other within himself. He has now internalized social attitudes. What was once external is now within himself; what others expected of him, he now expects of himself. He has, in ordinary terms, a *conscience;* Mead called it the "me," in contrast to the unsocialized "I," whereas Freud called it the *superego.* Conscience is simply the internalization of the norms of society. It enables the individual to respond morally to his own actions and thoughts, and to judge himself as he perceives he would be judged by the community. Such a capacity for self-judgment means the individual now has a self that has developed through the individual's social interaction with others. This self possesses a consistency, though not a perfect one, and this consistency gives an integration to his actions. Indeed, many social psychologists see the self as an *organization,* for the self-image that develops is always a somewhat consistent one. The individual organizes his actions and his responses into a pattern that fits the self-image he possesses.

The Meadian perspective on socialization lets us see how society "gets into" the person, so that self and society are inseparable phenomena. Furthermore, the process of internalization suggests that the individual becomes a self-conscious member of society by taking on the attitudes of the community in general. But Mead was insistent that this is by no means all that there is to the self; while clearly *social,* in being formed through interaction with others, it is not simply determined in every aspect by society. Mead's famous distinction between the "I" and the "me" was his way of distinguishing between two aspects of self: the "me" is the socialized side, made up of internalized attitudes, whereas the "I" is a spontaneous, creative, even impulsive side, a *self-interested* side that takes into account the "me" but is not entirely controlled by it. Sigmund Freud had a somewhat similar idea when he advanced the concepts of *id, ego,* and *superego.* The latter is the same as Mead's "me," the internalized values, society inside the person. But the id is that basic biological force of life that cannot be socialized, only channeled and restrained. The ego, in turn, is a reality-oriented, mediating mechanism that functions between the id and the superego.

Neither of these influential efforts to delineate the nature of the self in any way denies the fact that socialization is a process whereby the norms and attitudes of society enter into and become part of the person; yet neither Mead nor Freud grant to society any complete victory over the person. Each recognized an element of the individual that is not fully socialized, so that the conduct of the person can never be totally explained as conformity to the norms of society. Nor does society ever totally control the person.

Agencies of Socialization As a social-psychological process, socialization occurs in all societies, primitive or modern. Since no society can avoid providing for the care of the young, agencies of socialization are a basic part of the social structure of all societies. The *family* unit is the most obvious instance of an agency of socialization. Though the structure of the family varies from one society to another, some arrangement of familial relationships becomes, in every society, a basic group to which is assigned responsibility for the care and nurturing of the very young. The extended dependency of the human infant requires that its needs be met by others and for quite some time. But the family role is more than that of meeting the needs of a dependent child, it also assumes the responsibility of teaching the young moral behavior and of training it in socially valued skills. Accordingly, it assumes control over the young human, becoming the representative of society's authority and exercising the external control necessary before the internalization of norms occurs.

Nevertheless it is not sufficient merely to meet the needs of the new human and exercise control over him; the milieu within which this occurs is also important. The family can be viewed as the most significant of the *primary groups* within which the new human has a place. The notion of the primary group was a contribution of Cooley's, and he developed the idea from his observations of the behavior of his own children in the family situation.[20] He conceived of the primary group as the small, intimate, face-to-face group within which it was possible for the new human to be significant to others, to be loved and wanted, and to be treated compassionately. Within such a milieu, Cooley saw the growth of love and affection and the creation of the moral sentiments of a mature human being. The significance of the primary group for socialization, as he envisaged it, was that within it human nature comes into existence. By human nature, Cooley meant those "sentiments and impulses" that separate the human from the animal and are universally characteristic of mankind. In short, the primary group is the cradle of human morality and ideals, of the fostering of a sense of decency and worth that becomes part of the human being for the whole of his existence. By Cooley's definition, the primary group is not only sociologically instrumental in humanizing man, but it is undoubtedly the most morally valuable group known to man.

But the family is not the only primary group important for socialization. The *peer group* functions to complement the family in socializing the individual. This group is the play group for the child and the teen-age gang or clique for the adolescent. In the interaction in such a group, the highly personal authority of a parent is replaced by the impersonal authority of a group. It is the peer group that provides the experience of internalizing the generalized other. The peer group also provides significant experiences for the child in learning to interact successfully, to be accepted by others, and to achieve a status for himself in a circle of friends. Unlike the family circle, the child has no assurance of being accepted—he is not guaranteed a place as he is in the family.

There is another important difference between socialization by family and by peer group: the family's socialization prepares the child for participation in the society and into those segments of it—such as social class and ethnic groups—in which the family has status. But the peer group socializes the child to the world of children and adolescents and to the values and perspectives that age-grading produces.

---

[20] See Cooley, *Social Organization* (New York: Scribner, 1909).

The family and peer groups, then, are the significant agencies for the socialization of the child in society. They provide the small and intimate contexts of personal relationships in which personality is shaped, and a self is developed. Eventually, a fully socialized adult is ready to assume his place in society, familiar with its social roles and acceptable behavioral patterns, and has internalized the emotional and moral perspectives appropriate to the role-demands that society will make upon him. Other more formal agencies also share in this socialization of the child, but their total influence is much less than that of family and peer group. The school provides training and experiences that are often beyond the capacity of the family to provide in readying the individual to be an adult in society. But it seems to have much less impact in the teaching, formal or informal, of morals and values than do the primary groups.

Adult Socialization   The socialization process is not entirely a matter of the early, formative years of life. Certainly, the first recognition by social scientists of the importance of the process focused on the socialization of the young. Furthermore, many writers, both old and new, assumed that socialization in those very early years formed the character structure of a person into a firm and definite mold that was not to change throughout life. But recent research in sociology has been concerned with the idea that socialization is a continuing process that never ceases, and furthermore that processes of socialization during adult years are essential in modern, mobile societies. In more traditional societies, the early patterns of socialization can possibly provide both the skills and attitudes that carry the person successfully through life. But this can hardly be the case in those societies where a person's life-situation may change rapidly, and where as a result, the early agents of socialization can provide little specific preparation for later roles. A changing society can not provide socialization that is preparation for more than a few years ahead. Consequently, the movement into a new age-status often requires a *resocialization* to enable the individual to meet a new set of requirements for interaction. Adult socialization, which is always resocialization, becomes as important as the socialization of the infant and child.[21]

People who are oriented to mobility may very well be appropriate candidates for *anticipatory socialization,* that process of socializing to new roles and values prior to actual occupancy of the roles. Joining an organization and learning an occupation are examples of situations in which anticipatory socialization can occur. A number of recent studies on the learning of an occupation has made it evident that there is much more to it than learning skills and

[21] See Leonard D. Cain, Jr., "Life Course and Social Structure," in Faris, *Handbook of Modern Sociology,* especially pp. 290–292.

knowledge: it means the growth of an *occupational personality*.[22] The learner absorbs new attitudes and values toward the work and the interactional context in which the work occurs, and he also learns an entire set of status definitions that relate people to one another in the work situation. From this, he gains a new image of himself—an occupational personality—and an occupational ideology by which he can interpret the world around him.

Although social mobility may clearly accentuate the need for continuous socialization in modern society, there are also other circumstances of modern life that do so. In a society in which age-grading creates significant subcultural differences and varying life-styles, the process of growing older necessitates socialization to successive new roles and behavior patterns. Becoming a grandparent and retiring are new statuses for which the individual must be socialized. The adult couple whose grown children have married and moved away— "empty nest" is the symbolic term now defining this phase of family life—also face an age status that is relatively new in American life and for which, consequently, there is as yet little in the way of role models. Irwin Deutscher notes that much of the descriptive literature indicates that this is a difficult period of life, and that both theory and clinical experience suggest that most people will have difficulty in making the transition.[23] But Deutscher's study of a sample of urban middle-class postparental couples discovered that the change in their life "does not appear to have been insurmountable and the adaptations are seldom pathological."[24] There was anticipatory socialization— Deutscher spoke of "socialization opportunities"—made possible by such things as an acceptance of the inevitability of change, including that of the family cycle, the temporary departure of children for college or military service, and the intent of the mother not to be "the mother-in-law you read about."

The fact that socialization is not restricted to childhood but occurs throughout the adult years suggests that older conceptions of personality, particularly those that viewed it as rigidly fixed in the early years, originated in more traditional social structures in which the need for continuing socialization was less evident. Furthermore, we learn from this that human personality can be remolded and reshaped over time; this is significant for evaluating the problem of change in societies undergoing rapid and radical transition.

The Socialization of Generations A society can persist only by socializing each new generation into the culture and into the expectancies defining role-

---

[22] For an example of such a study, see Howard Becker and J. W. Carper, "The Development of Identification with an Occupation," *American Sociological Review*, 61 (June, 1956), 289–298.
[23] Irwin Deutscher, "Socialization for Postparental Life," in Arnold Rose, ed., *Human Behavior and Social Processes* (Boston: Houghton Mifflin, 1962), pp. 506–525.
[24] Deutscher, p. 509.

behavior. One generation follows another, and the society goes on. But the period in which one generation comes of age and matures may be one of significant historical change, creating a milieu that is very different than that of the preceding, or succeeding, generation. To come of age in a depression or in a great war is to undergo socialization at a time when major values and social perspectives are being radically altered, and when people develop new outlooks that they may carry through life. Sociologists speak of *political generations* as shaped in this way.[25]

Sociologists have given but little attention to generational phenomena, and the term, generation, has no precise meaning. Often it means those who have experienced at about the same age some major source of socializing influence: war, depression, social movements, or the innovation of new life-styles. In addition, it frequently is restricted to those in the late teens and early twenties, who have shared crucial experiences when they are first testing and trying out adult roles and when their anticipation of adult responsibilities and privileges develops in them a critical view of the society. If this is so, a socialized generation is not the same thing as a chronological generation. Karl Mannheim made just this point in suggesting the *romantic's* conception of a generation: time internalized, based upon a common sharing of qualitative experience and lasting just as long as its modes of expression prevail.[26] Nelson Foote said something similar when he argued that what separates one generation from another is "marked qualitative divergences, occurring rather suddenly."[27]

But the sociological issue of the socialization of generations focuses particularly upon the young. Bennet Berger points out that in America the "younger generation" is now defined as extending from early adolescence to young adulthood, suggesting an age-expansion of the generation.[28] On the other hand, he also argued that there was now reason to suggest that the span of a generation now may be only about a decade. In this latter case, a generation is being defined—as did Mannheim and Foote—in terms of those who share formative experiences. Student generations in colleges are even shorter than a decade. Many college professors viewed the college generation of the middle 1950s as apathetic and subdued, a "silent generation" created by the cold war and the McCarthy period of anti-communist investigations. It contrasted sharply with the renewed political activism and outspoken dissent of the 1960s among college students. The beatniks of the 1950s and the younger hippies of the 1960s developed yet another pattern, one of apolitical

[25] Rudolph Heberle, *Social Movements* (New York: Appleton, 1951).

[26] Karl Mannheim, *Essays on the Sociology of Knowledge* (New York: Oxford, 1952).

[27] Nelson Foote, "The Old Generation and the New," in Eli Ginzberg, ed., *The Nation's Children*, Vol. 3, *Problems and Prospects* (New York: Columbia University Press, 1960), pp. 1–24.

[28] Bennet Berger, "How Long Is a Generation?" *British Journal of Sociology*, 11 (March, 1960), 10–23.

protest and withdrawal from active involvement in the middle-class careers of an affluent society.

The qualitative meaning of generation, then, not only can define a shorter or longer period of time, it can also be defined to include only some of those who are the generation of age. The political activists and the hippies of the student generation of the 1960s constitute a significant generational experience, but many other college students knew little of either group. They escaped any socialization into the particular perspectives that characterized this generational grouping. And the working-class youth, who went, not to college, but to work and often to military service, were simply another generation altogether, so far removed from the college generations in socializing experiences that perhaps the only thing they shared was a common age.

MOTIVATION AND SOCIAL CONTROL

Socialization is significant in developing the intricate and subtle relationship of the individual to society. It serves to produce the type of individual who "fits"—who has the skills and values that enable him to participate in an ongoing social process; it is thus a means for achieving continuity in social order. Through socialization individuals internalize the values and norms of society and are able to exercise self-control. Yet no society ever relies entirely upon socialization. There are laws and customs, there are modes of enforcement of these, including sanctions meted out to violators, and there are agents and agencies of the society that assume major responsibility for seeing that the group's ways are upheld. In addition, in informal but no less compelling ways, any social group invokes pressures and demands upon its members as a price of acceptance in the group. All of this is *social control,* and every society manifests certain universal types of control. But modes of compulsion, with the threat of punishment, are not the only complements to self-control. In mobile and changing societies, in particular, there is the process of linking the individual to various kinds of social action by offering rewards for undertaking sustained activities or by giving people sufficient reason for doing things that are of value to the society, things not compelled or required either by custom or a sense of duty. This is the sociological and institutional aspect of *motivation.*

In the analysis of human behavior, motivation is usually treated as a *psychological* concept, a series of statements about the reasons why people behave as they do. The term has been complicated and rendered controversial by the diverse way in which the sources of motivation—both biological and psychological—have been sought, and by the fact that motivation is not a universal scientific concept. For obvious reasons, natural scientists do not make use of the concept. Nor has the concept seemed to be particularly useful in the explanation of behavior in traditional societies, where the reasons for doing the customary and well-accepted things seemingly need no formulation. In such societies, the interest lies more in the *how* rather than the *why* of behavior. For sociologists, concerned with the study of society, the interest in motivation lies primarily in the social inducements by which the actions of individuals are effectively linked to the social structure. Accordingly, sociologists look for whatever it is that induces individuals to play their roles in society according to established expectations, as well as for the incentives that are socially created, if not socially approved, to act contranormatively.

Motivation for Achievement   Of the several problems in motivation relevant to sociology, there is one in which sociologists have sustained a long interest. This is one where the linkage between person and society includes the need to specify motivation as an internalized attitude toward achievement, which enables people to mobilize their energies and organize their behavior to pursue difficult goals. In mobile societies, many but not all aspire for higher status. Those who have a strong need to achieve high status are motivated to pursue long-term goals, and this may serve to organize their entire life. It may lead them to defer present satisfactions, to work very hard and long for small immediate rewards, to endure discomfort and even hardship, all in order to realize the dream of some form of high social status.

The theme of "rags to riches" in American life has been a motive-inducing myth that has led generations of Americans to believe that a sustained effort on their part could lead to great personal success, if they also had the personal attributes of ability and moral character. This is the *Horatio Alger myth*, the story of the poor but hard-working boy who eventually achieves the pinnacle of success in American society.[29] An important element in this is the idea that the society is so organized that such motives can in fact be realized, that the effort will lead to success. There must be enough evidence of this if the myth is to be sustained, and if such a pattern of success-motivation is to be effectively inculcated in at least some of the younger generation. In mobile and changing societies, then, motivation becomes an important factor in mobilizing the interests and energies of individuals in activities that lead to personal achievement, and that also have significant social consequences for the society. In his highly provocative study, *The Achieving Society,* David McClelland related achievement motivation to economic development.[30] He and his associates and students not only carried out highly imaginative psychological experiments,

[29] Horatio Alger (1834–1899) was a writer of popular inspirational novels, whose name came in time to symbolize the myth.

[30] David McClelland, *The Achieving Society* (Princeton, N.J.: Van Nostrand, 1961).

but they also accumulated much historical evidence for the important place of motivation in the economic development of societies.

Perhaps the classic study of economic motivation is Max Weber's great work on the relation of Protestantism to the origin and growth of capitalism in the Western world.[31] Weber carefully documented the way in which religious interests provided motivation for economic behavior that, however unintentionally, promoted the development of capitalism. The Protestant entrepreneur intended by his economic action to demonstrate, at least to himself, that he was one of God's elect—Protestants then believed in predestination—and this he presumably could do by living ascetically, working hard, and becoming a success. This strong devotion to economic effort, coupled with the thrift and savings that his ascetic life brought about, produced a capital accumulation that led to more investment and the tremendous stimulus for economic action by which capitalism flourished.

One could hypothesize from such examples that under certain conditions there emerges in a society a personality type of the achiever, whose commitment to accomplishment may bring about significant social changes. McClelland and others have sought to provide a social-psychological characterization of this type of person. They have asserted that he is the product of a type of child-training that emphasizes at an early age independence, assertiveness, and mastery. Such children are expected quite early in life to make their own friends, know their way around the city, do well in competition, be active and energetic, and try hard for things for themselves. They are more likely now to be middle class than lower or upper, but it is doubtful if there is any necessary relationship to social class. Nonetheless, it is not difficult to understand the location of much of this type of child-training in a success-oriented middle class.

The conventional route to success in modern society, however, more and more requires other requisites than motivation—education and training, for example—that many who aspire do not have. For them, there have been alternate routes to status, such as the vast world of popular entertainment, including sports. Such professional sports as baseball and boxing once provided goals for the aspirations of lower status males whose athletic prowess was perhaps their only possible route to fame and fortune. The minor leagues of baseball and the small tank-town boxing circuits paid poorly, yet thousands of young men endured them while sustaining the hope of making "the big time." The old-time baseball managers had a word for them: they were "hungry." They could endure uncomfortable travel, poor accommodations, indifferent food, and poor pay, partly because they had little option for anything better, but primarily because they clung to the hope of achieving

[31] Max Weber, *The Protestant Ethic and the Spirit of Capitalism*, trans. by Talcott Parsons (New York: Scribner, 1930).

the success that went with the big leagues. The dream factory that is Hollywood has also nurtured and channeled such aspirations.[32] The myth of the young starbound actress discovered at a drugstore counter was sufficient to send thousands of young women to Hollywood to endure years of sacrifice in the hope of eventual discovery and stardom.

It is different now, not because the aspirations are not still there or because this route to social status is not still viable. But the minor leagues and small-town boxing clubs are gone, and the mode of recruitment has changed. Athletes are recruited off the college and high school campus and are paid bonuses; they expect to make it big in a shorter period of time or else to quit for whatever middle-class career is available. The young actresses for Hollywood movies and television are recruited less from behind a drugstore counter and more from college campuses, local television stations, and actors' training studios. But the world of phonograph records, oriented largely to mass tastes among adolescents, still provides an opportunity for someone to reach fame and fortune without much in the way of education, professional training, or even long experience.

Talent and Performance   Motivation for achievement, then, may be a socially viable way of encouraging the talent that is always present in some unknown quantity in any society. We recognize that a society can tap only a limited proportion of the human talent that is available, though a modern and developed society undoubtedly draws upon more of such talent than does a traditional one. But talent and performance are not the same. Every society is a pool of talent, a reservoir of human ability. It requires social organization, however, to find means and motivations for its development and expression and for its social use. Thus, motivation is a significant link between talent and performance. It constitutes the *raison d'être* that encourages talented people to mobilize their energies, to hold to their aspirations, and to make long-term commitments in seeking achievement.

But motivation needs to be seen in perspective. It constitutes the individual's reasons for linking to some processes in the society. But such processes need to be accessible to the individual. If they are blocked, if prevailing social structures drain off energy in other directions, or if established institutional agencies hamper and even threaten, then such talent is much less likely to result in performance. In the cases of social mobility that we mentioned, and in many others, the channels for mobility were there, and the encouragement of entrepreneurial or athletic or political or entertainment talent is a valued effort within American society. Indeed, the myth would have it that all

---

[32] Compare Hortense Powdermaker, *Hollywood: The Dream Factory* (Boston: Little, Brown, 1950).

successful Americans became so by a Horatio Alger process. In too many cases this was not so, but so powerful has the myth been that most men wanted to be thought of as having made it from the bottom up.

How a society can harness its human talent and shape social aspirations has also been demonstrated in recent efforts to improve scientific education in the United States and to encourage the development of technological and scientific talent. The political and ideological concerns of the society have placed great value on this kind of education, and not equally on others. Resources were therefore made available, and channels were created to funnel larger numbers of talented youngsters into careers in science. What may then seem at one level to be the personal decisions of millions of young men to seek a college education and pursue science as a career, may also be the consequence of deliberate efforts to induce motivations to choose one career over another, and to strive for a high level of personal achievement that is rewarding because it is valued by the society.

By the same token, socially encouraged motivations cannot be made meaningful and compelling to the members of a society if there is too great an observable discrepancy between motivation for achievement and structural possibilities. It has proven difficult, for example, in the past to motivate deprived Negro youngsters to evince an interest in education when they quite realistically assessed the actual opportunity for achievement to be low. Where a desire for achievement did become internalized in disadvantaged youngsters of any race, it often harnessed energy and talent into alternative channels, such as athletics, where the color line has been less of an obstacle. Sometimes it encouraged these youngsters to enter criminal and delinquent careers as still another alternate channel for social mobility.

Mechanisms of Social Control   A reliance on socialization and on motivation may be a primary means of assuring behavior for carrying on the society, or even for action that breaks ground in new directions of change and development; but these cannot provide complete assurance that such will occur. Social control becomes institutionalized, but it also emerges in certain normal processes found in all reasonably integrated human groups. It becomes institutionalized when formal mechanisms and procedures are created to contain action within established limits. *Sanctions* may be imposed on offenders, according to custom or law, and these can range from rebuke to the ultimate penalty—death. While only an official authority can invoke the sanction to deprive a person of his life, social groups have always had available as an ultimate weapon the ostracism or isolation of the offending person, who is simply no longer accepted as one of the group—who "dies" socially.

It does not require any official authority to invoke actions for the purpose of social control. Even the smallest of groups, or the most loosely organized, manages to do so. Such informal mechanisms as *ridicule* serve as effective threats to the group's esteem of the individual and thus to his self-esteem, threatening his good standing and personal reputation among others. It is because of this that *gossip* is an effective control mechanism, for gossip is talking about people in such a way as to threaten their reputations. To avoid gossip, then, compels the individual to avoid the conduct that would be a prime subject of gossip. An earlier generation of sociologists used to emphasize this form of social control, asserting that in the small rural community and cohesive neighborhood of the past the informal social controls, such as gossip, worked very well just because one lived entirely among people before whom one's behavior was always visible. These sociologists also made much of the fact that the anonymity and impersonality of the city made these very controls less effective, with a consequent irreparable loss in group control over individual moral standards.

It is readily evident that acceptance by one's peers can hinge on one's acting consistently with group expectations; in this manner the group has a control over the behavior of the individual. The more the individual values acceptance by his peers, the more he is susceptible to the pressures of the group. Most people can anticipate what the response of the group would be for any behavior that violates group standards, and this serves as a built-in control. Thus, groups always exercise control over members, and small and intimate groups, the primary groups we spoke of above, are in a strategic position to exact a far-reaching conformity from their members. We have then a paradox of human existence: that the individual may be most effectively controlled in that group in which he feels most free. His most valued group may be his most coercive, for he can least avoid living up to expectations in small and intimate groups. Because he has internalized the values of such groups, however, the controls may be self-controls, and he may not be conscious of just how controlled his behavior is.

To dwell upon the existence of mechanisms of social control seems to empha- size that the group demands conformity by the individual, and thus to deny the freedom and individuality that are such important values in American culture. But there is no freedom and individuality that exists outside of human society, and this polarizing of society against the individual distorts what is a real and yet difficult issue. Certainly, there is no absolute and complete freedom for the individual, for such would be anarchy and a negation of social order. As we have pointed out in a number of places, social order exists only because there is a consensus of expectations and a commitment to living up to these on the part of individuals. Socialization is one primary means by which human organisms are turned into human beings who love and care, have feelings and a moral sense, feel responsible for others, and take pride in what they do. Only in a context of social order is there such a thing as human nature, but that same context does put limits on behavior. A social order socializes its members to have an appropriate moral sense. However, socialization is always imperfect, and moral meanings also change; thus, the imposition of standards of behavior may indeed be experienced as compulsion. There is an eternal dilemma of constraint and freedom in the relation between the person and the group that cannot be adequately analyzed by polarizing the two.

CHARACTER AND SOCIETY

The interest of sociologists in such processes as socialization, motivation, and social control comes from a point of view that looks upon them as means of assuring continuity and persistence in social organization. How disparate and unique human beings conform sufficiently to expectations of behavior to insure the existence of social order is an issue that gives sociologists a reason for having some interest in the person. But the relationship of person and society is larger than what is subsumed by discussion of socialization, motivation, and social control. The way in which sociologists view socialization demonstrates the fact that they usually give primacy in their explanations to society, or to social processes and group organization, or to culture, and tend to see the individual person as a product of these shaping forces. Thus, persons are viewed as the *products* of group processes; an organism becomes a person only by socialization within a group context, and human character is shaped by the internalization of culture. Although sociologists readily acknowledge that each person is a unique individual, their interest is in the *common* features of personality shared by those socialized within the same culture.

By no means do all sociologists share an outlook that views the person as *only* a product of social organization, and thus posits a deterministic view of society as cause and person as effect. But even though many sociologists would explicitly deny such a view, it is nonetheless implicit in the mode of analysis they carry out. As noted previously, a major concern in the early days of sociology, particularly evident in the work of Emile Durkheim, was a determination to resist the reduction of sociological analysis to explanation by psychological variables. In addition, sociologists are generally committed to the concept of *social structure.* If socialization in different structural contexts yields different personality patterns, then it is not difficult to give primacy to society over the person. This viewpoint undoubtedly gets further support when the person is viewed within large structures, such as bureaucracies and nations, where it is difficult to see how the person can shape such organizations, but easy to see how these organizations can force the individual to adapt to their behavioral requirements. There seem, then, to be two basic (and closely related) ideas that dominate sociological thinking about the relationship between the person and society. One is that there is a close, functional fit between person and society; the other is that the person is a product of the way society is organized, and that people change in response to changes in the structure of society.

The Plasticity of Character   If there is one model of the person that dominates contemporary social scientific research, it is that in which character is essentially plastic, readily adaptable to a range of varied situations, responsive to behavioral cues from significant others, and receptive to new opportunities for socialization. In large part, social scientists have indicated that this is what modern social character is, and furthermore, that this is what it should be, given the nature of modern social organization. A more rigid character structure, it has been pointed out, is more likely to be characteristic of psychotics and bigots, for only these would remain rigidly the same in a segmented and complex world.

The best known work of our time in establishing this model of the person has been *The Lonely Crowd.*[33] In this work, Riesman outlined three types of social character: *tradition-directed, inner-directed,* and *other-directed,* which have become part of the intellectual vocabulary of contemporary life. His starting point was, again, the sociological aphorism that a society seems to get the type of character that it needs. A tradition-directed character was typical of a traditional society, where the same mode of organization, relatively unchanged, had existed for centuries, and where the major orientation of the person was conformity to a seemingly eternal set of traditions.

But tradition-directed merely completed Riesman's analysis; interest centered on his other two types. Inner-direction was that mode of conformity created by childhood socialization, in which the individual internalizes a set of values and moral standards, largely from the family, and utilizes these to guide and control his own behavior during his adult life. It is a mode of conformity for those transitional types of societies that are undergoing rapid change, and in which a traditional culture and a seemingly unchanging pattern of social life can no longer provide adequate behavioral guidance. The individual must be flexible enough to adjust to changing situations and to find or create new modes of behavior. But his direction for this comes from a secure set of internalized values, a firm moral orientation, by which he can find his way through a bewildering pattern of change in social life.

According to Riesman, the inner-directed character was typical of the United

---

[33] David Riesman with Nathan Glazer and Reul Denny, *The Lonely Crowd* (New Haven, Conn.: Yale University Press, 1950).

States in the nineteenth century, whereas the twentieth century has seen the emergence of the other-directed mode of conformity, particularly among the urban, college-educated, bureaucratically-employed middle classes. Here, a new type of society, highly urbanized, and incorporating people into large-scale organization, demands a highly flexible, continually socializing type of person, and this need is met by the emergence of the other-directed man. The other-directed man is the plastic and flexible type so current in contemporary literature. His character is particularly sensitive to the demands of peers and the expectations of the immediate situation, and he readily responds to the cues he expertly detects in the behavior of others. He is socialized early to be particularly dependent on the peer group, to be well-liked and accepted, and to make those adjustments in his own conduct that will insure his acceptance by his peers. His direction, then, comes less from parental values internalized in childhood than from a ready response to peers and to the larger contemporary world to which he is oriented through peers. The other-directed man is never certain of his own values and opinions; while the inner-directed man needs to be respected, the other-directed man needs to be liked.

It is important here to insist that Riesman defined all three of his types as "modes of conformity," since so much of the response to them has shown a strong preference for inner-directed over other-directed. The assumption has been that the former is a model of the independent and nonconforming person, so admired in a society where individualism is still a major value, and the latter is the conforming and hapless individual unable to withstand the demands of massive organization in contemporary life. But Riesman intended no such interpretation; instead, he was attempting to describe what seemed to him to be three different ways in which human societies obtained conformity from its members.

Riesman's work was deeply influenced by prior work on the linkage of character and society by Margaret Mead and other anthropologists studying primitive societies, and by the work of Eric Fromm and other European scholars repelled by the advent of naziism and seeking explanation for that event. But Eric Fromm's work and the study of authoritarian types also demonstrated strong value orientations implicit in such research, orientations readily apparent in the way readers responded to Riesman's three types.[34] These earlier, politically-oriented studies had been concerned with the way in which society produces the anti-democratic character, the influence of which is then to move society in such a political direction. Riesman was not so concerned with the problem of anti-democratic behavior, but there was nonetheless a significant comment on our society inherent in his work. He contributed to

---

[34] Eric Fromm, *Escape from Freedom* (New York: Holt, Rinehart and Winston, 1941).

a major discussion within social science and within the larger intellectual community of the character of modern, middle-class Americans in an increasingly bureaucratized world.

Eric Fromm and C. Wright Mills developed types quite similar to the other-directed person for the purpose of making a major critique of modern capitalist society, particularly American. Both of them emphasized the demands that the market economy places on character, and so Mills suggested a "competitive personality," and Fromm a "marketeer."[35] In both instances they gave prominence to the abuse and manipulation of personality for the sake of status and mobility, the loss of integrity by the person engaging in the act of "selling oneself" and thus turning one's own self into a marketable commodity. Perhaps Dale Carnegie's *How to Win Friends and Influence People* is the epitome of this idea, for what is meant is how to win friends *in order to* influence people.[36] Other people's personalities, as well as one's own, then become viewed instrumentally as manipulable objects in the pursuit of wealth and status.

While Mills and Fromm used the market as the context for interpreting modern character, one of the most successful books of popular sociology, William Whyte's *The Organization Man,* used corporate bureaucracy as the context for explaining the making of a pliable character.[37] This book makes explicit application of Riesman's typology to middle-level corporate executives, their wives, and their suburban lives, and then offers this as evidence of a vastly conforming trend in modern life. The impelling demands of bureaucracy on character had been spelled out earlier by Robert Merton, who outlined the pattern of a careful, cautious, unimaginative, rule-conforming mentality produced by conventional bureaucratic structure.[38]

Modal Character   These instances of a fit between character and social structure suggest another issue that only sometimes have sociologists examined thoroughly—the idea that there is some modal cumulation of personality characteristics to be found in members of a society or of subgroups within a society. Anthropologists have long collaborated with psychiatrists and psychologists to delineate the modal character of a culture, particularly in preliterate ones. But sociologists have doubted that similar generalizations can be made about modal character in large and complex societies, for the division of labor, the class structure, and, in general, the complexity of the social structure of such societies seemed to belie there being any significant common-

[35] Eric Fromm, *Man for Himself,* and C. Wright Mills, "The Competitive Personality," *Partisan Review,* 13 (1946), 433.

[36] Written in 1936, Carnegie's book sold in the millions and became the model of the effort to provide middle-class Americans with an easy formula for success.

[37] William H. Whyte, *The Organization Man* (New York: Simon and Schuster, 1956).

[38] Robert Merton, "Bureaucratic Structure and Personality," *Social Forces,* 18 (1940), 560–568.

ality of characteristics to be found in the general population. For that reason sociologists have demonstrated very little interest in studies of *national character,* for another the idea had an earlier and discredited association with racial psychology. In addition, the sociologist, Alex Inkeles, points out that "no one has ever tested a national population or even a major subpopulation using either an adequate sample or adequate psychological instruments."[39] Much remains, therefore, to be done before sociologists are likely to turn with any sustained interest to this issue.

Undoubtedly, for most sociologists (and anthropologists too), the accepted fact of a fit between person and social structure is seen as prime evidence of the powerful socializing effect of group life on the individual. But Inkeles and some others have raised further sociological interest in this relation: the effect of character on role performance and thus on possible integration and change in social organizations and institutions. This is the basic idea behind *The Authoritarian Personality.*[40] The roots of this imaginative work go back to the rise of naziism in Germany and the effort of a group of German social scientists to explain it by finding something in the German people that created a readiness to accept authoritarian rule and give up freedom. Their first efforts centered on the authoritarian family, to which they attributed the socialization of the German people into a national character that was predominantly authoritarian. Later, two of these social scientists emigrated to the United States, and in the 1940s joined with two American social psychologists to carry out the impressive study of the authoritarian personality.

The authoritarian individual is one who, by virtue of difficult, even fearful, experiences with other people is insecure, anxious, hostile, and always feels threatened. Central to his view of the world is a sharp distinction between the powerful, with whom he identifies, and the weak, whom he despises. The measurement of the authoritarian personality was done in a number of ways, but perhaps the most important was the *F-scale.* Authoritarians are the high scorers on this test, and democratic personalities are the low scorers. Those persons who scored high on the F-scale exhibited, among other traits, emotional rigidity, conventionality, emotional immaturity, and lack of insight.

Although the study was not based upon any national or subnational sample, many subsequent ones have sought to apply the F-scale in such a way as to determine the distribution of authoritarian individuals in the national population. High scores on the F-scale have been positively correlated with age, with personal maladjustment, and with conformity, while such things as intelligence, education, and social class are negatively correlated. Religiosity, how-

[39] Alex Inkeles, "Personality and Social Structure," in Robert Merton, Leonard Broom, and Leonard S. Cottrell, Jr., eds., *Sociology Today* (New York: Basic Books, 1959), pp. 267–268.
[40] T. W. Adorno, Else Frenkel-Brunswick, Daniel J. Levinson, and R. Nevitt Sanford, *The Authoritarian Personality* (New York: Harper & Row, 1950).

ever, yielded somewhat contradictory evidence. Note what this means: by the measurement of the F-scale, the younger, more intelligent, and better educated, who are usually also higher in class position are *less* likely to be authoritarian, whereas older and less educated people, particularly those lower in social status, are *more* likely to be more authoritarian. Generalizations such as these presume the validity of the F-scale as a scientific instrument, and there has been much effort to test its validity.

But sociologists are likely to be quite dubious about the assumption of these studies, namely, that a personality configuration is the key to behavior. It must be recalled that the original impetus of this problem was to understand the rise of German fascism. Sociologists believe that a complex historical event can not be understood as the outcome of a personality type; there are structural factors that promote or impede social change, and there are great national events that dislocate people and so disrupt their sense of security and their confidence in the future that they are rendered amenable to suggestions for more drastic political action. Also, the mere presence of people who are more authoritarian does not necessarily assure any particular consequences. The political sociologist Seymour Martin Lipset, for example, has suggested that strong social organizations that represent powerful identifying interests, such as labor unions and political parties, may successfully channel authoritarian responses into more democratic behavior.[41]

Does that mean, then, that the sociologist can ignore character as a psychological issue of no relevance to his analysis of structure and process? Many would say so, yet some sociologists, such as Alex Inkeles, hold the cautious position that character can be one factor under appropriate circumstances that can make a difference in social action. There are few studies however that support this position. One effort to do so is Daniel J. Levinson's study of the relation of authoritarianism to foreign policy.[42] He related the ideologies nationalism and internationalism to character to show that authoritarianism was related to nationalism, and equalitarianism to internationalism. Levinson felt that the authoritarians take an autocratic view of the world, and this includes their perspective on foreign policy. Their choice of ideology is a function of their character. (Note that Levinson's study made the value judgment that internationalism was the rational and democratic ideological choice.)

But the concern for the relevance of character for social action does not have to be pursued only at the national level, and in fact only infrequently has this been done. Inkeles points out that "within major subgroups of the population personality types may in fact be much less random than is com-

---

[41] Compare Seymour M. Lipset, *Political Man* (New York: Doubleday, 1960), pp. 97–130.
[42] Daniel J. Levinson, "Authoritarian Personality and Foreign Policy," *Journal of Conflict Resolution,* 1 (March, 1957), 37–47.

monly supposed," and he refers to studies of occupational groups by Anne Roe and Guy E. Swansom as evidence.[43] While here also there are too few studies to provide solid support for any proposition, these occupational studies and a few others suggest possible inferences about the relation of personality to social action. Inkeles cites particularly such a study as Gilbert and Levinson's of nurses' aides in a mental hospital.[44] Some aides were "custodial," meaning they were harsh and emphasized keeping good order, and some were "humanitarian," meaning they were more friendly to patients and concerned for their welfare. The custodialism of some aides correlated highly with authoritarianism as measured by the F-scale. This only confirms what many have long observed about such institutions as mental hospitals and prisons: they have attracted to various subprofessional custodial positions less educated, authoritarian types who then have an opportunity to exercise authority over powerless patients and inmates. The effect on the functioning of the institution is clear enough; an element of harshness in human relations enters in that is not intended or prescribed in the official code of the organization, and which may impede the achievement of its desired goal of therapy or reform.

To demonstrate the existence of modal character remains a major task for social psychology. Many sociologists doubt that there is enough sharing of personality characteristics in the large and highly differentiated structures of modern societies for it to be a significant issue in sociological analysis. That there will be a great deal of fit between character and structure can be expected, few sociologists would doubt. After all, people are socialized in interaction, and from such interaction they come to be the kind of people who share whatever values and norms governed the social relations in which they were involved. The danger in this is in possibly overemphasizing the fit and thus in creating the oversocialized image of man.

But *The Authoritarian Personality* and some other works have been concerned with something else, that of showing that a modal character is not merely a fit with social structure, but that it influences role performance in that structure and that it can influence the outcome of social action. Levinson's study was intended to show that the foreign policy of the United States was affected by the widespread distribution of authoritarian types in the United States, and *The Authoritarian Personality* was intended to show the anti-democratic potential of such a type. More modest studies purport to show that personality types recruited to particular occupations effect role performance and thus influence the consequential outcomes of the efforts of large organizations. These various studies, then, advance the claim that a modal character, some par-

[43] Inkeles, "Personality and Social Structure," p. 264.
[44] Inkeles, p. 65. The work referred to is D. Gilbert and Daniel J. Levinson, "Role Performance, Ideology, and Personality in Mental Hospital Aides," in M. Greenblatt and others, eds., *The Patient and the Mental Hospital* (New York: Free Press, 1957).

ticular configuration of the internal organization of a person, shared frequently in a human population, is a major variable to consider in the analysis of social action, or that some significant even if minority type (such as the authoritarian) can influence the outcome of social events. If the evidence makes a serious case for such an argument, it is still an argument, open to varying interpretations. And care must be taken in the logic of such an analysis. To say that authoritarians are prejudiced, for example, does not mean that all prejudiced people are authoritarians. Here lies disputed boundary between psychology and sociology and some still unsolved issues about how much of human personality must be taken into account by the sociologist in his analysis of social action.

Identity and Alienation   Evidently, the many studies concerned with the relation of character to society have stressed the fact that socialization leads to a good fit between the two. But in recent years some work has emphasized instead the tensions between individual and society and the circumstances under which no easy fit occurs. The pressing concern of recent generations has been with the impact of vast and powerful social organization on individual human beings, on the potential loss of integrity and individuality in the fact of conformity-demanding social structure, and on the hypnotizing sameness and routinization of life in mass society. Social scientists have responded with analyses that have found large and fascinated audiences.

The existentialist perspective that has inspired so much of contemporary critical social-philosophical thinking has sought to find ways to protect the "authenticity" of personal experience; during the 1950s and 1960s it has encouraged a withdrawal from involvement with the institutions of modern society. A pattern of life that emphasized a detachment from conventional institutional structures, particularly the economic and political, and a focus upon the immediate and private in human experience, was one major response to this issue. It found expression in a world-wide existentialist mood of youth, and it also affected social science. The argument that modern society forces a loss of identity for the individual, that he becomes a nonself, a face in a crowd, a number on an IBM card, turned the attention of many social scientists to the problems of *identity*.

What we know about the emergence of the self in the process of socialization suggests that each of us carries around a self-identity, an image obtained from a dominant group membership and our roles in that group. It might be occupational or class, possibly ethnic or racial, but whatever it is, the self-image is built from membership in a group that is of central value to the person. It is a group that provides the roots and source of individual identity —which only states in another way the idea that person and society are indissolubly linked.

The concern with loss of identity and the consequent anxiety of modern man is not directed at the loss of actual participation in social groups, but at the loss of central meaning and value attached to this participation. Though no one can escape the behavioral demands of those vast organizations that dominate modern life, many apparently choose not to make any significant identification with them. They remain uncommitted.[45] Indeed, to play it "cool" is just the idea of not becoming emotionally involved, of remaining somewhat personally detached. Although all men in modern society presumably face this problem of identity, many social scientists have been particularly concerned with youth, apparently with the view that it is the youthful generation that must find roles and meanings for itself in a highly complex society, and that many of them have great difficulty in doing so. In the words of Eric Erickson, whose writings first emphasized the problem of identity, youth often experience an *identity crisis,* a difficulty in knowing what combination of roles so fit their character that they offer a mode of participation in society that will allow them to become the persons they want to and to live in accord with the values they hold dear.[46]

Why can this happen? The efforts of social scientists to explore this dimension of modern life have been organized around the concept of *alienation.* The alienated person is one who feels *powerless* about the central situations of his life, who finds personally *meaningless* the values that are organizationally central to such situations, who, in short, is *estranged* from the social groups and organizations of modern social life in which he must necessarily be a role-player. The recent sociological studies have been concerned with the estrangement of youth, and also of delinquents and minorities, whereas the early sociological studies imputed alienation to the worker in industry. His presumed inability to control his own work environment, his loss of control over conditions of work, even over the very tools with which he worked, has led generations of thinkers since Karl Marx to select the worker as the epitome of alienation in modern industrial society.

Alienation as the negation of identity has been an approach built upon the assumption that an identity that provides a rewarding sense of self is essential for human existence, and is to be found only within the context of an organized social life. Thus, one's identity is inextricably bound up with contexts of social interaction. The social roles that channel our action and link us with society are then the behavioral patterns through which we can be identified by others and from which we can derive a sense of our own identity. That a rewarding sense of identity does not automatically come from merely any

[45] Kenneth Kenniston, *The Uncommitted: Alienated Youth in American Society* (New York: Harcourt, 1965).

[46] Eric Erickson, *Childhood and Society* (New York: Norton, 1950), pp. 227ff., and "The Problem of Ego Identity," in Maurice R. Stein, Arthur J. Vidich and David M. White, eds., *Identity and Anxiety* (New York: Free Press, 1960).

form of social organization is evident in the analysis of the impact that bureaucracy and mass society has on social character. Even though many times these analyses have overstated the case, perhaps because they have been motivated by strong adverse criticism of modern social life, they do indicate the complexity of the relationship between character and society, and perhaps more to the point, that social character is not something neatly stamped out by organizational cookie-cutters.

Yet the weight of most current sociological and social psychological analysis has been heavily toward asserting the priority of society over the individual, its control over his life, and its capacity to force an adjustment of the person to the extent of altering his character to suit the needs of organization. Only the research on alienation, and particularly on political alienation, which views the alienated as striking back at society in some fashion, interprets modern character as something other than a characterological fit with the demands of social organization.

The Oversocialized Conception of Man   By emphasizing the different nature of each, the analysis of the linkage of character and society can easily enough lose sight of the basic principle that Cooley uttered back in 1920: "a separate individual is an abstraction unknown to experience, and so likewise is society. . . ." "Character" and "society" are abstractions from the same social process, and to forget that is to reify them, to treat them as things, to commit what the philosopher A. N. Whitehead (1861–1947) called the error of "misplaced concreteness."

The concept of person or character, then, implies the idea of the socialization of the organism through the internalization of the culture. But this is always an imperfect process, and it would be an error of considerable magnitude to assume that socialization resulted in persons who had fully internalized the social values of the group and, therefore, had no other responses to experience than those that were appropriate to social roles. Furthermore, it is easy to assume that attitudes and values appropriate to roles constitute the only ones the person has. It is also easy to assume that just because a person's behavior is consistent with role expectations, he has fully internalized the appropriate role-values. None of these assumptions may be true. Many people conform to role expectations because of coercion, when the effective social controls permit them no alternative.

The concept of *role-distance* gives us a useful orientation by suggesting that there can be some psychological distance between the person and his roles, and that he can be quite conscious of this. Sometimes the internalization of variant and conflicting values in a heterogeneous culture permits a certain amount of distance from any one role. In turn, the segmentation of a complex society leads usually to a segmentation of self, in which never more than a limited aspect of a person becomes emotionally attached to a particular social structure. But this distance may also be viewed in terms of the "I" of which Mead spoke, or the ego of Freud—those aspects of the person that are not simply the social character created by internalizing the society's norms and values. Mead viewed the "I" as spontaneous and creative and, given the opportunity, capable of reorganizing the social process. Freud, in turn, viewed the ego as a reality-oriented mechanism that mediated between the id and the superego. In neither of these influential interpretations was the person regarded as synonymous with his internalized values. This reminds us again of Dennis Wrong's *oversocialized* image of man—the person so thoroughly socialized as to be indistinguishable from the role-player he necessarily is. So this discussion has come full circle from the first concern about the nature of human nature and of the person.

It is not to deny or even to underemphasize the great importance of society in shaping and forming social character by the socialization process to suggest that an adequate conception of human nature insists that man is always more than the roles he plays and the norms he has internalized. A consciousness of themselves and their lives with others enables men to respond to their own conduct in social situations as *experience*, which is to assess the meaning of what happened and to create responses that may not always be assigned by established social structure. When these new assessments are communicated and shared, new cultural perspectives have been created, and a potential for new modes of conduct is present.

This last point underscores another issue here. Most of the concern for the relation between character and society views the former primarily in terms of the individual—and to the sociologist that is a concern of psychology. But we are concerned with the fact that even the aspect of man not captured by internalization is still involved in interaction and communication through language. It is as conscious and communicating human beings, in collective dialogue, that men assess human experience, reassess it, and thereby evolve new modes of conduct and new types of social character, and find new ways to play old roles.

Drawing by Ross; Copr. © 1964 The New Yorker Magazine, Inc.

"I'm of two minds. On the one hand, it's difficult to breathe, while on the other hand, they've paid a whopping good dividend for thirty-five years."

Donald Reilly from LOOK 6–11–68

PART 2 SOCIAL GROUPS

1   2

1. A street roller-hockey game.
2. A father and his sons.
3. Vietnam: friends helping a wounded soldier.
4. Champs Elysées, Paris: demonstrating for better social conditions.
5. Harlem: "horsing around."
6. Track meet officials.

3

5

4

6

GROUP AND SOCIETY

7

Social life becomes organized, we saw earlier, when there are established ways of interacting that are indicated by such concepts as *role, relation,* and *structure.* When there is also persistent interaction among the same people, there emerge social collectivities, both large and small, for which such terms as *group* and *society* are used. A group or a society differs from a social structure analytically; it is a different "thing." Groups and societies exist by the coming together of an identifiable people who build and develop their social relations over time into a stable pattern—a social structure—and who identify to some extent with the others with whom they share this particular structure. Thus, a group *has* a structure, and this distinction between group and structure we need to keep in mind.

THE SOCIAL GROUP

Group is the one concept (with the possible exception of *society*) most commonly identified with sociology. It is an old term, which has persisted in the discipline, somewhat ambiguously symbolizing sociology's focus on man's collective life. Because of this, sociologists have sometimes been casual about what they mean by *group.* A rather simple but common definition is that a group is two or more people in interaction. But this is an inadequate definition just because it includes too much and is imprecise. A useful definition requires something more precise. A proper definition of group also requires that we indicate that mere aggregates of people are not groups, at least not in a sociological sense. A collection of people on the corner waiting for a bus, or just waiting to cross the street, barely aware of one another and certainly not concerned about one another, is not, sociologically speaking, a group. Nor is the group a *social category,* like all taxpayers, parents, or baseball fans. Taxpayers and parents are social roles by which people can interact with others in social groups. But all of them together, though having much in common, do not have a pattern of interaction. Baseball fans are an unorganized collectivity of people who share an interest; they can be the basis for a group, as a fan club, and they can become a public.

The sociological conception of group, then, has come to mean the following: *a plurality of people as actors involved in a pattern of social interaction, conscious of sharing common membership, of sharing some common understandings, and of accepting some rights and obligations that accrue only to members.*

People in social groups are conscious of belonging together in common memberships, and a group possesses some mechanism to determine who belongs and who does not. In formally organized groups, membership qualifications may be spelled out, and who belongs may be formally recognized by such means as membership rosters, membership insignia (cards, keys, rings, and pins), and access to privileges that go with membership. Even in groups that have no formal organization, the recognition of who belongs and who does not is crucial to the group's sense of its own existence. In small and informal groups, the conferring of recognition upon a person as belonging and another as an outsider may be carried out by forms of address and by obvious ways of inclusion and exclusion in the activities of the group. No human group has any particular difficulty in making an individual feel that he is not wanted, that he is not "one of the group." All social groups also have ways of inducting members into the group. These may be such simple formal processes as signing up a member and giving him a card or other insignia. Traditional organizations, such as fraternities, sororities, and honorary societies, may invoke elaborate ceremonies of initiation in order to place high significance upon the act of becoming a member of the group. These induction ceremonies are filled with symbolic significance and often strong affective expression.

Membership in a group relates people to one another in a way that is different than how they are related to others not in the group. Common membership subjects them to the expectations governing action in the group— its social norms—and to the culture that emerges from the interactions shared among the members. Members of a group, then, share a common set of cultural understandings about the meaning of membership in the group that emerges from their consensus about what the group is for—its functions and objectives.

This sharing of membership in a group, and a sharing of its common experiences, has the potentiality to develop a strong sense of group unity that is functional for the effectiveness of the group in its collective activities. An early American sociologist, Franklin Giddings, spoke of "consciousness of kind" to designate this sense of unity that common membership and common experience brings.[1] But the consciousness of kind that unifies group members, particularly against those outsiders who are seen as a threat to the group, cannot be treated sociologically as an automatic consequence of there being a group. Rather, it must be defined as a variable, present to a greater or to a lesser degree. Many large groups suffer an attenuated sense of belonging, for their members place only limited value on membership, and the heterogeneity of members tends to reduce any consciousness of kind. Also, the members of one group have membership in other groups, so that no one group may claim a total loyalty or a full commitment from the individual; that also reduces the power of the group over the member. Limited though it may be, however, membership in a group does bring some degree of consciousness of kind and some recognition of sharing with others the obligations that par-

---

[1] Franklin H. Giddings, *Principles of Sociology* (New York: Macmillan, 1896).

ticipation in a group requires. Without some consensus among its members as to its norms and its expectations of behavior—its definitions of its roles—there cannot be a group. This is the sense in which it is not merely a system of interaction, it is also a sharing of membership among those who interact in this way.

The Integration of Social Groups   Social groups, from the smallest to the largest, persist over time only when their members experience social ties that link them to the group and give them reason to belong. The problem of integrating its members into a relatively cohesive and functioning interactional system, then, is a basic problem of all social groups. A consciousness of such a problem is present in those large groups that make explicit provisions for recruiting, socializing, and rewarding its members. But even the smallest of groups can fail to persist, can literally disappear, if its members can find no reason to continue to interact with one another. This concern for the persistence of groups is evident in many ways. When an ethnic group worries that intermarriage of its young outside the group will weaken the group, there is manifested such a concern. When a church worries that it is not successfully reaching the young and also is not recruiting enough young people into the ranks of the clergy, such a concern is again evident. When a civil rights organization is warned that its talk of "black power" will scare off white supporters, there is another kind of concern about the persistence of the group.

Yet, there are situations in life in which the demise of social groups is accepted as natural and inevitable. The high school cliques that break up after graduation when its members scatter and lose contact with one another, the peer groups in the army that break up when demobilization comes—these are but two obvious instances of what happens almost every day without any effort to prevent it. So, the persistence of groups, then, is not a matter of planning or intending to continue the life of every group. As the old popular song had it: "Those wedding bells are breaking up that old gang of mine." People outgrow some groups and the group is lost, to be replaced by others.

In the preceding chapter, we discussed the relation of the person to society, stressing how he becomes integrated into society by virtue of *socialization,* yet how a society necessarily relies upon various modes of *social control* and invokes *sanctions* against those who violate its social norms, and also how a society encourages and develops certain patterns of *motivation,* such as that of achievement. At this point in the discussion, each of these can be referred to again, this time as evidence of group integration. Undoubtedly, one of the major sources of group integration is the socialization of its members resulting in an internalization of the values and norms of the group, a belief in its objectives and purposes, and a willingness to act consistently with the group's expectations of behavior. Efforts at social control serve to reinforce this *normative* integration of the group. Normative integration is also enhanced when the individual can be motivated to achieve something for himself that successfully contributes to the group's values and mode of existence, and when the group in turn can reward such activity. Thus, what we saw to be important in developing human personality and fitting the person to the group also is important in providing social integration for the group.

The normative integration of the group, then, is simply the acceptance by its members of group norms and the degree of their compliance. It is always a matter of degree, rather than an all-or-nothing affair. Small groups that are also homogeneous in membership are likely to have less difficulty with such norm-compliance and thus to be better integrated. Its members are more likely to evidence a higher degree of group solidarity and more of an identification with the group's objectives, producing what is called high *morale*. But large groups have a greater difficulty in achieving normative integration. For one thing, their members are likely to be more heterogeneous. Also, there will be subgroups that emerge within the large group, some of which will develop norms that are inconsistent with if not contradictory to the norms of the larger group. Some of these subgroups will develop from the heterogeneity of the membership, reflecting social differences significant in the larger society— race, sex, age, for example—that have been incorporated into the group. But other subgroups will emerge around the division of labor that occurs in a large group, where specialization of tasks and functions elaborates the structure of the group, making it complex and requiring a functional coordination and some specification of authority if there is not to be confusion and ineffectiveness and a working at cross-purposes. These two types of subgroups may overlap, as when particular functions are assigned to members by categories of age or sex or race.

The problem of the integration of the group, when we speak of large groups, becomes one of *functional* integration, the effective coordination of the human effort of its members, as individuals and as subgroups, so that their diversified and specialized activities support and supplement each other. This, as we shall see later, is the basic concern around which the concept of *bureaucracy* becomes sociologically relevant. It leads to problems of the replacement of members, the recruitment and training of new members, the assignment of people to positions, the criteria for differential rewards, and the legitimation of authority and decision making. It produces that explicit concern for the problems of the organization of the group that is one feature of modern social thought about management and administration and human relations.

Large social groups may then turn to an effective functional integration when size tends to lessen normative integration. Yet functional integration depends on a sharing of normative elements. There has to be some agreement on what is worth doing and some relative consensus on what are reasonable expectations for the actions of people functioning in social roles. Short of that, an organization must rely more on sanctions, and often coercive ones. An army that conscripts its members still tries to socialize them to the values it represents, even though it may be ready to enforce a strict discipline. A firm that employs people to do its productive work may rely to some extent on the fact that its employees simply need a job, and will perform their tasks in order to hold their job. Yet really efficient performance would seem to require that people share some values and norms about the job and are motivated other than by sanctions to act in ways that enhance group objectives.

SOCIETY

The concept of society (like that of group) has always been a central one in sociology; sociology has often been defined as the science of society. Nonetheless, what sociologists mean by society has often been left unstated. It has sometimes been a symbolic term, connoting the range of social phenomena that concerns sociology and signifying the web of relationships within which we interact with others. But it has also been given a more specific meaning in which it stands for the largest social group that encompasses all the other subordinate social groups organized by a people. If we remember that group was defined as "a plurality of people in patterns of interaction, conscious of sharing common membership . . .," then the conception of society as "the largest social group" is based upon the cultural act that turns a population into an identifiable "people." It occurs when a human population defines itself as culturally distinct from other people. The Hopi are a people, as are the Italians and the Irish, the English and the Germans, and the Americans. The inclusive networks of interaction among a culturally defined people sustain a complex social structure that provides for the totality of a way of life for that people. There are no larger groups of which these people are a part; this encompassing social structure is not a subordinate part of a more encompassing one. A society, then, is the social group that encompasses all other social groups that exist among a people.

Such a conception of society does not signify any given size; societies can be large or small. But in the modern world the trend is to large national societies that are politically organized and controlled by a nation-state, and that monopolize control over a given territory customarily inhabited by and identified with the people of that society. American society is such a politically organized society. But prior to the growth of the nation, societies were frequently smaller entities, in which the cultural definition of a people and their territory was not organized into a nation. A tribe, for example, may constitute a society, even though its membership may be only a few thousand people. In Africa, at the present time, former colonies have become independent nations. Their political boundaries were originally shaped by the way in which the colonizers seized territory, and often do not even now constitute any definition of territory customarily identified with a people. Usually, the area encompasses a number of tribes and their customary territories, and sometimes it cuts across traditional tribal territories. While these new nations exist as political units, the concept of nationhood has only begun to find cultural roots in the politically organized population, and tribal loyalties and identities are often still dominant. In short, new national societies are still taking shape, are still emerging out of old tribal societies. The tribe as a definition of a people is slowly giving way to a national definition that encompasses a large population. Inevitably, a great deal of social conflict often accompanies such nation building.

The Institutions of Society In the analysis of societies, sociologists invoke the concepts of *role, relation,* and *structure,* just as they do in the analysis of any form of social group. But in the analysis of society the concept of *institution* also comes into use. Like the concepts of group and society, institution is one of those older concepts that has long been closely associated with the discipline of sociology. In fact, just as it has long been called the science of society, sociology has also been called the science of institutions.

An examination of the sociological literature reveals two conceptions of institutions that are, in fact, more closely related than may seem apparent at first glance. Probably the most frequent conception of institution is that which begins with the idea of an *institutional norm* and defines *an institution* as a complex of such norms. Norms are institutional when they are relatively strongly supported by group consensus and when strong sanctions for violation are imposed by enforcing agencies. Institutional norms are quite *obligatory.* They are, indeed, what Sumner meant by the mores. A second conception of institution stresses, not the institutional norms alone, but also the social practices or activities that the norms govern. Here the emphasis is upon *institutional roles and relations.*

It should take but a moment's thought to realize that these two definitions are not incompatible. One calls institution the norms that govern action, the other calls institution the action itself; institution is clearly composed of norms and roles. But what neither one of these approaches does is tell us why some activities are institutionally normative and some are not. To answer that question, we need to bring into consideration two salient issues. One emerges from the nature of man and one from the nature of society.

The conception of man that undergirds contemporary social science, as we have already suggested, is one that asserts that he has no set of instincts which govern his behavior in some fixed pattern. Men must develop tools and techniques, modes of action, and styles of thought in order to create a social order. But the human mind can conceive of more than one logically possible way of handling or doing anything. And so it does, as cultural history and anthropology demonstrate convincingly.

Every society, secondly, constitutes an historic working out of a way of life, a set of human arrangements by which life is ordered and sustained. Even the most superficial survey of known societies tells us that societies do not make identical human arrangements. Rather, they manifest a wide and even contradictory range of cultural values and institutional patterns.

In order to sustain social order, every society must develop orderly ways of handling some problems that are universal, that is, are common to all societies. Each society, for example, develops a social arrangement to legitimize mating and the birth of the young, and then the care and socializing of the young. What we label *family* is such an arrangement, even though the pattern from one society may be very different from that of another. But there is no one way given in the genetic nature of man, no one way that is instinctively right for him. If some societies practice monogamy, others are polygamous. If most societies assign the obligation of fatherhood to the biological father, some primitive peoples do it differently, assigning this role to the mother's brother. But what is crucial here is that a society cannot follow several different ways. Social order requires that such a significant matter as the social control of mating and reproduction, and the consequent socialization of the young, be organized in some way that for that society becomes the right way, morally and intellectually.

One must remember, of course, that no one society ever conceives of all the logical possibilities, and many relatively isolated societies seem unaware of logical alternatives until contact with other societies is established. Therefore, no society ever chooses its institutional arrangements as a logical and rational process. Instead, each society has developed its own pattern out of the context of its own historic experiences, legitimated by the major values and assumptions of the people of that society. This is why there is a certain rightness in defining institutions as norms. It emphasizes the fact that a society develops its central values around some significant modes of action. These institutional norms are rooted in the fundamental value perspective of the members of that society, in its most basic conception of what is right and moral in life.

The making of institutions, then—the *institutionalization* of norms and actions —occurs in all societies as it shapes its own distinctive social structure around some salient, universal issues. At some crucial points it weds its deepest moral considerations to the behavior that is an answer to these issues. But what are the issues that give rise to the institutions? Our example has suggested that one issue is the problem of controlling the process of mating, procreating, and caring for the young. Every society has some one structural pattern for this, even though given societies devise different ways. But each society, in turn, invests this one way with strong emotional and moral feeling and invokes strong sanctions against violation.

But the institutionalization of kinship roles and norms is not the only instance of a social institution. There are several other universal issues, common to all societies, that produce that cluster of norms and roles we call institutions. One of these has to do with the fact that every human society has to organize its population to *work*, to *produce* the material goods on which life depends, and to *distribute* those goods in some manner deemed legitimate. The economic structure also becomes institutionalized around norms governing productive processes and the rights and obligations of people as participants.

Every society, in some manner, allocates *legitimate power*, which is *authority*, to ensure social control within a set of basic rules shared by the members of the society, thus protecting and guaranteeing social order. This is a structural pattern that provides means for invoking sanction against violations, for the legitimate use of force, for redefining and renewing the rules and agreements that bring consensus to the society, and for providing a means of legitimate decision making. This is the sphere of political process and structure and of *political institutions*.

The young in any society must be inducted into the culture, and trained both in values and in social skills. This is *education*. In most of the preindustrial societies we know about, this educational task was largely performed within the kinship system, and little of a separate structure for education developed. But in modern societies an *educational* institution of considerable scope has been developed.

In the case of education we can make a case for it being an institution in the modern world better than we can in the primitive world. But in religion, it is the reverse. We can make a case for the universality of the *religious institution* in primitive and preindustrial societies, but may be less sure of the existence of religious institutionalization in modern societies, where organized religion is detached from the state, and organized religious groups are highly competitive and are sometimes in conflict with one another. The basic issue that results in the institutionalization of religion is usually defined as the ritualistic and structural expression of those most fundamental beliefs, the underlying moral outlook that unites the society in a moral consensus. Nonetheless, we shall persist here in designating a religious institution, and at the appropriate place we shall turn our attention to the question of the institutionalization of religion in the modern world.

These, then, are the spheres of social relations, the patterning into social structure in any society that the sociologist usually calls institutions: the familial, economic, political, educational, and religious. Each of these is a complex of norms and structural patterns that emerge around issues central to the very organization of society: the assigning of responsibility for care of the young, the allocation of legitimate power, the provision for a legitimate structure for decision making and the like. There are, logically, a number of ways in which any one of these functions could be carried out, but out of its own historical experience a society develops one structural pattern which for its members becomes the morally right way and thus is sanctioned and supported. And the normative consensus is usually quite strong. This gives us the basis, then, for a definition of social institution as: *a normative order defining and governing patterns of social action deemed by its members as morally and socially crucial to the existence of the society.*

Because social institutions are supported by strong normative sanctions, they are the most stable elements of a social structure. They are more resistant to change. But this undoubted fact should not leave the impression that institutions do not change, because, of course, they do. They are slowly altered over long periods of time, accompanying other changes in society. What we call the Industrial Revolution was the slow transformation of society into a new kind of structure, including altered institutional arrangements. Sometimes change comes in the way we ordinarily call "revolution," swiftly and violently. In either case, the fundamental change that is involved when basic social institutions are altered and remade is revolution.

Types of Society The systematic study of society received impetus from the recognition that human society had been radically altered by the Industrial Revolution. The social thinkers of the nineteenth century recognized that the social patterns of traditional society had been disrupted, weakened, and dissolved. Conservative thought had lamented this disruption and had seen in it the breakdown of human society. In contrast, the classically liberal outlook had viewed the change as progress and as freedom for the individual from the dead hand of custom and tradition. Whatever the differences in interpretation, the breakup of the traditional culture and of the organization of society could be agreed upon.

The challenge to explain and understand the type of social life emerging from this dissolution of the old order led a number of social scientists in the nineteenth and twentieth centuries to develop a mode of social analysis that sought to contrast the basic characteristics of radically different social structures. They defined two types of societies, the traditional and the modern, which stood in radical contrast to one another. In part, these contrasting types developed out of a comparison of modern industrial society with an historically earlier type of social structure in Europe: the cohesive peasant village. But they were also shaped, particularly in this century, by comparison with the ways of life of contemporary primitives. Thus, we find there were two points of reference for drawing significant comparisons between modern society and older ones: in the Western world, the historically earlier pattern of peasant society, which was so radically transformed by the Industrial Revolution; and in the non-Western world, the type of society organized for precivilized man.

The terms *folk* and *modern* will be used here to refer to those ideal types that contrasted two forms of human society. Folk refers to one particular pattern for the organization of social life to be found extensively (though not universally) outside the Western world, and perhaps in the most isolated villages of European peasants. Modern, in turn, refers to the kind of society that the Industrial Revolution brought into being in Europe and America. In doing this, we have selected two terms out of a number that have appeared in the literature. *Folk* and *urban* are two comparable terms from the work of the American anthropologist, Robert Redfield, and it is his conception of folk that still dominates social-scientific thought.[2] Ferdinand Toennies spoke of *Gemeinschaft* and *Gesellschaft,* which the American sociologist, Robert MacIver, has translated as *community* and *association.*[3] Henry Sumner Maine (1822–1888), the English jurist and legal philosopher, spoke of societies characterized by *status* and *contract,* while Emile Durkheim used the terms, *mechanical* and *organic.*[4]

Folk and Modern Societies   The contrasting typologies of folk and modern are concepts intended to analyze as precisely as possible the great social transformation through which the peoples of Western culture have been moving in recent centuries. It is an analytical tool intended to highlight the essential elements that differentiate modern society from older ones. The terms are not to be taken as exact descriptions of any particular society; rather, in each case they are selections of some elements found in a number of similar societies.

Perhaps one point of contrast is *size.* Folk societies are typically small, whereas modern ones are large. The primitive or peasant village compared to the huge, sprawling urban metropolis is the relevant contrast. If the folk society is small, so are the social organizations that are its constituent parts: family and kinship groups, for example. The encompassing environs of the village, the structure of kinship, and the small primary groups of peers are the significant networks of social relations in which the functioning individual is

---

[2] Robert Redfield, "The Folk Society," *The American Journal of Sociology,* LII (January, 1947), 293–308.

[3] Ferdinand Toennies, *Community and Society,* trans. and ed. by Charles Loomis (East Lansing: Michigan State University Press, 1957). Robert MacIver, *Society* (New York: Holt, Rinehart and Winston, 1937).

[4] Henry Maine, *Ancient Law.* Original edition, 1861. (New York: Dutton, 1960). Emile Durkheim, *The Division of Labor in Society.* Trans. by George Simpson. Original French edition, 1893 (New York: Macmillan, 1933).

involved. Thus, relationships are more personal, for interaction occurs within small networks of persons on a frequent, familiar, face-to-face basis. Modern society, in turn, is made up typically of many large-scale organizations, particularly the bureaucratic. Bureaucracies organize the actions of many people on a quite impersonal basis, for people find it necessary to interact with others whom they do not know as individuals.

Kinship is a predominantly important group for the individual in a folk society. It is a cooperative group for meeting many needs and functions, including the economic, and constitutes a major source of security for the individual. Kinship obligations are binding, and family ties are close and secure. In modern society, however, the kinship group loses many of its functions, and the significance of kinship declines. The individual's kinship obligations are less. This decline of kinship signifies the replacement of the small, close, and secure structures of folk society by the large and usually impersonal organizations of modern society.

The folk society is an agrarian society, without mechanization and science, and consequently with little specialization in occupations or economic functions among its members. It lacks a complex *division of labor.* Economic tasks may be divided among men, women, and children, and differences in physical abilities may be recognized. But there is only a limited number of tasks to perform, and most members of the society know and understand these and share in the skills and competencies. A modern society, in contrast, offers an extensive and complex division of labor. Its technological development creates a wide variety of necessary skills, a vast number of occupations, and an indefinite narrowing of specialization.

Since the limited division of labor in folk society does not require of its members a great specialization of skills, knowledge, or ideas, the practical knowledge that people have, their ideas about the world, the standards by which conduct is normally guided and controlled, and the goals for the individual, are roughly the same for all members of the society. A folk society is *culturally homogeneous.* Modern society is *culturally heterogeneous.* The particular kinds of knowledge that specialization requires leads to a considerable differentiation of knowledge and ideas, and also to a wide range of cultural experience. Modern society thus becomes vastly differentiated within its structure, characterized by a large number of subgroups quite different from each other in the actions they display and the values they manifest. Thus, it is easier for a folk society to be cohesive and integrated than it is for a modern society; its typical modes of behavior are long established in custom and are a highly conventionalized way of acting. What one man does is what all men do, just as what one man knows and believes, all others do also. The people of a folk society act much alike, think alike, and so are much alike as persons. It is no wonder that in such a society, in which interaction is close and intimate

among its members and in which there is little if any interaction with outsiders, that there is a strong sense of belonging together.

A folk society is one in which *a sense of the sacred* is pervasive throughout
the life of its members and affects much of their activity. The long established
and uncritically accepted traditions of the society leads to a sense of deep
reverence for the ways of the group and a resentment that often brings on
severe sanctions if one questions the values so deeply imbedded in folk life.
Many kinds of social objects are invested with sacredness in a folk society
and are then kept away from the ordinary and profane, often by ceremony
and ritual. In a folk society, no activity is ever solely instrumental—a means
to an end—but is always valued intrinsically. In this way what is sacred
permeates all of life. But in a modern society, the realm of the sacred shrinks.
Tradition declines and with it the sense of reverence for established ways
and beliefs. Perhaps more to the point, modern society maximizes the instrumental and pragmatic, seeing a sharp distinction between means and ends.
Furthermore, the rationality that characterizes science and technology encourages a skepticism about untested claims, however sanctified by tradition,
and an attitude that welcomes new ideas and new knowledge.

In summary, then, folk society is a small and isolated society that lives
by traditional and conventionalized folkways, shared by all its members.
There is little division of labor and thus little social differentiation. What one
man does and knows, all do—and so the people of a folk society are remarkably similar in their actions, their beliefs, and their personality. Their social
relations are close and personal. A sense of the sacred pervades much of their
life, a life in which there is no consciousness of social change. There is social
stability and a common sharing of culture that helps to create a strong sense
of belonging together, as does isolation from and unfamiliarity with other
peoples and societies. A modern society, in turn, contrasts sharply with folk
society. It is a large and complex social organization with vast social differentiation, a multiplicity of social groups, impersonal social relations, and
social change that is not only an accepted fact but indeed frequently welcome
and sought for.

Feudal Society   Until recently, social scientists used the folk-modern typology
to analyze the difference between modern society and those traditional forms
of society that had preceded it. But, in fact, the idea of the folk society has
been most systematically developed by anthropologists through their study of
preliterate peoples. Widespread as it undoubtedly is, folk society as a type is
hardly representative of all human societies that preceded industrialization.
They are but small villages, and the territory of a folk society is a small area.
But long before the Industrial Revolution there were towns and cities and
there were societies with large populations covering a large geographical area.

Intermediate 50 societies group

Between the folk society and modern society, then, is another type, the *feudal*,[5] which continues to exist today.

Feudal society, upon inspection, reveals much that looks like folk society. There are the small peasant villages, relatively isolated, where life is regulated by customary ways, bound to tradition, and seems to have gone on unchanged for centuries. There is a folk wisdom handed down by oral communication, and there is social organization based upon kinship. But a closer look reveals some things not found in the preliterate societies the anthropologists describe. Often present in the peasant (feudal) village are people who are not peasants, though they may have come from peasant stock: priests, for example, who represent the religious faith that the peasants share with other peasants in other villages, and who provide one important link between the village and a larger society of which it is a part.

The village, then, is tied into a larger society, religiously, politically, and economically. The government in the feudal society includes the peasant village, but the seat of authority is in a distant city, and the lives of the peasants are governed by decisions made in remote towns by distant officials. Furthermore, they pay taxes to this authority and are controlled by its police powers. Then, too, some of what the peasant produces is taken to the markets of nearby towns, for the peasants of such a society support the small but dominant urban population. Since there is an urban population, though not an industrial one, the feudal society is more complex than is a folk society, and its people are more culturally heterogeneous. They are more differentiated by function and by typical experiences—there are peasants, artisans, merchants, clergymen, and a ruling elite. Tradition is important in a feudal society, and the sense of change is limited. But the same traditions are not binding on all, for the traditions of the peasantry exist alongside other traditions. There is literacy in a feudal society and, thus, a small but significant educated stratum. The man of knowledge in feudal society is most likely to be in the church, but there are also scholars who are not churchmen. There is also a greater differentiation of wealth and power in feudal society than in folk societies, where all are usually equally poor, and where power differentials are always small.

In feudal societies, the city is an urban center in which is clustered the small urban elite. It constitutes the point of contact between the society and the larger social world beyond its borders. It also sits astride the major transportation routes that link the urban elite to the peasants and to the lesser and provincial elites who reside in the provinces. The city offers an urban and civilized mode of life that contrasts sharply with that of the impoverished

---

[5] For a discussion of the distinction between folk and feudal, see Gideon Sjoberg, *The Pre-industrial City: Past and Present* (New York: Free Press, 1960).

and illiterate peasantry, whose status and life style is usually viewed with disdain by those in the city. Indeed, in a feudal society, the peasantry are closely controlled; land ownership belongs, not to them, but to provincial lords. They are forced to pay taxes, to pay rent in money or more likely in goods and services, and thus to yield a surplus that makes possible the existence of an urban population. Given the significant differentials in power, the peasantry yield up a surplus that they can ill afford and thus live in poverty that demands unremitting toil.

Societies in Transition   The folk and feudal societies of man's long past still abound in the world. Africa, Asia, and Latin America are great land areas mostly made up of such societies. But no longer do these societies continue as they once were; instead they are undergoing radical and often disruptive change. If they are not yet modern societies, they are no longer the folk and feudal societies they once were; they are societies in transition.[6] They are not yet modern, but they are *modernizing*.

These once traditional societies undergoing modernization offer to the student of society an almost endless laboratory for the study of human society and its social institutions, and they provide the opportunity to carry on the *comparative* study, which Durkheim said is sociology itself. In particular, modernization requires radical changes in the economic and political institutions, the development of a modern bureaucracy and an educational system. It requires urbanization and the development of an urban-based labor force. This in time brings significant changes in population composition and also in population trends. It brings into being such large-scale and secular groups as political parties, labor unions, and professional associations, which in turn compete for the loyalty and commitment of youth with such more traditional groups as tribes and villages, clans and kinship groups, and even the religious groups so often dominant in feudal societies. New systems of human recruitment and social control are created, and new modes of socialization (and resocialization) come into being. Formal and deliberately created social groups replace those traditional ones by which people are linked to one another, and the scale of organization increases sharply. This twentieth-century process of the transformation of human society from folk and feudal into modern societies is analyzed by social scientists in conceptual terms not unlike, but more sophisticated than those that nineteenth-century sociologists used in tracing the European transition from *Gemeinschaft* to *Gesellschaft*. From time to time, in the chapters that follow, some detailed attention will be given to these changes.

---

[6] It is common in social science to speak of *modernizing* societies; Gideon Sjoberg speaks of *transitional* societies; see his "The Rural-Urban Dimension in Preindustrial, Transitional, and Industrial Societies," in Robert E. L. Faris, *Handbook of Modern Sociology* (Chicago: Rand McNally, 1964), pp. 127–160.

Modern Society   The effort to characterize folk and feudal societies stems in part from a comparative analysis that is concerned with finding what is distinctive and definitive about *modern* society. As we saw earlier, sociology emerged from the intellectual concern with the problematic nature of modern society and was strongly influenced by the conservative response to industrialism as threatening the small solidary groups deemed essential to human existence. A first and more simple characterization of modern society, then, emphasized it being large and complex, industrial, urbanized, bureaucratized, with much of its social relations transferred from a personal to an impersonal basis. From the work of Ferdinand Toennies in describing *Gemeinschaft* and *Gesellschaft* as basic types of societies, several generations of sociologists have drawn a set of conclusions about the organization of modern society. They have emphasized the loss of personal relations and the complementary loss of social ties that bound the person to the society. From here it is but a short step to the perspective that defines modern society as *mass society,* a perspective that draws upon the weaknesses of modern society as highlighted by a comparison with an idealized version of folk society or of Toennies' *Gemeinschaft.* As Daniel Bell rightly notes, there is in the concept of mass society a confusion between "a judgment regarding the *quality* of modern experience," and "a presumed scientific statement concerning the disorganization of society created by industrialization and the demands of the masses for equality."[7] For the basic idea of mass society lies in the presumed failure of modern society to provide a communal context within which men can find meaning and value in their shared existence and can find solidary relations with others like themselves. Industrialism, it is charged by those who utilize the concept, has burst forever the small, closely-knit communities (*Gemeinschaft*) of the past and has left men unattached and unrelated, uprooted in a large and impersonal society that cannot command loyalties in the fashion of communal orders.

What joins together in the concept of mass society, then, is a tradition of sociological analysis that draws heavily from (but does not begin with) Toennies' social analysis and a tradition of social criticism that draws from both radical and conservative sources in the nineteenth century and to this very point of time in the twentieth. The first is an effort at scientific analysis that seeks to understand the kind of society that industrialism made possible, whereas the second is concerned with severely criticizing the quality of life in such a society. Both are relevant and worthy intellectual enterprises, but they are not identical. The result of merging them, however, has been a readiness in social science to accept uncritically the description of mass society as

[7] Daniel Bell, *The End of Ideology* (New York: Free Press, 1960), pp. 26–27.

composed of lonely and isolated individuals, a description, we shall see later, that sociologists also at one time applied to urbanism.

Although there is validity in the sociological perspective that points out how thoroughly mass society reflects the erosion of the primary and communal ties of traditional societies, it does not follow from this that modern society has become a void. Otherwise how do we account for the fact that despite almost a century of such analysis, modern society stubbornly refuses to collapse? It does not follow that the erosion of some traditional forms is not to be followed by the creation of new ones; to assume so is to deny to modern man the age-old capacity to create new groups and new social structures as a way of meeting change.

One of the basic tenets about mass society is that the individual becomes mass man, the isolated person bereft of meaningful social relations, and that this implies the dissolution of social groups, except for the large society itself and its centralized political institutions. But this does not describe modern society, which is a vast and complex network of social groups of all kinds and sizes: fraternal, civic, educational, community, professional, economic, political, ideological, and so on. All kinds of people belong to and participate in them, and through them they are attached to the large society. Robert MacIver calls modern society the *multigroup society* to give meaning to the idea of a complex network of interdependence built upon a vast number of social groups with overlapping memberships.[8] All men, at least, are not rootless and detached in modern society; most men, in fact, are linked to their society in a way that gives meaning to their lives and that ties them into normatively ordered relations with others.

Part of the difficulty in assessing modern society is that it is compared with an idealized version of *Gemeinschaft* and of folk society. The common version of the folk community present it as free of conflict and without the pressures and tensions that make life difficult for modern man. But this is utopia, not a real society. The anthropologist, Oscar Lewis, for example, revisited Tepoztlan, the first village that Robert Redfield had studied in formulating the concept of folk society.[9] His perspective found it to contain discord, criminal behavior, politically-generated violence, poverty, oppression, and interpersonal relations marked by fear, envy, and distrust. If folk society is presented in an idealized version, which ignores some of the harsher realities of life in primitive and peasant societies, so too is the version of modern society as mass society a one-sided view that points out the negative aspects but ignores the positive. Thus, Daniel Bell says,

[8] Robert MacIver, *The Web of Government* (New York: Macmillan, 1947).

[9] Oscar Lewis, "Tepoztlan Restudied: A Critique of the Folk-Urban Conceptualization of Social Change," *Rural Sociology*, 18 (1953), 121–134.

If it is granted that mass society is compartmentalized, superficial in personal relations, anonymous, transitory, specialized, utilitarian, competitive, acquisitive, mobile, and status-hungry, the obverse side of the coin must be shown, too—the right to privacy, to free choice of friends and occupation, status on the basis of achievement rather than of ascription, a plurality of norms and standards, rather than the exclusive and monopolistic social controls of a single dominant group.[10]

Similarly, the work of the sociologist Edward Shils has, for a quarter of a century, been concerned with how modern man is attached to modern society, particularly through the vital primary groups that emerge in large-scale organizations and provide an important source of linkage between the person and society. He says:

As I see it, modern society is no lonely crowd, no horde of refugees fleeing from freedom. It is not *Gesellschaft*, soulless, egotistical, loveless, faithless, utterly impersonal and lacking any integrative forces other than interest or coercion.[11]

Instead, Shils views it as integrated through the complex web of social ties—primordial, personal, sacred, and civil—which give it form and shape and a vibrant if often discordant existence.

It is held together by an infinity of personal attachments, moral obligations in concrete contexts, professional and creative pride, individual ambition, primordial affinities, and a civil sense which is low in many, high in some, and moderate in most persons.[12]

To interpret modern society as mass society, then, is to use a selective frame of reference that depends for its historic referent on a conservative, idealized, and historically inaccurate image of folk society. Such an interpretation ignores the fact that the individualism it worries about is also a creation of modern society, as is opportunity and mobility. Both scientific analysis and critical intellectual inquiry require a more balanced view of modern society than the concept of mass society gives us.

The Diversity of Social Groups   The types of social groups characteristic of folk society—kinship, clan, village—decline in frequency and significance in the transition to modern society. In turn, groups characteristic of modern society emerge, and typically these are large, formal, and specialized. The typically small structure of one type of society gives way to the large structure of another. Yet small-scale organization remains frequent and significant in modern society—families, friendship groups, work teams, and committees are

[10] Bell, *The End of Ideology,* p. 29.
[11] Edward Shils, "Primordial, Personal, Sacred and Civil Ties," *The British Journal of Sociology,* 8 (June, 1957), 131.
[12] Shils, p. 131.

examples. From *primary group* to *bureaucracy* may perhaps symbolize the range from small to large structures found in modern society, in which the increase in size as a quantitative change has qualitative consequences.

But from small to large size is not the only significant dimension in examining the range of social forms in modern society. Some social groups are highly cohesive and well-integrated, while others reveal a looseness of structure, a lack of cohesion, and no systematic organization. Primary groups display a high degree of consensus, and bureaucracies are highly organized. But modern communities are usually weakly integrated. Although bureaucracies are usually well integrated functionally, its members do not usually share high consensus, except on a very limited range of norms. Some of the differences in the function and integration of significant social groups in modern society need to be explored more fully. In the rest of this chapter, we shall examine that much analyzed phenomenon, the small group, and in the two chapters that follow we shall look at the large social group often deemed as typical for modern society, the formal organization (or bureaucracy), and then examine the community.

SMALL GROUPS

The recognition that the world is being constantly transformed by increased size and complexity of human organization has been a critical element in the sociological consciousness for over a century now. The concern for the possible deleterious consequences of this enlargement of man's social groups has dominated not only sociological thought but also a great deal of political, ideological, and philosophical thinking. It has created a denigrating perspective of the large organization, and particularly the bureaucratic one, and it has also led to a prevalent romanticization of the small group. This moral and often affective response to the increasing size of social groups has rendered more difficult an objective sociological analysis of the issue of size and complexity. The social values that seem to be threatened by growth in organization often intrude into the effort at social analysis, and the result is often more moral (and moralizing) than intellectual.

The conception of the small group as a scientific problem in sociology came only with the emergence of a complementary conception of large-scale organization, and particularly bureaucracy, as a scientific problem. The idea that size is a significant variable means that each type, the small and the large, differ in certain significant ways. Another way to put it is the idea that an increase in size has some definite qualitative consequences for organization. As groups increase in size, they change qualitatively—they are not only larger, they are a different kind of group. What these differences are that characterize small and large groups has therefore become an important scientific problem for sociology.

The roots of the sociological interest in the consequences of growth in group size go back at least to the early decades of the last century, when social thinkers were disturbed by the possible consequences of the industrialization of society: the loss of tradition and custom, of kinship and community, in the transition to new and larger forms of social life. Emile Durkheim's work signifies much of this concern. His analysis of the division of labor was intended to explicate some of the social consequences inherent in both increasing size and complexity of groups. He recognized the direction of social change in the Western world, and he shared with others a concern over the difficulties of consensus and integration when the typical mode of social organization was large and complex. Ferdinand Toennies' famous typology, *Gemeinschaft und Gesellschaft,* was also based upon a recognition that the major trend in the Western world was from small to large-scale organization, and his typology constitutes the basic intellectual assessment in the nineteenth century of the meaning of this change.

The concern of Toennies and Durkheim with small groups was specifically with the small community in contrast to the large urban complex, with the small society of traditional, agrarian life contrasted to the new industrial society of great magnitude. But a concern for genuinely small groups—those with only a handful of members—was first introduced into sociology by Georg Simmel (1858–1918), a German sociologist with a somewhat unsystematic but extraordinarily perceptive and innovative mind, who opened up a whole new set of issues for sociologists. He is the predecessor of that contemporary generation of social-psychologically oriented sociologists who are interested in careful and precise analysis of the interaction that occurs in small groups.

The Problem of Small Groups The interest of the sociologist in the study of small groups has broadened from earlier, more limited concerns, until now it is a major concern of contemporary sociology. It is important to indicate as precisely as possible the *sociological* problems the small group poses, for psychologists have also undertaken the study of small groups, particularly in laboratory and experimental situations, in order to study psychological problems. Perhaps the major interest of sociologists in the small group is still in the *primary group,* though this has gone well beyond the interest in socialization that led Cooley to "discover" it. A very considerable range of sociological research now gives much attention to a particular kind of small group that is also primary in Cooley's sense—the *peer group.*

The study of the primary group (including the peer group) attracts sociologists for several reasons. First of all, there is the continued interest in socialization, now including adult socialization, for which the primary group, in the form of family and peer group, is so relevant. Then there is the related interest in social control. Both of these issues are but two aspects, albeit central ones, in the larger matter of the relation between the individual and the group. The study of the small and primary group is an excellent context for exploring ideas about this problem. But another major problem for which the study of the primary group, particularly in the form of the peer group, is useful is the function of the small group within the structure of large groups. Here, small and large groups are not presented as opposite phenomena instead, large groups always subdivide into smaller groups of varying sizes, including some that are small and primary. In such large-scale organizations as factories, corporations, armies, and the like, the primary groups that indigenously emerge are significant for the intermediary functions they perform between the person and the large group. Both of these concerns about the primary group—as agency of socialization and social control and as intermediary between the person and the large group—suggest that the primary group is a significant type of social group even in modern society where large-scale social structure is so pervasive.

But the primary group is not the only concern with the small group that the sociologist has. He has also studied the small group under laboratory conditions to explore experimentally a range of problems in human behavior: norms and social control, decision making, group structure, morale and cohesiveness, leadership, democratic and authoritarian atmospheres, communication, task performance, and the effects of group size. In some of these studies, to be sure, the small group was hardly *problematic;* rather, it was merely a convenient context for easily controllable and thus potentially quite rigorous studies of human behavior, either individual behavior or group behavior. But in many others the nature of the small group was a foremost concern.

THE PRIMARY GROUP

For quite some time, the small group and the primary group were practically synonymous for American sociologists. Furthermore, the primary group was first thought of only as a socializing group, and so the primary groups were the family and the peer group of children. This limited conception of the primary group failed to see its significance in other spheres of social life. Therefore, the primary group had to be rediscovered several times in American sociology from the 1920s to the 1940s before sociologists had a full sense of its significance.

Perhaps the first rediscovery of the primary group came in the famous Hawthorne study carried out by Elton Mayo and his associates at Western Electric.[13] These studies of the behavior of workers on the job ran throughout the decade of the twenties and explored every possible influence on worker productivity and job satisfaction. It was only toward the end of years of careful research that Mayo, a psychologist, discovered that social relationships among workers was an important variable in their behavior; prior to that, he had been defining his problem as one of *individual* behavior, and thus had been seeking out various physical and psychological influences on the individual worker that affected his work performance. The discovery, then, that small networks of interpersonal relations among workers who interacted in a face-to-face situation had a great deal to do with their behavior came as a great and revealing discovery. The primary group among adults took on a new significance for sociologists. The Hawthorne study now is viewed as one of the great pioneering efforts in industrial sociology, and *Management and the Worker* is a classic in modern social science.

But the primary group was to continue to be rediscovered in still other contexts. In the 1930s, William F. Whyte studied the life-style and social behavior of postadolescent young men in a depression-poor Italian slum area of Boston, and from observations based upon actual participation he wrote one of the best one-man studies in American sociology, *Street Corner Society.*[14] Then, during World War II, the army-sponsored researches of social scientists on the attitudes and behavior of the American soldier led again to the discovery of another context—army life and combat—in which the primary group was a significant unit in understanding human behavior. The study that emerged from this research, *The American Soldier,* provided a detailed analysis of the primary group under the stress conditions of combat as well as its significance for the citizen abruptly conscripted into military service.[15] Studies made for army intelligence on the German soldier also provided strong evidence of the importance that the primary group has for army life.[16] More recent studies have predictably rediscovered the primary group among adolescents as a major factor in influencing behavior in the high school.[17] So, too, have delinquency studies discovered that delinquent behavior is very often a

---

[13] A detailed accounting of the study is Fritz Roethlisberger and William J. Dickson, *Management and the Worker* (Cambridge: Harvard University Press, 1947).

[14] Enlarged Edition. Chicago: University of Chicago Press, 1955.

[15] Samuel A. Stouffer and others, *The American Soldier: Combat and Its Aftermath.* Studies in Social Psychology in World War II, Volume II (Princeton, N.J.: Princeton University Press, 1949). See also Edward A. Shils, "Primary Groups in the American Army," in Robert K. Merton and Paul F. Lazarsfeld, *Continuities in Social Research: Studies in the Scope and Method of "The American Soldier"* (New York: Free Press, 1950), pp. 16–39.

[16] Shils, "Primordial, Personal, Sacred and Civil Ties," pp. 135–136.

[17] James Coleman, *The Adolescent Society* (New York: Free Press, 1961).

group-influenced phenomenon, and interpersonal relations in a primary group often have more to do with becoming delinquent than do the usual range of "background" factors.[18] The primary group, in short, has been rediscovered enough times in sociological research over the past thirty years for sociologists to develop a full appreciation of its importance in social life and of the scope of its functions in the organization of society.

The Meaning of Primary Group   A primary group is evidently a small group, yet not all small groups are primary; size is only one criterion. Furthermore, what is small has never been made explicit in sociological research or theory. The contemporary small group laboratory experiments seem to define a small group implicitly as one small enough for face-to-face interaction. But how small that is, is never stated; operationally, however, it would seem to be from two to twenty at the most, and most experiments rarely utilize more than five or six. What Charles Horton Cooley meant by a primary group, is stated as follows:

> By primary groups I mean those characterized by intimate face-to-face association and cooperation. They are primary in several senses, but chiefly in that they are fundamental in forming the social nature and ideals of the individual.[19]

He identified as the "most important" of these groups "the family, the play-group of children, and the neighborhood or community of elders."[20] It is evident from Cooley's own discussion, and from the subsequent discussion of others, that the primary group is regarded as a small and intimate group, within which highly affective relationships exist. Thus the concept of primary group gets at two things: a type of social relationship and the type of group within which this relationship is sustained. Let us look at each of these in turn.

The primary relation between human beings is probably best exemplified as that idealized one between mother and child, between lovers, between the closest of friends. It is a nonmanipulative relationship of love, of close affectional attachment, of emotional involvement, and it is never viewed instrumentally, as something useful and a means to some other end; rather, it is valued as an end in itself. It is a relationship, then, the existence of which needs no extrinsic justification; it is always of intrinsic value. It is also the kind of relationship that is *personal,* not *impersonal;* it is a relationship between particular persons, and each person is interested in the other as a person, not as an agent or role-taker of social organization. Such a relationship involves

[18] Albert K. Cohen, *Delinquent Boys* (New York: Free Press, 1955).
[19] Charles Horton Cooley, *Social Organization* (New York: Scribner, 1909), p. 23.
[20] Cooley, p. 24.

the whole person in all his human concreteness, not merely a segmented aspect of the self with whom another has to interact in order to carry out certain necessary functions. One consequence of this is that the affectional primary relation is *diffuse*—it is not explicitly limited to specific obligations that each has for the other. One cannot specify beforehand what a parent or a friend is limited to do for the other in the relationship. In this sense it differs from the *contractual* relationship that governs, say, the obligations of employer and employee to one another.

This being the nature of the primary relationship, the question then becomes: what is the kind of group that best sustains and makes possible such a relationship? It is here that the nature of the primary group becomes our concern. Knowing that the primary group is defined in terms of the primary relationship, we can then understand why it is regarded as small and characterized by face-to-face interaction, though neither of these two characteristics are peculiar to primary groups. Though size is a crucial dimension, a small group is not necessarily primary. A primary group must be small enough for each person to be a unique personality to the other. As a group increases in size, interaction ceases to be between total persons but between agents and role-takers, which is segmental interaction, for it involves only very limited aspects of the self. Thus, being small is a *necessary* element of a primary group, but it is *not sufficient* to produce the primary relationship.

Just as size is a necessary but not sufficient condition for a primary group, so is face-to-face interaction. Face-to-face interaction is that direct and unmediated social interaction of close physical proximity that makes most likely the developing of a primary relationship. Although perhaps not impossible, it is only in the rarest of known examples that relationships we call primary do not depend on the physical proximity that permits face-to-face interaction. The limitation on interaction that distance imposes severely hampers the likelihood of the relationship becoming primary. Yet, such physical proximity does not guarantee that a primary relationship will emerge. Face-to-face interaction occurs every day when people ride a bus, shop in a store, or otherwise carry on a wide range of interactions in conducting their daily business. These face-to-face interactions are passing and ephemeral and may have little meaning for either party; neither responds to the other as a unique person. This implies that the development of the affective relationship that is primary cannot occur when interaction is infrequent and sporadic; instead, it must be frequent and durable. People need to interact frequently over an extended period of time. The longer people interact in a face-to-face manner, the more intimately do they become related to one another, the better they know one another as persons, the more they become attached to and affectively involved with one another.

There are, then, three basic conditions for a group to be primary: small size, face-to-face interaction, and reasonably long duration. The family and friendship groups meet these conditions, and the neighborhood and the small community can also, though in the modern world they frequently do not. It is important to recognize that the pure primary relationship is but imperfectly embodied in primary groups. Primary relationships have no extrinsic intent or goal, have no social function other than the affective relationship of feeling and sentiment. Therefore, they are best realized in spontaneous, freely chosen, and informally organized groups. But few if any primary groups can be the pure embodiment of the primary relationship. The family, for example, is an institutionalized group, and even friendship groups that fall within the context of organizations or social classes will not escape the intrusion of the demands and restraints of society into the primary relationships.

The Family as a Primary Group   Cooley and Mead have made it evident that the social relationship by means of which socialization can occur is a primary relationship. Cooley in particular emphasized the family as the primary unit of society in which were created human relationships that were emotionally strong, warm, and personal; within these there could develop what he considered to be the basic human nature of man: the capacity to live, to sympathize, to feel that one belongs with others, to feel loyal, to respect and have self-respect, and to love. Because it socializes the young, the family is the one primary group that is consciously recognized as functional for society, and which then is explicitly provided for by society. Yet this process of institutionalization builds into the family some of the elements that violate the primary relationship and are characteristic of *secondary* groups (a concept sociologists have created to express the idea of groups opposite of primary). The family always has more formal organization than other primary groups; there is authority vested in parents and in the role of male head of the family, for example, and there is a division of labor that places specific functions on particular family roles. In this way, the family can become a *secondary* group. Nonetheless, the family's small size, its face-to-face interaction, and its longer duration are the conditions that encourage primary-group formation. Indeed, there are cultural expectations and values that support the family as a primary group and provide for a maximization of those primary qualities in the interaction that goes on within the family as a social group.

Nonetheless, the fact that the concept of *family* designates both a major institution in society and a primary group suggests that the analysis of the family as the latter is always an incomplete analysis. It must also be analyzed as an institutional arrangement in society for carrying out a number of societal functions, of which those that make of the family a primary group, such as socialization, are only some—other family functions would not require it to be a primary group. (That is why this book has a later chapter on the family as an institution.)

The institutionalization of the family, then, presents a possible threat to the supremacy of its primary relations. Perhaps this is seen best in premodern family groups, where an agrarian economy and the absence of urban occupations ties the individual solidly to the kinship group and makes him dependent on it for his major roles in society. Prior to industrialization, most people lived their lives in small and enduring groups—such as kinship and community—and relations in such a context were largely culturally defined and prescribed (and some proscribed); thus, these groups became conventionalized, and less natural and spontaneous than their primary character might lead one to expect.

Perhaps it is just because in modern society the individual is no longer so functionally dependent upon the family—he can always earn his living independent of family—that expectations of primary relations become paramount. People want a happy marriage and spontaneous evidence of love and trust. They frequently fail to realize that human relationships are also mediated through socially sanctioned norms and expectations. To be a good wife, a woman cannot merely love her husband and children. She is expected by her husband, but also by society, to perform certain functions, such as caring for children and for the house, preparing meals, and numerous other tasks; in turn she can legitimately expect her husband to be a good provider. Each partner to the marriage asks certain institutionally assigned functions of one another, and certainly can and does judge and evaluate one another, to some extent, in terms of how well they fulfill these role-demands. Nor does love necessarily conquer all or forgive all. In *Is Anybody Listening?* William H. Whyte dealt, in a revealing way, with the interaction of family and corporation and the consequences for that highly primary yet institutionalized relationship, marriage.[21] In particular, he pointed to the devastating effects upon those marriages where the woman would not or could not live up to corporate expectations about the role of the corporation wife. Yet, the corporation also recognized the primary nature of the family when it expected it to function as what Whyte called a "refueling station," a social group that provided the love and warmth that resuscitated the exhausted executive and readied him once more in energy and spirits for the daily business struggle.

However distorted the corporate view of the family may be, as a primary group the family does do more than socialize the young. It provides a significant set of primary relations that have enduring value in the life of the

[21] William H. Whyte, *Is Anybody Listening?* (New York: Simon and Schuster, 1952), Chapters 8 and 9.

individual. It is a refuge from the world of secondary and manipulative relations, a group in which the person is considered and responded to as a unique
and valued individual. In a world that is ever more large-scale and impersonally organized, it is the primary group dimension of the family that becomes
increasingly important.

THE PEER GROUP

The attachment of the person to the primary group makes him susceptible
to its pressures and demands, and so makes of the primary group an effective
agency of social control. How it controls the person and for what purposes or
ends then becomes an additional issue in the study of the primary group.
Another concern has been the question of whether or not the primary group
exerts control over the individual to support or to subvert society; that is, to
control his behavior in conformity with the norms of society or against such
norms. A more specific concern that is theoretically similar has been about
primary groups within large-scale organization, where management has viewed
them as acting either to control the individual to support the organization's
norms and goals or to violate them and thus to subvert the aims of the organization. These concerns focus on the place of the primary group within the
community and within large-scale organization and on its role as a mediating
agency between the person and the larger group. The ability of the primary
group to exercise effective social control is one aspect of this, but so is its
ability to socialize the person into new roles and situations. It is then not the
family but the primary group of friends and coequals, the *peer group,* which
becomes the focus of these concerns.

Unlike the family, the peer group is not institutionalized. Rather, it emerges
spontaneously and naturally from among the interactions of social equals,
who are thus likely to share the same life conditions. Unlike the family, also,
the peer group does not have the hierarchy that age grading and institutionalized authority bring to it, though peer groups do have leaders. It is the
equality of an age-defined status that makes a group of adolescents a peer
group, but it is an equality of work-status that makes a group of factory
workers a peer group.

The power of the peer group to control behavior and thus have some effect
upon what goes on within larger organizations has been explored many times
since Mayo and his associates first discovered the primary group as an organ-
izer and controller of work behavior. One of their most influential studies
was that of the Bank Wiring Room, where researchers found impressive evidence of the ability of the peer group to control behavior and thus affect the

pattern of behavior within the larger organization.[22] Careful observation of fourteen workers engaged in an interrelated production task revealed a pattern of organization that had spontaneously emerged among these workers and was upheld by norms of their own. This group organization existed within the pattern of formal organization created for the performance of the job by management, which established official norms for how work was to be done and what standards of output were to prevail. But the peer group set its own norms of behavior and, for example, developed such cooperative patterns as exchanging work assignments, even though this was officially forbidden. Most important of all, the peer group developed its own consensus about output of work, and each worker's behavior was governed by his own group's norms, not by those of management. These norms allowed less output than management wanted and from the official point of view, the peer group was responsible for a restriction of output. Furthermore, the group was remarkably effective in handling the individual who tended to stray from the norms of the group and increase his output.

A large number of factory studies by industrial sociologists have since documented the principle that workers will, on their own group intitiative, restrict output by setting production norms of their own and will then quite effectively control the behavior of individual workers. Nor can such group restrictions be easily seduced by managerial efforts to provide individual inducements and rewards for maximizing individual effort. Such efforts as piecework, bonus payments, and the like, have encountered the serious resistance of workers organized into effective peer groups. Furthermore, the recalcitrant worker meets the opposition of the group to his "rate-busting" performance and finds strong sanctions meted out. Punishment can take the form of ridicule, harassment, ostracism, and even physical violence.

The analysis of such research has often focused primarily on the demonstrated power of the peer group to impose group norms on its members in the face of and contrary to the official norms and regulations of the factory. But such analysis often provides too little emphasis on the fact that the peer group emerges naturally and spontaneously among those who share the same life-situation and environmental conditions—in this case, workers in a factory —and that it is a collective and cooperative effort to achieve a level of control over the circumstances of work that cannot be done by the individual alone. The emergence of work-restricting and regulation-violating conduct among workers testifies to the limited ability of such large and impersonal organizations to socialize its employees to its organizational norms and to a desire to conform to official standards of behavior.

An extended series of studies carried out on enlisted men during World

---

[22] Roethlisberger and Dixon, *Management and the Worker,* Part IV.

War II, and fully reported in *The American Soldier,* provided evidence that the peer group does not necessarily operate *against* the large-scale organization but may function to support it. It may be the peer group that effectively ties the individual into the larger group by giving him status in a set of primary relations. Indeed, for civilians conscripted into the army, the existence of satisfactory primary relations is a fundamental factor in their being able to function effectively in combat situations and withstand the strains and stresses, the fatigue and danger, of combat. Both American and German soldiers were influenced less by propaganda about the aims of the war, the meaning of the conflict, and the concept of the great causes at stake, than they were by a sense of loyalty and obligation to their comrades. Primary relations bound them closely to a few others with whom they shared hardship and danger, and made them reluctant to leave them or let them down. Thus, the rewarding interaction of comradeship was more important for morale than all the efforts to convince conscripted soldiers about the national or even international importance of what they were doing.

The German Army during World War II fought effectively and seemed to maintain morale until the very end, despite some sustained efforts at psychological warfare intended to weaken their resolve to fight on, particularly when there were serious reverses, and the war was going against them. A subsequent study found that the propaganda had little effect and that the German soldier, like the American, was bound into primary ties of enduring comradeship, and his loyalty held him to the task of combat and sustained his morale. This study revealed two types of primary ties that enabled the German Army to resist disintegration and remain relatively cohesive until the last days of combat.[23] One of these was among a "hard core" of Nazi soldiers, younger men who were enthusiasts for army life and had an ideology of community solidarity. They were unsparing of themselves and provided a significant model for other men around them. But they were never more than a minority of the German soldiers, and there were fewer of them as the war went on and conscription drew in more of the ordinary, non-Nazi German. For these ordinary soldiers, it was the highly personal ties within the small combat unit that held them to their task even when the German Army faced defeat.

If desertion can be taken as one index of social disintegration (as Shils and Janowitz did in this study), then the German Army resisted disintegration until the very last, for it had few deserters until then. Among those who did desert, a failure to assimilate into a primary group was the most important factor in their desertion, more so than any political dissent. In fact, anti-Nazi political dissenters did not desert, and when captured, justified this by refer-

[23] Edward A. Shils and Morris Janowitz, "Cohesion and Disintegration of the Wehrmacht in World War II," *Public Opinion Quarterly,* 12 (1948), 280–315.

ence to their sense of comradely solidarity. In a later study, Shils found that Soviet soldiers were much the same; their motivation for combat "drew relatively little sustenance from any attachment to the central political and ideological symbols of the society in which they lived."[24] Instead, motivation came from other sources, of which one was "the morale of the small unit, i.e., the mutual support given by members of the group to each other. . . ."[25]

These studies of men under combat are striking cases of the significance of primary relations for large-scale organization. The small primary groups that are first formed under conditions of army training develop into deep and lasting friendships and into a comradeship on which men's very lives depend, providing them with the rationale to endure danger and discomfort and frequently to risk their own lives for others. From the perspective of the army, their morale is higher, and their combat effectiveness is greater. In addition, these studies also underscore the importance of the primary group for sustaining the individual and giving him emotional support and security. Without the intervening group, the individual stands alone within the large organization, and isolated individuals are unable to resist organizational demands. But the support of the primary group also integrates them more effectively into the larger organization, enabling them to socialize effectively to its operations, to learn their way around, and soon to feel a normal part of it. Particularly when first becoming a part of a large organization, the individual feels alone and insecure—a stranger, uncertain about everything. The primary group that takes him in and "shows him the ropes" provides a sense of personal security that eases the transition to new roles.

This brings us around to our starting point. The socialized person has developed a human nature that now needs the emotional response and affection of others, the warmth and intimacy of close human association; without it, he suffers a sense of personal disorientation that may very well produce neuroses and emotional disturbances. But this developed need for human intimacy with some few others then has significant consequences for the participation of the individual in the group. Where his participation proceeds through such sustaining primary relations, he becomes an effective member of the larger group; where it does not, he is not effectively integrated into the larger organization, his own performance is lessened, and his personal well-being is hampered. Without primary relations, the individual has no strong sense of belonging to a group; not feeling a part of the group, he feels lonely. Thus, college freshmen and newly drafted soldiers can be homesick, feeling alone and unwanted, even when surrounded by many others. Being lonely is a

---

[24] Shils, "Primordial, Personal, Sacred and Civil Ties," p. 141.
[25] Shils, p. 141.

psychic, not a physical state of affairs. For college freshmen and new soldiers, this situation usually abates in time. They soon become friends with others in the same situation, and new primary relations are formed that serve to aid in integrating the new member into the large group.

Peer Groups and Subcultures   Although the peer group in armies and factories functions as a significant link between the individual and the organization, it can also serve to mobilize resistance to the official demands and requirements of the organization, providing the milieu of interaction within which counter-norms and values emerge and become operative in controlling human behavior. The peer group is located at the very genesis of those subcultures that arise and give concrete expression to the meaning of experience within large groups. Particularly within hierarchical organizations we find significant subcultural responses to the organization and its official creeds and aims, emerging from those who are in subordinate status: enlisted men in the army, workers in the corporation, and students in the high school or college. The existence of primary relations permits full expression of opinion and attitude that might otherwise be inhibited among impersonally related individuals, encouraging the communication of ideas about the meaning of experience. The emergence of the primary group may be a coalescence of relations among those who share similar experiences by virtue of similar status, and who share their positive and negative responses to the situations in which they find themselves.

When small peer groups emerge among enlisted men in the army or among workers in a factory, the larger aggregate of enlisted men or workers becomes an extended network of peers, among whom there is a sense of sympathy for shared status and a "grapevine," a communication network, that allows for a wider sharing of the norms. Thus, peer groups are an important and fundamental unit in the emergence of subcultures that challenge the power and the official norms and values of the more institutionalized groups and the great impersonal organizations of modern society. This generating of challenge and resistance to the established social structure is an important source of social change. This, in turn, depends upon the effectiveness of small peer groups for making possible the cohesion, solidarity, and capacity for organized action of larger networks of peer relationships. The sense of "we" that so closely identifies one with others, and which Cooley regarded as an indication of the primary group, flows out from the smaller and more intimate peer group to the larger network of peer relations. If these relationships are not so intimate and not always face-to-face, they are developed, nevertheless, in a perspective of empathy that enables individuals to view them as extensions of their primary relations, as interaction with others who share the same fate and life-circumstances as they do. Cooley, indeed, saw neighborhoods and communities as just such larger and somewhat more extended "we-groups" that are more primary than they are secondary.

Peer Groups and Adolescents   Understanding the significance of the peer group for the emergence of subcultures and thus for potentialities for change is necessary for understanding the relation of the peer group to the adolescent. The adolescent peer group is significant in the life-experience of the young person in modern society, for it partially detaches him from the influence of that other primary group, the family, and it serves to socialize him into an adolescent subculture providing a particular orientation to the larger world. Adolescence is an uncertain and insecure status in modern society, one that has never been precisely defined. The adolescent is neither a child nor an adult, and he is a minor (one not yet of adult status) in law. Unlike primitive societies, modern society lacks puberty rites and rites of passage, those cultural ceremonies that signify that the individual passes from one age-defined status to another. In this rather extended and ill-defined period of uneasy and uncertain transition to adulthood, primary relations among peers provides a context for ready acceptance by others and for an empathic sharing of the problems of growing up. Interaction by peers then produces groups that are highly valued by the individual; his own felt need for the group makes him particularly anxious to be accepted—thus, the commonly observed conformity of the adolescent to his group.

But the adolescent peer group has other functions, too. Like all primary groups, it socializes its members. This comes at a crucial time in the life of the individual, for peer group socialization now competes with and sometimes contradicts the socialization of the family. It socializes the adolescent to peer status and to a subculture that manifests the values and orientation of adolescents to a society they only fit into uncertainly and only understand imperfectly. In this way, it provides the adolescent with a means for coming to grips with the larger society in terms of resistance and challenge, even rebelliousness, that very few adolescents could possess individually. The sustaining support of peers and the emotional ties to a primary group are necessary elements in the generating of an adolescent subculture. The non-conformity with the adult world of official structures and established values and norms is then possible at a price of high conformity to the peer group and to adolescent values and norms.

There is a sociological similarity here with the peer groups of workers in factories and their subculture of resistance to the official authority and work standards of the corporation. In each case, the peer group is the core element in generating a perspective and orientation that gives expression to the meaning of the experience of these individuals of subordinate status to a situation over which they formally have little control. The network of group relations that emerge around primary group interests and the control over individual behavior then permits these subordinate persons to take back some control over their own life-circumstances. Workers impose their own production norms and restrict output to less than management wants; adolescents, in turn, find means for having adult-forbidden experiences (sex and smoking, for example), for resisting the work and study values that are official for the school, and for developing a set of their own values that center around personality development and around creating styles and fads that often repel and bewilder adults. The latter makes them consumer-oriented and active participants in the mass culture, which in turn is highly youth oriented.

THE STUDY OF SMALL GROUP BEHAVIOR

The interest of sociologists in studying small groups has focused primarily on the small peer groups, which are so significant in relating the individual to the large organization. As a consequence, most studies of peer groups have been conducted in the natural context of large-scale organization. But for quite some time now a number of sociologists have been undertaking the study of small groups under controlled laboratory conditions. In varied experimental ways, they have sought to observe human behavior as an outcome of the face-to-face interaction of a small number of persons, being primarily interested in the *forms* of behavior that emanate from the interaction, rather than in the *content* of the interaction. They are more interested in *how* the group interacts than in *what* it interacts about.

Although the interest in the forms of interaction in small groups is a fairly recent interest of sociologists—practically all research comes after 1950—it was Georg Simmel more than fifty years ago who first suggested to sociologists the value to be derived from such study. Simmel was perhaps the first sociologist to suggest that qualitative changes were introduced in social interaction as a consequence of a change in the numbers of the group, such as an increase from two (a dyad) to three (a triad).[26] He pointed out that the dyad differs from all other social groups in that the two members have to confront, not a collectivity, but each other. It is the one mode of group relations in which the individual member cannot have the collective majority arrayed against him and cannot, therefore, be subject to the control and restraint that the group can exercise over any one of its members. The dyad, Simmel ob-

[26] Georg Simmel, "The Number of Members as Determining the Sociological Form of the Group," *American Journal of Sociology*, 8 (1902–1903), 1–46, 158–196.

served, does not develop a structure that transcends its particular members and leaves them feeling dependent on the group. But the addition of one member that turns a dyad into a triad achieves a major qualitative change in the nature of the relationships involved. This is the smallest of social groups that can build a structure that attains some control over the individual. The highly imaginative and creative mind of Simmel was able to explore the immense range of relationships possible in the triad and not in the dyad, providing a powerful demonstration of a sociological analysis that does not resort to psychological reductionism. He demonstrated what happened when a third person was added to the former dyad, a consequence for the nature of inter-action that was independent of the psychological attributes of the participants.

Simmel also explored some implications of the increase in the size of groups. For one thing, in a small group the members have an opportunity to interact directly with one another, but this declines as the group increases in size, and interaction is therefore mediated through some structural mechanism. The larger group necessarily develops various mechanisms for patterning interaction, such as status and position and a role differentiation, that constitutes a division of labor. Furthermore, the smaller group allows for that intense interaction that creates a closer involvement of the person with the group, but the larger group cannot sustain this mode of interaction; thus a weaker and more seg-mental attachment of the person to the group occurs in larger groups. Yet Simmel also recognized the more coercive and closer scrutiny of the small group over its members, and the liberation from this made possible by an increase in group size.

Small Groups in the Laboratory   Within the last two decades there has been a vast amount of research on human behavior in small groups undertaken by both sociologists and psychologists; this has frequently taken the form of carefully designed experiments rigorously conducted under laboratory conditions. These groups, usually assembled for the purpose of the study, are small— rarely having more than a dozen members and usually smaller than that— and are involved in face-to-face interaction. But these are not primary groups, for there is usually no duration to their interaction beyond the experiment, and the relationships that develop are not deep and personal. Nonetheless, the exploration of human behavior in these small group experiments has proved to be a useful way of examining a limited range of problems, both psycho-logical and sociological, and certainly has made possible more rigorous control and measurement than is usually possible in the complex and often ambiguous environment of natural groups.

A pioneer in the postwar upsurge of small group laboratory research in American sociology has been Robert Bales of Harvard University. In 1947 Bales and his associates began a series of experiments in small groups. Each group was given a task to carry out to completion, which usually consisted of a set of facts about a problematic situation, and a request that the group review the facts and make a recommendation for action to an administrator. A research staff observed and recorded the interaction in detail as the group discussed, agreed, disagreed, and sought to arrive at a consensus.[27] The observations that were minutely recorded ignored the content of the discussion—the particular task was of no issue to the research—and concentrated on the forms of interaction that occurred. Bales and his associates worked out a set of categories for observation, beginning first with a distinction between verbal remarks that are responses to others, and the comments of others that elicit these responses. The reactions in turn become positive or negative, and the comments are either those that offered suggestions or asked questions. A further breakdown of these produced twelve interaction categories as follows:

A.	Positive Reactions	Shows solidarity
		Shows tension release
		Shows agreement
B.	Problem-Solving Attempts	Gives suggestion
		Gives opinion
		Gives orientation
C.	Questions	Asks orientation
		Asks opinion
		Asks suggestion
D.	Negative Reactions	Shows disagreement
		Shows tension increase
		Shows antagonism

A careful analysis of data taken from a large number of studies seriously challenged the common idea that a small group consists of a leader and several followers, and that the leader is the best-liked and most active member of the group and is regarded by the others as the best performer in whatever tasks the group undertakes. Consequently, the Harvard observers developed the hypothesis of two complementary leaders, an *idea* man who initiates problem-solving attempts, but who also disagrees more with others and shows more antagonism to others, and a *best-liked* man who offers responses that are

[27] Compare Robert F. Bales, *Interaction Process Analysis: A Method for the Study of Small Groups* (Cambridge, Mass.: Addison-Wesley, 1950). A good summary of subsequent research by Bales and his associates, on which the following discussion is based, is Robert F. Bales, "Task Roles and Social Roles in Problem-Solving Groups," in Eleanor Maccoby, Theodore Newcomb, Eugene Hartley, eds., *Readings in Social Psychology,* 3rd Edition (New York: Holt, Rinehart and Winston, 1958), pp. 437–447.

positive—he agrees, is supportive, and makes humorous remarks that release group tension. He also asks more questions. The interaction in the group seems to bring forth two complementary roles, "with the idea man concentrating on the task and playing a more aggressive role, while the best-liked man concentrates more on social-emotional problems, giving rewards and playing a more passive role."[28]

A further important finding of the research had to do with frequency of participation in the group discussion. *High* participators were more likely to be the specialists in problem-solving, whereas *low* participators specialized in positive or negative responses or questions. This seems to follow from the fact that those who make many problem-solving attempts necessarily talk a lot, whereas those who are liked best achieve that liking by providing positive responses to others, including letting them talk more. It would seem then that leaders must choose between task effectiveness and popularity. But this seems also to make no distinction between sheer amount of activity and the value placed upon it by the members of the group. However, Bales suggests that an examination of a number of studies indicates that three factors emerge when members of small groups rate each other or are rated by observers. He calls them *activity, task ability,* and *likeability.* In effect, the former distinction between sociability and task performance is altered by further dividing the latter into two: activity, the effort of the individual to stand out from others and achieve an individual prominence; and task ability, the effort of the individual to contribute to the attainment of group goals. Although these two may both imply high participation, the group recognizes the difference.

There seems to be no simple correlation among these three types. A high standing in one of these activities does not preclude a person achieving a standing in another, but over all the populations studied, there is no prediction possible of a man's standing on one by knowing where he stands on another. On the basis of this, Bales suggests five types of roles in small groups:

1. The *good leader* or "great man," a rare type that is high on all three factors.

2. The *task specialist* who is high on activity and task ability but is less well-liked.

3. The *social specialist* who is well-liked but ranked less high on activity and task ability.

4. The *overactive deviant* who is high on activity but relatively low on task ability and likeability.

5. The *underactive deviant* who is simply low on all three factors.

These studies by Bales and others at Harvard by no means describe all

---

[28] Bales, "Task Roles and Social Roles in Problem-Solving Groups," p. 442.

the kinds of research that has been carried on under laboratory conditions.[29] Other studies have observed the emergence of group norms as a consequence of social interaction and the function of these norms in patterning behavior. These studies have also observed the exercise of social control by the group over the individual, sometimes in quite ingenious experimental situations. Some experimental studies have gone further than have observations on natural groups that have strongly documented the conformity of the individual to the group. Everyone in the group does not conform completely, and some group experiments have discovered at least some of the variations. For example, there is much less conformity to group judgments when the object being judged is unambiguous, and the judgment is a factual matter—such as the size or shape of a physical object. There is more conformity to group judgment, in turn, when the object to be judged is ambiguous, as an art object. But even then very self-confident persons will be less swayed by others' opinions. This suggests that status differentials in natural groups may have significance for conformity and control. Also, when individuals have their opinions "anchored" in groups significant to them, they will be less swayed by the opinions or norms of other groups. Then, too, if a person finds support for his more deviant opinions from another person, it will increase his likelihood to hold out against group pressures.

These few examples can barely suggest the many observations about behavior in small groups that help to illuminate the nature and consequences of social interaction. Other studies have been concerned with problem-solving alternatives, democratic and authoritarian leadership, differences in communication networks, morale and cohesion, and problems of group size. However valuable these studies have been, there are still some apparent limitations on the study of small groups as an approach to the study of social order. The creation of artificial groups in the laboratory for experiments in interaction around matters that are of small (or even no) concern to the participants risks losing the very significance of the cultural milieu that surrounds so much "real" interaction and gives it its meaning. The study of human behavior *in vacuo* has advantages in creating a laboratory-induced control over all relevant variables, which is the ideal for scientific research, but such control may distort the research by losing the rich and ambiguous milieu that is the typical context for social interaction. An equally relevant problem is that of abstracting findings from the laboratory and applying them to larger con-

---

[29] For a recent review of small group studies, see A. Paul Hare, "Interpersonal Relations in the Small Group," in Faris, *Handbook of Modern Sociology*, pp. 217–271. For a collection of representative studies, see A. Paul Hare, Edgar F. Borgatta, and Robert F. Bales, eds., *Small Groups: Studies in Social Interaction* (New York: Knopf, 1955). For an excellent summary and evaluation of small group research and theory, see Michael S. Olmsted, *The Small Group* (New York: Random House, 1959).

texts. In short, how to generalize findings from laboratory research to the natural group settings for human interaction, and whether or not larger group structures can in fact be analyzed by the study of small groups, remains an issue of import about which sociologists as yet disagree.

It is readily evident that many such experimental studies have practical utility and application. Large organizations cannot avoid organizing people into smaller groups, and knowledge about modes of interaction and leadership that enhance cooperative task performance is thus valued. That is why industry has often cooperated with and supported such studies, and this is also why the U.S. Air Force has supported small group research, for effective team performance is essential for its operation.

THE VALUE PROBLEMS OF SMALL GROUPS

An earlier generation of sociologists worried that the increasingly large scale of social organization meant the demise of small, and particularly, primary groups to the detriment of all. However this has not occurred. Although it is true that the small community has often become the large city, and that more and more people live in these cities and work in large organizations, man's capacity to build primary relations with others and to construct small groups is not impaired. Most of all, what the earlier sociologists did not anticipate was the effective and meaningful existence of small groups within large-scale ones. Though small groups are, therefore, still a significant element in the organization of modern society, there are two basic value problems about such groups, the origin of which is rooted in the dominant attitudes about small groups in American society. One of these problems has to do with the widespread animus against large organization and the consequent romantic preference for the small group. This value orientation that says small is good and big is bad produces a distorted view of the function and meaning of group size in modern society. A second problem, which follows from the first, is the widespread modern effort to exploit this value preference as well as to manipulate primary relations for extrinsic reasons.

The Preference for Small Groups   For more than a century now, in the Western world, there has been a dominant perspective that has placed strong value upon the small and personal in human relations. Small towns are supposed to be warm and friendly, big cities cold and impersonal. No less today within the younger generation than with numerous thinkers of nineteenth century Europe, the growth of large and impersonal organization is viewed as dwarfing the individual and denying him his individuality. The widely expressed fear of sameness and uniformity, as well as conformity and the stifling of creativity, are seen as the inevitable outcome of the eventual dominance of society by bureaucratic structures. The existentialist perspective has given philosophic support to this conception of a loss of selfhood before massive organizations and thus a romantic preference for small-scale human groups. Yet such an ideological perspective distorts what we know sociologically about the significance of size for social groups. Most importantly, small groups are not inherently free and democratic; indeed, historically, political democracy grew with the urbanism of the Western world. Secondly, social controls are stronger and more effective in small groups; the individual is indeed freer in the larger communities than in the smaller ones. Not all large groups are bureaucracies with their efforts at centralized control, but even bureaucracies exert a control only within a narrow range of the individual's action. In short, the problem of human freedom and group size is much more complicated than the oversimplified generalization that bigness in organization thwarts individuality.

The illusion of the moral superiority of small groups persists nonetheless; but here again, the personal preference for those relationships that are warm and intimate, that are primary, confuses personal desirability with social function. An increase in the scope of organization enhances other values, such as efficiency and organizational effectiveness. Even impersonality has its functional value; it may be necessary to be impersonal on many occasions if people are to be able to interact effectively and efficiently in accomplishing some task. To speak of the warmth and personal relations of the small community is to stress but one perspective or but one side of the coin. The small community or any other small human group also exerts greater social control and "invades" the personality to a much greater extent. By being so concerned with the person, the small group exposes the private individual to the others; the more intimate the relationship, the less there is that is secret or entirely a private matter. Thus, all social relations cannot be primary without denying the privacy so essential to human integrity and the "authenticity" of the person so emphasized in existential analysis. The greater formality and impersonality of secondary social relationships have this value, then, of protecting the person against an invasion of his privacy of feelings and thoughts by others. Role taking in a complex society may very well mean that we don "masks" behind which our true feelings are often hidden, but this also serves to protect these intimate feelings from an exposure that might bring attack if they are deviant, thus serving to protect our very individuality. The more people know about what we think and feel, the greater is the pressure to think and feel as they do. The intimacy and greater concern for us on the part of our primary groups is thus associated with a greater control over our behavior. We are less free in those groups in which we are most accepted.

This, then, is the paradox of the contrast between the small and large in human groups, between the primary and the secondary. Although a world without the primary would be cold and humanly unbearable, a world that is only primary in its relationships would be small and confining, one in which the group dominated the person, and in which human individuality and personal freedom were largely unknown. It is part of man's historic record that he became freer and more of an individual when he won some measure of independence from the small and confining groups of kinship and village, some liberation from the exclusively primary context of human life. The very concept of the individual person as something separate from his social groups —both as a fact of life and a social value—emerged strongly in human consciousness only in the larger network of relationships in complex and segmented societies.

The Manipulation of Primary Values   It is the very nature of primary relations that they are not a means to some other end, but are of intrinsic value and an end in themselves. However, a manipulative tendency to convert primary relations to means to other ends and to exploit the value inherent in them is endemic in modern culture. It is a source of moral corruption that has been a frequent target for the social critics of a business and success-oriented civilization. The essence of this pattern is exemplified, as we noted earlier, in the now famous book title, *How to Win Friends and Influence People,* where winning friends here means to be able to influence people, a presumed formula for success. In American society, in particular, the cultivation of seemingly personal and primary relations, of an apparent friendliness that quickly moves to a first-name basis and declines to "stand on ceremony," has frequently shocked, confused, and sometimes alienated European observers. At its most obvious, this is apparent in aggressive salesmen who cultivate friendly and informal mannerisms. It is apparent in the behavior of those who cultivate "contacts," that is, "friendships" that give them privileged access to others for purposes of self-aggrandizement. It is apparent also in the behavior of those who join clubs and organizations that permit them to cultivate such contacts in an apparently private and more primary atmosphere. And it is apparent in the behavior of those who entertain in their home for business advantage, thus blurring the lines between the private world of friends and the more public world of business relationships.

This manipulation of primary relations is most crucial as a value issue in that set of circumstances in which people apply the *particularistic* values of primary and *Gemeinschaft* relationships to those who are considered by others to be operating on *universalistic* values. For example, to call on a friend for help is to appeal to a particularistic relationship—one cannot call on just anyone for that. But if one's friend holds a position of official responsibility, such as a law-enforcement officer, and one asks him to "fix" a ticket, then he is being asked to violate the universalistic norms of his office, which require him to treat all citizens equally and impartially. If a man seeks to get his company to employ a relative, then particularistic norms of kinship are confused with presumably universalistic criteria of impersonal selection of qualified persons for employment.

The concern for "contacts" and for "pulling strings" that marks so much American behavior is not only an effort to exploit primary relationships for personal advantage, with a consequent corruption of universalistic performance, but it is also associated with cultivating those primary relations at the outset for the very purpose of making use of them. But such relations are not then genuinely primary, for they do not meet the definition of being of intrinsic value, an end in themselves. Instead, they are pseudoprimary. A significant value problem lies in the fact that modern, complex societies encourage the manipulation of primary relations for personal advantage, putting tremendous pressure on individuals who are caught between the universalistic norms of their office and the particularistic demands of friends. One response to the widespread use of universalistic norms in large-scale organization is to seek inside advantage and special privilege by exploiting one's primary relationships. But to do that is to corrupt these universalistic criteria that presumably promote fair and equal consideration for all in an impartial manner. Thus, we become aware that these universalistic values are in fact the values of large and secondary organizations; small groups, in turn, promote a quite particularistic treatment of persons. What is legitimate *within* the group becomes corrupting of both relationships and persons when located in the context of a larger and more impersonal world. Such observations as these should make it apparent that the relation of social values to group size is a complex issue that is only obscured by a confusing emphasis upon the moral superiority of small and primary relations and groups over large and secondary ones.

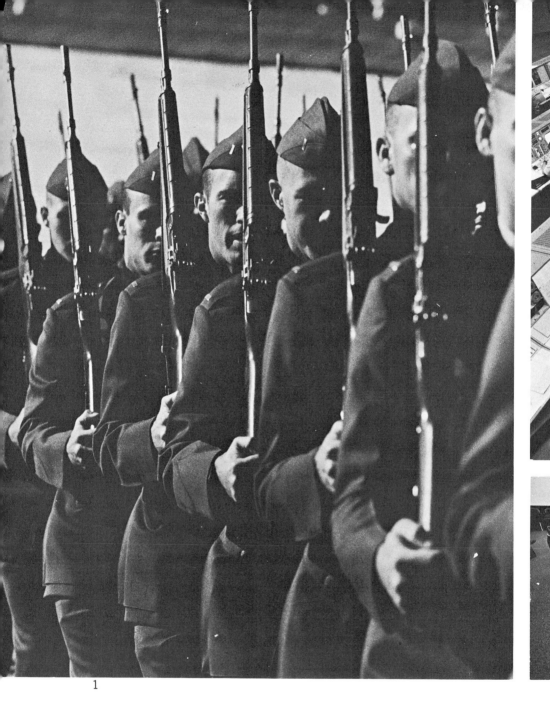

1

1. Marching soldiers.
2. Workers in a computer room.
3. A business conference.
4. George Tooker's painting, *Government Bureau*.
5. India: male and female construction workers.

4

2

3 5

THE FORMAL ORGANIZATION

8

In the modern world, the scale of social organization seems to increase steadily. Ever larger organizations rise to dominate the social landscape, commanding a greater share of the social resources, exercising ever greater social power, and proving to be effective and efficient mechanisms for organizing large and disparate aggregates of people into well-coordinated patterns of action in the pursuit of human goals. The sociologist's concern with the *size* of social groups, we observed in the last chapter, became a problem for sociology only when the large-scale group, particularly in the form labeled bureaucracy, emerged as central to sociological analysis. Max Weber's focus on bureaucracy concentrated on the rational coordination of behavior in large-scale organization and posited the view that this was a form that was increasingly to dominate the life of man.

To speak of large-scale organizations is to encompass a wide variety that differ among themselves in many ways. Political parties, business firms, voluntary civic groups, governmental agencies, hospitals, prisons, universities, and armies are all large organizations, different from one another in the goals they pursue, the kind and amount of resources they command, and the particular internal structure they develop. Nor are they all equally large, for what is large can be anything from a department store or a social service agency to the General Motors Corporation or the Department of Defense. Although variations in size and in purpose are important in producing differences in the way large groups are organized, what sociologists have been interested in primarily has been the tendency of large organizations to become *formal;* that is, to develop a formal structure, which is usually called bureaucracy. It is this that will be the central concern of this chapter. The sociological analysis of the bureaucratization of large groups has been accompanied by a widespread and pervasive social criticism of modern society—to which some sociologists have contributed—in which bureaucratization is viewed as one of the major problems. From this latter perspective, modern bureaucracy is not merely another form of social organization but an index of much of what is presumably wrong with modern society. Its growth and spread signifies to these critics the loss of community and the decline of personal relations, an increase in alienation, and a decrease in loyalty and commitment to social organization. It is part of the great social transition that has moved men from villages to cities, from being peasants to being workers, administrators, and professionals, a transition that has largely been viewed with great misgivings. Some idea of how the concept of bureaucracy fits into the historic moral concern may be useful before proceeding with the social-scientific analysis of formal organization.

The Bureaucratic Mystique   In an age of utopian dreams, men could conceive of attaining such control over their social organization that they could construct humane and rewarding social relations. But this is not a utopian age; indeed, it could be labeled anti-utopian, and the dreams of the future that modern Western intellectuals project are like the nightmare in George Orwell's novel *1984*. No amount of progress in material level of living or in science, not even modest progress in social science, has been able to stem the flow of social pessimism that has engulfed Western intellectuals in this century. Central to this pessimism and decline of hope in social progress has been the development of an involved social mystique about bureaucracy and the bureaucratization of modern society. Increasingly, bureaucracy serves as a symbol of a presumed process of social change in which man's hope for rational mastery of his environment for the sake of a freer social life goes sour. Instead, he is viewed as becoming increasingly imprisoned within the complex networks of modern bureaucratic structure. He is robbed of his hope and his freedom, and human rationality becomes, not his servant and tool, but a social form that reduces him to docility and subservience.

This mystique about bureaucracy constitutes a highly pervasive modern belief that makes of the word, bureaucracy, an evocative symbol for much of the existentialist mood about contemporary social life. Perhaps nowhere is the social scientist more at odds with contemporary intellectual life than in his own resistance to this mystique; instead, he constantly attempts to understand bureaucratic organization, and he refuses to accept a frightening image of modern man rushing through the bureaucratic grooves like rats in a scientist's maze. Although the social scientist uses the concept, bureaucracy, as a fairly precise and unemotional term to conceptualize a form of social organization, the more pervasive existentialist outlook projects a conception that is charged with emotional nuances. Thus, at the very outset, the social scientist has difficulty using the term as a scientific concept, and as a consequence, sociologists have increasingly come to speak of *formal* or of *complex organization.*

This mystique about bureaucracy attributes to it a dehumanized (and dehumanizing) quality that sometimes leads one to forget that organizations are made up of human beings. They seem, rather, to have a life and direction of their own and also to have a consistently destructive impact upon human relationships and human personality. An emphasis upon its size and its impersonality contributes to this image of a monstrous organization that engulfs the mere humans who come into association with it. This crushing and engulfing of the individual by the great organization is one of the presumed consequences of the bureaucratization of social groups and invokes a long familiar concern for maintaining the integrity of the person in the face of pressures by organization. Such a concern, indeed, invokes a conception of the person *versus* the group that Charles Horton Cooley criticized when he said that "a separate individual is an abstraction unknown to experience, and so likewise is society. . . ." Nonetheless, a dominant existentialist emphasis has indeed acted as if the individual were separate and unique from the network of social relationships within which he functions. The crushing of the individual by the organization then becomes a major theme that has had widespread ideological support throughout the Western world over the past century. The organization is viewed as destroying creativity because creativity is an attribute of the individual; the organization does not allow for that spontaneity and uniqueness of response from which creativity emerges. Organization, so goes the ideology, does its thinking by committee, and committees produce the answer that is a matter of common denominator and consensus.

If organization does not present a milieu favorable to the more imaginative individual and depresses the creative impulses in persons, it presumably also exacts a high degree of conformity. Organizations, it is said, create organization men—those men in grey flannel suits that presumably look alike, act alike, and even think alike, because they think organization thoughts, not their own. The conformity-demanding nature of bureaucracy, indeed, has been one of the central issues in the newer social criticism of the quality of American life. It has pervaded a critical American self-perspective at least since David Riesman's *The Lonely Crowd* projected an image of the dominant American character-type as *other-directed*. This issue of conformity ties in well with the position that bureaucracy is characterized by a deadening routine. That the routinization of functions is an intended aim of bureaucratic organization is quite correct, but this criticism goes beyond the intent to routinize for the purpose of efficiency. Instead, it defines routinization as a process of reducing behavior to a boring and meaningless standardization process that allows no innovation or individualizing aspect. Here is the crux of the idea that bureaucracy is a well-oiled machine which maximizes efficiency at the expense of the individual participants and which views them as cogs in a machine whose performance is to be routinized and standardized as much as possible. This notion of the evil of routinization leads inevitably to the moral charge that bureaucrats do not see people as people but rather as manipulable sets of skills and attributes that can be fitted into a complex machinery to perform certain standardized functions. People are treated in terms of their skills and their functions, not in terms of their personal and human attributes.

This, then, is the mystique of bureaucracy—a conception of a humanly created yet inhumanly effective organization that engulfs and crushes individuality, destroys creativity, exacts an inhibiting conformity, establishes meaningless and deadening routines of behavior, and ultimately treats its members, not as people, but as bundles of attributes that fit functional slots, as faceless numbers in a huge mechanism. Bureaucracy has become a term that conveys part of the image of the vast and complex social machinery of modern social life that has presumably gotten beyond humanly controllable dimensions, in which the individual and the unique is lost in the face of impersonal and standardized modes of behavior. The anonymity, the impersonality, the being a faceless number, all this is presumably typical of the modern experience of man, and bureaucracy, as a term, conveys some sense of the kind of social organization that typifies this mode of experience.

Yet there is, as we have suggested, a view of bureaucracy that is not consistent with this mystique. This is the interpretation of social scientists, who resist seeing bureaucracy in such uncompromisingly harsh terms and who have long sought to provide an interpretation that makes an objective assessment of the nature and meaning of the large-scale organization in modern life. Thus, we have two contrasting sets of interpretations of the bureaucratic experience in modern life; the one an existentialist critique that emphasizes the negative impact of large and impersonal organization on the human individual, and the other that pursues a scientific effort to understand how human action is ordered under conditions of large and complex organization. So pervasive and influential has been the first viewpoint that many social scientists have abandoned the term, bureaucracy, in order not to create the impression that they share in the same perspective on large-scale organization. Yet, their own work has not gone uninfluenced by this critique, particularly where they have concentrated on the so-called *informal* aspects of bureaucracy and on the relation of bureaucracy to personality. However, their basic effort has been an attempt to provide a scientific analysis, rather than a social critique of complex organization. The pervading moral attack against bureaucracy has complicated that task, challenging social scientists to delineate fully the consequences for modern man of living in a highly bureaucratized world.

THE PROBLEM OF FORMAL ORGANIZATION

The effort at a scientific study of large-scale organization has been central to sociological analysis at least since Max Weber wrote his famous analysis of bureaucracy. By now there is a well-established body of literature, a conceptual framework for interpreting human action within the context of formal organization, and a conception of the more fundamental scientific problems that are involved in making such an analysis. For the sociologist the problem begins with a concern for the social conditions out of which these formal organizations grow. Human beings shape social organization to meet human problems and to deal with recurring exigencies and issues. The kind of social organization called bureaucracy is a consequence of circumstances and problems that seem to be paramount in modern society. Bureaucratization, then, is a response to a set of conditions that encourages certain modes of organization and renders other modes of organization less effective. To approach it in this manner, as sociologists do, is to provide some objective and unemotional understanding of bureaucracy by seeing it as an outcome of a set of circumstances that compels a particular form of organization. It serves to emphasize that the bureaucratization of organization is not something brought about by bureaucrats, or by power-hungry men, but is a natural consequence of certain prior developments.

The starting point for sociologists has been the social conditions that generate bureaucratic structure, but they are even more interested in delineating the social structure that is the outcome of these preceding conditions. Max Weber gave to the discipline a conceptual model of bureaucracy that spelled out just what kind of behavior is characteristic of such a mode of organization. Since then, sociologists have been applying that model to a wider variety of situations than Weber studied and so have improved the generalizable quality of his model. Probably the modern corporation has been most extensively studied, but government agencies, social work agencies, school systems, hospitals, and a range of other organizations have also been scrutinized to delineate the particular pattern of organized behavior that is bureaucratic.

These, then, are two major aspects of what is problematic about large and bureaucraticized organizations for sociologists. They ask questions to determine the conditions that lead to the emergence of bureaucratized structures, and they ask other questions in order to know as exactly as possible what there is that is distinctive about a bureaucratic organization—what, in short, social scientists mean when they say an organization is bureaucratic.

But if large and complex organization tends to become bureaucratic, only some of its people—its top and middle-level administrators—are usually called *bureaucrats.* The pattern of organization and the complex and efficient ordering of action that administrators preside over is a rational process, which can be and usually is written down. But the large group of people who are the personnel of such organizations create their own pattern of interaction, a nonrational one that falls outside the formal structure and its provision for rational patterns of action. This includes the emergence of an "informal" side of bureaucratic structure and constitutes another major facet of the problem of formal organization.

If bureaucratization is the consequence of certain prior conditions, there are also consequences that flow from the bureaucratization of organization. There are problems generated from the very nature of bureaucracy: (1) its imposition of a highly rationalized view of society; (2) its capacity for great social power; (3) its distinctive bureaucratic view of man. Here is where the scientific analysis of bureaucracy touches that existentialist critique of bureaucracy, for social scientists too have been concerned with what bureaucratization does to people and with how bureaucratic organization inevitably creates a view of man congenial to its own purposes, though perhaps not congenial to those very men so viewed. These consequences are not only contained within bureaucracy. A society in which bureaucratic organization is pervasive does not remain untouched by it; bureaucratic modes of action and the human responses and resistances to bureaucracy diffuse throughout society.

The sociological analysis of formal organization, then, concentrates on these problems: (1) the conditions generating formal organization; (2) the formal structure; (3) the nonrational component of large organizations; and (4) the pervasive consequences of bureaucratization that serve to influence so much of modern society.

CONDITIONS GENERATING BUREAUCRACY

It is to Max Weber that we owe some insight into the historical factors in Western culture that are responsible for the pervasive spread of the bureaucratic form of organization.[1] Weber's encompassing scholarship created an historic panorama that enabled us to see major strands of ideas and values as well as institutions that accounted for a single phenomenon. Thus, he could relate bureaucracy to capitalism and its money economy and also to some major value orientations found among Western men. Though bureaucracy in some ancient forms has existed outside of a money economy (when payment was in kind), Weber showed how the development of a money economy facilitated the development of bureaucracy by permitting the payment of salaried officials who could count on the security of their position and thus on an opportunity for a career. Such officials were dependent on the organization and on their superior, yet were independent enough to carry out the particular assigned functions and to exercise judgment and expertise in doing so. The development of capitalism and of the modern state were also clearly related to the development of bureaucracy. The rational calculation of economic risks required not only a money system and a rational system of accounting, but also a political system that was not arbitrary and disruptive. Stable control of the economic and political conditions under which business flourished, then, demanded a rule of stable and accountable law and a system of officials who could be counted on to enforce law and ensure stability. In addition, bureaucracy needed a sense of discipline, specifically a self-discipline that permitted the bureaucratic official to be subordinate to the organization and even to the office he held. The Calvinism that Weber demonstrated as so

[1] Hans Gerth and C. Wright Mills, eds. and trans., *From Max Weber: Essays in Sociology* (New York: Oxford, 1946), Chapter VIII, "Bureaucracy," pp. 196–244, particularly pp. 204–209.

significant in the emergence of capitalism provided the ascetic discipline that permitted the selfless and disinterested conduct necessary for large-scale administrative efficiency.

Perhaps the basic reason for the pervasiveness of bureaucracy is given in Weber's statement: "The decisive reason for the advance of bureaucratic organization has always been its purely technical superiority over any other form of organization."[2] He goes on to note that bureaucracy compares with any other form of organization "exactly as does the machine with the non-mechanical mode of production."[3] Under some earlier and traditional forms of social organization, a concern for efficiency in organization was not paramount in human consciousness. But when social conditions generate complex administrative problems, when the sheer size of organization becomes a significant factor, an awareness of the problem of maintaining effective organization comes to consciousness, and bureaucracy develops. It develops because circumstances demand a concern for effectiveness in administration. After all, bureaucracy *means* effective and rational organization.

Some degree of bureaucracy was characteristic of great empires of the past. When control of long frontiers for defense or of waterways for subsistence was necessary, the complex administrative task generally brought into being a body of administrative officials and some methods for administering in routine and stable fashion, so that there was an accountability of these officials to the emperor, and some potentiality for calculating. For this reason, bureaucratic structures existed during the Roman Empire, and in civilizations such as the Chinese, the Byzantine, and the Egyptian.

The most systematic effort to deal with the most general conditions for the emergence of bureaucracy is that of S. N. Eisenstadt.[4] According to Eisenstadt, the most fundamental factor is a significant social change in the structure of a society, which releases human and material resources from their embedding in traditional, particularistic (kinship and ethnic) groups, bringing about a highly differentiated society that can no longer function primarily through the small, local structures usually characteristic of agrarian societies. Under that basic pattern of change, then, there emerges a set of conditions that in turn lead to the emergence of bureaucratic organizations. This begins with an extensive differentiation among major social roles and among such institutional spheres as the economic, religious, and political. These important social roles become allocated, not by membership in particularistic groups but by universalistic criteria (based upon competency and training) or by membership in professional, vocational, religious and "national" groups, not particularistic ones.

[2] Gerth and Mills, p. 214.

[3] Gerth and Mills, p. 214.

[4] S. N. Eisenstadt, "Bureaucracy, Bureaucratization and Debureaucratization," *Administrative Science Quarterly*, 4 (1960), 303–320.

Also, many new functional groups emerge, particularly economic and professional ones, that are not attached to the old particularistic ones. The pursuit of goals by these new groups goes beyond the boundaries of the older, more local groups, and there emerges a definition of the total community that reaches beyond the boundaries of the traditional one. The growth of a more complex and differentiated social structure from these developments produces an interdependence among separate groups and competition for the allocation of resources; this competition for resources and for manpower, freed from traditional localistic ties and functions, produces many regulative and administrative problems. From such conditions, bureaucracies arise.

The modern world with its advanced technology, mass markets, extensive communication systems, and mass production, faces the necessity of large-scale organization and great complexity of administrative problems in rendering all these into a controllable and accountable organization. As Weber has properly noted, "the great modern state is absolutely dependent upon a bureaucratic basis. The larger the state, and the more it is or the more it becomes a great power state, the more unconditionally is this the case."[5] Bureaucracy, then, is an indispensable aspect of modern society. A growth in size and in the complexity and differentiation of organization necessitates some processes whereby a stable and routinized administering process permits effective control and operation of the entire structure. This is the sense in which bureaucracy is a response to an organizational problem. Whether it be a factory, an army, or any process of organizing and administering the work of a fairly large and diversified number of people, those who seek to carry it out have to face a basic problem: what is the organizational form by which the efforts of this large number of people can be effectively coordinated into a common, productive effort?

It becomes immediately clear that effective relations must be established among people who do not have face-to-face interaction and whose relations are not primary. Thus, authority and control must be separated from the persons who exercise authority and their personal qualities. The traditional form whereby subordinates swore personal loyalty to a lord or chief will not suffice; responsibility must be vested in an *office*, not a person, and thus must be impersonal. Furthermore, if any calculable result is to accrue, it soon becomes evident that what those in authority expect of their subordinates cannot be left to chance or to older traditional expectations but must be rendered explicit. Consequently, traditional norms governing conduct are replaced by explicit rules. In like fashion, the chain of authority, necessarily more complex, must also be spelled out, so that who can do what and who takes orders from

[5] Gerth and Mills, p. 211.

whom is clear and unambiguous. In similar fashion, the effective coordination of work often compels a further division of labor that creates specialization, and the expertise that goes with it. Hence, bureaucracy itself provides the conditions favorable to specialization and so to the emergence of professionals and experts. Technical competence is increased.

But let us not continue now this line of analysis, for we do not want immediately to spell out the elements of bureaucracy but merely to make clear why it is that bureaucracy emerges. The conditions that give rise to bureaucratic forms of organization are those in which large numbers of people, dispersed somewhat in space, must be coordinated in order to carry out one or more tasks. When men become conscious of such a need and develop a highly rational process for creating and modifying organization fitted to the task of an effectively coordinated work-process, there are certain predictable elements that will always appear. An organization revealing these elements, we call bureaucracy or formal organization.

FORMAL STRUCTURE

The effort to create a rational organization that provides an efficient coordination of diverse human behavior toward a single objective leads to the formalizing of structure. We call it *formal*, following Weber, because of a process of rendering explicit and official the patterns of behavior worked out for effective performance. This results in a generalized model of formal structure. Today we are more likely to speak of this general sociological picture of bureaucracy as a *model;* Weber called it an *ideal-type.* By this term he did not mean something that was morally ideal; instead, he meant a *pure* type, an image of the structure drawn in terms only of its essential characteristics, unaffected by other complicating factors. Weber was using the term, *ideal,* in the sense of ideas, thus meaning the purely abstract idea of the phenomenon in question—in this instance, the purely abstract idea of bureaucracy.

The Weberian ideal-type sought to make explicit the essential features of bureaucratic organization. His analysis specified these: (1) the positions become explicitly defined *offices;* (2) the social relationships are inherently *impersonal;* (3) norms become explicit *rules* and *regulations;* (4) a high degree of *specialization* of function with utilization of criteria of *technical* competence; and (5) a formalized *hierarchy* of offices. Now let us examine each of these points.

1. Each person in a bureaucratic organization occupies an *office,* the duties of which are explicitly prescribed. A set of formally defined offices both define

and limit the duties and functions expected of its occupant. Furthermore, such a process detaches the office from the person; the office exists as an explicit definition of duties and functions, separate from a given office-holder. Bureaucracy differs from more traditional modes of organization in that the office does not belong to any person—no one has a special claim upon it by virtue of inherited position, special rank, or privilege. Rather, claimants for the office are those who possess the explicit qualifications that are based upon the defined duties and functions. This formal separation of office from person serves to free the organization from the power of or dependence upon any particular person, and provides for a condition whereby individuals become dispensable and replaceable actors in the organization, much like replaceable parts in mass-produced machinery.

2. It follows from the separation of person from office that the relationships that are formally prescribed are then relationships among offices, not among persons. Thus, the relationships necessary to carry out the tasks of a bureaucracy are *impersonal*. This ensures cooperation among persons who must interact to carry out their assigned duties, and their personal feelings for one another can then be subordinated to the demand of the office and formally contained so as not to impede or disrupt the formally required interaction. The spirit of impersonality is one of detachment and distance, enhancing the capacity to render rational and objective judgments, uninfluenced by likes and dislikes of particular persons. The rationality of bureaucracy is corrupted when technical competencies are influenced by quite personal responses to other persons. Weber made this quite clear: "The dominance of a spirit of formalistic impersonality, 'Sine ira et studio,' without hatred or passion, and hence without affection or enthusiasm." Impersonality promotes equality of treatment.

3. All social organization is normative, but in a bureaucracy the norms are spelled out, generally in written and codified form, in quite explicit sets of *rules* and *regulations*. The rules are specific, in that they apply to quite definite situations and circumstances, but are also general, in that they formally apply to all (or at least all office-holders within the scope of the rule) in an impersonal manner.

4. Bureaucracy develops a high degree of specialization of function and areas of *technical* competence. The selection of personnel for office then comes to be made in terms of technical and professional qualifications. This makes important the development of tests and other measures of technical achievement, by which the qualified can be certified. Any college student today is aware of how much of his life is governed by various kinds of tests.

5. The organization of a bureaucracy takes the form of a hierarchy of offices, with a chain of command and a centralization of authority and major decision making within a management or administration. Thus, bureaucracy makes explicit the location of authority and the range and limits of the

possible exercise of authority for any office. Every person in a bureaucracy is responsible *to* someone above him and is responsible *for* the behavior of those under his authority.

Authority, Rewards, and Communication Social scientists have analyzed formal structure around three major points: authority, rewards and communication. Weber's analysis emphasized belief in the legality of bureaucratic authority since it produced voluntary acceptance of orders by those within the hierarchy. There had to exist, according to the Weberian perspective, a value orientation among members of the organization that brought an acceptance of the legitimacy of authority in order to provide a reliable basis for stable and effective control. Weber's emphasis plays down the fact that bureaucracy also contains *power* that can be used to invoke sanctions against its members. Amitai Etzioni has examined bureaucracy with just such an emphasis upon power and the use of sanctions, and he argues that power becomes authority when the use of sanctions is accepted as legitimate by persons subject to them.[6] Also, the types of sanctions used—symbolic, material, and physical—effect the acceptance of sanctions, with physical sanctions least producing an acceptance of legitimacy and material sanctions next so.

Rewards The problem of rewards has been emphasized in recent organizational theory with the view that an adequate reward system is necessary to ensure adequate participation and performance in the organization by its members. Stanley H. Udy, Jr., in a study comparing organizations from a sample of cultures, suggests that a reward system does the following for an organization: (1) assures an adequate recruitment of personnel; (2) maintains an acceptable level of performance by members; (3) integrates the authority when higher officials control the rewards of members; and (4) assures adequate role differentiation by the manipulation of rewards to support the division of labor necessitated by technological developments.[7]

Communication No complex organization can function effectively—or indeed at all—unless it has assured channels of communication. A pioneering student of organization, Chester Barnard, has in fact made the existence of formal communication networks the central focus of his conception of organization.[8] He has insisted that channels of communication must be known to all participants, that each member should have access to the formal channel of communication, that the lines should be as short and direct as possible, and that

[6] Amitai Etzioni, *A Comparative Analysis of Complex Organizations* (New York: Free Press, 1961).
[7] Stanley H. Udy, Jr., *Organization of Work* (New Haven, Conn.: HRAF Press, 1959).
[8] Chester I. Barnard, *The Functions of the Executive* (Cambridge, Mass.: Harvard University Press, 1938).

those communicating should make use of the appropriate line of communication, not bypassing any link. Ideally, each member will have access to what he needs to know but will not be overburdened with extraneous information. Some small group research has sought to simulate communication processes in organization, comparing the effectiveness of one pattern against another. A well-known experimental model by Alex Bavelas has been used in a number of studies to demonstrate that groups are more effective in carrying out tasks where the communication pattern is hierarchical.[9] But two other students of organization, Peter Blau and W. Richard Scott, argue that this effectiveness of a hierarchical communication pattern applies to task-oriented groups where the coordination of persons is paramount, but that a free flow of communication is better in other organizational situations, such as the generating of new ideas or the working out of difficult problems not yet routinized.[10]

That communication is a basic process of organization is evident from more sources than these studies. The study of social organizations of any kind long ago revealed a close relation between communication and power. Gaining control over the communication system in an organization is a well-known way to get and retain power; a study of democracy in labor unions described the clear advantages that accrue to an incumbent leadership that has control over the official communication media of the organization.[11] In addition, the emergence of informal and extra-legitimate channels of communication in organizations indicates that formal communication networks are always supplemented and perhaps even replaced by informal ones. In some cases these informal channels may contribute to the effectiveness of the organization by making possible quick and efficient communication not possible by formal means, or by encouraging a sharing of information among those who have similar tasks and responsibilities. But informal channels that distribute unfounded rumors, particularly at times of change and tension in organization, can inhibit the effectiveness of the organization.

The Formalization of Organization   These several points constitute a conception of the formalization of organization. It is rendered explicit and unambiguous and thus highly rational; indeed, it can be put down on paper by reducing it to a chart that defines offices, codifies rules, specifies the flow of authority and the extent of responsibility, and indicates the technical competences that

[9] Alex Bavelas, "Communication Patterns in Task-Oriented Groups," *Journal of the Acoustical Society of America,* 22 (1950), 725–730.

[10] Peter M. Blau and W. Richard Scott, *Formal Organizations* (San Francisco: Chandler Publishing Co., 1962).

[11] Seymour M. Lipset, Martin A. Trow, and James S. Coleman, *Union Democracy* (New York: Free Press, 1956).

provide qualification for office. The problems generated by size and complexity of organization in the modern world tend more and more to produce this formalization of organization. Furthermore, such a type of organization has distinctive advantages over one in which the rationality and effectiveness of the organization must depend upon these developing over time among persons who interact frequently. For one thing, a formal organization does not depend upon the sentiments that the members hold toward one another and even discourages those positive sentiments that might interfere with professional discipline and objective judgment. The organization becomes independent of any particular person and can replace anyone and continue to function. A large formal organization is unlikely to be disrupted by the loss of even its top-ranking officer.

In the above discussion we have implicitly distinguished between bureaucracy and the organization. Bureaucracy is not to be identified with the substantive organization; rather, bureaucracy identifies an internal structure that large-scale organizations use in response to the problem of achieving effective integration in the face of both numbers and complexity. Any given organization, however highly bureaucratic it may be, is always more than a bureaucracy. As a total organization, concerned with a substantive set of goals and values, its bureaucratic processes constitute one major segment of its mode of functioning, but by no means all. In that sense, the study of large and complex organization is only partly the study of bureaucracy.

THE NONRATIONALITY OF ORGANIZATION

When an organization is viewed as a totality, there is always more to it than its formal structure, even though this rational dimension has been emphasized by students of organization. But organizations also display non-rational characteristics, and much sociological analysis concentrates on this dimension of organizations. Furthermore, as Sheldon Wolin makes clear in his fine history of organizational theory, many social thinkers have been concerned with possible *communal* qualities of organization, especially Elton Mayo, who saw in organization a social order to offset the anomie and disorganization of modern communities.[12] Nonetheless, what Alvin Gouldner calls the rational model of organization has dominated most sociological

---

[12] Sheldon Wolin, *Politics and Vision* (Boston: Little, Brown, 1960). For Mayo's conception of the communal potentiality of organization, see his *The Social Problems of an Industrial Civilization* (Boston: Graduate School of Business Administration, Harvard University, 1945).

analysis. Charles Perrow, another student of organization, labels this an "over-rationalistic view" of organization and says: "Actually, however, non-rational orientations exist at all levels, including the elite who are responsible for setting goals and assessing the degree to which they are achieved."[13] Some of these nonrational aspects are generated by problems inherent in formal structure; others emerge from human responses and intentions that lie outside the formal structure and are, therefore, often labeled *informal.*

Subgroup Sources of Organizational Conflict   If any formal organization were perfectly rational, its organizational effort would run smoothly and the relation of each subunit to the total organization would be harmonious. But such is rarely the case, and the existence of subunits in a large organization is always a possible source of conflict and competition that impedes the formal structure in realizing a totally rational effort. Specifically, the danger is that subgroups will pursue their own interests with too little regard for the equally legitimate interests of other subunits or for the welfare of the larger organization. Where competition among subunits is encouraged, for example, such competition can lead to a situation where each subunit will maximize its own goals at the expense of organizational goals. When this occurs, these competing subgroups may have entirely different conceptions of what the organization's goals and needs are. It is obvious that each subgroup will see the larger organization from the perspective of its own functions and interests and often will place a higher value on its own contribution and importance than the top leadership does.

Melville Dalton has explored just such a conflict in organization by describing the conflicts between line and staff officials of industrial management.[14] Staff organization is made up of research and advisory functions, whereas line organization is that vertical hierarchy which has authority over production processes. This difference in staff and line constituted such a different kind of functioning that friction emanated from that fact alone. Line officers regarded their authority as "something sacred" and resented the implication that they needed the assistance of less experienced newcomers. But staff officers thought of themselves as agents of top management, experts and managerial consultants who tended to approach middle and lower line officers with an air of condescension. The differences of function were exacerbated by social differences in the two groups. Staff officers, as research specialists, were better educated and younger than the line officers and had strong mobility aspira-

[13] Charles Perrow, "The Analysis of Goals in Complex Organizations," *American Sociological Review,* 26 (December, 1961), 854–855.
[14] Melville Dalton, "Conflicts Between Staff and Line Managerial Officers," *American Sociological Review,* 15 (June, 1950), 342–351.

tions—they "were markedly ambitious, restless, and individualistic. There was much concern to win rapid promotion, to make the 'right impressions,' and to receive individual recognition."[15] The frustrations of these young experts with the older and often resentful line officers produced a high turnover of staff personnel. Although staff officers had no doubts in their own mind of the great importance of their expert function, they also recognized that they needed to prove themselves to the line officers; they had to justify their existence. In their strong efforts to develop new techniques and get them accepted, they often displayed an impatience that only confirmed the suspicions of line officers that staff men were reaching for authority over production. Indeed, line officers worried that staff people, by virtue of their well-financed research, would undermine line authority. In turn, staff officers could not get a promotion except by the recommendation of influential line executives. In addition to all of this, the younger and better-educated staff researchers dressed and acted differently than did the line officers. They were meticulous in their grooming, used better English "and were more suave and poised in social intercourse. These factors, and the recreational preferences of staff officers for night clubs and 'hot parties,' assisted in raising a barrier between them and most line officers."[16]

The behavior of these staff officers in Dalton's study—trained researchers—suggests that professionally trained people may bring professional goals into organizations and these, as subunit goals, may influence the goals and activities of the larger organization. This theme is pursued by Charles Perrow in his study of voluntary general hospitals.[17] Perrow traced an historical trend in such hospitals from a domination and control by unpaid trustees, who were civic leaders and community representatives, to a control by the medical staff without whose highly technical skills the hospital cannot function. Such a change in organizational control also reduces the actual power of the hospital administrator, a nonmedical man concerned with administering the hospital as a total organization. Furthermore, it leads, in Perrow's terms, to a shift from *official* to *operative* goals, from the publicly proclaimed goals of the organization, on the basis of which community support is mobilized, to a set of professionally defined goals that determined in fact how the organization will operate. In a hospital, for example, the operative goals "are likely to be defined in strictly medical terms and the organization may achieve high technical standards of care, promote exemplary research, and provide sound training."[18] But such operative goals are not without consequences. Resources may be used for the benefit of private (paying) patients with less attention

[15] Dalton, p. 344.
[16] Dalton, p. 347.
[17] Perrow, pp. 854–855.
[18] Perrow, p. 859.

to such community problems as care of the medically indigent. So, too, there may be lessened emphasis upon preventive care or upon innovating new forms of patient care. From this may come in time a complexity in the responsibilities and functions of the hospital that the medical staff cannot in fact control, and domination of the hospital may be returned to the administrator. It is also possible that there will be a multiple leadership of trustees, medical personnel, and administrators. But the concern here is with Perrow's point that professionals may increasingly take over operative control of organizations as there accrues to them, by virtue of their professional skills and competences, a wider range of functions and responsibilities. Their own professional goals become increasingly the operative goals of the organization. Their professional interests shape the organization and they "may develop an identity and ethic which cuts them off from the needs of the community and favors specialized, narrow and—to critics—self-serving goals."[19] In the universities, says Perrow, the criticism of "emphasis upon research and overspecialization in graduate training at the expense of the basic task of educating undergraduates is a case in point."[20] But so is criticism of professionals in correctional institutions for being more interested in middle-class "neurotic" delinquents than in the much larger number of "socialized" delinquents from culturally deprived areas, and of psychiatric social workers more interested in attaining a status comparable to psychiatrists.[21]

Bureaucracy's Other Face   In his pioneering studies, Max Weber abstracted the formal processes that make bureaucracy a rational system, while leaving relatively unexamined the spontaneous and unplanned behavior that can be observed in any large organization. Contemporary sociologists, in turn, have been much preoccupied with discovering and describing this other aspect of organization, what Charles Page felicitously called "bureaucracy's other face," and what sociologists more conventionally call *informal structure.*[22] The vast array of data from sociological research about informal structure can be organized under two general points. First, there is that behavior that occurs as a consequence of continued interaction among the persons working in an organization, much of which is usually face-to-face, offsetting if not subverting the quality of *impersonality* that is central to formalization. Secondly, there are organizational problems that cannot be handled entirely by the formal processes; these problems then generate responses that lie outside the officially-prescribed behavior, but are no less essential for the effective functioning of the organization.

[19] Perrow, p. 862.
[20] Perrow, p. 862.
[21] Perrow, p. 862.
[22] Charles H. Page, "Bureaucracy's Other Face," *Social Forces,* 25 (October, 1946), 91.

However impersonal bureaucracy may be, the occupants of the offices of necessity must interact frequently with some others and so come to know them as persons, not merely as office-holders. As a consequence, they build a complex network of social relationships that are not formally prescribed; indeed, they may engage in behavior that violates some of the formal sanctions of the organization. Thus, as friends, they may "cover" for one another when they take time off the job that is not sanctioned, or they may provide one another with information about what is going on, creating informal gossip channels that circumvent the slower and less informative official channels. In short, people in interaction turn the abstract and formalized processes of rational organization into a complex, nonrational network of cliques, primary groups, informal communication networks, as well as informal channels of influence and advantage. If bureaucracy means a rational use of human beings as instruments of organization, informal structure means the very human effort to master and control the organization, or at least segments of the organization, to provide job security and to humanize its environment by those same human beings whom the organization would use.

This basic source for informal structure suggests there is reason for there being tension between the formal and informal structure. The intent if not always the result of formal structure is to maximize efficiency in organizational procedures in order to accomplish the basic tasks in as rational and effective a manner as possible. But the working personnel of bureaucracies may resist conforming fully to the organization's rules and procedures. When the informal network of relationships emerges among people who continually interact with one another, they are encouraged to act in ways that benefit their own interests rather than the interests of the organization. In a perfect bureaucracy, the members would have no interests other than the realization of the objectives of the organization, but in the real and complex world people are not merely office-holders, socialized completely to the demands of their official role. For one thing, they have a quite personal interest in their job-security and in advancement. Furthermore, particularly at the lower levels of bureaucracy, there is often a most imperfect sense of what the goals and objectives of the organization are. People invoke friendship as a way to get favors done, to get privileges of information or material resources; or otherwise use the primary relationship as a means of violating the bureaucratic rules for personal benefit. In addition, there is a very human resistance to being treated as a replaceable unit, a standard human item, in an organization. No amount of favorable or competitively advantageous personnel policies—better wages and salaries, retirement system, or generous vacations—can offset the resentment at being a faceless cog in a vast machine. This results in a thousand and one little ways in which people actively humanize the presumably impersonal environment of the organization. The development of primary relations running across the formal roles and relationships of the structure is one way; numerous small ways of managing not to conform to all the regulations is another.

At this point, it may be useful to cite the evidence presented in Chapter 6, particularly the section on the peer group. Peer groups in factories, we saw, emerged among those who interacted on a face-to-face basis; such a group then successfully asserted its own norms of production, effectively exercised control over the individual member, and imposed its own informal and unofficial standards and regulations on the work situation. In such fashion, the formal standards for work and the formal authority over work were successfully challenged and subverted by a quite informal but nonetheless real and effective structure of social relationships within small groups. A large amount of industrial research, beginning with the famous Hawthorne studies in the 1920s, has documented this process. (The reader might profit by rereading that section.) We also viewed peer group interaction as the basis for subcultures emerging among workers, soldiers, and students, who by virtue of the formal structure had little power and responsibility and thus little formal control over their life-circumstances within the organization. Their constant interaction as peers created a situation for developing a consensus of values and outlook on the organizational circumstances of their status, generating a capacity for united action to reassert control over their own lives by controlling some aspects of the way the organization imposed itself on them.

This tension between formal and informal structure is a tension between the effort at efficiency and effective performance on the one hand, and the effort, on the other hand, to resist being entirely an agent of the organization and instead to use the organization for personal or subgroup ends as well as to create a less impersonal atmosphere for the carrying on of organizational activities. But another tension arises from an almost opposite circumstance, in which it is by informal means that people try to get problems solved and activities carried on when the formally prescribed processes stand in the way. The intended efficiency of bureaucracy is not always that. There is the famous "red tape," which means a too complex process for getting things done—clearing with too many offices, or filling out too many forms. In particular, this may make it difficult to act quickly in sudden emergencies. Shortcuts are then devised, such as getting agreement informally and then carrying out the formal processes later. These violations of the formal procedures are not intended to subvert the goals but to carry them out by other means when the formal procedures are inadequate because of the following: (1) they move too slowly; (2) they are too complicated; (3) they are adapted to an earlier situation, whereas conditions have in fact changed; or (4) they are overly rigid when a degree of flexibility is needed. This last is an important point about bureaucracy. Rigidity in procedure is one of the potential deficiencies that can beset any well-established and well-running organization. But rigidity violates the modern conception of effective formal structure, which allows a range of operating alternatives to those skilled and professional personnel who have a responsibility for major administrative or technical functions. Informal structure, may, in effect, represent efforts of office-holders to get around rules and procedures that hamper effective performance and to devise less formal ways of achieving their assigned goals. Primary relations may enhance such effectiveness, even though the impersonal pattern of relationships is violated.

Rationality and Social Insulation   Max Weber recognized that if a bureaucratic structure was to maximize rationality it needed to be insulated in order to reduce the influence that the larger society had upon it. He suggested that officials be selected by free contract on the basis of their technical qualifications, and that their job should become their primary interest in order that they be free of what today we have come to call "conflict of interests."[23] But formal organizations are not always able to do this, and this inability may be greatest in those cultures in which traditional and particularistic relations still prevail and influence other social relations. James C. Abegglen found that in Japanese factories recruitment by education is importantly related to family status, and that the contract between worker and management is a lifetime agreement for both parties.[24] Both of these factors reduces the flexibility of organization in adapting to changes; hence, it is less rational. Monroe Berger, in turn, found that over 40 percent of the Egyptian civil service officials in his study believed that family connections, wealth, and social background should count in the selection of civil servants, besides the universalistic criteria of education and experience.[25] Berger reports that the performance of these civil servants often manifests a particularism in which friends and relatives receive favorable treatment. Thus, an insularity from such particularistic demands is most important in creating a professionally competent civil service in developing nations, but attachment to kinship and ethnic groups makes this hard to achieve. Nevertheless, developed nations are not free of these nonrational sources of behavior, either, as the frequent observations about the power of "old-school ties" in the British civil service suggests.

[23] Max Weber, *The Theory of Economic and Social Organization,* trans. by A. M. Henderson and Talcott Parsons (New York: Oxford, 1947), pp. 334–335.

[24] James C. Abegglen, *The Japanese Factory* (New York: Free Press, 1958).

[25] Monroe Berger, *Bureaucracy and Society in Modern Egypt* (Princeton, N.J.: Princeton University Press, 1957).

THE CONSEQUENCES OF BUREAUCRATIZATION

If bureaucracy is caused by certain prior conditions, it also has significant social consequences, both for organization and for society. It is the matter of these consequences that will be considered now. A world increasingly dominated by bureaucratic organizations is a new kind of world, one hitherto little if ever experienced by mankind. Bureaucracy itself, as we previously noted, is not new; there were bureaucratic structures in a whole range of ancient societies. Not the existence of bureaucracy, then, but the bureaucratization of society is what is new. Although there are myriad consequences that flow from the extensive spread of the bureaucratic form of organization, it seems possible to organize them under three major issues: (1) the rationalization of society; (2) the relation of bureaucracy to social power; (3) and the emergence of a new and significant bureaucratic view of man.

The Rationalization of Social Life   In Max Weber's analysis, bureaucracy became sociologically significant, not only because it was an increasingly dominant form of social organization in modern life, but also because its very dominance signified the increasing rationalization of modern life. A world grown more rational, we said in Chapter 2, was for Weber the most significant development in the history of the Western world. A rationalized world is one less spontaneous, less mysterious, more subject to rule and procedure. It is a world that proceeds in the face of custom and emotion, disregarding these to base action upon criteria related to the efficient attainment of given ends. As Weber pointed out, the rationalization of life proceeds in a number of different directions, but bureaucratic rationalization constitutes a major one. It is, though, by no means the only one; science, for example, is a major rationalizing force as well as a major force for rationality. Science strips the world of much of its mystery, and sometimes unintentionally, of much of its charm. It contributes significantly to that "disenchantment with the world" that we quoted Weber on in Chapter 2—and he was quoting Friedrich Schiller. It treats the world as a natural process that proceeds by rules of nature. Ultimately, if only all of nature's rules could be known to man, nothing would be mysterious. The more man-as-scientist penetrates into nature, the more nature becomes known and unmysterious, and much of the workings of natural processes become quite matter-of-fact.

It may be that science and bureaucracy are the most significant of the secular rationalisms at work altering the world. That science has an increasing impact upon the modern world is a truism that needs no elaboration here. But that bureaucracy is increasingly important in organizing the modern world may be superficially obvious and may be interpreted as a negative factor, without the full meaning of such an idea being evident. Bureaucracy is a rationalizing force because it seeks to order its own world in a systematic fashion, within a clearly defined set of rules and procedures applying to all possible behavioral situations. In short, it seeks to reduce the world to a calculated and predictable pattern, controlled by criteria that logically relate means to ends. Bureaucracy seeks to proceed in the most efficient and effective manner, not, therefore, necessarily in a customary or traditional manner. It is ever ready to discard tradition, it tries to repress the claims of sentiment, it abhors passion, and it ignores aesthetics. Bureaucracy encourages matter-of-factness in thinking, inducing a viewpoint that sees the world as a set of facts and things, which can be handled, manipulated, and treated in order to proceed logically toward goals. It has a place for the engineer but not the poet. In addition, it is bureaucracy that encourages expertise and the specialization that produces the role of *expert*. When bureaucracy proceeds in such a rational manner, it contributes significantly to a rationalizing of the world. Increasingly, the matter-of-fact attitude, the treatment of the world as an environment of objects and things, which behave according to natural rules and thus are manipulable and controllable, constitutes a secular rationality that is now an inherent part of modern thinking, not merely scientific thinking.

Bureaucracy and Social Power   Bureaucracy by design and intent is not democratic. To say that is not to criticize but rather to observe that one of the significant issues about the bureaucratization of society is the relation of bureaucratic structure to the distribution and exercise of social power in society. The hierarchical nature of bureaucracy has always concentrated authority at the top. This is so even when for reasons of efficiency there may be a decentralization of considerable authority to subordinate units of the organization, and when the professional expert may enjoy considerable autonomy in the performance of his functions. This means that a complex and efficient organizational apparatus is controlled by its top administrators, who are in a position to exercise power relatively independently of those to whom they are nominally responsible.

The theoretical argument for this was made back at the turn of the century by a European sociologist, Robert Michels, whose *Political Parties* is one of the classics of political sociology.[26] Michels advanced the thesis, known as the *iron law of oligarchy,* that organization always induced oligarchy (the rule of the few), and so democracy (the rule of the many) was an impossibility. The logic of his argument will be examined in detail in Chapter 16, entitled Polity and Power; here we want only to point out that Michels built a strong case for the autonomous power of those who served as the top permanent officers and controlled the organizational machinery. In this case, Michels was ana-

---

[26] Robert Michels, *Political Parties* (New York: Free Press, 1949).

lyzing the great mass political parties of the democratic left in Europe and attempting to show that, with the best intentions in the world and with a genuine commitment to a democratic philosophy, their leaders became an oligarchy that ruled the organization, rather than the "servants" of a ruling membership. In fascinating detail he showed how control of the apparatus of the organization made the leadership independent of the membership and the membership in turn psychologically dependent upon the leadership. A bureaucratized leadership always controls the paid personnel, the files and records, the material resources, the jobs, and can, therefore, utilize all of these for its own objectives. Such control gives it power vis-à-vis its elected superiors, on the one hand, and the voting body of citizens or member-delegates, on the other. In the same fashion, it becomes independent of a clientele whom it presumably serves.

When bureaucrats are full-time career officials of government agencies and their superiors are elected or appointed cabinet or ministry officers, the latter are often at a severe disadvantage in carrying out policy that the former oppose. The career officials' control of the organization permits them to effect considerable and often successful resistance. Seymour M. Lipset, in *Agrarian Socialism*, a study of the coming-to-power of a socialist party in an agrarian province of Canada, described the way in which conservative career officials effectively subverted the efforts of the newly appointed cabinet officers to carry out socialist or even reforming programs.[27] The cabinet officers depended so much on the bureaucratic machinery, as well as the knowledge and skills of the bureaucrats, that they were vulnerable to the resistance of these bureaucrats to radical political innovations.

Lipset's analysis suggests that bureaucracy can be a conservative force in resisting social change because a combination of power, based upon control and competency, and an ideological orientation may lead bureaucrats to choose a particular type of social policy. However, as Lipset notes, this can be changed by appointing new officials who have a different political ideology but the same professional competency. This suggests that the social origins and backgrounds of bureaucrats are relevant for the manner in which they provide professional service or carry out an administrative function, and that their particular ideological commitments may be highly relevant for the manner in which a program of social reform is carried out.

One study that has explored this issue in some detail, showing how compromises with original ideal aims is exacted by established bureaucracies, is Philip Selznick's *TVA and the Grass Roots*.[28] The existing agricultural bureaucracies in the Tennessee Valley—cooperative extension services, agricultural

[27] Seymour M. Lipset, *Agrarian Socialism* (Berkeley: University of California Press, 1950).

[28] Philip Selznick, *TVA and the Grass Roots* (Berkeley and Los Angeles: University of California Press, 1949).

colleges, and the Farm Bureau—were staffed by competent but quite conservative professionals whose own interests and those of their organizations were possibly threatened by the new TVA agency. The resulting struggle led the fledgling TVA to compromise with these established bureaucracies in order to develop its own program as one carried out in cooperation with "all the agencies concerned with and essential to the development of a region's resources: the local communities, voluntary private organizations, state agencies, and cooperating federal agencies."[29] The resulting vision of a grass-roots democratic partnership led the TVA leadership to adopt an ideology that co-opted many of these organizations into the programs of TVA, with results that compromised and altered the original goals. Indeed, the grass-roots ideology served to defend many adjustments and changes worked out, such as accepting a limitation on the participation of Negro institutions and developing a special relation to the American Farm Bureau. It also led the TVA, by virtue of its alliances with the Farm Bureau and the extension services of the land grant colleges, to oppose other New Deal agencies like the Farm Security Administration and Soil Conservation Service. The TVA also fought against "the policy of utilizing public ownership of land as a conservation measure and thus effectively contributed to the alteration of the initial policy of the Authority in this respect."[30] Also, after nine years of operation "the county soil associations handling TVA fertilizer were found to be still tools of the county agent system, to which the TVA test-demonstration program was delegated."[31] What the TVA gained from this was a set of powerful allies when the political climate was charged with severe opposition and also a *legitimation* of its program and of the organization itself in the area it served. But the price it paid for this was a serious alteration of its original goals.

Historical scholarship, too, has provided evidence of the power of bureaucracy. Many scholars, for example, have documented the rise of Stalin through his strategic position as secretary of the central committee of the Bolshevik Party and the control of the party machinery that this gave him. His ascent to power would not have been possible except that he was able to use this bureaucratic machinery to defeat opponents. Indeed, Communists have long recognized the importance of organizational bureaucracy as an instrument of power. Philip Selznick's study, *The Organizational Weapon,* documented the Bolshevik technique of capturing power within an organization to use it as a weapon in the struggle for power.[32] In this process, the offices of secretary and treasurer were more important than that of president, just because they led to control of the resources and the positions of the organization.

[29] Selznick, p. 37.

[30] Selznick, p. 263.

[31] Selznick, p. 264.

[32] Philip Selznick, *The Organizational Weapon* (New York: McGraw-Hill, 1952).

Although the career bureaucrat thus has an advantage over the appointed official who holds office for but a brief period of time, there does occur in some organizations a welding of elected and career officials into a single unit. Here is the case where, once elected to office, a leadership can then utilize the bureaucracy to ensure their own reelection time after time, so that nominally elected officials are in fact a permanent bureaucratic leadership. How is this possible? Michels first posed this issue and suggested some reasons. The very development of an organizational process of delegated power creates an elite who can manipulate both organizationally and psychologically to hold power and make itself seem indispensable. Its control, as we noted, over jobs and resources gives it a paid staff to work on its behalf. Its control over records and the membership roster gives it access to the membership that its critics often cannot equal. Its use of administrative secrecy and public relations enables it to present the best public case for its administration and makes it difficult for its critics to ferret out more accurate accounts of its performance. Much of this has been documented in *Union Democracy,* a cogent sociological analysis of a labor union.[33] It applied Michels' "iron law of oligarchy" to modern labor unions, where the assumption of office by one faction usually leads to a consolidation of power by effectively controlling the bureaucratic apparatus, so that control becomes permanent, and genuine democratic process is reduced. *Union Democracy* is a detailed analysis of a particular union, the International Typographers Union, which seems to be an exception to this usual oligarchic process. The authors studied the ITU, not to refute Michels' law, but to learn its limitations. Their major finding was that the ITU has institutionalized a two-party system, which ensures effective rather than merely token opposition to the incumbent leadership and prevents it from becoming an entrenched controller of the organization's bureaucratic structure.

Those who control a bureaucratic organization constitute a genuine elite of power, for large and efficient organizations are significant instruments of power, whether they are labor unions, political parties, corporations, trade associations, civic organizations, or government agencies. As Peter Blau, a leading sociological student of bureaucracy, said,

> . . . bureaucracies create profound inequalities of power. They enable a few individuals, those in control of bureaucratic machinery, to exercise much more influence than others in the society in general and on the government in particular.[34]

Bureaucracy, then, always constitutes a potential threat to democracy. A bureaucracy is not a democracy internally, and within a democratic nation

[33] See Lipset, Trow, and Coleman, *Union Democracy.*
[34] Peter Blau, *Bureaucracy in Modern Society* (New York: Random House, 1956), p. 116. This is one of the few studies that contains a chapter on democracy and bureaucracy. See Chapter 6, pp. 102–118.

its own functioning does not promote that social condition whereby sovereignty rests with all the people, and each citizen has an equal voice in the major decisions of the society. Against the concept of responsible *individuals* exercising influence, bureaucracy asserts the influence of *organization.* Against the idea of the validity of the sovereign voice of the *people,* it presents the testimony of the *expert.* Up against experts, mere people are amateurs and dilettantes.

Yet bureaucracies are not entirely anti-democratic in their influence. If they were, as Peter Blau observed, it would simply be a matter of endeavoring to abolish bureaucracies. Bureaucracies invoke rational employment policies based upon criteria of technical qualifications, which benefit minorities and threaten the advantages of class and status, kinship and community—the placement values of a more traditional era. Furthermore, equal treatment under law (or rule or regulation), and disinterested and equal treatment of all according to some objective criteria are universalistic values that bureaucracies readily accept. Large-scale organizations have by no means always effectively practiced these values in the face of contrary values of the community or society in which they function. But the point is that the attainment of such values is not contrary to rational bureaucratic functioning. Generally, it is not the bureaucrats who must be fought to get the acceptance of such values, but those influentials who have managed to maintain privileged actions against the rational criteria of the bureaucratic process.

The prevalence of bureaucracies may indeed be a threat to democracy, but this is an ambiguous matter, nonetheless. It will not save democracy merely to point this out. The modern world is very much a product of an "organizational revolution," as Kenneth Boulding called it, and the effective organization of a complex technology in a vast market system in societies that are huge compared to past ones cannot dispense with bureaucracy. It has become an organizational necessity, for this is unequivocally an organizational society and thus to a considerable extent a bureaucraticized society. In modern society, bureaucracy and democracy at best live in tension with one another, for they are two very different human systems. Bureaucracy is a system for the efficient organization of human action for explicit goals, and it uses human beings as experts who know better than any one else how to carry out specialized tasks. Democracy, in turn, is a system for governing by the participation and consent of the governed, and achieving the consent of the governed requires that dissent be allowed and indeed freely expressed in order that consensus by a majority be eventually attained.

The unintended but nonetheless real effect of the proliferation of bureaucracies, then, is to contribute to the creation of a hierarchical, authoritative, highly organized, and rationally planned world of large organizations, manned by administrative and technical experts with professional qualifications for what they do, for the judgments they render, and for the decisions they make or at least strongly influence. Such a world, however unintentionally, is not democratic. This concentration of power in bureaucratic organization has far-ranging implications that were not anticipated in a democratic theory whose basic ideas and values were rooted in the small-scale world of the eighteenth century.

A Bureaucratic View of Man   However impersonal it may seem to be, bureaucracy is nonetheless an organization of people. It represents an effort to be as rational as possible in organizing people to carry out specific goals. Coordinating human effort in order to be as efficient as possible has consequences for the people who are members of the organization, in the way they are treated and what they experience. Perhaps it is this dimension of bureaucracy that has most frequently been singled out in the avalanche of criticism directed at large organizations. Eric Fromm, C. Wright Mills, William Whyte, and others have long insisted that bureaucracy, by virtue of its emphasis on efficiency, calculability, and standardization, treats people as objects and, what is worse, induces such a view within the people themselves. Mills in particular has articulated the viewpoint that bureaucracy not only exploits the individual, but induces him to exploit himself as well as those with whom he interacts. The moral case here is one of *conformity*, for bureaucracy is accused of wanting highly conforming individuals because of its standard procedures. Nonconforming persons, who may also be the most talented, are presumably administratively hard to handle. The result is to encourage and reward conformity and to discourage nonconformity. (In Chapter 5, in the section on Character and Society, some of these arguments were covered in more detail; the reader might profit by rereading that section.)

The concern about conformity was a salient issue in the 1950s, but a more persistent intellectual concern has been that bureaucracy as a major index of the rationalization of the world presages the decline of the individual. Marx had pointed out that capitalism separated the worker from ownership of the tools he had to use in his work. Weber in turn made it clear that this was but one instance of a more general process, whereby the soldier no longer owned his weapons, the scholar his books, the scientist his research instruments, or the doctor his medical facilities. Factories, libraries, laboratories, clinics, and hospitals then are created in order to control and utilize these "tools" of the highly trained specialists, who in turn become the employees of such organizations. This separation of the individual from his tools is but one aspect of a rationalizing process, which encourages specialization and so also encourages the development of teams and teamwork. There are research teams for scientific research, and there are surgical teams for performing operations; indeed, large organizations develop teams for carrying on almost any skilled task. Teams permit an advanced specialization, which maximizes efficiency of operation and effectiveness of performance, but which denies the individual a sense of carrying out a complete and whole task, which as a finished object or completed endeavor is therefore solely his own. The artisan is replaced by the skilled participant in a group operation. For the individual, this process signifies a reduction in control over the nature and conditions of his job and his mode of work. It reduces his chances for giving to his work his own distinctive mark, for carrying it out in his own unique manner. Rather, the emphasis becomes one of his lending his skills in a group endeavor. From the time of Karl Marx, social critics of modern society have pointed to this loss of the individual artisan and his replacement by an organizational unit, and they made of it one of the strongest indications of the rationalizing trend in modern life; they have also used it as evidence of alienation.

In addition to rationalization, several other issues deserve notice. Although specialization creates experts, it also creates a range of functions that are largely unskilled but whose routine performance as part of a larger operation contributes to an efficient performance. The dullness and boredom of work for the worker of limited skills and small responsibility has been a central emphasis in much of this criticism. (Whether in fact the unskilled worker finds his highly routinized job boring is an empirical question that has only infrequently been tested.) In some cases, bureaucracy also serves to reduce the sense of ethical responsibility. This occurs where bureaucracy removes authority and with it responsibility from the person as an agent of the organization and circumscribes his behavior by rules and regulations. This induces the famous "buck-passing" by which individuals hesitate to go beyond the officially prescribed boundaries of their office and so pass on a difficult, a controversial, or an ambiguous case to a higher echelon—and this may be done for several successive levels. Furthermore, the shrinking of decision making and responsibility under a centralization of authority may also shrink at lower echelons any personal sense of responsibility for the consequences of behavior, exemplified in the person who carries out his instructions and defends his individual action by saying, "Don't blame me, I just work here." This is the ethic of the technician whose skill lies in *how* to do something, but who takes no moral responsibility for the consequences of what he has done.

Perhaps one of the strongest criticisms of bureaucracy has to do with the impersonal and "de-humanized" manner by which it handles large numbers of people, either as employees, customers, clients, or whatever. The assignment of numbers to people for the more effective processing of records is a technique determined by the effort to be efficient. But it leaves many people with the sense of having no personal identity within the organization, of not having a name or a face. The issue, in fact, goes further than that. In trying to find some efficient manner for processing large numbers of people, bureaucracy turns to any number of ways of scoring and measuring people. It utilizes IQ tests, aptitude tests, achievement tests, vocational tests, and many others. By means of such testing, people can be scored in some quantitative manner and thus ranked on a scale—quartiles, percentiles, and so forth. Such widespread use of tests has recently been under strong criticism throughout the United States, both in terms of scientific inadequacy and in terms of abuse and misuse of even the best of them, particularly when relatively inexpert people are employed to interpret results. But no amount of such criticism has substantially reduced the use of them, nor is it likely to do so. These tests serve a need for bureaucratic organization, in that they provide a quick and relatively inexpensive way to process a large number of people and to measure them in such a way as to make decisions. People are graduated and certified, given jobs and scholarships, promoted or demoted, and even deferred from military service, on the basis of their performance on impersonal, quantitatively scored tests. Not to employ these tests would require instead highly expensive, highly skill-demanding, and much slower methods for processing people and making decisions. Furthermore, in an era of science and rationalized methods, these tests provide a presumably objective method for selection, rather than the subjective method based on intimate knowledge of the person. This lends a scientific rationale to the process.

A view of man is inherently implicit in this procedure. For the needs of bureaucracy, people come in quantity, not singly. They are not persons, not individuals with a unique combination of characteristics, rather, man is seen as a bundle of skills and attributes, each of which is susceptible to measurement. Bureaucracy is not so much concerned with the person, but with *personnel*. It hires personnel to fit into specific slots on the basis of specific and quite limited capacities. For bureaucracy, man is a relatively fixed set of attributes that can be trained, molded, and fitted into round or square pegs. It is not that people who are also bureaucrats actually see other human beings in such a limited way. But in their bureaucratic functions the problems of efficiently handling large numbers of people impels them to adopt such a view of man. The field of education has clearly come to share such a view, and social scientists, particularly psychologists, have contributed their skills to developing the instruments for such attribute-measurement.

Organization and Personality   The concern for the impact of bureaucracy upon a prevailing image of man has been most evident in the work of gifted and sensitive social critics, some of whom have been sociologists. But a great deal of social scientific work has explored the relation of the person to the large, formal organization. This relation of organization to personality is a complex one that involves several dimensions: (1) the *selection* and *recruitment* of personnel, which in many cases may reflect the particular values of the organization and thus favor some types of persons over others; (2) the *social-*

izing experiences of individuals within organization that either lead them to share in organizational values and goals or frustrate them and drive them into conflicting action; and (3) the effort of organization to provide *rewards* that will motivate individuals to compliant and cooperating action.

The process of selecting employees of corporations on the basis of skill, competency, and training seems not to be sufficient for modern organizations, and many of them make use of various psychological tests to screen out those prospective employees whose psychological tests make them undesirable employees. Just what is "undesirable" remains unclear beyond the possession of those traits that suggest people with neurotic symptoms. William H. Whyte made a vigorous attack upon this process of psychological testing by large corporations and attacked the psychological testers themselves in his humorous essay on how to cheat on personality tests.[35] It is possible for organizations to select new members for attributes of dutiful job performance and passivity, with no deviant attitudes, but the results may produce unintended difficulties later. In his study of a bank, for example, Chris Argyris found that the selection of passive, introverted types as bank employees worked well enough while these people held lower positions, but that they made ineffective bank officers when promoted.[36]

The conscious or manifest socialization of members of an organization often has little result; for one thing, it is likely to be offset by socialization into the informal patterns of conduct and belief shared among members at a given level within the organization. An unconscious socialization, evident in the way people adapt to the organization over time, is more indicative of how the organization can influence personality. Unfortunately, there is little hard empirical evidence to follow up Robert Merton's suggestive observations that established bureaucracies—he was referring specifically to governmental ones—produce officials who are timid, compulsive followers of rules and regulations, unimaginative and afraid to innovate, but who display arrogance and haughtiness toward clients.[37] Although such martinet behavior by many officials is evident enough, we still need to know why some behave that way though others do not. In studying a state employment agency, Peter Blau found that status insecurity on the part of some officials make them more ritualistic and conforming in their behavior.[38] These were the officials anxious about the attitudes and opinions of their superiors.

---

[35] William H. Whyte, *The Organization Man* (New York: Simon and Schuster, 1956), Appendix: "How to Cheat on Personality Tests," pp. 405–410.

[36] Chris Argyris, *Organization of a Bank* (New Haven, Conn.: Labor and Management Center, Yale University, 1954).

[37] Robert Merton, "Bureaucratic Structure and Personality," in his *Social Theory and Social Structure,* revised edition (New York: Free Press, 1957), pp. 195–206.

[38] Peter M. Blau, *The Dynamics of Bureaucracy* (Chicago: University of Chicago Press, 1955), p. 188.

The most severe indictment of organization has come from a foremost student of organization, Chris Argyris, who has argued that a comparison of the literature on organization and that on human personality suggests a thorough incompatibility between the demands that organizations impose on participants and the needs of emotionally healthy individuals.[39] According to Argyris, the principles of formal organization expect employees to work in an environment that provides minimal control over their work situation, to be passive, dependent, and subordinate, to have a short time perspective, to perfect and value a few shallow abilities, and to produce under conditions that lead to psychological failure. Such demands as these Argyris sees as incongruent with those that healthy individuals are supposed to desire and as much more congruent with the needs of infants. Perhaps the fact that there is not more failure, frustration, and conflict than there is stems in part from the fact that real organizations are not the ideal formal organizations of the literature. Also, there are many people who are passive and compliant and whose own perspective makes them obedient of legitimate authority. Then, too, many studies reveal that working-class members of organizations, according to Robert Presthus, are "indifferent" to the organization, and find their major personal satisfactions in situations and groups outside the organization.[40] Presthus feels that the upwardly mobile in organizations tend to come from middle-class backgrounds, to fear failure, and to respect authority. But there is also now much evidence to suggest that different kinds of positions in organizations are more or less rewarding to members. Those most rewarding, according to Robert Blauner, are positions that give the individual control over the pace of the work process and over the technical and social environment in which he works, and that also gives him freedom from hierarchical authority.[41] When these are combined with integration into a work group, high prestige, and off-work association with members of an occupational community, one finds those workers who feel most rewarded and satisfied. Note that in the organization, the most significant factor is the degree of control that provides the worker with *autonomy* with respect to authority and the impinging environment.

The Problem of an Organizational World   Whatever may be the moral stance we take toward it, the fact is that we live in an "organizational society." The working lives of most of us are absorbed in large, bureaucratized organizations. The significant economic, political, and civic activities that shape decisions for the future are made largely by and through modern organizations. Yet as

[39] Chris Argyris, *Personality and Organization* (New York: Harper & Row, 1957).

[40] Robert Presthus, *The Organizational Society* (New York: Knopf, 1962).

[41] Robert Blauner, "Work Satisfaction and Industrial Trends in Modern Society," in Walter Galenson and Seymour M. Lipset, eds., *Labor and Trade Unionism* (New York: Wiley, 1960), pp. 339–360.

we saw there has been a profoundly negative response to this fact, resulting in a mystique that anticipates only an Orwellian future from such a process. For over a century now, this pessimistic prediction of the future of man in organizational society has been a cornerstone for an existentialist perspective that views, with deep moral and intellectual misgivings, the increasingly rationalized character of the world and its dominance by large and complex organizations. Nonetheless, the mystique offers an incomplete analysis. It erects a contrast between the individual, viewed as small and helpless, and the organization, seen as large and powerful. This selects one particular angle from which to view organization in order to make a moral case against it. But there is much more to be said about organization than that.

Not the least of what needs be said is that formal organization is an instrument by which modern society undertakes tasks of large dimension and efficiently accomplishes them. The gathering of human skills and technical resources into a single highly rationalized organization permits the effective exploitation of opportunities for technological development, for scientific advance, and for the mass production and distribution of resources that creates an affluent society. The destruction of large-scale organization would require a return to small communities, to a simpler and less productive technology, to lowered standards of living, and indeed to many of the conditions that prevailed in the nineteenth century. It is unlikely that the moral deficiencies and human problems of bureaucracy—real and compelling as these are—are going to induce a modern people to forego the obvious advantages of organization for a return to some version of a smaller and simpler life. The consequences of this are highly ambiguous. There are rich returns from bureaucratization in terms of a developed organizational capacity to build a more ample and affluent society, a society with a greater range of personal opportunities for an ever larger segment of the population. But there are also those consequences that have provided such a morally compelling case for the existentialist critics of modern society and have also provided the basis for what has been called here the bureaucratic mystique—a perspective that sees organization as the antithesis of individualism, of personal freedom, and of human creativity.

But the world is moving rapidly toward the image of the modern society, and the "development" of new societies in Africa and Asia is a process of developing rational organization in place of traditional tribal organization, of converting a traditional society into a modern organizational one. The case for returning to small-scale organization has no compelling support in modern life, however much a hearkening back to "the old days" may be a convenient and pleasant romantic escape for each generation. In this sense, the world of large and bureaucratized organizations has developed to a "point of no return" in human experience. The moral and ideological attack against the evils of bureaucracy has the merit of pinpointing those most compelling human problems that bureaucratization creates. But it offers no viable alternative. These problems cannot be ignored, they can only be effectively confronted. But they are going to be confronted and solved, if at all, by humanly imaginative alterations in the structuring of human behavior within formal organizations, not by attempting to eliminate them.

1. A park bench in California.
2. Suburban commuters in Hoboken, N.J.
3. A California beach, with a Con Edison plant in the background.
4. A new high-rise apartment house.
5. Air view of Salt Lake City, Utah.

4

3 5

THE COMMUNITY

9

Ever since that now remote time when nomadic groups ceased to wander and claimed one spot on earth as theirs, the community has constituted a major form for the organization of social life. And almost since the beginning of the discipline of sociology, sociologists have given primary attention to the study of community. Much of the sociological literature in America is about the community. The sociological study of rural life began largely as studies of rural communities, whereas the great flowering of empirical research in American sociology in the 1920s was the study of the endlessly varied aspects of one urban community—Chicago.

Perhaps the first community study by an American sociologist was J. W. Williams' study, *An American Town*, in 1906. The following year W. H. Wilson published *Quaker Hill*, Newell Sims published *A Hoosier Village* in 1912, and that same year Wilson wrote *Evolution of the Country Community*. Then in 1915 C. J. Galpin published *Anatomy of an Agricultural Community*, which established a whole new approach to the study of community; it stands as the pioneer in community studies in American sociology. What each of these several studies had in common was a deep concern that the obvious rapid urbanization of American life was irrevocably changing these rural communities.

Despite the long interest of sociologists in the community, there is no precise meaning of the concept. A common-sense meaning says it refers to locality: village, town, and city. But it is frequently used to refer to all those in a locality who share some common interest or identity: the Negro community, the Jewish community, or the business community. Others use the term to convey the idea of common interest or identity without a specific locality: the community of scholars, the community of science, or, in a reference to religion, the community of believers. Nonetheless, a conception of community as *locality* has been a central one for sociologists. Many sociologists, however, have insisted that a town or city is not in and of itself a community unless a *communal* aspect is present. This means a sense of community, a we-feeling, a conception of belonging together. Without this, so goes the reasoning, a locality is not a community.

COMMUNITY AS A SOCIOLOGICAL PROBLEM

The lack of consensus about the concept of community among contemporary sociologists, which is evident in speaking not only of rural and urban localities as communities, but of professional communities and ethnic communities as well, does not testify merely to the inability of sociologists to agree on what a concept is to mean. Rather, it suggests that an older conception of community has now ceased to have its once common meaning. The growth of cities, the decline of the rural village, and even the modernizing transition in Africa and Asia that is replacing villages with cities, suggests that the once common form of community, the traditional and cohesive folk community of the past, is passing away. There is *a decline of traditional community.* For the sociologist, this decline of community constitutes a major sociological problem.

If the sociologist must explain this decline of the traditional community, he must also explain the great urban localities that have replaced these disappearing traditional communities. The *urbanization* of society is a basic social process, worldwide in scope, from which develops a nation of cities and an urban-based population. Furthermore, the urbanization of society produces *urbanism,* the social perspectives and life-styles of city-dwellers that arise from the structure of the city. An earlier but still influential sociological position interpreted this phenomena of urbanism from the perspective of the folk community, viewing it with great misgivings. Understanding the decline of community, then, requires an understanding of urbanization as a major social process in the world and urbanism as a new way of life for modern man.

A related problem is posed by the effort to interpret the city in terms of the adjustment of population to space and the allocation of scarce resources. The emerging social organization of the city presumably could be understood as a social adjustment to a physical environment. From this perspective, the concern for the communal values that presumably united people into a community give way to viewing the community as a functionally interdependent system for the use of space and time by an interacting population. This is the *ecological* perspective on the urban community.

But these problems posed by the decline of the traditional community and the rise of the urban community hardly exhausts the sociological issues about community that have interested the sociologist. The development of *suburbs* around the central city is an ecological and structural differentiation within the urban patterning that has become socially and politically as well as sociologically important. To explain the emergence of suburbia and its particular patterning and development is one major problem; to relate its development to changes in life-style and class structure of American society is another, one that puts the problem of suburbia into a larger sociological context.

The emergence of suburbs around central cities indicates the growth of large *metropolitan areas,* and the giant metropolis suggests the full extent of the urbanization of an industrial society such as the United States. The complex interrelations between city and suburb, the shifting of population from one to the other, and the conception of the metropolis as a total entity, an interdependent system of communities functionally differentiated from one another then emerges as still another problem for the urban sociologist.

Lastly, there is the problem of the *urban crisis.* The rapid growth of suburbs and the seemingly unceasing spread of slums has called into question the very future of the city as we have historically known it. The goal of urban renewal has been to restore and revitalize the city by rebuilding its inner core and by replacing slums and ghettoes with new neighborhoods and commercial areas. The political effort has been extensive and the investment considerable, but the result as yet has not demonstrated beyond question that the city, as the center of a vast centralized urban complex, can be rescued from decay. The urbanization of a population in a modern society is assured, but that this urbanization will be characterized by the urban patterns that we have known historically is not so assured.

These, then, are the several major problems that the sociologist of the community inquires into. The decline of the traditional community is the first of these; then, the urbanization of the population, the urban community, the significance of suburbia, the growth of the metropolis, and the extent of the urban crisis.

THE DECLINE OF COMMUNITY

The emergence of the city and urban culture has occurred concomitantly with industrialization and thus with the decline of an agrarian economy and rural life, including the rural village. In Europe, this began some three centuries ago, with the movement of vast numbers of peasants to cities and factory towns, where they became urban workers. This was a tremendous uprooting process, in which former peasants lost any sense of being located in a stable and traditional community, organized around kinship, religion, and a common life.

A concern for the consequences of this decline of the traditional peasant community has been a feature of modern social science, particularly European, for over a century. It is but one dimension of the secular crisis that provided the social origins of sociology. Its significance lies in the relatively negative interpretation of this consequence of industrialization. The focus on this presumably declining community occurred in Europe at a time when thoughtful men were concerned about the apparently harsh and brutal life of the urban working classes. Their picture of the urban worker's life in European cities in the 1700s and 1800s seemed to contrast quite unfavorably with peasant life, with its closeness to nature, its stability of family life, its adherence to traditional values, its rootedness in a secure community. Such a contrast, of course, romanticized the traditional village and ignored the pervasive brutality and poverty of peasant life.

In America, in turn, the concern for community, and particularly for the declining rural community, emerged in response to observations on American cities in the late nineteenth and early twentieth centuries. The rapid pace of industrialization after the Civil War converted America into an industrial society in a few decades, and set in motion a rapid urbanizing process. Americans became city people in large numbers in a short period, moving to the city from farms and small towns. They were now urban-dwellers, but they had been socialized in their youth as rural people, and they frequently retained a rural social outlook and responded as rural people to the realities of urban life.

Drawing upon the intellectual inspiration of Ferdinand Toennies and other European writers, American sociologists created the idea of a *rural-urban continuum,* with two types of communities, the rural and the urban, at each extreme of the continuum. This typology was drawn in such a way that the rural possessed much of the following traditional folk characteristics of a community: (1) a simple division of labor; (2) a population small enough for people to know one another in personal and intimate terms; (3) enduring social values; (4) effective social controls binding the individual to the community; (5) strong kinship ties; and (6) its social life manifested a strong sense of local identity and sentiment. The traditional community provided the significant social relationships of its members. It possessed a distinctive local culture, when, as a small society in its own right, it was *autonomous*—it was independent of any larger social structure. As a small society, its internal patterns of interaction were decisive for the life-chances of individuals. The decisions that were vital to its way of life were decisions taken within the community. The legitimate authority exercised over the social life of the community was the traditional authority residing within the community.

The decline of local autonomy, concomitant with the rise of the modern nation-state, the market economy, and bureaucratic associations, is perhaps the most significant factor in distinguishing the contemporary locality from the community of the past. The extent of local autonomy in the eighteenth and nineteenth centuries has probably been overstated, but nevertheless the rural community approximated in some ways a localized society. Few modern communities can do so. The modern nation moves toward increasingly centralized political controls, and modern government penetrates into even the smallest of communities in numerous ways. Local independence of action is increasingly limited, local resources are increasingly viewed as inadequate compared to the richer resources of the welfare state. As a result, local government has only circumscribed powers and increasingly assumes responsibility only for a small range of services—streets, sewers, garbage collection, and zoning, for example. It goes beyond these only when the local situation is desperate—as when the loss of a local factory results in a vigorous industrial development program—or where federal or state government prods and encourages and assists, as in school consolidation and urban renewal.

Politically, local communities are not, and never have been, separate and independent governments. Their powers are granted by state government. Local school systems have increasingly been subject to the controls and standards of state boards of education. The local economy is absorbed into a national market, and its local enterprises are frequently the branch plants of large firms whose headquarters are elsewhere. Even the political life of the community may function through the local units of the Democratic and Republican parties, in addition local units of the NAM (National Association of Manufacturers), of the AFL-CIO, of particular national unions, and of various trade associations may be involved in both economic and political activities in the community. In each case, these local units operate within a framework of policy set down from state and national headquarters. There are numerous other examples possible: local churches affiliated with large denominations, local Boy Scout and Girl Scout organizations, local YMCA and YWCA organizations, local Red Cross chapters, local chapters of fraternal lodges, of veterans' associations, and of service organizations. Each of these may be conceived of as a "community" organization, and although its orientation may be toward local action, its basic policy and goals are not determined within the local community.[1]

These last examples are particularly relevant, for they are representative of those national organizations that depend upon the mobilization of local community support for the attainment of their organizational goals. Many of their volunteer supporters conceive of their own efforts as "community work," and so it may generally be regarded in the community. Nevertheless, control of the program and decisions over policy are not localized. The local community, then, can no longer be conceptualized by the sociologist as autonomous. The massive secular trends set in motion by industrialization and urbanization have been a movement away not only from the small, rural community but also from the self-contained society to the large, urban one. The growth of urbanism has been marked by a decline in the *communal* and the *autonomous* character of locality.

Some social thinkers, such as Elton Mayo, have suggested that the decline of kinship and community necessitates new forms of communal organization to provide organizing and cohesive values for a stable social life. Mayo, the pioneering social scientist in the study of factory life, suggested that what men had lost in the decline of kinship and community might be recaptured

[1] For a discussion of this issue as it pertains to conceptualizing community, see Roland Warren, "Toward a Typology of Extra-Community Controls Limiting Local Community Autonomy," *Social Forces,* 34 (May, 1956), 338–341. Reprinted in Roland Warren, editor, *Perspectives on the American Community* (Chicago: Rand McNally, 1966), pp. 221–226.

in the factory. There men might find a sense of community not to be found in the disorganized world outside the factory walls. Though few other social scientists were ready to find such moral substitutes for the traditional community, many were engaged in assessing the full meaning of the change that has so radically altered the nature of community. The locality is no longer the autonomous community of the past and indeed is no longer a significant membership group for many people. Instead, many people find that their community roles are less significant than are their roles in the nation, in large-scale associations, and in occupational and economic organizations. Social class, nation, and large-scale association supersede community as social structures decisive for the life-chances of individuals and thus as more controlling of their behavior and to which they feel more strongly tied. Morris Janowitz' term, "the community of limited liability," seems particularly appropriate.[2] No longer does community necessarily command the primary loyalty of the individual. We have seen happen what Maurice Stein has called "the eclipse of community."[3]

Bureaucracy, class, and *nation,* then, are three organizing modes of social life which transcend community and which provide a basis for uniting people in common interests, in common beliefs and values, and in common social perspectives. In the face of this, community recedes in its meaning to the individual, and it declines as a significant means for the organization of social life.

To say all this is not to deny that locality is still a dimension of human experience, and that much human interaction is yet oriented to local affairs. Sociologists continue to study those social relations, such as neighboring, derived from the sharing of a locality, without always being concerned with the concept of community. And many sociologists have continued to study locality while being quite unconcerned with the *communal* attributes once traditionally associated with the concept of community. They are studying the structure of locality: locality groups, relations, and organizations. Somewhat parallel to this has been the study of the city and urban life. Urban sociologists have developed the study of urbanism, usually without referring to community or making community a part of their conceptual frame of reference. In short, they have, implicitly or explicitly, regarded the city and urban culture as a new social phenomenon that is not community in the traditional sense of the term, lacking communal attributes, and having instead its own social characteristics.

These few comments suggest that sociologists have not abandoned the study of life in the locality, in the village, town, and city, but that they have some-

---

[2] Morris Janowitz, *The Community Press in an Urban Setting* (New York: Free Press, 1952).
[3] Maurice Stein, *The Eclipse of Community* (Princeton, N.J.: Princeton University Press, 1960).

times abandoned any reference to community in the older sense. Others have continued to use the concept of community as a basis for comparing rural and urban life, and (as we shall see below) as a basis for analyzing urbanism in terms of a loss of community. Clearly, then, there is some doubt about the sociological usefulness of the concept. For some, community does not exist in modern life, though towns and cities do. For others, the community, in the form of local organization, is no longer a significant social structure in modern society. Yet this ready dismissal of community as a significant context of social life leaves other sociologists concerned. They are not so sure but that community is still significant, though just how and in what way remains uncertain. Some have become interested in the growth of suburbia and profess to see in the development of suburban life a reassertion of stable community life, albeit in new, urban forms.

As long as man organizes his social life, he will arrange himself in patterns and clusters in space. His use of territory for residence and work produces social arrangements that vary from the most remote village to the gigantic metropolis. Historically, this social organization within space, or better, this spatial basis for social organization, from mud-hut village to skyscraper city, has been called community. But for most of mankind's social existence, a predominantly agrarian life put most men into small communities within which they lived out the span of their lives and within which they found the total range of their social world. Community set the limits and horizons of their existence. A social life so confined was a little society, a whole in itself, and not, in any significant social sense, a part of any larger form of social organization. However, the Industrial Revolution broke through this predominant pattern, and community in this sense ceased to provide the social context within which modern man lived out his life. This separating of communal existence from organized locality constituted the basis for community as a sociological problem.

Some Changing Perspectives on Community   In 1915, C. J. Galpin's *Anatomy of an Agricultural Community* broke new ground in the sociological study of the community by the innovative approach to the analysis of small agricultural communities in Wisconsin. What Galpin did was ask whether there was in fact a rural community, given the penetration by urban influences of rural life, and if so what were its characteristics. Earlier studies of rural communities had demonstrated that the rural community is vulnerable to penetration by the influences of an urbanizing society. Galpin set out to devise a careful measurement of the community relationships within a rural Wisconsin county. Wilson, in his *Evolution of the Country Community*, had defined a rural community as "an area within a team haul of a trade center." Galpin sought to improve on this by delineating twelve trade zones in a Wisconsin county, and went on to show that each village or town served as a center around which developed an area of trade and commerce. Within these trade areas were the functioning zones for such "institutions" as banking, newspapers, libraries, high schools, churches, and milk production. Galpin concluded that these were social services used by both farm and townspeople, and that they operated over a relatively fixed and determinable land area.

The work of these early rural community sociologists (Williams, Wilson, and Sims), culminating in Galpin's influential study, served to shape much of the study of the community, both rural and urban, that was to follow. Galpin's work defined two major emphases in the study of community that were to receive somewhat separate development in later studies:

1. His concern for the local "institutions" that provided social services for a local population, and in this way organized local social life, led to later studies that sought to detail the interdependent structure through which local community life took on organization. This approach has been utilized by both anthropologists in studying preliterate societies and rural sociologists in studying rural communities, but it has found its classic expression in *Middletown* by Robert and Helen Lynd, which is accepted as one of the classics of American sociology.[4] In *Middletown*, the Lynds sought to describe the daily life in a typical American city, the social routines of family and work by which life follows institutionalized patterns. The study is highlighted by a contrast of the business class and the working class, with the former seen as dominant in the institutional structures. The Lynds also gave careful and systematic attention to the social values of the community that served to legitimize its structure. This concern for the distinctive value orientation of the local community has been one of the features of this approach to the study of community.

2. Galpin's efforts to delineate the local area of a community, particularly as it extended out from a center, thus relating *people, land,* and *social organization* in an interrelated pattern, was a significant prelude to the later *ecological* studies of community that were to emerge from the study of Chicago and other urban centers. (A later section in this chapter examines the ecological approach to the community.)

Community Status   In the 1930s and 1940s, sociologists began to view community from the perspective of community status. In 1937, John Dollard published *Caste and Class in a Southern Town,* in which he studied a small community's social life from the perspective of Negro-white relations.[5] But the

---

[4] Robert and Helen Lynd, *Middletown* (New York: Harcourt, 1929).

[5] John Dollard, *Caste and Class in a Southern Town* (New York: Doubleday, 1957).

publication in 1941 of the first volume of the *Yankee City* series, *The Social Life of a Modern Community,* followed by the second volume, *The Status System of a Modern Community,* in 1942, provided a new focus of interest in the community.[6] A great deal of sociological research on community followed, most of it utilizing Warner's categories of "class" (community status) as a vantage point from which to analyze a contemporary community. These studies interpreted the status system of the community as a major factor in its social organization and thus depicted the distribution of prestige, life-style, and behavioral controls within the community as a consequence of it being stratified. The communities studied were usually small, ranging from under 10,000 to the 17,000 of Yankee City itself. Furthermore, most of them seemed to have relatively stable status patterns, so that an examination of community status provided a close look into the internal social life of a community.

This concern for rank and prestige in the community then led sociologists to note the dominance over community life exercised by those of high status. Robert and Helen Lynd, in reexamining Middletown during the depression, focused attention on the power of the "X" family in controlling the community.[7] August Hollingshead showed how status correlated with influence in affecting the educational process in the community, from the distribution of grades and scholarships to the decisions of the board of education.[8] From such concerns as these came in time an interest in community power. The first major sociological work from this new perspective was *Community Power Structure,* a detailed examination of the top elite of decision-makers in a large city in the South.[9] (The studies of community power will be the concern of a later chapter dealing with power.) The subsequent studies usually found a close relationship between status and power, with an elite of high status making major decisions for the whole community.

Such studies as these had one important consequence, whether intended or not: they destroyed any notion of the community as homogeneously integrated and constituting a "grass-roots" democracy. Rather, even the smaller communities were organized along lines of status and power, with a consequent differentiation of life-styles and life-chances. In every community there were privileged classes and disadvantaged ones; there was a power elite who made decisions, and a majority who were powerless and remote from involvement in decisions.

[6] W. Lloyd Warner and Paul S. Lunt, *The Social Life of a Modern Community* (New Haven, Conn.: Yale University Press, 1941); W. Lloyd Warner and Paul S. Lunt, *The Status System of a Modern Community* (New Haven, Conn.: Yale University Press, 1942).

[7] Robert and Helen Lynd, *Middletown in Transition* (New York: Harcourt, 1937).

[8] August B. Hollingshead, *Elmtown's Youth* (New York: Wiley, 1949).

[9] Floyd Hunter, *Community Power Structure* (Chapel Hill, N.C.: University of North Carolina Press, 1953).

Reconceptualizing Community   The trend from the 1930s to the 1940s was to study community in quite selective ways: as a system of stratification and as a power structure. More and more, sociologists seemed to be removed from a theoretical concern for community as such; rather, many of their studies simply utilized community as a context for studies of status and power. But by the 1950s some sociologists returned to the persistent question of what the concept of community now had reference to in the modern world and whether it was still a viable sociological term. They recognized that the community, as one type of human group, no longer could be viewed as autonomous and as existing in isolation. It exists, rather, in the context of a large society, and it is profoundly influenced by what occurs in that society. Nor can it any longer be viewed from the perspective of *Gemeinschaft,* the historic folk community. Even the smallest of modern communities is not a folk community, even though there may exist in such communities an ideology of rural and small town superiority over the city.

It remained for two quite urban (and urbane) sociologists, Arthur Vidich and Joseph Bensman, to provide the community study that ended forever in American sociology the illusion of the small town as a contemporary *Gemeinschaft.* Their study, *Small Town in Mass Society,* analyzed a small community in upstate New York.[10] The study stressed, among other things, the ideology of moral superiority and cherished life-style in a small community that was in fact dependent upon the larger society, and that had lost any significant capacity to make decisions about its own destiny. Vidich and Bensman's study made it quite clear that the small community in the modern mass society had no autonomous existence of its own, even though its local ideology maintained such an illusion. In keeping with the tradition of community studies going back to the 1930s, they demonstrated how the community was stratified, and they also described the community's power structure. In effect, *Small Town in Mass Society* ended in American sociology (possibly in American intellectual life) the capacity for romantic illusions about small towns as autonomous communal entities and as grass-roots democracies.

Such sociological strictures as these, however, are not intended to convey the idea that smaller communities do not differ in significant ways from larger cities. The greater functional differentiation to be found in the larger urban community creates a greater diversity of subgroups, cultures, and life-styles than does the small community. There is usually a greater ethnic diversity than in small towns, some small communities may be very ethnically homogeneous. There is also greater class and status variation in the larger city. Nonetheless, the effective penetration of all communities by the mass media,

[10] Arthur Vidich and Joseph Bensman, *Small Town in Mass Society* (Princeton, N.J.: Princeton University Press, 1958).

particularly by metropolitan newspapers and television, removes the cultural isolation that tends to make a small community an autonomous little society of its own.

As we saw, these concerns have led many sociologists to lose any theoretical interest in the concept of community and either to ignore it as a social phenomenon or simply to use it as a context for other sociological studies, such as those of status and power. Nonetheless, a number of sociologists have persisted in advancing a sociological position around the idea that *territoriality* remains a significant dimension of human experience. For example, Charles Loomis argues that: "Territoriality determines within limits, how much space each person or group may have, the frequency and intensity of interaction within the group, and the probabilities of systemic linkages between groups."[11] Any society has territoriality, but a community possesses *locality,* a geographical area within which a social life is organized and maintained. The physical nature of the area enters into the very nature of community life to some extent and becomes central to its existence. This locality orientation has become central to those contemporary sociologists seeking to find an adequate conceptualization of community that avoids the assumptions of value-consensus and a distinctive and shared culture that undergird the concept of the folk community. Even though, they argue, the modern community may not be a folk community, it is a social organization that emerges around the fact of locality in the lives of people; there is a social group that emerges from the sharing of locality and the social functions that must be performed among those residing in such a locality. Roland Warren defines community from this perspective as

> that combination of social units and systems which perform the major social functions having locality relevance. This is another way of saying that by 'community' we mean the organization of social activities to afford people daily local access to those broad areas of activities which are necessary in day-to-day living.[12]

Warren then organizes his study of community around five major social functions: (1) *production-distribution-consumption,* the economic organization of the community as local participation in the larger economic processes of the society; (2) *socialization,* here conceiving of the community as a unit of the society in transmitting values, knowledge, and acceptable behavior patterns to individuals; (3) *social control,* the means by which the group obtains adherence to social norms; (4) *social participation,* providing local access to involvement through a

---

[11] Charles P. Loomis, *Social Systems: Essays on Their Persistence and Change* (Princeton, N.J.: Van Nostrand, 1960), p. 37.

[12] Roland Warren, *The Community in America* (Chicago: Rand McNally, 1963), p. 9.

range of formal and informal organizations; and (5) *mutual support,* the providing of aid and assistance for one another, particularly in time of need. As Irwin T. Sanders notes in his book on community, Warren's perspective on community sees it as serving as "a mediating social mechanism between individual and societal needs."[13]

This conception of community answers for contemporary sociologists several of the critical questions that had been raised by sociologists who found an incompatibility between a traditional definition of community and the observable empirical reality of modern communities. Maurice Stein's provocative and critical study of the "eclipse" of community had stressed that urbanization, industrialization, and bureaucratization had so penetrated the local community that it had been effectively absorbed into a larger society, losing its local autonomy and furthermore losing its sense of common belonging and of local solidarity, and that it had broken into often hostile subcommunities. Vidich and Bensman made the same argument by documenting it with a detailed study of a single small community. This new conception of community accepts the "eclipse" of the traditional community with its strong we-feeling but posits a conception of *interdependence* that links the members of a community together in a common enterprise acting to carry out a number of local functions and activities. This interdependence of activities around a common locality serves also to restore the idea of a common locality to the concept of community. The argument that community might better be conceptualized without a geographical base had been advanced by those sociologists who asserted that the significant ties that bind men together in the modern world are not those of locality. Melvin Webber, for example, has argued that community can be "without propinquity" because technological developments now permit the spatial separation of people who are closely related.[14] Furthermore, this argument points out that the community of residence of an individual is not necessarily the same as his community of work or of play and recreation. Webber distinguished between "place community" and "interest community" with the idea that the latter does not require people to be located in the same locality.[15] An acceptance of the fact that the social organization of people in modern society occurs through large-scale organizations that reach across local communities suggests that community in the sense of locality is no longer a dominant form of social group in the lives of men today as it was for so long in human experience. Nonetheless, men are still grouped in localities, and there is social organization that develops in response to the problems of locality

[13] Irwin T. Sanders, *The Community,* (2nd ed., New York: Ronald, 1966), p. 52.
[14] Melvin M. Webber, "Order in Diversity: Community Without Propinquity," in Lowden Wingo, Jr., ed., *Cities and Space* (Baltimore: The Johns Hopkins Press, 1963), p. 23.
[15] Webber, p. 29.

interdependence. It is the recognition of this that leads sociologists to treat the locality as a still relevant theoretical problem in sociology. No one who examines the now critical problems of the urban community and the desperate efforts to remove the ghetto and to rebuild the city can seriously argue that locality is irrelevant to modern experience.

THE URBAN COMMUNITY

To speak of the urban community is to join together two terms, *urban* and *community,* that do not fit together by an older and more traditional conception of community. But the modern community is increasingly an urban one, and no analysis of modern community life can avoid taking full account of what the urbanizing process has done to the modern community. The efforts of sociologists to take such account has meant noting the radical transformation in sheer size that has occurred over the past century or more, and the fact that residence in urban places is now characteristic of more than half of all Americans.

The Urbanization of the Community   For sociologists, the analysis of modern society has focused persistently on that complex and ever changing phenomenon: the city. The growth and spread of the city and its urban way of life is a process of urbanization, a process that has continued relentlessly throughout the decades of this century. Modern society is increasingly an urban society; even now, about two Americans out of three are urban, and more than half live in metropolitan areas of over 100,000 population. Furthermore, the trend continues to run strongly in that direction. The continued industrial and technological transformation of modern society promises only further urbanization of its population.

The recognition that the industrialization of society has been accompanied by urbanization should not lead us to think that cities are anything new in man's existence. The emergence of cities some three or four thousand years ago has been documented from historical records as well as archeological evidence. Men have built and lived in cities for centuries now, but usually only a small part of the population inhabited the city, whereas the majority lived an agrarian life in the surrounding countryside. Cities could not emerge, however, until certain specified conditions made it possible. There had to be a sufficient surplus of food and other resources that permitted some small segment of the population to engage in nonproductive activities; at first, this segment was probably a priesthood, which became in time an administrative and political elite. But there also had to be a level of technology and of social organization that permitted the city to have sufficient control over the country-side in order to insure its own existence. Armies and bureaucracies, then, came to be essential units in the social organization that made the city possible.

In Europe, the fall of Rome brought urban decline; cities did not become significant again in Europe until the return of trade and commerce about the tenth century. Then, cities grew up around the walled towns that were the administrative centers and defensible strongholds for the feudal aristocracy. Gradually an urban population of artisans and merchants built the great medieval cities that nurtured a distinctly urban culture and way of life.[16] Throughout the Middle Ages, however, these cities were small by contemporary standards and grew slowly. For example, Florence in 1388 had a population of 90,000 and Venice in 1422 had 190,000. London in 1377 had only 30,000, but by 1801, as the major city of the most industrialized country in the world, it had 865,000 inhabitants.[17] Thus, the great cities of the Middle Ages were modest in size compared to those of the twentieth century.

The Industrial Revolution was, among other things, an urbanizing revo-lution; it sharply altered the rural-urban proportion by urbanizing an ever larger proportion of the total population of every industrial society. Prior to 1850 there were large industrial cities in the Western world, yet no society had so concentrated its population in cities to an extent sufficient to call that society *urbanized.* Even by 1900, probably only one society—Great Britain—could be called urbanized. But now all industrial societies are urbanized, and there is an accelerating world trend toward global urbanization. The growth of the urban population in the world is greater than that of population growth in general, even though world population has grown rapidly since 1800. Accord-ing to Kingsley Davis, the world's population living in cities of 20,000 or more has increased from 2.4 percent in 1800 to 9.2 percent in 1900 to 20.9 percent in 1950. Comparably, the world population in cities over 100,000 increased from 1.7 percent in 1800 to 5.5 percent in 1900 to 13.1 percent in 1950.[18]

The United States, now a highly urbanized society, has only been so for a few decades. According to the first census taken in 1790, only 5.1 percent of the population was urban. In 1860, at the outbreak of the Civil War, the urban population was 19.8 percent, which means that at that time more than four

---

[16] For a classic analysis of medieval cities, see Henri Pirenne, *Medieval Cities: Their Origins and the Revival of Trade* (Princeton, N.J.: Princeton University Press, 1925).

[17] Kingsley Davis, "The Origin and Growth of Urbanization in the World," *American Journal of Sociology,* 60 (March, 1955), 432–433.

[18] Davis, p. 433.

out of five Americans lived in a rural place. But only a decade later, by 1870, the urban population was 28.2 percent, evidence of the accelerating effect that war often has upon the urbanization of industrial societies. By 1900, 39.7 percent of the United States was urban and by 1920, after World War I, the percent had risen to 51.2. It is about the time of World War I, then, that the turning point was arrived at—more than half the population of the United States lived in urban places. By 1950 this figure had reached 59.0 percent.[19]

In 1950 the Bureau of the Census recognized that its definition of *urban* had become inadequate and, that as a consequence, it was underenumerating the urban population. The main concern was the growth of a considerable urban fringe around central cities that remained unincorporated yet had the density and related social characteristics of an urban place. Therefore, the old census definition of urban—all places incorporated as municipalities provided they had a population of 2500 or more—was replaced with a new definition. Now urban is defined as all those places of 2500 or more people, as it was before, plus two new categories: (1) the densely settled urban fringe around cities of 50,000 or more, and (2) unincorporated places of 2500 or more people outside the urban fringe. The urban fringe is defined as continuously built-up areas outside the major cities which have an average density of about 2000 persons per square mile. As a consequence of this new definition of urban, the 59.0 percent urban of the old definition in 1950 became 63.7 percent. The United States was evidently more urban than had been apparent. Seven and one half million people were added to the urban category—and subtracted from the rural one—by this redefining process.

The rapid urbanization of the population in this century was hardly unique to the United States. In 1951 82.9 percent of Scotland's population was urban, making Scotland the most urban nation in the world. England and Wales (treated as a single entity) was 80.7 percent urban. More than four out of five Britons live in an urban place. Israel, with 77.5 percent of her population urban in 1951 was third, and Australia was fourth, with 68.7 percent urban in 1947.[20] Another measure of urbanization is the percent of the population living in cities of 100,000 and over. The United States ranks fourth in this category, behind England and Wales (51.9 percent), Australia (51.4 percent), and Scotland (50.7 percent). The figure for the United States was 43.7 percent and for Israel it was 39.9 percent.[21]

[19] For a discussion of urban growth in the United States, with the above and additional data, see Donald J. Bogue, "Urbanism in the United States, 1950," *American Journal of Sociology,* 60 (March, 1955), 471–486.

[20] The source for these data is Donald J. Bogue, *The Population of the United States* (New York: Free Press, 1959), p. 34.

[21] Bogue, p. 34.

URBANISM AS A WAY OF LIFE

The decline of the traditional community with the onset of industrialization and the consequent growth of large urban centers led sociologists to search for a framework from which the city could be interpreted. Using the city of Chicago as an urban laboratory, an industrious generation of sociologists at the University of Chicago, notably Robert Park and Ernest Burgess, carried out a pioneering series of research studies on city life: the ethnic communities, the slums, the criminals, the rich and the poor, the taxi dance halls, the Jewish ghetto, and so on. In all of this, they treated the city, not as a single cohesive community, but as a series of communities, natural areas, and local groups, each an entity in itself and each lacking a conception of the city as a whole. The image of the urban community implicit in the Chicago studies was eventually provided a brilliant and influential interpretation by Louis Wirth. In 1938 he published an essay, "Urbanism as a Way of Life," whose very title became a common phrase among sociologists, a symbol of a point of view that what was significant about the city was its distinctive way of life.[22] Wirth defined the city as "a relatively large, dense, and permanent settlement of socially heterogeneous individuals." Thus, he postulated three basic characteristics: *size, density,* and *heterogeneity,* and then proceeded to derive the characteristics of urbanism from them.

The relatively large *size* of the modern city, according to Wirth, produces a wide range of social differentiation in occupations, cultural life, personal traits, and ideas. A diversity of backgrounds weakens the bonds of kinship and neighborliness, as well as the sentiments generated within a folk tradition. People cannot base their social relationships on personal knowledge and familiarity of one another, and the result is a segmentalization of relationships and roles and the emergence of secondary rather than primary contacts. Most daily relationships are impersonal, superficial, transitory, and segmental. Even though the individual in the city, Wirth says, may have gained liberation from the controls of intimate groups, he loses "the spontaneous self-expression, the morale, and the sense of participation that comes with living in an integrated society."[23]

According to Wirth, the city concentrates large numbers in a limited space, producing a *density* from which certain sociological consequences flow. Differentiation and specialization are necessary consequences of this, and thus,

[22] Louis Wirth, "Urbanism as a Way of Life," *American Journal of Sociology,* 44 (July, 1938), 1–24.
[23] Wirth, p. 13.

density reinforces numbers in producing diversification and complexity. This produces specialized areas of the city, each different in its use and in its resulting social and cultural characteristics. The closeness of people who are not tied by bonds of sentiment produces competition, aggrandizement, and mutual exploitation, which can be controlled by such formal means as rules and laws. Movement throughout the congested city brings friction and irritation, and close contact among unrelated people brings about reserve and increases the likelihood of loneliness.

The *heterogeneity* of the city, in turn, Wirth credits with fragmenting memberships and loyalties, since each individual associates with a number of groups, but each such group is related to only a segment of his personality (as parent, worker, taxpayer). City people are transitory, even within the city; group membership changes, and organization is hard to maintain. The typical city-dweller is a renter, not a homeowner and not a stable, long residing neighbor. Nor is he able to develop a conception of the city as a whole or his own place in it. Lastly, Wirth sees urbanism as destructive of individualism, producing a leveling and depersonalization of human beings. The individual cannot receive individualized service or attention from facilities and institutions; instead, such service is directed to the typical and average, subordinating the individual and the unique to the mass characteristics of urban life.

The view of the city that emerges from Wirth's analysis is characterized more by what it lacks than by what it possesses. The city is not an integrated community, it seems not to have found an adequate and meaningful replacement for the traditions and sentiments of the rural community, and its residents lack even a conception of the community as a whole. The language of the essay is negative: segmentalization, depersonalization, weakened bonds of kinship and neighborliness, superficiality, impersonality, transitoriness, frictions and irritations, aggrandizement and mutual exploitation, leveling and depersonalization, and loss of spontaneous self-expression, of morale, and of a sense of participation. The reader is overwhelmed by such words, and the total effect is to create an entirely negative image of the modern city. In "Urbanism as a Way of Life," Wirth summarized and synthesized so ably the character of a whole generation of sociological thought on city life that his article became a standard sociological statement on the city and on urbanism for a succeeding generation. It was not until the 1950s that a younger generation of urban sociologists began to develop a newer point of view that modified to some extent the image of community in dissolution.

A New Look at Urbanism   The reassessment of the image of urbanism that has emerged in recent years constitutes a stock taking of what sociology knows about the city and city life and what it sees as important and most relevant. One dimension reassessed has been that of *primary relations*. The emphasis on the impersonality, transitoriness, and superficiality of social relations suggests that primary relations decline under conditions of urbanism. There can be no question but that there are more impersonal relations in the city and that a larger proportion of any one person's social relations are impersonal in nature. But recent urban research suggests that many urban people do find satisfying primary relations in the city. Industrial sociologists have pointed out the network of primary relations that occur in work situations; other sociologists have documented the vast network of social organizations of all kinds to which Americans belong and within which personal relations are established. The older view asserted that primary relations were a product of neighborhood patterns; that in the city neighboring declines, and people are simply less able to know one another well. They unite, instead, in terms of shared interests; and interest groups are large and impersonal, with only a segmental involvement of the person.

But where and how do urban people form primary relations, develop friendships? If neighborhood is no longer a significant basis, urban people find other sources. They develop friendships out of acquaintances made within their profession or occupation, their place of work, their membership in church, labor union, fraternal lodge, business organization, or political party. Interest groups provide the context within which urban people sort out those congenial few who form a small circle of primary relations.

The *neighborhood*, however, is still a source of primary relations for many. It is true of any urban neighborhood where stability of residence prevails, but it is particularly true of the old ethnic neighborhoods. In such neighborhoods, some residents develop closer and more intimate relations with some other neighbors. This occurs more in neighborhoods of single-family homes than in apartment house areas, and more in home-owner neighborhoods than in rental areas. It is also more characteristic of working-class and lower middle-class neighborhoods than of upper middle-class ones.

But the established neighborhoods of the city provide more than a context for primary relations. Many of them, and particularly the ethnic ones, constitute small social worlds of culturally homogeneous people; they are *urban villages*.[24] Herbert Gans studied an Italian working-class community of Boston, an "ethnic village" of people who isolate themselves from significant contact with other urbanites, except in places of work. Their way of life is based on primary groups and kinship within the structure of the ethnic group; it lacks the anonymity and secondary group relations that Wirth emphasized, and it is weak in the frequency and influence of formal organizations. Its members possess an in-group outlook that makes them suspicious of people and activities outside their own group. Thus, their lives are characterized by a great deal of

---

[24] Herbert Gans, *The Urban Villagers* (New York: Free Press, 1962).

isolation from others, even though they live in close physical proximity. They set up social barriers that others cannot cross. Furthermore, this pattern of urban villagers prevailed in American cities in Wirth's day even more than in contemporary cities. Wirth recognized this when he said that "two groups can occupy a given area without losing their separate identity because each side is permitted to live its own inner life and each somehow fears or idealizes the other."[25]

The neighborhood has another sociological meaning, too. Neighbors and neighboring, in the sense we have been speaking of above, refer to the small immediate circle of homes. But *neighborhood* often means to these same urban (and suburban) dwellers a larger physical area, such as a recognized section of a city, a subdivision, or even a suburb. The name of the area suggests a level and style of living and thus serves to symbolize something about the status level of the person. The widespread economic homogeneity of urban social areas makes possible large, identifiable neighborhoods with a specific status image. In addition to homogeneity of income and social class, such areas may successfully practice the exclusion of Negroes, perhaps of Jews, and sometimes other minorities as well.

During and just before the 1920s, the Chicago sociologists focused their attention on the transient and unattached individuals—the new arrivals from the farms and small towns, particularly the young, who lived in rooming houses and hotels and looked for the chance to make their fortune in the city. A concern with such a category of people led to an emphasis upon the decline of *kinship* under urbanism. However, more recent sociological research suggests that the unattached individuals removed from family connections are less prominent in the city now than they were in the first quarter of this century. Wirth's references apply to an earlier historical period in the development of the American city. These same individuals married and raised children in the city, their children have grown up and married, and new kinship patterns have been established. For example, sociologists at the University of Michigan have studied family life in Detroit; the analysis they give is quite different from that of the Chicago school in the 1920s. A study of Detroit area people in 1955 reveals that 66 percent of them got together informally with relatives at least once or twice a week, and 28 percent did so almost every day.[26] Only 17 percent reported not meeting with relatives at least once a month.[27] Such data as these do not bespeak the decline of family and kinship under conditions of urbanism.

---

[25] Louis Wirth, *The Ghetto* (Chicago: University of Chicago Press, 1928), p. 283.

[26] Detroit Area Study, *A Social Profile of Detroit, 1955* (Ann Arbor, Mich.: Institute for Social Research, University of Michigan, 1956), p. 23.

[27] *Social Profile of Detroit*, p. 23.

These few comments on the sociological reanalysis of urbanism bring out two basic criticisms of the point of view about the city held by an earlier generation of sociologists. In the first place, it was clearly somewhat anti-urban, possessed of a vocabulary of disorganization, and reflected rural values and perspectives in interpreting urbanism and the city. Secondly, "Urbanism as a Way of Life" describes American cities in their periods of early growth, when their social structure reflected the rapid influx of unattached migrants from rural America and from Europe. When the city is viewed at an historically later period, and the anti-urban values of a rural romanticism have declined, then it appears to be a less disorganized context for human experience. This conception of the city as disorder dominated the American sociological perspective during the 1920s and 1930s. Yet such a perspective is inadequate. The city is a complex organizing process, a form of social order with its own kind of social structure. Furthermore, much of the research of the Chicago school treated the city as earlier sociologists treated the village, as an autonomous process. But urban communities, perhaps even more than the rural villages of the past, are responsive to the larger society of which they are a part; they are not independent of major sources of change within the society and they are closely interdependent with the complex structure of the society.

The Ecological Approach   A contrasting approach to the study of the city defines community from a perspective which seeks to relate people (population) to land (physical environment), and to interpret man's social organization as a consequence of human adjustment to environment. The study of *ecology* is a major concern of biology, and the concept was borrowed from that discipline by sociologists seeking to understand the internal organization of the city as a problem of the adjustment of concentrated population to relatively scarce land. Suggested first in Galpin's work, it was explicitly developed at the University of Chicago in the 1920s.

If human ecology borrowed its basic concept from biology, it turned to classical economics for a model from which to develop a set of assumptions. A concern with the distribution of scarce values has long been the focus of classical economic analysis of capitalism. Competition in a free market has been conceived as the way in which values are established and then distributed among claimants. Human ecology conceived of the city as a limited array of space, the social use of which is distributed in some organized way as a consequence of competition. The competition for space in the city produces a *segregation* of people and facilities. Thus, at the center of the city is the principal business district (frequently called "downtown"), which is the centralization in a relatively small space of major commercial functions. The processes of segregation and centralization produce areas inhabited by specific categories of people—the poor, the wealthy, the immigrants, the Negroes, the Jews—as well as areas given over to specific social functions: factory districts, theater districts, shopping areas, and the like.

The most influential attempt to give sociological expression to these processes of segregation and concentration in urban space was the famous *concentric zone* theory of the city developed by Ernest Burgess in 1925.[28] Burgess postulated the idea that one could abstractly visualize the city as a series of concentric circles, each circle being a different zone of functional use of space in the city. The zones were as follows: (1) the central business district; (2) the zone of transition, the old area of residential deterioration just beyond the downtown area, an area of social disorganization, high in proportion of family-less people, of physical and mental disease, a center of vice and crime, in effect, a slum; (3) the zone of workingmen's homes, largely constituted of second-generation immigrant settlement; (4) the zone of better residences, namely, the middle-class area; and (5) the commuters' zone, the middle-class residential area in the suburban belt around the city.

Burgess's theory has been criticized as describing Chicago, which served as the model for the theory, but not necessarily other cities. In addition, it has been indicated that cities in other cultures were so constructed that they did not develop along the pattern of concentric circles. Other American sociologists, notably Homer Hoyt, have developed other theories to provide an explanation for the same phenomenon, though Burgess's has remained the best known. Hoyt's theory postulated *sectors* instead of zones. A more complicated, *multiple nuclei* model has been developed by Chauncey D. Harris and Edward L. Ullman (Figure 1).

The real value of Burgess's theory was that it was not only an attempt to explain the city, but in particular an effort to explain the growth of the city. Burgess conceived of the city as growing out from its center, as pushing out to its periphery as population grew, and demands for space increased. The theory implicitly recognized the aging process of areas and neighborhoods as leading to physical deterioration. As a result, original residents or business users of the area moved out to newer areas where land was not yet used up. Left behind were old and worn areas and those categories of people who could not successfully compete for the newer. *Invasion* and *succession* were the terms used to describe this process of change in residential and business use of urban space. Thus, as time goes on, a middle-class area of fine, large homes ages, and the economic value of the homes declines. At some point a social group of lesser economic status begins to move in—invasion—and when they have become the dominant residential group, succession has occurred. In this way,

[28] Ernest W. Burgess, "The Growth of a City: An Introduction to a Research Project," in Robert Park, Ernest W. Burgess, and Roderick D. Mackenzie, *The City* (Chicago: University of Chicago Press, 1925), pp. 47–62.

an area may change from white to Negro, from an older immigrant group to a newer and economically poorer one. Those who move out in the face of invasion form new areas farther out; the movement to the suburbs is one index of the invasion and succession process having gone to the point where the central city has now used all available land space. The search for new space, particularly by the economically affluent, now goes on largely beyond the city limits, in the surrounding countryside.

The value of the ecological perspective, then, has been to enable the sociologist to focus on the city as a dynamic and changing phenomenon and to trace many changes made apparent by the way men organized life within the limited space available. It focused analysis on "natural areas," on areas as

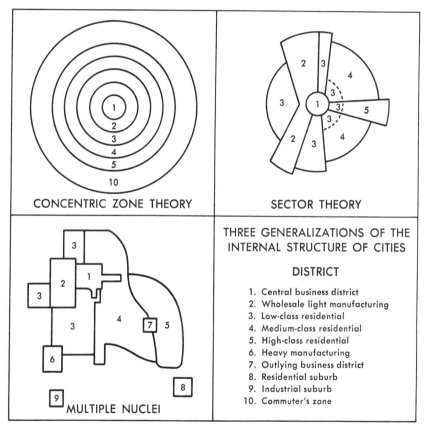

CONCENTRIC ZONE THEORY

SECTOR THEORY

THREE GENERALIZATIONS OF THE INTERNAL STRUCTURE OF CITIES

DISTRICT

1. Central business district
2. Wholesale light manufacturing
3. Low-class residential
4. Medium-class residential
5. High-class residential
6. Heavy manufacturing
7. Outlying business district
8. Residential suburb
9. Industrial suburb
10. Commuter's zone

MULTIPLE NUCLEI

FIGURE 1

Adapted from Chauncey D. Harris and Edward L. Ullman, "The Nature of Cities," *The Annals of the American Academy of Political and Social Science*, CCXLII (November, 1945), 13.

clusters of homogeneous people (the same race or ethnic group) as well as on areas of functional concentration (the garment district, the central business district), created, not by authority or law and pertaining to no legal or political boundaries, but emerging from the adjustment of people to environment in a milieu in which the processes of segregation, centralization, and concentration operate.

The competition for space within the city suggests that the major factor in the ecological patterning of a city is a *rational-functional* one in which specific activities are located on sites that give access to necessary facilities: transportation, materials, and the like. Factories may be located near railroad spurs and truck routes, shopping centers near residential concentrations yet convenient in terms of access by major thoroughfares, and apartments conveniently located for shopping and access to major work centers, while being away from factories and related facilities. This leads to patterns of segregation in land use for purposes of residence, recreation, business, and manufacturing, and, in large cities, even more specialized segregative patterns: theater districts, hotel areas, bohemian areas, and the like.

But sociologists have never accepted the idea that such functional-rational criteria alone are decisive for ecological patterning. Ever since Walter Firey's study of Boston, in which he demonstrated that high status families chose to remain in the older residential areas (such as Beacon Hill), the place of *values* (other than rational ones) in the allocation of space has been central to the ecological study of the urban community.[29] Status considerations, for example, may thoroughly disrupt a strictly rational ecological process. Such considerations as a desirable view, scenery, an elevated or commanding site, a spacious area, a comfortable distance from "nuisance" activities, a desire to remain close to others of similar status, and a desire to locate in areas of high reputation, are mentioned by Alvin Boskoff as some of the major status motives for retaining land use that defies the rational-functional criteria.[30] On the basis of this, Boskoff argues that there is an *orthodox* ecological model, in which the rational-functional criteria are dominant in determining the pattern of land use, and a *symbolic* model, in which there is no apparent organization, and zones and sectors are hard to identify.[31] He characterizes the symbolic type as

a continuation of early ecological patterns or a reflection of organized resistance to the liberation of rational, competitive motives in allocation of land. In place of zonal and sector developments, the symbolic type is compounded of a series of

[29] Walter Firey, *Land Use in Central Boston* (Cambridge, Mass.: Harvard University Press, 1947).
[30] Alvin Boskoff, *The Sociology of Urban Regions* (New York: Appleton, 1962), p. 108.
[31] Boskoff, pp. 110–112.

nuclei, which are maintained in roughly their traditional form by the stubborn immobility of high status families.[32]

In the symbolic model, residential areas of both high and low status are evaluated in terms of how they have been used historically in the past, and they are not assessed as areas to be exploited for private gain.

The ecology of an urban community, then, is a dynamic process of adjustment and accommodation among competing claims for a limited land use; what prevails in a community at a given point in its history is a compromise among rational factors, on the one hand, and status and other symbolic considerations, on the other. What has prevailed in the past becomes a source of influence on decisions taken for future development. Whereas rational factors seem often to have been dominant in ecological actions, symbolic interests have often intervened, more in some cities, less in others. To cite Boston and New Orleans as major examples of urban communities in which symbolic interests have seriously modified the rational-functional criteria is to suggest that in old, historic cities, status considerations may link with an interest in historic values in the struggle to retain certain areas and protect them from economic and status decline. There are some notable examples of rescuing declining areas from slum or near-slum status in older cities, of which upper-status Georgetown in Washington, D.C., is one. In American cities, in particular, an appreciation of old historic areas and old landmarks has recently become more influential in offsetting the strictly market orientation that so often has either permitted steady decline and transition to a slum or has moved in with bulldozer to raze old structures in order to build new ones.

THE SUBURBAN COMMUNITY

The sociological study of the community now must turn its attention to the suburban community, for suburbs have proliferated in America in recent years, inducing considerable sociological interest as well as extensive comment both popular and intellectual. Among many cultural critics, suburbia has become a symbol of middle-class life-styles. Its development housing, its homogeneous population, its reduction in urban diversity have all been taken to exemplify a tendency to sameness and conformity in American life. Thus, the suburban community has been less sociologically examined than it has been criticized as a manifestation of much that is undesirable in the affluent middle class.

[32] Boskoff, pp. 110–111.

Suburban Growth   Suburban residential development outside a large city is not new; in the early 1800s, English industrialists moved their family residences out of such early industrial cities as Manchester and Liverpool in order to escape the filth and the fetid air. Residence beyond the city limits for the more prosperous of the city's industrial and financial leaders was a well-developed pattern in the United States before the turn of the century. The growth and declining exclusiveness of the suburban community has been a function of local transportation. At first, suburban residence beyond the city was limited to those upper income people who could afford the private transportation, the time spent in travel, or the train fare necessary to commute to the city. With the growth of railroads, suburban communities sprang up along railroad lines; the typical upper-middle class suburbanite was a commuter. Probably through the 1920s, most suburban residents commuted by train to the city. With the growth of motor transportation and the mass consumption of automobiles, suburban communities were no longer confined to railroad lines, and a much larger space around the periphery of the city became potentially available for residential development. Commuting became a matter of driving one's own car or taking the bus. With car and bus transportation available to a much broader stratum of people, so too was the opportunity for suburban residence.

In the United States, suburban development accelerated rapidly after World War II. There were a number of economic factors that account for this. New housing had been but a trickle during the war years and had been only moderate in the 1930s, a depression decade; there was, then, a pent-up demand for new housing. The years after the war were relatively prosperous years, as well, with high employment; thus there was a more widespread capacity to consume new housing than probably had hitherto existed in American life. In addition, the delayed marriages and resumed family life of servicemen meant an upsurge of new families needing housing. These circumstances, then, were propitious for a great increase in the construction of new housing. But why did this occur in suburban areas? Why not in the city? By the end of World War II, most larger American cities had exhausted the available land space and population potential of the central city. Additional population and housing growth had no alternative but to spill into the area surrounding the city. Then, too, the construction industry was now ready to change from the individual, handcraft construction to the mass construction of homes. Only outside the central city was there land available for large housing developments.

To this point, then, we can explain the growth of the suburbs by such factors as: (1) the development of modes of transportation; (2) the demand for and supply of new housing; and (3) the exhaustion of land space in the central city. These constitute the social conditions, primarily economic and ecological, that account for the growth of suburban residential communities at a greatly accelerated rate in the United States since World War II. But these factors only set the framework within which the sociologist asks his questions and pursues his inquiry into the nature of suburban life. In short, after a set of objective conditions ensure the acceleration of suburban growth, the sociologist wants to know what the structure of social life in the suburban community will be. He wants to know who suburban dwellers are, how they differ from city dwellers, and what new styles of life are manifest in suburbia.

Who Goes Suburban? The analysis of the conditions giving rise to mass suburbia development suggested that suburban living was once largely the exclusive prerogative of the wealthy, but that the motorization of the population brought suburban living within the means of many less wealthy people. Certainly, the mass construction of housing in suburban developments signifies that the suburb is no longer a symbol of upper status. Yet, this "democratization" of suburbia has not gone so far as to make it equally accessible to all economic levels. Although blue-collar workers have joined white-collar workers in moving to the suburb, and large metropolitan areas now possess working-class suburbs, suburban residence has, nevertheless, become most economically accessible to middle-income people. The lowest income levels are excluded from the suburban housing market.

The rapid influx of young couples into new suburban housing after the war gave many suburban communities a rather unique age-structure. The adults were young, and their children were preschoolers or at elementary school age. In such communities there was a less than average number of unmarried, of middle-aged and older, and of teen-agers. During the 1950s, suburban subdivisions made up almost entirely of young couples between twenty-five and thirty-five years of age, with an average of three to four children under ten years, could be found around every major metropolitan area in the United States. To be sure, such a unique age-structure is unlikely to maintain itself over time. The couples grow older, and their children grow into teen-age. New families moving in bring in younger children, however, and thus a wider range develops in both adult and child age-structures. However, there is some limitation on this. In white-collar, middle-class suburbs, where young executive and professional people live, occupational advancement means higher income, resulting in movement to new residential areas that symbolize the social mobility achieved. Under such conditions, one can expect a high rate of movement out and, in turn, an inward movement of new young couples still at the earlier stages of their occupational career. In this way, some suburbs can be expected to retain something of the unique age-structure developed at the outset. However, in working-class suburbs, where social mobility is less evident, our sociological expectation would anticipate a gradual movement toward a wider age-distribution.

The economic character of the contemporary suburb, namely, mass-produced housing, produces an apparent economic homogeneity. Houses of the same price, carrying similar mortgages, are inhabited by people with similar incomes. While there can be a considerable range of occupations, both blue-collar and white-collar, there is only a limited range of income level. The cost of the housing sets a minimum, and when people move well beyond the income level symbolized by the cost of housing in a suburban area, they move to higher-priced housing. Yet a similar income level may in fact be a superficial similarity, obscuring such significant differences as the presence or absence of mobility aspirations and opportunities.

What so often makes a suburb look homogeneous is an effective limitation on accessibility to the suburb by people of particular racial or ethnic categories. Of these, the most significant is race. The new suburbs have been almost entirely white, and Negroes have been blocked in efforts to find suburban housing even when their income, education, and occupational levels were the same as those whites residing in the community. Suburban communities of an even higher economic level have often practiced other exclusions, most particularly that of Jews, but sometimes also of southern and eastern European groups, such as Italians, particularly where ethnic cultural characteristics, as in speech, are still evident.

Who does go suburban, then? The young, the more economically secure, the socially mobile—these find suburban living most accessible and most congenial to their interests and values. Obversely, suburbia excludes the poor, the older, and the social minorities, and these people in turn constitute a significant segment of those left behind in the movement out of the city. This tells us, in objective terms, about the selective process that goes on in sorting out the urban population for suburban residence. But sociologists press their inquiry even further. They want to know what suburbia means to those who choose to live there, and what values are given objective expression by the modes of life evident among the new suburbanites.

Suburbia as a Search for Values Sociologists bent upon probing into the significance of the new suburbs have interpreted suburban living as a sometimes unclear but always persistent attempt to find new values in American life and to evolve a style of life that gives expression to those values. The sociologist, Wendell Bell, has tested in research the proposition that the move to the suburbs gives primary expression to the value of *familism*.[33] Familism as a value means, in the words of sociologist Nelson Foote, ". . . the self-conscious recognition of family living as a distinctive and desired activity— quite different from operating a family business, 'raising a family,' or visiting

[33] Wendell Bell, "Social Choice, Life Styles, and Suburban Residence," in William Dobriner, ed., *The Suburban Community* (New York: Putnam, 1958), pp. 225–247.

relatives. . . ."[34] Bell points out that the high valuation on family living given concrete expression in early marriage, the short childless period after marriage, and the child-centered family life, is chosen as a value over other possible alternatives. In the suburbs, then, higher than average economic status, a decline of ethnic identification and clusterings, and a strong familistic orientation mark a distinctive suburban life-style. The choice of a smaller suburban community as a setting for a familistic style of life can have associated with it, according to Bell's research, a concern for community as well, expressed in such indexes as greater community participation and a sense of belonging to the community.

This approach to the meaning of suburban life creates an image of its desirability to working-class and middle-class American adults who are primarily family-centered in their own values. It is more desirable as residence because it is inhabited more by people like themselves in social status and in values, because physically it is cleaner and fresher than the city, and because it offers both now and in the future a "better" situation for children. One reason it seems better for children is that it offers them friends and associations that meet parental standards set by criteria of status and status-related values.

The Suburban Neighborhood The long-established sociological interest in the neighborhood and neighboring goes back to those studies of small rural communities, in which the neighborhood as a primary group that exercised strong social controls over individuals was contrasted with the anonymous urban residential area. The denial of genuine neighborhoods in the city was a feature of the early urban literature in sociology, and the idea that the suburban pattern would now foster neighboring arose again, particularly from William H. Whyte's influential study of such patterns in Park Forest, Illinois, a middle-class suburb near Chicago inhabited largely by mobile young executives.[35]

Recent suburban research suggests that new suburban developments manifest a high degree of neighboring of a more intimate and intense kind than is found in older, settled neighborhoods. And lastly, the neighborhood remains a source of primary relations for the woman, who in her combined roles of housewife and mother is confined to the local neighborhood much more than is her husband. This last point is quite important. Women, it would seem, still manage to develop primary relations in the neighborhood. They do so because they need to, since the neighborhood is their working and living habitat. It is, of course, easier for women to utilize the neighborhood for

---

[34] Quoted by Bell, in Dobriner, *The Suburban Community,* p. 227. The quotation is from Nelson Foote, "Family Living as Play," *Marriage and Family Living,* 17 (November, 1955), 297.

[35] William H. Whyte, *The Organization Man* (New York: Simon and Schuster, 1956), Part VII, pp. 267–404.

primary relations when their neighbors are similar to them in income and economic level, in age, and in a common concern about caring for small children (thus, the childless woman might find it harder to make friends in the neighborhood). Men, in turn, find less need to utilize the neighborhood as a source of primary relations, for they have many other avenues open to them, and, of course, they spend less time in the neighborhood. Neighborhood friendships among men seem to develop most frequently under a specific set of conditions: new suburban neighborhoods of younger men, where much borrowing of tools occur, as well as assisting one another in putting in lawns and doing the numerous other things that suburban residents must do at the beginning. If men do not utilize the neighborhood in the same way as do their wives, they nonetheless recognize its meaning for women, and they too find a value in neighboring. Good neighboring may not mean close friendship, but it does mean friendliness, and it means assistance in time of crisis. Given the absence of close kin for the typical suburbanite, suburban dwellers need to be able to turn to neighbors in an hour of crisis.[36]

The sociological functions of the neighborhood change under suburban living, and while the old rural form of a close-knit neighborhood may not reappear, a new form of neighboring does. It is a source of friendly aid on matters pertaining to the maintenance of house and yard, a source of assistance in a time of crisis, and a source of more definitely intimate and personal relations for women during the day, which does not necessarily extend to couples.

Suburbia as Anti-City   In analyzing human behavior in terms of motives, one can get caught on the "push-pull" problem. Do people act in some particular way because they are *pulled* in that direction by positive factors, or are they *pushed* by the desire to escape undesirable features? Something of this is involved in the attempts to analyze the movement to suburbia. Suburbia pulls people because of what it has to offer, but the city frequently pushes them out, as well. They flee the city to escape features they regard as undesirable. People may leave the city to escape its noise and congestion, its dirt and untidiness, its crowdedness and apartment living. New suburban developments offer opportunities for more space and greenery, cleaner air, and it is farther removed from the source of urban dirt—factories and industrial processes.

However, the city is more than physically unattractive to many people, it is often socially unattractive as well. The city possesses slums and slum dwellers, poor whites and Negroes recently arrived from the South whose less educated children threaten the academic level of the city's public schools. Negroes

---

[36] For a cogent analysis of the meaning of neighboring for the middle class, see Ruth Useem, Duane Gibson, and John Useem, "The Function of Neighboring for the Middle-Class Male," *Human Organization*, 19 (Summer, 1960), 68–76.

and slums, racial conflict and large relief rolls, juvenile gangs and criminal violence, these are some of the negative symbols of the city which lead people to seek the suburban life. Thus the statement so frequently met in research reports, the desire to be among people "like themselves." This means people of the same income and education, the same racial stock, as well as the same cultural interests and life-styles, thus the rigid barriers to suburban penetration by the poor and by social minorities.

The problems of contemporary American cities are large and difficult, and no easy solution lies at hand. Much of the movement to the suburb can be interpreted as an escape from all of this, as a shedding of social responsibility for the larger and more difficult problems of American life. It can be viewed as an attempt to create small enclaves isolated from the problems of urban-industrial existence, while enjoying its amenities and advantages. Suburbia as a way of life, then, can be interpreted only in a larger urban context. What it represents as a selective process and as life-style can only be understood if we examine the urban pattern from which suburbanites come. The selective process and the life-style emphasize what is to be found and created in suburban life, and what is to be escaped from and left behind in the central city.

The emphasis on familism, on middle-class consumption, and on new life-styles tends, whether the social analyst means to or not, to present positive images of suburban life. In turn the emphasis on leaving behind the poor and the minorities, on creating enclaves of better educational opportunity for children, on narrowing friends and associates to people who are culturally most like oneself, creates a negative image of suburbia that emphasizes concerns of status and advantage, a narrower, less challenging existence, in which family life and private concern and leisure pursuits project what David Riesman called the "sadness of suburbia . . . an aimlessness, a low-keyed unpleasure."[37] Whether one interprets the sociologists' data on suburban life in more positive or more negative accents, it is possible to read into it a significant choice that mid-twentieth century Americans have made among the alternative potentialities for community life in the urban context. If David Riesman is correct in asserting "that the suburban styles of life tend increasingly to become the American style, with ensuring loss of certain kinds of diversity, complexity, and texture, . . ." and if there is relevance to his comment that today's suburbs signify, "in their familism and search for community, a tacit revolt against the industrial order, . . ." then a sociological concern for analyzing the particular constellation of values that shapes the suburban community becomes one of the most challenging research assignments of the contemporary sociologist.[38]

[37] David Riesman, "The Suburban Sadness," in Dobriner, *The Suburban Community*, p. 377.
[38] Riesman, p. 375.

Suburbia: Myth or Reality?   Not even the careful work of competent sociologists has managed to avoid contributing to a pervasive myth of suburbia, somewhat like the mystique of bureaucracy, though in fact not sociologists but many kinds of social critics have been most responsible for giving to suburbia an unflattering image of affluent, status-conscious America in its new residential life-style. In the first place, this new myth presents a highly selective view of suburbia as the residential site for the youthful and mobile middle class who are but temporarily there, for their mobility will lead them to move on. Suburbia, so goes the myth, has developed a hyperactive social life, which includes both intensive neighboring with a loss of personal and family privacy and an active organizational life that reflects every conceivable kind of shared interest in the community.

All this is possible, the myth says, because the suburbanites are a very homogeneous people: (1) they are about the same age; (2) they are at about the same point in family cycle with children about the same age; (3) they have similar education and jobs, and (4) their social aspirations and values are the same. Such a pervasive similarity then produces a "classless" community—really a one-class community. It also results in a similar life-style that suggests a conformity in values and behavior. Since the men of suburbia commute to the city for work, suburbia by day is a community without men. Commuting to and from work takes more time away from the family and increases the responsibility of women for the care of children. On Sunday, suburbia makes real its "return to religion," where local churches are not only religious shrines but also local civic organizations. Furthermore, the myth has it that urbanites who have become suburbanites take on the values and life-styles of their new community, so that in politics Democrats become Republicans, and a more active political involvement characterizes all those who dwell in the suburb.

The characterization of this conception of suburban life as simply a myth has been suggested by a number of sociologists.[39] There are now two important empirical studies. Bennet M. Berger studied a blue-collar suburb of former city-dwelling workers, while Herbert J. Gans has undertaken perhaps the most ambitious and thorough analysis of a suburban community that we have in the sociological literature, *The Levittowners*.[40] Perhaps the starting point of this is the discovery that the suburban community is not exclusively middle-class. There are now numerous blue-collar suburbs, and many large middle-income suburban developments attract a range of social classes to them. In his study, Gans carefully documented the working class, lower-middle class, and upper-

---

[39] The above comments draw upon Bennet M. Berger, "The Myth of Suburbia," *Journal of Social Issues*, 17, No. 1 (1961), 38–49. See also Dobriner, *The Suburban Community*, pp. xxi–xxiv.

[40] Bennet M. Berger, *Working-Class Suburb* (Berkeley and Los Angeles: University of California Press, 1960). Herbert J. Gans, *The Levittowners: Way of Life and Politics in a New Suburban Community* (New York: Pantheon, 1967).

middle class types of suburban residents within one community, as well as the variations in aspirations, life-styles, family-styles, political orientation, and degrees of community involvement to be found within it.

Nor does the physical and social similarity of many suburban communities markedly differentiate them from many urban neighborhoods. There, too, many men commute to work, and many urban residential blocks are filled with identical housing. This pattern is no invention of the suburban developer, though often he has available a much larger tract of land to fill with such identical dwelling-units. Indeed, Gans has made the point that the significant differentiation in urban social patterning is not city and suburb but the inner city and the outer city, for many middle-class neighborhoods in the city are no different in any way from suburban ones.[41] The same charge of conformity could be made here, and this similarity in physical and social patterning is hardly new.

Such criticisms as these of the prevailing myth of suburbia is not to deny the accuracy of the observations and writings that gave rise to the myth. Rather, it is necessary to point out the highly selective sample of suburban communities on which generalizations about suburbia were based. They were middle-class suburbs of young, mobile executives, narrower within the economic and occupational range than is true for many other suburbs. As Berger notes, the myth of suburbia has been based largely upon analysis of life in Park Forest, Illinois, Levittown, New York, Lakewood, near Los Angeles, and a suburb of Toronto called "Crestwood Heights."

That suburbia exacts conformity and a common life-style from its inhabitants has promoted the idea that it turns Democrats into Republicans. But Berger found that the automobile workers in his study who had moved to a new suburb continued to vote Democratic. Gans has documented in even greater detail that politics, family patterns, and life-style are not thoroughly altered by a movement to suburbia. Where there are changes, Gans notes, they are likely to be a kind desired and intended and made possible by just such a movement. Furthermore, the workers and the lower-middle class of suburbia are not mobile, they know it and do not absorb the life-styles of rising, better educated executives. Berger found that most of his workers did not belong to any organization besides the union, though Gans found a plethora of civic organizations going on in Levittown.

The Functions of the Myth   However much the myth of suburbia distorts somewhat the reality, it is nonetheless a pervasive one, widely repeated in intellectual essays and more popular magazine articles. Why has it been so

---

[41] Herbert J. Gans, "Urbanism and Suburbanism as Ways of Life: A Re-evaluation of Definitions," in Arnold M. Rose, ed., *Human Behavior and Social Processes* (Boston: Houghton Mifflin, 1962), pp. 625–648.

pervasive? Among those for whom this critical and negative view of suburbia is functional, according to Berger, are sociologists and other students of contemporary life, and he quotes David Riesman, who said of the authors of *Crestwood Heights* that they "collide, like Whyte, with a problem their predecessors only brushed against, for they are writing about *us*, about the professional upper middle class and its business allies."[42] This is appealing, says Berger, but more importantly,

> the myth of suburbia conceptualizes for sociologists a microcosm in which some of the apparently major social and cultural trends of our time (other-direction, social mobility, neoconservatism, status anxiety, etc.) flow together, and may be conveniently studied.[43]

The widespread acceptance of the myth can also be attributed to its popularity with those middle-class critics of American society who are in some degree left-wing or formerly left-wing, and who find in the myth a source of *cultural* rather than political criticism of the American middle class. Suburbia then, notes Berger, becomes a scapegoat, and "we achieve ritual purity without really threatening anything or anyone—except perhaps the poor suburbanites, who can't understand why they're always being satirized."[44] A cultural criticism is both acceptable and safe, says Berger, and he quotes Edward Shils who observes that a cultural critique may be all that is possible now from the standpoint of a left-wing perspective. Berger then makes this telling comment:

> There is irony, therefore, in the venom that left-wing critics inject into their discussions of suburbia because the criticism of suburbia tends to become a criticism of industrialization, 'rationality,' and 'progress,' and thus brings these critics quite close to the classic conservatives, whose critique of industrialization was also made in terms of its cultural consequences.[45]

THE METROPOLITAN AREA

The movement of people from the city to the suburb is not a new development, but it has proceeded with an accelerated pace in recent decades. As a consequence, it has become increasingly necessary to look at the larger area of population that contains both a city and its suburbs, for the urban population now spreads out from the city into a hinterland, formerly but no longer

[42] Berger, "The Myth of Suburbia," p. 44.

[43] Berger, p. 45.

[44] Berger, p. 46.

[45] Berger, p. 46.

rural, frequently larger in physical area than the central city, and sometimes equal to or even surpassing the city in population. The term, *metropolitan*, refers to a concentration of urban population distributed among a central city and a complex of smaller satellite cities and villages surrounding it. The most frequent term is *metropolitan area*, rarely metropolitan community. The term is indicative of the contemporary tendency to regard the metropolitan complex as simply a large area of physical space and population, but not to view it as possessing the social organization of a community.

The need to view the urban pattern of settlement as extending well beyond the incorporated city led the Bureau of the Census in 1950 to create several new categories for gathering data about urban and rural residence. There is, in the first place, a new definition for *urban*, as we saw previously. Secondly, *urban area* was defined, in brief, as including a central city plus all the contiguous area with densities of about 2000 inhabitants per square mile. Thirdly, the standard metropolitan area, now called the *standard metropolitan statistical area*, includes one or more cities of 50,000 or more, the one or more counties in which they are located, and any adjoining counties that by certain social and economic criteria are dependent upon the central city (or cities). Then, fourthly, there is the *standard consolidated area*, which is composed of contiguous standard metropolitan statistical areas. For the purposes of the 1960 census, only two such areas were designated, one for "New York-Northeastern New Jersey," and one for "Chicago-Northwestern Indiana."

The Changing Metropolitan Population   The rapid postwar growth of the suburban component of the metropolitan area has meant a significant shifting of population within metropolitan areas, even as more and more Americans move into such areas. Data from as brief a period as the 1950s gave us graphic evidence of what has been happening. The data in Table 1 tells us that the largest gain in population in that decade occurred *in* metropolitan areas but *outside* central cities. In 1950 36 million people lived outside central cities but in metropolitan areas (and were 24 percent of the population), whereas in 1960 there were 64 million such suburbanites, and they were now one out of every three Americans. Note that central cities gained 10 million but declined as a proportion of the total. Even this is deceiving, for many of the larger and older central cities of the United States, particularly in the North and East, lost population in the decade, but newer cities in the Southwest gained considerably. Table 2 reports this decline in the population of these cities. Note too in these data that nonmetropolitan America also declined proportionately, and only gained 3 million in a time when America was increasing by 41 million.

The 1960 census also recorded for the first time the fact that in some metropolitan areas more people live outside the central city than live in the central

TABLE 1   POPULATION IN METROPOLITAN AND NONMETROPOLITAN AREAS, UNITED STATES: 1950 AND 1960

	1950		1960	
	Number (millions)	Percent of total	Number (millions)	Percent of total
Metropolitan	86	57	124	64
Central Cities	50	33	60	31
Suburbs	36	24	64	33
Nonmetropolitan	65	43	68	36
Total Population	151	100	192	100

SOURCE   for 1950: Conrad and Irene B. Taeuber, *The Changing Population of the United States* (New York: Wiley and Sons, 1958), p. 140; for 1960: U.S. Bureau of the Census, *Current Population Reports,* Series P–20, no. 151.

TABLE 2   POPULATION DECLINE IN SELECTED CITIES, 1950–1960

City	1950 Population	1960 Population	Population Decrease	
			In numbers	Percent
Boston	801,444	697,197	104,270	.130
St. Louis	856,796	750,026	106,770	.124
Buffalo	580,132	522,790	57,342	.098
Detroit	1,849,568	1,670,144	179,424	.095
Pittsburgh	676,806	604,332	69,093	.102
San Francisco	775,357	740,316	35,041	.045
Cleveland	914,808	876,050	38,758	.041
Philadelphia	2,071,605	2,002,512	69,093	.033
Chicago	3,620,942	3,550,404	70,538	.019
New York	7,891,957	7,781,984	109,973	.014
Cincinnati	503,998	502,550	1,448	.003

SOURCE   U.S. Bureau of the Census, *U.S. Census, 1950 and 1960*

city. This was not true, however, of New York, Baltimore, Chicago, Minneapolis-St. Paul, and Milwaukee. These metropolitan areas still had in 1950 a majority of their population within the central city. But Detroit no longer had, nor did Los Angeles, Philadelphia, San Francisco, Boston, Pittsburgh, St. Louis, Washington, D.C., Cleveland, Newark, Buffalo, Cincinnati, or Kansas City, Missouri. In some of these areas, the suburban population of the metropolitan area had become as high as three out of every four persons: 75 percent of the Pittsburgh area residents lived outside Pittsburgh, for example. The figure was 73 percent for Boston, 76 percent for Newark, while it was 60 percent for San Francisco, 64 percent for St. Louis, and 62 percent for Washington, D.C. Data such as these suggest how powerful the current of migration is from central city to suburb, when at the same time Americans are becoming increasingly urban.

Race in the Metropolitan Area   If the movement to suburbia is a selective one, among other selective criteria a significant and potentially controversial one is *race*. Suburbia has been overwhelmingly a white community. In fact, by 1960 more whites lived in suburbs than they did in central cities. Given the large white exodus of recent decades, the nonwhite proportion of the central city could not help but increase, even if there were no more in-migration of non-whites, and this is not the case. As a consequence, Negroes are becoming an ever larger proportion of the population of the central city, and in one city, Washington, D.C., they were a majority by 1960. Since Washington is a federal city without home rule and largely controlled by a Congressional committee, this event went largely unnoticed, for it did not have any immediate impact. Table 3 records the proportion of Negroes in those American cities in which Negroes number more than a quarter of a million. The election of Negro mayors in Gary, Indiana, and in Cleveland, Ohio, in 1967 testifies to the

TABLE 3   UNITED STATES CITIES WITH MORE THAN 250,000
NONWHITE RESIDENTS: 1960

City	Nonwhite Residents (in thousands)	Percentage of City's Population
New York	1141	14.7
Chicago	838	23.6
Philadelphia	535	26.7
Detroit	487	29.2
Washington	419	54.8
Los Angeles	417	16.8
Baltimore	328	35.0
Cleveland	253	28.9

SOURCE   U.S. Bureau of the Census, *U.S. Census of Population: 1960*, Vol. I.

political implications of white exodus and Negro increase in the central city. The basis of real political "black power" lies in the potentiality for Negroes to control central cities by democratic processes in the near future.

The Unity and Disunity of the Metropolitan Area   For some purposes, the metropolitan area can be (and is) treated as an organized community. It is a single trading area: one or more daily newspapers serve its population; large department stores deliver to the suburbs as well as to the central city; supermarkets, drug stores, and banks operate a chain of branches throughout the area. Indeed, the residents of a metropolitan area do not hesitate to cross political boundaries when it seems to be to their advantage as consumers. The services basic to an interacting and interdependent population are also provided on an area basis: (1) water and sewage; (2) public transportation; (3) gas; (4) electricity; and (5) telephone. Cultural activities may be centered in the central city, but they are supported by a metropolitan clientele. The symphony orchestra and musical concerts, the art museum and art exhibits, the legitimate theater and art films need a broad middle-class clientele to sustain them, and this clientele is found throughout the metropolitan area, particularly in the middle and upper status suburbs.

Increasingly, the major voluntary welfare activities, united for fund-raising purposes under the red feather symbol, serve an entire metropolitan area and raise funds from this same area. Some of these agencies may concentrate their services on the poor and dependent and thus expend most of their resources on a clientele located in the central city's slums. But other services, such as that provided by a family counseling agency, a mental health clinic, or such youth services as the Boy Scouts and Girl Scouts, may service a more heterogeneous clientele, and, in the case of youth services, a clientele that is predominantly middle-class, which means more service to the suburbs. Lastly, the major hospitals are usually located in the central city but provide hospital service to the entire metropolitan area and are in part sustained by civic funds raised throughout the same area. These examples document the simple point that for many significant purposes the metropolitan area is organized as an interdependent system. In particular, the provision of important human services is organized on a metropolitan basis when these services are not political or governmental, but are either provided commercially or are sustained by voluntary civic action. (The extension of city-owned water and sewage facilities to the metropolitan area is an exception to this general process.)

Politically, however, the metropolitan area is not one community but many. It is fragmented into numerous small political subdivisions that defy any effort at creating a rational structure for handling the numerous problems that face the entire metropolis. Most of these problems seem to require joint action for solution, and this is hampered by the existence of so many political jurisdictions.

Those who want some kind of political unification of the metropolitan area do so because they want to create a basis for rational action. A fair distribution of the tax burden and an efficient use of taxes, as well as unified action on such pressing metropolitan problems as water, expressways, and similar services, become the major objectives to be sought through political unification.

But the effort to promote political unification is a cause that attracts as yet only a small number of civic leaders and urban professionals; the vast majority of suburban dwellers are thoroughly opposed to any such unification with the central city, or even with other suburbs. An ideology about the value of suburbia as small community and grass-roots democracy, not unlike the small-town ideology that Vidich and Bensman reported about Springdale in *Small Town in Mass Society,* persists in the face of the logic about the insuperable problems and the need for efficient use of resources. It is not the attachment to values of *rationality* and *efficiency* that attract suburbanites, even those who are organization men and operate in terms of these values in their daily jobs. Whatever may be the myth that social scientists and cosmopolitan intellectuals have about suburbia, the suburbanites have a different kind of myth, one that asserts that suburbia is community and independence and autonomy and local democracy, values rooted deep in the American experience. "If these values were not dominant," says Robert Wood, "it would be quite possible to conceive of a single gigantic metropolitan region under one government and socially conscious of itself as one community."[46]

To the civic, professional, and political proponents of metropolitan unification, the political divisions of the metropolitan area are an irrational structure based only upon petty jealousies and parochial interests. Robert Wood expressed the position of many in saying:

> A theory of community and a theory of local government are at odds with the prerequisites of contemporary life and, so far, theory has been the crucial force that preserves the suburb. There is no economic reason for its existence and there is no technological basis for its support.[47]

Yet there is reason for the persistence of small suburban communities. The ideology (or theory) that suburbanites hold utilizes some hallowed American traditions to defend the existence of independent suburban communities, however inefficient that may be. Undoubtedly, suburbanites believe their own myth about independence and grass roots. But this ideology, like many other, conceals group interests. Most important of all at the present time, suburbs are selective about who gets in; they have managed to erect firm barriers

[46] Robert C. Wood, *Suburbia: Its People and Their Politics* (New York: Houghton Mifflin, 1958), p. 18.
[47] Wood, p. 18.

against Negroes and other minorities. The more economically advantaged suburbs now maintain the best public school systems, and their academically excellent high schools offer the best access to the more preferred colleges and universities. The reputation of a preferred suburb is a mark of status for its residents. These and other reasons suggest the stake that a suburbanite has in the existence of his suburb. The myth he perpetuates rings the bell on some hallowed values, but his interests are in the prestige and advantages that the particular selectivity of a suburb has to offer, as well as simply in a place to live that is newer and seems more desirable than his former residence in the city. When Robert Wood says, "There is only the stubborn conviction of the majority of suburbanites that it ought to exist, even though it plays havoc with the life and government of our urban age," he ignores the social interests of suburbanites that are served by not having political unification.[48] If suburbanites value these interests in status and advantage in the urban environment more than they value rationality and efficiency, then their action is not irrational when seen from their perspective. The suburban ideology of localism defends the stake that people have in their status in a particular suburban community. For that reason, for some time to come we will have metropolitan *areas*, not metropolitan *communities*.

THE URBAN CRISIS

The problems of urbanization and urban structure have become an important issue in American life in recent years, as they have in almost every industrial society. Intellectuals have addressed themselves to the cause of cosmopolitan values, and social scientists have dissected the urban pattern and predicted its future development. Urban planners have come into being as a profession of urban experts seeking to maintain and renew the city as an historic pattern of human settlement. The cause of decaying and troubled cities is represented politically at the highest levels of the federal government; there is now a Department of Urban Affairs. In turn, the Congress appropriates large sums of money to finance programs of urban renewal. All of these representations of urban concern testify to the common recognition that cities are in trouble; it is an inescapable fact that there is an urban crisis.

Urban Renewal   For about two decades now, urban renewal has been a means by which cities can plan and carry out ambitious projects for renewing the

[48] Wood, p. 18.

city with the federal government underwriting much of the major original expense. These federally-supported efforts at urban renewal testify to a sustained concern for revitalizing the central city. In particular, the funds and tools of urban renewal have enabled city administrations to clear away slum areas close to the central business district, and to use the recaptured area as a new commercial area or for a new residential area particularly appealing to upper-middle-class professional and managerial persons, whose employment is likely to be in downtown itself. Younger people who do not yet have children, or do not want them, or older people whose children are grown and no longer at home, are the ones who can be lured back to the center of the city.

Central cities have come to recognize the strong and compelling power of values the very opposite of familism and small community as useful in their rebuilding. A *cosmopolitan* outlook for many middle-class Americans makes the central city exciting if it offers the opportunities for such leisure patterns as fine restaurants, theaters and nightclubs, symphony orchestras and art museums, as well as fine shops. The luring of visitors and conventioneers to the center of the city has now become a major consideration in rebuilding the central city; increasingly, its ecology, architecture, and cultural offerings are redesigned with maximum concern for appeal to the cosmopolitan tastes of visitors and its own upper-middle class residents.

There is no assurance, however, that cities can rebuild successfully on the basis of cosmopolitan values alone. A city is more than its central business district; it, too, has residential neighborhoods, and it must offer an environment for family life if it is to retain population. The effort to save the major American cities is an effort not only to attract a middle classs back to the city, but it is also an effort to revitalize a central business district and to rehouse its poor and, thus, do away with the ugly slums that steadily threaten to engulf the city. But despite a great deal of earnest effort and a vast amount of political organization and financial investment, there is yet no assurance that the central city can be saved, even though a failure to do so will create a political crisis of massive proportions to test as never before the problem-solving capacity of American democracy.

The Inner City   The crisis of the city is not a crisis of the entire city, but a crisis of the *inner city,* the area beyond the central business district that includes transient residential areas, slums, minority ghettoes, even some Gold Coasts. In many cities the inner city now extends for miles. One dimension of this crisis is that present development suggests that the inner city may someday be coterminous with the central city. What is not inner city—the outer city—is much like the suburbs in social character, so that, as Herbert Gans observed, the real distinction in urban life is not between the central city and the suburbs but between the inner city and the outer city, regardless of where corporate boundaries may fall.[49]

In the contrast of inner and outer city are two social worlds, two congeries of compatible life-styles. Gans sees several types of people who are inner-city dwellers.[50] One of these is the *cosmopolites,* those students, intellectuals, writers, musicians and artists, and some other professionals, who find in the city a compatible cultural milieu. They are usually childless. Another is the "ethnic villager," who lives in a still solid ethnic neighborhood and who isolates himself from others. Then there are two groups of disadvantaged who cannot escape the city: the *deprived,* the very poor and the non-whites, and the *trapped,* those usually older or otherwise disadvantaged people who are left behind when a neighborhood is invaded by a lower-status group.

To a considerable extent, then, the enlarging inner city contains many people who lack the political organization and the social power to give effective expression to their own interests. Only in the rapidly increasing concentration of Negroes in the inner city is there a likelihood of powerful political organization. But this may come to mean that inner city will come to signify *black* and outer city *white.* The assuming of political control in the central city by militant Negroes then will pose an unheralded crisis in American urban affairs. There will be greater resistance to even mild forms of suburb-city cooperation, and there may be a political effort to wrest control from Negroes. In this sense the race crisis in America is an urban crisis, and the urban crisis is a race crisis; the two issues cannot be separated.

Decentralization   There is another compelling issue that raises some fundamental questions about the form that urbanization may take in the future. The basic assumption behind the current conception of a metropolitan area is that of a central city and its suburbs, gradually thinning out to open country. Thus, the centrality of the city gives it organizing functions in coordinating a large urban complex that is viewed as roughly a circular pattern. However, new trends in urbanization, evident to anyone who studies census statistics and maps, suggest that such an assumption can be called into question. Urban sprawl has gone to the point where one metropolitan area merges into another, and large metropolitan belts and corridors are now growing rapidly. In this pattern, is a central city any longer central? Furthermore, the advance of modern technology obviously no longer requires the centralization of the contemporary metropolis, just as the growth of suburbia once meant that we no longer required the concentration of population within the confines of the

---

[49] Gans, "Urbanism and Suburbanism as Ways of Life: A Re-evaluation of Definitions," pp. 635 ff.

[50] Gans, pp. 629–632.

city. The major expressway networks, whose construction is now aided by the federal government, are having a further impact on urbanization: urban building increasingly clusters along such major transportation routes with a further decentralizing of the city.

It is not impossible to conceive that by the end of this century the heavy burden of renewing the inner city, the unresolved tension of race, and the decentralization of functions once located in the central city may make financially and politically possible the virtual abandonment of the central city, or at least a willingness to leave it as the inner city of a large metropolitan community that is served by newer centers. Already the building of completely new cities, though as yet without any impressive results, has captured the imagination of many city planners and others, who are intellectually ready to confine the historic city to the dustbins of history, an archaic and obsolescent form that has served its purpose. But before or even while this is happening America must yet confront what the inner city represents: the communal patterns for poor people and minorities who have no access as yet to varied community choices that the metropolitan area offers. What America finally learns to do about poverty, and how it finally manages to resolve (if it does) the tension of race may have more significance for the future of community than anything city planners or urban renewers dream up on their planning boards.

Nonetheless, the dreamers dream and the planners plan, and the urban future hints of as yet undreamed possibilities. A more decentralized as well as a more rationally and aesthetically planned urban environment for the future implies radical innovations in the creation of urban environments. It also suggests radical redefinitions of the meaning of community as an integrating pattern of social life. Even as the urbanization of modern societies continues, new vistas of urban utopias offer some of the most challenging and imaginative reconstructions of the city. The radical redesign of spatial arrangements and architectural forms for urban living is not only one of the twentieth century's most exciting frontiers into the future, but it has also become one of contemporary man's most promising efforts in his long and often defeated attempts to create a society that brings within reach the values he would choose to live by.

"Oh, I beg your pardon! I thought you were extinct."

Drawing by B. Tobey; Copr. © 1956
The New Yorker Magazine, Inc.

PART 3 SOCIAL STRATIFICATION

1

1. Slum children in an empty lot.
2. Society group at a museum art exhibition.
3. Schoolboy in Somerset, England (Wells Cathedral in the background).
4. Taking it easy on a store porch.

2

3 4

CLASS AND
STATUS

10

In any human society men rarely, if ever, accept all others as social equals. Instead, they engage in a complex process of creating and elaborating forms of behavior and speech that symbolize some as more prestigeful, influential, powerful, or affluent, and they build into their social structures those inequalities of material and psychic assets that set some off from others in persistent distinctions of higher and lower rank. However much we may berate this process as snobbery or as based upon false values, it permeates the organization of social life. To the sociologist, the perpetual pursuit of the symbols of prestige, the sometimes ignoble scrambling for a position in a human pecking order, and the struggle of social classes seeking to enlarge their share of social rewards at the possible expense of others, all constitute the complex and fascinating substance of social stratification.

We are all aware of the reality of stratification; it is too persistent and obvious to deny recognition. Indeed, our vocabulary is filled with terms that give recognition to status: *big shot, VIP, leading citizen, common man, rank and file, influential person, leader, ordinary people, high society.* In the modern world of corporate and governmental bureaucracy, social stratification is pervasive: there are officers and enlisted men, upper and lower echelons, executives and clerks, supervisors and workers, top management and middle management. The social positions of industrial society rank above or below one another, no less so than they did in ancient and medieval societies.

Not only our vocabulary but our behavior expresses our perception of stratification. In a thousand different ways during any one day we can observe people being courteous to and considerate, even solicitous, of the admired and prestigeful ones. We can observe them being respectful, even obsequious, to the powerful and affluent. Sometimes we can observe the resentment and hostility that the have-nots feel toward the haves. The presence of rank is everywhere in society, and no one is unaware of it. However much modern men may profess a belief in equality, inequality is built, in myriad ways, into the structure of society—and that is what social stratification is all about.

THE PROBLEM OF STRATIFICATION

During periods of relative stability in human history, the existing patterns of social stratification seem to be part of the natural order of things. Most men take it for granted and do not ponder on its nature, and the myths that legitimize it are widely even if never completely accepted. But in periods of change and unrest, the order of things that make some men superior in power and privilege is questioned and challenged. So it was in the secular crisis that accompanied the industrialization of Europe, where the "privileged orders" that existed for so long lost their power to a rising bourgeoisie, and their privileges were dissipated before the political attacks of democratic populations. A new generation of secular men no longer took the old order of social rank for granted and even dared to ask if rank in any form was justified. From there they went on to ask if the division of men into unequal classes was even necessary in society, and some men dreamed of the possibilities of a classless society where all men would be truly equal.

Because some secular thinkers came to believe more in social equality and less in privilege and inherited rank, the nature of social stratification became a sociological problem. Those who advocated the equality of men claimed that social inequality in the form of inherited position and privileged birth was not a necessary part of society. They also disputed the ancient ideas that those born to high rank were "naturally" superior people, or that any segment of the population possessed "naturally" superior qualities or attributes and the rest of the population naturally inferior ones.

This provocative challenge to ancient concepts of privilege and rank was one of the more intellectually daring and revolutionary lines of thought to emerge in the secular crisis. It opened up for critical analysis the entire spectrum of stratification in its myriad dimensions. For the discipline of sociology, stratification became a highly problematic, demanding, and difficult issue. One major reason it was difficult was because sociologists could not easily extricate their analyses from ideological defense of or attack upon social rank. The defense of social rank was a cornerstone of nineteenth century conservative thought, whereas the attack upon the privilege and power of social class was a central concern of radical ideology. At the outset of the discipline, then, sociological inquiry has focused upon the basis for the stratification of society. What was it about man and his social life that created this ranking process? Was it inevitable and natural to a society, as the conservatives claimed, or could men choose to create classless societies as the radicals asserted?

This first and basic problem, however, led quickly to others. Two related problems emerged from the empirical observation that social stratification took many forms; a look back in time suggested many ways that men had stratified their societies, and a look across the globe only confirmed this: there was much variation in stratification in the many different societies now existing. Sociologists explored the vast range of social forms manifested by stratification. They recognized that social ranking in ancient Athens would not be the same in a medieval peasant village or in a modern industrial nation. The form in each case would be indigenous to the particular society. Did this mean an endless array of forms of stratification, or were there some major types of stratification, derived from some universal basis of stratification?

This interest in the many forms of stratification was not some dry and scholarly interest, but rather a vital interest in finding a perspective from which to understand the still emerging class structure of industrial society. Class as a form of stratification was the primary interest. Marx had focused upon the class structure of industrial society as a key to its development and its eventual change, relating it to the economic organization of the society and the division of labor. His perspective dominated European thinking, but in the United States there was resistance to accepting his or any perspective that gave validity to the concept of a class system. These two contrasting views and others as well then give conflicting interpretations of what stratification looked like in modern society, for each selected out different aspects to "see" and report. As a consequence, sociologists struggled from the outset with the problem that there was much apparent variation in stratification *within* modern society, as well as from one society to another. This multidimensionality of stratification then became a third sociological problem, for which the work of Max Weber and W. Lloyd Warner have been particularly relevant.

The concept of class in something like the Marxian sense—a stratification derived from the economic organization of society—has long been central to the sociologist's interest in industrial society. Such concepts as *middle class* and *working class* suggest major groupings that are a consequence of the industrial division of labor, though a changing and fluid set of groupings lacking the rigidity or the religious justification found in older historic systems. Much sociological analysis, then, has focused around this fourth sociological problem: the complex, fluid, and ever-changing class structure of a modern society.

For American sociologists in particular, this concern for the modern class structure has provided the basis for still another though closely related problem; the fact that many differences in action and belief correlate with social class. To the sociologist primarily interested in these other phenomena, class is an independent variable by which he can account for much of the social difference he finds. But to the sociologist primarily interested in stratification, these differences, viewed as *correlates* of class, tell us much more about how the social classes differ from one another, particularly in *life-chances* and *life-styles*. To a considerable extent they function as indexes of social inequality.

Lastly, the fluid nature of the modern class structure indicates that the rigidity of older systems is absent. People do not retain the class position into which they are born; they are mobile. This *social mobility*, viewed as both fact and ideal, poses fascinating questions about how people move up the class order and even how some move down. It constitutes a persistent problem for sociological analysis.

These, perhaps, are the dominant lines of inquiry that sociologists have directed toward the problem of stratification. They have been asking one fundamental question—what is stratification?—and attempt to answer it by seeking out the basis for stratification and the dominant forms that stratification takes in society. From these they have gone on to several other problems: the multidimensionality of stratification; the class structure in modern society; the correlates of class; and social mobility.

THE NATURE OF SOCIAL STRATIFICATION

That some men are rich and some are poor, that some are privileged and others are not, that a few are admired and most are not and some even are despised, is a fact of social life evident to men throughout history. There is, apparently, never an equal distribution of the goods and opportunities in a society; in the language of Max Weber, the *life-chances* of persons are not equal. Differences in the distribution of life-chances create stratification; those who share the same set of life-chances are a stratum among several strata.

The recognition that inequality in the distribution of life-chances is a substantial feature of every social structure has ancient roots. Men have addressed themselves to it for centuries; there is discussion of it in the Bible, the classical Greek thinkers spoke of it, as did medieval thinkers, and in modern times the issue has been a paramount one. But the discussions about it have always centered around a major dispute between those who accept the inequalities of society as both just and necessary, and those who decry them as both unjust and unnecessary. There has, then, been both a *conservative* and a *radical* view of stratification in human thought for centuries, an inequalitarian and an equalitarian view. This dispute is no nearer settlement today, and even as in the past, the different perspectives about it have influenced modern thought, including sociological theories of stratification.

The Conservative View   The acceptance of some form of social stratification usually goes with the acceptance of the prevailing *status quo*, in the contemporary idiom, the *establishment*. It was a strong feature in ancient Hindu writings, and Aristotle strongly defended both private property and the institution of slavery. His defense of slavery, on the ground that some men are naturally free and others are not, suggests that the defense of social inequality has often been rooted in conceptions of natural human differences that presumably warrant socially established differences of power and privilege. Though both conservative and radical views of stratification have been part of Christian history, over the centuries the established church has usually sought to provide justification for the established inequalities of society.

In more recent times perhaps the most powerful argument in behalf of stratification has been provided by the nineteenth-century Social Darwinists, who used Darwin's evolutionary theory to argue that evolutionary selection enables those with more talent to fare better than the less talented; thus, they constructed an argument that inequality in social positions reflects the natural differences among men. Among American sociologists William Graham Sumner vigorously argued such a position.[1] While the Darwinian argument has lost intellectual acceptance over time, an alternative argument developed by the Italian social thinker, Gaetano Mosca, in response to the challenge of socialism and the emergence of mass working-class parties in Europe, has remained influential.[2] Mosca argued that the necessary political organization of society necessarily results in inequalities in social power. Mosca sees society as always divided into the rulers and the ruled; also, the ruling class will always be economically privileged.

The Radical View   The contrary thesis that inequality is neither just or necessary has persisted as a counter-argument over the centuries. Early Christianity contained many such equalitarian views, even before that Old Testament prophets such as Micah railed against the wealthy as greedy and oppressive. In contrast to Aristotle, Plato argued for a common ownership of property. If the Christian Church has been conservative and has accepted the established inequalities of medieval society, radical Christian sects have constantly emerged to challenge such inequalities and to criticize the church in doing so. The Anabaptists and the Waldensians, for example, became the object of forceful repression for their revolts and became persecuted heretical sects. A criticism of established inequalities came from the seventeenth-century Levellers and the Diggers, and later from the new Methodist sect, and from the Salvation Army, which at the turn of the century appealed to the depressed urban groups and voiced a strong criticism of the churches for condoning urban poverty and suffering.

In the tradition from medieval to modern society, the scholarly work of such men as John Locke and Jean-Jacques Rousseau was important in undercutting such ideas as the divine right of kings and in making more acceptable the idea that sovereignty rests in the people. But the major onslaught against the conservative view of stratification came from Karl Marx; with Friedrich Engels he wrote the *Communist Manifesto* in 1848, a pamphlet that provided an impressive intellectual analysis in plain language of the causes of social inequality. For Marx the social classes were both the units of historic change and the oppressive divisions within society created by the economic (productive) system. The desirable goal of human freedom and equality was not

[1] William Graham Sumner, *What Classes Owe to Each Other* (New York: Harper & Row, 1903).
[2] Gaetano Mosca, *The Ruling Class* (New York: McGraw-Hill, 1939).

to be reached until the proletariat had arisen in revolution to abolish capitalism and to create a truly equal and Communist society; only then would men escape the inevitable pattern of change induced by changes in productive system to go from one system of class oppression to another.

The Functionalist and Conflict Theorists   Modern sociology in recent years has relived much of the historic intellectual clash over the conservative and radical views of stratification. The sociological versions of the conservative argument as to the necessity and inevitability (and so the justness, by implication) of stratification has come from the *functionalists*, a group of sociological theorists who argue that stratification arises from the needs of society, not of the individual. In an influential and controversial article, Kingsley Davis and Wilbert Moore stated the functionalist argument for viewing stratification as a nearly universal feature of human society, essential to its functioning.[3] They argued that in every society there are some positions that are of the greatest importance for society and that require the greatest amount of training or talent. To ensure that these important positions are filled by qualified persons, there must be inequalities in the distribution of such social rewards as income, status, and power. In a later work, Davis called stratification the "unconsciously evolved device by which societies insure that the most important positions are conscientiously filled by the most qualified persons."[4]

The challenge that this functionalist thesis generated among sociologists was considerable, and produced a literature that was a running argument among sociologists for over a decade. Some of those simply pointed out that there is much empirical evidence about the distribution of social rewards, particularly income, which simply does not support the position that the greatest reward goes to the most qualified to perform the most needed functions. But the most developed position was from the *conflict* theorists who see society, not as a functionally integrated system but as an arena of combatting groups in which social power is the significant key to the distribution of social rewards. Conflict theorists give emphasis to struggle and to conflicting group interests and to the coercion of one group by another, and the emergence of what Weber called "structures of domination."

Toward a Synthesis of Views   Not all sociologists have simply been protagonists of one position or the other, even when the weight of their argument supported one position. Some clearly sought for what was sociologically basic

---

[3] Kingsley Davis and Wilbert Moore, "Some Principles of Stratification," *American Sociological Review,* 10 (April, 1945), 242–249.
[4] Kingsley Davis, *Human Society* (New York: Macmillan, 1949), p. 367.

in both positions as a way to move out of the theoretical impasse. Dennis Wrong, for example, a critic of the functional view, noted that critics of the functional view of stratification

> have succeeded in showing that there are a great many things about stratification that Davis and Moore have failed to explain, but they have not succeeded in seriously denting the central argument that unequal rewards are necessary in any and all societies with a division of labor extending much beyond differences in age and sex.[5]

The German sociologist Ralf Dahrendorf, a conflict theorist, viewed functional and conflict views as two different views of the same reality, with a resolution of the differences to come in some future theory.[6]

The idea that a synthesis of these conflicting views might be possible was suggested by the late Polish sociologist Stanislaw Ossowski who argued that both functionalist and Marxian (conflict) views are fundamentally correct, though they present but partial views of the complex reality of stratification in modern societies.[7] But the most ambitious American effort to provide a synthesis has come from Gerhard Lenski.[8] Lenski has created a *distributive* theory that rests upon a set of postulates about the nature of man and society. He conceives man to be a social being who must live with others in a society, but who, when faced with decisions, will always choose his own or his group's interests over others. Since most of the things (material and nonmaterial) men strive for are in short supply, there is always a struggle among men in every society. Furthermore, says Lenski, men are always unequally endowed by nature for this struggle and tend anyway to be creatures of habit and custom. In turn, he argues that societies vary considerably in their degree of interdependence and integration, and that there is no such thing as a perfect society in which the actions of all parts are completely subordinated to the interests of the whole.

These assumptions provide Lenski with a basis for what he calls the *two laws of distribution.* The first of these is that men will share the product of their labors to the extent required to ensure the survival and continued productivity of those others whose action are necessary or beneficial to themselves. The survival of mankind depends on its compliance with this law, for this is the fundamental idea of the necessity of human cooperation. Also, this

---

[5] Dennis H. Wrong, "The Functional Theory of Stratification: Some Neglected Considerations," *American Sociological Review,* 24 (December, 1959), 773.

[6] Ralf Dahrendorf, *Class and Class Conflict in Industrial Society* (Stanford, Calif.: Stanford University Press, 1959).

[7] Stanislaw Ossowski, *Class Structure in the Social Consciousness,* Sheila Patterson, trans. (New York: Free Press, 1963).

[8] Gerhard Lenski, *Power and Privilege: A Theory of Stratification* (New York: McGraw-Hill, 1966). For the following discussion, see particularly Chapters 2 and 3.

law dominates in those technologically simple societies with little or no sur-plus of goods; it is in such societies as these that we can expect to find no social stratification, though there may be a simple division of labor, such as by sex and age.

But when the technological capacity of the society and the division of labor produces a surplus, then the second law of distribution applies: power will determine the distribution of nearly all of the surplus possessed by the society. Lenski says "nearly all" because he gives credence to the play of altruism for accounting for a small part of the distribution. On the basis of his assump-tions about the nature of man, Lenski sees him as struggling over the surplus produced, and it is those with power who are able to obtain the largest share. Furthermore, the greater the surplus, the more will be distributed by social power. The power that gives a group a larger share of the goods of a society is then also the basis of *privilege,* defined as possession or control of a portion of the surplus produced by a society; privilege is thus a function of power.

To say that power will decide the distribution of the surplus does not say who has power or how it is gained. Lenski notes that there is great variation here, and one source of this variation is the technology of the society. Socie-ties vary from hunting and gathering societies to modern industrial ones; Lenski classified societies on the basis of technology to establish the major variations in distributive systems. But even within these major categories, there are differences in distributive systems that are due to a wide set of other factors.

Might and Right   To explain stratification in terms of the two variables of power and privilege, and to make power the key concept, should not give the impression that force or coercion is all that is involved. To be sure, the capac-ity to use force is fundamental to the ability to use power, but what always happens in societies is that the distributive system becomes *legitimized.* What unequal distribution power has made possible then comes to be viewed as right; legitimating myths about superiority in skills or about ability or about greater risks or investment serve to justify the inequalities of distribution. Even men of modest means are likely to believe that natural and social dif-ferences warrant social inequalities. Nonetheless, the legitimacy of the pre-vailing myth is always stronger with the more advantaged than with the disadvantaged.

Lenski's effort to develop a theory of stratification marks a major step for American sociology in recognizing the basic relation of stratification to power. Marx, of course, had always done so, and so had Max Weber, and many American sociologists seemed to accept Weber's definition of class and his distinction between class and status. Despite this, the study of stratification for many American sociologists had become the measurement of *prestige,* particularly occupational prestige. The study of stratification in the community often became also a study of relative prestige rankings, with little attention to issues of power and privilege. For Lenski prestige is largely a function of power and privilege in societies of substantial surplus. Indeed, on the basis of the work of Otis Dudley Duncan, Lenski claims that most (five-sixths) of the variance in occupational prestige "is accounted for, statistically, by a linear combination of indicators of the income and educational levels of the occupations."[9] Since he views education as a *resource* (thus a form of power) and income as a *measure* of power and privilege, he interprets most of the variance in occupational prestige "as a reflection of occupational power and privilege."[10]

THE STRATIFICATION OF INDUSTRIAL SOCIETY

The effort to determine what is most distinctive about the pattern of stratification in industrial societies led sociologists to look back in time and abroad to other, non-Western societies to gain some perspective. The *caste* system of India and the *estate* system of the Middle Ages in Europe provided two major reference points for distinguishing the *class* system of modern industrial societies from that of other societies and for emphasizing certain of its basic features. The perspective invoked was at the macro-societal level, comparing major types of societies and the stratification systems within them. Each of these—class, caste, or estate—was interpreted as a major organizing pattern for its society.

Caste   The concept of caste refers to the permanent, relatively rigid form of social stratification best exemplified by India. The social strata are ranked in a rigid order of superiority. The various castes are closed off to one another so that an individual cannot in principle change his caste designation (though in practice the principle is sometimes violated). Since the castes are endogamous (meaning marriage occurs only within the group) intermarriage is not available as a way of changing caste position. The individual is born into his caste—this alone determines his group membership. Each caste is usually an occupational group, whose interaction with others is strictly limited, so much so that low castes are "untouchable" for higher castes.

In India, which has had the world's most fully developed caste system, this division of castes into occupational groups finds strong support in the sacred

[9] Lenski, pp. 430–431.
[10] Lenski, p. 431.

Hindu literature, and the rigidity of the caste is due to the Hindu religion. Economic organization alone could not provide the almost complete separation of the castes from one another, nor is it likely that political organization could do so. But the Hindu religion provides a supernatural explanation, not only for the origin of caste, but for its persistence as well. It sanctifies and justifies the order of castes; its doctrine of the elect and the pale, of cleanliness and uncleanliness, its conception of the sacred and the profane, are all infused into the caste system. Caste imposes duties and obligations on each person; no matter how lowly and menial such duties are, the Hindu religion provides a religious basis for observing caste patterns and for not violating the provision and rules of caste order.

In a society as large as India, the caste structure turns out to be highly complicated. There are four basic castes: the *Brahmins,* or priests (who are the intellectuals); the *Kshatriya,* or warriors; the *Vaisya,* or merchants; and the *Sudra,* or peasants and workers. There are also the *outcastes* or *untouchables,* those who have lost their caste status or are descendants of those who have, usually for violations of the rigid codes governing caste behavior. In 1931, the last date for an enumeration, the untouchables were 20 percent of the Hindu population; the Brahmins were 6 percent.

But these basic castes only begin to indicate the nature of the caste order. The census of 1901 listed 2300 main castes and these in turn are divided into subcastes, sometimes several hundred of them for a single main caste. Furthermore, over many centuries, numerous local variations of the caste system have evolved, so that there is not a uniform distribution of castes throughout India.

Estate   In contrast to caste is the estate, a form of stratification historically associated with medieval Europe. Like castes, estates are a series of social strata rigidly set off from one another. Although their rigidity is not enforced by the sanctity of religion, they are supported by law and custom. A hereditary, landed aristocracy is the upper class of the estate system, with the clergy closely associated. Below them are merchants and craftsmen, then free peasants, and at the bottom are the serfs, when serfdom exists.

Both custom and law provided strong barriers to mobility, however, it did occur from time to time. Unlike the caste system, mobility was not forbidden by religion. A serf might be freed by his master or gain his freedom after running away and staying uncaught for a given number of years. An able peasant lad might climb in the church hierarchy, a commoner who had distinguished himself might be knighted by the king, or a wealthy merchant might arrange the marriage of his daughter to a not so wealthy aristocrat.

What made the estate system so static and rigid was an economy based overwhelmingly upon a technologically simple agriculture. An agrarian system with a large peasantry and a relatively low level of productivity did not provide for an expansion of occupations or for much opportunity for individuals to move from one social level to another. This was reinforced by customs associated with inheritance of status and with laws that established the particular rights and privileges of each social level.

In Europe, the estate system was the stratification pattern of feudalism. As a structure of social relationships, feudalism emerged in small, relatively isolated, agrarian societies after the fall of the Roman empire. The estate was originally a two-class system, organized in a master-servant relationship. The oath of fealty that *commoner* (lower class) took to *nobility* (upper class) bound the two together in a relationship in which both classes were obligated to one another and both had a set of rights, though these were by no means equal. The mass of commoners were peasants, with the addition of a small number of household servants, laborers, and others attached to the noble family for personal service, and who were usually drawn from peasant families.

Class   When *class* is viewed in contrast to caste and estate, the emphasis is upon the contrast both with the religious sanctioning of caste and the relative rigidity of caste *and* estate. From this perspective, a class system is *open;* it is not closed off by religion. In addition, classes are not separated as sharply from one another, either by law or by culture. Intermarriage across class lines is not limited by law, though it may be so by practice and custom. An open class system is a set of social strata that are not reinforced and made rigid and fixed by either religion, law, or even significantly by custom.

This contrast with caste and estate tells us but little about social class, but the contrast does emphasize that major forms of stratification have emerged in and are a significant part of the social structure of quite different types of society. Each is closely related to the economic system and to the division of labor (the role differentiation) of its society. The beginnings of industrialization in India has put a severe strain upon the ancient caste system, though it has not yet eliminated it. Though new occupations and professions require new sets of relations, the caste system has shown a remarkable capacity to adjust to social changes of considerable scope. It will not survive unchanged as modernization continues in India, but a modified system of caste may yet survive, at least for a long time, and be adapted to a more modern society. The estate system of Europe, in turn, has vanished with the feudal world, as the powerful force of industrialization radically modified the structures and institutions of both Europe and America. The modern class system emerged with industrialization, and whenever industrialization occurs, old systems of stratification give way to new ones—the new one is always some version of a class system.

Social Class in Industrial Society   The emergence of an industrial class structure can be seen best among those Western societies whose technological and social innovations first gave the Industrial Revolution impetus. The estate system of feudal Europe flourished after the fall of Rome until commerce returned to Europe about the eleventh century. In time a pattern of commerce emerged in medieval Europe. With this, a class of merchants and artisans emerged who lived in towns, and who were "free men" in that they were not bound be fealty to serve feudal nobility. These merchants and artisans were a middle class, located between the large lower class of peasants and the upper class of landed nobility. The impact of industrialization on feudalism and on medieval class structure was not felt immediately or even in a short span of time. Rather, industrialism moved slowly this first time in history, for inventions and their social use and adaptations to their possibilities and their consequences had to evolve in the perspective of changing human experience. The changes briefly detailed here took in fact at least three centuries.

During this long span of time, two distinct class roles emerged. One was the capitalist *entrepreneur,* who put up the capital for an enterprise; he thus had ownership of the machinery and materials that went into the production of goods. These goods he then sold for profit on the market. He was the owner-operator, who combined in his person the functions of managing and of capitalizing and owning the business. Of course, most such businesses were modest, with only a few employees; they were small business by today's standards. One sociologist, Daniel Bell, has called this *family capitalism* to express the idea that ownership of the enterprise was contained within the same family, so that security of class position was obtained by the inheritance of property.[11] The ownership of a business meant that such people were self-employed, and their income was derived from profits. Also, they were a class of employers, even though on the average they did not employ large numbers.

The contrasting class role in industrial society was that of the *worker.* He was employed to work in the factories and shops and to operate the machinery by which goods were produced, and he was paid a wage for his work. He did not own the machinery that he operated. He was an employee, and he was propertyless in the sense that the tools of production belonged not to him who used them but to the entrepreneur.

The industrial process under capitalism with its private ownership of property, then, created two new classes, a *middle class* of owner-operators and a *working class.* Under earlier industrialism, these classes were rather clearly separated. One class earned profits, the other wages, one class was self-employed and employed others, the other was one of employees. Wages were relatively low under early industrialism, and a considerable difference in standard of living separated the two classes. The ownership of property, specifically the tools of industrial production, and the independent status of self-employment,

---

[11] Daniel Bell, "The Breakup of Family Capitalism," in his *The End of Ideology* (New York: Free Press, 1960), pp. 37–42.

as well as the authority inherent in being an employer, were the symbols of middle-class status. The ownership of property symbolized independence; it also was made to symbolize ability, responsibility, and moral character, the very values stressed by the middle class in its self-image.

The industrialization that produced a middle class of property owners and a working class of wage-earners served also to destroy the upper class. This term originally applied to a landed aristocracy, a class that monopolized the functions of political management and decision making. This ruling class derived its wealth from the ownership of vast agricultural estates in an agrarian society. Their way of life provided the only opportunities for leisure and classical culture found in such agrarian societies. Industrialization seriously undercut the privileged position and entrenched class power of the aristocracy. Land became subordinate to industry as a source of wealth. The democratic political revolutions that accompanied the Industrial Revolution were the means whereby the emerging middle class challenged and finally overthrew the ruling aristocracy. Without significant wealth or power, the upper class slowly deteriorated, even though the titles of noble rank were still kept and still used. But no longer did these titles provide privileges, power, or wealth; the titled nobility no longer constituted a particular social class in society.

Karl Marx: The Significance of Social Class   Of all the great nineteenth-century students of industrial society, perhaps none gave such emphasis to the importance of social class for both understanding industrial society and for predicting its future course as did Karl Marx. When he said that "the history of all hitherto existing society is the history of the class struggle," he seemed to be associating social class with conflict and revolution, with social antagonism and constant struggle between existing social classes. This association of class with conflict and revolution is one major factor in the controversy about Marxian thinking; at the same time it is one important issue in the attempt to define and understand the significance of social classes in society, particularly in modern industrial society.

Although Marx's conception of class has been one of the most significant and controversial attempts to tell us what class is and what its significance is for society, a specific definition of social class at one point in time was never given in his writings. It requires, therefore, a somewhat careful reading to understand what he meant by class. At the outset, he seems to specify that a class constitutes those persons who share the same function in a society's organization of production. Marx sees the division of labor made necessary by the particular technology creating what he called a "mode of production"; that is, a social arrangement or set of social relationships among men as workers. It is this cooperation of men in the division of labor, making use of whatever technology is available to them at their particular stage of history, that separates them into different functions, such as peasant and landlord, worker and bourgeois, and this provides the fundamental basis for the existence of social classes.

In a footnote to the first page of the *Communist Manifesto*, Engels, Marx's lifelong associate, characterizes class in the following way:

> By bourgeoisie is meant the class of modern Capitalists, owners of the means of social production and employers of wage-labor. By proletariat, the class of modern wage-earners who, having no means of production of their own, are reduced to selling their labor power in order to live.

However, the *Manifesto* is a pamphlet calling men to revolutionary action; it was not intended by Marx as an analytic or scholarly discussion of class or of any other issue. But this reference to class does, at least, hint at elements that appear in his more scholarly works. Note the reference here to only two classes, set off against one another. Note also the reference to the class of wage-earners "reduced" to selling its labor power in order to live. This idea of one class exploiting another is basic to Marx's analysis of social class.

Marx did not limit his conception of class only to those who share a similar function in the mode of production. This situation only creates the possibility for the development of class. Rather, Marx believed that an individual's participation in the production process provides him with a crucial life-experience, one that shapes his beliefs and strongly influences his behavior. Perhaps the most significant aspect of this experience is conflict and disagreement over the share that the individual receives for his participation in production. Thus, the element of conflict and hostility between those in different positions in the production process emerges. At the same time those who share similar positions come to share similar attitudes, a process fostered by frequent communication and interaction with one another. Out of this emerges a consciousness of class position, an awareness of common economic interests and of a common condition of being oppressed by another social class. In time, this leads to common political action directed against the oppressing class. One of Marx's infrequent definitions of class says much of this:

> Insofar as millions of families live under economic conditions of existence that divide their mode of life, their interests and their culture from those of other classes, and put them into hostile contrast to the latter, they form a class.[12]

This hostility to an oppressing class is, for Marx, a necessary aspect of social class. It is its common interest in opposing the oppressing class that unites a stratum of workers or peasants into a social class. Otherwise, as Marx saw it,

---

[12] Karl Marx, *The Eighteenth Brumaire of Louis Bonaparte* (New York: International Publishers, n.d.), p. 109.

they are in individual competition with one another. He puts it quite suc-
cinctly: "The separate individuals form a class only insofar as they have to
carry on a common battle against another class; otherwise, they are on hostile
terms with each other as competitors." While it is common to assert that Marx
is an economic determinist, this conception of class is *political.* A social class,
in his conception, exists only insofar as an economic stratum is aware of and
is prepared to struggle for its economic interests against another class: ". . . the
struggle of class against class is a political struggle."

Marx made a significant contribution to the sociological analysis of social
class; even the controversy his ideas created have produced criticism and
analysis that has yielded a better understanding of class in industrial society.
His exploration of the basis of class structure in the organization of production has given us a basis for a sociological conception of class, even if we do
not accept his own definition. His emphasis upon class consciousness has raised
a major issue about the awareness that people have of their class position.
This emphasis upon class consciousness and class conflict has focused the attention of social scientists on the conditions under which social classes will organize politically to advance, by whatever means, their particular common
interests, as they may define them.

The American View of Class Marx's analysis of class in industrial society
helped to make the concept of class significant in European thought, but in
the United States there has been a stubborn resistance to conceding the reality
of social class or to acknowledging that any permanent and enduring social
classes exist here. In part this resistance stems from a belief that an emphasis
upon social class sounds too Marxian, placing too much credence on the part
that class and class conflict play in human affairs. The concept of class is not,
however, inherently radical, and Marx was not the first to stress its importance
for human society. Classical conservative thinkers of the nineteenth century
stressed the importance—and the social value and moral rightness—of a stable
class order. But whereas conservative thought emphasized the contribution of
class to social stability, the Marxian analysis stressed class as a source of
conflict and social change.

The association with Marx is not the only or even necessarily the basic
reason for the American resistance to the concept of social class. Fundamentally, it would seem to involve the violation of a historically significant image
of America held by millions of middle-class Americans; namely, that of a
society in which there are no class barriers to upward advancement. This
image may or may not be factually true. What is important is that millions
of Americans *believe* it to be true, and because they do, they resist giving any
salience to class as a part of the social reality of American life. Accordingly,
the American ideology has been inconsistent and ambiguous in its orientation

to social class. Americans have not readily recognized the importance of social class in industrial society, or at least in America, and they have often been unwilling to admit that America even has a class structure. The fluid, open, and free character of American society is presumably validated by the lack of clearly developed social classes.

At the same time, many other Americans assert that this is a middle-class society because the vast majority, they feel, are middle class, or at least because they think of themselves as middle class. Those who claim this are likely to point to a Gallup Poll that asked a nation-wide sample of Americans: "To what social class in this country do you think you belong—the middle class, the upper, or the lower?"[13] Americans responded as follows:

Class	Percent
Upper Class	6
Middle Class	88
Lower Class	6

However, in 1945, a psychologist, Richard Centers, asked a national sample of males to choose one of four classes instead of the three used by Gallup: middle class, working class, lower class, and upper class.[14] The results were as follows:

Class	Percent
Upper Class	3
Middle Class	43
Working Class	51
Lower Class	1
Don't Know	1
Don't believe in classes	1

A radically different pattern of class identification among Americans results from a different use of terms. It is not hard to glean from such research that Americans are particularly reluctant to identify themselves as lower class, but that working class is a respectable and acceptable term for half of the American population. To the student of society, this is a simple but important lesson in the methods of social research. In the Gallup survey of 1940, a large majority of Americans chose middle class as their identification when asked to choose from three terms: upper, middle, and lower. However, when a fourth term, working class, was introduced, the choosing of class position changed radically. But the student should notice here that the people doing the re-

---

[13] George Gallup and S. F. Rae, *The Pulse of Democracy* (New York: Simon and Schuster, 1940), p. 169.

[14] Richard Centers, *The Psychology of Social Classes* (Princeton, N.J.: Princeton University Press, 1949), p. 77.

search supplied the class terms, and those answering could only choose from those three or four.

But what would happen if we merely asked people what class they thought they belonged to and let them supply their own terms? This was done in a *Fortune* survey[15] Besides the four terms used above, Americans spontaneously called themselves such things as these: best, highest, upper middle, above average, in between, moderate, laboring, poor, poorest, and others. Furthermore, more than one-fourth of the sample could not spontaneously come up with any term that described their own class position.

These data would seem to suggest that in American culture the language of class is suspect because it is the language of economic interests and of social conflict. Many Americans have an image of their society as so fluid and open in its class structure that no really fixed social classes exist. Thus the widespread use of the term, *middle-class,* and the lack of a consistent class vocabulary in America does not provide an objective description of the American class structure, but it does tell us something about the American conception of and perspective on social class.

These data from national polls go back almost three decades, and so they may no longer be as indicative of the American perception of class as they were at the time. In recent years, the recognition of poverty and race and the persistence of ghetto life for millions has made many middle-class Americans sensitive to the fact that to be middle class and live in suburbia is to enjoy a relatively privileged class position. It is doubtful that most Americans are as innocent of the fact of class and its relevance for social inequality as they once were.

THE MULTIDIMENSIONALITY OF STRATIFICATION

One reason that class differences in America could be less than obvious to middle-class Americans was that stratification was frequently interpreted in ethnic and racial terms. These other forms of social stratification overlapped with, but were not identical with social class. Native Americans could look down upon "foreigners," whites upon Negroes, Anglo-Americans upon Spanish-Americans, and so on. In the same fashion, there could be groups of high prestige in a community, yet the source of their prestige might simply be an old family background, as W. Lloyd Warner reported in Yankee City. More educated people are likely to gain prestige from that fact alone, and occupations can be ranked on a scale from highest to lowest in the prestige accorded

[15] See *Fortune* Magazine, February, 1940.

them by the general population. These few instances—and others could be cited—suggest that there can be diverse bases for social stratification in a modern society. Whether the concept of social class then appropriately incorporates all forms of stratification, or whether class is but one of several ways of stratifying, becomes a conceptual issue of importance. However sociologists choose to define class, the complexity of stratification is evident enough, It can and does take myriad forms; men can be counted upon to find numerously diverse ways in which to create social rank and to claim greater prestige or privilege than others.

Of the major sociologists besides Marx who have contributed to a theory of stratification, Max Weber has been most significant in taking account of the complexity of stratification and suggesting such forms as *class, status,* and *party.*[16] Among American social scientists, the social anthropologist W. Lloyd Warner has studied stratification in the community and has attempted to incorporate several dimensions of stratification into a concept of class.[17] These two social scientists are the most significant contributors to the difficult issue of the multidimensionality of stratification.

Max Weber: Class, Status, and Party   Although sociologists are by no means agreed as yet on a vocabulary of stratification applicable to our or any other society, the clarification of terms has been strongly influenced by Weber's work, particularly his distinction between class and status. Even those who do not follow Weber's analysis have nevertheless used it as a point of departure.

Class   Weber is in the main stream of traditional social analysis when he asserts that the *economic* organization of a society provides one basis of stratification. It is obvious to everyone that income provides a simple ranking process, yet income alone has never provided a satisfactory basis for defining social class. Often skilled workers and even unionized, semiskilled workers in the large, mass-production industries earn as much if not more than many people in white-collar occupations. Although reports about the income of factory workers are exaggerated, it is a fact that the incomes of factory workers and many white-collar workers overlap. Income alone, then, is not an adequate means for ranking. But Weber and many other social scientists have specified the *source* of income as a criterion of rank: the combination of what people do in the division of labor (occupation) or of what they own (property), as well as what they earn (income), provides a more adequate and revealing conception of stratification in economic terms.

[16] Max Weber, "Class, Status, and Party," in Hans Gerth and C. Wright Mills, *From Max Weber: Essays in Sociology* (New York: Oxford, 1946), pp. 180–195.
[17] W. Lloyd Warner, Marcia Meeker, and Kenneth Eels, *Social Class in America* (Chicago: Science Research, 1949).

However Weber was not content merely to define class by economic criteria. Rather, he thought it important to point out that people were in the same *class situation* when their occupation or ownership of property under the conditions of commodity or labor market gave them a similar chance, however large or small, to obtain some of the things valued in a society: material goods; physical health; education; travel; leisure; and exposure to a wide range of highly prized social experiences. Some people have goods to sell to others, and it is this that determines their *life-chances*. Other people sell their skills or labor on a labor market to available employers. Still others, such as professionals, offer highly valued and relatively scarce services to a clientele. Each of these constitutes a different "class situation." For Weber, class is a collectivity of people who share a common set of life-chances as these are determined by property, occupation, and income. His specific definition is:

> We may speak of a 'class' when (1) a number of people have in common a specific causal component of their life-chances, in so far as (2) this component is represented exclusively by economic interests in the possession of goods and opportunities for income, and (3) is represented under the conditions of the commodity or labor markets.[18]

Weber recognized the varied ways in which the possession of property or goods by those who "do not necessarily have to exchange them" gave them an advantage in the market over those who had to sell their goods to survive or who had no goods but only their "services in native form." Weber sounded not too different than Marx when he said: " 'Property' and 'lack of property' are, therefore, the basic categories of all class situations."[19]

Status As distinct from class, status refers to the ranking of social groups *by prestige and honor*. There must be both a *claim* to prestige and a *granting* of prestige. Such a necessary process requires, first of all, a recognition both of the agreed upon criteria for prestige and honor and the opportunities for interaction by means of which claims to honor based on these criteria can be observed and evaluated. As a consequence, status stratification is frequently local in nature, in contrast to the broad, societywide nature of social class.

A *status group* can be said to exist when a number of individuals occupy a similar position in the prestige ranking of their community, and when they recognize each other as equals and interact regularly with one another. They form friendship circles, dine together, belong to the same organizations, encourage the intermarrying of their children, and otherwise exhibit a common *style of life*. A style of life common to a group provides a basis for both inclusiveness and exclusiveness; that is, for defining both who belongs and is

[18] Weber, "Class, Status, and Party," p. 181.
[19] Weber, p. 182.

accepted as a social equal and who does not and is left out. If Weber was not content to define class in terms of economically situated roles, but pointed out that people shared a common class situation in similar fashion, he conceived of a *status situation* as one in which a positive or negative *estimation of honor* determines to some extent the life-chances of people.

Status does not operate independently of social class. Most frequently members of a status group also belong to the same social class, since the style of life usually requires a particular economic level or amount of income. It is difficult to develop status groups among individuals whose class positions diverge widely, since their social experiences are so varied, their social values cannot be homogeneous enough to maintain a distinctive style of life. If Jews and Negroes, for example, have been ethnic and racial status groups, it is because all Jews and all Negroes have in common the overriding importance of an oppressed status, and because there has historically been only a limited range of class positions available to the large majority of Jews and Negroes. Most Jews have been urban middle class, most Negroes have been lower class. Furthermore, status groups develop a style of life that may in time usurp privileges for themselves; in doing so they may interfere with the pure workings of the market. These groups may also seek to limit economic opportunities in order to maintain the exclusiveness of their own group. But even when others attain their economic level, they may not confer on them an equal status. The plight of the *nouveaux riches* in lacking family background, proper "breeding" and "taste," and the like, is a familiar example.

Party   What leads Weber to put party with class and status in his distinctions about stratification? For Weber the three phenomena are linked by virtue of the fact that they are all aspects of social power: "Now: 'classes,' 'status groups,' and 'parties' are phenomena of the distribution of power within a community."[20] In a brief commentary appended to his discussion of class and status, Weber observed that parties "live in a house of 'power.' "[21] They are organized to acquire power, that is, "toward influencing a communal action no matter what its content may be."[22] They may recruit followers from either classes or status groups and thus be concerned with representing such interests, or they may become neither class or status parties exclusively, which is usually the case. Parties vary, notes Weber, according to whether stratification is by class or status, for they vary according to the "structure of domination," since they are always "structures struggling for domination."[23] Thus, parties are linked to classes and status groups, for to speak of these phenomena is

[20] Weber, p. 181.
[21] Weber, p. 194.
[22] Weber, p. 194.
[23] Weber, p. 195.

to speak of power and of how the structure of domination reflects the struggles of parties in a context of class and status.

W. Lloyd Warner: Class as Community Status Among American sociologists, the best known and most influential conception of social classes has been developed in a series of community researches by an anthropologist, W. Lloyd Warner. These studies, of which the series about Yankee City are the most famous, have probably influenced the thinking of more American sociologists about the nature of class and stratification than any other single approach.

Warner's research began with the idea that the *economic* factor is the fundamental one controlling the society and thus is basic to stratification, but his research, he felt, did not bear this out. Rather, the picture of the "class" system that emerged from the study only imperfectly correlated with economic position. For example, in Yankee City, the very top class (the upper-upper class) was not the economically dominant segment of the community, rather its members were descended from the original families who settled the community some three centuries ago. In turn, some quite wealthy and powerful individuals whose families had a shorter history in the community, but who had only (more) recently acquired their wealth ranked below them.

Out of his discovery that higher status in the local community does not necessarily go to those with the predominant economic position, Warner developed a conception of social class that he called *evaluated participation.* This means that the way in which an individual participates in community life—as that participation is evaluated by his peers in the community—is the basis for his class position. Such a criterion stresses knowing the right people, knowing how to "act right," knowing how to spend money, belonging to the right kind of associations, the area in which one resides, how long one's family has been in the community, and the like. Warner developed a sixfold classification by taking the familiar terms, upper, middle, and lower, and dividing each of them into an upper and a lower. Thus, there is an upper-upper class, composed of the community's elite of long-standing, its old ruling families of high prestige, and a lower-upper class of rising families with newly-won wealth, eager to win social acceptance. The upper-middle class constitutes the established business and professional people, and the lower-middle class is made up of varied white-collar people, small businessmen, and skilled workers. The upper-lower class is made up of skilled and other workers who are "respectable" though poor and hardworking, whereas the lower-lower includes the most economically depressed whose way of life is not respected by other members of the community.

This problem of accurately describing the prestige ranking of a local community has opened up a fascinating if sometimes confusing aspect of the issue. Sociologists have discovered that if they seek to develop a picture of the prestige system of the community based upon what the people in the community itself say, there is no necessary consistency or close agreement. For one thing, only in a very small community can each person know all the other persons (or at least all other families) well enough to rank them against one another. Secondly, the status system itself limits interaction and familiarity, so that a person of highest status in the community may not recognize any significant distinction between some of the lower ranks. He may see only three or four ranks instead of six. In the same fashion a person of low status may have only a blurred notion of prestige ranking at the upper levels of the community. Nor are they necessarily agreed upon criteria for establishing several ranks.

To meet some of this difficulty in studying stratification in the community, Warner developed a newer method for class placement, which he called the Index of Status Characteristics (ISC). The index is composed of four items: *occupation, source of income, house type,* and *dwelling area.* These are intended to be a set of objective criteria applicable to any American community. The first two are economic and are objective; they can be applied by an outside investigator and are not subject to variations in local definitions of prestige. But what is a more prestigeful type of house or a higher status neighborhood can be influenced by local definitions of prestige. Warner's ISC is a conscious effort to include both economic and noneconomic characteristics in determining status. He identified himself as among those writers who "argue that class is a multifactored phenomena."[24] But Warner's effort was to find a way to include the several relevant factors into a single hierarchy of classes, and this brought upon him the criticism of those who, following Weber, felt that different orders of stratification should be identified. C. Wright Mills, for example, charged that Warner "indiscriminately absorbs at least three items, which, when considering 'stratifications,' it is very important to separate analytically."[25] He then indicated he meant Weber's class, status, and power.

Marx, Weber, and Warner: A Comparison   The different manner in which Marx, Weber, and Warner sought to analyze social stratification might seem to differ considerably and thus to create confusion as to what the sociology of stratification is all about. There are some very real differences in their analyses that cannot be overlooked or underemphasized. Yet, a closer inspection will reveal significant points of comparison.

Weber's analysis is regarded as classic among sociologists just because he separated class from status and allowed for an analysis of stratification that permitted taking into account all three dimensions. His conception of social class is built upon the dimension of unequal rewards; he sees class as the

---

[24] Warner, Meeker, and Eels, *Social Class in America,* p. 129.
[25] C. Wright Mills, review of W. Lloyd Warner and Paul S. Lunt, *The Social Life of a Modern Community, American Sociological Review,* 7 (1942), 264.

(always unequal) distribution of life-chances as these are determined by the opportunities of the market. Status, in turn, is concerned with social groups that claim social prestige (Weber speaks of honor) and that evidence a pattern of homogeneous behavior—what he called a *life-style*. Sociologists have appreciated this capacity of Weber's to distinguish among the distinct dimensions of social stratification and thus to account for a wider range of observations about stratification than other analysts. Class and status as two distinct processes of stratification, as Weber has defined them, have proven to be quite adaptable to contemporary stratification situations and, for many sociologists, these have become the significant concepts to be used in stratification analysis.

Karl Marx, in turn, also built his conception of class upon the unequal distribution of social rewards and emphasized that the unequal distribution was unjust—that one class was being exploited by another. Marx's philosophical as well as revolutionary interest in class as the basis for the struggles that changed society focused his analysis almost exclusively upon class. He did, however, point out that a social class shares a common mode of life. Furthermore, when its social interaction has created a consciousness of its own class interests, it has become ideologically homogeneous. Understandably, status groups not grounded in economic organization held little interest for Marx, and thus one finds his approach unconcerned with the analysis of status.

Warner's contribution focuses upon the two dimensions of prestige ranking and homogeneous behavior. His conception of class contrasts sharply with that offered by both Marx and Weber, but it is clearly very close to Weber's concept of status group. If we recognize that when Warner speaks of classes he is referring to status groups in the small community, we find no necessary discrepancy between his work and Weber's. Indeed, he has provided the sociological literature with rich and rewarding studies of status in the American community.

However, where Warner differs most from both Marx and Weber is in their conception of stratification as related to power and domination and thus to the establishment and maintenance of inequalities in society. Warner shifted the emphasis to social ranking by a set of criteria that put some people above others in prestige. But for both Marx and Weber prestige clearly follows from power and privilege.

SOCIAL CLASS IN MODERN SOCIETY

Although the multidimensionality of stratification in modern society must always be kept in mind in order to analyze what is a most complex phenomenon, class is the primary stratum. Anchored in the commodity and labor markets of the modern economy, class exists only because there are different life-chances in relation to these markets. Those who share a similar life-chance, who are, in Weber's term, in the same class situation, constitute a social class.

Historically, the social classes of modern society have developed slowly from the earlier patterns of class found in the medieval economy, and they have been remarkably sensitive to changes wrought by modern technology. Here, surely, is one of the most visible and measurable examples of the alteration of social structure in societies with advanced technology, where scientific progress leads to technological innovation with consequent impact on the processes of occupational and professional specialization. As industrialization advanced, as large industrial organization replaced the many, smaller family enterprises, as capitalism changed from the competitive, laissez-faire model of the eighteenth century to twentieth century capitalism with giant corporations in monopolistic and semimonopolistic positions, a modification of class structure occurred.

The Middle Class   With the growth of large-scale enterprise there came a marked increase in the proportion of salaried employees. One increase was in administrative and managerial personnel; a large enterprise not only needs more such individuals, it apparently needs a larger proportion of such persons. In addition, the large enterprise employs larger numbers of people who perform technical functions: engineers, production experts, research scientists, and accountants. In time, new professional functions have emerged: time-study; wage-analysis; personnel; public relations; customer relations; advertising; marketing; sales; and so forth. Associated with this growth of the large enterprise was the growth of the office and the increase in white-collar positions, particularly for women. Over the last eighty years, then, we have observed not only an increase in the labor force, but a change in it: the emergence of a wide range of white-collar positions and an increase in the proportion of white-collar employment. Many of these positions are technical or specialized, others are administrative or managerial. They are salaried positions, and the individuals are employees; as such, they are not middle-class in the nineteenth century sense of the term; they do not derive income from profit nor own the business. Yet they are not in the same stratum as wage earners. Their positions require more training, and as highly specialized persons, they will likely work with less supervision or direction than will workers. Or they may exercise authority over other persons in managerial capacities. Furthermore, their compensations, on the average, exceeds that of the working class.

This is a middle stratum, yet it violates the older conception of middle class. Nonetheless, these newer middle-class positions, in the United States at least, outnumber the older form of middle class. Consequently, sociologists have found it useful to recognize an old middle class and a new middle class.

Middle class, then, is a term that might more properly be used in the plural. The old middle class is made up of those whose relation to property is one of ownership, who operate their own individual or family enterprise, and whose income is derived as profit from the ownership and operation of such a business. In addition, old middle class includes the "free" (self-employed) professionals, who "hang out their shingle" and conduct a private practice in law, medicine, dentistry, and the like. Their income is derived from the fees of their clients. The new middle class, in turn, is a term covering a wide range of salaried, white-collar positions. The salaried manager or executive, the technical specialist, and the salaried professional make up this class. A combination of skill and specialized knowledge are necessary for these middle-class occupations, some of which are professionalized, all of which are specialized and skilled. People in these occupations are hired for a salary by others to perform technical and managerial services.

It is worth noting that occupation alone does not determine class position, at least does not distinguish between old and new middle class. For example, two men might both be barbers. But if one owns his own shop and has one or two other barbers working for him, he is a small businessman, whereas the other barber, who is employed at a wage or salary, is not. Their occupation is the same, but their class position is not. Similarly, a lawyer with an independent practice is old middle class, but a salaried lawyer working for a corporation or a large law firm is a salaried professional of the new middle class.

The old middle class has been in decline throughout this century, while the new middle class has been in relatively rapid expansion. When the social scientist Peter Drucker called this an *employee society*, he was referring to the growth of a great middle class of salaried employees, who, along with the working class, made up a large majority of people, whose livelihood depends on their working for some employer, which is more likely to be an organization than a person, an organization managed and operated by persons who are themselves employees.[26]

Upper and Lower Middle Class   If we can make a distinction between old and new middle class, we can also make a distinction between upper and lower middle class, though perhaps not as precisely; such a distinction can at best be only a rough one. But it is not difficult to imagine an upper middle class of salaried professionals, managerial executives, and other college-educated professionals, on the one hand, and independent professionals and owner-operators of larger businesses, on the other. The large white-collar army of

[26] Peter Drucker, "The Employee Society," *American Journal of Sociology,* 57 (January, 1953), 358–363.

sales and clerical personnel make up a lower-middle class, as do those small merchants, businessmen and small farmers, who own and operate the numerous little businesses. Between the lower and upper ends, there is a middle range, too, and indeed, one could probably draw a number of finer lines if one wanted a more precise demarcation.

Working Class   Since the worker in modern industry never was self-employed, the distinction between old and new, as in the middle class, has never applied. There have, however, been a plurality of working classes. Perhaps the basic working class, under industrial conditions, has been made up of those semiskilled occupations directly involved in operating the machinery of industrial production. But there has also always been a class of workers, such as tool and die workers, highly skilled and usually much better paid; they have been the "cream" of the working class. On the other extreme, there is a class of unskilled laborers, employed in factories and in service industries, whose training and experience count for little, and whose wages and security of employment are both low. One can also note the existence of a shrinking class of domestic servants, though such a form of employment involves a large number of unskilled and untrained Negro females. In the agricultural area, farm laborers, including migratory workers, also constitute one kind of lower working class.

These distinctions suggest that, like the concept of middle class, the working class should be viewed in the plural. A skilled class of craftsmen, separately organized in craft unions, and a larger class of semiskilled operatives, constitute the major divisions of the broad stratum of blue-collar workers in industrial society. The semiskilled also have been organized in mass unions in America since the 1930s, in Europe even earlier. Below them are an array of more disadvantaged categories, inclusion of which in the working class only causes confusion. The unskilled and the underemployed at the bottom of industrial society's economic strata suffer by comparison with the working class in social power (they are not usually organized), in income, and in job security. Their ranks are now increased by the addition of many dispossessed by mechanized agriculture (and mechanized mining in Appalachia) from rural America; a disproportionate number of them are Negroes. This lower class (or under class) with only a marginal status in the market economy has become a central issue in America since poverty has become a national issue. (We shall examine this in detail in Chapter 13.)

Is There an Upper Class?   The assertion that the working class and the middle class were the two basic classes to emerge from industrialization, and that industrialization gradually undercut the upper class, the landed nobility, seems to imply that no upper class exists in industrial society. Certainly, no aristocracy does. Because of this the term upper class has had no consistent meaning. Some would argue that historically the upper class passed out of existence. Others apply the term to those who are the wealthiest.

An upper class, if one exists, ought to be distinguished from upper-middle class by income, by power, by privilege, by style of life, and by function in the division of labor. Does such a class exist in the United States? Sociologists are not yet prepared to give a definitive answer, but their discussions divide between two perspectives. One perspective sees an old upper class of families of great wealth, usually of inherited income derived from extensive invest-ments and property holdings. Great family fortunes have been built up in the past, and when they are manifested in ownership of property and diversified investments, they are not easily dissipated. These families are characterized by a distinctive life-style, for family wealth, family lineage, and unique pat-terns of socialization create a relatively exclusive *status group*. Although such status groups can easily be identified locally, a national status group is harder to identify. And no longer, in a mass society, is such a status group the exclu-sive arbiter of tastes and styles.

The other perspective focuses on power and attempts to identify the emer-gence of a new *managerial class*. The now well-recognized distinction between ownership and control in private industry is the basis for defining this new class who assume the corporate decision-making function without possessing ownership. James Burnham predicted its emergence as the ruling class of industrial society, the makers of a revolution different than Marx predicted.[27] But C. Wright Mills argued that the considerable incomes of the new man-agerial class permit them, not to displace the propertied elite, but to merge with them "into the more or less unified stratum of the corporate rich."[28] Mills' own study spoke not of class but of a *power elite*, made up of the corporate rich, the top political leadership, and the military elite, who in a unity of interest and ideology have come to dominate America. This, however, is not an upper class so much as it is a convergence of dominant elites from the several major spheres of power in the society. Lenski objects to overemphasizing the unity of these elites, and particularly insists on the continuing need to distinguish analytically between the managerial class and the propertied elite, on the grounds that membership in one category does not automatically confer membership in the other, and that "where dual membership is not held, we recognize that a basis for conflict exists."[29] The military, in turn, undoubtedly possessing an enlarged power to make war has not, however, been able to translate this effectively into the power to increase its own share of the national income.

[27] James Burnham, *The Managerial Revolution* (New York: John Day, 1941).
[28] C. Wright Mills, *The Power Elite* (New York: Oxford, 1956), p. 147.
[29] Lenski, *Power and Privilege*, p. 360.

Trends in Class Structure One clear trend in the development of the class structure of industrial societies is the development of the new salaried classes, to the point (in the United States, at least) where they now account for a larger segment of the population than does the old middle class and the upper status based upon ownership of property. Accompanying this has been an expansion of the number and proportion of white-collar positions, and thus an increase in middle-class positions. These two trends are related, of course, in that the expansion of middle-class occupations largely occurs in the new middle class.

Since the class structure of industrial society is a direct product of its division of labor, anything that is likely to alter the division of labor will have direct influence on social class. Technological developments that eliminate occupations and create new ones change the division of labor and thus the class structure. In part the emergence of new middle-class positions arises from the development of new professional and technical fields; these are most likely to be salaried positions, requiring considerable training, in large private and public organizations.

One potential consequence of improved technology, including automation, is its effect on the structure of existing jobs and its creation of new ones, thus, further altering the class structure. From the present perspective, still early in the social development of automation, we can anticipate the growth of more technical positions and the decline of many working-class occupations. Automation, from one perspective, only continues the trend away from manual and physical labor by replacing human labor with mechanical labor. The introduction of mass production techniques once created many semiskilled jobs and a semiskilled class of machine operators—production and assembly line workers in factories—mitigating the formerly sharp distinction between skilled workers on the one hand and unskilled workers on the other. Now, automation finds ways of replacing the formerly large number of semiskilled workers in the production process, in turn creating skilled, technical positions, although much fewer in number, which deal with the operating and maintaining of automated processes. Even white-collar positions in offices, particularly female clerical ones, are changed and sometimes eliminated by automation. Automation can take over many bookkeeping, recordkeeping, and other functions so necessary for the administration of large enterprises.

THE CORRELATES OF CLASS: INDEXES OF INEQUALITY

In much of sociological research on class in American sociology, indexes of class—education, income, occupation, or some combination of these—have often been used as an independent variable in the explanation of some other phenomena. By this means sociologists have accumulated a great deal of information about the *correlates* of class; that is, those phenomena that correlate, positively or negatively, with class ranking. If, for example, social participation correlates positively with class, this suggests that the lower the class position, the less social participation.

Although not always intended as such, much of these data on the correlates of class provide substantiating evidence on the unequal distribution of life-chances in American society and so document the inequality that is the very meaning of class. Other data, in turn, provide considerable information on the social differences in beliefs, behavior patterns, and cultural outlooks of the several classes, documenting the idea that each class manifests a distinct life-style.

Life-Chances   Weber's concept of life-chances, we have seen, refers to the opportunity to acquire the valued material and nonmaterial rewards of the society. For Weber, the very essence of class was the unequal distribution of these life-chances. Income, of course, is one major kind of social reward, but there are others as well, including the chance of avoiding some of the greater hazards of life. Among some of the life-chances that are so unevenly distributed are the following:

1. The chance for a long and healthy life is not one that comes equally to all in any society, not even the United States. A longer life expectancy is correlated with social class, as is a higher level of health.[30] This is obviously because of differences in economic resources in paying for medical care, as well as the educational advantage of knowing about the need and importance of medical care, nutrition, and habits of health.

2. What is true for health and life is also true for mental health. People at the lower levels of social class have a better than average chance of becoming a psychotic patient in a mental institution, whereas those at the upper levels have a less than average chance.[31] Class differences are also evident in the treatment given to the mentally ill. The higher the class position, apparently, the better the psychiatric treatment; more frequently are such advantaged people treated at private hospitals and given psychotherapy, whereas lower-class patients are sent to public institutions, where care is less adequate because of overcrowding and under-staffing, and they are not as likely to receive prolonged psychotherapy or even any therapy at all.[32]

---

[30] Kurt B. Mayer, *Class and Society* (New York: Random House, 1955), pp. 33–34. L. Guralnick, "The Study of Mortality by Occupations in the United States" (Washington, D.C.: National Office of Vital Statistics, September, 1959).

[31] Compare Robert E. Clark, "Psychoses, Income, and Occupational Prestige," *American Journal of Sociology*, 54 (March, 1949), 433–440.

[32] Compare August B. Hollingshead and Frederick C. Redlick, *Social Class and Mental Illness* (New York: Wiley, 1958).

3. The chance for a college education, despite financial aid and publicly subsidized universities, decreases as one goes down the class structure.[33] This is partly a matter of financial means, partly a matter of class differences in instilling academic skills and motivations and providing hope and encouragement for those who sense the odds are against them.

4. The chance to escape imprisonment for criminal activities improves as one moves up the class ladder.[34] The common impression is that the lower class is more criminal; but the measurement of "more" or "less" criminality is a difficult thing. Generally, the lower class commits crimes of violence against persons and property which receive public attention and fit a common-sense notion of crime. Also, the class status of an accused person has a bearing on his treatment in the judicial process. The dispensation of justice, in terms of the likelihood of being arrested and convicted and in terms of the severity of punishment meted out by the court, seems to vary with the social class of the alleged offender.

These few examples suggest that the chances to live longer and in better health, to retain one's sanity, to get an education, and to stay out of prison, are better for those of higher class position than they are for those lower in the class structure. These are only a few of the more provocative examples, but sociological research provides the documentation for many other differences in the class distribution of life-chances.

Life-Style   What Weber called life-style has reference to the ways in which classes and status groups develop a mode of living, a cultural pattern of action and sets of beliefs. Each of the social classes develops a life-style of its own, and each of the classes manifests a distinctive *world-view*, a way of looking at life that expresses its particular social experiences and its relation to other social classes. Much of the work of W. Lloyd Warner and others who have utilized his approach have provided rich descriptions of the life-styles of social classes. They have described the pursuit of leisure and forms of recreation, aesthetic tastes and preferences, ways of entertaining, religious differences, moral outlooks and political values, and also patterns of family life, marital relations, and child raising, of social classes. (See Chapter 13, The Family, for some discussion of this last issue.) In particular, the family patterns of the working class and the lower class have intrigued middle-class sociologists, and a considerable literature has proliferated. Herbert Gans' recent study of Levittown, New Jersey, is a sophisticated sociological effort to explore, among

---

[33] For a review of evidence, see Mayer, *Class and Society,* pp. 34–38. See also Elmo Roper, *Factors Affecting the Admission of High School Seniors to College* (Washington, D.C.: American Council on Education, 1949).

[34] Compare Warner and Lunt, *The Social Life of a Modern Community,* pp. 375–376; also, John Useem, Pierre Tangent, and Ruth Useem, "Stratification in a Prairie Town," *American Sociological Review,* 7 (June, 1942), 341.

other things, the particular relation of three classes—working class, lower-middle class and upper class—to the life and politics of an emerging and growing community, and to explore conflict and cleavage about community policy that is generated by different class outlooks and aspirations.[35]

Ideology and Politics   Class as a source of ideological belief points up one of the older ideas about class, namely, that social classes possess distinctive ideological interpretations of society. In the United States, sociologists have found that people are more conservative at the upper levels of class and more liberal, or even radical, at the lower levels. There is nothing either new or startling in this observation. However, more recent research in political sociology has required some modification. It now seems valid only to assert that the lower the social class, the more liberal or radical are people on *economic* issues, whereas those of higher class position tend to be economically conservative. Thus, working-class Americans support social security, labor unions, and government regulation of business, as well as government programs of social welfare. Middle- and upper-class Americans, in turn, are much less in favor of these, and many even oppose them. But middle-class people are more liberal than working-class people on such social issues as civil liberties and civil rights.

The differences in ideological beliefs characteristic of different social classes lead directly to a concern with political, economic, and other social behavior based upon these beliefs. Working-class people in the United States join labor unions as a means of collectively rather than individually improving their economic position. Most of them vote for the Democratic Party in preference to the Republican Party. By their votes, they support stronger measures of economic and political control effected by the federal government.

Significant for the exercise of power in American society is the fact that there is a rough correlation between social class and amount of voting. The lower one goes in the class order, the smaller the proportion of people who vote, and they do so with less regularity. This is why many politicians believe that a heavy turnout of votes is always to the advantage of the Democratic Party. This is also why politically active labor unions put so much effort into getting workers registered to vote.

The pattern of less frequent voting by those lower in the class order is parallelled also by their less active participation in various forms of political, economic, and other social action. Working-class people belong to fewer organizations than do middle-class people, attend less frequently those organizations to which they do belong, and less frequently hold any elected or appointed position in the organization. Thus, the vast range of voluntary associations in

[35] Herbert J. Gans, *The Levittowners* (New York: Pantheon, 1967).

American society are largely sustained and manned by middle-class Americans. Some sociological research has discovered that large numbers of working-class people belong only to a church or a labor union, or possibly both, but not to any other of the social organizations to be found in the community. This lesser participation in political and civic life by working-class people diminishes the significance of their considerable numbers. In like fashion, the greater participation of the middle-class maximizes their potential influence in the political process.

Life-Style and Inequality   That differences in life-chances constitute indexes of inequality is easy enough to understand, but it is surely not so obvious that differences in life-style among social strata can stand as indexes of inequality. Not all of the varied aspects of life-style are indexes of inequality, but many are, or at least they function as such. Some of them, for example, become in effect social stigmata of lesser class position: modes of speech and grooming and tastes are socially ranked, and those associated with higher classes are always more prestigeful. Indeed, mobile people often need to shed such mannerisms that give away their lower class origins if they are to assimilate into a higher class position. Only those later generations safely secure in high status can usually afford to acknowledge, even point out, their humble origins.

Other aspects of life-style are indexes of inequality in that they serve as disadvantages for that class, whether in promoting class interests or in enhancing the mobility of its members. The educational choices of factory workers' sons, for example, often serve to be so practical as to limit their occupational choice and their consequent life-chances. The lesser involvement of working-class people in civic life reduces their political effectiveness, particularly in the community, whereas the greater involvement of the middle class enhances their influence beyond their numbers. Their educational style also provides a greater sophistication about processes of political conflict and change and a greater capacity to deal effectively with them for their own interests.

SOCIAL MOBILITY

Compared to castes and estates, social classes in industrial societies are relatively *open*, so that an individual's class position is more likely *achieved* than it is *ascribed*, that is, assigned to the person by virtue of the family into which he was born. Social mobility is this process of individuals either moving up or down the class hierarchy, though most discussion tends to focus upon the upward process. Although social mobility is present in all societies to some extent, it is both visible and approved in an open class society to an extent undreamed of in such closed systems as castes and estates, giving rise to pervasive expectations and aspirations.

But it is not expectations and aspirations that make mobility a reality, it is the change in occupational structure that enlarges the range and proportion of middle-level occupations while perhaps reducing the relative proportion of the lower ones. By moving peasants into urban occupations and by enlarging the middle class through the development of manufacturing processes, the transition from an agrarian to an industrial economy provides social mobility not imagined before.

But industrial change does not stop there. Rather, advanced industrial countries move beyond manufacturing to develop the tertiary branch of the economy: trade, transportation, communication, and personal and professional services. At the same time, agricultural employment declines, manufacturing usually remains steady in absolute numbers but declines proportionately. This newer area provides a greater proportion of employment, more of it white collar and middle class. All our evidence indicates that tertiary employment provides distinctly higher earnings than does agriculture and manufacturing.

This pattern of analysis links mobility or its absence, or varying degrees of mobility, to certain key variables in the economic structure of the society. A society that is industrializing is a society that is opening up new forms of industrial employment and is creating social mobility. An advanced industrial society, by technological and commercial change, upgrades its population by expanding the proportion of middle-level occupations. This suggests, further-more, that social mobility is rooted in the industrial characteristics of its society, particularly its technological developments that produce transitions from one form of employment to another, generally reducing physical and unskilled labor and creating more skilled forms of occupational service.

Presumably, this is true of any industrial society, whether that society is capitalistic or not; therefore, social mobility would of necessity occur in socialist and communist societies as well as capitalist ones. The Soviet Union is perhaps the test case of this idea. It has undergone rapid industrialization since the Russian Revolution in 1917, the Bolshevik leadership being intent on changing a largely agrarian society into an industrial one. In the process, millions of peasants have been employed in urban occupations, and higher education has increased considerably as a necessary source for training large numbers of people for varied technical and professional fields. The industrial-ization of the Soviet Union simply created a great middle stratum where it had not existed before.

Mobility and the Family   The family is usually regarded as the social unit through which an individual is placed in the class structure. If the child assumes his father's occupation, then he also remains in his father's social class, and family succession of occupation becomes a means of limiting mobility within a class structure. Mobility is always limited in any society by a process of *social inheritance.* In nonindustrial societies, this may constitute the major process for locating individuals in the social structure. A son inherits his father's occupation, property, titles, and social status. Although industrial societies do not fix and thus guarantee that a son will inherit his father's social status, they do not eliminate social inheritance as a significant process for the placement of people in the class structure. In a capitalist society, the inheritance of property occasionally ensures occupation and social position for some. Such status by ascription puts these positions beyond the competitive achievement of another person. A successfully competitive father, for example, may bequeath a son a fortune and a business. What was once won by competing against others is now passed on noncompetitively.

Even where the family cannot transmit property to the next generation, it nonetheless seeks to maximize the social chances of its children. Middle-class people are likely to seek preferred educational opportunities for their children, to teach them what they believe to be the attributes of successful people, and in other ways increase their children's chances of being mobile. Even having fewer children may increase the chances of a family to do more for those children it does have, and in all industrial societies the upper economic levels have fewer children than do those of the lower economic level.

For the nonpropertied classes, particularly, education is a necessity in the mobility process. Educational opportunities have never been equally open to all economic levels, though the growth of public education to the university level has widened the chances for an education and has no longer made it the class privilege it once was. In the nineteenth century, one gained entrance into the middle class by accumulating some modest capital; in the twentieth century, a college education more and more becomes the "social capital" necessary to make one's way into the middle class.

Even when those of higher social status are not entirely conscious of striving to improve the mobility chances of their children, thus somewhat reducing the mobility chances of others, they nonetheless do so by their very style of life. A child of a professional man is exposed to a cultural milieu and a pattern of attitudes and values that are appropriate to and expected of one at that class level. Such a child has a distinct advantage over the child of the factory worker, who must learn later in life all these cultural attributes that characterize the style of life to which he aspires.

The advantages that many middle-class parents seek to give their children are often just that, *advantages* in the chance to be mobile. Although a head start in the race to get ahead does not guarantee winning, it is not surprising that the children of the middle class constitute a disproportionately larger segment of the successfully mobile, and that many more are upwardly mobile than are downwardly mobile. Numerous studies by sociologists have demonstrated that the sons of white-collar fathers have a better chance of being mobile than do the sons of blue-collar fathers. The chance to be mobile may be present for all, however, it is never present to the same degree.

Social Mobility in America and Europe   Americans not only believe that mobility is a fact of life in American society, they also believe that the chance to move up is greater in American society than in European ones. Furthermore, Europeans also seem to believe this. Does such a view rest on solid evidence? What is a widespread impression is not necessarily a fact. It is not easy to make any precise assessment of this, for data that allow accurate comparative analysis are hard to come by. In the 1950s, Seymour M. Lipset and Reinhard Bendix pioneered an effort to undertake such a study,[36] and a great deal more subsequent research has followed.

Given the fact that existing international data did not allow a refined breakdown, Lipset and Bendix divided their data into a simple manual-nonmanual distinction for a number of industrial countries. They computed three rates: (1) the proportion of all sons of manual workers who are in nonmanual occupations—upward mobility; (2) the proportion of all sons of nonmanual workers now in manual occupations—downward mobility; and (3) an index of total vertical mobility, obtained by combining both upward and downward mobility, and expressing that as a percentage of the total number of sons in each national sample. This last index proved to be fairly narrow, from 31 percent for Germany to 23 percent for Switzerland.

More recently, Lenski has computed a similar manual-nonmanual index based on data from a variety of sources, and he lists the United States as first with a mobility rate of 34 percent.[37] But five other countries—Sweden, Great Britain, Denmark, Norway, and France—are only a few percentages below that. The consistency in data such as these has led to the conclusion that mobility is fairly similar in industrial societies.

Nonetheless, there are differences, too, and an interest in the similarities may very well overlook some important variations. For example, the United States and Great Britain are quite similar when one measures mobility across the manual-nonmanual line. But in Great Britain, this means that the sons of manual workers can move into white-collar positions at the middle level, but not into more elite positions. In the United States, however, there was more mobility from manual to elite positions. The elitist group in Britain is

---

[36] Seymour M. Lipset and Reinhard Bendix, *Social Mobility in Industrial Society* (Berkeley, Calif.: University of California Press, 1959).

[37] Lenski, *Power and Privilege,* p. 411.

still largely self-perpetuating, or only open to penetration by other middle-class persons.[38] What is more true of Britain than of the United States, however, is still largely true of both societies: upward mobility for manual worker's sons is largely into the more modest white-collar positions, and mobility into the upper, elitist levels of occupations is most possible for those who start half-way up the scale.

Mobility in America: Fact and Belief   This effort at comparative international research on social mobility in industrial societies has not confirmed the idea that in the United States there is an opportunity for getting ahead that is simply not present in other countries. Rather, mobility seems to be a function of the industrialization of the society, modified, no doubt, by still persisting status factors (as in Great Britain) that still make for some national differences. But this is still much different than the belief about America that both Americans and Europeans share. How, then, can we account for this solid belief?

One factor is the stronger belief in America in the social value of mobility. Undoubtedly, social opportunity has been a major American value. It has been proclaimed in our popular literature and is an integral aspect of what has been called "the American way of life." Then, too, the experience of European immigrants in finding a relatively higher standard of living in the United States than in Europe has possibly contributed to such a belief, even though such an experience is not in fact evidence of *mobility* but rather of *improvement* in the standard of living. To millions of Americans only a generation removed from Europe, and for whom Europe was the point of reference, the comparison between living standards experienced there and then achieved in America seemed to substantiate the idea that America offered an opportunity not available in Europe. Opportunity, in this sense, did not mean mobility.

It is also just possible that, from a historical perspective, there was greater social mobility in America than in Europe in the last decades of the nineteenth and early decades of the twentieth century. America entered into a period of rapid industrialization after the Civil War that lasted until the end of the century. During that period, it was catching up with the major industrial nations of Europe, and this expanison of industrial organization set in motion a tremendous transition in America's class structure, including the rapid development of an expanding middle class.

Whatever the facts about social mobility in America, the belief in mobility and in the right to an opportunity to be mobile is a sufficiently important American value, one that can and has been used as a criticism and an impetus for change and reform. But recent sociological analysis has made us

---

[38] S. M. Miller, "Comparative Social Mobility," *Current Sociology,* 9 (1960), 1–172.

aware that not all Americans strive to be mobile, though we possess as yet no measurement of just what proportion of the population that might be. We do know that they are drawn from the lowest levels of the class structure and disproportionately from the ranks of minority groups. This suggests that those who are the most disadvantaged may be primarily concerned with the day to day struggle to earn a living, and may find in the harsh reality of their existence little hope for aspiring to anything better.

A more interesting sociological problem, however, concerns the response of those who do aspire to mobility but either fail in their efforts, or who at the start lack such a necessary prerequisite as an education to get any consideration in the competitive struggle for individual position. What do people do in a modern society when they believe in mobility but cannot achieve it? One possible response, of course, is to regard oneself as a failure. This means that one continues to believe that the opportunity is there and assumes that not having made the grade, one is lacking in either the ability or the drive to succeed. Such a response is highly self-punishing, and many people hedge at assuming that it was simply a matter of their own deficiencies. An alternative response is to alter one's aspirations by expecting and being satisfied with much less than one once hoped for. An individual lowers his aspiration level to fit the modest gains in status he can realistically accomplish. Or he can modify his belief in the mobility process by insisting that chance plays an important part. The only difference, he says, between himself and a more successful person is a "lucky break."

In an interesting study of automobile workers, the sociologist Eli Chinoy found that they frequently did not expect mobility for themselves, yet did not lose their faith in opportunity in America.[39] As Chinoy reports, although they did not believe that they were going to escape from factory work or move up in the factory, they had strong hopes that their children would be able to rise into middle-class occupations. What they had done was transfer their mobility aspirations from themselves to their children. Whether these expectations for their children were realistic or not, such a transfer enabled them to continue to believe in opportunity in America, even for working people.

Between those who are successful and those who are not, but who find ways of adjusting to it that are not punishing, is a quite different category: those who are mobile but not in the conventionally expected way. "Success" in the American process of mobility generally means mobility within the conventional occupational structure of society. In particular, it means creating and building a business, moving up in the hierarchy of managerial positions in corporations or other large-scale organizations (military, corporate, governmental, or educational), or achieving recognition within a profession. But a movie or

---

[39] Eli Chinoy, *Automobile Workers and the American Dream* (New York: Random House, 1955).

television star, a professional boxing champion, a professional baseball or football star, are successes, too, for they have been mobile, even if not along the conventional routes. A man who has achieved high political office, or who is a successful operating professional politician, is also a success. So, too, is a high ranking labor leader. And can not the same be said for those who rise to the top of the great syndicates of organized crime?

Popular entertainment, professional athletics, politics, labor, and organized crime, then, are each an avenue for career mobility in American society. A successful entertainer or athlete can attain wealth and public fame. Through labor, politics, and organized crime he can attain power. Through popular entertainment, professional athletics, and politics, he may be able to win social acceptance from the more conventionally successful and so ensure middle or upper status for his children. It is difficult for labor leaders to win such acceptance for themselves, but it is possible for them to transfer such middle-class status to their children. The leaders of organized crime find it most difficult of all to win social acceptance for themselves, and difficult but not impossible to do so for their children.

Social mobility through these avenues does not require the usual pre-requisites of education and training, for those who have ability or talent of some kind but lack much formal training, a career in one of these ways may provide success when nothing else would. This fact explains why so many of the successful in these fields come from lower status backgrounds and indeed why so many come from minority groups. Entertainment and athletics are characterized by less discrimination than many other spheres of modern social life. If a Negro boy can box well or play basketball, football, or baseball in professional fashion, his skin color will not keep him from a professional career. Then, too, lower status people provide a large part of the audience for professional athletics and popular entertainment, they also constitute the supporting public for urban political organizations, they are the membership of labor unions and much of the clientele of organized crime. This close association means that many young people of lower status can see the success of a local boy who made it in athletics, in entertainment, in politics, in labor, or in organized crime. It is from among these that they may find relevant models to provide a source of aspiration and hope—and the kindling of ambition to "make it big."

STATUS IN MODERN SOCIETY

Status, according to Max Weber, is concerned with the distribution of honor, and it is to be distinguished from social class, which is based upon the economic structure of society. Though status is not independent of social class, it is a separate phenomenon in the stratification of a society. Class and status are interlinked because status groups rarely include people from a broad range of social classes. The mode of life of a status group is likely to be strongly influenced by the amount of income as well as by the occupation and property ownership of its members.

But the fact that people have the same class position does not put them in the same status groups. In the first place, a status group recognizes who belongs by extending to them prestige and honor, and this is not usually accorded to people merely because of their class position alone. In Yankee City, Warner and his associates found that the highest status group in the community possessed prestige and honor because its members were descendants of the original families who settled the town some three centuries ago. They were no longer the wealthiest families, and they no longer had significant property ownership in the community. But their claim to prestige had not yet been damaged by their loss of economic position. Furthermore, there was an exclusiveness to such a status group that could not be changed. One either was a descendant of the original settlers, or one was not. Also, since the original settlers were of old Yankee stock and were Prostestants, this made it impossible for the more recent immigrant groups and the Catholics to make similar claims for prestige.

The Status of Old Families   Observers of "high society" have long noted that what the French call the *nouveaux riches,* newly rich persons, are not usually accepted by the old established families. Although the *nouveaux riches* may have won the class position of these old families, as defined by income, occupation, and property, they have not been educated to the style of life, and thus may find that they are not accepted. However, their children may be able to claim such acceptance, because they can be educated to the style of life and because, unlike their self-made fathers, they did not have to work themselves up from a lower social level.

In these and other instances of high status groups, we see that they are marked off from others, not only by a higher class position, but by a style of life that has to be learned, often from childhood, in order to develop competence in it.[40] It not only involves such things as private schools, a social debut for young ladies, and vacations spent abroad or at notable resorts, it also means many subtleties of attitude and behavior: correct forms of dress and grooming for varied occasions; familiarity with theater, dance, and art; and a vast range of other small details that make up a complex and distinctive style of life. One characteristic of a status group is the attempt to monopolize all of these

---

[40] See E. Digby Baltzell, *The Philadelphia Gentlemen* (New York: Free Press, 1958); also, Warner and Lunt, *The Social Life of a Modern Community.*

symbols of the style of life and not to initiate into it just everyone who has attained a certain class level.

Education in the United States, and probably to some extent in any industrial society, has long been recognized as an instrument of class mobility. But long before education served such a more democratic function, it was closely related to the exclusiveness of high ranking status groups. The tremendous prestige accorded some private American colleges, especially some on the East coast, arises only in part because they are academically excellent; it also comes from the fact that they have been the preferred educational institutions for some of the nation's traditional high status groups. In some status groups, education at any Ivy League school is practically an essential; it is part of a style of life. In the same manner, such upper-status groups have traditionally avoided public schools and have sent their children to private "prep" schools. Their presumed academic superiority to public schools is as much a rationalization as a reason; at such schools the children of upper status families mingle together, and at the same time are kept away from the more varied group that would ordinarily be found in a public school. In addition to the academic program, then, such schools also teach the behavior and attitude appropriate to high social status.

Clearly enough, then, one function of education can be to train individuals to the style of life of the status group. Where the symbols of status are thus acquired only over long years of training, going back to childhood, they are not easily learned by others and, therefore, serve effectively to close off membership in the status group to all but those who come from already socially accepted families. When such a restriction of membership is possible, a status group may live and marry entirely within itself. Indeed, such groups often place great emphasis on intermarriage, taking great pains to limit the marriage choices of their children. All the exclusiveness of interaction, of course, restricts marriage choices, anyway.

In the discussion to this point, we have emphasized and used examples from groups of high social status. Such groups are frequently in a somewhat better position to monopolize a set of status symbols and restrict their membership to a limited proportion of those of upper class position. But status groups range from the highest level to the lowest, and there are many life-styles that status groups develop and by means of which they confer prestige on individuals.

Glamour: A Status Aggregate The high status of old families has received much sociological and journalistic attention: New York's 400, the proper Bostonians, Philadelphia gentlemen, Yankee City's upper-upper class, and the like. But much less sociological analysis has been given to a relatively newer form of status, the *glamour status* emerging from the varied forms of popular culture in modern society. Particularly the movies and more recently television, and also professional sports, have created elites of glamorous personalities who are better known to the broad mass of Americans than are any other category of influential Americans, including top political and governmental leadership.

Unlike the status groups of old families, glamour status does not refer to a social group in the sociological sense. The individuals do not display a lifestyle inaccessible to others and certainly not one for which they have been trained from childhood. Nor is membership restricted by the recognition extended by the group itself. For the life of glamour, recognition is extended by large publics through the mass media. It is by becoming a glamorous success in the eyes of these publics that earns one status; the recognition or lack of it by others of such status is of little importance. Glamour status is therefore not a status *group* but a status *aggregate*.

Glamour status is rarely achieved by descent. Being the child of a glamorous personality does not seem to offer any particular advantage. Indeed, a successful career in the great world of popular entertainment, including professional athletics, is open to those who have the skills and appeals that attract a box-office public, and race and ethnic status is rarely a barrier. (But this must be qualified: such professional sports as tennis and golf are still difficult for Negroes to get into, and the color line in baseball has only been broken for about two decades.) Unlike the world of business and the professions, the upper levels of the world of glamour are as accessible to Catholics as to Protestants, to Jews as to gentiles, to Italian-Americans as to old Yankee stock, to Negroes as to white.

Furthermore, such status is precarious. If not attained relatively early in one's career, it is unlikely to be attained at all. And age, even middle age, threatens a glamour personality's status, for a fickle public is likely to turn to newer and younger personalities. The life of glamour is more emphatically youth oriented than any other phase of life in modern society.

Community Status   Status is often a local matter, and in small towns, and older, more stable ones, we can observe a series of socially ranked status groups. Warner's study of Yankee City, as well as studies of many other small American communities, such as Elmtown[41] (a Midwestern town of about 6000), and Old City[42] (a Southern town of about 10,000), have given sociologists an excellent picture of how status operates in the small community. Frequently, as in Yankee City, an "upper-upper" group is made up of old residents of considerable wealth or preferred occupations, of particular ethnic

---

[41] August B. Hollingshead, *Elmtown's Youth* (New York: Wiley, 1949).

[42] Allison Davis, Burleigh B. Gardner, and Mary R. Gardner, *Deep South* (Chicago: University of Chicago Press, 1941).

stock (usually old American), and of a particular religion—Protestantism. Other status levels in the community are characterized by different economic levels, by different ethnic origins (descent), by different religious affiliation, and, in each case, by its own life-style.

Religious, Ethnic, and Racial Status   Religion and ethnicity provide criteria not only for status in the community but also in American society. The Jews, for example, are a group whose ancestry and traditions go far back in time; they have a specific identity, and they are more culturally homogeneous than many ethnic groups. At the same time they are subject to discrimination by both Catholics and Protestants. Thus, Jews develop an organizational and community life that parallels that of other middle-class groups. They create their own associations and clubs, their own welfare organizations, indeed, all the organized forms of social life in a typical community. We are not concerned here whether they do so by choice or because they are denied access to other groups. Both reasons, in fact, are present. However, such historically rooted separateness not only gives the Jews a sharp sense of separate identity and status, it also gives others a conception of the Jews as a separate status group.

If Jews have been historically urban and middle class, the immigrant of the last seventy or so years in America has usually been a working-class person. If higher status frequently goes to those who established the community, or at least are long settled there, low status frequently goes to those who are the most recent arrivals in the community, especially if they enter the community at a low economic level. This was usually the case with the European immigrant, especially the great mass of immigrants who came from eastern and southern Europe after 1880. Relatively unskilled at first, largely from rural, peasant backgrounds, speaking little if any English, they clustered in immigrant colonies in America's rapidly growing industrial cities and soon constituted status groups that ranked low in the community.

The relationship of these two status groups (Jews and European immigrants) to social class provides an interesting contrast. The Jew is already a middle-class person but has been confined to certain occupations and industries with that class. Discrimination for the Jew blocks him from equal access to the total range of middle class occupations. For the immigrants, striving for improved social status has meant striving for class mobility, that is, to move from low economic position to a higher one. In the process the mobile ethnic may not only move from working to middle class, he may move out of his original ethnic group.

When we speak of Jews and European immigrants, we have reference to *cultural* criteria for distinguishing one status group from another. Religion and the traditions of the original culture serve to distinguish these groups from the religious and cultural traditions of the earlier settlers and residents. But in the case of the Negro, *racial* criteria for status enter into the issue. Race is a biological factor, and what race means to the scientist is often quite different from what it means to the man in the street. Yet race provides a criterion for status, when, whether scientifically valid or not, the members of a society *evaluate the biological differences in terms of superior or inferior.* This may mean that they may impute to race social differences (such as mental ability or moral character) that are not in fact empirically verifiable by scientific standards. But if people *believe* that such differences exist, they act accordingly; thus, the social consequences are real enough, whether or not the basis for the behavior can be scientifically validated.

When criteria of status are racial, religious, and ethnic, and when those who rank low by such criteria are disesteemed by others and are denied the life-chances accorded others, we have *minority status* and *minority groups* with associated *prejudice* and *discrimination.* America has been struggling with the problems of minority status, but the issue is not peculiar to America; it is a worldwide matter that assumes increasing importance.

Status and Social Chance   In distinguishing between class and status, Max Weber asserted that people are in the same class situation when their ownership of productive property or their occupation, under prevailing market conditions, determined their life-chances. In speaking of status groups, he referred to the distribution of honor accorded those who effect a particular style of life. But status groups also influence the individual's life-chances. Preferred educational opportunity for traditional high status groups, for example, serves not only to train its members to a style of life, but it also opens doors to career opportunities not available to others.

We could cite many examples, but one or two will do. For instance, when a Jewish student finds it more difficult than others do to get accepted into a professional school because of the operation of covert "quotas," then his Jewish status has limited his life-chances despite his substantial middle-class status. When white workers resist the movement of Negroes into semiskilled and skilled jobs hitherto held only by whites, then racial status rather than class works to determine social chances. Whenever the world is divided into "white" jobs and "Negro" jobs, an individual's life-chances are determined, in part at least, by his racial status. Accordingly, in analyzing industrial societies, we find it useful to distinguish between class and status, for they clearly constitute two different bases for the determination of life-chances. Being Negro and being a well-trained professional are, for the individual, two different ways in which his social chances in life may be effectively influenced.

However, in preindustrial societies, where traditional modes of stratification fuse class and status, this distinction may not be relevant. Where there is little mobility, and thus where the same set of families occupies a particular class level from one generation to the next, the social interaction among them develops a commonly shared style of life. Peasants, artisans, merchants, and aristocrats, in a feudal society, not only exist in different class situations, but they also exhibit a style of life common to those in the same class and quite different from other classes. Therefore, class and status sometimes merge into a single pattern of stratification, particularly in those traditional societies where there is little, if any, social mobility. On the other hand, under conditions of relatively rapid social mobility, class and status diverge, and people in the same class situation belong to different status groups. Weber recognized this when he observed:

> When the bases of the acquisition and distribution of goods are relatively stable, stratification by status is favored. Every technological repercussion and economic transformation threatens stratification by status and pushes the class situation into the foreground.[43]

[43] Gerth and Mills, *From Max Weber: Essays in Sociology,* p. 194.

1 2

3

1. Alone in a crowd.
2. Puerto Rican girl in front of New York grocery store.
3. South Carolina gas station rest rooms.
4. Boys near Mobilization for Youth Center in Spanish Harlem, N.Y.
5. South Africa: a special "Keep Off the Grass" sign.
6. A city boy.

4 5

6

MINORITY
GROUPS

11

Of all the patterns of inequality found in human society, none is more controversial today than that which designates some in society to have fewer life-
chances because of race, religion, or national origin. This is not an issue
confined to the United States; rather, the conflict over status and the distribution of life-chances among different racial and ethnic groups has rever-
berated around the world during the past two decades. Despite the fact that
colonial rule, and with it the domination of nonwhites by whites has ended
in most of Asia and Africa, the issue of racism is stronger now than ever.
Racism has become a worldwide issue, associated with the efforts of new
nonwhite nations to develop new ideologies appropriate to their problems.

In the United States, the status of religious, racial and ethnic groups has
been a persistent and difficult issue, of which the status of the Negro has been
the most basic issue. A major social movement concerned with changing now,
not later, the pattern of race relations in American society has been the major
domestic issue during the 1960s. It has generated more social conflict, more
national soul-searching, and more efforts at amelioration and change, than
has any single issue since the labor movement of the 1930s.

MINORITY GROUPS AS A SOCIOLOGICAL PROBLEM

The several sociological problems focused on the minority group constitute
an extension of the problem of social inequality. Racial, ethnic, and religious
groups as minority groups are *status* groups. Status groups, however, are not
independent of class, and the origin of most minority groups is in class situations. All status groups, Weber noted, are intimately related to class situations,
and there can be no understanding of minority groups unless their relation to
the inequalities of life-chances by class situations is also understood. A first
sociological problem, then, has always been to define minority status as one
significant form of social stratification and to recognize its intimate connection to class and power. It is important to emphasize that, for in the United
States much of the sociological and social-psychological literature has stressed
the prejudices of the majority group and the creation of a minority by virtue
of the disesteem in which the minority is held. This tends to define the problem as one in which differentials of prestige create differentials in privilege;
it ignores the possibility that it is differentials in power and privilege that
create differentials in prestige.

For sociologists, the pattern of discrimination in so many areas of social
life, but particularly in education, employment, and housing, has been described in great detail, both as local and as national processes. The concern
for the *structure of discrimination* has given a distinctive sociological focus to

the problem of minority status, for it is in the processes of discrimination that majority-minority relations are established and that minority status comes to mean differentials in life-chances. Following that problem, there is the issue of whether or not a minority group then is differentiated from a majority group by the values and meanings it gives to its way of life—in short, its culture. That ethnic groups possess a culture of their own is unquestioned, for the very definition of an ethnic group includes this idea. But the idea of a minority group culture (or subculture) earns no agreement among sociologists when applied to the life of the Negro in American society.

In the the United States, it is in the area of race relations that change and conflict is most evident now as it has been for some time and as it will probably be for an indefinite future. Race and racism in American society is a source of severe tensions. However, significant changes, including first the emergence of a civil rights movement and out of that a militant black movement constitute what is now most dynamic, changing, and controversial about race relations.

Lastly, the American social-scientific literature on minority problems has been strongly social-psychological, thus consistent with the American outlook. It has taken a long time for sociology to develop a theoretical focus on minority groups in which the concept of prejudice is no longer so preeminent and in which the prejudicial attitudes of individuals are not viewed as the central problem. This theoretical focus defines the problem as the structure of group relations organized around differentials of life-chances defined by racial or ethnic criteria. Such a structure of group relations occurs when a structure of domination becomes a structure of discrimination. All of this is not to say that prejudice is an irrelevant matter; what has been problematic has been determining just what the relevance of prejudice is, and how the existence of prejudice relates to minority status.[1]

MINORITY STATUS

The term *minority* is often used to designate those members of society who cannot participate fully and equally in all phases of social life because of race, religion, or national origin. But the meaning of the term often remains ambiguous and confusing because minority has a quantitative meaning that

[1] For a succinct review of the contemporary sociological approach to the study of minority groups, see Peter I. Rose, *They and We: Racial and Ethnic Relations in the United States* (New York: Random House, 1964). For one of the first efforts to insist upon viewing minority status in a context of social power, see Raymond W. Mack, *Race, Class, and Power* (New York: American Book, 1963).

most readily comes to mind. Many Americans are likely to speak of the white majority because they constitute more than half the population, and speak of Negroes as a minority because they constitute less than half the population. But America is a society with many categories of people, distinguished from one another by economic, occupational, political, religious, and other social differences, and almost all of these categories are but a small minority of the population. To state the issue in this way suggests immediately that such categories as Negro and Jew are minorities for reasons other than number. As a concept, minority must designate something besides the relative proportion a category of people constitute in a population. When we speak of minority groups and minority rights, we have reference to problems of *social status* and only incidently and secondarily to an issue of size and number.

Minority Status and Social Power The pattern of majority-minority relations in any society is not to be explained primarily in terms of some set of prevailing prejudices; rather, minority status can be understood only as one kind of social inequality, and this is a structural arrangement that is sustained by more than just attitudes. Indeed, the domination of a minority group by a majority group cannot occur except through the exercise of *social power*. To be a majority group and to confine a minority group to a subordinate position within the social structure requires the majority group to have the instruments and mechanisms of power necessary to sustain its dominant position. To discriminate in employment requires that the majority group have control over the distribution of jobs. To discriminate in education requires that the majority group control the educational process.

It is this process of discrimination that creates a minority group. The very act of discriminating—in jobs, housing, income, social services, and education— constitutes the social process by which a racial or ethnic group is converted into a minority group. The mere holding of prejudicial attitudes by one group toward another does not make of the recipient group a minority; such a situation merely indicates the existence of group hostility. Thus, Negroes develop attitudes of resentment and hostility toward whites, but whites do not become a minority because of this.

Given such a pattern of relationships as acts of discrimination bring about, it is understandable that the majority group will possess a set of *cognitive* and *affective* states that support the relationships between the two groups. It will possess, first of all, a set of beliefs that will validate its own majority status as well as the minority status of the other group. Its own history, the two different cultural experiences of the groups, and group stereotypes that assert the superiority of the dominant group, will all be utilized by the majority to create a set of viable cultural myths that serve to rationalize their dominant status. This is more than prejudice; rather, it is a complex cultural pattern of beliefs, attitudes, and expectations that are erected to provide justification. This cultural pattern not only defines the group that is the object of discrimination; it also defines the majority group to itself. A flattering self-image, a positive self-stereotype, an attribution of positive and desirable characteristics to itself, is also part of the cultural process. Thus, to make the issue all the more difficult, one of the consequences of the whole process is that the majority group becomes committed to cultural myths of its own superiority, which can then be seriously threatened by any action to lessen discrimination.

If one of the consequences of the fact of being majority is a highly positive self-image, one of the consequences of being minority is to experience a negative self-image. The imposition of minority status on a group means that they cannot fully escape the definitions and viewpoints imposed on them by the majority group. But the psychological injury done to the process of personality-development for a minority group is only compounded by the manner in which discrimination serves to validate the claims of inferiority of the minority made by the majority. When a minority group is denied equal educational opportunity, on the grounds that they are intellectually inferior, then this poorer education will result in their doing poorer work as measured by various forms of academic achievement, and even in their scoring lower, on the average, on IQ tests, since IQ scores are not at all independent of cultural achievement. This lower academic performance and lower average IQ scores will then be used as evidence of less ability. In short, what occurs here is what Robert Merton once called the "self-fulfilling prophecy."[2] The majority group asserts that the minority group is inferior and incapable of achievement, then acts in a discriminatory fashion to ensure that such inferior performance will be the outcome. (This is not to say that they consciously intended it to be this way, or even are aware of the workings of the self-fulfilling prophecy.)

Types of Minority Groups   What are the types of groups that most frequently become organized into majority-minority relations? An examination of the historical record tells us that dominant social groups have defined minority groups in terms of a very few criteria, of which the important ones have been *racial, ethnic,* and *religious.* But a majority group cannot discriminate against a minority group unless it can distinguish that group from other groups, including its own. Thus, the minority group must be identifiable in some highly visible way.

Race   The most obvious case of a physically visible minority is that of race. Yet, even this is not perfectly so. In those instances, which always occur in

[2] Robert Merton, "The Self-Fulfilling Prophecy," *The Antioch Review,* 8 (Summer, 1948), 192–210.

multiracial societies, where some people are racially mixed, they may very well look so much like a member of the majority group that they cannot easily, or even at all, be recognized as a member of the minority group. Thus, there are American Negroes who cannot be distinguished from whites. The Nazis could not tell Jews apart from other Germans, so they required them to wear a Star of David.

Of course, these racially mixed people may even be biologically more of the majority than of the minority group. But what is biologically the case is not necessarily socially the case. In any society in which the majority group institutionalizes and legalizes majority-minority relations by racial criteria, it provides some social and legal definition of where the biologically in-between ones belong. Usually, it relegates them to the minority group. It does so because it believes in genetic differences, and so from its perspective a mulatto or half-caste is still inferior, for his blood carries the "contaminated" blood of the inferior people. The Nazis in Germany defined as Jewish anyone who had even one Jewish grandparent; similar definitions have been applied by whites in defining who is a Negro.

Ethnic Groups   Ethnic groups are visible only, if at all, by *cultural* rather than racial criteria. This means that their cultural origins are quite different from that of the majority group. For example, the historically significant ethnic groups in America have been those nineteenth and early twentieth century immigrant groups from Europe, particularly those from eastern and southern Europe, who were visibly different by virtue of their cultural patterns and life-styles.[3] They spoke a language other than English, they dressed differently, and their customs and ways of life contrasted sharply with the customs and life-styles in America. When they clustered together in ethnic ghettos, they maintained for several generations a life style that made them culturally visible. Even when their use of English, as in the next or later generations, was not noticeably different, their names were identifiably ethnic, whether Irish, Polish, or Italian. Indeed, last names as identifying ethnic status has remained a significant factor, even when speech and other identifiable characteristics no longer make people so visibly different.

The history of the ethnic minorities in American society has been one of assimilation and acculturation, thus, the gradual loss of group identity.[4] The

---

[3] A Pulitzer Prize-winning history of these immigrants to American society, including an excellent study of the development of ethnic communities, is Oscar Handlin, *The Uprooted* (Boston: Little, Brown, 1951).

[4] The best discussion of assimilation in the sociological literature is to be found in Milton M. Gordon, *Assimilation in American Life: The Role of Race, Religion, and National Origins* (New York: Oxford, 1964), especially Chapters 3 through 6.

idea of America as a "melting pot" has long had strong support as a major value orientation in this society, with the goal of gradual absorption of varied ethnic groups into the major American cultural pattern. What has been a goal to many has also seemed in fact to be the actual historical process: as the old ghettos disappeared and the younger generations lost much, if not all, of their ethnic identification. The rapid decline of the numbers and proportion of foreign-born, as recorded in the United States census, constitutes one kind of significant datum about the disappearance of ethnic groups in America. But sociologists may have been too ready to write off ethnic groups as no longer a significant part of American social life. Nathan Glazer and Daniel Moynihan studied ethnic groups in New York City and came to the conclusion that they were very much "alive" yet, that an identification with ethnic groups was still quite meaningful to many, and that ethnic groups were significant units of the political structure of New York City.[5]

However, this fact does not necessarily mean that these ethnic groups are any longer minority groups. Certainly, Americans of Polish and Italian descent no longer face the kind of discriminations that were often met by the first generations of their groups. Although not all discrimination may have disappeared, it is no longer the significant element it once was. Nonetheless, a certain sensitivity to the former minority status remains with most ethnic groups—witness the sensitivity of Italians to references to gangsters and organized crime.

New Ethnic Groups   If older ethnic groups seem to be less visible than they once were, new ones continue to emerge in American society. The Puerto Ricans in New York City[6] and Mexicans in Los Angeles are two such examples. Here are two groups that are both culturally and racially distinct from the main Anglo-Saxon patterns of American origin. In Britain, immigrants from the British West Indies, who are now British citizens, constitute a new racial minority that has brought Britain all the problems of urban racial tension that the migration to Northern cities by Negroes has brought American society.

It seems to be the nature of the social processes of migration, settlement, gradual assimilation, and then social mobility, that minorities enter a society at the lower levels of the class structure and in time find the opportunity to

[5] See Nathan Glazer and Daniel Moynihan, *Beyond the Melting Pot* (Cambridge, Mass.: The M.I.T. Press and Harvard University Press, 1963).

[6] On Puerto Ricans in New York City, see Oscar Handlin, *The Newcomers: Negroes and Puerto Ricans in a Changing Metropolis* (Cambridge, Mass.: Harvard University Press, 1959). For a perceptive journalistic description of Spanish Harlem, see Dan Wakefield, *Island in the City* (Boston: Houghton Mifflin, 1957).

move upward. This creates the need for others to fill these lower class positions, and opens the way for new migrant sources. In the United States, the movement from the rural South to the urban North has been characteristic of both Negroes and whites. Most attention has been given to Negroes, but the movement of whites has also created what might be regarded as something close to a minority group when such rural whites, lacking formal education and bringing a rural, mountain-bred life-style inappropriate to urban life, find themselves labeled "hillbillies" and treated in discriminatory fashion.

Religious Minorities   In the long history of man, the tensions among religious groups and the persecution by the religiously dominant of other religions has been a prominent issue. In the United States the division between Christians and Jews and the Christian division between Protestants and Catholics has frequently led to relations of majority and minority. The settlement of New England by Protestants and their clear numerical domination in the early days of the young republic led most nineteenth century Americans to believe that America was a Protestant country. Certainly, before the Civil War Catholics experienced not merely discrimination, but outright violence and persecution.[7] Anti-Catholicism was a major issue in the presidential elections of the 1840s, and the Know-Nothings of that day made religious prejudice a politically viable issue.

Catholicism in the middle of the nineteenth century, however, was the faith of only a small proportion of Americans. But in the great wave of immigration from eastern and southern Europe in the 1880s, millions of Catholics entered the country. They became so much more numerous that in some of the larger cities, such as Boston, they became the numerical majority. Nonetheless Catholics were not a clear-cut group of their own in the period from the 1890s to the 1930s; instead, they merged with ethnicity and class. Since the majority of the newer ethnics were Catholic, and since they were also largely urban working class, the Catholic Church in America during this period was primarily a church of working-class immigrants. The result was a minority status in American society that was an historical blend of ethnicity, class, and religion.

Since the 1930s, this pattern has been undergoing change. Social mobility has brought a decline of ethnic identification and of cohesive ethnic communities and a process of movement into the middle class. With it has come a considerable diminution of religious discrimination for Catholics. The election in 1960 of John F. Kennedy to the presidency of the United States marked an end of significantly effective anti-Catholic political discrimination in the national politics of American society.

[7] See John Tracy Ellis, *American Catholicism* (Chicago: University of Chicago Press, 1956).

The Jewish Minority No discussion of minority groups would be complete without reference to the Jewish group.[8] The Jews are one of the West's more persistent minority groups. They have existed for centuries in various societies, taking on some of the characteristics of the host society, yet always remaining something of a group apart as much by choice as by the desires of the dominant group.

Although Jews are indissolubly linked to Christians by a common religion tradition from Jesus Christ back to the Old Testament prophets, they are more than simply a religious group. They have maintained over centuries a culture that is rich and living, which has sustained them through the vicissitudes of mistreatment and persecution. In Europe, the Jews historically performed occupational functions of an urban kind, and their presence in cities was often tolerated only on condition that they live separately. Frequently this meant in a walled-off part of the city—this was what *ghetto* first meant.[9] If the ghetto was segregation enforced by gentiles, it was also a form of protection; Jews were safe from molestation behind its walls. In smaller towns and cities of Eastern Europe, Jews were often the target of violent actions, the scapegoats of others' class and group frustrations, and were often literally driven out and forced to move on. These *pogroms* were responsible for the emigration of Russian Jews to the United States in the nineteenth century.

Nothing in human experience testifies more emphatically to the evil that men can do to one another in the name of group superiority than what the Nazis did to the Jews in Europe. During the 1930s many Jews were put into concentration camps and all others were forced to wear the Star of David as an insignia of inferiority (and identification). Then during the war came the frightful gas chambers and the almost total extermination of the German Jewish community. Not even the attainment of a Jewish homeland—the state of Israel—after centuries of striving could diminish the horror for Jewish people of this most atrocious event in their long history of suffering.

What testifies to the particular nature of the Jews as an ethnic minority is their refusal to give up their identity; that is, their disinclination to assimilate and so their persistent efforts to maintain the integrity of Jewish culture and the Jewish group. The survival of Jews as a human group after centuries of persecution and mistreatment speaks to their belief in their own existence. They have always taken a position in favor, not of assimilation, but of *pluralism*—a state of society in which culturally distinct groups can maintain their

[8] For a study of Jews in American society, see Nathan Glazer, *American Judaism* (Chicago: University of Chicago Press, 1957); also Marshall Sklare, ed., *The Jews: Social Patterns of an American Group* (New York: Free Press, 1958).

[9] For an understanding of the ghetto in its origins, and a detailed study of the Chicago ghetto of the 1920s, see Louis Wirth, *The Ghetto* (Chicago: University of Chicago Press, 1928).

identity and pursue their own interests without suffering for their separateness by discrimination. It is to be understood that this is an ideal, not a description of social reality.

RACE AND RACISM

Throughout history minority status has only sometimes been racial in character, but race has become strikingly salient in the world in the twentieth century. The collapse of European colonialism has ended white domination of nonwhite peoples in Africa and Asia. The resulting change has produced charges of *white racism* directed at Europeans because of their treatment of the nonwhites. This is also frequently heard in the United States in reference to domestic Negro-white relations. Although it is clear that there has been a Western racism, racism is not an invention of Western peoples. It has appeared from time to time elsewhere, even in Africa prior to the coming of the white man. Nonetheless, there is a pattern of racism peculiar to the Western world that has been particularly important over the past century and has been the most pervasive and powerful racist ideology the world has apparently seen. Although its roots go back to the slave trade, according to Pierre L. van den Berghe, Western racism only emerged as a distinct ideology in about the 1830s and 1840s and reached its peak between 1880 and 1920.[10] It has since entered a period of decline, but it remains alive and cannot be expected to be gone for still three or four more decades.

The emergence of Western racism, says van den Berghe, requires the presence of racially distinct groups, different enough so that at least some of their members can be readily classifiable.[11] But these visible group differences must overlap with dissimilarities in status and culture and a situation of established inequality. These conditions most likely occur when groups come into contact through migration, when one group invades another people's territory and enslaves them, or when one group "imports" another as slaves or as an indentured alien group. Yet, as van den Berghe points out, even though these may be situations of rigid stratification and even of brutal treatment of one group by another, they do not always produce racism. The prevailing ideology may be a highly ethnocentric one, proclaiming the cultural superiority of the dominant group, still a racist rationalization may not emerge. The efficient causes of Western racism, van den Berghe argues were: (1) its congruence with capitalist exploitation of the New World and of colo-

---

[10] Pierre L. van den Berghe, *Race and Racism: A Comparative Perspective* (Wiley, 1967), p. 15.

[11] This paragraph draws from van den Berghe, pp. 13–18.

nial expansion in Africa, where slavery had to be rationalized; (2) its congruence with a dominant form of Darwinism, which made radical ideas seem scientific; and, paradoxically, (3) the Enlightenment ideas of freedom and equality; these ideas could only be violated (and they were) to justify slavery if some distinction were drawn between men and submen. When the latter occurs, there emerges what van den Berghe calls *Herrenvolk* democracies, which are democratic for the master race but tyrannical for the subordinate race.

Types of Race Relations   When social stratification is by racial criteria rather than cultural criteria, the system is more rigid and lacks the flexibility that would be present if cultural criteria prevailed. Cultural criteria can be learned, and individuals can then move from one group to another, but race can be the basis for a rigid system of ascriptive status. However, this requires that the visible racial differences be defined as constituting races of unequal attributes. As van den Berghe says, we can speak of racism only "when group differences in physical traits are considered a determinant of social behavior and moral or intellectual qualities."[12] The pattern of race relations is always unique to some extent to each society, reflecting both its history and its particular culture. But that does not spare us the necessary task of discovering some commonalities among the many societies in which two (or even more) major racial groupings have functioned in some kind of a dominant-subordinate relationship. We follow van den Berghe at this point in finding it a useful distinction between *paternalistic* and *competitive* types.[13]

Paternalistic Race Relations   The paternalistic type of race relations is characteristic of complex but preindustrial societies in which an agriculture economy requires a large supply of field hands who are utilized as forced labor or even as slaves. There is a wide gulf between two racial castes in this system, they live very different and very unequal lives, even though they live in fairly close intimacy. The dominant racial group is often but a small numerical minority, which develops an explicitly defined master-servant type of relationship. This is rationalized by an ideology that is not one of racial hatred or hostility but is rather a benevolent despotism (except in the face of rebellions) —an ideology that claims a paternal care and responsibility for a subordinate group defined "as childish, immature, irresponsible, exuberant, improvident, fun-loving, good humored, and happy-go-lucky; in short, as inferior but lovable as long as they stay in 'their place.' "[14] The antebellum United States

[12] van den Berghe, p. 23.
[13] van den Berghe, pp. 25–34.
[14] van den Berghe, p. 27.

is one of a number of societies in which such paternalistic race relations have prevailed; it was also to be found in such preabolition regimes in northeast Brazil, the Western Cape Province of South Africa, and the West Indies; in colonial regimes using forced labor, and in the *encomienda* system in Spanish America.

Competitive Race Relations   The contrasting pattern of competitive race relations occurs in industrial, urban societies where the dominant group is more likely to be a majority, or at least a large minority, and where the *class* differences of the industrial society enter into the contrast between the castes, in that there is a *greater* range of income, occupation, and education within each caste than there is between the castes. The caste etiquette of the master-servant relations break down, and it is replaced by competition between the subordinate group and the working class of the dominant group. New efforts at social distance produce physical segregation in several forms, including the urban ghetto. The ideology changes also, its paternalistic view is replaced by one in which hatred replaces condescension.

Conflict is endemic in such a system, for it is an effort to have racial castes in an otherwise open class system that is also free and democratic. Industrialism tends to cut across racial lines to create political and economic interdependence, but the racial process itself separates, producing a *segmentation without differentiation*, namely, a duplication of communities and institutions. These two processes then pull in opposite directions and are the source of some of the major strains and tensions in such societies.

The United States and South Africa have been the two large *Herrenvolk* democracies in which this competitive pattern of race relations has prevailed, and their development showed much similarity until about the time of World War II. In South Africa in 1948 the Afrikaner Nationalists came to power and instituted a system of severe and repressive *apartheid* (separation), moving back to a situation of even less rights and less opportunities for racial minorities. In contrast, the United States moved through a process of change in which programs for increasing desegregation, integration, and expanding civil rights, under white leadership, made definite if not large gains. The Supreme Court decision of 1954 ended the constitutionality of segregation in American society. Although its enforcement in more than token terms was slow to come, the expectations it created, when not soon fulfilled, were a substantial factor in the Southern civil rights movement that developed after 1960.[15]

From 1960 through 1965 a major southern-based civil rights movement

[15] For a good review of the events of the late 1950s and early 1960s, see Louis E. Lomax, *The Negro Revolt* (New York: New American Library, 1963).

undertook significant forms of demonstrations against the prevailing pattern of race relations in the South. The basic pattern was nonviolence, and the major leadership came from the Reverend Martin Luther King. But a new and militant generation of very young activists pressed for the political organization of rural Negroes. This new generation emerged from these years of struggle unconvinced that nonviolence was necessarily the best way to carry on the cause or that active white leadership was of any value; indeed, the latter became defined as a deficit in the struggle for Negro freedom and equality. However well-meaning, white leadership was viewed as inhibiting the development of indigenous Negro organization and leadership.

From Protest to Black Power   The first cries of *black power* from young leaders in the South created only confusion and led to varying interpretations of what was meant. Only after some time and further development of civil rights militancy did it become apparent that a new phase of race relations in American society has opened up. For one thing, a new black leadership became painfully aware of the fact that little substantial gain in economic status had been achieved by Negroes since World War II, that the income gap had widened, and that both school and residential segregation had increased, not decreased. Furthermore, any real gains in social power seemed illusory; power still seemed to rest with whites. In response to this, a new assertion of militant leadership was not simply more militant; instead, it reoriented civil rights activity to a new set of goals.

A major component of the new pattern was an emergent *black consciousness,* a new awareness of the specific and special interests, values, and destiny of black Americans, and a new consciousness of and pride in their own racial nature.[16] This is a major social-psychological and cultural transformation for the American Negro. Much of the social scientific literature of the preceding several decades had emphasized the psychological injury sustained by the Negro by virtue of discrimination and segregation, and of being socialized into the values of the dominant group. It was argued that the Negro could not avoid feeling that white was better than black, thus always feeling ashamed of his color. The result was an ambivalence in self-perception, a combination of both self-regard and self-hate. An inferior social status, it was argued, always left a *mark of oppression.*[17] But now black Americans have created a new conscious pride in race, a sense of personal and group worthiness, and

---

[16] For a discussion of this by a thoughtful leader of the new movement, see Nathan Wright, Jr., *Black Power and Urban Unrest* (New York: Hawthorn, 1967).

[17] See Abram Kardiner and Lionel Ovesey, *The Mark of Oppression* (New York: Norton, 1951).

they have discovered an identity not thought possible only a few short years ago. Yet, there is reason to believe that the resources for personal dignity and group pride have always been there; what was required was a structural context for its emergence from the ghetto into the open, and the opportunity for its development and maturity.[18]

One major component of this transformation was a rejection of the former goal of integration, for if integration meant giving up one's newfound racial identity, the new black American wanted none of it. It was not integration that was the concern now, but desegregation, where this meant a blockage to opportunity. This in turn, however, did not mean any enforced integration. One of the new black spokesmen, Nathan Wright, Jr., said: "Negroes do not need the presence of white people either to give them worth or to learn."[19] So, just thirteen years after the Supreme Court decided that segregated schools harmed Negro children, a new leadership proclaims that Negroes do not need "the presence of whites" in order to learn.

But the transformation of the Negro into a self-conscious and prideful black American (still far from completed) is not the only significant change. On the group level, the recognition of the need to build a *black community* complements the recognized need to be self-respecting individuals. The term, black community, is now a new and compelling symbol with variants of meaning. But there is one thing that is basic: the enlarged capacity of Negroes for shared collective action toward determining their own destiny. Thus, black community is not a place but a communal sense of belonging together, and this means all blacks, not just those in the ghetto. It means a collective base for community action and a basis for power to change the pattern of white domination. So, black community as a term is both symbolic of new hopes and aspirations and of new group pride. Pragmatically it is a call to developing a capacity to act together so that Negroes can decide their own destiny.

The emergence of a new social movement, then, has had three components: a black consciousness; a black community; and a militant black leadership seeking somewhat different goals. But like any social movement, it is not neat and consistent; there is some confusion over goals, both short-run and long-run. In particular, there is a range of positions from the black revolutionary one that has given up on America, to the militant black community approach that, for all its bitter criticism, has not given up on America. (These variant ideological positions of the contemporary movement will be explored in Chapter 21, Social Movements and Ideologies.)

[18] See Robert Coles, "It's the Same, but It's Different," in Talcott Parsons and Kenneth Clark, eds., *The Negro American* (Boston: Houghton Mifflin, 1966).
[19] Nathan Wright, Jr., *Black Power and Urban Unrest*, p. 131.

The crux of minority status is the capacity of one group to impose discrimination upon another. Discrimination, in turn, is that behavior which denies to some people opportunities for status and reward solely because of their belonging to a particular group or category of people, usually a racial or ethnic one. Discrimination is thus differential treatment; some categories of people are treated by a different set of criteria than are others. For example, a man may be accepted as qualified for a job if he has the necessary training, experience, and skill. If he is disqualified, however, because of his race, this is discrimination. The color of his skin is not a formal qualification for a job; if people are to succeed on their merit, skin color would not be applied as a qualification. This suggests that usually certain institutionalized norms are invoked in an open-class society, such as extending occupational opportunity to a person on the basis of merit or ability. Discrimination exists when these norms are violated.

Some social scientists have argued that we can define discrimination as invoking *irrelevant* criteria. They are irrelevant because they have nothing to do with the capacity of the person to qualify for the opportunity. Occupational training and experience are relevant criteria for a job, as is academic performance for admission to college. These are the kind of criteria by which one would distinguish between the qualified and the unqualified. All those who qualify by such criteria could normally be expected to perform in a satisfactory manner. A man's religion or skin color is irrelevant when determining the criteria by which such opportunities can be rationally allotted. It neither increases nor decreases the probability of his being able to perform satisfactorily.

Segregation   Segregation occurs when the races are physically and socially separated in the use of the services and institutional facilities of the community. It may constitute separate seating on trains or buses, separate waiting rooms in bus and train stations, separate dining facilities, separate recreational facilities, such as parks, golf courses, and swimming pools, separate churches, separate schools, separate seating areas in theaters and auditoriums, and separate residential areas.

Segregation reduces contact and association between the races. Accordingly, it is likely to be most rigidly maintained in dining and traveling, in recreational facilities, as well as in churches and schools. These are the occasions where social contact, if it were to occur, would be on an equal basis; that is, the social roles involved in interaction in these situations would not be likely to place people in superordinate and subordinate positions. In turn, segregation is less obviously characteristic of economic situations. When Negroes are employed as domestics by white families, or when they are employed as workers in various kinds of business firms, a strict and rigid separation of races cannot be practiced. But the interaction that does occur can be in a superordinate-subordinate relationship. The situation of white employer or supervisor and Negro employee does not encourage social intimacy or an equality of interaction.

In the Republic of South Africa segregation is carried out as a matter of national policy, more thoroughly and consistently than anywhere in the United States. The policy of *apartheid* has been followed since 1948. As national policy, it reflects the religious and social ideas of the Boers, white Europeans of Dutch descent who settled in South Africa some three centuries ago, and it calls for the most rigid segregation of races that is feasible.

Just how rigid a segregation is feasible in a modern society is a sociologically moot point, and apartheid, as a national policy, has provided South Africa with numerous difficulties. In the first place, the African Negroes have at times strenuously resisted, sometimes violently, the attempts to deprive them of any freedom of movement, particularly the requirement to have a kind of passport as a basis for traveling in towns and to and from jobs. Secondly, by making the movement of Negroes less free and by isolating their residence on the very edge of the city, the functioning of the economic system has been rendered less efficient. And the use of African Negroes as a source of cheap labor places definite limits on the extent of apartheid.

While South Africa struggles with the difficulties of apartheid, the official policy in the United States of America has increasingly become one of desegregation, that is, the removal of segregated practices. Since segregation has been largely, though not entirely, legally established in the southern states, it is there that the impact of desegregation has been felt. The significant legal act against segregation was the Supreme Court decision (*Brown v. Board of Education of Topeka*) of 1954. This historic decision ruled unconstitutional the whole involved legal and social structure of public school segregation that has been carefully erected in the South after the Civil War, and which had been legitimized by the Supreme Court in 1896, in the case of *Plessy v. Ferguson.* That decision had established the principle that "separate but equal" facilities were not a violation of civil rights. In practice, it is difficult to ensure that separate facilities will be equal, even when such is intended. But over time many southern states did not seem to manifest any such intention, and inequalities in such basic facilities as schooling developed and continued as established practice.

After World War II, many southern leaders anticipated that the South would be attacked in the federal courts for the failure to maintain equality among separate facilities, and some cases before the Supreme Court in the late forties and early fifties did hinge on just such a matter. But in the 1954

decision, the Supreme Court took the position that separate facilities are unequal by their very nature, that the very act of separating school children is
to imply that some are superior to others, and thus not to be mixed. It is
important to note that the decision referred to public schools, supported by
public funds; and in subsequent decisions, the Supreme Court has ruled that
other public, tax-supported facilities also cannot be separated by race: parks,
beaches, swimming pools, and golf courses fall in this category. By the same
token, the decision does not apply to any private facilities. The import of the
Supreme Court decision is that segregation is a form of discrimination. As
such, it is held to be a violation of civil rights when it involves the use of
tax-supported facilities or when it has to do with practices guaranteed as rights
in the Constitution.

The Forms of Discrimination   Discrimination can and does take many forms,
but there are a few modes of discrimination that are significant, even crucial,
because the entire structural arrangement of majority-minority relations depend upon them. They are the key to the advantages and domination which
discrimination gives to the majority. In the same manner, they are definitive
of the negatively privileged status of the minority group.

Employment   Discrimination in jobs is primary; by such means a minority
group is denied equal opportunity for social mobility. The generally superior
economic status of whites, or gentiles, or Protestants, is buttressed by practicing discrimination in employment. In this manner, Negroes in America
have remained largely a lower class people, and Jews, who are urban and
middle class, have found it difficult to move from the older urban occupations to the newer middle-class skills and forms of employment.

In America, as in any industrial society, the kind of job or work one does
is an important focus for social status. To discriminate against a group in
the allocation of jobs and work opportunities is to deny to them an opportunity
to share in the "American dream," the belief in the chance to improve their
lot in life. For the American Negro this denial of equal opportunity in the
economic order is an embittering reality that permeates every facet of his
life. It undercuts ambition, for why be ambitious when opportunity is limited?
It subverts an interest in education, and Negro adolescents make up a disproportionately high proportion of high school "drop outs." And it corrupts
conventional moral values, for these are identified with respectable social
status; but if attaining such a status is severely inhibited by economic discrimination, then the related moral values have less meaning.

Education   Discrimination in schooling has taken the direct and obvious
form of segregated schools in the South, where Negro schools are less well supported and qualitatively inferior. In the North, differences in educational

quality for Negroes and whites is not legally supported or even official policy, but it is nonetheless a reality. Schools become predominantly Negro because they are located in Negro residential areas, and thus segregation in schooling follows segregation in housing. When such schools prove to be inferior to others, it is difficult to demonstrate this to be a matter of deliberate discrimination; rather, it seems to be an unintended consequence of the whole larger pattern of discrimination in society. Its inferiority may be a consequence of (1) the subverted academic ambition referred to above; (2) the large number of Negro children whose early schooling was in the rural South; or (3) the difficulty that white, middle-class teachers have in stimulating an academic interest in Negro lower-class children (and frequently in lower-class white children as well). Beyond the elementary and high school level, discrimination in schooling may take more covert and subtle forms. An older controversial issue was the existence of a *quota* system, by which members of minority groups are granted admission to colleges and universities, particularly professional schools, but were kept to a certain number. However, the low proportion of Negroes in major colleges and universities is the result of their earlier educational disadvantages, which prevents most of them from qualifying.

Politics Discrimination in political activity has meant an effort to limit the participation of a minority group in the political process, first in voting, and second in holding political office. Of all minority groups, it is the Negro who has experienced the most persistent efforts to deny him the opportunity to exercise his right to the franchise. Such denial was not usually experienced by the European immigrant, even though, as an alien, he had to go through the involved process of becoming a naturalized citizen before he could qualify as a voter. Nonetheless this attainment of citizenship was encouraged rather than hindered by the political leadership of Northern cities, for the low income urban immigrant was one major source of support for the political machines that governed these cities.

To prevent Negroes from voting, a wide range of techniques have been used. The poll tax has put a financial premium on voting, thus discouraging the poor, both white and Negro. A more sophisticated technique has been to set up a literacy requirement, or a requirement to demonstrate some familiarity with the Constitution and the American system of government. White election officials could then fail Negroes, even educated ones, while passing semi-educated poor whites. Recent civil rights legislation has succeeded in reducing this practice.

Denial of political rights to a minority is a denial of political power. As long as free elections exist, minority groups can translate their grievances and demands into political goals. Nor do they need to possess greater numbers to do so. Rather, they can make the difference in otherwise close elections, providing the margin by which one party or the other, one candidate or the other, wins. Given freedom to vote, therefore, a minority group can mobilize its members behind a determined leadership and learn to exercise genuine political power. The elimination of other forms of discrimination—jobs, schooling, housing—can then become significant goals for which such political power is effectively exercised.

Discrimination in jobs, in schooling, and in political rights have all been the object of national attention from time to time. Discrimination in jobs received particular attention in the 1940s, both during and after World War II, when there was much concern with the possibilities of fair employment legislation at the local and state level. Discrimination in schooling has been a primary issue since the 1950s, particularly after the 1954 Supreme Court decision. In the late 1950s, the discussions in Congress preceding civil rights legislation, and the establishment of a Federal Civil Rights Commission, has once more given political rights national attention. In fact, Congressional legislation and vigorous action by the Department of Justice has sharply increased Negro voting. As a consequence, a few Negroes have already won political office in Southern states.

Housing Discrimination in housing is primarily a matter of segregation. The restriction of the Negro to residential areas marked off for him, and his exclusion from most of the residential areas of the entire community, particularly the better ones, is a pattern of segregation not legitimized by law. Nonetheless it is supported in effective practice by realtors, home financing institutions, property owners associations, and the majority of white home-owners and residents.

The rapid movement to the suburbs in recent years has been predominantly a white movement; Negroes have rarely had an opportunity for suburban housing. The result has been twofold. First, the large suburban ring that has grown up around the central city, sometimes exceeding it in population, has been a new white line of resistance to Negro movement, creating behind it a pattern of white suburban communities each relatively homogeneous in economic status. The once pervasive and extensive middle-class residential area of the city, from which immigrants, Negroes, and the lower class were effectively barred, has in effect been transferred to the suburbs. Secondly, the greater the white flight to the suburbs, the wider the economic array of housing available to Negroes in the central city, reducing to some extent the intense pressure on a limited supply of housing that once was so characteristic of the Negro ghettos. In short, the boundaries of the old Negro ghetto have been burst, and middle income Negroes in particular have found it possible to locate housing commensurate with their class status. As Negroes have moved rapidly into once white neighborhoods, the whites, who only a few years ago lived miles away from Negroes, now find them only blocks away. Furthermore, they learn that Negro children attend the same school their own children do. Frequently, this accelerates the white movement to suburbia.

However the movement of Negroes beyond the boundaries of established ghettos has proceeded differently in different cities, and some cities, such as Chicago, reveal a much higher degree of racial segregation than do others. Data from the 1960 census reveal the following proportion of Negroes in each of these cities who live in census tracts where more than 90 percent are also Negro—it is thus a measure of concentration and so of segregation:[20]

Chicago	65.6
Baltimore	56.8
St. Louis	43.9
Philadelphia	39.2
Detroit	29.1
Los Angeles	20.5

The significance of discrimination in housing lies in the particular urban meaning of neighborhood shared by its residents. Neighborhood is no longer a small and closely integrated area of homogeneous neighbors; rather, it is a larger residential area of the city, in which one shares residence with others who are presumably the same kind of people. More importantly, it is the location of family life and a major locus for the interaction of children. Here they find their peers with whom they share socialization into the culture. Thus, the neighborhood is a social setting for family life, and a context in which children share significant experiences. As a consequence some of the strongest efforts to segregate have occurred along residential patterns.

White middle and upper-middle-class neighborhoods in any American city are highly preferred residential areas. They are generally newer (there are exceptions to this), with better housing, aesthetically more pleasing, and generally better serviced. They are further from industry, less crowded, with less traffic, and altogether possess more of the desirable attributes people seek in housing. These preferred residential areas generally reflect the economic patterns of the community; they are available to those who can afford to purchase or rent property in them. But discrimination precludes Negroes, even affluent ones, from sharing in this preferred residential pattern. Thus, many middle-class Negroes may find it difficult to get very far away from the slums, and thus also difficult to get their children into the better public schools. (School administrators deny that there are better or worse public schools in the same system, but both Negro and white parents know better, or else they would be less concerned with the problem of pupil assignment.)

[20] Source: U.S. Bureau of the Census, *U.S. Census of Population: 1960*, Vol. I.

THE MINORITY SUBCULTURE

Any minority group sustains a set of experiences that has considerable influence on its collective viewpoint toward the world. After all, it views the world from the perspective of disadvantage, discrimination, and expressions of prejudice. It constantly experiences rebuff and rejection, and its self-esteem is persistently threatened by its interaction with the majority. There are a number of consequences of this. One is that the selective and limited participation of the minority group in the majority-dominated society results in a particularly selective socialization (of the minority group) to the values and perspectives of the dominant culture. Where discrimination is effective against social mobility, for example, a minority group is not going to take seriously such a majority idea as "hard work and ability will bring success." Indeed, a minority group is likely to protect itself from such ideas by withdrawing from the success mythology that works so effectively to provide mobility aspirations and achievement-motivations for the dominant group. The psychic pain that discrimination brings, as well as outright insult and ego-injury, leads to selective withdrawal from numerous common institutional involvements and commitments by the minority. This means a very selective pattern of social experience within the society, with a consequence for the social outlook and social values of the group.

A minority group learns to adapt itself to the social situations which the majority group controls. They learn those behavioral patterns that the majority group demands and expects, performance of which ensures their very survival. They become skilled in assuming a social mask that enables them to interact successfully with the dominant group, while yet retaining another self that the mask conceals. What this often means, for example, is that whites who employ or otherwise have frequent occasion to interact with Negroes, but always in a dominant-subordinate relationship, believe that they know what the Negro is like from the frequency of their interaction. But in fact they have seen only a psychic mask and a social performance by the Negro that he knows will be acceptable to the white. They have seen the Negro in the role he creates for his interaction with whites, a role tailored to white expectancies.

In addition, the minority view of life reflects the particular set of disadvantages and hardships that the majority imposes upon it; it becomes a philosophy that emanates from a particular kind of social experience. This view of life includes a distinctive view of the dominant group, of the kind of people they are, of how they behave in given circumstances, and of the gap that exists between what the dominant group thinks of itself and what it does or is, as the minority knows it.

The minority culture always includes those values and beliefs, religious and philosophical, that enable it to survive in the face of hardship, and give it a rationale for living in the face even of oppressive and demeaning circumstances. Any minority culture is always disproportionately creative, as oppression, hardship, and disadvantage serve as the crucibles for artistic creation and expression. It is no accident that in the United States, Jewish literary artists are found out of all proportion to their numbers. Negroes, out of an oppressive existence, have given us the deeply moving Negro spirituals, as the religiously musical expression of rural Negroes. Urban Negroes, in turn, have created jazz, that most distinctly American style of music. That jazz no longer belongs only to Negroes, and indeed to a great extent may have been usurped by talented whites, in no way alters the fact that its invention was a consequence of Negro experience. And jazz is still associated with a subculture of rejection of the bourgeois world of middle-class respectability.

The culture of a minority is also always shaped by its lessened opportunity to share in the larger culture, by the restriction of its chances to enlarge its scope of social interaction. Minority group members, therefore, tend necessarily to interact predominantly with one another, in their own organizations and churches, their own neighborhoods, even their own (in the sense of segregated) schools. Thus, they frequently exist in social enclaves in the larger society— ghettos—and this fosters particular experiences that help to shape a minority culture.

To speak of a minority subculture is to specify those cultural creations of a people that come directly from their minority experience and status. Thus, such a subculture does not necessarily constitute the full cultural patterns to be found among a minority people. American Negroes, for example, are American as well as Negro, and they possess many of the same cultural elements as do white Americans. In fact, some sociologists have insisted that there is no Negro subculture in the same sense in which there is a Jewish subculture, because historically the Negro's experience of coming to America as a slave occurred in such a manner as to strip him effectively of his native culture. The profound psychic shock of capture and the transition into a particularly brutal and demeaning slavehood seemed to destroy the Negro's self-identity and to detach him from his traditional culture. The culture that came to be his, then, was American culture. He took on Christianity, the English language, and his new identity was symbolized by a name borrowed from the white culture.

In contrast to this, the Jewish people have a rich cultural tradition and way of life of their own that has survived untold hardship and migrations. Although it clearly reflects the fact of minority existence, of ghetto life, and of being a stranger in an alien land, Jewish culture is rooted nonetheless in an historic experience of a people who have held tenaciously to their identity. It is not a culture that can be described only in terms of minority experience. Then, too, European immigrants to the United States became ethnic groups who also experienced discrimination and the status of a minority. Their ethnic subcultures were ways of life that encompassed much of the values and life-style of the culture they had left behind. Only to a limited extent did such ethnic subcultures express minority experience.

It is the difference between the Negro culture, on the one hand, and the Jewish and other ethnic subcultures, on the other, that has led some sociologists to assert that Jewish culture is a genuine culture, but that the Negro has no genuine culture of his own, only American culture. It is certainly true that the Negro is culturally American, but it is also true that he has assimilated American culture from the selective perspective and experience of a greatly disadvantaged minority. Indeed, one important difference between the Jew and the Negro is that the Jew has the resources of his own culture to fall back upon in the face of persecution and oppression; his identity as a person is sustained by cultural definitions that can not be taken away as long as Jews maintain their group identity. The Negro, in turn, has always suffered from problems of identity and has had to find his identity in the face of, and out of the experience of, a minority relationship. In this sense, his own unique interpretation of American life is a minority culture.

One obvious meaning of the militant Negro revolt of recent years is the creation of still another subcultural pattern among Negroes. In part it is a search for identity that seeks cultural roots in Africa. It is also an assertion of individual equality in terms of a refusal to don the Uncle Tom masks of the past and act the subservient and even obsequious role required of him for so long. The Negro has been liberated from some of the more oppressive behavioral requirements of the past while not yet achieving equality. Out of such a difficult situation his strivings for a new place in American society are creating a new culture that manifests his unmistakable assertions of dignity and equality and also of black solidarity and community.

PREJUDICE

The frequent reference to prejudice as well as discrimination in the controversy over minority status often serves to becloud the issue as much as to clarify it. For one thing, these are negative terms, and most people will deny that they are prejudiced or that they discriminate. In addition, these are emotionally-loaded words, so that their use in objective discussion is frequently difficult. In fact, the terms often become epithets rather than analytical concepts. Lastly, much discussion frequently uses the two terms interchangeably, as though they were synonyms for one another. But in fact they are two different concepts, with different meanings and referents.

Social scientists speak of *prejudice* when referring to attitudes and feelings; thus, prejudice refers to the psychological aspect of the problem of minority status.[21] Many students like to point out that prejudice means *prejudge,* that is, to make judgments of people prior to any actual experience with them. In order to prejudge, one must treat people as single instances of *categories.* For example, one encounters a Negro, and before any interaction with him, judges him to be a certain kind of person just because he is a Negro. Behind such action lies a set idea of what kind of people Negroes—all Negroes—are. This set idea is a *stereotype,* a mental image that attributes certain social character-istics to a group, but does so in an oversimplified and distorted manner. Thus, whites have a stereotype of Negroes, gentiles of Jews, Protestants of Catholics. The image of the gangster as dark and swarthy, with an obviously Italian name, is a common American stereotype.

A stereotype is not neutral. Rather, it presents a "good" or "bad" image, and thus one that evokes favorable or unfavorable judgments. Neither are the social characteristics attributed to people in a stereotype culturally insignificant or morally trivial; instead, they are always significant in the system of value-judgments of those holding the stereotype. For example, the stereotype of the Negro attributes moral weakness and a tendency to criminal behavior to that group. Morality and criminality are the bases of quite significant moral judg-ments, about which people are capable of feeling strongly.

Prejudice, then, refers to attitudes and feelings which operate from stereo-typed images of categories of people, and as a consequence allow no consider-ation of individual differences. To the prejudiced person, all Negroes are alike in the characteristics attributed to them in the stereotype. Thus, the prejudiced person responds in advance with typical attitudes and emotions toward any given Negro he may encounter. This implies a certain rigidity in the attitude. But prejudice is more than a rigid attitude. Fundamentally, it has an *affective* component, feelings toward others, and a *cognitive* component, an idea about the group that is usually expressed in the stereotype.

The Relation of Prejudice to Discrimination   What is the relation of the one to the other? The folklore and common sense response of our culture would be that *prejudice causes discrimination.* This is an argument so basic to an Ameri-can perspective, and seemingly so obvious to many, that too few have ever questioned it. To the social scientist, however, the relation of prejudice to discrimination is not at all obvious, and he does not take it to be a simple

[21] The outstanding work on prejudice is still Gordon Allport, *The Nature of Prejudice* (Cam-bridge, Mass.: Addison-Wesley, 1954).

one-to-one relation; that is, every act of discrimination is a consequence of a prejudicial attitude. Instead, he views the relation of prejudice to discrimination as complex and as thoroughly entangled with other relevant variables. It operates within the context of the prevailing culture and within the framework of a given social structure.

Most simply put, to say that prejudice causes discrimination is to say that *attitude causes behavior.* To the sociologist, this is saying that attitude is the only independent variable necessary to explain behavior as a dependent variable, or, that variations in behavior are to be accounted for by variations in attitudes. But the fact that attitudes and behavior are correlated does not make one the cause of the other. Therefore, the fact that a person has attitudes appropriate to his behavior does not mean that those attitudes caused the behavior. For one thing, people learn and internalize culturally defined attitudes appropriate to situations and the behavior expected in those situations. Cultural expectations are manifested both in culturally approved behavior and supporting attitudes. A more relevant point, however, is simply that each person in an organized society must from time to time behave in ways that are expected, even demanded, and he does not have the choice of acting in terms of his own attitudes. Thus, a prejudicial attitude could cause discriminatory behavior only if the person with the prejudice were free to act toward the other person solely in terms of his attitudes. And this is exactly what so often is not the case.

The sociologist, Robert Merton, once suggested the following diagram for this issue, where P is prejudice and D is discrimination, + means the presence of, and — the absence of:[22]

	P	D
1.	+	+
2.	—	—
3.	+	—
4.	—	+

The first two cases say that where there is prejudice, there is discrimination, and where there is not prejudice, there is not discrimination. Empirically, we can observe many instances of these, and it does not surprise us to find such consistency. But are the other two empirically possible? Can there be prejudice without discrimination, and can there be discrimination without prejudice? The answer, of course, is yes. Prejudice without discrimination occurs when the prejudiced person cannot discriminate. Thus, an employer who cannot refuse

[22] Robert Merton, "Discrimination and the American Creed," in Robert M. MacIver, ed., *Discrimination and National Welfare* (New York: Harper & Row, 1949), pp. 99–126.

to hire because of race, an admissions director who cannot deny admission to a student because of religion, a restaurant owner who cannot refuse to serve someone because of race, are all instances where prejudice does not cause discrimination. Law or official policy may preclude such behavior.

Furthermore, such examples suggest the opposite as well. Much discrimination, when it does occur, is not so much the behavior of individuals with prejudicial attitudes, as it is behavior determined also by policy or law. Thus, it is equally true that an act of discrimination may be less the result of a person's own attitudes and more a consequence of prevailing local policy or law, informal pressures, cultural expectations, or long-standing customs. In short, discrimination has to be explained in terms of group processes and structure as well as the culture of the group, rather than solely in terms of individual attitudes. Nor can we overlook the use of social power to support or countervail law, policy, or custom.

From this perspective, changing discriminatory behavior does not necessarily depend upon the long and slow task of changing attitudes. Indeed, the emergence of new attitudes may very well be a consequence of acting in new situations; that is, situations in which the behavioral patterns have been altered. Children, for example, who are socialized in integrated classroom situations, and know no other, will develop attitudes appropriate to such a structure of social relations. Also, alterations in behavior may be brought about by law, or by new organizational policy, which in turn may be the consequence of court decisions, the application of strong pressures, or shifts in social power. It may be useful to restate the point made above that no discrimination is possible against a minority unless the discriminators have the power to carry out their discriminatory behavior. But social change may bring a loss of the power to continue long established discrimination. All of this is not to argue that the existence of prejudice is irrelevant; it is only to make the point that a simple prejudice-causes-discrimination position is hardly an adequate explanation for what are very complex and involved phenomena. If changes in attitudes will bring about changed behavior, so too will changes in behavior bring about changed attitudes.

If prejudice itself does not cause discrimination, one might ask, what (if anything) does it do? What is its function in the relation of minority to majority group? One function of prejudice is to provide a rationale or justification for discriminatory behavior. For example, the late Ruth Benedict argued that racial beliefs and prejudices came *after* the onset of the slave trade, specifically, in response to the attacks upon it as inhuman and un-Christian.[23] Racist beliefs emerged, she argues in effect, to justify already

[23] Ruth Benedict, *Race: Science and Politics* (New York: Viking, 1940), Chapter VII, "A Natural History of Racism."

existing behavior. Pierre L. van den Berghe, we saw above, made a similar argument. Majority-minority relations, therefore, are rooted in an historically shaped cultural stereotype of a minority people held by a majority group. In cases of racial patterns, in the United States and elsewhere, the majority frequently holds a basic conception of the inherent, biological inferiority of the minority group. When this constitutes a firm social belief, it provides for the majority group a perfectly logical basis for its discriminatory behavior. It justifies differentials in educational opportunity, for why extend equal educational chances to people who are unequal in ability? It justifies a denial of voting rights, for why extend the franchise to people who do not have the intelligence to understand the political process? It justifies job discrimination, for why extend job opportunities to people who do not have the ability to hold a job demanding skill and ability?

If the function of prejudice is to provide the justification and rationale for discriminatory behavior, what, then, is the function of discrimination? We can answer that by asking, what does discrimination *do?* What a group does when it discriminates against another is to set up social mechanisms by which it allows differential access to the rewards of a society. It makes race or ethnicity a major determinant in the distribution of the life-chances of members of the society. But such a discriminatory process does not occur without creating cognitive and emotional defenses among the members of the dominant group. This prejudice is not merely an *individual* attitude but is also *collective,* a shared cultural belief.

THE FUTURE OF MINORITY GROUPS

There is no inherent rule of nature that prevents a majority group from dominating a minority to an infinity of time; but human time spans are quite finite, and history tells us over and over again of the rise and fall of structures of domination. We live in a time when old dominations are being overthrown, and when racial domination may just possibly no longer be a viable process in human society.

What happens to a minority group when, willingly or not, the majority yield its domination? We spoke above of assimilation, acculturation, and the American conception of "the melting pot." This is one alternative, in which a minority disappears from the human scene as an identifiable group by being absorbed into the majority. This has already happened to many of the European groups that settled in America, and the process continues, even if more slowly than once imagined.

It is not difficult to recognize that the assimilation of one group by another proceeds more easily when they are of the same race and even when they are of the same religion. Europeans are racially, culturally, and religiously the same as Americans, for Americans are the descendants of earlier European migrants. But Negroes are of another race, and Jews are a religious and cultural group that lived in ghettos and remained unassimilated in Europe for centuries. Need they be assimilated to escape minority status? And do they want to be assimilated, to give up their own identity?

Over the past several decades, the idea of *pluralism* has been suggested by many as an alternative to assimilation. This is simply the idea that America can be a nation of plural but coequal racial, religious, and ethnic groups. It suggests that Jewish culture is worthy in its own right, and Jews have a right to maintain the integrity of their own culture. To suggest assimilation into the majority culture is to imply the superiority and desirability of the cultural ways of the majority, and to denigrate the contrasting cultural life of the minority. But a new sense of appreciation of the diversity of cultures, a new value orientation to ethnicity suggests to some that the loss of diversity through assimilation will lessen the cultural richness of American life.

But the crux of pluralism lies, not in whether the majority sees the preservation of diversity as a cultural asset, but whether the minority group sees it as a viable and meaningful objective. The Jewish community has long accepted pluralism as a dominant value, for it constitutes a way in which the Jewish group can maintain its own integrity, while continuing to have an equality of life-chances in the society. Perhaps more significantly, the new Negro objective of a black community, the often aggressive rejection of the goal of integration of the "white liberal" leadership of civil rights, the explicit call for separatism by some militant leaders, and the new pattern of cultural preference for things black and African, suggests that a racial version of pluralism may be emerging as a new and significant aspect of American race relations.

Whatever the difficulties of such an objective, it suggests possibilities for race accommodation in the United States that are not yet apparent in South Africa. There a dominant white group has severely curbed the demands and aspirations of a numerically larger non-white group by coercive force and terror and by a denial of civil rights. To many scholars this suggests that any resolution of race relations in South Africa may only come in a "blood bath" of violent conflict involving the support and cooperation of the new black nations to the north of South Africa. In Great Britain, in turn, the development of race relations seems much like that in the United States some thirty or more years ago, and Britain may have to go through the same difficult set of experiences that the United States has.

Whatever the different national experiences, race relations in the twentieth century is the dominant form of relations between minority and majority groups. The effort to resolve the abrasive tensions of race will go a long way to create the pattern of social order to be found in modern societies at the end of this century. One does not have to believe in the elimination of inequality to envision the possibility of a world in which race does not connote racism and minority status.

1

2

1. Vagrants on a New York sidewalk.
2. Slum living in Atlanta, Ga.
3. Backstreet basketball in Harlem.
4. Indiana hillbillies.

3 4

THE LOWER CLASS
AND THE POOR

12

Undoubtedly the most problematic dimension of stratification in modern society is the troublesome presence of people who are poor. The pervasive fact of poverty stands as a silent but impressive rebuke to all the images of affluence and leisure that such a society projects. Although sociologists have long displayed an interest in those who are both economically and culturally impoverished and in a low status in society, this concern has been somewhat uneven. In the last two decades the illusion that poverty is vanishing in the United States has encouraged a shift of sociological attention from the poor to newer interests in the changing patterns of middle-class life. The newer middle-class concerns—bureaucracy, suburbia, and education—and the problems of leisure and affluence have increasingly preoccupied the time and attention of sociologists. There is an exception to this: sociologists have sustained an interest in the socializing and educational experiences of the children of the poor and disadvantaged, as well as in the delinquent behavior of adolescents from the lowest stratum.

But in more recent years, the problems of poverty have taken on a new and compelling interest for sociologists. The cumulative impact of research findings from such diverse fields as mental health, juvenile delinquency, slums and urban renewal, and social welfare has contributed to the development of a more adequate sociological perspective on the poor. But the newer focus of attention on the poor has been stimulated primarily by the central place given to the problem of poverty by the new programs of the federal government. The "war on poverty" has enlisted the intellectual concerns of social scientists.

The rediscovery of poverty as a pervasive phenomenon in the United States is a most recent event. Perhaps it can be dated, somewhat arbitrarily but conveniently, from the publication of *The Other America* in 1962 by Michael Harrington, a youthful journalist and intellectual radical. His provocative portrait of the extent and nature of contemporary poverty in America not only created renewed interest in the poor, but in fact corrected the widespread impression that poverty was largely an outmoded pattern in affluent societies.[1] The prosperity and affluence of the postwar decades did indeed foster the unsupported myth that poverty was no longer sufficiently extensive or deeply enough rooted to be a significant social problem for American society. In his influential and prescient book on postwar America, *The Affluent Society*, John Kenneth Galbraith, a distinguished social scientist, had advanced just this viewpoint.[2]

Galbraith asserted that poverty is no longer "a massive affliction" in our society, and that its occurrence has been reduced to two hard-core categories:

---

[1] Michael Harrington, *The Other America* (New York: Macmillan, 1962).

[2] John Kenneth Galbraith, *The Affluent Society* (Boston: Houghton Mifflin, 1958).

(1) the "insular poverty" of those who live in such poorer regions as the rural South and such depressed areas as West Virginia, areas which have not yet managed to share in the opportunities of the postwar economy; and (2) "case poverty," due to individual defects of the person—poor health, mental deficiency, excessive procreation, alcohol, insufficient education, or inability to adapt to the discipline of modern economic life. These people, according to Galbraith, had failed to do what everyone else had succeeded in doing, namely, master his environment. What Galbraith gave lucid expression to, however, was not a documented fact but a powerfully dominant image about the relative insignificance of the matter of poverty in America. Four years later, when Harrington captured national attention with *The Other America,* a whole series of economic studies on low income and unemployment had provided a stubborn, undismissable body of evidence that poverty, extensive and un-remitting, was a simple reality of contemporary society that no amount of reference to "affluence" could hide.

THE SOCIOLOGICAL PROBLEM OF THE LOWER CLASS AND THE POOR

In this chapter we speak both of the *poor* and of the *lower class;* a word here is necessary concerning vocabulary. The lack of a standard class vocabulary in the United States is reflected in the frequent failure of sociologists to agree on terms for social class but particularly to distinguish between *working* class and *lower* class. Thus, the recent "rediscovery" of poverty became for sociologists the discovery of a stratum of society that earned less income and was less secure than the stable working class. Many sociologists then simply spoke of poor people and of poverty. For others this has provided the opportunity to press for adequate sociological distinctions among the strata that are not middle class. The poor and the lower class, then, are not entirely adequate as synonyms for one another, but in fact the lower class are poor people, though whether all poor people should be called lower class is something else again; to do so may obscure some important differences among those who are poor.

To explain and understand the poorest people as a distinct and differentiated stratum in society has long been a goal not only of sociologists but also of intellectuals and writers, radicals and reformers. For the sociologist, however, the problem of explaining those who are lowest in the class structure of society is difficult to do. In the first place there is a need to understand those *structural* characteristics of the society that produce a lowest stratum who get the smallest share of what a society has to distribute. However, it is also important to the sociologist to determine the social and cultural attributes of this lower class—its life-style, its values and world-outlook, and its relations to the other classes of society.

What makes this difficult to do is the existence of a long heritage of prophetic interpretations and ideological explanations that stand as a ready-made context from which the sociologist can only with the greatest difficulty escape. And these perspectives provide completely contradictory interpretations. One is critical and negative and morally rejects the lower class as worthy of any respect. The other is romantic and positive and attributes morally admirable and politically significant qualities to these most disadvantaged segments of society. In neither case, however, do these perspectives yield interpretations with enough empirical accuracy nor are they sufficiently objective to satisfy the sociologist seeking an understanding of the life-conditions of those at the very bottom of society. What they provide are not so much explanations as moral and political rationalizations for the behavior of other social classes toward the poorest people in society.

It would seem that the effort to understand what poverty and lower-class status mean as a sociological problem begins with an examination of these historic and still viable perspectives. By such a process we can distinguish the contemporary meaning of poverty from its historic connotations, this will then permit an examination of the structure of poverty at the present time. Then it becomes necessary to move to the question of the lower class. This requires distinguishing working class from lower class, not merely in structural terms but also in cultural terms: values and ideology, life-style and world-outlook. Only such a careful distinction permits an adequate definition and description of the lower class as one among several classes in American society. Lastly, we turn our attention to the problems of social change, with a dual emphasis on the efforts to alleviate the plight of the poor and on the issue of the class consciousness and political potentialities of the lower class.

Perspectives on Poverty and the Lower Class

The Critical and Negative Image Throughout the long development of industrial society, and even before, the dominant middle-class image of the poor was a morally critical one. Furthermore, the rapid pace of industrialization within the past 150 years did little to change the perspective so dominant since the seventeenth century and originally manifested in the Elizabethan Poor Laws. These laws adopted during the reign (1558–1603) of Queen Elizabeth in England established local, community responsibility for whatever welfare measures were necessary for the care of the poor and dependent. However, more importantly, they asserted that any condition of personal dependency was the fault of the individual so dependent, an indication of morally defective character.[3] Viewing poverty as evidence of sin was a central ethical strand in an emerging entrepreneural world-view evident among the Protestant middle classes in England and Germany. There was no room in this ethical outlook for sympathy for the lower class; instead, they were held responsible for their own plight by virtue of their immorality. Yet, however reluctantly, the Elizabethan Poor Laws had established community responsibility for the poor and also had recognized that at least some poor, such as widows, orphans, and the handicapped, were not necessarily personally responsible for their dependent status.

But during the 1820s and 1830s, in both the United States and England, a middle class committed to the philosophy of laissez-faire worked politically to reduce public responsibility for the poor. Such major intellectual figures as Thomas Malthus and David Ricardo had created the ideological rationalizations for such action, and Social Darwinism provided a full justification. The poor were forced to shift more for themselves or to be dependent on private charitable projects, usually operated under religious auspices. In America the philosophy of the 1830s governed the welfare aspect of relations between the classes until the 1930s, though in England and most of Europe a new approach to welfare had been developed by the end of the nineteenth century. It was not until the Great Depression of the 1930s that a national welfare program in the United States brought some modifications of this ancient pattern of welfare, and even this was resisted by many middle-class Americans.

Although the details may vary slightly over time, this middle-class perspective on poverty has changed but little over the last several centuries. It speaks in moral rather than economic terms; it claims that the lower class lacks the qualities of moral responsibility and individual initiative, as well as personal pride and independence, that the middle class sees as being its own primary virtues. Therefore, this perspective insists that the plight of poor people is their own fault, a consequence of defects of moral character.

The Radical and Romantic Image   In contrast to this dominant perspective that sees the poor as the victims of their own moral failure, the last century and a half has witnessed a singularly impressive tradition of intellectual dissent and revolutionary criticism of the class structure of industrial-capitalist society. This tradition has produced radical and romantic interpretations of poor people and their life, attributing to them positive moral qualities presumably lacking in the middle class itself. Poor people are deemed to be honest, frank,

---

[3] For a full review of the origins and development of welfare as one aspect of the development of industrial society, see Harold L. Wilensky and Charles N. Lebeaux, *Social Welfare and Industrial Society* (New York: Russell Sage, 1958).

and unaffected, devoid of the hypocrisy and pretentiousness its critics claim mark the moral quality in the life of the respectable and affluent classes in society. From Saint Francis of Assisi to twentieth century beatniks and hippies, voluntary poverty has been viewed as a virtue, and renunciation of material gain has been a morally acceptable way of criticizing and even rejecting the allegedly corrupting consequences of the material life. To seek identification with the poor and downtrodden can be either a moral or a political act of protest, but it always involves a distinctly romanticized conception of these people.

Socialism, too, has created a highly approving image of the poor, this time a politically radical one. The impoverished and downtrodden have been looked upon by socialists as a potentially revolutionary class that will, in good time, revolt and overthrow the ruling class and then create a new and better society. From this perspective the poor are the historic *proletariat,* to whom are imputed the moral attributes of a social class fighting, in the name of all humanity, to build a better world; in turn, the middle classes are made to symbolize all the negative qualities of a dying society.

The underlying assumption of these romantic and radical conceptions of the poor is that poverty can be ennobling and productive of those very moral qualities that elude affluence. That these ideas can be found in both Christian and Marxian thought, in both political and apolitical perspectives, testifies to its deep-rootedness in Western culture. But the pervasiveness and persistence of the idea of the nobility of the poor in Western thought is no more necessarily accurate than is that middle-class view that sees the poor as causing their own poverty by the defects of their character.

However contradictory these two ways of looking at the poor may be, they have one thing in common: they define the poor as the moral antithesis of the middle class. Where the view of the middle class is positive and self-laudatory, the view of the poor is morally negative; but where the perspective of the middle class is morally and politically critical, the poor are elevated to a high moral plane and given an historic political role in the transformation of society. In each instance, the middle class is judging itself when it seeks to find a perspective for understanding the poor, for it needs to be remembered that the radical perspective is as much an intellectual creation of the middle class as is the other.

These traditional perspectives on the poor are rooted in a nineteenth century assumption that the working class are the poor people, and so little distinction between a working class and a lower class was made; the two terms were used synonymously. Yet sometimes a distinction did creep in, such as that between the proletariat and a *Lumpenproletariat,* the latter term designating the poorest and most dispossessed elements of the society, the socially alienated and disorganized segments at the very bottom of the class structure. Marx sometimes referred to the *déclassé*. For labor and radical leaders of the nineteenth century, these lowest in the class structure often appeared as agents of the enemy, for they could be recruited as strike-breakers, as *agents provocateurs*, resorting to violence to oppose the actions of organized segments of the working class.

The Changing Poor   The conception of who the poor are has undergone considerable change over the past century. At least three images of the poor have existed in the past, none of which is particularly relevant today: the poor as working people; the poor as immigrants; and the poor as the unemployed in a depression. One hundred years ago, industrial society was still a society of relative scarcity, rather than relative affluence. Its technology and production methods, relatively crude by contemporary standards, required a large mass of untrained and unskilled workers, who, as a corollary, were quite lowly paid. Being poor, then, was the lot of the working people of society; it was the common condition of a large social class, and it was philosophically accepted by workers and middle class alike as the lot in life for most men.

Toward the end of the nineteenth century, an increasing awareness of the debilitating consequences of urban poverty became a new element in the social consciousness of the middle classes. Particularly in England and the United States, middle-class reformers publicized the social conditions of the poor and pressed for reforming legislation. Such works as Charles Booth's *Lives and Labor of the London Poor* in England and Jacob Riis' *How the Other Half Lives* in America gave explicit descriptions of how the urban poor lived, and conveyed to sympathetic people some sense of the deprivation that accompanied their lot in life.

Although the image of the working class as the poor people in society was general throughout industrial societies, the image of the poor as immigrants was particular to the United States. After about 1880, a last great wave of immigrants from Europe, including, for the first time, large numbers from eastern and southern Europe, poured into America's expanding cities as part of a vastly increased industrial labor force. Many were peasants, few had any industrial skills—they were a ready source of cheap, unskilled labor. Since the immigrant was a particularly visible segment of the industrial poor, poverty and immigrant status were soon associated together in the American mind. Both of these images—of the poor as working class and as immigrants—were to fade as they became less congruent with reality. In particular, the European immigrant managed to effect enough social mobility so that he was less frequently defined as poor. Furthermore, in the last twenty-five years, the economic status of the working class has improved to that point where working class is simply no longer identified with poverty.

During the 1930s, poverty became identified with *unemployment* as a temporary status, to be remedied with the return of normal business and employment. Such unemployment cut across class lines, and the experience of poverty was shared by millions of both white-collar and blue-collar workers. As a result, the image of who the poor were was broadened to include many who were not lower class; also, it involved less of the moral blame that had long stigmatized the lower class. Yet, there was still considerable middle-class ambiguity about poverty and the poor. The recognition that millions were poor because of depression unemployment and for no personal failing only partially obviated the older idea of poverty as a condition induced by personal failure to be sufficiently moral, hard-working, and responsible.

The depression years were a time of resurgent romantic and radical perspectives on the lower strata, both in the United States and Europe. In the United States, a reinvigorated labor movement organized mass industrial unions. In the process the often violent struggles of labor and management helped create considerable liberal middle-class sympathies for workers as underdogs, giving new currency to those perspectives that saw in class struggle the violent shaping of a new society. But by the 1950s this was a fading dream, no longer evident in a society in which government increasingly extended its responsibility for social welfare, and in which now well-established labor unions seemed to be less a social movement than a self-interested bureaucratic structure. There was an observable liberal and intellectual disenchantment with organized labor, and the search for the potential sources for significant change in the world shifted to other matters: race, as a last domestic issue; and the large and vastly unexplored worlds on the non-Western continents.

It was in this milieu of changing intellectual focus and concern that the poor slipped out of public view, and it became possible to entertain the comfortable illusion that poverty was an issue of the past in modern society, though clearly still a major issue in those modernizing societies where limited resources made being poor the lot of the vast majority. Therefore, when a concern for poverty became a part of a renewed social consciousness in American society in the 1960s, an awareness that the conditions of poverty are probably not the same today as they have been, and that the poor are probably not the same people as they once were, made necessary the task of determining just who the poor now are.

THE STRUCTURE OF POVERTY

The poor and the lower class constitute those people who are located at the lowest level of the class structure, who have the lowest incomes, the poorest paying jobs, and who experience the most economic insecurity. Whatever may be their attributes as people, the sociologist is compelled to recognize that they are a distinctive social stratum, a differentiated segment of modern social structure. Although an individual might possibly move out of such a category, the category itself continues to exist. Moving up to the working class for some lower-class people does not remove the class as a whole; its existence is a consequence of the structural arrangements that unequally distribute life-chances.

The Economics of Poverty   In a time of relative affluence, it is not necessarily apparent that large numbers of people are poor and, to a considerable extent, they are not as visible to the middle classes as they once were. They are confined to ghettoes or to rural pockets hidden from view from the great expressways. Many middle-class travelers no longer come into the city by train, which once always passed through some of the poorest sections of a city. It is this lack of easy visibility, for example, that during the 1950s could sustain the myth that there were no longer any substantial number of poor. Their rediscovery has still left open two issues: what income level defines poverty; and how many poor are there?

How Poor Is Poor?   What kind of income defines one as poor is clearly a relative matter, for the income that would provide a decent standard of living two decades ago will not do so today. What is poverty, then, has to be tied to the always changing and mostly rising standard of living. Most economists and others seeking to define poverty have worked with data from the Bureau of Labor Statistics, for it is this federal agency that provides a measurement of the cost of living in American cities. (Cost of living increases for workers provided through their union contracts are usually based upon BLS figures.) Throughout the 1960s, based upon current living costs, the poverty line was drawn at just about $3000, even though BLS estimates of a "modest but adequate" budget for a city family of four to purchase a representative list of goods and services would require more than twice this amount. The economist Leon Keyserling has insisted that an income under $4000 is poverty and from $4000 to $6000 is deprivation. Why can we not establish a rigorous and unarguable figure? We cannot because what is an *adequate* income is a value judgment, and people have defined varying levels of living as "necessary" for a family. Nonetheless, there is now a reasonable consensus on $3000 as a good minimum definition of poverty in the United States.

How Many Are Poor?   By whatever standard poverty is measured, there are many millions of Americans who are poor. How many these are depends both upon how poverty is defined in income and the application of this standard to demographic data about population and family size. One scholar, Oscar

Ornati,[4] defined poverty at three income levels. By his first level of minimum subsistence of $2500 for a family of four, he determined that there were 20 million poor in the United States in 1960. But this figure jumped to 46 million at his second level of minimum adequacy of $3500. This second level of poverty included 26 percent of the American population in 1960, and Ornati compared that with 27 percent for 1947. The level of poverty has not changed much in postwar America. Although the estimates of the number of Americans who are poor necessarily varies with the way poverty is defined, that at least one out of every five Americans is poor seems now to be fairly well agreed upon.

The New Poor To speak of "new" poor is not to imply that these people were not poor before, or that all those who were poor in the past have escaped into affluence. Instead, it is only to suggest that the designation of poverty today fits a constellation of people quite different from those so designated for the first half of this century. The structure of poverty has undergone considerable change, and some very recent efforts by social scientists have been intent upon measuring that change.

The analysis that social scientists seem to have found most fruitful in attempting to differentiate the poor from others specifies a set of structural categories that delineate the changing conditions in the American economy that make for poverty. The advance of technological change, for which the term *automation* often serves as a symbol, effects the *displacement* of workers, and this occurs in both rural and urban forms of employment. There are farm workers displaced by mechanization and the growth of the large farm, many of whom then move into urban slums. There are urban factory workers whose unskilled and more probably semiskilled jobs have been eliminated by technological changes. Thus, one major category for the creation of poverty is the continuing displacement of workers by technological changes.

A second major category has to do with the fact that the rising standard of living and the rising level of income, the new levels of wages and salaries, have not included all areas of employment. There are low-paying industries in the United States where people working a forty-hour week for fifty weeks still cannot earn an income that takes them out of the poverty category: restaurants, hotels, laundries, farming, agricultural processing, and retailing are some of the more important ones.

There is, then, a significant shift in the labor market from the first half of this century. Increasingly, technological skills are needed to hold any job at all, or at least those jobs that pay an income above the poverty level. To be

---

[4] Oscar Ornati, "Poverty in America," in Louis A. Ferman, Joyce L. Kornbluh, and Alan Haber, *Poverty in America* (Ann Arbor, Mich.: University of Michigan Press, 1965), pp. 24–39.

able to find a place in that labor market, or to hold one's place in it, is to have access to an opportunity structure that makes possible a regularly improving share of the rewards, economic and other, that an affluent society has to distribute. Not to be able to find or hold a place in that labor market is to be cut off from access to opportunity, and thus to make poverty a condition of life that threatens to endure and become permanent.

But who are the people whom the structural changes put at such a disadvantage? Although the displacement effected by technological change can strike at random across American society, there is nonetheless a discernible pattern of who are most likely to be affected and who least so. The chances of getting access to the opportunity structure are least for certain definable categories of people: the nonwhite; the uneducated and untrained; and those families with a female head. Also, age is a factor that is related to poverty, and in two ways. Older people, particularly those over sixty-five years of age, are often without adequate savings to keep pace with rising living costs, and they are at a severe disadvantage in finding employment in a labor market that uses age as a criterion for employment. Although Social Security and now Medicare have lifted many aged people from the very bottom levels of poverty, it has still left a large number who fall short of levels of adequacy and comfort.

But it is not merely those in the older age brackets who suffer disproportionately from poverty; so do those who at an early age assume the responsibility of family head. Young families headed by males between the ages of fourteen and twenty-four make up a disproportionately large segment of the poor. In these cases, youths who have left school and married early are without sufficient skills to find regular employment or to find employment outside of the low-paying fields.

Here then is the beginnings of a profile of the poor: the nonwhite; the rural migrant; the technologically displaced; the elderly; the young and untrained worker; and those families depending on female employment. There are also concentrated among these the functionally illiterate, those whose education has been so meager that for all practical purposes they are illiterate. The people who find themselves in one or another of these categories are not there by choice; they have not opted for poverty over affluence. But neither are they in any ready position to choose to be anywhere else. Poverty is not simply a situation of having little income; it is, instead, a patterning of life that those who dwell in it can do little about.

The Poverty Trap   The poverty in which several million American families find themselves is sustained and reinforced by a set of conditions that are beyond the scope of the individual to alter. The "new" poor are trapped in a structure of poverty that confronts them at several different points. A small supply of income is only one factor; there is a pattern of built-in disadvantages of jobs, housing, schooling, and consumption that serve to reinforce the inhibiting incapacities that beset the poor.

The poor live in slums, whether urban or rural. As a community and neighborhood, slums create several disadvantages: (1) the housing is poor and deteriorating; (2) the social environment is bleak and unrewarding, yet confining and limiting for both children and adults; (3) less is offered in the way of recreational and educational services; (4) the area is threateningly high in physical disease and conditions injurious to health; and (5) as a ghetto of the poor, it renders them conveniently less visible to the more affluent. The poor, it seems, inhabit a social environment that offers little that is positive or rewarding and much that is debilitating and destructive. In particular, the large urban slums are frequently so expansive a physical area that children and even many adults may have little opportunity to get beyond its environs for any other kind of social experience.

Housing is one of the major expenses of life that provides particularly difficult problems for the poor. Slums by definition are areas of inadequate housing, and the United States Census records that substandard housing still exists in substantial amounts in American cities. Places like Harlem and comparable Negro ghettos are simply large areas of deteriorated and still deteriorating housing. The poor either accept the inadequate housing, or else they pay comparably more for housing than anyone else, as much as a third of their income. To do so, they sacrifice clothing, medicine, or other important consumer items.

If the poor can purchase adequate housing only at a serious sacrifice of other of life's necessities, it is also the case that most of their consumer purchasing is done at a disadvantage. Slum landlords are not the only exploiters of the poor; slum merchants are, as well. In his revealing book, *The Poor Pay More*, David Caplovitz has documented the fact that the poor pay more for goods of poorer quality than do any other group of people in the city.[5] They are victims, in the first place, of an inability to be sufficiently mobile within the community to do comparison shopping. More to the point, they have only little cash on hand, and their credit is nonexistent in most stores of the community. But there are merchants who specialize in selling on credit to the poor, despite the obvious risks, and manage to make it a profitable enterprise. The fact that the poor are frequently unsophisticated about credit and prices and are as hungry as other Americans for such durable goods as furniture, television sets, and radios creates a set of circumstances in which their effort to share in the affluent society's consumption patterns renders them

---

[5] David Caplovitz, *The Poor Pay More* (New York: Free Press, 1963).

vulnerable to effective economic exploitation. And this only increases their entrapment in the world of poverty.

In the case of housing and consumer goods, the poor pay more for less, but in the case of schooling, the poor must simply accept the quality of schooling that the community makes available to their children. And the poor get inferior schooling. This is strongly denied by public school authorities, but a sociologist specializing in the relation of education to social class, Patricia Cayo Sexton, has documented the class inequities of urban public schooling in her book, *Education and Income.*[6]

The inability of the poor to have access to equal education only adds further to their already significant educational disadvantage: the poor are largely the uneducated, the untrained, and the unskilled. One of the few aspects of the position of the poor that has received national recognition is that their lack of education is now a severe handicap, when once it was not. The school "drop-out" is not new; the children of the lower class have long failed to complete twelve years of schooling. But once there were the unskilled jobs of the community available to them, and now these are the jobs that are gone, by virtue of technological change.

Still, the poor compound their difficulties by failing to complete education through high school in far greater proportion than any other group in the society. The children of the poor perpetuate the lack of education of their parents and, in a technological and affluent society, this is the most effective way to perpetuate poverty. To say that the poor fail to complete an education is not to imply a criticism. It is simply to state a fact of great importance. The attitude of the children of the poor toward school is often negative, but then so is the experience of schooling a difficult and often penalizing one for them. It is a simple fact, stated here without any intention of moralizing or attaching blame, that the middle-class institution, the public school, has not yet coped successfully with the problem of the lower-class child.

The structure of poverty does something else to the poor besides compounding a network of disadvantages in housing, consumption, and schooling: it constitutes a pattern of life that takes a personal toll in physical and mental health. Chronic ill health plagues the poor, and they are more susceptible to contagious diseases. A recent series of provocative studies on the relation of social class to mental health also demonstrated that the poor suffer far more from emotional difficulties—from neuroses and from psychotic disturbances. However, they get little attention from psychiatric facilities until they reach that serious point where they are disruptive in their relations with others and must be hospitalized.

[6] Patricia Cayo Sexton, *Education and Income* (New York: Viking, 1961).

THE WORKING CLASS AND THE LOWER CLASS

For many American social scientists, there is a middle class and a lower class, and little distinction is made within the range of varied occupations and life-styles to be found outside the middle class. But the new concern for poor people has made these social scientists aware of what others have known: that the terms *working class* and *lower class* do not refer to the same social phenomena. In Chapter 10 we noted the need to speak in the plural of working classes in order to make sense of the array of occupations, life-styles, and life-chances to be found in the vast blue-collar world. Some of these would be lower class.

The working class is made up of those in manual occupations outside of farming. Its life-chances are dependent upon a job involving a limited range of manual skills. Within the working class there is a skilled class of workers whose earnings are measurably higher than others, and whose life-chances are protected by craft unions that control the apprenticeship system as well as access to the occupation. Historically, the larger semiskilled working class has suffered from a greater supply of workers than jobs, so that the free play of the labor market would normally bring wages down to a subsistence level. But the labor movement emerged among workers as far back as the eighteenth century, creating unions that sought to prevent any labor being available to employers below a given level of wages. In the twentieth century, the organization of the working class into unions in the democratic industrial societies is quite far-reaching and inclusive. Unions constitute one of the significant means by which the working class has sought to have some control over the distribution of life-chances. But another means, as Lenski notes, has been political organization.[7] The working classes in most democratic, industrial societies support a party of the left—Communist, Socialist, or Labor. In the United States the Democratic Party has been the working man's party. Through these parties workers try to control politically some of the factors affecting their life-chances that they cannot control in other ways. Lenski observes that "the efforts of working men's parties are aimed largely at making the distribution of goods and services subject to political, rather than economic, determination."[8]

The lower class, in turn, is made up of those unskilled and irregularly employed workers, including the unemployed, whose life chances are distinctly less and whose economic interests are protected neither by effective union organization nor by political organization. Not all unskilled workers are lower

---

[7] Gerhard Lenski, *Power and Privilege* (New York: McGraw-Hill, 1966), pp. 379–380.
[8] Lenski, p. 380.

class, for some work in unionized industries and are paid higher wages and have relative job security. But most unskilled workers have no such advantages.

This structural differentiation into these two classes suggests a stable working class characterized by a subculture that reflects both its social position in the society and its relation to other social classes, and a lower class with a life-style marked by its many disadvantages and insecurities. Herbert Gans has appropriately assessed the culture of a class (or *subculture* as he calls it) as a *response* to the *opportunities* and *deprivations* that people encounter.[9] Thus, each culture is

> an organized set of related responses that has developed out of people's efforts to cope with the opportunities, incentives, and rewards, as well as the deprivations, prohibitions, and pressures which the natural environment and society—that complex of coexisting and competing subcultures—offer to them.[10]

Gans thus sees the culture manifested by a class as closely related to the structural patterning that defines the class in occupational and income terms. "In each of the subcultures life is thus geared to the availability of specific qualitative types and quantities of income, education, and occupational opportunities."[11]

The Culture of the Working Class   The complex patterning of working-class life cannot be described in full here; rather, we intend only a brief description of some major *themes* of working-class life, drawing for this purpose upon Herbert J. Gans as well as S. M. Miller and Frank Riessman.[12] Gans' work gives particular emphasis to the *family-centered* life of the working class, a fact that also emphasizes the ethnic origins of much of the American working class. Its way of life is largely based upon social relationships among family and relatives; close friends are included in the family circles and become, as people say, "like one of the family." The extended family pattern encourages mutual aid and cooperation. Miller and Riessman further develop the ethnic, immigrant origin of so much of the working class to stress the *traditionalism* of workers: a patriarchial family pattern that is not child-centered like the middle class and is characterized by a sharper separation of sex roles. Similarly, the worker expects his children to obey, is less of a permissive parent, and likes discipline, structure, order, organization, and strong leadership. Yet, he is also *person-centered* and makes a poor bureaucrat; he relates himself to people, not to roles or offices. He likes easy, informal relations, and his "horse-

[9] Herbert Gans, *The Urban Villagers* (New York: Free Press, 1962), pp. 249–252.
[10] Gans, p. 249.
[11] Gans, p. 249.
[12] Gans, *The Urban Villagers*, Chapter 11; S. M. Miller and Frank Riessman, "The Working Class Subculture: A New View," *Social Problems,* 9 (Summer, 1961), 86–97.

play" at work expresses his preference for a human quality to his relationships on the job as well as off.

Because he is a traditionalist in many spheres of life and possesses a traditional attitude toward discipline, he has seemed to some social scientists to be authoritarian. But this is more likely to be merely a consequence of his "conventional" character—authoritarians are supposed to be conventional—and of the stronger value placed upon discipline. Workers also measure higher on prejudice scales, but working-class prejudice is not evidence of a racist ideology so much as it is a response to the economic threats that minorities have often posed for them. Indeed, *stability* and *security* are persistent themes of working-class life, for the threat of unemployment and loss of income is never absent, even in "good times." The concern to achieve security has led many workers to refuse promotion to foreman; this contrasts with the middle-class striving for mobility. Workers do not share the middle-class interest in a life-style that emphasizes status and prestige and "getting ahead." They are quite anti-snobbery and resent status pretensions on anyone's part.

The worker is not uneducated, but he is not well-educated. He appreciates the importance of education for his children, but he feels estranged from the teacher and the school. This alienation also affects his view of politics, which is negative, and by and large he is not greatly interested in politics. Yet he votes his economic interests, where he is likely to be most liberal, though he is quite conservative on other, mostly noneconomic matters. The American working class seems not be to *class-conscious* compared to European workers, a fact that has encouraged many efforts to either explain or disconfirm this fact. However, John C. Leggett's research in Detroit has discovered a relationship between a more militant class-consciousness and economic insecurity, suggesting that, as in the 1930s, an increase in unemployment and job insecurity can turn politically moderate workers into militant class radicals.[13]

The Culture of the Lower Class[14]   The social world of the poor is unremittingly harsh and provides little reward for any human effort. It sustains a meager material existence and provides little on which to nurture the human ego. Yet the lives of the poor are not entirely without meaning and significance, at least for them. Like any other people, the poor build their lives around the fixed conditions of their existence.

The term *the culture of poverty* has recently been introduced into the sociological vocabulary. It has enjoyed a quick and widespread acceptance as an

[13] Compare John C. Leggett, "Economic Insecurity and Working-Class Consciousness," *American Sociological Review,* 29 (April, 1964), 226–234.
[14] This section has been drawn largely from Gans, pp. 245–246 and from Walter B. Miller, "Focal Concerns of Lower-Class Culture," in Ferman, Kornbluh, and Haber, *Poverty in America,* pp. 261–270.

apt term to define the culturally shaped response that poor people make in situations of poverty to the pattern of opportunity and deprivation that is offered them. Not all sociologists use the term, or feel it is adequate, but it has become the widely accepted way to refer to the patterning of belief and attitudes, the values and social perspectives of the poor. What is ambiguous about the term is that it suggests a cultural pattern characteristic of all those who are poor. But not all poor have the cultural attributes found in the culture of poverty. Some poor people whose incomes have once been more adequate—technologically displaced workers or retired people—have the social outlooks of other social classes. And some poor hope and strive to rise to the level of the stable working class—their outlook on life is atypical for the world of poverty. The attributes of the culture of poverty are peculiar, then, to some but not all of those who happen to be poor. What is required is a lifetime of experience with poverty, poverty as a permanent condition of life and accepted as such. What social scientists have been calling the culture of poverty is that subcultural pattern of the permanently poor—the lower class. The culture of poverty is simply a new and more fashionable name for the lower-class subculture as found in the United States, but apparently, from what little evidence we have, it is also characteristic of the lower class of other societies. The essential pattern of lower-class life, and its social perspectives, can perhaps be best covered by considering it under three major headings: male and female; the context of living; and outlook on the larger society.

Male and Female The life of the lower-class male is more representative of the subculture of this class than is that of the female. Perhaps nothing distinguishes the lower class from the working class so much as the difference in family life and the consequent difference in the typical modes of behavior of male and female. Whereas the working-class family is stable and encompassing, providing the intimate context for most human associations for its members, the lower-class family is a weak and uncertain unit. The role of the male is so frequently marginal that the lower-class family is often a female-based unit. The male is often peripheral to the day-to-day life of the family, taking little part in the raising of children and extending little if any affection or emotional gratification to his wife and children. He inconsistently provides some economic support, and he is husband, or at least a sexual partner, more than he is father. The stability, to the extent that there is any, of the lower-class family depends, then, on the female. The woman tries to create some routine and stability for the family. She is much nearer to working-class values in her outlook, and she attempts to encourage her children to seek a more stable mode of life.

There is a segregation of the world of male and female in the lower class that is far more thorough than that of any other class. Thus, for the female, there is the peculiar situation of gravitating between the working-class environment of routine and stability she seeks to effect in the home (though not usually with success) and the lower-class culture she shares in her involvement with her husband; sometimes this involves sharing in the pursuit of excitement and the difficulties that may follow any such escapade. The lower-class male culture permits little of tenderness and affection, and thus the sexual relationships of the lower class reflect it. Women are more likely defined as sexual objects, targets for sexual conquest, and less likely seen as total persons, with minds and emotions.

Much of the observation of social scientists on the life of the lower class has been made on the urban male, usually on the younger male. These men are least successful in the world of work and are not usually steadily employed. Nor do their values give primacy either to work itself or to steady employment, and education does not have the value or prestige it has in the rest of society. The life of the lower-class male is oriented to action rather than to routine, to excitement where possible, even when, and possibly just because, the seeking of excitement may mean violence and law-violating behavior. The search for "thrills" involves the extensive use of alcohol, gambling, and sexual adventures. Such activity often means involvement with law-enforcing agencies as a logical outcome of the pursuit of excitement.

The lower-class male affects an attitude to his own world that requires a stance of *toughness,* an emphasis upon male virility, upon physical (including sexual) prowess, and upon being daring and fearless, and a complete and unforgiving disdain for anything that could be defined as weak, effeminate, or timid. But he also prizes being "smart," which means to outwit others and to gain objects from others by a verbal adroitness; in short, he admires "conning" people and despises "being taken." This may explain why lower-class males have so often been recruitable as strike-breakers or as violent agents on behalf of other class interests. Lower-class males display a greater concern over masculinity than do the males of any other class. This seems to be related to the female-dominated family life in which they were reared and the lack of a male family head, a father, from whom to learn a more typical and responsible version of the male role.

Lower-class males also seem to prize their independence, and their own talk asserts their dislike of controls, of authority, and of any restrictions on their behavior. This, alone, would help to account for their failure to assume the responsibilities and thus the more controlling discipline of being a father and family head. Thus, there is readiness to assume the role of the rebel against authority. However, the anthropologist Walter Miller has argued that the lower-class male's emphasis upon this autonomy is an overt pattern of behavior that conceals a covert tendency to seek out the very controlling environment he most strongly denounces.[15] Miller argues that such people mentally connect authority and nurturance, and that being controlled or restricted comes also to mean being cared for. Thus, there is an element of seeking dependency that is only masked by a pose of tough rebelliousness.

Lower-class culture, in its male aspect, at least, is given to illegal behavior. Legality is a pattern consistent with middle-class values, and so the lower-class male in pursuit of his own class goals may seem to be criminal, malicious, and deliberately refusing to conform with middle-class ways. But lower-class culture is not merely a reversal, a cultural opposite, of middle-class culture; its illegal behavior is more likely to be an unintended consequence of its pursuit of its own way of life.

The Context of Life   Poor people are necessarily involved in a day-to-day concern about living, a struggle against difficulties from which there is no release. The lower class is not involved in any realistic struggle to escape their circumstances; as a result, they focus a great deal of their interest in life on the details of their own life circumstances. They know intimately the nature of their own existence; contrastingly, they have but little knowledge, or access to knowledge, of the larger world outside their immediate environment. Their interest is largely confined to themselves and their own fate, their family and peer groups, and to the neighborhood that serves as the circumscribed environment within which their interaction with others occurs.

For poor people, their response to their world is in quite concrete and personal terms. They focus attention on the immediate, in all its concreteness of detail. The vocabulary of lower-class people is dominated by concrete terms, and the abstract expression is a less frequent element of their mode of communication; thus, they tend less to generalize. Their response to the life about them is in terms of the sensory and intimate, for there is a compelling immediacy about the demands of life at the lower-class level.

A way of life immersed in the immediate does not suggest any large concern for time. The poor live life *now*, in the present, and their sense of time is largely restricted to that; they have little sense of a time span that includes the past or the future. This orientation to time reflects their very real sense of the futility of planning ahead or of anticipating anything very promising or rewarding in the future. Trapped in the immediate pressures of an unrewarding environment, lower-class people take whatever chance for enjoyment they can now. As a consequence, they often seem to middle-class people to be spendthrifty, to squander any resources that might come to them and not to postpone pleasure for the sake of saving; in the language of the psychologist,

---

[15] Walter B. Miller, "Focal Concerns of Lower-Class Culture," p. 268.

they do not *defer gratification.* An inability to defer gratification has been more frequently labeled as typical of the lower class than almost anything else. For many social scientists this is the one outstanding characteristic that makes them unlike the middle class.

But some sociologists have argued that perhaps too much emphasis has been put upon this one issue.[16] For one thing, the ability to defer gratification until some future time, to plan for a future, to forego pleasure in the present for the sake of the future, and to resist impulse now by a future-oriented self-discipline, all this, long defined as the values of the middle class, is hardly descriptive of that social class any longer. The middle class now buys on time, goes into debt, complains of not having enough income, sometimes moon-lights, and increasingly middle-class women enter the labor market to bring home a second paycheck because the family's life-style exhausts the primary one.

But perhaps the most telling point that these sociologists make is that the comparison between the deferred gratification of the middle class and the nondeferred gratification of the lower class may be an invalid comparison, one made from a middle-class point of view, neglecting to see what is involved from the perspective of the lower class. As they point out, a comparison of the middle and lower classes on the matter of deferred gratification can only be valid if it is assumed that the objects deferred are equally valued, if defer-ment imposes the same loss or suffering or pains of denial, and if there is the same probability of achieving the gratification in the future. But the lower class may not place the same value on that for which the middle class defers, it may cost the lower class much more to make such a deferment, given its lesser resources, and it may have much less chance of attaining the deferred value or have much less confidence in its ability to attain it. Although an emphasis on nondeferment of gratification for the lower class contrasted to the deferring of gratification on the part of the middle class may well be a meaningless comparison, the fact remains that the lower class does live in the present, and it does take advantage of present opportunities for pleasure now, not later. The essence of the argument is that it becomes quite under-standable why the lower class does not defer gratification, and there is no reason to expect them to.

Outlook on Society   The poor today are often charged with being apathetic and unwilling to do anything for themselves. This charge of apathy comes from middle-class people who invoke a conception of voluntary action as a

[16] See S. M. Miller, Frank Riessman, and Arthur Seagull, "Poverty and Self-Indulgence: A Critique of the Nondeferred Gratification Pattern," in Ferman, Kornbluh, and Haber, *Poverty in America,* pp. 285–302.

legitimate expectation of how people act upon their problems in a democratic society. But such an expectation assumes both the capacity to act effectively and the holding of an expectation that such action will likely bring fruitful results. The lower class lack the kind of experiences in society that develop skills in carrying out collective forms of organization and civic action, and they possess no confidence that any action by them will change their lot in life for the better. Such an effort is regarded as futile from the very start. For this reason, the concept of apathy may be inappropriate; what appears as apathy to middle-class eyes may be the result of a sense of futility and resignation to one's lot in life.

The world to the lower class appears hostile and threatening, and they feel weak and powerless in the face of stronger forces. Furthermore, these more powerful forces are always a threat, promising harm, only rarely good. They cannot be trusted and must be guarded against. Thus, the poor are reluctant to join organizations, even organizations that promise to help them. Their experience with those who have promised to help them has rarely been rewarding; these helpers, particularly those who manage the welfare agencies, effect a control over them, make demands, and interfere in their lives. They become a beneficial enemy, but an enemy nonetheless. In addition, of course, all around the poor are those who try to exploit or cheat them.

Such a definition of reality as the poor possess leads to a negative and hostile attitude to the world, particularly to all those who do not share the same fate; for these, there is suspicion and resentment. The sense of being unable to control one's own life leads to the idea that the controlling forces lie in a coercive and arbitrary environment. In the face of that, one can easily become pessimistic about doing anything and fatalistic about one's lot. Such a point of view also makes more understandable the more extensive use of alcohol, particularly for males, of the occasional outbursts of violence and of the deep interest in gambling. This is nothing new to our time or unique to the American poor. For example, among the impoverished workers of Manchester, England, in the nineteenth century, there was a saying that gin was the poor man's escape from Manchester; the middle class, of course, could get away on weekends and holidays. Gambling, in turn, is endemic among the poor in many cultures and is a manifestation of their strong belief in luck.

Except for the known historical information about drinking, violence, and gambling, this social portrait of the poor is the product of research on the American poor carried out by American social scientists. As a picture of the poor, then, it may be true only for the American poor; our information from other cultures is very fragmentary. Nevertheless, the anthropologist, Oscar Lewis, in *The Children of Sanchez*, has given us a moving portrait of the lives of the urban poor in Mexico and has written of them in these terms:

. . . a strong present time orientation, with relatively little ability to defer gratification and plan for the future, a sense of resignation and fatalism based upon the
realities of their difficult life situation, a belief in male superiority which reaches
its crystallization in *machisme* or the cult of masculinity, a corresponding martyr
complex among women, and finally, a high tolerance for psychological pathology
of all sorts.[17]

While undoubtedly there are considerable variations among diverse national
cultures in the subculture of the lower class, the situation of poverty and
powerlessness, wherever found, probably contributes to a cultural pattern much
like the one we have described for the poor of the United States today.

The Poor and the Lower Class   One of the persistent questions that has beset
those sociologists studying poverty and lower-class life is whether the culture
of the lower class, as we have described it above, fits all those who are poor.
Walter B. Miller asserts that it applies to about 15 percent, or 25 million
Americans, who comprise a "hard-core" lower-class group.[18] However, he also
notes that there are probably at least four to six major subtypes, including
some that would place a higher value on "law-abiding" behavior. The structural pattern of an impoverished lower class American probably covers a
somewhat wider range of cultural patterns than this core pattern.

In response to this concern, S. M. Miller developed a typology organized
around an economic-occupational criterion, *security-insecurity*, and a life-style
criterion of family pattern, *stability-instability*.[19] By combining these into four
logical possibilities, Miller created a typology of four lower classes. These are
(1) the *stable poor,* who have economic security though low-paying jobs but
have stable families; (2) the *strainers,* who are economically secure but have
unstable families; (3) the *copers,* who are economically insecure but have stable
families; and (4) the *unstable,* who are economically insecure and have unstable families. These are the hard-core poor who constitute the problem as
it is often seen by social scientists and by welfare professionals, particularly
in the city. The first category, the stable poor, is probably most frequent
among the rural poor, and it should be remembered that most of the poor
live in rural America. Furthermore, these stable poor are a rural lower class
that manifest only some of the cultural aspects of the lower class we spoke
of above. The *copers,* too, among whom are many downwardly mobile, are less
involved in such a culture, for they often bring to lower-class life the values

---

[17] Oscar Lewis, *The Children of Sanchez* (New York: Random House, 1961), pp. xxvi–xxviii.

[18] Walter B. Miller, "Focal Concerns of Lower-Class Culture," p. 261.

[19] S. M. Miller, "The American Lower Class: A Typological Approach," *Social Research*, 31
(Spring, 1964), 1–22.

and perspectives of those social classes from which they have moved. Not all those who are poor, then, share fully in the pattern of values that we have called the lower-class culture.

THE LOWER CLASS IN A CHANGING SOCIETY

One of the significant discoveries coming from the new concern for poverty has been how little the large edifice of welfare institutions has done in altering the depressed status of the lower class. These are structures created in the 1930s and little changed since then. They were instituted on the assumption of that time that the welfare needs in the vast majority of cases were a consequence of the temporary unemployment of the depression. As they now operate, however, all of the poor do not benefit by these welfare institutions. The permanently unemployed have exhausted unemployment benefits, and, being jobless, are not paying into the OASI (Old Age and Survivors' Insurance), commonly called social security. The millions who are employed, but at low wages, do not qualify for any welfare benefits, except eligibility for public housing. Perhaps the major source of welfare assistance for the lower class has become ADC (Aid to Dependent Children), which provides minimum support for families lacking a male head and breadwinner. The local public welfare rolls constitute the other major support for the unemployed poor.

Social scientists have recently been giving emphasis to the findings of various kinds of social research that point up the fact that the experiences of the lower class with all the social institutions and organizations of society manned by middle-class personnel, including the welfare agencies, are unrewarding and threatening to their self-esteem. Middle-class personnel as gate-keepers often can and do effectively screen out the poor, making easy access to the services of the institution difficult for them. The very "red-tape" of the welfare bureaucracy also discourages and inhibits. To their own disadvantage, then, the lower class often withdraws from such institutions as schools, social agencies, neighborhood houses, and the like.

The middle-class world of social institutions and the lower-class world of social deprivation are two distinct social worlds. If the lower class does not always understand the intentions and meanings of middle-class institutional representatives (sometimes they do only too well), these middle-class agents do not understand the social perspectives and values of lower-class people, and their often earnest efforts to help frequently prove ineffective. As a line of analysis (and also criticism), this theme of misunderstanding between the classes places most of its burden on the middle class; after all, it is they who are attempting to reach out to the lower class, and it is they who might be expected, by virtue of superior education, to understand. The implication is that an understanding of the poor by the middle class is possible and that, if it is done effectively, they can then proceed to act toward the lower class in such a way as to change its position in society. The social change that is envisaged is primarily one of change from the lower class to a middle-class or at least a working-class perspective and pattern of behavior; a change from lower-class people relatively alien to the society into working-class people integrated into the system of values and aspirations that guide the lives of the majority in society.

Whether or not the lower class can be appealed to and thus motivated by middle-class values is a continued source of discussion and argument among social scientists and also among professionals concerned with various programs intended to assist poor people. Some assert that the poor should not be asked to change their values or their life-style; this criticism comes from those who tend to romanticize the poor and it constitutes basically a criticism of the middle class itself, an argument that middle-class life-styles do not warrant extending to other social classes. But the more relevant criticism is that the lower classes—and the working classes, too—view the world from a different perspective than do the middle-class professionals who are the caretakers of the major service institutions of modern society. Herbert Gans calls these caretakers *missionaries* when they seek to build middle-class values and behavior patterns among their lower and working-class clients.[20] Although they genuinely wish to serve their clients' needs, their avowed objectives would require insight into and some empathy for lower-class life, but this seemed always to be lacking among these professionals. Their inability to understand the cultural perspectives that made lower-class behavior meaningful then led them to believe that the failure of lower-class people to learn middle-class ways was "pathological," an individual consequence of the deprivations imposed on them by living in a slum. The professional position that disadvantage and lack of education prevent people from following middle-class patterns is a common one among the professionals of service agencies and is shared broadly in the middle class. This position ignores the culture that such a people have developed as a response to the middle-class institutional world; furthermore, it provides a justification for these agencies to teach and build middle-class values among the poor. Thus, the continuity of many programs to help lower-class people is a continuation of the professional-client relationship, one in which the poor are necessarily *dependent* upon the middle-class professionals and their organizations.

But no amount of help for the lower class can be successful without their

[20] Gans, *The Urban Villagers*, p. 143.

cooperation. However, the lower class tends to withdraw from contact with the middle class and to have little confidence in programs directed to an indefinite future; their powerless involvement with even benevolent middle-class professionals is a demeaning experience, and not all are benevolent. Asking the lower class to develop middle-class motivations is a major barrier to its effective involvement in most programs. Furthermore, many of the new programs do just what the older ones did, namely, make the powerless poor dependent on the powerful agents of the society who have the sources of help to dispense.

But making the poor less dependent in attitude and outlook and thus encouraging the development of a capacity to act on behalf of themselves is not easy to do, for any kind of assistance to the lower class is still invariably a system of controls over them, and even benevolent and reforming middle-class agencies are not likely to relinquish such controls easily. Yet these very controls ensure the continued dependency of the lower class and the concomitant sense of powerlessness that impedes all effort to change them. It may be, then, that any ultimate solution to the position of the lower class in society may depend on types of social action that reduce their dependency on powerful and controlling agencies, enhance their capacity to act, and develop their confidence that such action will produce rewarding outcomes.

For such a solution there is a need for very different kinds of strategies for attacking poverty. Most of all the middle class must be willing to relinquish some of its power over the lives of the lower class and seek instead to involve them in social relationships that give them an obvious (to them) stake in programs and actions, and that also give them channels of communication and access to decision-making centers in the society. Such a strategy clearly has political implications, for it suggests that effective measures to reduce poverty may finally come only when the poor are sufficiently organized and thus sufficiently powerful to force changes in the opportunity structure of modern society. Some recognition of this has led the current federal anti-poverty programs to require that the poor be included in community efforts to build programs to cope with poverty. That such a stipulation had to be specified, and that it has been so politically and professionally controversial is testimony to the strangeness of the idea. Certainly, the lower class to this point has been defined as a dependent and subject population, *for* whom things may be done, but not *by* whom anything is done. For social workers and for all the professionals of the bureaucraticized welfare services they are a client-population. The professionals act to, act on, act toward, and act in behalf of their clients, but the clients do not undertake any action by themselves.

The magnitude of this task is evident when one scans the complexity of poverty and the enormity of the sense of helplessness and cynicism that marks the lower-class view of the world. But to say the task is impossible invites comparison with action for civil rights. Poor and uneducated Negroes in the cities have learned to have hope where they had none before, have learned to defy and challenge segregation and white power where they never did before, and have learned to demonstrate in the face of opposition and threats where they never dared before. There has developed a capacity for action in these people who seemed the least likely candidates for becoming self-activating.

The whole self-image and self-esteem of Negroes has been redefined by their involvement in successful action programs. Not only have they achieved gains in civil rights, they have achieved gains in their sense of being worthwhile persons and of being genuine participants in the society. What poor urban Negroes can do is therefore not beyond the capacity of other poor. There have been some few cases of success in involving the poor in action programs; although the number is yet limited, the point is that it can be done. More to the point, the new style of black power among urban Negroes, most of whom are lower-class, may provide the source for significant lower-class power generating effective demands to eliminate the structural sources of poverty.

An affluent society, shaped by an advanced technology, finds in the presence of poverty and the lower class an embarrassment that is not so evident in other societies. In a technologically advanced society there is no useful social function for the lower class, and their very numbers testify to a waste of human lives. But also it is an embarrassment to all the claims of affluence, education and opportunity, and the better life for all, that are made in behalf of such societies. The existence of a lower class is nothing new; but the idea that there need not be one is new. What happens to the position of the lower class in American society may then be one of the most significant social changes in the continually modifying structure of modern industrial societies.

"Even though there's no chance of a meaningful dialogue at this time, your mother and I want you to know that the channels of communication are always open."

From *Here It Comes* by Lee Lorenz,
copyright © 1958–1968
by the Bobbs-Merrill Company, Inc.,
reprinted by permission of the publishers.

*"Know what Ah miss? Ah miss that soft, sweet singing.
That's what Ah miss."*

Drawing by Ed Fisher; Copr. © 1956 The New Yorker Magazine, Inc.

PART 4 INSTITUTIONS AND SOCIAL STRUCTURE

1

2

1. Nigeria: a king and his wives.
2. Washington Square, N.Y.: a family outing, plus one.
3. Puerto Rican family in New York.
4. Suburban scene.
5. Mother combing her daughter's hair.
6. Mother with infant and dog.

3

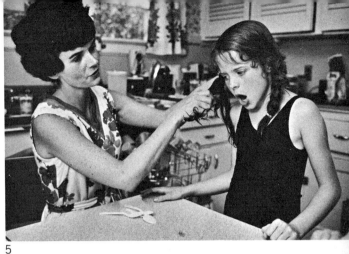

5

4

6

**THE
FAMILY**

13

Down through the ages, so it has seemed, the family has been a fundamental and persistent social group, a basic social institution at the very core of society. The values institutionalized in the family have long been regarded as important enough to warrant strong measures against any behavior that violated them. Not only has the family been defined as fundamental to the existence of society, but it has been viewed as a source of morality and decent conduct. It has also been defined as a primary force for controlling behavior and civilizing the human animal.

However, when men have talked loftily about *the* family, they have in fact meant the Western family and perhaps only the middle-class Western family—and they have confused *that* family with the family everywhere. The Western family is but one form of the family, however, and the vast exploration by anthropologists into the organization of human life tells us that what may properly be called *family* appears in a wide and varied set of social patterns. There is no one common arrangement among all peoples of the earth, no one set of human relationships that is universally defined as properly familial.

Men have often talked about the universal character of the family, about how essential it is for civilization, and about family as an institutional necessity if there is to be society. They have often been moved to say these things just because they have begun to fear that such an appreciation of the proper place of the family was no longer so commonly accepted and taken for granted, and because the family seemed to them to be in danger of losing its central institutional place in human affairs. This gloomy prediction of the decline of the family, with fearful consequences for human society, has indeed helped promote some of the sociological inquiry into the family as a human group and a social institution.

THE FAMILY AS A SOCIOLOGICAL PROBLEM

As long as there has been sociology, the family has been regarded as a social institution and a significant social group. Nonetheless, early sociologists gave little direct attention to such smaller social units as the family in their analysis of society. In the late nineteenth and early twentieth century the study of the family was carried on by anthropologists and archeologists, who examined it in preliterate culture as well as in ancient civilizations. A great amount of data about the family in other times and places, though primarily Western, was amassed in G. E. Howard's *History of Matrimonial Institutions Chiefly in England and the United States,* published in three volumes in 1904. By the turn of the century the study of the family was well established in the burgeoning social sciences, and there was as well a highly relativistic perspective that recognized great differences in the family in different places and at different times. Perhaps Edward A. Westermack's *The History of Human Marriage* was the climax to this relatively objective, historical, anthropological, as well as relativistic approach to the family. When American sociologists, particularly after 1920, gave serious attention to the family, a strong basis for a comparative perspective on the family as a social institution had already been established.

From then until now, the study of the family as a sociological interest has flourished; there has been a vast amount of research on the modern American family and a steady stream of textbooks on the sociology of family and marriage. During this period certain persistent sociological problems have remained in the forefront of scholarly concern: (1) the universality of the family; (2) the family as a social institution with appropriate social functions; (3) industrialization and the changing modern family; (4) the effect of stratification on the family; (5) the relation of family status to other social roles of women; and (6) the future of the family in advanced industrial societies.

The concern about the universality of the family and the family as a social institution reflects the basic scholarly interest in the family as a human pattern appearing in (presumably) all cultures, however varied its form and functions. The very process of defining the family in universal rather than the particularistic Western terms depended upon an adequate description of what appeared to be the family structure in all known human societies, past and present. However, the American sociologist has been primarily interested in the modern American family, and particularly in the middle-class family. His concern for the effect of stratification upon the family, in turn, is evidence of the sociologist's sensitivity to the possible error of defining the urban, middle-class, American family as *the* American family; thus, it introduces a comparative note to research within the context of American society, encouraging the comparison of the family at different class levels.

Then, lastly, the concern about the relation of industrialization to the family reflects a persistent interest in the long-term effect of industrialization upon the structure of the Western family and the deep concern over its possible disorganization as an institution, if not an actual group. This concern also reflects the treating of the family as a social problem in modern society. Here are expressed those long-felt fears that the primacy of the family both as an institution, as an agent of socialization and of social control, are adversely affected by the political, economic, and technological changes which so radically alter traditionally folk societies. It is in this same context that the position of women is so frequently reviewed. Their status is compared to that of women in earlier, more agrarian periods when the several roles of the woman as wife, mother, and housekeeper were all family-linked, and her access to the outside world was much more limited. Thus, changes in family structure have been regarded as central to changes in the status and roles of modern women. Furthermore, industrialization and technological change are continuing processes, with still further unanticipated effects upon the family.

THE UNIVERSALITY OF THE FAMILY

To say that the family is universal is to say that its definition encompasses those several characteristics of the family that are to be found in all known human societies. Furthermore, it is also to say that there *is* some such social structure or at least some social processes that can in fact be found universally. The strong moral value placed upon the family in Western culture is no guarantee that the family as Western men have known it, or even something like it, will be found in all other societies. The case of its universality, then, is in one instance an empirical matter; it is to say that as a matter of fact the family is found universally, though in variant form. But it is also a theoretical matter, and the common theoretical position is that the family is universally necessary because it fulfills certain basic functions for the maintenance of social life. Combining these two, the empirical and the theoretical, then goes like this: there are certain basic functions that must be fulfilled in any society, and there is a basic structural unit, consisting of husband, wife, and children, called a *nuclear* family, that can be empirically observed in all societies that carry out these functions. The functions are: (1) permission of sexual access between adults; (2) legitimate reproduction; (3) responsibility for the care and upbringing of children; and (4) cooperation as an economic unit, at least in consumption. This has been the highly influential thesis advanced by the anthropologist, George P. Murdock.[1] These four functions, apparently agreed upon as universal by social scientists, point up one important factor: every known human society regulates and controls in some institutionalized manner the relationships of the sexes and the provisions for mating for the purposes of reproduction. Even the so-called "primitives" define who may have sexual access to whom—it is the crassest form of ethnocentrism to believe that only "civilized" societies have normative regulations about sex.

When the legitimate sexual access of male and female carries with it the society's recognition of the right to have children, the resulting relationship is *marriage*. Murdock's effort to define family led him to define marriage more narrowly, namely, that there also had to be cohabitation in the same household and some degree of economic cooperation. However, there are known exceptions to this: in the Israel *kibbutz*, for example, there is no specific eco-

[1] George P. Murdock, *Social Structures* (New York: Macmillan, 1949).

nomic cooperation of husband and wife. The marriage of male and female as a socially recognized right then permits the assignment of responsibility for the care and upbringing of the resulting issue of such a union, in short, for the *maintenance* and *socialization* of the child. The economic cooperation that Murdock believed to be universal is related to this responsibility for socialization, for it implies a cooperation in providing for the needs of dependent children.

If there is any quarrel among social scientists about the universality of the family, it seems to lie, not in the matter of the basic functions used to define the family, but in the existence of a basic concrete social unit that embodies these functions. There is not even disagreement that it is a small and kinship-based unit; but there is disagreement that it is universally the nuclear family unit of husband-father, wife-mother, and son and daughter. The disagreement is empirical, there are simply well-known examples of societies in which this nuclear family unit is not the group for carrying out at least all of these functions. We have cited the *kibbutz* as not exemplifying economic cooperation as a separate unit, but also in the *kibbutz* the mother-father unit does not raise and train the children; this is a communal responsibility. In China (at least prior to 1949) the economic cooperation and the education of children was carried on within an extended family group rather than the smaller nuclear unit. These few examples suggest there is an extremely varied patterning of human relationships that makes possible the carrying out of these four functions. Thus, it becomes sociologically necessary to distinguish between those defined processes, here called "functions," and a concrete form of social group that embodies these functions. It is clear from anthropological research that no one concrete form of human group is essential to carry out these functions, and therefore no one concrete group is universal.

This requires a theoretical distinction between the family as an *institution* and the family as a *social group*. As an institution, the concept of the family refers to those processes or functions mentioned instituted in any society for sexual control of mating, reproduction, and the care and socialization of the young. There is a range of structures by means of which these functions can be carried out, and it is not necessary that *one* structure be designated for all the necessary functions, or that such a structure have *only* these functions.

As a social group, the concept of family refers to a small, kinship-based interacting unit, within which at least some of the functions are carried out, and within which at least some of the socializing experiences of the child occur. Although the nuclear family is widespread, its make-up is not; among the Nayar of India, for example, the resident family group consists of brother, sister, and sister's children. The father of the children resides elsewhere and is not part of the family as a group, though he is part of the institutional arrangement for mating and procreation.

In a recent review of the literature of family and marriage, the sociologist Morris Zelditch, Jr. asserts that there is no one concrete group that can be called "family" and so he turned to an earlier definition by the great functional anthropologist, Bronislaw Malinowski, to find what is universal.[2] Malinowski proposed that *legitimacy* is the institutionalized family norm, for the concept of legitimate birth is universal. Legitimate birth places the child into an ongoing social structure in an appropriate set of relations to others. It establishes his rights and his status with others; his rights include the right to inheritance, to education, to being cared for, and to succession to status in the society. Thus, according to this perspective, for a family to exist, there must be a *pater role*, which determines the status, rights, and obligations of a child socially defined as pater's, and, in turn, which assigns to the pater responsibility for that child. Zelditch suggests that what is "subtle" about this definition is that, despite the Western use of the term, *pater,* the conception of family does not require that pater be a male, be one person only, or be the one to provide instruction for the child. Rather, says Zelditch, pater need only supervise the child and be responsible to society for the way the child conducts himself.

As Zelditch correctly points out, this conception of the family presumes that "every society has some conception of legitimate birth," and where there are known societies, such as Haiti, where well over half the births are illegitimate, "it is open to serious question whether illegitimacy is everywhere defined, or everywhere defined as morally wrong."[3] The widespread pattern of illegitimacy among Caribbean societies—there are at least eight with illegitimate birth rates of over 60 percent—provides a testing ground for this proposition, for at first blush the evidence would seem to suggest that there was no belief in legitimacy of birth when illegitimacy is so common. But the careful work of a sociologist, William J. Goode, seems to make quite clear that the evidence from the Caribbean countries is not to be taken as evidence contradicting the universal existence of a conception of legitimate birth.[4] Rather, Goode found that legitimate birth was recognized and valued in these countries, but that illegitimacy was a consequence of family disorganization among lower-class families. No new structures had emerged to take the place of older courtship practices, which had broken down. Furthermore, Goode discovered that women enter these "consensual" unions only when marriage is not immediately possible, and that eventually a marriage does take place.

The family, then, is a universal process in human society. What is *not* universal is the form of the family as it is known in Western society, or indeed

[2] Morris Zelditch, Jr., "Family, Marriage, and Kinship," in Robert E. L. Faris, ed., *Handbook of Modern Sociology* (Chicago: Rand McNally, 1964), pp. 680–733.

[3] Zelditch, p. 682.

[4] W. J. Goode, "Illegitimacy in the Caribbean Social Structure," *American Sociological Review,* 25 (February, 1960), 21–30.

the particular form to be found in any society. What is universal is that every society sanctions mating between male and female, which gives legitimacy to the birth of a child, thus establishing some way (and there are varied ways) in which the child is given status and rights in the society and in which responsibility for the child is assumed by someone.

An appreciation of just how varied in form the family can be is an essential element in a sociological perspective on the family, even if one's concern is only with the nuclear family of Western societies. A gloomy prediction of the collapse of the family has often come from those who implicitly defined the family in terms of the particular historic forms known in Western culture. Thus, the advent of significant changes has been interpreted as disorganization and the loss of a basic institution, with presumably dire consequences to follow. What follows below is a brief discussion of some of the major variations, though by no means all, which will give some better idea of just what *variation* in the family really means.

Mate-Selection   In any society mate selection is never a chance procedure, but only in some societies is there a notion of romantic love as a basis for a *free* choice of mates by the individuals themselves. In a large number of traditional societies, mate-selection has been a prerogative of the family. These are often crucial and complex decisions for families, involving many economic and prestige interests, since inheritance of status and property may be associated with marriage. In those cultures in which the choice of a mate is crucial for the family system, it is, therefore, not likely to be a free one. But regardless of whether it is free or not, the selection process in many societies is also governed by rules of *endogamy* and *exogamy*. An endogamous rule prescribes that the individual must marry *within* a defined group (a tribe or clan, for example), whereas an exogamous rule specifies that the individual must marry *outside* the social group (the kinship group or the clan).

In folk societies, rules of endogamy and exogamy are formally prescribed and are a part of the traditional culture. In modern societies there are few formal requirements, yet there are powerful informal expectations of endogamy and exogamy that often exert an implicit choice on young people. Race and religion are obvious examples of this, particularly race, for interracial marriages have long been formally proscribed by law in some states of the United States; recently, these laws have been invalidated by civil rights decisions of the Supreme Court. Yet the strength of these endogamous rules does not rely on legislation but rather on widely diffused informal expectations; severe sanctions are often invoked for violation, such as ostracism and disinheritance from the family. Though perhaps less binding, an endogamous expectation to marry within one's *religious* grouping also has strong influence on marriage selection. Less obvious but no less significant is an informal endogamous rule about *social class*. The parents of an eligible daughter, in particular, are usually concerned about the class standing, now and potential, of the young man that would marry their daughter.

Where the choice of mate is tied up with the social interests of the family as a unit, and particularly its economic interests, the selection of a bride for an eligible male may be negotiated in accompanying economic terms. Thus, there may be a bride-price, which means that the male's family must pay the bride's family, or the bride may provide a dowry. In other cases, there can be an exchange of goods between the families. Societies in which these processes prevail often have a specialized role for the negotiation and arrangement of marriages.

Forms of Marriage   The Western form of marriage is *monogamy,* but this is by no means universal. Many societies in the world have sanctioned *polygamy,* where a plurality of mates is possible. We are likely to think that polygamy means a man has several wives, but the term also covers the situation where a woman has several husbands. *Polygyny* is the term for a man having several wives, and *polyandry* the term for a woman having several husbands. Polygyny is far more common than polyandry, and it occurs in societies in which men have superior status and are the source of authority in the family. Yet even in societies which sanction polygyny it remains an ideal that only a minority can ever attain. To marry several women means to be able to support several women as well as their children, and thus a polygamous man is wealthier and of higher social status. Indeed, having several wives is often an important index of status. The lot of the common man is to be able to afford but one wife. Polyandry, in turn, is a very infrequent form of marriage and is usually associated with poor economic conditions. It occurs in western Tibet, among the Marquesans of Oceana, and also among the Todas of India. In the latter case, the several husbands are usually brothers. The existence of polyandry is not associated with a dominant position for the woman but rather with situations of scarce resources, in which men are apparently compelled to share a wife.

Rules of Authority, and Residence   Where authority in the family is vested in the male head, the family is *patriarchal.* This is the Western tradition; indeed, wherever the male is dominant, this is the family pattern likely to exist. Usually closely associated with this is a patrilineal tracing of descent through the male side of the family. Inheritance of name and property, for example, are frequently patrilineal. Where a newly married couple are required to take up residence in or near the residence of the male's family, the rule of residence is then *patrilocal*. Obviously, there are also *matriarchal* systems of authority for the family, there are *matrilineal* systems for descent and inheritance of status, and there are *matrilocal* rules of residence. But there are also rules which are neither. The tracing of descent may be *bilateral*, as it is, though imperfectly, in American society—imperfectly, because we are patrilineal in such things as transmitting names. But we do relate the child relatively equally to each line of his descent; he has four grandparents, for example, and our rules of descent do not favor one over the other. Furthermore, the rules of residence for us are neither patrilocal nor matrilocal, but *neolocal;* the new couple chooses a place of residence by other criteria. Authority in our system is still largely formally patriarchal, but in practice the trend has been largely in the direction of an equal relationship, concomitant with the relative equalization of the status of women. There are class variations in this, however, with the middle-class family nearer to the pattern of equality.

Divorce and Remarriage   Whatever the form of marriage in a society, every society must have rules concerning continuity of the marriage and also about remarriage. Divorce is a socially sanctioned dissolving of the marriage between living partners. In many societies, divorce has been easy to obtain, and there indeed may be no necessary expectation that a marital liaison be permanent. But other societies have placed a religious sanctification on marriage, and strong sanctions, including no customary or legal provision for divorce, have been placed against breaking a marital union. In other societies, divorce rights may rest with the male only, with both partners, or even with the female only, as can be found in at least one primitive society.

Where marriage is based upon free choice and deep emotional attachment, and where the nuclear family maintains a separate family residence, divorce is disrupting to the lives of children as well as parents. In such societies it is never highly favored or easily obtained. Careful legal controls are developed to ensure the economic support of the woman and children. But where marriages are not based upon love and the liaison is not based upon strong emotional attachment, and where children are secure within an extended family, as in many tribal societies, divorces may be an easy matter, decided by the partners themselves. Where religious belief and rule forbid divorce, other kinds of sexual liaisons outside of formal marriage may develop, particularly where, among the upper status, the marriages are not love affairs but family-arranged liaisons of convenience. In France and in Latin America, some wealthy men maintain a marriage and a home but also frequently support a mistress.

A more important issue for any society is the marital future of males and females when their partner dies. In many traditional societies, neither male nor female could survive economically without a partner, and thus remarriage was always provided for. Perhaps the most striking instance of this is the situation whereby a man is expected to marry his brother's wife, if the brother should die. In this way the woman and her children are provided for in advance.

Marriage and Family: A Variable Process   These few comments have pointed out the major forms and rules governing marriage and family life in the human species. There are minor variations on even these. But what is important is that the vast range of known examples tells us, most clearly and simply, that no one pattern or rule is *inherently* natural to man. However strange, morally wrong, or even repulsive, any one of them may be to some, it has seemed to be right and natural to others. To say this is to assume a culturally relativistic posture and argue that men have developed a range of forms out of their experience and in response to conditions and problems that they faced. No one alternative, of all the known ones, necessarily seemed more naturally right than others, except to those who developed it from their historic experience.

This last point needs to be underscored. A scientific cultural relativism rests upon a position about the nature of man, about what is part of his inherent nature and what is his experientially developed culture and human nature. But one cannot, by agreeing with this, then leap to a *moral* position that any alternative is as good as another and, by that, seek to justify patterns of sexual behavior that have been institutionally proscribed. Various alternatives developed in different societies each have their logic and rationale in the context of cultural values and historic experience of that society, and each form fits in with the pattern of other forms that make up the larger structural arrangement governing marriage and family. Furthermore, each one of these is also rooted in a wider pattern of economic and social relationships and an accompanying cognitive structure of assumptions and values that "makes sense" to the participants.

SOCIAL FUNCTIONS OF THE FAMILY

When examined as a social institution, the family is viewed from the perspective of its relation to society. As a social institution, it is a structural arrangement, an organized means for carrying out certain functions necessary for the continuity of society and for the maintenance of social order.

What are those functions so necessary for the society that are carried out by the family? It is a matter of consensus among sociologists to specify four: reproduction, maintenance, socialization, and placement.

Reproduction No human society, no matter how primitive, fails to control the reproductive process in some fashion. Marriage, as we saw above, is a social sanction for sexual union that leads to procreation. To that extent it represents a control of sex as well, but it does not follow that all societies therefore restrict sexual intercourse to married partners. Again, within a wide range of variation, there are societies that permit premarital intercourse and others that do not restrict sexual relations to married partners only. The control of sex is a wider and only partly related matter to that of control of the reproductive process. Whatever may be the way in which any society allows sexual relations, it does provide a process for designating and sanctioning mating for reproduction. What follows from this is that the offspring of such matings are then legitimate, and responsibility for their care can be assigned within a kinship structure, according to the institutional rules of that society.

Maintenance The human young is helpless for a longer period of time than any other animal and requires constant care. His needs must be attended to and he must be supported, even though he cannot contribute in any way to his own support. Some set of relationships and some designated responsibilities must then be assigned to adults to see that this is done. Again, the family, whatever its structure, is the organized unit for carrying out this function.

Socialization The responsibility for ensuring the socialization of the young is always explicitly designated, for this significant process cannot be left to chance. The very continuity of the society depends not merely upon the reproduction of the species, but also upon a careful social induction of the young into the society and its varied social groups. It is the family unit—and usually, though not always, the mother and father—who spend the time necessary to see that the young learn the skills and knowledge sufficient to take their place as adults in the society.

As we examined it previously, socialization was interpreted primarily as a *social-psychological* process whereby the new human organism became a person; without the socialization that human interaction provides, he would remain an organism or at best a haphazardly learning animal. But our perspective here is *institutional*, emphasizing that the socialization of the young is also necessary for the continuity of the society. It is the means by which the members of a society are adequately replaced by the oncoming generation. As a consequence, socialization is no haphazard or implicit process in any society. There is much deliberate effort to teach both skills and norms and so to inculcate both the values and the techniques that enable an individual to become an adult member of the society. Although much learning can and does occur outside of any family group, particularly in modern society, socialization remains a primary family function.

Placement   A legitimate birth provides a specified relationship of a child to others and places him in a kinship system. Through that he is then placed in the larger groups of the society and is assigned a status. The family as a persistent social unit used to provide the sole training for status; in the peasant family the boy learned to be a tiller of the soil, in an artisan's family he learned to be a craftsman, whereas in the aristocrat's family he learned to be a cultivated gentleman and a ruler of others. In modern society, where achieved status is so much more relevant than in societies of peasants, artisans, and aristocrats, the placement function is nonetheless still important. The present complex problem of educating the children of the poor—the culturally deprived—demonstrates quite well that birth into a middle-class family in modern urban America means a preparation by the family, through sociali- zation, educational opportunities, and social class experiences, for a position in the middle class and in the mobility process, even though not into the specific occupation of the father.

Legitimacy in birth, as we saw, is necessary for placement in the society; thus, the vested interest that all societies have in legitimacy. In many societies some process of *succession,* the transmission of status from father to son, or at least from one adult to his legitimately designated successor, is one major way of placing the young person in the status system of the society. So is *inheritance,* the transmission of property from one generation to another, a process that is often tied up in complex institutional rules. A third way is *descent;* the place- ment of the young in wider social groups, such as kinship, ethnic, or tribal. In modern society an informal process of descent serves to locate people in political parties, occupations, churches, and even colleges, so that, for example, they become Republican, lawyers, Episcopalians, and graduates of an Ivy League college, because that is where family tradition places them.

The Affectional Function   When sociological analysis of the family focuses upon the contemporary family—and particularly the American family—then there is an emphasis upon what has been called "the affectional function." The argument here is simple: the intense and close interaction of children and parents in a separate household creates a small, primary unit that is the major source of sustaining affection for both parents and children. The modern American family, in particular, is frequently geographically removed from other kin, and this intensifies the familial interaction that occurs within the conjugal unit of mother, father, and children occupying a common household. However, this is not to make the affectional function a universal one for the family. Rather, the affectional function becomes peculiarly that of the modern, urban family. In the more extended family of agrarian societies, the primary interaction even within a common household or a series of related and closely located households extends over a wider range of relationships, and the provision of affection and intimacy may not be as dependent upon a smaller set of relationships.

Because of this function, the modern family carries a particularly heavy burden, for it is the social unit from which people expect love and affection; thus, adults demand, not a marriage, but a *happy* marriage. That this is not easy to attain or to maintain, once attained, can be seen by the relatively high divorce rate. But that divorce does not disabuse people of this ideal or completely disillusion them can be seen also in the fact that most divorced Americans remarry. It is commonplace to relate this emphatic expectation of love and affection in marriage to a romantic myth that is regarded as of peculiarly strong quality in American culture, sustained by all the outpourings of mass culture. This is simply a way of saying that it is not a *universal* characteristic of the family, not even in the Western world. Romantic love does not everywhere provide the means of mate-selection and the basis for marriage. Among the rural Irish, for example, ever since the devastating potato famine of the 1840s, marriage generally occurs quite late, and a bride is carefully selected for a now quite mature son by his father, based entirely upon social and economic considerations. As noted before, a "marriage of convenience" is common among French upper bourgeois, for again considerations of status, family honor, and economics dictate the choice, not love. This then often leads to other alliances that are tolerated as long as they are discreet enough to bring no public shame on the family.

This emphasis upon the affectional function of the family has two dimensions. First, it asserts that *universally* the intimate interaction of parents and children, or at least that frequent and intimate interaction that occurs within some circumscribed circle of kin, creates a basic *primary* group that generates the deepest of human feelings of love and affection (and possibly also hate) that are significant in providing a context for the socialization of children. But, secondly, there is today among American families a very high *expectation* of happiness to be derived from the intimate and primary character of family relationships, particularly the marital. This happens as adults increasingly see in the family a fundamental source of primary response to a world more and more impersonal in its relationships.

The central argument underlying this latter point—that the American family places high expectations of happiness in marriage and family relationships—rests upon an analysis of what has happened to the family over the past century or so, largely as a consequence of industrialization. This revolutionary process has, so goes the analysis, significantly altered the family, just as it has other social institutions. In particular, the thesis is that the significant change in the family is one of a loss of central functions with a concomitant change in the relationship of the individual to the family.

INDUSTRIALIZATION AND THE FAMILY

A common perspective for viewing the family today is to see it as a social institution that has undergone radical change by virtue of the industrialization of society. Thus, what it is today is highlighted against what it was in the past. The common theme of this analysis is the *decline of social functions* that belong to the family as a major consequence of the structural changes producing an increasingly large-scale, more technological society. A generation back, sociologists frequently viewed this development with misgivings, seeing in the loss of functions a decline in the central institutional importance of the family. One prominent feature of such analysis was to suggest that the family was passing "from institution to companionship," as suggested by Ernest Burgess and Harvey J. Locke in the title of their book.[5]

This sociological perspective focused, first, on a conception of the agrarian family (even into the nineteenth century) as necessarily the center of life for the individual, who was in fact highly dependent upon the family. The family possessed major *economic* functions, for the agrarian family was a *productive* unit, organized by a division of labor to operate a farm. The occupation of the person, except for the few who went into religious institutions or the cities, was therefore tied in with his family status and could not be carried out except through the family as a work-group. This economic dependence upon the family was the source of family authority and control over the individual. But also, since the family was a unit of production as well as consumption, since the family organized work and owned land, its own continuity, power, and economic well-being meant that family interests took precedence over individual desires. The individual was locked into a demanding kinship structure of duties and obligations that extended beyond the immediate (nuclear) family to a wider network of kin.

In agrarian society there is less specialization than in urban society, and thus the family performs many functions that have since become community or societal responsibilities. It not only socializes the young, it provides much of the other training the child will receive. In fact, among European peasants,

---

[5] Ernest Burgess and Harvey J. Locke, *The Family: From Institution to Companionship* (New York: American Book, 1953).

where literacy was for a long time uncommon, there was no significant training outside the family. A boy was going to be a peasant, and how better to learn than by working with his father at a young age. A girl who was going to be a wife and mother in a peasant family learned best working with her mother, assuming at a young age responsibilities in the care of the young and tasks related to maintaining the household. Out of this developed something of an age-graded division of labor. An agrarian society had no structure for welfare or social security; the family maintained the aged, nursed the sick, buried the dead, and provided for the mentally or physically crippled. The kinship system also had to ensure support for widows and orphans and also had to provide a place for the occasionally unmarried woman. Given this, one can understand the growth of a moral outlook that made kinship a most binding and obligatory relationship, regardless of what personal feelings the members may have had for one another.

In an agrarian society, then, the extended family was an institutional structure developed to carry out a whole set of *life-maintaining* activities—what sociologists conventionally call *functions.* Its particular pattern of organization was a consequence of the centralization of a whole range of social functions in one social group. The centralization of socially necessary activities then made the family an *institution,* not merely a social group, and one that many could legitimately feel to be *the* central institution in society.

The transformation of society by industrialization thoroughly altered the set of institutional arrangements that had given to the family a complex and authoritative institutional structure. Perhaps the first thing was the development of a technology that took work out of the home and into the factory; as a consequence, the family ceased to be a productive unit. Work, located elsewhere, became in time the almost sole responsibility of the father, and this separation of family and occupation had a number of consequences. For one thing, children were no longer economically necessary, as they had been in agrarian society, where a father without sons might not be able to maintain himself. In the family as a unit of consumption they were mouths to feed, and the reward for having them was no longer in economic values. In this pattern is the source of the self-induced limitation on family size by mobile, middle-class families, who find that children are competitive with other values, and who thus clearly balance off the reward of having children with other material and psychic rewards available in modern society.

A loss of economic function, then, transforms the family. Such a change accounts for the decline of the extended family system of kinship obligation and the emergence of the small, nuclear family that maintains a separate and independent household. Such a family often reduces considerably its interaction with other kin, since its dependence on kin has been reduced. Similarly, the kinds of occupational training and more advanced education required for an industrial society has led both to the emergence of separate, specialized institutions of schools and universities and to the loss of education as a primary family responsibility. This means that *socialization* is no longer a family monopoly; instead, it is necessarily shared with schools as formal institutions and with the peer group culture that abounds in the context of the school.

Children in an industrial society do not in large part succeed to the same occupational roles as their parents. Even when they do, it is not the parents who control entrance to the occupations, though in some few cases they may be able to exert influence for preferential acceptance of their children. Their pursuit of careers and education that were perhaps not even known or available to their parents also makes them somewhat independent of the family. Their occupational future is not bound up in the family, and the family has little control over it, except where there is a family business. The overall consequence of this is a lessening of family control over the individual, a shrinking of its relevance for various areas of his life, and a diminishing of those obligatory bonds that knit together a kinship structure.

What is left is a social group that still performs those core functions of the familial institution—reproduction, maintenance, socialization, and placement—even though socialization is a function shared with other institutions. The loss of economic functions, then, has changed the family, and these changes are still going on. Nonetheless, the recognition of even radical change in the family does not justify the pessimistic view of the past generation that saw the family as breaking up and losing its central importance to society. Modern Americans marry and establish families as much as ever—more so, in fact, since the census records fewer unmarried adults than ever—though the social unit established is not modeled after the agrarian family of the nineteenth century. If modern people still marry, reproduce, and bring up children, under the vastly altered circumstances of a highly technological society, they obviously find some value in it. In no way, for the purposes of education or occupation, for sex or prestige, do they need a family. But the intimate, shared interaction of a small family unit has become a highly desired experience that almost all seek. A happy marriage and a happy family life may, indeed, be difficult to obtain, but in a world more and more rendered impersonal and bureaucratic it is an intimate set of relationships and a modern form of belonging to a primary group that almost all seek to create for themselves.

STRATIFICATION AND THE FAMILY

The processes of industrialization and urbanization have so altered prevailing family types that the large, extended farm family of the past is no longer the typical family in American society. Instead, sociologists invariably single out the urban middle-class family as the "typical" family and also as the significant one. However predominant in its numbers and its influence and however much it may be held up as a model in the mass media and the marriage manuals, the urban middle-class family as a prototype does not exhaust the range of family types to be found in American society. The stratification of American society into various classes and status groups has its effect upon the family; variation in stratification yields variation in family types.

The sociological analysis of the relation of stratification and family has focused primarily upon the familial function of placement. The family places the child in status positions within the society by such processes as *descent, inheritance,* and *succession.* The latter in particular means the transmission of status. As noted before, even in the mobile society of today the family's placement function is no less important, even though the son may no longer inherit his father's occupation or indeed any other element of his status in the community.

In all stratified societies, where major social class differences occur, family occupies a position within one of the social classes, and we speak, for example, of middle-class or working-class families. Do we mean anything more by that than that the father can be classified middle-or working-class? Apparently we do, for families seem to vary by class in ways that are significant for the life-chances of their offspring. By and large, even in mobile societies, the family acts as a stabilizing factor in the class structure, for it is through the family that most individuals are placed in the class structure, tending to get the same position as their parents. In part this is done because the family has the resources, the knowledge, the "contacts" and influence, to locate their children in class positions similar to their own. An upper-class family, of course, and even a middle-class family knows how to choose educational lines of greatest advantage or how to gain entry into the corporate structure through personal contacts. Even skilled workers often manage to get their own sons preferential entry into an occupation, where access depends on getting into an apprenticeship program.

These are the factors that have made family more important in small towns than in big cities, more important for those of higher social status than for those of lower status, and have been more important in the past than they are now or are likely to be in the future. Yet this does not reduce the importance of family for placement in social class, for the socialization of the child by the family transmits the attitudes and values, modes of individual behavior, and life-styles that are typical of the parent's social class. By virtue of socialization, then, the child becomes a person whose very approach to life makes him an appropriate member of a given social class.

Because the family naturally and unconsciously socializes the child into the values and life-styles of its social class, sociologists have concentrated on variation by social class in the family's socialization of the young and particularly in its child-rearing practices. Yet the effort to contrast the middle class with the lower class on child-rearing practices has proven to be scientifically controversial and theoretically difficult. During the 1940s the work of such prominent social scientists as Allison Davis and Robert Havighurst demonstrated that middle-class mothers followed a rather rigid, inflexible schedule of feeding, attempted toilet-training early, and sought early attainment of habits of cleanliness.[6] Lower-class mothers, in contrast, seemed to proceed flexibly without a rigid schedule and to allow greater freedom for impulsive and even aggressive behavior.

For a decade or so, this interpretation of class differences in socialization was widely accepted in social science. It was supported by a then prevailing perspective that viewed critically the apparently rigid and demanding character of middle-class child-training, in contrast to the presumably freer and relatively permissive child-rearing practices of lower-class people. The latter practices were credited with developing personalities who acted more spontaneously and responded naturally to sexual desires and to impulsive expressions of aggression. Arnold Green's influential essay provided a more general theoretical support by delineating sources of tension between middle-class parents and their children.[7] Green suggested that the source of neurosis was in the anxiety of the middle-class child about his relations with his parents. Their love for him seemed to be conditioned upon his adequate performance of parental expectancies, which in turn were shaped by their orientation to the competitive milieu of the middle class and their practice of constantly comparing their children to others.

Despite the scientific merit of the research that drew this contrast there lurked throughout it an implicitly unfavorable contrast between the classes, in which the lower class emerged as natural and spontaneous, whereas the middle class appeared to be reared in an atmosphere of impulse-renunciation, rigid controls, and anxiety over interpersonal relations. In the lower class, children were accepted naturally and allowed to act somewhat uninhibitedly, but in the middle class, child-rearing seemed to be oriented to the potential achievement and mobility of the children. Behind the surface of scientific research was a moral criticism of middle-class devotion to success and social status.

Later on, however, new research seemed to suggest just the opposite: it was the middle class that appeared permissive and less demanding in its child-rearing practices, whereas the lower class seemed rigid and demanding, exerting

---

[6] Allison Davis and Robert J. Havighurst, "Social Class and Color Differences in Child-Rearing," *American Sociological Review,* 11 (1946), 698–710.

[7] Arnold Green, "The Middle-Class Male Child and Neurosis," *American Sociological Review,* 11 (February, 1946), 31–41.

strong parental controls and insisting on strong conformity to parental demands and rules. Urie Bronfenbrenner, a social psychologist specializing in the problems of socialization and family relations, analyzed the seemingly contradictory findings in a definitive essay and pointed out the middle-class child-rearing practices had, indeed, changed.[8] It seemed that since World War I, parents had been geared to professional advice, particularly that of the highly influential manuals published in successive editions by the U.S. Children's Bureau, as well as to such authorities as Arnold Gesell and Benjamin Spock. Changing advice had brought changing practices.

In unraveling the effect of social stratification upon the family some problems are due to both methodological and conceptual difficulties in making the contrast between any two classes, such as middle class and lower class. How social class is defined, so that how respondents in any study are then classified, is one matter of importance. For example, the effort to contrast the middle class with a stratum below it in social rank often leads to lumping together people sometimes labeled lower class and sometimes working class. But this confuses two distinct class levels in the society, whose family patterns are quite different. Many of the family studies revealed a stable working-class family in which parents not only made strong demands on their children, but also were gradually learning the child-rearing styles of the middle class.

Classes are wide and varied strata, and research oriented to the legitimate task of finding *inter*class differences may tend to slight *intra*class differences. Thus, the assumption that there is *a* middle-class family may give insufficient attention to differences in family patterns *within* the middle class. A study in the Detroit area by Daniel Miller, a psychologist, and Guy Swanson, a sociologist, deliberately sought to compare "entrepreneurial" and "bureaucratic" families in their orientation to child training.[9] In effect this was a comparison of families of the old middle class and the new middle class.

What they discovered was that the new middle-class, ("bureaucratic") parents taught their children the importance of adjustment, security, and getting along with peers, an orientation consistent with the newer child-training literature and fitting in with an "organization-man" perspective of the world. The old middle-class, ("entrepreneurial") parents, in turn, instilled in their children a more active and manipulative approach to life in which the child learns the necessity of strong aspirations and hard striving toward his goals. These are the familiar historic values of the Protestant Ethic, and they are also the child-training values found in the professional literature of twenty and thirty years ago.

[8] Urie Bronfenbrenner, "Socialization and Social Class Through Time and Space," in E. E. Maccoby, T. M. Newcomb, and E. L. Hartley, eds., *Readings in Social Psychology* (New York: Holt, Rinehart and Winston, 1958), p. 400.

[9] Daniel R. Miller and Guy E. Swanson, *The Changing American Parent* (New York: Wiley, 1958).

In the same sense, the working-class family and the lower-class family are not to be confused. The former is a stable family unit that emphasizes its own respectability and demands obedience, whereas the latter are often unstable units because of the uncertain relation of the male head. It is here that is found, particularly in the Negro lower class, the matri-centered family in which parental authority is weakly exercised, and what cohesion exists in the family is due to the mother.

These researches in the relation of stratification to family child-rearing practices have largely centered around one major issue: the extent to which one or more classes are the source of a more inhibiting and constraining mode for the socialization of the young. The early research first said that it was the middle class that was inhibiting and that the lower class socialized its children in a freer and more permissive way. The idea has been that the impulse-inhibiting atmosphere produces less psychically free individuals, less able to create new modes of behavior and thought, thus more in need of authority-sources to guide their own conduct. It was readily assumed that a more permissive socialization process would create less repressed and inhibited personalities. But what purported to be a scientific contrast was also quite clearly a criticism of the middle class in terms of a value orientation that presumed that a freer and more permissive socialization produced a more adequate and a "better" personality. If one tries to sort out this research, several things are evident. First, the very criticism of the middle class became integrated into the professional literature that the middle class read and took seriously, and a significant shift in its child-rearing practices toward a less inhibiting and more permissive pattern occurred. Secondly, the difference between the middle class and other classes on this matter was primarily based upon research on middle and lower classes, not the working class, whose child-rearing practices were not, in fact, any more uninhibiting and permissive than the middle class, though its emphases were different. Thus, there are two differences here: (1) there is a change over time, particularly within the middle class to a greater permissiveness and a less inhibiting and constraining milieu for the child; and (2) there are important intraclass differences. For the lower stratum, there is an upper blue-collar level, a working class, whose demands on their children do constitute a more constraining atmosphere demanding inhibition of impulses. However, *lower* in the blue-collar level and *higher* in the white-collar level, in the lower class and the upper-middle class, there is a more permissive atmosphere that allows a freer expression of aggressive impulses.

Now we have reached that point where a reassessment of the value of permissive-oriented socialization is underway, and a recognition of the importance of the relation between externally-imposed authority and internal controls is appearing in the even newer professional advice. Furthermore, a more detailed examination of the less inhibited socialization of the lower class indicates that they do not enjoy a rich inner life but are oriented to the immediate and concrete, the personal, and the sensory; they also have difficulty in developing a time perspective, an appreciation of the complex, or a capacity for abstraction.

Class and Ethnicity   An emphasis upon class-based differences in the family stresses the family as a socializing agency, but it tends to obscure other forms of status as differentiating the family. Within the United States, the still meaningful ethnic differentiation, though clearly intertwined with class, has nonetheless given us ethnic family types. In particular, the peasant origin of many ethnic families has meant a tradition of a strong and cohesive family, with meaningful interaction along lines of extended kin. Even though the urban environment may not seem to be as conducive to retaining such a pattern of family life, there is still evidence of much rich and complex family life, particularly at the working-class level.

Where class and ethnic culture meet in the same families, they modify one another. Perhaps one of the best expositions of this has been Herbert Gans' *The Urban Villagers*, a study of working-class Italians in Boston. Gans described their family type as one between the modern, and particularly middle-class, *nuclear* family and the *extended* family typical of peasant societies.[10] The *households* are nuclear, in that a single nuclear family lives separately, but the family maintains a rich and meaningful set of relationships with kin, particularly among adult brothers and sisters and their spouses. There is, however, less interaction across the generations, with the important exception of the mother-daughter relationship, which remains close even after the daughter's marriage. She usually locates her new home close to that of her mother's. The extended family pattern provides much of the social interaction for the adults, and they also depend upon one another for advice and help. Thus, interaction outside the family is limited by the high degree of interaction within it.

The relationship (in Gans' study) between the sexes, however, contrasts sharply with that of the middle class. First of all there is no easy interaction between the sexes, and men much prefer to interact only with men. Even within the same house, or within the same room, the men will speak to the men and the women to the women. Communication across sex-lines, therefore, is limited, and men particularly feel ill at ease at this, feeling that women talk faster and are more skillful at it; women, in turn, depend upon this ability to talk their husbands into whatever they want. In husband-wife relations, there is what Gans called a *segregated* relationship, in that there is a

---

[10] Herbert J. Gans, *The Urban Villagers: Group and Class in the Life of Italian-Americans* (New York: Free Press, 1962).

clear differentiation between the tasks and duties of husband and wife, and thus much less, if any, of the *joint* relationship that characterizes the middle-class marriage. Husbands rarely assist in household duties, and women do not even feel it would be right to ask them to do so. Women assume entirely the very large task of caring for children, leaving perhaps only more severe punishment to the father. This family pattern that Gans so vividly described was both ethnic and working-class. Gans, indeed, feels that the class dimension is the more important, and his ability to compare the family pattern there with the working-class family elsewhere, such as in England, testifies to how much of the type is a consequence of social class.

The Negro Lower-Class Family   Of all the issues relating family to stratification, probably none has commanded more attention in recent years than has the Negro lower-class family residing in the urban slum. Social scientists, legis-lators and policy makers, social workers and social reformers, and Negro intellectuals and civil rights leaders, all have debated the problem of the Negro slum family. The controversial issue has been whether this family structure should be viewed only as an outcome of the Negro's economic deprivation, or whether, once established, its inadequate socialization of children further contributes to the Negro's problems.[11]

The Negro slum family is a distinctive variant on the Western family: the major issue is the Negro *mother-centered* organization. Historians and sociolo-gists have documented the impact of slavery upon the Negro family, particu-larly the difficulty that Negro slaves had in maintaining a full nuclear family when their status as chattel property led to their being sold and thus disrupt-ing stable family relations. "The mother-centered family with its emphasis on the primacy of the mother-child relation and only tenuous ties to a man, then, is the legacy of adaptations worked out by Negroes during slavery."[12] After emancipation, this family pattern served well in the often disorganized social conditions that Negroes experienced in the late nineteenth century, yet rural Negroes have been able to maintain full nuclear families more often than have urban Negroes. It is the move to the city that has produced the conditions that led to a high proportion of mother-headed families. Thus, the U.S. Census in 1960 reported that 47 percent of urban Negro families with incomes under $3000 were headed by females, as against 8 percent of those earning over

---

[11] This recent focus on the Negro slum family is consistent with the long established emphasis upon the importance of stable family organization in the sociological literature, as well as the particular concern that goes back more than half a century about the problems of family disorganization.

[12] Lee Rainwater, "Crucible of Identity: The Negro Lower-Class Family," in Talcott Parsons and Kenneth B. Clark, eds., *The Negro American* (Boston: Houghton Mifflin, 1966), p. 167.

$3000.[13] (When this is contrasted with white families, where 38 percent of those with incomes under $3000 are mother-headed, as against only 4 percent of those with incomes over $3000, the case is strong for insisting that this is first a *class* pattern, secondly a *race* one.) Based upon these data Lee Rainwater claims that "it seems very likely that as many as two-thirds of Negro urban poor children will not live in families headed by a man and a woman throughout the first eighteen years of their lives."[14] The frequency of the mother-centered family among Negro urban poor, however, does not mean that such a pattern is preferred or regarded as ideal. Lower-class Negroes know that their family pattern is different from the rest of society, and they often regard the stable family pattern of the working class as the desired one. But the life-circumstances of these people make it too difficult to sustain such a pattern, and the mother-centered family is a cultural adaptation of poor Negroes to the facts of their existence.

The lower-class Negro household run by a woman provides a minimum of effective control over children, both outside the home and even within the home as they grow older. The pregnancy of teen-age daughters that may or may not result in marriage rarely results in the daughter leaving home; instead, the family simply becomes three-generational. Within the limits of her resources, the mother succeeds in maintaining a household and socializing her children; she perseveres without a husband, and one consequence of this is the much greater independence that lower-class Negro women have from the male sex. They have learned not to count on men, and this in turn means a devaluing of the status of men. The inability of lower-class Negro males to hold regular employment severely limits their opportunity to provide regular support for a woman and her children. Indeed, a woman can receive AFDC (Aid to the Families of Dependent Children) if she has no male support, and this encourages unemployed males "to disappear" in order that their family can receive support.

Much of the controversy over the Negro slum family hinges on the evaluation made of the quality of family life and of the socializing of children in a fatherless family. The criticism that such a family pattern is inadequate has brought a defensive response asserting that this presumes that the middle-class family pattern is the only desirable or worthy one, and that the fatherless family of the slum is not the social disorganization that middle-class whites always see. But much of this misses the point and only reflects the contemporary sensitivity to black-white relations in America.

What is relevant is that the mother-centered family is a cultural adjustment

---

[13] Cited in Rainwater, p. 169.
[14] Rainwater, p. 169.

to situations of economic deprivation and the denial to many Negro men of access to the job market on any *regular* basis. It constitutes an achievement under circumstances of severe deprivation to create even a weak family structure, and it provides experiences that are valued by Negro slum-dwellers. But there are severe disadvantages. A significant one has to do with the roles of males and females. The very demands of running a family has given strength to the woman as well as an independence from the male, and a maturity that the male frequently fails to achieve. A great deal of research on this pattern of family life makes one central point: that the Negro male suffers for this family arrangement by a failure of his masculinity. For one thing, there is no adequate male model such as the one a father usually provides for his sons. Secondly, as Rainwater's fine study makes clear, the very pattern of family and neighborhood life is destructive of the necessary search for identity that all maturing persons go through. Children in the Negro slum do not learn to regard themselves as part of a "solidary collectivity." The pattern of family quarreling denies worthy identity-claims as hostile family members vent degrading verbal (and sometimes physical) aggressions on one another. Women in anger will demean the masculinity of young males. That same male, forced into only unskilled, poor-paying jobs, is often treated with little if any respect in the larger community, as well. Thus, within the Negro slum community and within the larger society the Negro male finds no respected male role, and the mother-centered family in which women dominate and men have no stable place only further denies to him the possibility of validating his masculinity in ways that are respected and understood in the society. The consequence is then to find other ways to do so: in sexual prowess and in violence, for example, but these are destructive. But if the Negro male suffers for this pattern of socialization, so do the females; no child growing up under such circumstances can escape its impact on the shaping of his personality. Rainwater notes that

> Negro slum children as they grow up in their families and in their neighborhoods are exposed to a set of experiences—and a rhetoric which conceptualizes them— that brings home to the child an understanding of his essence as a weak and debased person. . . .[15]

Among those social scientists who accept this analysis there is controversy about the mother-centered slum family when the issue of social action for accomplishing change is raised. Should this family pattern be a target of such remedial action as family counseling, family therapy, education for family living, and so forth? Must the family be strengthened, particularly in regard to developing acceptable male roles, before Negroes can cope successfully with

[15] Rainwater, p. 194.

their problems? One significant answer is yes, arguing that the weak family structure of the Negro slum family inhibits the capacity of Negroes to act effectively; therefore, that family pattern must be changed directly. Yet Rainwater asks, "Can an army of social workers undo the damage of three hundred years by talking and listening without massive changes in the social and economic situations of the families with whom they are to deal?"[16] His own suggestion, like that of many others, is that primary emphasis needs to be given to Negro male employment and to income maintenance for mothers. The debilitating effects of extreme poverty must be overcome before there can be any stabilization of slum family life. But there must also be the development of a new and meaningful pattern of education for slum children, as well as new modes of participation for Negroes that permits them to pursue aggressively their own self-interest, and that also develops pride in group identity. Such an argument as this does not make the family a direct target for change but seeks instead to create the social conditions under which a pattern of family life that Negro slum-dwellers fully recognize and prefer is capable of emerging.

WOMEN: FAMILY ROLE AND SOCIAL STATUS

Throughout history the basic organization of the Western family has rested upon the division of roles between male and female, upon the differential assignment of functions to each, and also upon the overtly stated superiority of males. Indeed, women in classical Greece and Rome were deemed inferior creatures and their subordinate status reflected it; at one time the Roman father and husband held practically life-and-death power over both his wife and his children. Although there was a gradual change over the centuries, the significant transition in the status of women has come since and as a consequence of the Industrial Revolution; its impact upon the structure of the family could not but help affect the role of the women in society. Yet, despite quite radical changes, the status of the woman much more than that of the man is bound up in her female capacity for childbearing and in her traditional role of wife and mother.

The Weaker Sex   Over the centuries the male sex has offered varied rationalizations for subordinating women, and much of it has rested upon the dubious assumption of women's inherent inferiority. That women are *physically* a weaker sex is no universal idea, for though men have been the warriors and athletes, peasant and native women in many cultures have performed hard, manual

[16] Rainwater, pp. 195–196.

labor. Whatever the superior *muscular* capacity of men, women are apparently superior in other ways; the female organism has a better survival capacity than the male, and nature apparently compensates for this by having more males born than females. Whatever advantage nature gives to the male sex here, however, barely lasts into early adulthood; by about age twenty-six in the United States, there are as many females as males.

Rationalizations about the physical and intellectual inferiority of women no longer have the same credence that they once did. The long struggle for equal status for women has brought them the vote, property rights, and an equality in civil status before the courts of the land. Yet it would be incorrect to assert that women are equal to men in every phase of modern social life. Job discrimination for women still exists, no less so in middle-class occupations than working-class ones. Indeed, women still do not find it easy to gain access, both educationally and occupationally, into the historically male professions—and college teaching is one of them.

Home versus Career   Since the turn of the century, the problem of the woman in society has been one of home *versus* career. Most of the discussion has tended to polarize the alternatives available to women: marriage, with a home and children, *or,* singleness and a career (though in some cases a childless marriage was regarded as possible). As a consequence, employment was long regarded as appropriate for women for the few years prior to marriage, and, of course, for spinster school teachers. This was to a great extent the actual pattern, and prior to World War II the majority of employed women in the labor force were single and under twenty-five years of age. With few exceptions, they left their jobs upon marriage; indeed, many pre-World War II employers would not retain women after marriage.

During the early part of the century, and particularly during the 1920s and 1930s, a greater opportunity for a range of careers for women gained headway. Pioneering generations of women broke barriers in professional and business occupations. Yet World War II brought a new pattern of earlier marriages, earlier birth of the first child, and an increase in the average number of children born to young middle-class women. The sharp increase in the postwar birth rate was a consequence of this pattern. By their own choice women still seemed to place high priority on the conventional wife-mother role.

Education for Women   This concern about careers for women has particular relevance for the question of education for women. Resistance to equal educational opportunities for women has long been predicated on the assumption that education has an economic payoff in careers, and if women are bound only for marriage, then extended education seemed unnecessary. But perhaps a more crucial issue has been the effect of a college education on the self-image of women. It is the educated women who have worried most about a career versus marriage and who have been concerned about making some valid use of the talent and knowledge acquired in college. It is they who have chafed at being "merely a housewife," and have talked about being "unfulfilled" with the routines of motherhood and housekeeping. Many of them have solved their problem by finding part-time employment that makes good use of their skills. Others have simply worked while raising one or two children; nursery schools and baby-sitters and housekeepers have helped. The more frequent pattern, however, is a new life-cycle for such educated women, involving a college education, employment until marriage and even after, usually until the birth of a child, then a full-time motherhood role while the children are growing up. For many of today's younger-marrying women, this role may come when they are in their twenties and early thirties. Then, lastly, comes a return to the job market for a full-time career.

Vocation and Avocation   But for many women, particularly upper-middle-class ones, the delayed-career pattern may be inappropriate or simply undesired. For them there is still an older model of a spare-time avocational career: a busy social and civic life, and these two may be considerably intertwined. Church, civic, and charitable organizations have long looked to middle-class women for the skills and energies to carry out campaigns and to assist in operating the organization. From the League of Women Voters to the March of Dimes, there is a wide range of socially acceptable functions for the skills and talents of women. Increasingly, such women are politically active, manning offices, getting signatures, and undertaking the many other unpaid tasks that go with politics.

Class Differences   The concern about careers and education for women and about the status of women in modern society is particularly significant with regard to middle-class women. Social class differentiates not only the behavior and life-style of women, but their very aspirations and hopes as women. The wives of workingmen do not usually have the training for careers and cannot even easily imagine what a career would be. Their own perspective is more closely rooted to the wife-mother role in the working class.[17] Furthermore, they are more conventional in their acceptance of their role, of its obligations and demands on them, and of the relatively sharp separation between the

---

[17] For a description of the life and values of the working-class woman, see Lee Rainwater, Richard P. Coleman, and Gerald P. Handel, *Workingman's Wife: Her Personality, World, and Life Style* (New York: Oceana Publications, 1959). Also, Mirra Komarovsky, *Blue-Collar Marriage* (New York: Random House, 1962).

work-role of the man and home-role of the wife. Neither are they joiners and civic-doers—nor are their husbands, either. They live lives less involved in and less related to the larger world, whose agencies and institutions are, from their perspective, manned by the trained and verbal professionals of the middle class.

Women in the Labor Force   Yet even among working-class women the work-role penetrates into their lives in a way it did not in the past. In the United States work has now become a more significant aspect of the lives of more women than ever before. More women work today than ever in the past, but working women are not randomly distributed among the female population. Working women are now, on the average, older women, with many of the married ones no longer raising children, and divorcées and widows who often must work out of necessity.

However there are two other factors about working women that need to be understood. Women are employed either out of necessity or at least to add to the family income; this economic motive is much more important than any concern for "fulfillment" and for a rewarding career, even though in some cases an economic motive and such a career may very well go together. But for most women they do not. The reason for this is simply that the world of jobs is still male controlled, and female employment is still predominantly in traditional lower-paying female jobs. In 1962, women accounted for 69 percent of all clerical workers, and 98 percent of all household workers. They were 28 percent of all factory workers, and 39 percent of all professionals. However, the latter category includes teachers, social workers, and librarians; women are still scarcer in the more prestigeful professions.[18]

THE FUTURE OF THE FAMILY

The once pessimistic forecast about the future of the family, so common a generation ago, has now given way to a perspective which acknowledges that the family indeed remains a central institution in modern society, the primary agency for reproduction and for the socialization of the child. But there is still much about the future of the family that is highly problematic. There has emerged a newer pattern of younger marriages, with a related style of having children sooner, generally while the mother is still in her twenties. A consequence of this has been a rapid increase in the birth rate, creating the concern about population growth and the possibilities for birth control.

[18] These figures on women in employment are from the *1962 Handbook of Women Workers* (Washington, D.C.: U.S. Department of Labor, 1963).

The New Familism   A new pattern of family life was well under way in American life before there was any serious recognition of it. It evidently first emerged during and just after World War II, but the changes then were attributed to the war itself and regarded as only a temporary hiatus in the more familiar pattern of middle-class family life. But by the 1950s, it became clear that something different characterized the marrying and family style of young, middle-class Americans. By the 1920s in the United States, the urban middle class had evolved a recognizable family pattern that differentiated sharply from the rural family, on the one hand, and from the urban working class, on the other. It was marked by a delay in marriage until college was completed and even until some economic security had been obtained. As a result the average age of marriage for the middle class was in the mid-twenties for women and the late twenties for men. Furthermore there was usually some delay in having a first child, and family size was held down— two or three children, at most, and many having but one.

This was the pattern that changed so abruptly about the time of World War II. First, marriage came at a much earlier age; there was no waiting to be economically established. Then there emerged the pattern of the married college student and also of the wife working to support her student husband. It is perhaps difficult for today's students to realize how radically different the college campus became. Prior to World War II, the married student was a rarity, and indeed many liberal arts colleges would not allow students to marry and remain in school. Nor did colleges provide housing for married students—this is a postwar phenomenon. The earlier marriage was also associated with less delay in having a first child, with a somewhat closer spacing of children, and with an increase in family size to establish a new middle-class pattern of three or four children, not merely one or two.

The fact of marrying sooner and having children sooner and having more of them is evident enough from the statistical record. But what such factual evidence does not tell us is why. Well into the 1950s many presumed experts in both demography and family were arguing that what had occurred was simply a temporary interruption in a long run decline in the birth rate, due largely to the war and also somewhat to postwar prosperity. However, it is now time to recognize that such objective facts as availability of jobs and higher salary levels do not alone adequately explain what has happened. These make it possible for people to marry younger, but they do not compel them to do so. It now seems necessary to examine the values about marriage and family among the contemporary generation of young middle-class Americans.

That there has been a new-found value upon family living, a value of *familism,* has been argued by such sociologists as Wendell Bell and Nelson Foote. (This was discussed in relation to the movement to suburbia in Chapter 8.) Bell argues that the earlier marriage, the shorter childless time span after marriage, and the child-centered family life now typical of young suburban-dwelling Americans is evidence of a major choice of values, a familistic orientation chosen over other competitive values of status and life-style. Some hard, objective facts—recorded as statistics in census figures about age and marriage, age of mother at birth of first child, number of children born to a woman— provide documentation for the change in family patterns among the American middle-class. Although harder to do so, it becomes necessary to understand this process as not merely a response to changing conditions such as war and prosperity but also a change in values about marriage, family, and having children.

This is as far now as sociological analysis based upon empirical observation will take us. The inquiring mind, however, will still ask: *why* have values about family changed? There has been much speculation on this, pointing to the Cold War and to the uncertainties of life in a world constantly threatened by nuclear holocaust. Others have suggested that familism is a response to the impersonality and anomie of a bureaucratized world, a refuge in a primary group where love and intimacy are paramount. Such speculation is useful, though it remains just that—imaginative speculation, not empirical evidence. It is useful if it suggests where we might look for clues, or in what context of social change we might expect to test hypotheses about the resurgence of a familistic orientation.

The Family in World Perspective   The realization that the American family has adapted to the circumstances of industrialization and urbanization, and that its decline as social institution is a premature decision for social science has led to a new interest in the meaning of family in a changing society. But what is true of the United States in this case is also true on a world basis; the family is changing from old forms and patterns and adapting to the kind of society that is coming into being everywhere. The industrialization of the world is accompanied by the emergence of the conjugal family on a world basis, with a diminution of the extended kinship relationships so predominant in more traditional family forms. William J. Goode emphasizes that this conjugal family pattern is in itself a world revolution in family structure, but that also it is a factor in the world revolution that is the transition to the modern, industrial society.[19] As a part of that revolution the conjugal family emphasizes the freedom of the individual to choose his own life and control his own destiny. "It releases people from older family rigidities, and contributes to the development of the society and economy which in turn yield more

---

[19] William J. Goode, "The Family as an Element in the World Revolution," in Peter I. Rose, *The Study of Society* (New York: Random House, 1967), pp. 528–538. This article is a reprint of a pamphlet of the same name published by the Institute of Life Insurance. For a fuller exposition of Goode's analysis of the family in a world-wide perspective, see his *World Revolution and Family Patterns* (New York: Free Press, 1963).

opportunities for its members."[20] This revolution toward the conjugal family
with its greater personal freedom is not, however, necessarily welcomed by all,
who see, instead, "freedom's other face, which is irresponsibility, disorganization,
and the personal burden of failure."[21] Freedom of choice always risks the pain
of failure and disappointment; and the shrinking of kin ties reduces the sense
of responsibility that family members have for one another.

Goode's argument proceeds on the generally accepted premise that the
family in some modified pattern has survived the major social changes into
industrialization, and has a future in modern society. Perhaps the only significant contrary voice on this has been that of Barrington Moore,[22] who has
challenged this idea and suggested instead that the family may not survive as
an institution. He follows Bertrand Russell in viewing the family from an
evolutionary perspective that raises the possibility that it may be an obsolete
institution or become one before long. He argues that there are conditions that
"make it possible for the advanced industrial societies of the world to do away
with the family and substitute other social arrangements that impose fewer
unnecessary and painful restrictions on humanity."[23] Moore, a student of
totalitarian society, is unimpressed by the usual arguments that the Soviet
revolutionary experiment demonstrated the necessity of the family as an institution. Instead, he feels that in its early days the revolutionary leaders had too
much to do to be concerned with the family, and that in time "Soviet totalitarianism may have succeeded in capturing the family and subverting this
institution to its own uses."[24]

Moore's basic argument is that there is no necessity for the family today, and
that many of its basic features are outmoded and useless, if not worse. The
obligation of affection among kin, for example, he characterizes as "a true
relic of barbarism."[25] He regards the contemporary role of the wife and
mother as one which makes demands impossible to meet, children as often a
burden to parents, the troubles of adolescence as evidence of the family's
"inadequacy in stabilizing the human personality," and motherhood as frequently a degrading experience. He does not even believe that the necessity
of affection and love for the infant requires family, though he does recognize
that the present bureaucratized setting for nurses now precludes the necessary
warm and affectionate structure. But Moore again follows Russell in regarding this as a solvable problem, suggesting radical and perhaps yet un-

---

[20] Goode, p. 537.

[21] Goode, p. 538.

[22] Barrington Moore, "Thoughts on the Future of the Family," in his *Political Power and
Social Theory* (Cambridge, Mass.: Harvard University Press, 1958), pp. 160–178.

[23] Moore, p. 162.

[24] Moore, pp. 162–163.

[25] Moore, p. 163.

thinkable arrangements for child-rearing that would free most people from what have been burdensome if also rewarding relationships. His conception of a world revolution toward the freedom of the individual then goes much further than does Goode's idea of the conjugal family pattern. Undoubtedly, Moore's projection for the future of the family runs counter to that of practically all sociologists who have written on the subject and his conceptions of future institutional arrangements not only violate presently held strong values but seem to go somewhat beyond the empirical basis for adequate scientific prediction. Moore, in turn, feels that contemporary students of the family "are doing little more than projecting certain middle-class hopes onto a refractory reality."[26]

Nonetheless, Moore's voice is a lonely sociological one; those sociologists who study the family project a more positive view of the future of the family. They are intrigued with the new familism that has become an evident value perspective in American society since World War II. They are also interested in the new way in which the concern for birth control, planned parenthood, and limits on population growth have renewed an interest in the relation between the family and government; with the latter as the maker of societal policy.

The Family and Social Policy   The new familism induced an increase in the American birth rate that helped focus attention on what has now been called on a world scale the *population explosion*. The neo-Malthusian fear that the world simply cannot support an unlimited number has hastened a social concern about limiting births. Birth control, once so controversial an issue that political leaders stayed away from it, has now become social policy in many parts of the world, including the United States. *Family planning* has moved from a planner's dream to a central concern of social policy. That strong efforts are being made to plan family size testifies to the accepted institutional place of the family; its functions are still reproduction and the socialization of the child. It is on these functions that new social policies proceed: (1) to seek to control family size by various measures of birth control; and (2) to encourage a climate for socialization consistent with the latest in professional conceptions of what is ideal.

It may very well be, then, that the twentieth century has created a new aspect of family life—the direct intervention into family size and modes of socialization through various social measures and extensive family education. In the past societies have always supported the family in its traditional patterns. But what is new is the effort to set a pattern for the family as a matter of social policy. The consequences of this cannot yet be anticipated, for the

[26] Moore, p. 161.

social knowledge that would predict the complex outcome of family planning as national policy lies in the future. Perhaps this knowledge will come only after the facts, whatever they may be.

The family as we have known it in Western culture has survived some radical changes in human life without being abandoned or losing its central place as a social institution. It has, however, undergone considerable modification, and there is every reason to anticipate that some further changes will occur as the world responds to the threat of over-population. But these are *changes* in structure and in values, not the *decline* of the family, which a pessimistic view only a generation ago confidently predicted. As a social institution and as perhaps man's most valued primary group, the family still has a significant future place in human society.

1. A grade school dancing class.
2. Columbia University graduation.
3. Dr. Rufus E. Clement, President of Atlanta University.
4. Job Corps program: training in a supermarket.
5. High school class discussion group.
6. A public school class gets an inside view of a police station.

4 5

6

EDUCATION

14

Prominent among the massive trends of this century is the growth of a complex and bewildering web of institutional arrangements called education, commanding an ever larger share of the resources of the society and affecting in varied ways more and more persons for longer and longer periods of their lives. It interlocks with economic and technological structures, with political structures and elites, and with economic development and world affairs in a manner never dreamed of a few decades ago. Assuredly, education is one of the great, central activities of modern society.

There was a time, not so long ago, when education could be thought of as a morality-sustaining institution, functionally necessary for transmitting the culture and some requisite skills, but sharing with religion that curious status of being carefully sustained, symbolically praised, but largely outside the mainstream of relevant adult activities that counted as "really" significant. "Those who can, do; those who can't, teach"—this misguided aphorism not only expressed a widespread contempt for teaching as an occupation, but it also conveyed the anti-intellectualism of a business-dominated society. But this is no longer the case. Two major and interrelated events have changed the whole nature of education and moved it to the foreground of institutional arrangements. First, an educational system that benefited the few has been replaced by mass education, a transformation not yet complete, as rising college enrollments indicate. Secondly, a highly advanced technological society has an imperative, compelling need for highly trained people and for educated people to man the major institutions of society. To educate the many is necessary if all are to find a useful status in modern society. To educate new elites to higher technical and intellectual levels is also necessary if modern society is to make use of advanced technology and science, and if it is to construct integrative rather than conflicting relations with other societies in a rapidly changing and frequently volatile world.

Previous generations of sociologists gave but limited attention to the processes of education, so that the sociology of education is but a recent interest for sociologists. There is every reason to believe, however, that the sociological analysis of education will be a major concern of sociology in the decades ahead.

EDUCATION AS A SOCIOLOGICAL PROBLEM

The sociology of education has extended considerably its scope of analysis since the late Willard Waller wrote *The Sociology of Teaching* in 1932.[1] Earlier concerns with teaching as a social process, with the social roles of the teacher,

[1] Willard Waller, *The Sociology of Teaching* (New York: Wiley, 1932).

as well as with the functions of the school, have been enlarged to include the complex issue of the relationship of education to the other institutions of society, particularly the economic and political, as well as to the systems of stratification, particularly class and race. Sociologists have recently displayed a strong interest in the *internal* organization of education, with particular concern for the subcultures of students in high school and college. Much less attention has been given to the study of the college and the university, but a sociology of higher education has become a recognized need by sociologists. Although the newer interest of sociology in education is developing sociological specialists, other sociologists, particularly those concerned with social class and minority status, have contributed to our understanding of the educational process from their own particular perspective. Nor has there been lost the older concern for the functions of education and thus its relationship to society.

In one sense, the field of education may not be an appropriate subdivision of the field of sociology—education is not a conceptual distinction within the theoretical approach of sociology. Its varied phenomena can be subsumed under the sociology of formal organization, of social groups, of subcultures, of cliques (small groups), and of stratification. As an area of specialization, therefore, it is not conceptually distinguished from other areas, but is simply one of several, like medicine, law, and industry, to which sociological analysis can be applied. But the process of educating people is one of the major tasks in any society, and it has become a rapidly changing and profoundly complicating one for modern society. There is legitimation, therefore, in there being such an *institutional* field of study. Indeed, if there is anything that links the older study of education with the burgeoning works of a newer generation, it is this institutional approach that is concerned with education as a set of *functions* necessary for society, thus making it a universal process in human society. To be sure, as a differentiated institution, separate from family and work structures, education is a distinctly modern phenomenon. More to the point, the kind of simple statement about the functions of education that sufficed for any earlier generation will no longer do, for the complex process that is education in contemporary American society takes on many tasks hitherto unimagined and serves a wide and heterogeneous body of people in most diverse ways.

A concern for the functions of education in modern society focuses on the relation of education to its environment and the processes of mutual influence that go on. Perhaps one of these, however, stands out: sociologists concerned with stratification and minority status, with occupational access and achievement, as well as social psychologists studying child development, have all found significance in the relation of education to social stratification. Seemingly, class and ethnic structures, and racial status as well, differentiate the opportunities for education and also differentiate the manner in which the educational structure makes available its resources. Such an issue strikes at a significant value in a mobile society—the belief in equality of educational opportunity. Much of the ideological rationalization for differentials in status in American society rest upon the belief that even the poor and disadvantaged have an equal opportunity to be educated and thus to be mobile. Evidence that this might not be so damages that belief. It then raises the issue of who controls education—the relation of education to power.

Historically, most of the effort to study education as an institution and as a social process has concentrated upon the first twelve years of education, with much less attention given to the study of the college and the university. Although there are some similar problems and issues and some general functions typical of all education, *higher education*, nonetheless, possesses issues peculiar to itself. The study of higher education has then understandably emerged as a significant subarea of the sociology of education, only partially related to the traditional concerns of that field.

These several issues and areas of study, then, constitute what is now most problematic for sociology about the field of education: (1) the *functions* of education, particularly under changing circumstances in which it is no longer obvious just what these functions now are; (2) the complex involvement of education with the processes of *stratification*, particularly as these bear upon the issue of equality of educational opportunity and the position of disadvantaged children; and (3) the emergent giant that is *higher education* with its still changing and as yet unclear but nonetheless central place in the organization of modern society.

THE FUNCTIONS OF EDUCATION

The universal functions of education are to socialize the young and to transmit the culture to the next generation. Transmitting the culture has meant to teach norms and values, to teach knowledge, and to train the young in applicable and usable skills. Any society does this, but the traditional, preindustrial societies did so without developing a specialized institution: a school set aside from other groups, with a specifically identified group of specialists called teachers. Most preindustrial societies have been nonliterate, at least for the mass of the population, and of course many have been preliterate. Literacy, prior to the industrialization of society, was not essential for the mass of the population, and so any specialized education became a prerogative of particular groups in the society: (1) priests and others who were the literate ones of the society; (2) the aristocratic and ruling stratum; and later, (3) merchants and others involved in commercial transactions.

But a modern, industrial society simply cannot function with illiterates. More to the point, modern society increasingly requires people with higher levels of literacy and higher levels of technical training. Thus, education as a mass process becomes a prerequisite for the functioning of modern society. The continuing increase in specialized and advanced education for ever larger numbers produces a large and complex educational process, highly differentiated internally as it responds to the demand for a rich variety of specialized curricula. The consequence of this has been a varied and diversified set of educational agencies in, for example, the United States.

The Diversity of Educational Forms   Education in the United States has been both private and public, specialized and comprehensive, centralized and decentralized—a bewildering variety of forms and patterns that continues to grow and change. Historically the major responsibility for education has been public, however, there have been two major forms of private education that have persisted and even grown somewhat over time: private schools for upper strata and parochial schools for particular religious groups. The Catholic Church has developed the largest network of parochial schools, from the elementary to the university level.

According to the Department of Health, Education, and Welfare, there are nearly 2000 units of higher education, divided among universities, liberal arts colleges, teachers colleges, technical schools, junior colleges (a rapidly growing category) and some others: theological schools, art schools, and the like.[2] Although the largest single group is the liberal arts college—there were 760 in 1962—it is some 140 growing universities that are the symbols of what higher education is becoming in the modern world: the *multiversity* with its vast body of students and its complex research structure only partially related to the process of teaching.

There has never been a national system of educational control in the United States; rather, counties, townships, and cities have operated public school systems, and churches and other private groups have operated private schools. The result has been a great diversity in the quality and in the opportunity for educational advantage. Even within the same state, schools range in quality from the best to the poorest. Nor does a single control ensure equality and sameness of performance; within large cities, schools in slums are generally inferior to schools in middle-class neighborhoods. The legal right to operate schools in the United States is much more decentralized than in most other countries, a fact that accounts for much of the diversity in form and quality to be found in American education. But so does the American effort to extend

[2] U.S. Department of Health, Education, and Welfare, Office of Education, *Higher Education*, No. 17 (Washington, D.C.: Government Printing Office, 1961).

education on a mass basis and to provide some kind of education for a diverse array of talents, interests, and learning abilities within a heterogeneous population.

However, diversity in education is also a consequence of a differentiation among educational units that is, in turn, a consequence of specialization. In general, the American elementary and high school have been comprehensive schools, providing within the same unit and in the same building the major forms of study available to students. Such a school is comprehensive in that it takes all students, regardless of the social strata of their origin, nonetheless an informal and even concealed specialization may operate. Most obviously, a specialization of programs into commercial, vocational, and college preparatory separates students into different educational experiences. Furthermore, in large cities schools located in middle-class neighborhoods may in fact specialize as college preparatory, though ostensibly all curricula are available. Even more so, many upper-middle-class suburban high schools are almost exclusively college preparatory schools; graduation from one of these is an excellent access to preferred colleges and universities. Such specialization as this, however, is clearly related to problems of status, and reflects pressures of the local stratification process. Diverse and varied at the historical outset, then, American education has continued to display variation and specialization, and new demands and functions merely increase the diversity.

The Transmission of Culture   Throughout human history, the one broad and enduring function of education has been to act as the agent of society in transmitting the culture. Education has been caretaker of the culture, particularly its central values, and it has complemented the family's socialization function by inducting the young into the normative order. The new members of any society enter it in a culturally barbaric state, and the long task of inducting them into a normative order must begin soon after birth. At one time, the relatively undifferentiated character of traditional societies enabled kinship and community to do this, but the highly differentiated and technological complex society has come necessarily to rely upon a specialized institution.

The educational process begins for the very young as a fairly common and comprehensive emphasis upon normative training along with basic literacy skills. As the child advances through the educational process, two things occur: there is a shift from the early emphasis upon the normative and there is the introduction of more specialized training; education becomes less a common and comprehensive process. The decline in the emphasis upon the normative is followed by an enlargement of the teaching of knowledge, though the normative is by no means absent here. Indeed, values may play a large part in selecting both the kind of knowledge to be taught and the perspective from which it is taught. The teaching of a society's history and thus its self-image and conception of its place in the world and its relation to other societies is a case in point. In the modern world, as education continues, the teaching of specialized skills becomes increasingly dominant within the process. The more advanced education is, the more does it become specifically related to qualification for professional occupations.

The Decline of Moral Authority   By virtue of the emphasis upon a normative orientation as a first aspect of cultural transmission—really a process of continuing the socialization begun in the family—the school has long been regarded as a significant source of moral training. There was highly pronounced emphasis upon this moral task in American education from elementary school through college in the nineteenth century. The private liberal arts college in the United States, which has no obvious counterpart in European education, was largely begun under church auspices, and the professional training it accomplished was related mostly to teaching and preaching—to turning out teachers and clergymen. The moral controls of such colleges were rigid, and their frequent location in small towns and rural areas was a deliberate effort to isolate them from the more secular, urbanizing influence of the city.

There is, however, an unmistakable trend away from this emphasis and a distinct loss of moral authority. Emile Durkheim, perhaps the only one of the great founders of sociology to be intensely concerned with education, depicted the teacher as primarily a moral authority, both by virtue of experience and as an authority of the culture.[3] But this interpretation would seem to hold best in a traditional society, where the teacher was seen as the representative of society and its cultural values by both the students and their parents. In modern, technological and mobility-oriented societies, such traditional moral authority for the teacher dissolves. There are several reasons for this. The relation of the teacher to the student becomes increasingly one of the teacher having control over the social chances for mobility, a "gate-keeper" to educational advancement so necessary for attaining higher status. Also, in a more educated society teachers are no longer the unique symbols of moral authority and intellectual competence that they once were, thus they no longer so adequately represent the culture in the eyes of others. Furthermore, the subcultures of youth, manifested in influential peer groups, now successfully compete with and challenge the traditional moral authority of the teacher.

This last issue is crucially important, for it suggests that there are significant noneducational structures in modern society that nonetheless perform educative functions. For a broad mass of youth, the significant one is the mass media

[3] For Durkheim's conception of education, see his *Education and Society* (New York: Free Press, 1956).

of entertainment—primarily radio, television, movies, and the record industry—which combines instruction and education. Much of the adult critique of these modes of youth entertainment have been oriented to questions of taste; but perhaps the primary issue is the extent to which there is significant cultural transmission by these mass media—not only taste, but perspective and normative outlooks, life-styles and cultural choices. Whether such media merely sensitively reflect and give expression to cultural patterns emergent within a new generation, or whether instead they create and transmit them to a readily responsive youth poses a causal question that cannot now be answered. Whatever the causal process may be, however, the mass media enter the picture as a major competitor with the school for a source of moral influence over youth and thus as a major competitor with the school and the teacher for moral authority.

The significance of this development lies not only in the diversification of socializing influences upon youth, but also in the fact that the more local and immediate sources of cultural indoctrination—family and parents, church and community, school and teacher—lose some influence to new sources of influence that are not responsible to or controllable by the older forms of family, church, and school. As *agents* of society, teachers could mediate between the child and the larger world, selecting what of the cultural tradition was to be transmitted and thus effectively controlling (though never completely so) the way the individual was to be culturally introduced to his society. But the mass media are a revolutionary change, in that the mediating agent is displaced; these media reach *directly* to the peer groups and to the adolescents, and increasingly even to preadolescents. Nor is their primary concern or interest that of cultural transmission or moral instruction. These occur more as the unplanned by-products of a process in which the material for cultural transmission is selected less by normative criteria or by any conscious evaluation of their moral influence than by their mass appeal and their commercial marketability. The new definition of the young as distinct and specialized markets for consumption is the prime factor in the mass media seeking them out as targets and finding what is appealing to the young.

Perhaps nothing disturbs the basic function of cultural transmission by the institution of education as does this growth of a mass media that is not normatively regulated, and indeed that has not been consciously assigned such a function within the society. It throws into critical relief the whole issue of whether the culture is to be transmitted effectively within the framework of recognized institutions, or whether a disparate set of unlinked and unregulated structures and processes are to carry out competitive, even contradictory cultural transmission, with whatever unanticipated consequences. But one consequence that not only can be anticipated but can be observed is what

Burton Clark calls "a crisis of authority" as "a fair characterization of the role of the teacher in much American education."[4]

This moral crisis is not the only way in which the function of cultural transmission has been altered by new developments. Another lies in the vast increase in the scope of the culture that education is expected to transmit in some fashion, so much of which is now specialized. Increasingly, education must treat its clientele as not one group but as a set of heterogeneous groups, with quite variant demands on the educational process. The pressure for specialized knowledge and related skills competes with the older value on general education and its basic assumption—that there is a basic core of values and knowledge that all ought to learn. Particularly at the higher levels of education do these two aspects of education create intense pressures on the shaping of curriculum and the determination of educational goals and content.

Education and the Economy   The development of a modern economy by the process of industrialization has had a radically marked effect upon education. As work shifts from primarily manual skills, traditionally acquired within the family, to mental work that requires nonfamily training, new and demanding educational requirements for work emerge. As a consequence, education increasingly reflects the demands of the economic system, and becomes the major agency for supplying the economy with the types and amount of human skills essential for its operation.

The simple literacy that was sufficient a century ago has long since been replaced with a "functional literacy" that means being able to read instructions, blueprints, application forms, newspaper want ads, contracts and mortgages, licenses and permits, traffic signs and advertisements. For an increasingly larger segment of the population, qualification for employment requires even higher levels of literacy and general knowledgeability, as well as specific training within an occupational specialty. In industrial societies, then, education becomes the major agency in the society for supplying the trained personnel needed by an advanced (and steadily advancing) technology. What people can do is increasingly defined by what education they have, and certification of education becomes a sine qua non for status placement.

Within recent decades, the problem of unemployment in the United States has centered less around the swings of the business cycle and more around the problem of technologically displaced labor, on the one hand, and undereducated and untrained labor, on the other. Old occupations are abolished by modern technology, and whole industries undergo revolutionary transformation

---

[4] Burton Clark, "Sociology of Education," in Robert E. L. Faris, ed., *Handbook of Modern Sociology* (Chicago: Rand-McNally, 1964), p. 765.

in their occupational structure. The many who are less skilled give way to the few who are highly skilled. The arduous and demanding task of retraining workers for new occupations has emerged as a matter of national concern and responsibility.

Perhaps even more difficult is the task of utilizing those members of the society who are "functionally illiterate" or who have no marketable occupational skills. The school "dropout" is one such example. There are still many youths who leave school before graduation, without having developed any skill for which there is demand. Despite the widespread publicity about it, the dropout is not a new phenomenon; rather, it represents a changing definition of a long familiar and well-established process, that of leaving school at the earliest allowable age. Such a process once induced no particular problem and indeed served to provide the economy with an adequate supply of willing young workers at a host of unskilled tasks. What is now critical is that while the supply of early-school-leavers continues, the supply of unskilled employment has sharply decreased. Although these young people are added to the *supply* of labor, they are not added to the *employed* labor force. Indeed, not only are they not employed, they are largely unemployable, for in a skill-demanding economy, they have no skills.

If the lack of education severely limits the life-chances of the uneducated, and if the acquisition of an education is the major instrumentality for social mobility, then the level of education attained is a crucial matter in the life of any person, and education as a social process becomes of increasing concern to everyone. It is no longer the concern or the privilege of the few but necessary for all. Education in industrial society is necessarily mass education.

In modern society, then, education and occupation are closely tied together, for educational achievement is the major access to preferred occupational roles. The great expansion in college enrollments has been in the professional and occupational programs, not in liberal arts; and even many liberal arts programs have sought to justify themselves on the grounds that they, too, are good occupational training. The shift away from the undergraduate liberal arts programs over the past decades has moved at such a pace that by the end of the 1950s two out of three college students were in occupational programs as compared to liberal arts.[5] In this way, the demands of the economy have a profound effect upon the structure of education. Its changes in curriculum, its efforts to upgrade academic and technical performance, its struggle to provide functional literacy for the most educationally disadvantaged, its response to the demand for more scientifically trained, all these and other changes are indexes of education's sensitive response to the changes in the occupational requirements of a modern economy.

[5] F. C. Pierson, *The Education of American Businessmen* (New York: McGraw-Hill, 1959).

Education: From Local to National   In a society that has long held up the value of local political control and independence, education has been primarily a local enterprise, particularly at the precollege level. This contrasts with Europe, where education has been under national control and thus much more reflective of national policies, as in France, or in Sweden, where the schools are nationally financed but administratively decentralized. In the United States, the consequence of local control has meant an emphasis upon a decentralization of education, with local resources supporting a locally controlled school system responsive to dominant local needs and values. Indeed, a sensitive reaction to local interests to the point of being dominated by them is encouraged by the dependency of local educational systems upon local political control.

Localism in education produces diversity, and it also provides an opportunity for innovation, for the absence of centralized controls from the top permits independent choice of alternative directions of development. Yet, an effective use of the opportunity to innovate, as Burton Clark points out, requires that there be certain conditions.[6] He points out J. Ben-David's example of major universities that are free of central control and can compete for top scientific personnel. However, this requires that there be a visibility of major personnel and the reputational system of scientific "stars" on which the universities depend for their own prestige. These conditions are unlikely to apply at the secondary school level, where, instead, there is no national visibility and no national system of academic prestige and reputation.[7]

This localistic pattern in education was functionally adaptive to a society that was primarily localistic or at best regional in its economic structure, such as was the United States in the nineteenth century, when the majority of its population engaged in agriculture, and much of its developing industry was still small and geared to local markets. This has no longer been so throughout most of this century; however, it has only been recently that American society has been consciously sensitive to the maladaptive function of educational decentralization. An educational system adapted predominantly to local interests is not consistently responsive to national interests. In the years since World War II, the demands upon education have been discussed almost entirely in terms of the needs and interests that are society-wide, not local.

A rising national consciousness about education has produced efforts to provide more coordination and to link education with national interests. Education has become a matter of national policy and is receiving a steadily increasing share of national resources. The rapid growth of the U.S. Department

[6] Clark, "Sociology of Education," p. 752.

[7] Clark, pp. 751–752. Clark's reference is to J. Ben-David, "Scientific Productivity and Academic Organization in Nineteenth Century Medicine," *American Sociological Review,* 25 (December, 1960), 828–843.

of Education into a position of leadership in education, with resources for the support of varied types of programs for the development of quality education, is a development less than two decades old. The National Science Foundation has undertaken a national program for upgrading science training, as well as an extensive support of scientific research in universities.

Along with the federal government, which has actively thrust itself into a coordination of educational programs across the nation, there are other factors that have worked against the traditional decentralization of education in American society. Private foundations, for example, throughout this century have undertaken various projects intended to improve quality or to innovate in the area of curriculum, and education has come to depend upon these organizations for support for innovative efforts that could not be locally supported. Increasingly, state governments have acted to minimize local differences through state certification of teachers, some common course requirements, and also through allocation of tax funds for education. Thus, state departments of education (sometimes called public instruction) have long been a major force for providing a more equal, less differential local pattern of education.

The teacher training institutions have exerted a significant role in promoting certain common standards that reduce local differences, in particular by their being the source of the supply of trained teachers. The old-fashioned normal schools, often created to develop a local supply of teachers, have long since given way to colleges of education that are now increasingly included within universities. Also, the professionalization of teachers and educational administrators has introduced national standards that serve to put pressure upon local boards and to protect both teachers and administrators, in turn, from local pressures. More and more local systems must conform to now nationally accepted professional standards in order to compete successfully for good teachers; thus, *professionalization* creates a certain degree of professional autonomy for educators and promotes a national standardization of education.

In a formal sense education is still decentralized, but strong pressures for centralization are operative. The flow of new resources from state and national agencies makes education responsive to these more distant groups and by virtue of that responsive to national interests. In a complex but highly influential way, new mechanisms have been created that pressure a nominally localistic and pluralistic educational system to coordinate their varied efforts toward the creation of an educational process that is increasingly oriented to a national perspective of what the educational institution should be doing.

All of this has occurred without a great national debate over the issue of local versus federal control, though, to be sure, there has been consistent political action to oppose the growth of federal educational programs and to champion the cause of local, grass-roots control. But localism is no longer the untarnished ideological issue it once was, not even at the local level. Local people have often felt caught between limited resources and expanding educational intentions that only outside assistance could make possible. Furthermore, the weakening of local power has come from a variety of sources, of which the federal government is only one. It has come about through the growth of state and national professional organizations, through increasing state control and support, and also through the efforts of national foundations to promote educational improvement. Lastly, the decline of small, almost neighborhood-size school districts by consolidation into larger, more efficient schools that can provide a more specialized and better quality education has been a major blow to the ideology of localism in education.

STRATIFICATION AND EDUCATION

Those who constantly urge young people to continue their education are fond of quoting statistics to prove the economic value of education; also, the expanding programs of university-level training are closely linked to white-collar professional training. A wide range of sociological research has documented the complex interplay between education and social stratification; certainly, status placement is one of the significant social functions of education.

The complex linkages between education and stratification have been pursued by sociologists along two lines of theoretical inquiry. One—and perhaps the major one—has been around the hypothesis that stratification serves to distribute educational opportunity and accessibility unevenly, reflecting the stratification of the parental generation. In short, it is the idea that the children of the poor and uneducated get a poorer education and the children of the affluent and educated get a better education. Such an hypothesis explores the function of education as a social institution, acting primarily to stabilize the class structure by allocating educational chances according to family status, thus producing successive generations of high-status families with high education and low-status families with little education.

However, a society increasingly technological cannot merely stabilize the generations; rather, the transformation of the occupational structure thrusts education into the task of developing the mass training of middle- and high-status persons. Thus, consciously or not, education becomes an instrumentality for selecting, training, and placing persons in occupations higher than those of their parents. Education then becomes the institution most relevant for social mobility. This encourages sociologists to pursue a different hypothesis about the relationships between education and stratification: that the educational process is the major mechanism for social mobility.

The Opportunity to Be Educated   When the sociologist August Hollingshead wrote *Elmtown's Youth,* his picture of the pervasive influence of the stratification of a small town upon the educational process carried on in the local high school came as a shock to many.[8] Hollingshead not only made it clear that social class differentiated the lives of the community's adolescents, but he also depicted how the school acted toward its students in ways determined more by their social class position than by their qualities or abilities, even to the point of the distribution of grades and scholarships. In such a community, school was subservient to the local community, and for the adolescent the school experience differed in no significant way from experience outside of school: the children of the lowest stratum were as disadvantaged in school as they were in the community.

That there is a strong link between education and social status is a matter of common observation, and recent social research has been concerned with exploring the complexity of this relationship. Is education shared unequally because of what Hollingshead found in Elmtown, namely, that the social advantages of high status included preferential experiences in school? Or do the children of low status fail to take advantage of educational opportunities that may be available to them? There are certain objective facts about this issue that are evident enough. Status correlates negatively (inversely) with school dropout and correlates positively with those who aspire to go to college. Several studies have demonstrated that family position weighs considerably in the aspiration to go to college, though none of these studies agreed on what relative weight to give to family position and what to the ability of the student.[9]

But the family is not the only index of the effect of status on educational aspirations. Havighurst and his associates in their study of River City found that children tended to reflect the educational values of the neighborhood.[10] These different neighborhoods constitute what A. B. Wilson called "climate of aspiration";[11] they are a consequence of the educational segregation created by placing schools in neighborhoods of varying social status. The aspiration climate is lower in low-status neighborhoods and higher in high-status ones. Although

[8] August H. Hollingshead, *Elmtown's Youth* (New York: Wiley, 1949).

[9] Examples of such studies are: J. A. Kahl, "Educational and Occupational Aspirations of 'Common Man' Boys," *Harvard Educational Review,* 23 (1953), 186–203; William H. Sewell, A. O. Haller, and M. A. Straus, "Social Status and Educational and Occupational Aspiration," *American Sociological Review* (February, 1957), 67–73; and Natalie Rogoff, "Local Social Structure and Educational Selection," in A. H. Halsey, Jean Floud and C. A. Anderson, eds., *Education, Economy and Society* (New York: Free Press, 1961), pp. 241–251.

[10] R. J. Havighurst, P. H. Bowman, G. P. Liddle, C. V. Matthews, and J. V. Pierce, *Growing Up in River City* (New York: Wiley, 1962).

[11] A. B. Wilson, "Residential Segregation of Social Classes and Aspirations of High School Boys," *American Sociological Review,* 24 (December, 1959), 836–845.

there is much homogeneity in the class levels of such neighborhoods, there is sometimes variation, too. Thus, working-class boys in a predominantly middle-class school are likely to raise their aspirations, but these same aspirations will usually be depressed in a slum-located school.

Family, then, measures as a significant factor in educational aspiration when it reenforces neighborhood, as is usually the case; here one gets a cumulative effect of family and neighborhood. The peer group, too, serves to reenforce aspirations; peer group and neighborhood are both extra-familial factors whose impact is mutually reenforcing, since the neighborhood is the ecological context within which specific peer group cultures are generated. The school reflects the climate of neighborhood and peer group and so adds cumulatively to the mutual reenforcement of the aspirations of students.

Negroes make up a disproportionately high percentage of school dropouts, and their educational level is below that of whites. Under the segregated schooling that long prevailed in the United States, officially in the South and informally elsewhere, Negroes received an inferior education. Racially segregated schools have simply been poorer schools, and children in these schools are not given the same opportunity to learn to the same level as white schools. The inescapable fact of being in an obviously inferior school backed by the organized power of the community has depressing effects upon attainment and aspiration, which then may be used as evidence of the inferiority of Negroes to justify having inferior schools in the first place.

The pattern of the segregated inferior school has been a result of official action in the South. In the North, however, the pattern has been that of the ghetto school, where the large Negro area, coinciding with slums and lower-class status, has inferior schools, even though this may be officially denied. Here class and race link together to provide an overwhelming context of family life, neighborhood, peer groups, and school that neither encourage nor support high aspirations and indeed depress any expectations of educational achievement. A personal sense of inferiority is often developed in such atmospheres; at least, it is difficult to escape it. When this last situation occurs, class and race are so thoroughly interwoven that it is not always obvious which is the significant factor. However, a number of studies have indicated that class is more relevant than race, and that the low educational achievement and depressed aspirations of Negro youths is better accounted for by their class origin and the social disadvantage that goes with it than by race. In fact, the situation also holds for lower-class whites. Race, however, adds cumulatively to and renders more difficult the problem of low status and its negative effect upon education.

When low social origin acts to produce an inferior education for those of low status, two interlinked processes occur. First, the children of the lower strata are defined by particularistic criteria (as race, ethnic, or class), which ascribe to them inferior qualities or attributes, so that the school treats them as inferior from the outset. The very definition of their inferior nature serves to create weak self-images as well as little belief that academic achievement is a rewarding activity for them. Their failure to perform well then only serves to provide justification for those who had said they could not—an example of what sociologists call the *self-fulfilling prophecy*. Secondly, children from low-status parents acquire their social values in an environment in which those of the school are largely absent. Academic achievement, aspiration for high social status through educational achievement, and the discipline necessary for academic performance—these values are not cultivated in the families, the neighborhoods, and the peer groups of the lower class. Even the working class has limited educational aspirations, though increasingly it has recognized the importance of more education and has raised its aspirations. What it is important to recognize here is that this differential distribution of educational achievement by social class means that education becomes a mechanism whereby ascribed status, whether by class or race, is translated into achieved status in the occupational structure. The advantages of one generation become the opportunities of the next. Yet the American system of public education does not permit recognition of this process; claims to equality of educational opportunity must be symbolically upheld. This is achieved by the *open door* policy of junior colleges,[12] as well as by the policy of some state universities to grant admission to almost any graduate of a high school within the state. These large numbers of students below the middle class who cannot succeed or at least cannot earn a college degree do not recognize the class basis of their academic failure because they are *individually* eliminated by low grades and by counseling them out. This is what Burton Clark calls *cooling them out*. By this means, public educational institutions make social inequality legitimate by individualizing failure.

However, subtle means of concealing class advantage in education is only necessary in those societies in which the value of equal educational opportunity is publicly avowed. In many societies of the world, even industrial ones, this is still not the case. In western Europe education is still organized so as to reflect the demands of dominant social classes for schooling according to social origin, thus providing different preparations for different social positions. In Britain the "public" (actually private) schools for the upper class continue, although there has been strong pressure to move to more equal schooling. Actually in Europe it is in Czechoslovakia, Yugoslavia, and other eastern European countries that the effort to create new comprehensive schools to serve all social classes for all modes of educational achievement has been most effectively developed. There has also been a strong development in Sweden, but the movement is comparatively weak in Britain and France.

[12] Burton Clark, *The Open Door College* (New York: McGraw-Hill, 1960).

Status and the Assumption of Educability   From kindergarten to high school, from the classroom to the laboratory, the school is organized in order to effect learning. Yet it is a sociological truism too little explored that how it is organized has some bearing on the learning process. There has been a long series of issues within education about certain differentials in internal organization, such as separate classes for the better students, but sociologists have rarely been involved in such analyses. They have, however, studied the school in such a way as to throw some light on certain aspects of the school as a learning environment.

The Assumption of Educability   One most basic issue has to do with the assumptions that teachers and educational administrators make about the *educability* of their students. Here, again, is where the issue of social status intrudes into the schools. In this instance, teachers often assume that lower-class or Negro children either are unwilling to or cannot learn, or both. In a large number of "inner city" schools in America's larger cities, there are classrooms where no real education is attempted by teachers who assume that their charges are incapable of learning. Whatever their other limitations, there are no children who do not soon sense this implicit evaluation made of them. Their own resentment often results, of course, in disciplinary problems, in anti-school attitudes, and in early dropout. Many of the bitter attacks upon such inner city schools in cities like New York and Chicago in recent years originate in the Negro community's resentment at what it feels is the failure of these schools to make an adequate effort to educate their children.

The assumption that some children, by virtue of race or class, are not educable has no scientific warrant. The vast number of intelligence studies on school children compared by race and class have led psychologists, anthropologists, and sociologists to take about as firm a position as they can without being scientifically dogmatic. The very real measurable differences between middle-class and lower-class children on IQ tests, as well as the differences between white and Negro children, are to be accounted for, not by innate differences in ability, but by differences of cultural exposure and learning opportunities. Also, differences in the aspiration to learn are a consequence of cultural experience and training. But none of this denies the fact that many white, middle-class teachers *believe* that there are real differences. Also, many of them cannot learn to accept the cultural patterns of class and race that are strikingly different from middle-class culture, and their negative reactions create serious barriers between them and their students. The consequence is a pattern of nonlearning classrooms where teachers do not teach, students do not study, and the educational process does not educate anyone.

These conceptions that teachers hold are also widely shared by others in the urban community, and the result is often a serious discrepancy in the quality of education afforded children of different social classes and racial groups.

Patricia Sexton has reported in detail the class inequities of one large city school system.[13] In 1962 John E. Coons, a law professor at Northwestern University, prepared a report on racially segregated schools in Chicago for the United States Commission on Civil Rights.[14] He reported that in 1961–1962 in Chicago schools (1) there were 30.95 pupils per classrooms in white schools and 46.8 in Negro schools; (2) there was an average appropriation of $342 per pupil in white schools, but only $269 in Negro schools; (3) the proportion of uncertified teachers was 12 percent in white schools, 27 percent in Negro schools; and (4) there was an average of five books per pupil in white schools, two and a half in Negro schools. Such data as these help to document the fact that the same school system systematically allocates less teaching resources to those lowest in the class structure of modern society, even though this may be contrary to any public policy and can never be publicly acknowledged.

There have been two responses to this. One has been among social scientists, who have first documented the differences in educational opportunity, and the particular disadvantage of the child deprived at the very outset. But they have gone beyond this to explore means by which such differences can be altered, not merely by an equal allocation of resources, but also by the development of a classroom in which learning does take place.[15] To do so they have emphasized how much there must be an accounting of the class and racial subcultures of the children and thus some altering of the conventional material used in middle-class classrooms. It is also evident that what is needed are teachers whose very assumptions about lower-class children begin with a recognition of their educability, yet are also aware of the cultural disadvantages that these children bring to the school.

A second development is evident as yet largely only in New York City, where there is a strenuous effort by the Negro community to influence the education of their children. They have vigorously protested every evidence of neglect and failure to teach and have forcefully insisted upon more Negro teachers and principals; more importantly, they have insisted upon having a voice in the decisions that effect their children's education. This has induced a major effort to decentralize the complex bureaucratic structure of New York City schools and provide a basis for parents to share in decisions about the educational process.

[13] Patricia Cayo Sexton, *Education and Income* (New York: Viking, 1961).

[14] Cited by Patricia Cayo Sexton in her article, "City Schools," in Louis Ferman, Joyce Kornbluh, and Alan Haber, *Poverty in America* (Ann Arbor, Mich.: The University of Michigan Press, 1965), pp. 240–241.

[15] See, for example, A. Harry Passow, ed., *Education in Depressed Areas* (New York: Teachers College, Columbia University, 1963); also, Frank Riessman, *The Culturally Deprived Child* (New York: Harper & Row, 1962).

Education and Social Mobility   In a changing and mobile society, education cannot continue to practice in unaltered fashion these processes of defining the educational chances of children differentially by reference to the already existing status of the parents. The process of social mobility, as we tried to make evident in Chapter 10, is not merely an *individual* matter, though that is the way the American ideology defines it, but it is also a *societal* matter. Social mobility is not merely *opportunity,* it is also a process of selectively moving large numbers of people upward in status in order to fill the social positions created by the rapid expansion of the middle class. Mobility, then, is not only possible, it is necessary in a society in which positions are shrinking at the lower class levels and expanding at the middle levels. This process of selectivity determining who moves up from the lower ranks rests largely with the educational process. It has the task of raising the general level of education of all in a more technological society and of sifting out and encouraging aspirations in some who will then move up and fill in the newly expanded ranks of the middle levels.

It has long been conventional to view the stratification order as a pyramid, in which the social positions are fewest at the top and most frequent at the bottom. But this crude model probably only roughly fitted society in its earlier industrial phase. Prior to industrialization, the mass at the bottom of society would be better pictured as a large rectangular block capped by a small pyramid, so few were there who were above the status of peasant. The later industrial pattern is not a pyramid either; rather, the pyramid is radically modified in that the broad base shrinks and the middle expands. It is the shrinking base that makes up those social positions that require little or no education, whereas the expanding middle requires even more education than was true a generation ago.

Education, then, has two tasks in this changing structure of increased mobility: (1) it must locate and educate more people at lower status levels for higher status positions; and (2) it must increase the general level of education at practically all class levels in the society. Studies by W. Lloyd Warner and J. C. Abegglen have carefully documented the increased education of top business executives in the United States, for example; in 1952, only four out of a hundred had less than a high school education, while more than half (57 percent) were college graduates.[16] Twenty-five years before that, slightly more than a quarter of them (27 percent) had less than a high school education and only about a third of them (32 percent) were college graduates. These figures are now almost 20 years old, and the trend indicated there has undoubtedly continued. The executive ranks of the large American business

[16] W. Lloyd Warner and J. C. Abegglen, *Occupational Mobility in American Business and Industry, 1928–1952.* (Minneapolis, Minn.: University of Minnesota Press, 1955), p. 108.

corporations are increasingly held by college graduates, and movement up the managerial ladder now requires a college education as a starting point.

What is true for managerial status in American society is equally true for a wide range of other occupations, too. In response to this steadily increasing demand for technically and professionally trained people, as well as to the increasing pressure for higher educational opportunity, American education has gone through several major phases of development, each one adding substantially to the proportions of Americans who seek and obtain higher education. A first phase, developed in the United States during the nineteenth century, is one that all industrial societies experience, that of a mass literacy as a common level for the entire population. No industrial society can develop without this basic level of education.

But education development in advanced industrial societies does not stop there. A second stage is the development of *universal* secondary education, which then alters the secondary school's former role of only preparing students for entrance to a college; it must now serve a large number of students who are not going to college. The United States began this phase before World War I and had completed it by World War II. Since then, the United States has moved into a third phase in which some phase of higher education becomes a universal goal. During this century the United States has moved steadily in the direction of ever larger numbers entering college. At the turn of the century only 4 percent of those age 18 to 21 were in college; this figure doubled about every 20 years, so that it was 16 percent in 1940. It has been estimated that by 1970 almost half (47.6 percent) of those 18 to 21 years old will be enrolled in a degree-granting college.[17]

Comparable data from other industrial nations suggest that although they still lag behind the United States, they are moving in the direction of expanding university enrollments. In Britain many new universities are being built, though only about 8 percent attended a university full-time in 1961; the projected goals for 1980 is 18 percent, which is about where the United States was at the end of World War II. Some expansion in enrollments without comparable expansion in faculty, classrooms, lecture halls, and laboratories, or in other physical facilities, was one important factor in the student unrest manifested in German, Italian, and French universities in the spring of 1968.

This expansion, however, does not necessarily do away with unequal chances; it merely increases the opportunity for a university education for all social classes. Data by Dael Wolfle indicates that the proportion of those entering college by occupational categories of parents ranges from 67 percent for professional and semiprofessional, 50 percent for managerial, 48 percent for

[17] Martin Trow, "The Second Transformation of American Secondary Education," *International Journal of Comparative Sociology*, 2 (1961), 144–166.

sales, clerical, and service, and 26 percent for manual occupations.[18] A quite comparable pattern was reported for Britain, except that the proportion in each or similar categories was considerably lower. Nonetheless, data examined over time document the point that the expansion of higher education has been accompanied by a narrowing of the gap in the chances of the social classes. There is a movement toward an equalization of educational opportunity, but the factors that make for differences in such chances still constitute a stubborn resistance to the dream of equal opportunity, even in the United States.

Although a college education becomes increasingly an essential component of a mobile career, it is not a matter of indifference as to what college the aspirant attends. "Success" as measured by position and salary accrues most to graduates of Ivy League schools, particularly Harvard, Yale, and Princeton. This obvious "success" dominance of Ivy League schools may be only partly a matter of their very real academic quality and superior preparation of their students. Their very selective process, their high percentage of sons of established families of wealth and influence, suggests that the ascriptive processes that operate at the lowest levels also operate at the highest levels: old established families of wealth and education have close connections with the best educational facilities. But the educational success of their children can then only be partially attributed to education. Even when such graduates do not come from wealthy families, the prestige of the degree gives them considerable advantage over others in attaining the best positions. There is a comparable situation in Britain; the former monopoly on university education of Oxford and Cambridge has been broken, but their preeminence makes their degrees far more valuable than those from the "red-brick" universities.

But this is a special though by no means unimportant issue in the larger matter of educationally-sponsored social mobility. The rapid expansion of state universities and the rapid growth of community colleges is not simply because people want mobility for their children; it is also because this society needs to train on a mass basis for the filling of a vast range of middle positions in the society. Under these circumstances, family and other factors of social origin loom as less significant, and the educational process can less and less operate with ascriptive definitions of status. Instead, there must be an expansion of those who are defined as *educable,* and the increased utilization of universalistic criteria for admission *must* be complemented by achievement criteria in awarding degrees and effecting job placement. The *"must"* in the previous sentence is not a moral imperative, but only what has to be done if education is to provide rationally for the necessary social mobility required

---

[18] Dael Wolfle, "Educational Opportunity, Measured Intelligence, and Social Background," in A. H. Halsey, Jean Floud, and C. Arnold Anderson, eds., *Education, Economy and Society* (New York: Free Press, 1961), p. 230.

by a technically advanced society. Thus, education becomes less subservient to local interests and less a monopoly of the already privileged as it seeks out the talented and the potentially talented from whatever social levels are their origins.

The Control of Education   Whether public or private, the school system (or systems) of a society are subject to controls exerted from outside the educational process itself. To a considerable extent education has been a process of preparing young people to meet requirements set down by other institutions of the society, and the changes in educational standards are a response to changing demands within the society. But within a context of stratification, there is an unequal capacity within the society to exert influence upon the educational structure and to make it more or less responsive to the demands and interests of various status groups and classes.

Historically, the established elites and privileged groups in society have exerted control over education in two ways. First, they have in some manner differentiated an educational process for their own offspring, usually in distinctive schools and universities, such as the English public schools, the German law faculties, the Ivy League universities, and the elite prep schools. Secondly, they have exerted a strong ideological control over the content and subject matter of the educational process of the other social classes. They have sought to make that education a practical one, with an emphasis on docility and loyalty to the established order. But in the twentieth century the emergence of a more complex society has undercut somewhat the once strong control of established elites, and even higher education has changed accordingly. New elites have emerged that are now closely involved in the corporate and governmental power structures, and a technical and scientific training is the basis of their own social origin. These elites come from various social strata. Education functions as the selecting and training process by which young people of diverse social origins can be mobile and enter these new elites.

This transition is simply one aspect of a more diverse pattern—that of the growth of a large *new* middle class of educated people who recognize that education is the source of their own status and mobility, and that of their children as well. It is these people who, in the United States, have supported a broadening of educational opportunity, particularly the vast growth of public higher education. It is also these several strata that have constructed the superior suburban high school systems that have frequently equaled if not surpassed the best prep schools in the preparation of university students.

The growth of a new middle class is accompanied by an increased *professionalization* of the occupations of the middle class, and this professionalization in turn has a significant effect upon education and upon the controls exercised. In the first place, it tends to bring professional criteria to bear upon education and thus to give more control to various professional organizations. This means a proliferation of significant control agencies, including accrediting agencies, the impact of which is that control is exerted over substantive curriculum matters by agencies outside the school system or university. Frequently a board of education or a board of trustees has no choice but to meet such requirements in order to qualify its program, and its own official authority may no longer be the effective decision making.

The professionalization of occupations has a further significance: the professionalization of the educational process itself. The persistent effort to raise the professional standard of teaching in the United States has been accompanied by the growth of professional organizations and then of professional power. Increasingly the professionals within education have more scope and influence over the educational process. The most recent development, however, is a segmentation within the professional structure of education, in which classroom teachers have organized separately from professional administrators in order to advance their economic interests. Previously, the complex structure of professional educators organized in the National Education Association included everyone from classroom teachers to superintendents, though there were separate divisions for specific functions. But this meant that administrators, who hired and promoted teachers, were in the same organization—and in many school districts membership in NEA was formally or at least informally required—resulting in a domination by administrators that made NEA a professionally oriented, but ideologically conservative organization. Thus, increased professional power has induced the specific development of "teacher power" with accompanying economic action, including strikes, a pattern of behavior previously defined as unprofessional. But teachers are responding to an anomaly of professional status: an insistence that by function and training they are professionals, but by pay they are at best skilled workers. They have sought to remove this anomaly by adopting the orientation of skilled workers. The labor-affiliated teachers organization, the United Federation of Teachers, has become the representative of teachers for bargaining purposes in a number of larger cities, such as New York City and Detroit.

Such developments as these have accordingly attenuated the once very real control over education at the local level by local elites. State governmental control over the licensing of teachers and state-supported teachers' colleges, as well as state funding of education, has removed some political control from the local to the state level. But when state power is institutionalized into a state department of education staffed by professionals, professional control is extended and strengthened by governmental backing. The tenure and pay of teachers is less and less under the meaningful control of local systems, for they now must meet market, organizational, and legal demands. And the content of education, furthermore, is increasingly standardized by national conceptions of what is regarded as "good" education. Here the standard-setters are both professional organizations and other major groups that with foundation or federal funds innovate new programs in teaching or in course-content that alter old ways in education. Keeping pace in order not to disadvantage their children requires local systems to adopt new methods and programs. Yet local control of education is not simply becoming a myth, even though it is in considerable decline; the still considerable diversity in the range and quality of local educational systems testifies to the fact that local control still functions to differentiate education. The United States is still far from a common national pattern that is characteristic of some European countries.

Is There a Coming Meritocracy?   It should be apparent that perhaps the most significant change in education is one from a bastion of class privilege to a democratization that increasingly selects on the basis of ability and aspiration. To be sure, as yet the children of the affluent have the advantage even here, for they come from homes where the importance of education is understood and appreciated, and where the young are strongly socialized to expectations of educational achievement. But increasingly the modern educational system rationalizes the process of social mobility, finding new social mechanisms for offsetting the disadvantages of low social origin: the Head Start program for lower-class preschoolers is but one example.

Difficult as may be the problems of rendering equal the educational opportunities of all children, there can be no doubt that a belief in discovering and educating the talented and the more intelligent is a major rationale for new programs of educational innovation. Also, it has become a major rationalization of the modern, bureaucratic middle class that they hold their positions by virtue of achievement, not ascription, and that they have risen by their own merit, not by ascriptive advantages of race or class. Furthermore, it is now a prevailing belief that this is exactly how the high and responsible positions in a modern society should be filled, for then merit demonstrated by education and occupational success will give a society the best leadership. It is seen as more fair and more just than older systems of inherited position, since it produces a more equalitarian and more democratic society, as well as a more rational and intelligent one. But what kind of a society would it be if all positions were selected on merit alone, and the entire educational system were geared to the selection and training of the more able for the superior positions in the society? Would it be the intellectual utopia many have dreamed about?

Since there has never been such a society, there are no historical models to study, and social research on present society can offer only slight clues. Nonetheless, a highly imaginative British sociologist, Michael Young, has tried to think through what would seem to be the necessary sociological outcome of such a gradual process over more than a century of development.[19] His satirical analysis, written as a kind of social science-fiction account from an imagined future perspective, explores the social structure of such a society and the new form of stratification that emerges in a *meritocracy*. He probes the weaknesses of such a society, the tensions and cleavages that cannot be forever covered up and finally burst forth into an open conflict that surprises and dismays the meritocracy (just as the Negro rebellion has surprised and dismayed the dominant whites in the 1960s in America). Young is not arguing against a society utilizing merit over social inheritance as a mechanism for placing people in the highest positions in society. But he does use a vivid sociological imagination to show that such an historical process is no road to utopia. Rather, it creates a society with its own internal tensions and problems, like all human societies.

HIGHER EDUCATION

Ever since Thorstein Veblen penned *The Higher Learning in America*,[20] a scathing indictment of business domination of American universities, the place of higher education in the changing American social structure has been an issue that has concerned scholars and academicians in many fields. Yet little empirical research has been carried out; only recently have we gone beyond the keen observations of lifelong participants in the academic process.

There have been a number of studies recently of college students, their attitudes and opinions, and changes in these as a consequence of college experience and also of what happened to them after college. But there have been fewer studies of colleges as educational organizations and of their faculties. David Riesman reviewed the wide variation in the patterns of colleges and universities in the United States,[21] and several studies explored the issue of academic freedom during the 1950s, an issue that arose as one consequence of the McCarthy period.[22] Sociological studies more particularly geared to

---

[19] Michael Young, *The Rise of the Meritocracy, 1870–2033.* (London: Thames and Hudson, 1958).

[20] Thorstein Veblen, *The Higher Learning in America* (New York: B. W. Heubsch, 1918) and (Stanford, Calif.: Academic Reprints, 1954).

[21] David Riesman, *Constraint and Variety in American Education* (Lincoln, Neb.: University of Nebraska Press, 1956).

[22] See Richard Hofstadter and Walter P. Metzger, *The Development of Academic Freedom in the United States* (New York: Columbia University Press, 1955); Paul F. Lazarsfeld and Wagner Thielens, Jr., *The Academic Mind* (New York: Free Press, 1958).

the academic process have been fewer. Logan Wilson's *The Academic Man* remains one of the few studies that concentrated on the academic role;[23] more recently two sociologists, Theodore Caplow and Reece McGee, focused on a more limited issue, the recruitment of academic talent.[24]

The Origins of the Modern University   The university is an ancient and prestigious structure, which has survived over centuries of radical transformation of society, from medieval to industrial. Yet rarely has it led in that transformation; instead, it typically has followed changes originating elsewhere in the society, and often only after considerable resistance. Medieval universities were closely tied to the religious structure. But even after they had freed themselves from close religious control, universities resisted being too closely tied to the emerging economic structure of the new industrial society; in particular they resisted assuming any vocational training. The concept particularly strong in Britain, though sustained as well in continental Europe and America, was that the university's proper function was the education of the *cultivated* man rather than the *specialist,* and, as Max Weber noted, this has meant training men for membership in highly esteemed status groups.

However, in the early 1800s significant changes in the European university began to occur, and a new type of university emerged.[25] Wilhelm von Humboldt established a new university at Berlin in 1810, and others followed in other German cities. Within a decade or two they became centers of *scientific* learning in which the laboratory became as important as the lecture hall. So prestigious did German universities become that thousands of American and British students went to Germany for their education, and from the 1860s until the outbreak of war in 1914 the German university was the most esteemed in Europe and the most imitated.

The German model of the university stimulated significant reform in both Britain and the United States. In Britain there was severe resistance to introducing research as an instrument of education at Oxford and Cambridge, though new universities had already been established at Manchester and London after the German model. The British universities, however, *adapted* to the German model, they did not fully adopt it. They retained the tutorial system so identified with Oxford and Cambridge, and they also retained their strong control over the student and his education, which gave him no freedom of choice but instead prescribed almost every aspect of his education. Humboldt had envisioned a quite different process, and German universities prac-

[23] Logan Wilson, *The Academic Man* (London: Oxford, 1942).

[24] Theodore Caplow and Reece J. McGee, *The Academic Marketplace* (New York: Basic Books, 1958).

[25] The following historical observations are drawn from Eric Ashby, "The Future of the Nineteenth Century Idea of a University," *Minerva*, 6 (Autumn, 1967), 3–17.

ticed it, making them much less committed to a position of *in loco parentis.*

The German model of the university stimulated much educational reform in the United States, too. Americans educated in German universities took the leadership in reforming American universities: Charles Elliot at Harvard; Henry Tappan at the University of Michigan; Andrew Dickson White of Cornell; and Daniel Coit Gilman of Johns Hopkins. The American environment allowed considerable borrowing but in the end produced its own kind of university. The graduate school, for example, developed as a parallel to the German institute. But, as Eric Ashby notes, there are two important differences. One is that American universities have not practiced the restrictive admissions that German universities did. Secondly, American universities are of different qualities, and there is no common level of examining for degrees among them, as there is in Germany (and Britain and France as well). Thus, the United States possesses universities with a wide range of quality, and the B.A. degree from one university does not mean the same as it does from another.

The problem of restrictive admissions has now become a severe one throughout the world, for the aspiration for a university education is common throughout the modern (and modernizing) world; it is the one relevant route to status and position in modern societies and to elite status in the modernizing societies. The result is a tremendous pressure to accommodate ever more students. In Britain the response has been a moderate enlargement of positions by creating more universities but a still restricted admission based upon merit as measured by examination. This restricted process results in 85 percent of British university students attaining a degree, compared to less than half of beginning university students in the United States. In the Soviet Union, in contrast, admission to higher education is closely geared to that society's manpower needs, so that only about 10 percent receive a university education; the other 90 percent are trained in highly specialized but educationally narrow technical colleges. Furthermore, only about half the students in the Soviet Union study full-time. Thus, the Soviet Union has been less responsive to individual aspirations, and it has sacrificed education for an emphasis upon technical training.

In the European universities, this pressure of number has created a critical issue, in that more students have been admitted than can be adequately accommodated. The outbreaks of protest in German, French, and Italian universities that became so violent in the spring of 1968 is at least partially rooted in the inadequate physical and teaching resources of the European universities. In addition, in France and Italy the protest also stems from the ancient and unchanged curricula that these universities maintain and their considerable irrelevance to the technical and educational needs of a modern society.

The Changing American University   Thorstein Veblen's dour analysis remains relevant today, even if its details apply to an earlier era, for the issues to which he addressed himself have remained central for over a century: the relationship of the university to society, and the degree of autonomy and independence of the university from other institutions and agencies. Veblen's critique was directed against control by businessmen as he saw it operate at the end of the nineteenth and opening of the twentieth century. Before that there had been an extensive period of domination by churches and religious leaders, for churches pioneered in establishing colleges in America from the seventeenth to the nineteenth century. But as higher education became more secular and more public, businessmen replaced clergymen as the influential members of boards of trustees. Nor were administrators chosen most frequently from the ranks of the faculty. At first, college presidents were also clergymen and then businessmen, though there were always some outstanding exceptions to this, particularly at some of the most distinguished universities.

The absence of power by the faculty of an American college or university was historically rooted, then, in the circumstances of their origin, and this contrasted sharply with the European university, where there was and is a strong and ancient tradition of faculty control. In American colleges and universities today there is much more faculty control. This growth of more faculty control is only one manifest change in American universities and colleges, and Veblen's perspective no longer represents as relevant a statement of the central issue. Larger and more diversified than they once were, universities can no longer be effectively governed by boards of trustees that meet only a few times a year.[26] Bureaucratic processes have come into being here as in other large organizations, and a university administration grows to assume the detailed tasks of running a big organization. But a necessary decentralization of authority and the recognition of specialization also enhances faculty control, often vested in a faculty government. In particular, a significant tradition is that only academic people are qualified to make judgments on strictly academic matters, such as curriculum and degree requirements. Also, the selection of faculty is often left largely to the departments, and their official recommendations to administrators are usually the effective decisions.

The pattern of strong faculty control is most characteristic of the higher quality colleges and the larger and more influential state universities, which often serve as models of what a college or university should be. They stand at the head of a procession. But as David Riesman made so clear, the procession is no straight line. Some institutions may be trying to imitate a model

---

[26] For a recent study on governing the university, see Nicholas J. Demerath, Richard W. Stephens, and R. Robb Taylor, *Power, Presidents, and Professors* (New York: Basic Books, 1967).

set by a prestigeful school, when that school has already moved away from it by responding to new demands and social changes.

The Multiversity   Clark Kerr, a distinguished social scientist and a former president of the University of California, coined the term *multiversity* to give expression to the radical transition in the fundamental character of the large American university.[27] What he meant was that "university" no longer applied as a term, since there was no longer a single center of values and tasks to which the organization was dedicated. The varied functions and responsibilities of the university gave it multiple goals and a highly diversified academic effort. For one thing, it is the large public universities that have expanded to accommodate increased enrollments in their undergraduate divisions. But they have also grown as the major centers for training graduate students and thus for producing professionals, scientists, and scholars in greater numbers than before. Related to this is the university's major function as a producer of knowledge; the university is the major source of scientific research.

The new American university is beset with a series of problems that have ancient roots, but which are also greatly exacerbated by recent rapid growth and evolution from a somewhat simpler form and smaller, more manageable size. Of the several issues, there are perhaps two more relevant ones: the problem of bureaucratization and large size, and the tension between teaching and research.

There has been a vast increase in students at American universities; campuses that contain 25,000 or more are no longer uncommon. Not only, as we see below, does this diversify the student subculture into several, but it also makes difficult the maintaining of a single, cohesive sense of student life—and perhaps no desire among many that there even be one. But thousands of students on any large campus face a problem of being a nameless face in a huge student body, unknown but to a few friends, and seemingly unable to find means for more personalized interaction with faculty. It is this alienated condition that most observers credit for so much of the student rebellion that first manifested itself at the University of California at Berkeley.

However, it is not merely numbers that render the relationship of the student to the faculty so impersonal and frequently bureaucratized. In the large American university the student is by no means the only concern of the faculty and perhaps not the primary one. The vast research enterprise that large universities carry on now creates a different type of role for the professor that competes with his teaching role. Indeed, for most professors, the rewards of his occupation—recognition in his profession, publication of his work, offices in professional societies, and awards and honors—come, not from teaching,

[27] Clark Kerr, *The Uses of the University* (Cambridge, Mass.: Harvard University Press, 1963).

but from research and the publication of research. A great teacher is great only on his campus, but an outstanding researcher can have a national—even an international—reputation. He may then travel to conferences as a new part of the expense-account stratum, and his well-funded research may provide him with assistants, another office, secretarial help, and a light teaching load, or even no teaching; none of this may be available to the teacher-professor.

As researchers, consultants, and professional experts in every possible area of human knowledge, university professors now have a new and complex role, the multiple demands on which place less and less premium on teaching and so enlarge the social distance between them and the undergraduate students. Indeed, many such outstanding professors do not teach undergraduates at all, dealing only with graduate students. This means they are specialists teaching only future specialists.

A vast commitment to the production of new knowledge and to the expert guidance to its use in society has become a major function of the modern university. This is not a development invented by universities simply for their own benefit. Rather, it is a response to the demands of a highly technological society for more expertise and particularly for more scientific knowledge. As a result, the federal government has become, through its various agencies and institutes, the major support for scientific research in the United States. Most large universities operate expensive research facilities funded by contractual grants from federal agencies, plus additional funds from private foundations.

The involvement of the university with external tasks detracts from its capacity to fulfill its older, internal function of teaching. There is a strain among competing demands for one central resource: the limited time and attention of the faculty. This is a resource that cannot be expanded quickly. The consequence is a structural tension as universities seek to fulfill their historic obligation as teachers and transmitters of the cultural tradition, while continuing to serve the needs of a technologically advanced society by constantly creating new knowledge.

A modern-day Veblen would probably not turn his sardonic analysis on the relationship of the university to the business community, but would instead focus on the close relationship between the federal government and the university research function, and the manner in which this relationship possibly overshadows and even injures the carrying out of the teaching function. (In Chapter 17, this issue will be examined from the perspective of science and government.) Nor would he find it accurate to portray the faculty as dominated against their will by the business community; rather, today's university faculty increasingly enjoys the perquisites and life-style of upper-middle-class status, but not equal monetary rewards.

Our latter-day Veblen would then find that the faculty offers no unified criticism of the university, nor have they any single conception of what the modern university should be. Many of them are highly trained specialists more closely related to their specialized profession than to the university as an educational entity. Their more *cosmopolitan* perspective is primarily oriented to the larger world, and this differentiates them from the *locals* who are primarily oriented to campus affairs and events.[28] But even the professional specialists have little in common, for each is ensconced within his own specialty and unfamiliar with that of others. Furthermore, those in the professional and applied fields are less closely related to the traditional scholarly functions of the university and more committed to new tasks and the pursuit of new knowledge. In short, all the variation and diversity of modern education is reflected in the strains and tensions that make the modern university no longer a unified educational organization but rather a diversified and poorly integrated complex, contrasting the ancient scholarly commitment to conserve the culture with the new demands for scientific knowledge and technological innovation.

Subcultures and Learning   What learning goes on within a school or college is very much influenced by the subcultures that emerge among its interacting participants, both students and faculty. The norms and values, sentiments and traditions that emerge outside of the formal structure and serve to organize behavior vary considerably, however; they differ in content and in influence, there is one subculture or several, and they reflect in varying degree the influences of the larger society. Like all subcultures, they may be supportive of the formal structure, or they may be subversive of it.

In the small residential liberal arts college, the subculture of the students has often reflected their close interaction, their localized isolation from the larger society, and often their relatively homogeneous background. But the modern world makes it difficult for any one subculture to dominate. The increased size of educational structure, its specialization of functions, and the heterogeneity of those it serves tends to fragment it into a plurality of subcultures. No one perspective is the point of view of all the social actors in the structure, and no one set of values and sentiments commands the loyalty of all. The diversity and complexity of the modern educational structure is reflected in the diversity of subcultures within it.

However much people may talk of an "ivory tower" to express the idea of isolation of the educational structure from the presumably more "real" world, it is rarely so isolated, and perhaps much less so now than in the past. As education expands to meet the professional needs of a highly technological economy, it is more thoroughly linked to the larger society; as its expansion

[28] Alvin W. Gouldner, "Cosmopolitans and Locals: Toward an Analysis of Latent Social Roles," Part I, *Administrative Science Quarterly*, 2 (1957), 281–306; Part II, *Administrative Science Quarterly*, 2 (1958), 444–480.

incorporates into student life a wider and more heterogeneous body of students, selected from a broader range of social strata, it finds the ivory tower permeated by the bearers of the outside culture.[29]

Subcultures, then, can originate around quite varied interests and perspectives among both faculty and students, and in large universities there is no campus-wide culture that includes everyone. This has been possible in small, residential liberal arts colleges, particularly where social interaction is largely confined within this localized setting, and also where the college is relatively independent of the larger, immediate environment and thus is semi-autonomous. Its very traditions may emphasize its difference from the society and maximize those qualities that set it apart and make it distinctive. Where this distinctiveness is in terms of intellectual and academic superiority and high quality, the subculture may reflect a selective admission process and serve to break the ties of these students with home and community, orienting them to a new world of quite different cultural and intellectual values. At the other extreme from this are the locally controlled community colleges with commuting students, where community sentiments prevail, and the subculture of the students reflects more the norms and interests of youth culture disseminated by the mass media.

The Four Subcultures   Perhaps the most influential sociological conception of student subcultures and its meaning for the learning experience has been provided by Burton Clark and Martin Trow, in a perceptive analysis of four undergraduate subcultures: the collegiate, the vocational, the academic, and the nonconformist.[30]

The *collegiate subculture* is maintained by those who look to college primarily for its social life, with studies secondary. This "Joe College" type, so well caricatured by countless Hollywood movies, has been a persistent feature of American colleges since before the turn of the century. It has most often been the perspective of the sons of affluent Americans, for fraternities and sororities, weekend dates and proms are costly features of the requisite social life.

If the collegiate subculture is the oldest one, the new, rising subculture is the *vocational.* It is the subculture of those who regard college as a means of acquiring an occupation, although their perspective toward their studies is serious, they prefer vocational courses over liberal arts. Vocationally oriented students are more likely to be working part-time, commuting to college, and thus much less integrated into any campus life. Students from the lower-middle and working-class families, where a college education is the one big

---

[29] For an excellent study of peer groups and subcultures in the American high school, see James S. Coleman, *The Adolescent Society* (New York: Free Press, 1961).

[30] Burton R. Clark and Martin R. Trow, "Determinants of College Student Subculture." Unpublished manuscript, (Center for the Study of Higher Education, University of California at Berkeley, 1960).

chance to be mobile, figure more numerously among the vocationally oriented. This subculture is a pragmatic one in which there is both little time for fun and games in college and little awareness of or interest in the intellectual and scholarly aspects of campus life.

A third subculture patterning for college students is the *academic* one; here, the academic role of the faculty provides the significant model. Students study hard, get good grades, win scholarships, and enter graduate school. They enter the world of ideas and scholarship under the tutelage of their professors. The educated middle class is largely the source of these students, and their strong academic performance makes them attractive to the academically strong liberal arts colleges, where the academic subculture is frequently dominant.

Lastly, there is a *nonconformist* subculture, which has come to be more significant in the changing university than it was in the past. Like the academics, the nonconformists are seriously interested in ideas, but they are much more critical of the academic process and care less for grades and conventional performance. They are interested in art and literature, or in politics, as these function in the larger society. They are highly critical of the college administration and perceive it as representative of the "establishment." This nonconforming pattern attracts the rebellious students; it gives them a cultural milieu and set of values from which to manifest their idealism and their rejection of much of the contemporary culture.

These four subcultures have different effects upon the college as a learning environment. The older and now declining collegiate subculture, in effect, subverts serious learning and creates a tension between the academic values of the faculty and the nonacademic values of students. In those colleges in which this type has been dominant, the faculty developed an orientation of taking seriously and, in effect intentionally lecturing to only the occasional serious student. The vocational subculture, in turn, supports serious classroom work but confines itself to that learning which is explicitly vocational, reflecting the enduring tension between professional and liberal arts education.

The academic and nonconformist subcultures are more supportive of learning, but with quite different emphases. The former encourages students to study hard, learn well, and accept the academic values of the professors. The latter, in turn, provides students who learn but who are often quite critical of the official learning environment. As measured by grades, the nonconformists are not always the "good" students, but they provide much of the critical political and intellectual leadership in the student body, and they are the main link between the American intellectual community and university students. The dramatic instances of student "rebellion" at Berkeley, Columbia, and elsewhere in recent years has come from the student "activists" who are nonconformists. They have led the action for student rights, for campus protest against the draft and the war in Vietnam, and for active support for civil rights. Also among them are those collegiate experimentalists who have first tried LSD and other "consciousness-expanding" drugs. If the nonconformists are never a majority, as so many are quick to point out, they are nonetheless the active and influential student group on campus. What they do serves to shape the cultural perspectives and values of other students, particularly those serious students from the academic subculture. Indeed, the nonconformists recruit new adherents from among the ranks of the academics.

The Dissenting Academy Throughout American higher education new currents of change that threaten many established assumptions are developing. Until now only C. Wright Mills' *The Sociological Imagination* was a critical dissent from within academic ranks of the major trends that had professionalized the faculty and linked physical and social research with the major power centers of the society. But now his critical posture finds support from a wider range of young faculty who have subjected their professionalized and often tamed disciplines to highly critical scrutiny. Such a book as *The Dissenting Academy,* a series of essays critical of the teaching of the humanities and social science, represents the first response of a new generation critical of both academia and the society that so generously supports it.[31] Beneath much of the verbal and ideological confusion stands one fundamental issue: what kind of a university is it to be in what kind of a society? The close tie of universities to the Department of Defense, the heavy dependency upon the federal government for research funds, the dominance of research and graduate teaching over undergraduate education, and the failure to teach Negro history and cultural life, are some of the campus issues that have motivated efforts for change. These issues are critical both of the contemporary American university and the contemporary American society that it serves.

Thus, the American university, like its European counterpart, enters into a new critical era of change and reformation, with its outcome quite uncertain. It is evident that the university now constitutes a community in which there is centered much of the criticism of modern society: (1) its bureaucratization; (2) its patterns of inequality; and (3) the crass quality of much of modern culture. But there is also criticism of the university itself and of how it relates itself to the larger society. There is criticism of the *irrelevance* of much teaching and research for the lives of students and for the critical events of the society. The new dissent within the academy asks that universities redefine their conception of public responsibility, and that they become centers of social change, even radical change. These dissenters press for the independence of the university from other power centers and established institutions of the society.

But modern universities, and especially public ones, are now such integral

---

[31] Theodore Roszak, ed., *The Dissenting Academy* (New York: Pantheon, 1968).

parts of modern society and perform such critical functions for it that they cannot simply cease to perform the many teaching and research functions that make "multiversities" of them. Thus, universities are now beset by conflicting and competing demands from within and without, and their academic leadership is struggling to balance them off in such as way as to continue to serve modern society; while preserving their ancient function of detached scholarship and critical analysis. To do that the university must preserve its carefully developed and hard-won *autonomy* that enables it to sustain critical roles and to utilize its academic freedom to analyze and criticize other social institutions. How that can be done will be a major preoccupation of the academic community for several decades.

THE FUTURE OF EDUCATION

It is now apparent that modern society demands new and higher levels of expertness and training, and the underdeveloped societies place strong emphasis upon education as one significant feature of their modernizing transition. Education is no longer an institution associated with unmarried female teachers and harmlessly erudite old professors. It now commands a greater share of available resources, and its leadership is a new and significant elite in society. The general level of education steadily advances, and the man of the future is going to be an educated man. The effect of this is as yet unmeasured, but some studies indicate now that the college-educated population differs significantly from the less educated one in important attitudes and values, as well as in such characteristics as reading more, being better informed, and being more interested in significant social and political events. Furthermore, the educated will more and more engage in a constant exposure to education, to *continuing* education that will last a lifetime. Ever new knowledge must be constantly learned, and thus an education will never be regarded as "finished," as it is today.

The dominant power long vested in the political and economic institutions are no longer alone decisive for education. Although education is thoroughly involved in the very warp and woof of modern society and is committed to functions decisive for the very future of that society, control no longer will rest entirely in external power structures. Shaped by varied and often competing, even conflicting, forces that are operative in a diverse and changing society, education in turn is becoming a decisive and influential institutional complex for shaping the future of modern man and his society.

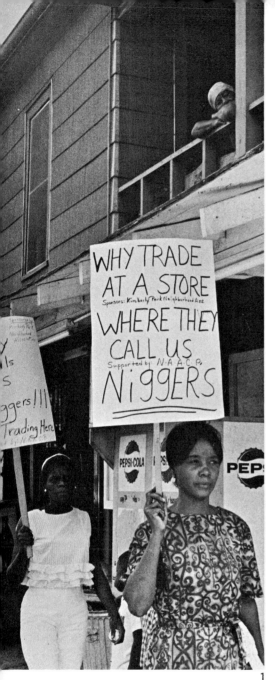

1　2

1. Winston-Salem, N.C.
2. Strikers picketing The New York Times.
3. An Italian immigrant in his shoe-repair shop.
4. A stockbroker's office in Detroit.
5. A debutante party.

3 4

5

ECONOMY
AND SOCIETY

15

From time immemorial, men have toiled; by the sweat of their brow they have wrested a living from a sometimes resistant and always capricious environment. They have cultivated, domesticated, and mined; they have become skilled with their hands, and they have fashioned tools and constructed machines in order to master the physical environment and provide themselves with the resources to sustain life. At no time has the work they have done been an activity merely economic; instead, it has always been intricately related to the total life of man within society. Economic activity has always come to have other meanings, moral and normative, religious and political, and to be closely involved in the distribution of status and prestige.

The growth of industrialism and capitalism in the West has gradually differentiated the economic institution from the other institutions of society; it is in the West that a developed conception of *the economy* as a distinct entity is most evident. With the growth over centuries of industrial capitalism, its distinct market economy encouraged the idea that the economic sphere was relatively separate from other spheres, both as a factual condition and as a moral theory of society. The liberal model of society was fashioned from this idea about the moral value (in terms of freedom and individualism) of a society in which relations among the institutions were minimal.

The presumed separate and independent activity that is economic has led to the development within the past century and a half of a social scientific discipline concerned exclusively with such activity: *economics*. As a result, sociology has tended to treat economic matters lightly and one-sidedly, so that the development of a sociology of economics, concerned with the place of the economic institution in the total fabric of society, has never been developed. Sociologists have, however, concerned themselves with the nature of industrialism and the factory system, and industrial sociology, as a thriving area of sociology, has explored the structure of social relationships within factories and within industries.

THE ECONOMY AS A SOCIOLOGICAL PROBLEM

The one-sided interest of sociologists in the economy has led them to study industrial relations and the social structure of work, while doing little with the larger issue of the place of the economy in the structure of society. Yet the *economy as an institution* is a central issue for sociology. As an institutional arrangement, economic activity carries out functions vital to the total ongoing activity of society.

The economist perceives the economy as independent and autonomous, a rational process for producing and distributing goods; but the sociologist sees it as one significant human activity among others, influencing these other activities and in turn being influenced by them. It is the very nature of the sociologist to ask questions about how economic activity and economic structures correlate with noneconomic processes: political activities, religion, and kinship, for example. This issue is particularly relevant in industrial societies, where the differentiation of the economy from other institutional orders is so pronounced. Thus, *the relation of the economy to the social structure* constitutes a major area of sociological inquiry.

The *relation of technology to social life* also constitutes a major area of sociological inquiry. Changes in technology that create new occupations and eliminate old ones have *social* consequences of considerable magnitude, both within the structure of work and within such aspects of the society as stratification and the existing system of occupations. What is called *automation* is the latest technological pattern that has radical implications for social structure.

Lastly, the economic processes of the society are a natural context for examining sociological problems of *integration and conflict.* There are several reasons for this. For one, a conception of economic *interests* has long dominated Western social thought and has been regarded as a prime mover of men and thus a source of conflict and difference. It is not only Marxian ideology but indeed most Western thought that has assumed that economic interests are of paramount importance, a source of consensus and cooperation, as well as of conflict and differentiation. All of the great ideologies of the past century were more or less oriented to the primacy of the economic.

Consequently, sociologists, as other social scientists, have seen in economic action and belief much that is relevant for the study of conflict and integration. Economic conflict has been endemic throughout the history of industrialization. The *integrative* function of the economic institution is a more complex issue, however, yet sociological thinkers since Spencer and Durkheim dealt with the issue, as did Marx in a somewhat different way. Economic action continues to provide the context in which sociologists ask questions about ideology, both divisive and integrative in its effects, about the management of tensions in industrial society, and about the effort to build an integrative pattern of "human relations" in work situations.

The pattern of modern economic organization has until recently been found only in Western industrial societies. But since World War II there has been a significant effort to develop this pattern in the economies of the newly emerging nations of Africa and Asia, now that colonial status has largely disappeared. But *economic development* turns out to be a difficult process, one that cannot be accomplished without significant change in the traditional structure of these societies. What is needed to bring about the modernization of these societies is then primarily a sociological issue of structural change; economic development rests upon complex social processes, and the sociologist finds himself studying such development simply as the key process of modernization.

These, then, seem to be the major problematic areas of the economy around which the concern of sociologists is centered: (1) the economy as a social institution; (2) its relation to noneconomic institutions and spheres of society; (3) the social impact of technology; (4) the problems of conflict and integration; and (5) economic development.

THE ECONOMY AS AN INSTITUTION

In any society, the economy needs to be viewed for sociological purposes in two related ways: (1) as a complex process for accomplishing certain functions for that society; and (2) as a social process thoroughly interwoven with the noneconomic processes of the society. The economist is concerned with those activities having to do with the production, distribution, exchange, and consumption of scarce goods. In modern society he assumes this to be a relatively independent process, at least to the extent that the major variables used for explanation are strictly economic. Thus, he conceives of a market process that is independent of the other institutional structures of the society; basically, it is a mechanism for responding sensitively to the supply and demand for goods and for using supply and demand to set prices and wages.

Throughout the development of economic theory, a central intellectual construct has been a postulate of *rationality*. The model of rational man in economics is the assumption that in any situation of economic choice, the individual will behave so as to maximize his economic position. This model has been a useful analytic device for the study of economic behavior. But for the sociologist, deviance from rationality is not merely a matter of ignorance or error but is also indicative of noneconomic values and norms that are so influential in controlling and directing human behavior.

Although it is easy enough to challenge the validity of the concept of rational man, particularly as the notion of a universal psychological motive, it can, as Neil Smelser points out, be regarded as an *institutionalized value*, a standard that serves to control behavior and is held as a widespread expectation by businessmen.[1] The institutionalization of economic rationality in Western life can be seen in such things as an assumption of acquisitiveness in man, an encouragement of such an attitude in businessmen, and in the

---

[1] Neil Smelser, *The Sociology of Economic Life* (Englewood Cliffs, N.J.: Prentice-Hall, 1963). p. 34.

treating of both the natural environment and man himself as commodities that can be monetarily valued in terms of supply and demand.

This model of rational man is an analytic technique of modern economics devised as a tool to explain the workings of the market in a capitalist economy. But the industrial capitalism that modern economics explains is not the only economic order that men have devised, either in the past or the present. Specifically, modern capitalism, as Max Weber's great historic researches made clear, is a particular form of capitalism; earlier forms existed prior to industrialization and under a different set of conditions. Thus, modern *capitalism* as an organization of economic relationships developed along with *industrialism,* but these are distinct phenomena. Capitalism is an organization of the economy, and includes such things as free labor, the free market, private property, and competition among relatively equal economic units. Industrialism is an organization of production, a system of social relationships adapted to the logic of technology and machine-production, and includes a technologically determined division of labor, occupations, and such organized units as factories. A society can be both capitalist and industrial, but it need not be both. The Soviet Union is industrial without being capitalist, and much of the industrialization that is proceeding among the new nations in Asia and Africa is noncapitalist.

The Economic Functions   For any human population, there must be a means for satisfying those material wants—food, shelter, and clothing—without which life could not be sustained. In all human societies, then, there is some social organization that is concerned with the carrying out of activities that provide the basic material sustenance of life. This social organization is a cooperative and interdependent process by which many different persons contribute in some manner to a total task of producing and distributing goods. What is sociologically relevant about this is that there is social organization—roles, norms, and social relations—for the economic activities. The effort to provide subsistence, then, reveals the same process of allocating people to social roles and providing normative controls as does any other sphere of social life.

The *productive* processes lead to the organization of work, which in turn produces a division of labor and a system of occupations. Work is usually done in social groups, whether that be the family, the small household unit, or the factory. Although the existing state of technology is clearly a major determiner of the division of labor and thus of the type and size of social units, other factors, such as values, also have some influence on the way in which work is organized.

The *distributive* processes are those social processes that are concerned with the relevant claims of each person to the products of the collective efforts of the group. To this point in human history, goods have always been *scarce,* and so distribution has always been necessarily unequal. The problem of distribution, then, is very much a problem of evaluating competing claims for shares of goods. But social power also is a determiner of the process of distribution, and the value system that prevails may be the one sustained by those who have the power. The distribution of goods, then, always rests upon a distribution of power and upon a system of values about who is entitled to what share for what justifiable reasons. Necessarily, in complex societies, there is pervasive conflict over the legitimacy of the system of distribution.

Economists usually speak of production, and *consumption*, the using up of that which has been produced. Only in a most limited way has economic theory provided for the effect of cultural factors and social structure in explaining consumption, though Alfred Marshall (1842–1924), one of the great names in economic theory, did recognize that many of the wants of people are socially structured. But one who did give recognition to the structuring of consumption process was that most sociological of economists, Thorstein Veblen (1857–1929), whose concept of *conspicuous consumption* asserted that people consumed visibly in such a way as to signify to others their social position and indeed to lay claim to such position.[2] Such behavior was particularly true of the very rich, whose expenditures went beyond sheer subsistence needs. In short, where affluence permits more choice, group-based standards of taste and style strongly affect the patterns of consumption. Modern advertising and most modern merchandising operate practically upon this idea. Yet, despite the ground-breaking thrust of Veblen's influential idea, little more has been done on the social and cultural factors affecting consumption. Certainly, sociologists have been almost entirely concerned with the productive function. They have been less concerned with the problems of distribution, which perhaps less easily lend themselves to analysis and are freighted with difficult problems of conflicting values.

Property   Fundamental to the economic institution is a conception of *property*. Again, property rests upon the conception of scarce resources, for if resources were unlimited and inexhaustible, no one would need to claim ownership of anything, and conceptions of property would be academic. The most common confusion about property is to conceive of it as a material object—land or tools—when the concept in fact refers to the *rights* to material objects. This right to goods or resources finds its expression in the value system of the society, in its norms and customs, and becomes an institutionalized expression of how the goods and resources of that society can best be utilized. The definition of property that prevails in a society, then, springs out of the very structure of the society and out of the cultural experiences of the group.

---

[2] Thorstein Veblen, *The Theory of the Leisure Class* (New York: Random House, 1931).

Property rights, then, are normative definitions sustained by collective agreement within the society and backed by legitimate forms of power and authority. Indeed, property only exists because there are collective agreements about rights to scarce resources. This is no less true of private property, which allocates such rights to individuals. But a person has private property rights only because the laws and courts of the state will protect and enforce such rights.

If property is a system of rights that is socially defined and enforced, it also follows that such rights are always limited. It is a misconception that private property means that the owner can do anything he might choose with his property, though what limitations prevail depend upon the social value and relative scarcity of the object of the rights. Laws have long regulated the moral use of property, and in the modern world there is a whole set of restrictions on private owners: fire and health regulations; zoning ordinances; safety regulations; these and other social controls specify limits on the right to the object that the private owner enjoys. Furthermore, property may be taken for public use, under controlled and specified circumstances, as when buildings are taken in order to build highways. Lastly, taxes are levied and if not paid, property rights may be forfeited.

Types of Property   Private property is but one form of property rights, and even a society that maximizes the value of private ownership necessarily also makes use of other forms of ownership. Among traditional societies there has often been operative a *communal* sense of property, in that land for tilling or for hunting may be regarded as the right of the group as a whole. *Public* ownership has meant the placing of rights to resources in the name of a political collectivity: the state or some subgrouping of the state. Socialization of the "means of production" has been a basic postulate of socialism's conception of the necessary transformation of legitimate rights to access and use of these basic resources. Indeed, this has been the key principle in Marxian socialism and perhaps the basic issue in the great ideological debate of the nineteenth century. However, the fundamental issue was sometimes obscured by verbal jousts and ideological semantics. From the Marxian perspective, two assumptions were made: first, that the right of private property created two basic classes, those who owned property and those who did not, and the former had power as a consequence of having property. On this issue, the Marxian position is sociologically sound: the right of property does create power for its possessors over those who are propertyless. Control of the scarce resources necessary for human subsistence has always created a powerful social class in any human society, whether agrarian or industrial. A second assumption was that ownership meant actual control and operation. From a nineteenth century perspective, the bourgeois property owners were also the operating entrepreneurs, the "bosses," who had functional responsibility for the daily operation of the business. But it is just this assumption that has been called into question in the twentieth century, a development signified by the rise of the corporation.

The Separation of Ownership and Control   The invention of the legal corporation created a significant means for raising capital for investment, for it permitted the pooling of the capital of many, instead of relying on the capitalizing abilities of the few rich, while yet protecting these many investors by limiting the liability of ownership they incurred. But it had one other social consequence of major significance that few realized at the time. The dispersal of ownership among a large body of stockholders tended to separate ownership from the actual, operating control of the enterprise. Increasingly, actual decision making rested with *management,* which not only directed and supervised the employees in the internal daily operations but also made fundamental policy decisions for the firm. The emergence of a professional management exercising decision-making power for which there is no legitimacy under the existing conception of private property is then one of the profound changes of modern times. This had already largely occurred before it was obvious to scholarly observers. Although first noted in a government monograph based upon Congressional investigation in the 1920s, the first full statement of the change was presented in 1933 in what is now a classic of modern social science, *The Modern Corporation and Private Property* by A. A. Berle and Gardner Means.[3]

It has always been the case, of course, that property rights do not necessarily include use. Property can be loaned, rented, leased, or otherwise used by others. But these have always been provided before, and did not seem to alter the basic significance of property ownership. But the separation of ownership and control in the modern corporation does. Basically, it challenged the Marxian assumption about the need to change ownership, for it has now become apparent that what the Marxians were concerned with was control. The nineteenth century assumption that ownership meant control could no longer be taken seriously.

Ownership in the industrial system may be largely a legal fiction that has significant ideological and political function, symbolizing the dominant political ideology of the society but not the actual directive processes. If the stockholder in the United States now merely regards himself as an *investor,* not an owner, so, too, public ownership of the means of production in the Soviet Union does not place actual control in the hands of the "public."

[3] A. A. Berle and Gardner Means, *The Modern Corporation and Private Property* (New York: Macmillan, 1933).

Rather, control there has been in the hands of the Communist Party, and its only effective challenge comes from a rising professional management.

In the nineteenth century the challenge of socialism was manifested in the symbolic pairing of capital and labor; but in the twentieth century the contrast is between management and labor. The older pairing implied a fundamental conflict, for it seemed to say that the interests of propertyless workers were necessarily opposed to the private ownership of the means of production. But a conflict of management and labor is more restricted, confined to pragmatic decisions about wages and working conditions, and at the most, over differing definitions of the on-the-job rights of both groups.

ECONOMY AND SOCIAL STRUCTURE

It is a sociological truism that the economic processes of a society are in some manner linked to other social processes. However segmented and differentiated a society may be, it is nonetheless also the case that these differentiated segments are only relatively distinct; they are also linked with each other to make of a society a single interdependent process. Modern society seems to differ from traditional ones specifically in this process of greater differentiation and segmentation of the "parts" of the society. Its specific institutions are no longer as integrated into single concrete human groups but are manifested in separate ones: families, factories, schools, government agencies, and so forth.

Yet the disconnection is only partial and may be less than is apparent. This would seem to be the case for the economy, the separation of which from the other institutions has for so long been taken for granted (thus permitting a specialized discipline of economics). However, the economy is linked in varied and numerous ways with the other institutions of society, having influence upon them and in turn being influenced by what goes on elsewhere in the society.

The Differentiation of the Economy   An analysis of the relationships between the economy and other facets of social structure hinges on one basic idea: that the modern trend is an increasing differentiation of the economic processes into separate institutional arrangements and economic groups, less attached to the social processes and values of other institutions. In traditional societies the communal outlook does not permit the pursuit of economic gain at the price of other values, and it relates economic activity more closely to religious conduct and family activities. The principles of modern analytic economics, then, have been developed to explain an economy that is a highly differentiated social structure, operating with a monetary system of exchange, an elaborate credit system, and a market organized around a price structure. These principles do not apply to all those traditional societies, whether peasant or proletariat, in which these conditions are not present.

Anthropologists studying "simple" societies often cannot even clearly distinguish an economic activity from a religious or political one. One of the first anthropologists to study primitive economies, Bronislaw Malinowski (1884–1942), found that the economic processes of the Melanesian tribes were thoroughly interwoven with the entire social life of the society.[4] Kinship was crucial in the organization of work, and there was communal labor based upon the obligations of kinship. Furthermore, assistance in building a canoe, for example, did not proceed in ways familiar to modern industry but was a communal enterprise without economic motives and with no wage payments. The place of magic in providing an integrative force by giving psychological confidence in the craftsmanship that went into the construction of the canoe was emphasized by Malinowski. He also described forms of gift giving that proceeded according to such noneconomic factors as custom and ceremony. Marcel Mauss (1872–1950) surveyed a vast range of anthropological literature in *The Gift*, in order to analyze ceremonial gift giving in primitive societies.[5] Mauss found that he could not account for the giving of gifts as a utilitarian exchange process; rather, gift giving was primarily a symbolic process that served to reinforce the integration of kinship or tribal units.

But these anthropological studies are of preindustrial, relatively undifferentiated societies in which the economic activities cannot be clearly distinguished from noneconomic ones. In the long transition to modern society, in turn, there has been an extensive differentiation of specific societal functions, and sociologists have developed their discipline around this complex segmentation. Although the differentiation of institutions and groups from one another has been a general process, differentiation in the economic sphere has been particularly related to the *rationalization* of modern life that Max Weber so thoroughly analyzed.[6]

Weber's analysis of the emergence of modern rational capitalism, in fact, is probably the most thorough effort to see the social conditions on which such a system rests. What Weber and others have related to us has been the gradual freeing of economic groups and activities from the network of customs, obligations, and religious values that once governed it and so tied it in closely to other institutions. Instead, economic activity has been rationalized by

---

[4] Malinowski's work on primitive economics is to be found in *Argonauts of the Western Pacific* (London: Routledge, 1922) and *Coral Gardens and Their Magic* (London: G. Allen, 1935).

[5] Marcel Mauss, *The Gift*, trans. by Ian Cunnison (New York: Free Press, 1954).

[6] See Max Weber, *The Theory of Social and Economic Organization*, trans. by A. M. Henderson and Talcott Parsons (New York: Oxford, 1947).

establishing criteria that maximized efficiency and from this economic productivity. This was accomplished by defining land and labor as commodities—
as objects which could be monetarily valued in terms of supply and demand
—and ignoring any other normative meaning that might be placed upon them.
Considerations of custom and sentiment, morality and belonging, had to
give way to the norms of the market and the impersonal and rational criteria
that governed production and distribution. Such relative autonomy not only
made paramount the rational standards of the market and the status to be
derived from making money, it also lessened the control of other institutions,
such as religion for example, which had long been the source of moral guidance.
Also, it gave a powerful dominance to the economic institutions and served
to reshape society around the demands and values of a rationalized economic
process.

Religion in the Economy   The reciprocal influences of religion and economy
have centered on the Weberian thesis concerning the place of religion in
generating values that either support or restrict significant patterns of economic
behavior. Max Weber undertook what is still the most extensive and penetrating study of the relationship between religion and economy. The impetus
for Weber's study was to show that religion was one significant factor (though
by no means the only one) in explaining economic behavior. To do this,
he undertook a massive comparative study of religion and economy in several
non-Western societies and in western Europe, to test specifically the proposition
that religious values either generated support for or hindered the emergence
of capitalism.[7]

In *The Protestant Ethic and the Spirit of Capitalism,* Weber's basic thesis was
that early Protestantism independently generated an ethical outlook and a
religious orientation to the world that created a mode of economic behavior
for early capitalist entrepreneurs which permitted both a break with feudal
economic patterns and the subsequent development of modern rational capitalism.

A more detailed analysis of the religious sources and meanings of the Protestant ethic will be discussed in Chapter 18, here the emphasis is on its economic
consequences. Weber asserted that early Protestantism generated an orientation
that encouraged self-discipline and hard work, initiative and material acquisition, and an individualism that encouraged competitive practices. The early
bourgeois Protestant was encouraged to work hard at the occupation to which
God had called him, and to live ascetically. His asceticism generated the famous

[7] Translations of Weber's comparative study of religion are primarily these: *The Protestant
Ethic and the Spirit of Capitalism* (London: G. Allen, 1930; New York: Scribner, 1958); *The
Religion of China: Confucianism and Taoism* (New York: Free Press, 1951); and *The Religion of
India: The Sociology of Hinduism and Buddhism* (New York: Free Press, 1958).

Puritan virtues of frugality and self-denial; the pleasures of the flesh were taboo. His hard work and self-discipline led to economic success, yet his asceticism would not permit him to spend his gain for his own worldly enjoyment. So his wealth became capital accumulation that was reinvested, leading to expansion and development. Thus, religious motives served to produce the economic behavior that led to the development of capitalism.

This contribution of Protestantism to the development of capitalism was not an intended one; the early Protestant theologians, such as Calvin, had no idea of encouraging any particular economic order. Yet their teachings led to a religious view of the world that encouraged significantly new modes of economic action. What Protestant ascetism encouraged most of all was a profoundly rational view of the world, and particularly of the economic sphere, in which the mastery and control of the physical environment and the social world became a dominant motivation.

Religion in a Secular World   The Protestant ethic was the orientation of men who were in the world but rejected its worldly values and symbols of success and in time profoundly changed that world. But as the world became more consistent with the Protestant ethic, the very religious values became a set of cultural values gradually detached from religion. Increasingly the Protestant ethic was a secular view of the world, its original religious source in decline. The descendants of the originators were hard-working businessmen, less ascetic in nature and less given to rejecting the world. The "spirit" of capitalism that Protestantism helped stimulate and develop tended, in the most capitalist and Protestant countries, to develop a church whose teachings were supportive of the middle class and business, and whose message was less and less comprehensible to the working classes. Such a pattern, however, was by no means confined to distinctly Protestant countries; in those Catholic countries, such as France and Italy, where industrialization also developed, the church lost much of its significance for the working classes as well. This loss of the working classes by organized Christendom has been one of the great moral crises for the churches of Europe.

But even more basic, perhaps, has been the development under rational capitalism of an economic order that is guided by its own normative system and is no longer under the moral guidance of religion. It is the economic order of modern society that has been its most rational and secularized sphere, detached from the traditional moral values of the culture that find their most profound expression in religion.

The Economy and Politics   The term, laissez-faire, was an expression of a basic value of the liberal ideology that supported capitalism. It was one dimension of a larger orientation, which suggested that a free society was promoted by the separation of the religious, economic, and political institutions of society. Laissez-faire, specifically, was an admonition that government let the economic order alone, except for the enforcement of laws against criminal and fraudulent behavior.

But now, this laissez-faire orientation does not apply, not even in the United States. Government regulation of various forms of economic activity is now well-established, but its significance lies in two spheres. One of these is the development of a vast *welfare* program that mitigates the impersonal effects of the market on those subject to low income and unemployment, and offers a basic line of social security for all. The other is the regulation of money, credit, and investment by various measures in order to limit the once more radical swings of the business cycle.

These changes suggest that private economic power concentrated in the corporation is no longer either unregulated or unchallenged. The concentration of political power in government and the concentration of powerful bargaining power in labor unions constitute *countervailing* power blocs that put limits upon the immense power of the corporation, but which also give control over vital decisions to large organizations, not to individuals.[8] This indicates that the economy has now been subject to *politicization,* and the differentiation of the economy from the polity in classical liberal theory is no longer as much a fact of life as it once was. There is now *political economy* in modern industrial societies. Economic policy is a central concern of government, and the major elite of American economists now constitutes a group of advisors to the president of the United States, not to corporation leaders.

The Economy and Kinship The impact of an industrializing economy upon the structure of the family has perhaps been the central concern of sociologists when posing questions about the relationship of the economy to kinship. Rarely have they asked questions, in turn, about the impact of family and kinship upon the economy. Yet there is a considerable anthropological literature which suggests that in nonindustrial economies kinship acts as a limiting force upon the economy. The obligations of kinship may assign economic roles and tasks, and the kinship system is a source of aid for the individual. In such societies, economic demands are rarely viewed as imperative enough to take precedence over the obligations of kinship.

In the study of industrial society, the one issue has been, as we have already noted, the impact of the economy upon the family, instituting the long controversy about the decline of the family and its disorganization that was reviewed in Chapter 13. But in the development of industrial capitalism, the

---

[8] This is John Kenneth Galbraith's thesis in his *American Capitalism: The Concept of Countervailing Power* (Boston: Houghton Mifflin, 1952).

family has played an important role. Great mercantilist families pioneered in overseas trade and consolidated large family enterprises through the inter-marriage of children. Much of the early history of Western economic develop-ment can be written in terms of the great interlinked families that owned and operated the banking and mercantile houses of Europe.

Yet, as Daniel Bell has noted, the growth of corporate capitalism has meant the decline of family capitalism.[9] Corporate capitalization far exceeds the resources of even the wealthiest of families. In fact where there is a refusal to extend the enterprise beyond the family, as has happened so often in France, there is a limitation on economic development. The French business family has been reluctant to go outside the family for capital, to recruit executives, or even to separate family and business bookkeeping. The result is to maintain an exclusively small family business, which lacks the desire to recruit "new blood" (except by intermarriage) or to adopt any of the rational capitalizing and accounting procedures so relevant in the development of corporate capitalism.

As differentiated as a modern economy may be, and as specialized as may be the social units (factories, banks, and so forth) by which economic activity is organized, the economic order is nonetheless linked in innumerable ways with various noneconomic institutions and activities. It has a pervasive influence on many noneconomic activities and in turn is influenced by these. We have briefly reviewed only some of these, to give some conception of the mutual interrelation between economic and noneconomic factors in the organization of a society.

TECHNOLOGY AND THE DIVISION OF LABOR

All of the great social thinkers have recognized the relevance of technology for the division of labor and the division of labor, in turn, for producing social differences that generate problems in integration and conflict. Karl Marx placed singular stress on the development of technology as crucial in shaping a division of labor that formed the social classes whose ultimate conflict, he said, would lead to the revolution that would change society. Among American thinkers, the economist-sociologist Thorstein Veblen gave most attention to the significance of technology for social life. Veblen was impressed with the idea that the logic of modern technology induced a rational mind, the kind that characterized engineers, scientists, technicians, and skilled workers, in contrast

---

[9] See "The Breakup of Family Capitalism," in his *The End of Ideology* (New York: Free Press, 1960), pp. 37–42.

to the nonrational mentality of farmers, unskilled workers, bankers and profit-oriented businessmen.[10] He felt that work habits and the mentality induced by modes of work was a major socializing experience for the individual, crucial in shaping his outlook on life and even his fundamental perspective on human society.

Veblen defined profit-capitalism as basically an irrational mode of behavior that would in time be replaced by the rational mentality induced by modern science and technology. Although he never went as far as Marx in predicting a social revolution, he did outline a social stratification that put engineers and other rational-minded occupations and professions on one side, against capitalists, farmers, unskilled workers, and all those others whose work-patterns did not induce such a rational mind, and who were still wedded to traditional, magical, and exploitative orientations. His work led others to expect a "technocracy," a society dominated by the rationally, technically trained segments of society. Thus, Veblen differed from Weber and other European thinkers in viewing quite hopefully the increasing rationalization of the modern world.

Work and Technology   In traditional, preindustrial societies, the organization of work is so interwoven with the larger organization of the society that they can only be separated analytically. Tradition specifies the allocation of tasks, with sex, age, and social rank as common determinants, though sometimes differences of skill may be relevant. Even when the division of labor requires some leadership and direction, this usually falls to a tribal leader or kinship head; that is, to someone whose social position of leadership is in a noneconomic unit. In such traditional contexts, work is usually carried on among people who spend their whole life together, and it is within a context of diffuse primary relations that norms governing work relations prevail. Even in the craft system of the Middle Ages, the shop was small, and the relations among masters, journeymen, and apprentices were close and personal. Despite his very real authority, the master craftsman was hardly master in his house; he was bound within a customary network of rules and regulations, and the journeymen and apprentices worked under the protection of strong craft traditions.

However, the introduction of an industrial technology radically altered the customary pattern around which work was organized. Work was removed from the household of craftsmen and peasants and organized around more complex machinery located in a central place; thus, the factory came into being. Neither the paternalistic authority of kinship nor the guild-based authority of the master craftsman prevailed any longer. Industrial capitalism replaced these with a rational system of control organized around two imperatives: the char-

[10] See *The Instinct of Workmanship* (New York: B. W. Heubsch, 1922), Chapter 7, pp. 309–311.

acter of the technological system; and the impersonal processes of supply and demand in a capitalist market. Work relationships were often shaped by how men were grouped in order to use the new machinery efficiently. The daily routines of work and the individual's claim upon a job were unprotected by custom, by the traditional power of a guild, or by the moral authority of a church. Instead, the principles of supply and demand impersonally set wages and determined if there were to be any job security. In addition, the authority of the employer was supreme, yet he did not have to assume any responsibility for the welfare of his workers.

The Social Consequences of Technology Industrialization brought about a social reorganization of work impelled by the introduction of new and complex machinery, before which all other historically known technologies seem primitive and crude. What is significant for the student of society is not the technology itself, but the vast social consequences engendered by the change from simple to highly productive technology. As machinery or tools, technology never stands alone; it is always part of a social context that includes the social uses to which it is put; the social value placed upon its productivity; the socially trained expertise that operates it; and the knowledge out of which it was created. Indeed, any definition of technology needs to include not only the technological instruments but also the technical knowledge required to produce and use them.

Perhaps the most significant social consequence of modern technology is that it creates an intricate division of labor, for technology requires numerous specialized tasks. The days of the old craftsman who made a total object with a few tools and his remarkable skills are gone. Now, the man-made object is the end-product of a vast system of production that involves many skills and specializations; each person contributes but one small part to the finished product. But technology is also determinative of other human actions. It affects the pacing of work and the level of skill that must be acquired, and most importantly it strongly influences the character of social interaction that can occur in the work situation. The spatial arrangements of machinery either permit much interaction or inhibit it by spacing men too far apart. Thus, the social groupings permitted by the technical arrangements affect the development of modes of interaction, patterns of communication and, thus, the emergence of small groups that control individual behavior and have some effect upon job performance.

Probably more than any one other factor in modern society, technology shapes and reshapes the occupational structure. Every change in technology modifies occupations, even eliminates some and creates new ones. Early industrialization created a small elite of technically skilled occupations and a large number of unskilled ones. Increasingly, technological changes created more and more semiskilled occupations found in mass production. Now the most advanced technology is eliminating these positions and creating a smaller number of more technically demanding jobs.

Automation   The social consequences of technology have been made vividly apparent in recent years by the development of automation. Automation is not merely a more advanced mechanization. It involves two principles: a continuous process of production, whereby machine-controlled parts move from one point to another without being touched by human hands; and, secondly, self-control by means of a feedback process, in which machines provide information on which decisions can be made, such as the decisions ordinarily made by inspectors or maintenance men.

The controversy over automation has been about the displacement of labor. There is no doubt that automation eliminates many of the machine-operative positions that once provided most of the jobs on an assembly line. Its long-run consequences on the need for labor are not yet quite clear and are still subject to contradictory interpretations. But it is quite evident that automation reduces the need for lesser skills and increases the need for more technically skilled people. Within the factory, technicians will replace unskilled and semi-skilled positions. Furthermore, the automating of the industrial process will lessen the amount of physical labor and shorten the workday and workweek.

Perhaps one of the most significant consequences has to do with the degree of control over the job exercised by workers. William Faunce's influential study of automation suggests that one of the profoundest effects will be on the nature of social interaction on the job.[11] He found in an automated automobile factory that there was little interaction among work groups and that work groups were smaller than in nonautomated factories. Further, automated work seemed to require more interaction with superiors, reducing interaction with peers. Faunce suggests that the primary group, which regulates behavior and controls job performance, may come to be less significant when automation reorganizes work. Since machines are controlled automatically, work groups will have less control over output, and even worker morale will have less influence on productivity. Thus, much of what industrial sociologists have taken to be determinative of the level of productivity may cease to be so, and a reassessment of the work group in industry may be in order. If this turns out to be so, we have a striking example of the impact of technological change on social organization.

[11] "Automation in the Automobile Industry: Some Consequences for In-Plant Social Structure," *American Sociological Review,* 23 (August, 1958), 403–406.

CONFLICT AND INTEGRATION IN THE ECONOMY

From the very outset of our study, we saw that the emergence of industrialism created deep concerns about the integration of society; sociology as a discipline was born from that problem. Any analysis of the economic order brings to the fore the problems of conflict and integration in industrial society. Some of the most bitter struggles that have occurred in industrial societies have been between workers and their employers. Workers have organized for power into unions and sometimes into worker-based political parties. The history of organized labor is a history of struggle, much of it violent and bloody. Also, during the nineteenth century and the first third of the twentieth, the great ideological struggles have centered on the nature of the economic order: communism, socialism, and capitalism.

The Division of Labor   That the integration of human society is related to the division of labor is an observation long existent in the history of social thought. Emile Durkheim made it an organizing idea in the development of sociology when he analyzed comparatively the significance of the division of labor in traditional and industrial societies. In his great work, *The Division of Labor in Society,* published in 1893, he contrasted the *mechanical solidarity* of traditional societies with the *organic solidarity* of modern industrial ones.[12]

In the traditional society the division of labor is minimal, often only between the sexes or by age, so that Durkheim felt that such a homogeneous society was composed of structurally identical kinship units; any one of them could replace any other in the division of labor. In such a society the basic values are shared collectively, for there is no social differentiation to produce value differentiation. The integration of the society follows from this homogeneity of social roles and social values. Furthermore, since variation is so little experienced, it is taken as a threat. Therefore, a deviation from established norms, said Durkheim, results in harsh and violent reaction against the offender. This mechanical solidarity is best represented in *repressive* law, which is law that demands a single conforming pattern of behavior from all members of the society. Such a society subordinates the individual to the common standards of the group.

In modern society, however, Durkheim saw the division of labor as creating a society of highly differentiated groups, with a plurality of economic and political interests, specialization of functions, and wide heterogeneity in values

---

[12] Emile Durkheim, *The Division of Labor in Society,* trans. by George Simpson (New York: Free Press, 1949).

and attitudes. Such a society is highly interdependent. The repressive law that is a strong social constraint no longer has the backing of collectively shared values, and so collective restraint decreases, allowing greater individualization and a variety of life-styles. In such functionally differentiated societies, Durkheim and other earlier sociologists saw serious problems of integration. It was true that there was a complex interdependency among the differentiated units, for none of them could exist alone. But was interdependence a sufficiently integrating force? That Durkheim was not confident that such was the case can be seen in his development of such ideas as *restitutive law* and also *anomie.*

Durkheim clearly viewed the problem of integration as *the* basic issue in the study of human society. The unrestrained individualism that much of the individualistic and laissez-faire ideology had advanced, represented best in sociology by the work of Herbert Spencer, Durkheim viewed as a threat to social integration. He believed that the only workable individualism was one that avoided any claim to the right to pursue immediate desires without regard to others. Thus, he spoke of restitutive law as that law which restored to the individual what was rightfully his, and which thus protected contractual and functional relations in an interdependent society of differentiated and socially free individuals.

Durkheim's conception of anomie conveyed a notion of a state of normlessness, a social condition in which collectively accepted norms no longer governed social relations and individual human behavior. Durkheim was talking about the breakdown of societal integration, an idea, when called *social disorganization,* which was highly influential in the development of American sociology. It reflected a pessimistic outlook on the social consequences of industrialization, of which the division of labor was a preeminent one. Indeed, the reader need but recall the discussion in Chapter 2 about the overwhelming concern for the destructive impact of industrialization on the more traditional, *Gemeinschaft* type of society, to note again how much the change to a modern economic order raised the issue of integration as a serious intellectual concern for an entire pioneering generation of sociologists.

Ideologies and Values   When problems of control and integration press themselves upon people, the relations of social structure to social values will be unclear, and ideologies will emerge to state the relationship in a way that promotes and justifies group interests. Thus, ideologies can serve as a moral and social justification for existing social structures, and they can also serve as a source of moral attack upon the existing order of things.

Perhaps the foremost sociological study of the control function of ideology is Reinhardt Bendix's *Work and Authority in Industry,* a comparative study of the use of ideology by management to justify its pattern of authority within the factory.[13] Bendix focused on the problem of getting workers to accept the authority of management within the framework of institutional and technological requirements that prevailed in a society. Thus, his analysis is a preeminent attempt to delineate the justifying force of ideology.

Counterideologies have flourished at two levels. Labor unions have challenged the authority of management, at least in all aspects affecting workers, and have developed an ideology that justifies their own existence in terms of the right of workers to act freely in their own behalf. It also projects a view of the union as fighting for social justice for otherwise powerless workers. A second level of ideological attack has been that sweeping rejection, not only of managerial authority, but of the entire social structure on which it rests. Communism and socialism have attacked the institutions of private property and of capitalism, and have called for a new social order in which the worker would be no longer subject to the control of his employer.

The Economic Basis of Conflict   One does not have to be a Marxist to recognize an economic basis for conflict. Indeed, many historians and other scholars with no Marxian assumptions have written of peasants struggling against landlords, workers against employers, the poor against the rich, and even of nations fighting over economic stakes: (1) access to markets and raw materials; (2) land; (3) trade routes; and (4) sources of food for their population. But Karl Marx has been the one major thinker who most systematically developed a conception of economically based conflict as a philosophy of history and a sociological conception of social change. In Chapter 10, we reviewed Marx's conception of the class structure as based upon the existing technology and the social relations among men in the use of that technology. What is relevant is that Marx thought there was a logical consistency between the technology and the social relations of men using that technology, which, however, did not last. Changes in technology produced strains and inconsistencies in the set of economic relations, but those whom the system advantaged and who held social power were unwilling to accept the next set of social changes logically dictated by the newer technology. Eventually, those who would gain by change recognize their interests in a new social order and bring it about by a revolutionary struggle.

Marx thus felt that all societies were historically unstable and carried within them the seeds of their own destruction. For capitalism, the "seeds of destruction" were the pursuit of profits by exploiting workers, and the cycles of boom and bust to which the capitalist market was necessarily subject. The increasing misery that befell the proletariat would eventually make them sufficiently conscious of how their interests were subverted by capitalism; then an eco-

---

[13] Reinhardt Bendix, *Work and Authority in Industry* (New York: Wiley, 1956).

nomic stratum of workers would become a social class that would organize politically in order to carry on a revolutionary struggle. Marx's conception of the class struggle is that such conflict is inevitable, and that the *interests* of workers and capitalists are inevitably caught up in irreconcilable conflict. These interests lead men to struggle to shape quite different kinds of societies, and through this struggle societies are changed. Thus, for Marx, conflict is the significant source of historical change; to deplore conflict is to argue for the dominance of established patterns and to fail to understand how society changes.

As a perspective on society and on social change, Marx's position contrasts quite sharply with that of those modern social theorists who have posited an essential harmony of interests and a consensus of values among the members of society. It also stands in contrast to the position of those industrial sociologists whose work has been concerned with developing workable human relations in industry to reduce conflict and build cooperative relations to ensure a maximum of productivity.

The Management of Tensions   The growth of unions as legitimate social organizations, with a legitimate function in society defined and protected by legislation, and the development of intricate mechanisms for negotiating industrial disputes, has lessened the influence of and the commitment to class-based ideologies, particularly where they served to mobilize people for social conflict. Now, both the ideologies of labor and management must adjust to the new legal order that insists on there being bargaining in good faith and on the creation of contractual relations. This means that new social mechanisms, such as bargaining elections, federal mediation of prolonged disputes, and union-management contracts, have become institutionalized in a society that in fact recognizes the necessary interdependence of its distinct functional groups. A new viewpoint now insists that such groups develop modes of "antagonistic cooperation" and constantly renew their set of contractual relations. Although hardly irrelevant, ideology plays a muted role in a society that has constructed social mechanisms for managing the tensions between workers and managers and thus for reducing industrial conflict.

Human Relations   The emergence of stable unions and new, socially supported mechanisms for managing tensions has been accompanied by a new and powerful ideology of "human relations in industry." It has developed most extensively in the United States, supported by the numerous in-plant researches of a burgeoning industrial sociology. Its distinctive feature is a set of assumptions about what is important in the behavior of workers and what is not. It originated in the work of Elton Mayo and his associates in the famous Hawthorne study of the 1920s (discussed in Chapter 8), where a shift from a concern with the individual worker to a concern for the work group and the relations of the immediate work environment brought into being a whole new analytical approach.[14] This new approach contrasted sharply with an older orientation that interpreted industrial conflict as being rooted in economic interests; thus conflict was regarded as a natural state of affairs that usually leads to institutional change. The new approach to the study of industrial relations clearly was more sanguine about conflict and also was often characteristic of social scientists whose liberal philosophy made them more sympathetic to workers and unions than to management. The human relations approach, in turn, has accepted the existing framework of institutional arrangements, or at least taken them for granted, and has focused on the interaction of workers and managers in the work situation. It has sought to find the conditions that generate cooperation, good morale, rewarding social relations on the job, and then high productivity as a consequence of these.

The rediscovery of the *primary group* among workers is the key intellectual issue in this approach; a cooperative and cohesive work group provides a source of friendly interaction for its members, an identification by the individual with the group (a "we-feeling"), and leads to the emergence of a sense of shared goals and to norms that control the behavior of group members. Industrial sociologists, following the intellectual leadership of Elton Mayo, have argued for the importance of the group in industry, even though the emergence of an informal group may in fact subvert the official norms and goals. But the art of human relations has become a process of seeking to link effectively the work group to the goals of production, largely by the exercise of supervisory leadership schooled in "human relations" and by thus creating an environment that reduces friction between group norms and official goals.

Needless to say, an element of controversy has hung over this aspect of industrial sociology. It has been accused of harboring an implicit ideological approach that favors management—of seeking to maximize production (a managerial goal), of favoring harmony and cooperation over conflict and change, and in general of being what Harold Sheppard called a "managerial sociology."[15] The emphasis in industrial sociology is on studies that have such a practical utility, and the fact that access to factories for research can only come through management, has made it difficult to distinguish between the genuinely scientific findings of industrial sociology and the ideological element that has been there since the 1920s.

Perhaps the crucial issue has been that so much of industrial sociology has

[14] This has been reported in the classic volume by F. J. Roethlisberger and William J. Dickson, *Management and the Worker* (Cambridge, Mass.: Harvard University Press, 1947).
[15] Harold Sheppard, "The Treatment of Unionism in 'Managerial Sociology,'" *American Sociological Review* 14 (April, 1949), 310–313.

been an in-plant sociology; it has taken as "given" the larger institutional context in which on-the-job relations occur. Furthermore, industrial sociology has clearly not shared the general Marxian assumption that there is an inherent conflict of interest between workers and managers, and that it is this conflict that results in significant institutional change. For Marxians conflict is to be as appreciated and valued as is cooperation, and one is not to be regarded as of higher value than the other or as more natural to the human condition.

Work and Alienation   One consequence of the Protestant ethic has been to view work as the central life interest of industrial man; it is his dominant and rewarding role, and other roles and social relationships are subordinate to it. Max Weber asserted that the Puritan viewed work as his "calling," hard and methodical labor thus came to be regarded as doing God's will. Men were integrated into society through the significant moral and religious meanings placed upon work.

But it was Karl Marx who raised an even more fundamental issue that has persisted in the analysis of industrial life ever since, the argument that the industrial worker under capitalism was *alienated* from his work.[16] Contrary to most assumptions, Marx's central concern was not the inequity of material rewards but the act of turning work into meaningless, alienated labor, transforming man into a "crippled monstrosity." Marx always opposed the lifelong involvement of a man in one occupation, but the situation was rendered worse when this one occupation was but a single small part of a complicated productive process. Whatever the poverty and hard labor of his life, a medieval craftsman at least controlled his own work, and produced by his labor a product that manifested his skill.

For Marx *specialization* was not the wondrous mechanism of the modern age but a crippling influence that forced a man to subject himself to processes not of his own making. This is the significance of Marx's famous statement that under communism,

> society regulates the general production and thus makes it possible for me to do one thing today and another tomorrow, to hunt in the morning, fish in the after-

---

[16] Karl Marx's discussion of alienation in relation to the division of labor under capitalism was written when Marx was but twenty-six years old and preceded the development of his mature thought as presented in *Capital*. While long ignored, this discussion recently received much attention, particularly because of the renewed interest in the process of alienation. See *The Economic and Philosophic Manuscripts of 1844*, edited with an introduction by Dirk J. Struik (New York: International Publishers, 1964). For a cogent analysis of the manuscripts from a contemporary perspective, see Erich Fromm, *Marx's Concept of Man* (New York: Ungar, 1961); and also Robert Tucker, *Philosophy and Myth in Karl Marx* (New York: Cambridge, 1961).

noon, rear cattle in the evening, criticize after dinner, just as I have a mind, without ever becoming hunter, fisherman, shepherd or critic.[17]

Alienation, for Marx, meant that man does not experience himself as fulfilled in his work, and the product of his labor is a thing apart from himself. Man has become a *thing* and has lost his individuality.

Whether the modern worker is as estranged from work as Marx believed remained largely a matter of conjecture until now. Many middle-class observers have long believed that boredom and dissatisfaction with the repetitive job is a natural outcome of modern, assembly-line work. But this may have been only a projection of middle-class attitudes. Until recently there has been a paucity of facts and a great deal of philosophizing about whether workers can find a meaningful identity in work. One relevant attack upon this problem has been by Robert Dubin, an industrial sociologist, who attempted to determine the "central life-interests" of industrial workers.[18] His research supported Marx by discovering that the central interests of workers were not in their work; rather, workers found their preferred human associations outside of the job. He also found that less than 10 percent of workers preferred the informal relationships of the job to other possibilities. But workers do place higher value on the work organization than they do on other organizations in which they have membership. Dubin felt that the worker had a well-developed sense of attachment to his work and work place without being totally committed to it.

The most thorough sociological effort to study the problem of alienation in work has been by Robert Blauner, who compared his own empirical research to other known data bearing on this problem.[19] Blauner's major innovation was to make *type of work* a significant variable; thus, he contrasted craft work with machine tending and then assembly work and lastly with a continuous process industry, such as the chemical industry, where work is highly automated. He discovered a regular progression of feelings of greater alienation, particularly powerlessness and meaninglessness, from craft work, where it was low, to automobile assembly work, where it was highest, with a reversal under the newer circumstances of automated continuous production. Where alienation was little apparent, as in the first and fourth cases, workers felt that they had a control over their job, were freer from close supervision, and were not mere appendages to the technological process. What Blauner's work optimistically suggests is that the apex of alienation from work may have been reached in

[17] Karl Marx and Friedrich Engels, *The German Ideology* (New York: International Publishers, 1947), p. 22.

[18] Robert Dubin, "Industrial Workers' Worlds: A Study of the 'Central Life Interests' of Industrial Workers," *Social Problems*, 3 (1956), 131–142.

[19] Robert Blauner, *Alienation and Freedom: The Factory Worker and His Industry* (Chicago: University of Chicago Press, 1964).

the mass, assembly-line production process, and its replacement eventually by automated processes may produce work environments less conducive to feelings of powerlessness and meaninglessness in work, less isolating and estranging. But, of course, this may hold only for a technical elite of highly skilled workers and not for others.

A work such as Blauner's follows an argument that goes back to Karl Marx in anticipating increasing alienation as craft work declines, and machine tending and assembly work increases. However, a much newer interest has been that which suggests that a fundamental shift in the value of work is occurring in industrial society, and in all occupations, not merely among industrial workers. Work, it is claimed, is no longer the central life interest of most people in such a society, and the interests of affluence and leisure come to predominate. David Riesman has been foremost among those who sense a perceptible shift from the older religiously sanctified value on work as a calling, to leisure pursuits as the sphere of life that can provide a significant meaning for living.[20] Certainly, mass culture is oriented to the world of leisure, not the world of work, and the most sought-after experience for youth are those of leisure, not of work.

What seems to be recognized here, though yet but dimly, is a new view of life that reacts strongly against both the bureaucratization that dominates work and the highly rationalized approach that, while maximizing production and profits, treats people as commodities or as things, as objects, not as subjects. The great receptiveness of so much of the younger generation to the philosophical message of existentialism occurs just because this philosophy has been generated out of reactions against the rationalization of life. It is this bureaucratized and rationalized nature of work that has resulted in a search for meaning in life in other spheres of social interaction. Even Blauner found that strongly cohesive relationships in ethnic groups or in communities mitigated against the sense of alienation that the work situation induced in machine-tending or assembly-line workers.

ECONOMIC DEVELOPMENT

Throughout the existing non-Western world there is underway the modernization of these hitherto traditional societies, and the central process by which this occurs is economic development. Although there is now much concern with processes of modernization, the impact of Western societies on non-Western

---

[20] See his remarks in various of the essays in his *Individualism Reconsidered* (New York: Free Press, 1956).

ones is centuries old, and none of these traditional societies undertakes the modernizing route untouched; they have all long since absorbed some modern cultural elements. Furthermore, modernization is undertaken in societies that vary greatly in cultural traditions and social organization, from the least modern to great nations that once were colonial societies, such as India. Thus, there is no single process called economic development and no one route to status as a modern society; rather, each society develops its own historical path and makes choices among very real alternatives toward some particular version of modernity.

Most of the contemporary social-scientific literature on economic development stresses two basic issues: the *conditions* necessary for economic development, including the impediments to creating these conditions; and the *consequences* of such development in the change from a traditional to a modern social structure.[21] For modern economists, the rate of economic growth is determined by four variables—natural resources, capital for investment, labor, and entrepreneural talent—which in turn are related to several other variables: savings; inflation; balance of payments; foreign aid; size of population; and rate of population growth. In traditional societies capital for investment is scarce, for the income level of the society is low, and this same low income discourages investment, for it signifies a low buying-power. The nonindustrial mode of production means a low level of productivity, which reflects the low level of capital investment, reflecting, in turn, that there is little inducement to invest. Each variable supports the low level of the other in a circular pattern impeding economic growth.

Economists concentrate upon the interaction among these economic variables, whereas sociological analysis stresses how each of these is determined in part by sociological variables. For example, the value system of traditional societies may place great emphasis upon channeling savings into unproductive forms, such as savings in jewelry, in grain, or in cash that are hoarded or used unproductively in various status-processes, where a generous demonstration of assets is essential for individual or family status. Neil Smelser cites Richard Lambert and Bert Hoselitz[22] as asserting that funds spent on marriage and death ceremonies in India, if spent instead on productive capital assets, would have increased investment by more than 50 percent. It is the long-established extended kinship system that is so frequently regarded by sociologists as the major impediment to economic growth. Kinship systems in

---

[21] There is an extensive literature on economic development, even by sociologists. For a brief introduction to the problems and to some of the more relevant literature, see Wilbert Moore, *Social Change* (Englewood Cliffs, N.J.: Prentice-Hall, 1963), Chapter 5, "Modernization"; also, Neil J. Smelser, *The Sociology of Economic Life* (Englewood Cliffs, N.J.: Prentice-Hall, 1963), Chapter 5, "Sociological Aspects of Economic Development."

[22] Smelser, *The Sociology of Economic Life*, p. 104.

peasant societies often make difficult the recruitment of labor for industrial occupations, for attachment to kin and to land render difficult the commitment to mobility and to the wage-earning industrial role, as well as to the discipline of work and regulation by time schedules required of industrial processes. The prevalence of clocks in modern society bespeaks a sense of time and a regulation of life by precisely measured increments that is culturally strange to people in peasant societies.

Many peasant and tribal societies possess a complex institutional structure built around religion, community, and kinship that reduces the likelihood of there emerging the kind of motivation for innovation and creativity to be found in the role of the entrepreneur. Max Weber's study of the emergence of Western capitalism under conditions in which the Protestant ethic created the motivation for capital accumulation as well as worldly economic success has been a major intellectual perspective for relating the emergence of the economic entrepreneur to religious motivations, or the absence of such a role to the absence of such motivation. Weber also sought to show that in India and China religion failed to provide any such motivation and indeed provided religious values that severely impeded the emergence of capitalism. For many modern students of economic development, this issue of the highly motivated, actively innovating entrepreneur (though now secular), the creative person breaking with traditions and established custom, is the key variable in the transition from traditional to modern society. Everett Hagen has put such emphasis upon the creative entrepreneur as to suggest that his emergence is the single decisive factor,[23] whereas Wilbert Moore notes that

> some degree of "achievement orientation," of ambition for personal betterment and the acquisition of the education and skills to further that ambition, must exist in some groups and spread rather widely, if sustained growth is to be accomplished.[24]

But for such a student of economic development as Moore, achievement orientation is not the only value change necessary. The need for individual mobility and for the process of selecting people by merit conflicts with kinship and other values, so that "extensive value changes are the most fundamental condition for economic transformation."[25] But Moore sees other changes in social institutions as necessary for development: in *property* institutions in order to mobilize land and capital for new productive uses, as well as changes to make *labor* mobile. Other needed changes include creating a commercialized system of *exchange,* institutionalizing *rationality* so that some sectors of the

[23] Everett E. Hagen, *On the Theory of Social Change* (Homewood, Ill.: The Dorsey Press, 1962).
[24] Moore, *Social Change,* p. 96.
[25] Moore, p. 93.

population become committed to science and technology and whatever else promotes planning for economic growth, and developing *political stability.*[26]

The necessity for political stability links the economic and political processes in a common emphasis upon development. A key factor in development is the emergence of political elites committed to modernization and capable of mobilizing their people, often by the value of *nationalism.* The sweeping power of national identification in new societies often serves to legitimize new political authority sufficiently to enable it to challenge and disrupt the traditional order. Political elites are crucial in non-Western societies in making up for the lack of the emergence of something akin to the generating force of the Protestant ethic in the Western experience. What does not emerge indigenously from within the culture they supply by political inducement and control, and there is often a forcing of change in such societies, a deliberately induced pressure to break into the traditional structure of the society.

This requires not merely political stability but also a concentration of political power that frequently motivates new political elites to abandon or ignore democratic processes before democratic structures have been institutionalized. The impulse to modernize rapidly, rather than taking three centuries, as did the Western world, impels these political elites to seek a concentration of political power and to combine nationalist and socialist ideologies into a home-grown ideology supporting forced modernization under authoritarian processes. Most Western social scientists seemed to have accepted the idea that rapid modernization can only be accomplished forcefully and nondemocratically, and then *after* modernization has been achieved, democracy and liberty can emerge. This is the intellectual position supporting authoritarian regimes in developing societies.

Only a few intellectuals and social scientists have scrutinized these assumptions or examined them against the developing record of new societies. One who has done so is the sociologist William McCord, whose *The Springtime of Freedom* is a reasoned argument against authoritarian rule in developing societies.[27] Authoritarian regimes, argues McCord, are not any more likely to enhance economic growth than more democratic ones; they are "no panacea for poverty." McCord suggests several dangers as an inherent part of politically authoritarian systems:[28]

1. A government controlling all resources can expend them as it chooses, wisely or unwisely. Being authoritarian is no guarantee of wisdom, and Indonesia is a prime example of a regime frittering away a society's riches and creating a severe economic crisis.

---

[26] Moore, pp. 94–95.
[27] William McCord, *The Springtime of Freedom* (New York: Oxford, 1965).
[28] McCord, pp. 240–246.

2. The more coercion and pressure a government applies, the less its citizens trust it and the more they conceal profits and falsify reports, thus crippling efforts at rational planning, for such efforts consistently lack accurate information.

3. In the disunity characteristic of developing nations, political coercion invites sabotage of the system by disaffected elements, as when state directives are ignored, and goods are smuggled out to other markets.

4. In the long run, authoritarianism "stifles the spirit of inventiveness and innovation so necessary to economic growth." Creative intellectuals leave, and so may the entrepreneurial talent, as has happened in Ghana. McCord sums up his carefully developed position thusly:

> Solely in terms of economic performance, the record of authoritarianism does not lend itself easily to the contention that total political control over a society represents the soundest approach to economic development.[29]

But whatever political form best provides for economic development, the need for relative political *stability* is recognized by all students of the developing process. Yet the often rapid and radical disruptions of old cultural patterns and of the traditional solidarities of kinship and community create dangerous potentialities for social disturbance and civic unrest. As a consequence, new elites seek, in various ways, integrating mechanisms that will supplant older ones. The ideology of nationalism and common membership in a dominant political party is one major effort, but others are needed. New agencies for welfare and assistance and for providing aid and information emerge, both locally and nationally, as new differentiated structures to specialize in some of the services once performed in the diffuse structures of tribe or kinship. But as Thomas Hodgkin points out, there may be great instability in these new integrative structures: labor unions may become political parties, or religious sects become political clubs.[30] Once integrative structures may become sources of dissension and conflict.

The dangers of modernization are exacerbated by the fact that the process always occurs *unevenly,* altering some traditional structures more than others. When that is so, the faster the rate of change the more severe are the disruptions. In addition, there is not simply conflict between traditional values and structures and new activities and norms and the structures that develop and support them (these latter being the highly differentiated structure of modern societies), but into this conflict come also new *integrative* agencies that have been instituted to take care of the disruptive consequences of the inno-

---

[29] McCord, p. 244.

[30] Thomas Hodgkin, *Nationalism in Colonial Africa* (New York: New York University Press, 1957), pp. 85 ff.

vating structures. "The result is a three-way tug-of-war among the forces of tradition, the forces of differentiation, and the new forces of integration."[31]

Perhaps the most severe and repressive kinds of conflict generated from the disruptions accompanying economic development are those in which economic interest or cleavage coincides with political, religious, or ethnic cleavage. In former colonial nations, natives have often been allocated only the lowest and unskilled economic positions, while other ethnic groups, as the Chinese in much of southeastern Asia, have been allowed to function as merchants, traders, money-lenders, and the like. Thus, when conflict emerges, economic issues assume racial and ethnic aspects that arouse diffuse group hostilities and invoke intense group loyalties.

The Complexity of Economic Development   If economic development is the key process in the modernization of traditional societies, it is evident that this is not a narrowly defined economic process. In order for there to be such development, there must be the radical altering of old structures and the building of new ones. Those traditional groups such as kinship, whose diffuse loyalties and moral obligations impede the development of mobility processes and aspirations must give way to new patterns that encourage individuality, the pursuit of a career, and the development of an achievement orientation. Thus, economic development requires new men—mobility aspirants and ambitious entrepreneurs—and new values, as well as new structures as a context for both new men and new values. What has to happen then is nothing less than the revolutionary transformation of a traditional society into a modern one. The process of change touches every aspect of life.

A society is a relatively integrated and interwoven social structure, and there is some reasonable complementarity and cohesiveness to its institutional ordering of activities and values, some consistency to its complex organization. When an old economic order is deliberately changed, so is much else in the society. When a new economic order is instituted, there must be much else that is also new in the total social order, and an altering and adapting of that which survives from the older patterns of life. In studying the economic development of various traditional societies at this point in history, the sociologist has an unparalleled opportunity to trace the complex interplay among economic and noneconomic factors that provides the integration of a society; he also has the opportunity to explore the processes of change that begin at one point and ramify to the other interrelated subsystems of the society. It is this conception of the economy as a subsystem of the total society that warrants the sociologist developing a sociology of economic life. *Homo oeconomicus* is but another limited version of social man.

[31] Smelser, *The Sociology of Economic Life*, p. 113.

A Final Note on Economy and Society   For man throughout history it has always been necessary to work, and the resources that sustained life have always been scarce. Although industrialization vastly increased man's capacity to exploit and master the natural environment, it did not make goods so abundant as to negate economic theories based upon the assumption of scarcity. But the future holds a promise that such a world of abundance and plenty may be coming into being, and the compulsions of labor and the organization of work may no longer dominate the time, interests, and values of men as they have in the past. Neither may the control of economic resources lead to such dominating power as occurred under the capitalism of the nineteenth century. Increasingly more rationalized and mechanized, demanding greater technical and professional skills, and thus greater education, the new technology may nonetheless be producing a world in which the economic order itself is a less dominant and compelling institution than the type that led Marx and so many others to build theories of society predicated on the dominant, causal place of the economic order. It behooves the student of society to recognize that new and unanticipated models of society may be necessary to explain the type of society that emerges from the revolution instituted in human affairs by modern technology and its source of ideas and principles, physical science.

1. Suffragettes (1910s).
2. Students confronting the National Guard during the 1968 Democratic Convention in Chicago.
3. President Kennedy leaving a joint session of Congress.
4. Nonviolent protest in San Francisco.
5. Rally against the Vietnam war.
6. New York Mayor John V. Lindsay (second from left) enroute to City Hall.

5 6

THE POLITICAL ORDER

16

No more persistent and troubling issue has plagued the study of society than has the concern for the place of power and authority in a social life no longer rendered cohesive and stable by common traditions sanctified by shared values and similar life-experiences. Modern society has struggled for three centuries to find new secular modes of cohesion and stability comparable to the unifying function of religion in the Middle Ages.

The study of political power and political institutions is usually regarded as the province of *political science,* particularly since the political processes, like the economic ones, have been regarded as sufficiently differentiated from the rest of the social structure to warrant separate study. Unlike the sociology of economics, however, *political sociology* has a more viable and comprehensive tradition that goes back to the founders of the discipline. Nonetheless, the very existence of political science has led sociologists to neglect certain aspects of the political process, such as the state and the law and other formal mechanisms of political control.

The origins of political sociology lie in the once controversial intellectual distinction between *state* and *society.* Ancient and medieval thought concerned itself with the civic order and the political community to which all men belonged. There was no conception of the state as separate from the rest of society. This idea emerged only during the sixteenth and seventeenth centuries with the breakdown of the cohesive feudal order. *General* sociology originated in this conception of society as an institutionalized process independent of the state, and *political* sociology emerged around the concern for the relation between the state as the political institution and the other social institutions. Such a sociological perspective viewed the state as but one institution in society, and society was seen as the more encompassing social process. Yet this was but one side in an historic intellectual controversy, in which many noted thinkers from Bodin to Hegel tried to formulate a conception of the sovereignty of the state and its necessary domination of other social institutions.

Most early sociologists were on the side of society in this controversy. But sociology has simply outgrown the issue by viewing it as a matter of posing the issue incorrectly. State and society are not two independent entities, and it is not a matter of which is to be dominant. Yet the underlying concerns which generated that issue for the intellectuals of a bygone era remain: the problem of the cohesion and consensus that makes legitimate authority possible and the problem of the capacity of a society to contain and control the conflict and cleavage that can potentially turn any society into warring camps.

THE PROBLEM OF POLITICAL ORDER

To sustain a workable, viable society, there must be social order; indeed, as we observed early in this book, society *is* social order. The consistent ordering of social relations is sustained in traditional societies by the largely undifferentiated structure that socializes each person to the same set of values and norms and involves him in the same network of kinship obligations and structural dependencies. Tribal law, as Durkheim noted, is repressive, but in large part the functioning social order of such societies is so effectively sustained by shared values and a coherent way of life that little if any differentiated political structure emerges. But in a modern secular order, a political differentiation is but one more aspect of a general social differentiation of structures and institutions. The political process becomes an identifiable segment, separate from the economy, from education and religion, and from family. It involves power and authority and the complex structures organized for decision making. Power, authority, and decision making, in fact, are what the political order is all about. It is also, however, about the acceptance of political structures as legitimate by the members of the society, and, in addition, about some conception of who has the right to exercise power and make decisions.

The political order, then, reveals to sociological observation a pattern of social organization, just as does any other aspect of social life. One major issue for the political sociologist, therefore, is to understand how social power is organized into political structures that relate significantly to other structures and institutions of the society. The state itself, and other smaller units of government, constitute one major pattern of political organization; what the sociologist is concerned with here are not the formal characteristics of government—that has been the scholarly preoccupation of political scientists—but the relations of the state, as the central focus of political power, to the organization of social life that prevails in that society.

Any viable political structure is supported by a political culture, a body of values, norms, and myths that serves to legitimize the structure and provide normative support for those who act to carry out decisions made within it. Thus, *legitimacy* is a crucial issue in understanding political structure. But whatever the source of its legitimacy, a political order may be authoritarian, and undoubtedly most historical examples known to us have been. They can also be totalitarian, as we have learned from twentieth century experience. Indeed, the inability of democratic governments to sustain themselves in Latin America and Africa has made it evident that a democratic order exists in a state of tension, and there are apparently conditions under which it cannot successfully be sustained. One provocative direction for political sociology, then, has been to understand *the social conditions under which a democratic order can prevail.*

Those political sociologists concerned with the conditions for democratic order have also been the ones largely concerned with *the relations of social class to political order.* The work of Karl Marx has created a Western tradition in which the economic and the political are viewed as highly integrated, so that dominant social classes control, not only the productive processes of the society, but the political organs as well. A revolutionary change, then, must originate with those occupying subordinate roles in the economic structure, who organize politically and, through the seizure of political power, wrest economic control from ruling classes. Marx's challenging conception of how societies are organized has thus raised provocative problems about the relation of class structure to political order, and generations of political sociologists have wrestled with the issue ever since.

Closely related to this issue is the question of *elites in society and their relation to power and the political process.* The ancient notion that a society is governed by elites has retained intellectual currency down to the present generation, and there is a significant sociological tradition from Gaetano Mosca to C. Wright Mills that views power as monopolized by elites, so that society is always divided between the few who rule and the many who are ruled.

Although all political structures are supported by some conception of their legitimacy, there are always some who do not accept the legitimacy of prevailing political institutions and thus do not feel constrained to pursue political goals within the rules of political action accepted by others. Such a disjuncture in values and perspectives then produces, particularly at crucial times of strain and tension, an *extremism of either left or right,* or both, which threatens established political order and brings conflict and cleavage into the open and makes it part of the political struggle.

These several issues which have been the central concern of political sociology—the organization of power into political structures, the conditions for a democratic order, social class and politics, elites and power, and political extremism—are by no means disparate issues, but rather are all different facets of the problem of political order: the capacity of a society to contain and control the conflict and cleavage that is always potentially disruptive and to provide instead legitimate and institutionalized means for carrying out political decision making and exercising authority.

SOCIAL POWER AND POLITICAL STRUCTURE

The central concept of political sociology is *power.* Yet it has been difficult to make power an object of dispassionate study, so moral and ideological are the connotations long fixed to the term. A moral suspicion of power as inherently "bad" has dominated Western thought since Machiavelli, in the fifteenth century, advised the prince on how to rule effectively; the historic liberal theories have treated power as a threat to freedom and individual liberty. Indeed, in the context of earlier liberal thought, almost any form of social organization spelled power and thus a coercive denial of men's liberties.

Whatever its other meanings, this intellectual orientation has made it difficult to treat dispassionately the problem of power in society and the function of the political institutions.

The Concept of Power   What is power? A search of the literature reveals that social scientists have used the term in diverse ways. Many have treated power as a scarce object, like any material good, so that there is a total sum of power, and more power for one group means less power for another. This view, often an assumption rather than an explicit definition, is frequently associated with a definition of power as control over the behavior of others. The difficulty with this simple enough definition is that it includes such a wide array of social phenomena—the control of a child by his parent, or of an employee's work by his employer—that it encompasses much that is not political, except by stretching the definition of politics. This definition is also undifferentiated from what has long been regarded in sociology as *social control*.

A much older approach to the concept of power is that of a *power elite*, a small group that controls the positions of authority and monopolizes the processes of decision making. What is now important about this approach, however, is that it also implies a conception of power as *decision making*. Although it assumes that decisions are monopolized by an elite, it does recognize there is a decision-making process. One has only to separate the concept of elite from the concept of decision making to have a more general conception of power that reflects the perspective of most social scientists today. When power is defined as decision making, it then is defined as a social process, not as an object or "thing" divided among power-holders. Thus, to speak of someone "having power" is an elliptical way of saying that he is a participant in a decision-making process. To say that some people are "powerful" is also an elliptical way to say that they may effectively control decision making or at least have a very strong influence on what decisions are made.

By the making of decisions is meant the established process for reaching *consensus* among those who participate in decisions. Every society thus develops a set of political institutions wherein normatively defined processes regulate and control the disagreements, conflicts and contested interests that eventually produce a decision. In modern societies elaborate and complex organizations, such as legislatures and political parties, are developed to give structure to the political process.

Power, thus, is never to be conceptualized apart from *authority*, which is the *right* to make a decision. When a president vetoes a bill, he exercises the authority of his office, as does the legislature when it votes on a bill. The city councilman and the mayor, the governor and the senator, all these are political roles in which is vested authority. Thus, authority means *legitimacy*, the normative right to make a decision that is based upon an acceptance of the claims of the decision-makers that their decisions are morally binding on all members of the social organization. Max Weber has indicated that in stable social orders legitimacy of authority may be *traditional*, as in the authority of a tribal chief, or it may be *legal-rational*, derived from laws, charters, and constitutions, and thus accepted as legally binding.[1]

Yet no theory of social power stipulates that only those with authority are *exercisers* of power. The formal designation of authority simply provides focus to a complex process of reaching decisions that involves other actors in the process. A crucial element, then, is the idea of *access*, the ability to reach and influence those who have authority. Those who have access are *influentials*, and some influentials, such as party bosses, lobbyists, and businessmen are often regarded as having more to say about decisions than those who possess authority. There are kinds and degrees of influence. First, there are those who actively seek to affect the outcome of a decision. There are others who participate indirectly because their possible reaction is taken into account in advance; to the extent that a predictable public disapproval will negate a possible decision, such a public has access to decision making.

A popular and common version of power denigrates the significance of authority and claims that "real" power rests in the hands of dominant influentials, an elite possibly not even known to the larger public. Officials are then often regarded as mere puppets who respond to the orders of party bosses, the requests or advice of lobbyists, or the demands of economic influentials. Even sociologists studying community power have usually looked for influentials who make up a power structure; thus, they tend to leave unstudied the formal system of authority in the community.

However weak the system of authority may be and however dominant a structure of influence, the exercise of power still cannot dispense with legitimate authority. For if it does, then decision making by powerful people can only be regarded as a system of coercion. All authoritarian systems of the past claimed legitimacy, whether by divine right of king, or whatever. Even modern totalitarian systems develop and propagate a rationalizing ideology to justify the monopoly of power by the party. Legitimacy must be established, else the exercise of power stands before all men as mere force and coercion. There are no ruling elites that have not justified to themselves and the world their seizure of power. Terror and coercion may well be effective instruments of power in nondemocratic orders, but they are not in themselves sufficient basis for a stable political order.

Decisions, then, must always seem to be the act of those who hold the sym-

[1] See Max Weber, *The Theory of Social and Economic Organization*, trans. by A. M. Henderson and Talcott Parsons (New York: Oxford, 1947), p. 328.

bols of authority. Other actors with access to them interact in situations of conflict or negotiation to produce a decision. These others are influentials, and they exert *influence* and *pressure*. The distinction between these two terms is not always easy to make in the concrete situation, but in the abstract we can define influence as the ability to affect a decision by virtue of a superior claim to consideration of or deference to the expressed attitudes or interests of a member (or group) recognized as legitimate by decision-makers. City councils, for example, have usually regarded as legitimate the attitudes and interests of businessmen, taxpayers, and property owners, and there may be considerable overlap among these categories. Pressure, in turn, is the ability to affect a decision by the threat of consequences injurious to the person or social position of the decision-makers. Thus, a group can exert pressure by threatening to withhold political support or to give it to the opposition. Our recognition that power is a complex social process of decision making then suggests such a definition as this: power is the distribution of influence, pressure, and authority within a social system for the making, legitimizing, and executing of decisions.

Most sociological research on power has been concerned only with the *making* of decisions, but their *legitimation* and *execution* are equally significant aspects of the exercise of power. Least attention has been given to the problem of the execution of a decision. Yet, a decision is not a decision until it has been carried out. Perhaps only in the literature on bureaucracies has there been recognition of the problems involved in the execution of decisions. In the middle level of bureaucracies, officials can significantly modify or even subvert a decision taken at higher echelons, so that the decisive outcome is simply not what was intended when the decision was made. By the same token, an anticipation of the difficulties involved and the resistance likely to be aroused by unpopular decisions are often factors taken into consideration in the making of decisions. Note that the execution of decision is a responsibility of authority; here again, the neglect of the study of authority by sociologists has provided an incomplete analysis, one that focuses largely on the question of who are the decision-makers and answers this by identifying the influentials.

When power is viewed as decision making, then, it can be viewed as a complex process essential within a society and always legitimized by the existence of authority. Governments and parties exist to provide an organized and legitimate structure for reaching consensus within the society on issues about which decision need be made. But more than this political structure may be required to ensure that a society possesses the consensus necessary for political efficacy. Given the proliferation of social groupings in modern society, how is that possible? No definitive answer can yet be given to such a fundamental question, for in effect it asks about the basis of social order in a highly differentiated society, and it asks about the presence of values and perspectives that cut across such differentiating processes to provide sources of consensus in the political order.

A tentative answer at this time must point to the fact that differentiation also implies interdependence:

> It is the social and economic interdependence of the subgroups within society which, through the agencies of communication and cultural transmission, generates and sustains the consensus at the foundations of political order.[2]

Undoubtedly the sources of common information and perspectives in the society are crucial here, and these are the public schools and the mass media. However, little research has been done by sociologists on either of these agencies as sources of political education and information. Greer and Orleans suggest that what few studies exist indicate a simple vocabulary that "flattens, blurs, and personalizes public issues, resembling strongly the results of experimental rumor diffusion."[3] Some other social scientists have examined mass culture as a purveyor of evocative symbols that organizes a consensus linking various subgroups of society, but as yet little has been done to explore the idea of a common and widely shared *political culture* that unifies the diverse segments of a complex mass society.

The State and the Party   Although the analysis of the state as a formal structure of authority and a process of public administration is the task of the political scientist, the political sociologist cannot be indifferent to the conceptual nature of the state. In modern society the state is an inclusive group from which, in fact, there is no escape, and to which all other social groups are subordinate. As Robert Nisbet points out, the dominant position of the state is related to the decline of once inclusive systems, such as kin, guild, locality group, and church.[4]

Sociologists most frequently use Max Weber's definition of the state: a political organization that claims binding authority and a legitimate monopoly of force within a territory.[5] Such a definition requires that one recognize, as did Weber, the struggle among politically oriented contending groups within the state. Of these, one of the most significant is the *political party*, that rational association "oriented toward the acquisition of social 'power,' that is

---

[2] Scott Greer and Peter Orleans, "Political Sociology," in Robert E. L. Faris, ed., *Handbook of Modern Sociology* (Chicago: Rand McNally, 1964), p. 811.

[3] Greer and Orleans, p. 811.

[4] Robert Nisbet, *The Quest for Community* (New York: Oxford, 1953).

[5] Hans Gerth and C. Wright Mills, eds., *From Max Weber: Essays in Sociology* (New York: Oxford, 1946), p. 78.

to say, toward influencing a communal action no matter what its content may be."[6] As Weber said, parties "live in a house of 'power,' " and "are always structures struggling for domination."[7] Political parties are social organizations for mobilizing citizens for political action; perhaps their main contention is over the selection of those who will occupy positions of authority, thus giving to some groups superior access to the decision-making process.

The Functions of Political Structure   The long moral suspicion of power in Western culture, and the association with it of ideas about conflict and coercion, has obscured the recognition of the fact that authority, as *legitimate* power, is a process as essential to society as the economic process for meeting sustenance needs. Power has to be *institutionalized*, and political institutions are normatively sanctioned processes for carrying out three essential functions:

1. To maintain social order within the society, by containing conflict and cleavage within manageable bounds so as to maintain the basic values that underlie the fundamental structures of the society;

2. To provide adequate means for adopting new policies and modes of action that permit the society to undertake orderly processes of structural change; such processes then render rational and controllable society's adjustment to a changing technical, economic, cultural and even physical environment;

3. To protect the society by war and diplomacy from *external* threats in its larger social environment.

The first and second functions hopefully make a point that is often missed when sociologists relate the political process to social order. The internal conflict and threat of social cleavage that can rend a society must be managed; but it is essential to recognize that this can only be done when the political process is cognizant of the *substance* of the dispute among conflicting groups. Social order is not effectively maintained by coercively denying the expression of differences in interests and values. Instead, an effective social order is maintained when a social consensus is achieved among contending groups, by finding the grounds for acceptable social change. Social order is not to be confused with the maintenance of a status quo.

The more effective the mechanisms for bargaining over conflicting interests and the easier the access to the locus of decision making for all groups, the more effective is the political process for maintaining social order; also, the more stable is that order. A political structure that cannot successfully resolve difficult problems will lose the support of those for whom the resolution of

---

[6] Gerth and Mills, p. 194.
[7] Gerth and Mills, pp. 194–195.

the issue is vital; they will withdraw their acceptance of it as legitimate, and may then engage in action that lies outside the normatively supported processes for engaging in conflict. In American race relations the onset of a high degree of militancy by civil rights groups follows from much frustration in their efforts to win equal status for the Negro by engaging in the usually accepted modes of political action and representation.

THE CONDITIONS FOR DEMOCRATIC ORDER

One of the most bitter experiences of the twentieth century has been to learn that the world is not and perhaps cannot ever be "safe for democracy." Furthermore, democracy is not merely endangered by external threats from totalitarian sources; the enemy resides within the gates, as well. The mere profession of democratic values or lip service to its symbols is no guarantee of a fundamental commitment. Political sociologists, and other social scientists as well, have long been concerned with determining the social conditions that make a democratic social order possible.

The Threat of Total Power   One of the great classics of political sociology is *Democracy in America* by Alexis de Tocqueville, a book that is remarkably contemporary in its significance today, yet was written more than a century ago.[8] De Tocqueville, a Frenchman of aristocratic origin, visited the United States in the 1830s, intent on observing the democratic process as it functioned in this new nation. He had accepted the inevitability of the French Revolution while yet sharing a conservative anxiety about the potentiality for amassing total power in the governments of new, industrial nations.

As a political sociologist, de Tocqueville recognized the central trends of modern society: industrialization, bureaucratization, and nationalism. He also recognized that these processes were bringing the lower classes into politics, and thus politics was no longer the prerogative of aristocratic elites. He did not expect to turn back the clock, nor did he share in the liberal illusion that a society could be created which possessed mechanisms that rendered unnecessary the organization of social groups with conflicting interests.

Half a century or so later, when industrialization had wrought its remarkable changes in society, Emile Durkheim[9] also faced the issue, seeing the possi-

---

[8] Alexis de Tocqueville, *Democracy in America,* Vols. I and II (New York: Vintage Books, 1954).
[9] See Emile Durkheim, *The Division of Labor in Society,* trans. by George Simpson (New York: Free Press, 1947); also, *Professional Ethics and Civic Morals,* trans. by Cornelia Brookfield (New York: Free Press, 1960).

bility of totalitarianism in the expanding domination of the nation-state. The trends he discerned then have continued, made necessary by the powerful demand for national coordination and by the fact that the liberal value prescribing a sharp distinction among political, economic, and other segments of the society is less and less a description of reality. Economy and polity are now integrated as a political economy, and there is an increasing concentration of decision making at the national level. Significant decisions that affect the life-chances of all citizens are increasingly political and increasingly national, with private and local structures declining in their capacity to render or even participate in these decisions.

The solution that de Tocqueville offered to the dangers of concentrated power was the conception of the *pluralist society*—one in which there are several sources of power other than the state, and in which there is a potentiality for engaging in conflict and struggling for goals against other groups. Thus, conflict becomes *positive* in its functions and is an insurance against the domination of society by a single center of power.

De Tocqueville thought that in America he saw in the *local, self-governing community* and the *voluntary association* the significant sources for a pluralism of power. These were to create active sources of political engagement, experience, and training for citizens, and so to be an independent source of politically capable leadership. They were also to generate new centers of power that could contest both among each other and with a limited state for a basis for a democratic consensus.

What de Tocqueville was basically concerned with was the existence of centers of power intermediate between the individual citizen and the nation-state. As an unorganized mass, aggregates of individual citizens could not counter the centralized power of the state. Intermediate political organization that had free access to masses of citizens and opportunity to organize them to engage in political contest, whether in competition for office or in conflict over policy, was a guarantee of a democratic society. This conception of the pluralist society has become by now one of the major intellectual perspectives on modern society and at the same time the definition of one of political sociology's most significant problems. De Tocqueville clearly saw value in conflict, yet recognized that it had to be kept within bonds, and, indeed, had to culminate in consensus. Thus, he did not view conflict and consensus as polarized, but as complementary processes that *in balance* made possible a democratic social order.

However, one of the hopes that de Tocqueville saw in the American system, local self-government, has been less and less significant as a source of independent social power. It has clearly declined as an autonomous unit in society. Furthermore, local government is often mostly responsive to local dominant majorities and the local elites based upon them which often choose *not* to act upon major issues, such as race, housing for the poor, and the like. In the metropolitan areas of the United States, the shared powers of a pluralistic society produce a proliferation of local governments that cannot act effectively upon metropolitan problems and yet prevent the development of a metropolitan polity responsible for the whole urban area as an integrated entity.

The voluntary association, however, has remained a significant source of power; the right of association guarantees that any kind of social value or shared interest allows the coming together of interested persons and permits them to mobilize others for bringing pressure on places of authority. Furthermore, this makes *political* many private organizations that are not ordinarily so defined: chambers of commerce; labor unions; manufacturers' associations; civic groups; taxpayers' associations; veterans' associations; and almost any other organized interest in the society. These groups are then *parapolitical.*

Like de Tocqueville, Durkheim looked for the solution to the threat of totalitarianism in the development of a political process that would give to the parapolitical the ability to be intermediary and thus protect the individual from the state; whereas the state in turn would uphold those civil liberties that would protect the individual from oppressive local government, that "tyranny of democracy" that de Tocqueville warned about. Thus, Durkheim in effect took a *federalist* position, much like that developed by James Madison, the father of the American constitution, one that allocates real authority and capacity for action to the several states, that separates the economy and the polity, and that denies the full concentration of power in any one branch of the federal government, as well as allowing a major role for a plethora of political forces.

Yet, as William Kornhauser notes, the mere fact of a multiplicity of associations in a society does not necessarily provide the conditions of pluralism that assure a democratic order.[10] The population of a society could be organized into a set of associations that manifested the cleavages of the society but provided no sources of consensus. Kornhauser feels that what is required for a pluralist society is a *multiplicity of affiliations,* wherein no one group is *inclusive* of its members' lives. Thus, trade unions have members of various ethnic groups and religious groups, churches cut across class lines, and political parties draw from a heterogeneous range within the population. Such extensive crosscutting affiliations prevent one line of social cleavage, such as class, from becoming dominant. But if, on the one hand, the members of the working class are organized into labor unions, vote heavily Democratic, belong predominantly to the same ethnic and civic groups, and are mostly Catholic, and, on the other hand, the middle class votes Republican belongs to completely

---

[10] William Kornhauser, *The Politics of Mass Society* (New York: Free Press, 1959), pp. 80–81.

different ethnic and civic organizations, and is mostly Protestant, the cleavage of class so coincides with other affiliations that conflict is exacerbated, and consensus is difficult to achieve. Pluralism assumes that voluntary associations develop memberships that cut across group identities, thus weakening their hold on the individual and providing bridges across class cleavages.

But the theorists of pluralism also make an assumption about voluntary associations as intermediate organizations—that they are reasonably equal to one another in the capacity to influence decisions—that is unlikely to be so. The pluralistic conception of society has often ignored the vast differences in size, in material resources, in public prestige, in access to loci of decision making, and in ideological advantage that accrue to some. Pluralism is then no guarantee against a preponderant domination by corporate power structures over economic decisions that affect the lives of all members of the society.

Voting The process of democratic selection of decision-makers by voting is one of the key elements of a democratic order. Voting becomes the resolution of conflict that is manifested in contesting political parties; the electoral process, including the campaign that precedes voting, is a basic social mechanism for giving expression to existing conflict and for providing a source of social consensus. Yet, as Seymour Martin Lipset points out, the study of voting, one of the major research activities of political sociologists, has rarely been designed to investigate the problem of conflict and consensus.[11] Instead, most studies of voting have been studies of individual voting behavior, a social-psychological investigation of how the individual makes up his mind about voting. Such studies have explored the context of family and peer groups within which the individual engages in an interpersonal exchange about politics, leading to a gradual crystallization of voting preferences generally consistent with these. Many of these studies have been of natural small groups, and they have been studies of the *voter* rather than of voting as a social process. They have been concerned with how group affiliation and interpersonal interaction within limited contexts serve to affect individual decisions.

Lipset also points out that these studies have emphasized cleavage along class, ethnic, and religious lines, and how the family and peer group socialize the person to commitments that reinforce that cleavage. Where persons are caught on cross-cleavage memberships, as workers who are Republicans, Protestants who are Democrats, Catholics who are Republicans, the cross-pressures they are subject to when class, religion, and ethnicity pull them in different directions more often than not results in their not voting; in effect,

[11] Seymour Martin Lipset, "Political Sociology," in Robert K. Merton, Leonard Broom, and Leonard S. Cottrell, Jr., *Sociology Today* (New York: Basic Books, 1959), p. 92.

they opt not to choose and thus not to alienate themselves from their most intimate groups.[12]

Apathy   The character of American elections, in which two parties compete for votes within the same groups, and in which only in national elections does even 60 percent of the electorate exercise its franchise, has led to a familiar criticism of the American democratic order: that *apathy* produces a low and possibly unrepresentative vote. There is perhaps no more frequently expressed value in American society than that everyone should vote; apathy is unequivocally regarded as a danger to democratic order. That only a national presidential election can bring out over half the registered voters is pointed to time and again as evidence of weakness in the American political process.

But there is no empirical evidence to support the idea that democracy is stronger if electoral participation is complete; instead, there is at least some evidence to suggest the contrary.[13] Situations in which the rate of voting sharply increases are situations of intense conflict, one in which there is a *decline* in consensus and a potential breakdown in the democratic process. A decrease in apathy and an intense increase in voting, for example, accompanied the rise of Naziism in Germany in the 1930s. The failure of an election to attract the vast majority of voters may be evidence that there is no *intense* dissatisfaction with the state of things.

American studies of voting permit us to distinguish between voters, those who fairly regularly cast their votes, and nonvoters, those who rarely do. It is these nonvoters who must be lured to the polls if a presumed apathy is to be overcome, and voting is to reflect almost complete participation. But these empirical studies show that nonvoters are more likely than voters to be authoritarian in their outlook, to be indifferent to if not opposed to democratic values, to prefer "strong" (meaning authoritarian) leadership, and to oppose civil liberties for radicals and political dissidents. Nonvoters, then, are more likely to be politically alienated, not only from the political process but from the democratic values that underlie it; inducing them to vote may represent no gain in the conditions for a democratic order. Studies of local elections, where voting normally runs quite low, have revealed that any high turnout is the result of the participation by those who are least committed to the local community. Thus, it is also likely to be a negative vote, and evidence for this seems to come from analysis of referenda, such as on school bonds and

---

[12] This persistent observation was reported in the earliest of the voting studies. Compare Paul H. Lazarsfeld, Bernard Berelson, and Hazel Gaudet, *The People's Choice* (New York: Columbia University Press, 1948).

[13] See Lazarsfeld, Berelson, and Gaudet, p. 95, for a reference to the literature that tests the relevance of apathy for the political process.

fluoridation, where a higher vote increases the negative vote and defeats the measure.[14]

Apathy, then, is a concept that does not do justice to the problem of political participation. Full participation and high voter turnout is likely to mean that at stake is an issue that strains the existing consensus in the community and induces high levels of protest and negative voting. But, at the same time, such occasional elections serve as a rough measure of the extent of the uncommitted and alienated, who normally find no reason for electoral participation. Clearly, a democratic order cannot survive too large a segment of the community who are so alienated. Although their nonvoting may conveniently contribute to the stability of the democratic process, their very presence is indicative of sources of malintegration and dissensus that the democratic process may be failing to resolve. As tensions grow and the numbers of alienated voters increase, there may occur a serious conflict that may extend beyond an election and require more than an election to create a new basis for social order.

Bureaucracy and the Political Order Few studies in political sociology have sought to determine the significance of bureaucratization for the democratic order, even though sociologists generally assume, with Weber, that increasing bureaucratization is a dominant feature of modern society. Nonetheless contemporary students of bureaucracy have rarely applied the analysis of bureaucracy to the political order. But Weber was keenly aware of the significance of bureaucracy for the political process, and specifically for the democratic order. Unlike Marx, he did not view the conflict between capitalism and socialism as the central problem of modern politics. Socialism, Weber thought, would only extend the bureaucratization encouraged by capitalism, and thus further, not alter, the rationalization of society that he viewed as being the basic process in the modern world. Yet Weber was able to suggest an integrative function to bureaucracy when it diffuses to the entire society the bureaucratic norms that call for equal treatment before the law and also encourage the wider acceptance of achievement criteria for selection and promotion—merit, in short, rather than inherited position and advantage.

One can argue, as Seymour M. Lipset does, that bureaucracy provides a context of political neutrality that reduces political conflict, for the bureaucrat is an impartial expert, not a partisan.[15] Thus, impartial experts in government can perform two integrative functions for democratic society. First, they can provide a stable and routine administration of established political functions, rendering less disruptive the change of power from one party to another. Secondly, they can reduce conflict to administrative decisions and expert judg-

[14] For a brief review of such studies, see Greer and Orleans, "Political Sociology," pp. 819–820.
[15] Lipset, "Political Sociology," p. 102.

ments, thus making sources of conflict more manageable and less disturbing within the social order.

Perhaps the outstanding American example of this is the construction of a complex social mechanism of federal mediation for resolving labor-management conflicts and insisting upon a resolution that embodies a workable consensus in a binding contract. This has created a body of experts—both within and without government—that can be called upon to provide a technical skill for resolving a dispute and finding the grounds for consensus. By this process the issues that are always a source of conflict are removed from the political arena and cease to be the basis for conflicting ideological positions taken by political parties. A possibly disruptive issue within the political process is then minimized.

But, as Lipset also notes, this stabilizing effect of bureaucracy can also be viewed as conservative in its significance for the political process, and so it will be by those interested in social change. In his *Agrarian Socialism,* Lipset described how a socialist party in Canada, after having won office, was then thwarted in carrying out its program by the resistance of the permanent bureaucracy of civil servants.[16] Weber recognized that control over administrative implementation of decision making was decisive for political power, and he was pessimistic about the chances of democratic politicians to keep such control from the permanent bureaucrats. Although bureaucracy may be stabilizing and a mechanism for reducing conflict, this, in Weber's view, did not make it supportive of democracy. His ultimate view about the impact of bureaucracy upon democracy was pessimistic, and his conception of the major political issue of our time was the prevention of a bureaucratic domination of all of social life.

CLASS, STATUS, AND POLITICS

The relation of the stratification order to the political order has been a central concern of political sociology, as it was paramount in the theories of many earlier social thinkers. Stratification can lead to the social cohesion and class solidarity of those who share common interests, but this same class solidarity then induces conflict with other classes. Stratification, in short, is a significant source of political conflict and a basis for the struggle for power.

Of all those sociological thinkers who have viewed class as productive of social conflict, the major theorist has undoubtedly been Karl Marx. His analysis

[16] Seymour Martin Lipset, *Agrarian Socialism* (Berkeley, Calif.: University of California Press, 1950).

of social class, as we saw before, emphasized not only the social differentiation into economic strata that was a consequence of the division of labor but also the emergence of a consciousness of class interests that turned these economic strata into social classes. When men realized their common economic interests, class emerged as a *political* phenomenon, constituting the basis for a political solidarity that made class conflict possible. For Marx class was inherently and necessarily a *dividing* process, a source of cleavage and conflict. This was so, not only because class represented the most basic interests of men, but also because the class structure was, in Marx's view, fundamentally a process for the exploitation of man by man. Men had to struggle to escape the oppressive power of other men who lived off their labor.

From this same perspective Marx viewed the state, not as a political structure for maintaining social order, but as the "executive committee" of the ruling class. The state was simply the organized political power by which the dominant class could control the other classes in society and legally protect its own interests. The processes of *legitimation,* for Marx, were clearly the fraudulent *myths* that concealed class interests; the emergence of class consciousness on the part of oppressed classes always meant a recognition that the ruling myths were lies and thus an ability to see clearly the naked class interests these myths were meant to conceal.

Marx had no interest in democratic order or in the problem of maintaining consensus as a basis for social order. For him all known human societies were characterized by constant conflict, and this conflict was the source of social change that brought new social structures into being. He did not, like de Tocqueville, see conflict as balanced by consensus; rather, conflict always led eventually to an open struggle that revolutionized the class order. This process would not cease until a communist society produced a social order that did away with classes because it did away with the division of labor from which they emanated. By the same token the elimination of social classes not only would end the class struggle, it would also make possible the "withering away" of the state, since there would be no need of a political organization to protect the interest of a ruling class.

It was natural, then, that Marx's analysis focused only upon the sources of conflict and cleavage, not on consensus. He was concerned with the solidarity of the classes and their capacity for cohesive organization that made possible effective struggle against other classes. His pervasive influence on political analysis has been extensive, affecting the ideas of many who were not Marxians; in particular, it has tended to give emphasis to the idea of class as inherently a source of conflict and also to the idea that, logically, political parties should represent the interests of specific social classes. Even political sociology has developed around a greater interest in the sources of cleavage than in the possibilities of consensus.

Social Class and Political Party   For a long time, American political parties somewhat puzzled European intellectuals, whose conception of the party was largely shaped by the Marxian perspective. Unlike the European ones American parties were not working-class parties and middle-class parties, nor did they espouse a distinctive class ideology or champion any revolutionary change. Many American intellectuals, particularly those liberal in their politics, shared the European viewpoint and wished for a logical division of American political parties between, most likely, a Democratic Party that represented workers, poor farmers, and Negroes and other minorities (without the conservative Southerners), and a Republican Party that represented business, wealth, and established interests. Then, one party would be logically radical, or at least liberal, and pursue changes that benefited the workers and minorities, and the other party would be naturally conservative and defend the interests of business, wealth, and property and oppose most changes.

But American parties have never been that logical; even though *most* workers and *most* Negroes are Democrats, and *most* businessmen are Republicans, *not all* are. Both parties seek votes in the other groups in order to achieve a majority. The large group that has no irrevocable commitment to either party forces each to seek its support and moderate their ideological claims. The same thing happens in Britain, where the Labor Party must seek middle-class support to win a majority; this struggle for a middle group moderates the parties and reduces the differences between them.

When political parties draw their support exclusively from one social class, they then become class parties, located on one side of the class cleavage of the society; their ensuing political activity accentuates the cleavage and pulls the political conflict to extremes. But when both parties compete for the votes of the same groups, though winning them unevenly, their differences are moderated and a political consensus is possible. Both (or several) parties can more easily abide by the election result, too, for defeat in an election does not imply the complete loss of the program of a social class.

Historically, American political parties have always been based upon a multiplicity of social groups and classes and have reached across the class and group cleavages of American society for support. The strict adherence of European parties to class and ideology, in turn, has been considerably muted in the postwar years, so that the British Labor Party, for example, earnestly woos the middle-class voter. To say that the two-party system of the United States is unique in developing a politics that bridges social class would be untrue, for it would be untrue to deny that class does constitute a major grouping for political interest. If all workers do not vote Democratic, most do, and that fact is significant in determining the character of both the Republican and Democratic parties.

Robert Alford has undertaken to compare the relations of class to politics in what he called the Anglo-American democracies: the United States, Great Britain, Canada, and Australia.[17] He found that voting by social class was highest in Britain, next in Australia, then lower in the United States, and least in Canada. In Britain, a fundamental class cleavage still forms the basis for the Labor and Conservative parties, even though somewhat muted now; this is also somewhat modified by the regional cultures of Scotland and Wales, and also by a religious differentiation. In Australia, not as class-divided politically as Britain, the Roman Catholics make up a deviant group, not voting as do others in the same class position. Although Australia is a large country, regionalism is not a significant factor in its politics. The United States is marked, by comparison, by a great diversity of support for the two major parties. The Southerner's historic association with the Democratic Party, and the tendency of Catholics also to be Democrats, seemed to Alford to be the major deviancy from the national voting pattern. Thus, both regionalism and religion were modifying factors. Canada, in turn, has even less of a class-based politics than does the United States. The support for national parties in that country is organized almost entirely around regional and religious cleavages, which have superseded the cleavages of class. In Canada, in short, the fundamental political division is between an Anglo-Protestant majority and a French-Catholic minority.

Participation and Interest   All politicians know that there are differences among the social classes in both interest in and participation in politics. It is a truism of American politics that a heavy vote favors the Democrats, since it is the workers and poor who vote less consistently. In general, persons of higher social rank participate more in politics; those of higher income and better education are not only more politically involved and vote more frequently, they are also better informed. But there is more to it than that. The selection of candidates and political leadership in general also manifests the fact of status. In the United States, the Democratic Party, even with a large working-class base, tends to select candidates from the middle class. Even in labor unions, leadership comes more from the ranks of the more skilled, and within most civic organizations the leaders are generally of higher social status than the average member.

This relationship of status to participation seems to hold also outside the United States, though not to the same extent. Where political parties are more clearly class-based, the way is open for those of lower status to achieve positions of leadership. Even in the United States, where a political party or labor

[17] Robert Alford, *Party and Society* (Chicago: Rand McNally, 1963).

union or civic protest organization needs to mobilize the lower social ranks and minorities, there is increased opportunity for people from these ranks to become spokesmen and representatives.

The absence of people of low social rank in positions of leadership in the United States has become a controversial issue in the 1960s in both race and poverty. Many critics of present programs have asserted that neither the poor nor the ghetto-residing Negroes are represented by their own kind, and that those who presume to speak for them do not do so legitimately. The effort of Congress to ensure representation by the poor in the War on Poverty produced strenuous objections by urban mayors, for their political control of the program was threatened, and the local power structure was endangered. But what is perhaps more relevant is that the increasing metropolitanization of the urban settlement is creating large legislative districts of poor and of ethnic and racial minorities, ensuring their representation in city, state, and federal politics by persons of their own selection if not from their own ranks; this also ensures that their conscious interests will be translated into political demands.

These class differences are not confined to voting and representation; they are equally manifested in the judicial process. The court system in the United States is predominantly white and middle class, and the actions of the court reflect that fact. Negroes, for example, often receive longer sentences for the same offense than do whites. That the poor and the minorities receive less favorable treatment by the police has been documented for more than one American city.[18] In recent years, the tension between police and Negroes has been one of the most exacerbated issues of civil rights. In the several riots that occurred in Negro ghettoes during the 1960s, the police were often forced to turn to militia to restore order, so intense was the enmity between them and Negroes. Since the protection of person and property is a major function of the state, class and status differences in the administration of justice suggests that political power is related to the class and status structures of the society. Although American democracy may be pluralistic, this pluralism does not provide equal access to power for all, and it may also provide a consensus to exclude some. In this sense a white consensus has effectively excluded Negroes from sharing in decision making and from having their interests count. This is the sense in which Negroes have been "second-class citizens"; so also have the poor in an affluent society.

The differential participation of social strata in politics is often treated as an individual matter, but as Herbert Blumer once noted, little participation

[18] See William S. Robinson, "Bias, Probability, and Trial by Jury," *American Sociological Review*, 15 (February, 1950), 73–78; Walter Reckless, *The Crime Problem* (New York: Appleton, 1950); and William A. Westley, "Violence and the Police," *American Journal of Sociology*, 49 (July, 1953), 34–41.

aside from voting and shopping occurs outside of a group context.[19] Many studies by both sociologists and political scientists have portrayed the politics of medicine, agriculture, veterans' benefits, and the like, as the process by which some organized groups manage to carry their demands through the decision-making process. This approach sees *interest groups* rather than individual citizens as the key unit of the political process. Much decision making goes on between elections, and frequently on issues on which the electorate is unheard or on which they have no opinion. This is not to say that interest groups always work against popular opinion; rather, they frequently base themselves upon articulate constituencies, and they often exploit grass roots sentiments and prejudices as well as the frequent indeterminancy and indecisiveness of the electorate.

Many who follow an interest group interpretation emphasize the power of such groups to control decision making. C. Wright Mills' study of a national power elite suggested a convergence of major interest groups at the top level of society, while Hunter and others have done the same in studying community power.[20] But still others have suggested that a proliferation of interest groups can also produce a stalemate; David Riesman spoke of veto groups for this situation,[21] while Samuel Lubell's studies have been concerned with the lack of a decisive majority that produces an indecisive balance of power in Congress.[22]

ELITES AND POWER

There is perhaps no more persistent idea in the history of thought concerning political institutions than the concept of *elite*. Almost all social thinkers in all times and places have been able to identify elites who exercise power over masses; not even the historic emergence of democratic society nor of equalitarian values has disabused social thinkers of the idea that political control always rests in the hands of an elite. Indeed, that an elite exists even within a nominally democratic structure has been one of the influential ideas of political sociology.

Three political sociologists whose lives spanned the period of the late

[19] Herbert Blumer, "Public Opinion and the Public Opinion Polls," *American Sociological Review,* 13 (October, 1948), 542–549.

[20] For discussion of these studies, see below.

[21] David Riesman, with Nathan Glazer and Ruel Denny, *The Lonely Crowd* (New Haven, Conn.: Yale University Press, 1950).

[22] Samuel Lubell, *The Future of American Politics,* 2d ed. (New York: Doubleday, 1956); also *The Revolt of the Moderates* (New York: Harper & Row, 1956).

nineteenth and early twentieth centuries—Gaetano Mosca, Vilfredo Pareto, and Robert Michels—pursued this theme of elite power and its relations to liberal and democratic institutions. Their pioneering work created one of the major dimensions along which political sociology was to follow.

Gaetano Mosca (1858–1941) wrote a major historic thesis, *The Ruling Class*, devoted to establishing, by erudite historical scholarship, that all human societies were always and everywhere ruled by a controlling social class, and thus human society always divided between the rulers and the ruled.[23] At the same time, he documented the fact that every ruling class creates a *legitimation* of its power in terms of the dominant values prevailing in the culture, as when kings presume to rule by the will of God and elected presidents by the will of the people. But Mosca's argument that there is always a ruling class was hardly an original idea; it had probably been taken for granted by scholars for centuries. However, his detailed documentation amassed an impressive range of supporting historical data, and the timing of his study coincided with serious intellectual concerns about new forms of political power and the potentialities for democratic order.

Vilfredo Pareto (1848–1923), one of the major figures in the development of sociological theory, taking the existence of a ruling class for granted, concentrated his study on the selection and change of elites, and contributed the famous phrase, "*the circulation of elites.*"[24] Pareto was basically concerned with the consequences of "open" and "closed" elites; they are open when access to elite position is possible for men of nonelite origin, and they are closed when an elite class monopolizes elite positions for those born into that class. Pareto saw no elite as having any monopoly of brains and skills, and thus a stable political process required that the ruling elite co-opt into its own ranks the best talent from the ranks of the nonelite. Yet the tendencies to closure are always strong in elites, for their very processes of legitimacy often impute superiority to themselves and an inferiority to subordinate classes. *Aristocracy* emerges when an elite becomes closed, imbues itself with definitions of superiority, and provides for legitimate succession only by birth within its own ranks. When the inevitable decay of aristocracy produces cleavage and dissension within its own ranks, new elites emerge from other classes to give leadership to revolutionary change. An old elite will then lose its ruling position, and a new ruling class will emerge.

Michels: the Law of Oligarchy   "Who says organization, says oligarchy." With these famous words, Robert Michels expressed in modern language an ancient pessimism about the capacity of men to achieve freedom and demo-

---

[23] Gaetano Mosca, *The Ruling Class* (New York: McGraw-Hill, 1939).

[24] Vilfredo Pareto, *Mind and Society* (New York: Harcourt Brace, 1935).

cratic order within social organization.[25] Oligarchy, the rule of the few over the many, he considered to be an inevitable outcome of social organization, and his "iron law" of oligarchy was a sociological formulation of this idea. Michel's argument has two major aspects: first, he argues for the necessity of leadership, and secondly, he tries to show how such leadership becomes an oligarchy. Michels argues that leadership is necessary in any group that organizes for collective action, for this requires a division of labor and an assignment of specialized and skilled functions on behalf of the group to some of its members. Leadership *roles* necessarily emerge from this problem.

But why does this necessitate oligarchy? First of all, because the delegation of tasks and authority to a leadership places in its hands a concentration of skills and prerogatives that others do not have. Leaders become specialized in carrying out tasks that others know little about, and the experience of being a leader sets these members apart from the others. However, leadership also makes possible an internal power. It affords the opportunity to build a staff of people who are loyal, it gives control of the channels of communication, and it permits a monopoly of access to the members. Only the leaders control the membership files, the official records, and the treasury, and without in any way being dishonest or illegal, they can use these to their own advantage.

Any theory about oligarchy, however, must also account for the followers. Michels saw the mass of membership of any large social organization as contributing to the emergence of oligarchy because of their indifference to running the organization and their unwillingness to become greatly involved. Furthermore, Michels argued, the members appreciate the greater skills and ability of leaders and they feel beholden to them, thus the members have no inclination to prevent their leaders' growing power.

The manner in which a leadership becomes self-perpetuating has consequences for the organization. An oligarchic leadership becomes conservative and cautious, and it develops interests of its own that may be quite different from the formally stated objectives of the organization. The more that these organizations grow and prosper, the more do they become stable and bureaucratic organizations, and the more do their original goals to effect radical change in society diminish. Michels had studied the great socialist parties of Europe, which, as they became more oligarchic, became less revolutionary.

Social organization, then, creates a set of conditions that makes oligarchy possible. Michels' formulations did not require any psychological explanations, such as a lust for power or a desire to dominate, though he did sometimes talk in this manner; instead, his perspective is basically sociological, for he interprets oligarchy as an inevitable outcome of a set of structural conditions that begins

[25] Robert Michels, *Political Parties* (New York: Free Press, 1949). This book was first published in 1915.

with the division of labor. Nor does his theory require any moral charge against leadership. Oligarchy is not the intent of leaders, nor did Michels doubt the commitment to socialism or the personal integrity of these men. Oligarchic leadership is not a consequence of having immoral leaders win out over moral ones.

Community Power Elites Among contemporary American sociologists, a renewed interest in social power has focused upon the community rather than upon the larger society. American sociologists apparently look upon the larger society as too large and complex a structure for present methodology to handle; but the community is apparently a manageable context for the more rigorous study of a complex and difficult phenomenon. The study of power in the community has centered around the approach developed by Floyd Hunter, a sociologist, and criticized by Robert Dahl, a political scientist.[26] In *Community Power Structure,* Hunter describes in detail an economic elite— mostly corporation executives and bankers—who by informal communication and because of a similar social point of view agree on the major decisions affecting the lives of all the citizens of the community. Yet this elite is not known to the community, for its members do not usually hold official positions, and its decision-making activities are not publicly visible.

Power, then, seems to be centered at the very top of the social structure in the hands of the community's economic elite. This small elite is able to exercise social power because of its control of the community's economic resources: the banks and credit, the corporations and jobs. The elite decides, but others, whom the community thinks of as community leaders, then go about the task of carrying out the decision, including mobilizing community support. These community leaders, including elected public officials and the heads of the well-known large organizations of the community, are not, according to Hunter, decision-makers in their own right. They are, rather, men of second and third rank in the power structure, whose function is to carry out decisions, not make them. Hunter sees the Chamber of Commerce and the numerous civic organizations as instruments for the execution of decisions made by the elite at the top of the power structure but not as channels of influence. This leads to the inference that these organizations are not controlled by their membership but are used, instead, to control that membership, in the sense of mobilizing their support for decisions made by the elite.

Hunter's method for discovering the power structure of a community has been labeled the "reputational" method; basically it consists of creating a

---

[26] See Floyd Hunter, *Community Power Structure* (Chapel Hill, N.C.: University of North Carolina Press, 1953), and Robert A. Dahl, *Who Governs? Democracy and Power in an American City* (New Haven, Conn.: Yale University Press, 1961).

list of persons whom knowledgeable individuals assert are the most powerful
or influential ones in the community and then interviewing them. Thus he
interviews those who have the reputation of being influential. This approach
to the study of community power has become a source of considerable controversy among social scientists, particularly between those who have followed
Hunter's method in studying power, and others, such as Robert Dahl, who have
offered alternate approaches. Dahl and his students have asserted that there
is not in fact a small, cohesive decision-making elite in the community; they
have criticized Hunter's "reputational" method for centering on *who* the
decision-makers are but not on *how* decisions are made. In turn they have
insisted on the importance of observing the *issues* in the community over which
decisions are made and of observing the decision-making *process* that occurs.
They note that the same people are not necessarily involved in the different
areas of decision making—education, city government, and community welfare,
for example. From this perspective one gets a different image of community
power structure, one much less monolithic, with a less close relation between
power and status and a wider citizen participation in decision making.

Sociologists as well as political scientists have offered criticisms of Hunter's
method and have conducted other studies of communities which reveal a less
monolithic image of power than Hunter does. From such research several
significant points emerge:

1. Hunter's conception of community power was probably influenced by
the particular southern city he studied. It was characterized by an absence
of two-party politics, there was not a strongly organized working class with
influential union and political leaders to speak for them, and the economic
leaders were men who not only managed large-scale enterprises but also owned
them. This particular constellation of factors would produce a somewhat more
concentrated, less shared in, process of community decision making than in
other types of communities.

2. Hunter's reputational method of asking only who are the most influential
persons in the community and then interviewing them about their activities
may produce the very image of power that Hunter gives us. In turn, asking
what the *issues* are; where in the authority structure (city government, board
of education, community welfare council) such decisions are made; who then
is involved in the social interaction at each different locus of decision making;
and what are the varied influences and pressures that produce decisions, tends
to give a less monolithic image of community power. It appears instead as a
more complicated process characterized by wider community participation.

3. Both approaches to the study of community power may be so intent on
observing the immediate participation of influential persons in decision making and the mechanics of how decisions are made that they neglect other
relevant variables. The cultural climate of opinion, for example, may be more

permissive or more restrictive; in one community decision-makers may be more free to innovate and change, in another more bound to operate within a prescribed framework of customs and values.

This spirited exchange of ideas about community power structure has been an excellent example of the scientific criticism and dialogue that has yielded a much better idea of just how power is structured in the community, and a recognition that variations in the structuring of power occur as a consequence of variations in the organization of community life. Yet the question of whether social power is always exercised through an elite remains an unresolved issue. Most sociological studies have been on the community level, a noted exception to this, however, was the late C. Wright Mills' *The Power Elite*, a sociologically bold and imaginative effort to delineate the power structure of modern American society.[27] Mills described an elite of top leaders in industry, labor, government, and the military who were united by a common ideological outlook.

But Mills' analysis has been controversial in social science and in the intellectual community. Many social scientists have insisted upon a more pluralistic view of social power, in which a wide and diversified array of interest groups have access to places of authority and manage to bring pressure upon official decision-makers. The complexity of the decision-making process and the fact of social change, it is felt, renders unlikely the capacity of a single elite to control all decisions. At the same time no one argues that all groups have *equal* access to decision making. A conception of an arena of decision making in which a small number of conflicting elites struggle to control the pattern of decision making emerges as a position somewhere between Hunter's and Mills' idea of a single elite and the contrasting notion of a shifting array of participating groups. This seems to be the notion of power in American society that John Galbraith offered with his conception of *countervailing power*.[28] Galbraith argued that the large bureaucratic organizations of modern America had rendered archaic the idea of a society of separate individuals who by individual votes made the society's decisions. The individual had been replaced by the organization. But, said Galbraith, when power concentrated in one large form, as it did first in the United States in the big corporation, this necessarily produced countervailing power groups, such as big labor and big government. Decision making, then, became a matter of conflict and negotiation among these organized giants.

The critics of this position have not disagreed with Galbraith's thesis about the growth of large power structures dominating decision making, but they have quarreled with the implication that all of these power structures are

[27] C. Wright Mills, *The Power Elite* (New York: Oxford, 1956).
[28] John K. Galbraith, *American Capitalism: The Concepts of Countervailing Power* (Boston: Houghton Mifflin, 1956).

equal in their capacity to participate in decision making. Specifically some critics see Galbraith's book as a liberal effort to provide a new rationale for bigness and concentrated power in American society, and thus to make it seem that the concentrated power of big business is no greater than the power of labor, for example.

THE POLITICS OF EXTREMISM

A democratic order can be conceived of "as a social mechanism for resolving the problem of cleavage and integration with a minimal use of force and the maximal emphasis of consensus of values."[29] It is a set of "rules of the game" for containing conflict within reasonable bounds, yet providing for social change and thus a resolution of issues that are the source of conflict. Such a democratic order cannot function unless the *legitimacy* of these rules is accepted by all the political actors. This is the basic normative expectation of democratic process: that all participants will confine their struggle to legalized methods and that they will accept the democratically regulated outcome, thus permitting victories, defeats, and shifts in power. This latter expectation also means that any "losers" in the struggle are not "liquidated" as "enemies of the state" but are protected by constitutional rights that permit them to rejoin the struggle. The political "outs," in other words, are only out of office, not out of society or out of their freedom or even their lives.

But at all times in democratic societies there are those whose political conduct suggests that they do not accept the legitimacy of these rules. They may not accept the necessity for a political tolerance of other groups and classes, expressing, instead, an authoritarian outlook on the world and on the political process. Or, they may be unable to accept as legitimate either the goals of a group that require a drastic change in some long institutionalized sector of society, or the rise in influence of a group that had once been powerless, such as workers or minorities. This is the problem of *extremism* in politics. Extremist political groups do not fit within the established framework for political action because their goals or their methods, or both, fall outside that which has become normatively defined as legitimate.

Extremism is thus a conception of politics rooted in the notions of an inclusive democratic process that tolerates divergent values and goals as long as individuals and groups play politics by the democratic "rules of the game" and so accept the legitimated process to attain influence and achieve their objectives. As used by political sociologists it is a normative term that designates those who are either to the left or right of an inclusive democratic mid-

[29] Lipset, "Political Sociology," p. 92.

dle, and whose political outlook supports a change in the rules of the game to create a more authoritarian state and to deny equal access to the political structure to all social groups. There is always the possibility of applying the term to the demands of previously excluded groups, who understandably may be unimpressed with the legitimacy of a structure that has denied them access. Such groups may be *radical* without being extremist and may be struggling for an even wider inclusion of groups in the democratic process and for an even more representative and responsive democratic order. Their successful inclusion in the democratic order then reduces their own critical stance toward the social order and gives them a stake in the existing structure. What once seemed radical, as labor unions did to many middle-class people in the 1930s, comes in time to be viewed as part of the "establishment" to a generation come of age in the 1960s.

The Appeals of Extremism   As it would to any ordinarily curious mind, the question as to what kind of people are extremists has occurred also to social scientists. But the effort to find an answer has led to several different approaches that are not completely compatible with one another. There are at least three that deserve notice. There is first a social-psychological approach that tries to determine the *psychological* characteristics of those people who respond most favorably to the symbolic and ideological appeals of extremist parties. The answer is found in identifying those who are least committed to the existing social order, uprooted, frustrated, and disappointed in life, in short, the *alienated*, who have little confidence in the stable social order and are ordinarily the least politicized.[30]

Such an analysis is sociologically inadequate if it remains *psychological* by identifying the problem as one of pathological personality types. It can only become a sociological problem by inquiring into the social conditions that induce a sense of alienation from the social order, thus locating those processes of social change that lead to *group* dislocations as well as the emergence of extremism in specific groups and classes.

Extremism and Status   A second approach does just that; it identifies some specific category of people—a social class or status group—as alienated and then as being intolerant and authoritarian. Perhaps the most controversial effort of this kind was Seymour Martin Lipset's analysis of "working-class authoritarianism."[31] Lipset argued that the conditions of lower-class life generated an anti-democratic authoritarianism and an anti-intellectualism that

---

[30] See Kornhauser, *The Politics of Mass Society,* for an extended discussion of this process.

[31] Seymour Martin Lipset, *Political Man* (New York: Doubleday, 1960), Chapter IV, "Working-Class Authoritarianism."

made such people responsive to extremist slogans as long as these were un-complicated, black-and-white explanations of a complicated world. The social ignorance and lack of education of the lower strata, according to Lipset, makes the sophisticated norms of democracy beyond their understanding. Thus, the seemingly historic liberalism of the working class is presumably misleading. It is only liberal on *economic* issues but illiberal on *social* issues, such as civil liberties and the rights of minorities.

Why has the working class then not always been on the extremist side? Lipset argues that working-class organizations, such as labor unions and labor or socialist parties, have been institutions well integrated into the democratic order, and the loyalty of workers to their organizations has kept them within the social order rather than politically outside of it. These organizations pre-sumably provide institutional sources of protest that keep the authoritarian and undemocratic attitudes of workers from having social effect.

Yet such explanation may not be sufficient. A careful examination of the thesis of working-class authoritarianism raises three critical questions:

1. The argument is based upon survey data from opinion polls, in which lower-class people always answer questions in such a way as to appear more illiberal and intolerant than the middle class. The educated strata are sophis-ticated enough to give the "right" answers to these questions and never acknowledge any racial or religious bias. Lipset acknowledges that British workers admit to anti-Semitism and the middle class does not. However, it is the Labor Party that elected several Jewish members to Parliament, and always from non-Jewish, working-class districts, whereas the middle class elects no Jews. The evidence from social surveys, then, on such highly intense mat-ters as prejudice and related attitudes may be often unreliable.

2. Lipset's unqualified vocabulary lumps together working class, lower class, and lower strata and fails to make any rigorous distinction between a stable and integrated working class and an unintegrated lower class; the latter group has historically provided the source of the "know-nothings" who have often acted violently in situations of political and social stress.

3. Although an alienated lower class has, indeed, often been highly intoler-ant and unpermissive in its political orientation (but also often politically passive and uninvolved), these people have not been the only ones attracted to extremist movements; thus, this lowest level of the stratification order can-not constitute the only social conditions that generate extremism in politics.

The Potentiality for Extremism   These criticisms lead naturally to a consider-ation of a third approach which defines the potentiality for extremist action in any group or class. Extremist politics will emerge in any group when its social position is seriously threatened, and it finds itself frustrated in trying to make the established political system work for it. Interestingly, Lipset is also one of the political sociologists who has pointed out that changing social conditions can generate extremism in any social class.[32] In Germany in the 1920s and 1930s the social conditions following World War I drove millions of middle-class people into fascism. Rudolf Heberle traced a close connection between the rise of national socialism in Germany and the threatened interests of small farmers and businessmen.[33] Since none of the existing parties seemed to speak for their interests, these groups moved toward a new party that promised a radical counterattack upon secular society. But as Heberle points out, this was not simply a defense of economic interests; it was also a defense of a way of life, the collapsing rural and small town society of the past.

In the early 1950s in the United States, the onset of McCarthyism similarly generated most support among small businessmen. The fears and frustrations that McCarthy most appealed to were those of the small town small business-man and the farmer, who saw their way of life under attack from immigrants and Jews, from big business and big labor, and from city politicians, and Eastern intellectuals and professors.[34] Huey Long in the South had a similar appeal in the thirties, and the Ku Klux Klan has always attracted such support, though its emphasis has been heavily on race. Thus, what has been called the "radical right" in the United States is basically an "old" middle-class manifestation of extremism in response to massive social changes that have shifted power and prestigeful life-styles to other groups.[35] There are also regional differences in the support of this extremism; the South and Southwest have generated support for this extremism among those who are fundamentally Protestant and oppose the liberal, socially conscious Protestantism found in the urban North.

Extremism, then, can be generated in any status group or social class in society, when the social conditions are appropriate. Social changes generate cleavages and conflict when once socially advantaged groups lose power and prestige to new social groups. When the threat of lost position or lost opportunities generates deep concern, there may be strong efforts to return to an earlier status quo or otherwise to bring changes that will restore power and status. When this cannot be done within the established political order, demands for changes that go beyond what has been institutionalized bring a new, extremist phase to the political process. But it is not only these long-

---

[32] See Lipset, Chapter V, " 'Fascism'—Left, Right, and Center."

[33] Rudolf Heberle, *From Democracy to Naziism: A Regional Case Study on Political Parties* (Baton Rouge, La.: Louisiana State University Press, 1945).

[34] For research documenting support for McCarthy, see Martin Trow, "Small Business, Political Tolerance, and Support for McCarthy," *American Journal of Sociology*, 64 (November, 1958), 270–281.

[35] For a series of perceptive essays from this perspective, see Daniel Bell, ed., *The New American Right* (New York: Criterion, 1955).

established groups that generate extremism; disadvantaged groups finding opportunities for new gains may also generate extremist tendencies if their efforts are continually frustrated, and they begin to feel they cannot achieve a desired status within the established framework for political action.

Revolution and the Totalitarian Left The social cleavages that generate the political extremism of the right are rooted in the shifts to a more urban, more secular middle-class society and the threat this poses to older status groups and life-styles. But the effort to create a revolutionary left is rooted in somewhat different concerns and developments. In the United States and even in Europe since World War II the "spectre haunting Europe" of a working-class revolution under communist leadership has seemed to be remote. But in the 1960s a New Left in both the United States and Europe has revived old dreams of revolution by depressed social classes, this time the urban poor, the "exploited" students, and the Negroes.

Whereas those concerned for democratic order sought ways to breach cleavages and reduce class and group polarization, the revolutionary looks for the cleavages that seem most persistent and most exploitable and seeks to exacerbate them by ideological attacks and direct action. The revolutionary interpretation does not make the normative judgments about extremism discussed to this point, but seeks instead to find ways to organize the alienated and to detach them further from their precarious commitment to the social order. Its organizing problem is often the apathy and disinterest in politics of such groups; its tactics, therefore, are directed to *confrontation* by direct means with authorities to press strong demands, so that refusal or only vague assurances will hopefully further polarize the alienated and discontented from the established order. In addition if illegal means bring reprisals and there is violence and arrest, there is opportunity to make accusations of police brutality and to widen support.

These tactics are designed to sharpen cleavage and polarize what seems from this leftist perspective to be almost a monolithic unity in society. It is intended to *politicize* the affected groups; that is, to get them to view more issues and events in political terms, and to *radicalize* them, to get them to adopt a more radical political view that accomplishes the polarization of disaffected groups from the social order. This effort to induce conflict often strains severely the tolerance of democratic order for dissidence and protest. It also arouses the antagonism of others, particularly the more conservative segments of the society; the consequence is a threatened "backlash" of political demands for more repressive measures against revolutionary protest, which in turn creates a strong counterattack upon political officials. There is then not one cleavage separating the disaffected from the established, but three camps in contention, with a threatened polarization of the extremes, in which the democratic order can then be a casualty of the resulting political struggle. Much of the viability of democratic politics depends upon preventing just such a polarization that destroys the legitimacy of the moderate democratic processes. Yet such politics must practice a wide tolerance of those more extreme elements without letting them destroy the democratic process. It must also respond sensitively to the grievances and demands of the disadvantaged and disaffected, for the democratic process, must prove itself effective if it is to be legitimate for masses of people. No system can expect to command the loyalty of people it cannot serve.

A FINAL NOTE: CONSENSUS AND CLEAVAGE

The sociologist, apparently, cannot avoid studying politics if he would study society, for society is a delicate balance among conflicting forces, an arena of groups contending for dominance in status and power; thus, conflict is always endemic within it. The sociology of politics is the study of the conditions by which men in society can contain conflict within accepted and legitimized processes and arrive at consensus. A political order sustains a social order, and a society is politically stable when its political institutions are accepted as legitimate by its members. But political stability is a fragile and precarious thing, for social cleavages and incipient conflicts beset any human society, and men in conflict will remain within the established processes for resolving differences only so long as they believe that these processes are viable ways of gaining their ends.

FIRST PICTURES FROM EUROPE VIA TELSTAR

U.S.NAVY

U.S.NAVY

1

2 3

1. First television picture from Europe via Telstar.
2. Training astronaut.
3. Influenza vaccine production: swabbing eggs with an antiseptic solution.
4. Curbside student reading a science book.

4

SCIENCE
IN SOCIETY

17

It would be unimaginable today to attempt to conceptualize the nature of modern society without accounting for the influence upon it and the place within it of modern science. Science is not merely a highly rational activity of immense practical consequence for almost every phase of man's life, it is a major institutional structure within modern society. It is also a revolutionary force for radical change in society, it provides cultural criteria for legitimizing belief and behavior. It is a contributor to and supporter of the rationalizing trend that is the basic mark of the secular society. Furthermore, it is also a powerful ideology and world-view for interpreting the modern world, shared by scientists and many others.

But the society within which science is so well established constitutes a social milieu that supports the values and activities of science and in turn shapes the kind of researches that science undertakes. In the nineteenth century science was largely conducted within universities, and its funding was meager. Men of science worked alone or with the aid of a few assistants and apprentices, and few of them were concerned with or in any way involved in the practical application of science. However, today science is an expensive investment, heavily funded by the government. The lone scientist in his own small laboratory is a rarity; scientists now work in large scientific-research organizations in cooperation with many others. And a very large part of the scientific effort is now concentrated in a diverse array of applied areas. There is, evidently, a reciprocal process at work here, a constant interaction between science as an autonomous process and the society within which it is established. If it is true, as it clearly is, that science has been one of the major shapers of modern society, it is equally true that modern society has organized and developed science to suit its pragmatic demands for an effective, rational, problem-solving instrumentality.

The Sociology of Science   Despite the generally acknowledged importance of the place of science in modern society, it has never become a central concern for sociology. There is still only a small (though growing) body of sociologists who pursue the study of science as an institution. This is not because scholarship has neglected science; quite to the contrary, the history of science is a small but flourishing scholarly enterprise. Indeed, many of the historians of science have contributed to the development of the sociology of science, particularly by their efforts to determine the specific social conditions that made science possible.

The sociologist of science is not concerned primarily with the substantive nature of science but rather with the complex relations between science and society. His starting point in his recognition that science is a human activity and, no less than any other human activity, is a social process. It has a history of development, it flourishes in some kinds of societies and not in others, and it has a normative order and an ethical outlook. Being a scientist is a career and a professional occupation, there is organization to carry on scientific research, and there is also a community of scientists whose interaction sustains science as a culture.

The Nature of Science   If one were to ask, what is science?, there are a number of legitimate answers. One common one is to define science as a logical mode of inquiry for discovering valid knowledge. A second answer would be in terms of what science knows—science as validated *theory*. Of these two, one stresses science as the inquiring *process*, the other as the cumulated *result* of that inquiry. But an answer can also be given by delineating the particular set of *values* that distinguishes science from other human activities. Furthermore, these values become institutionalized and operative only in an organized context of roles and relationships, structures and social groups, basically relevant for modern society. Science, from this perspective, is *institution* and *structure*.

When the natural scientist talks about science, he does so primarily in terms of method and theory, though he will frequently acknowledge the defining character of scientific values. He is less likely to perceive of science as social structure, or at best but dimly recognize what that means. But, for the sociologist of science, it is this aspect that defines science as an object of sociological inquiry. Science is more than method and theory; it is a complex and extraordinarily influential social process in modern society, and the role of the scientist is now one of the more important roles in the organization of that society. The student of modern society has no choice but to examine science as one among the major institutional structures accounting for the nature of modern society.

THE PROBLEM OF SCIENCE IN SOCIETY

What is *problematic* about science for the sociologist originates in the observation that science is a social process, one among other structural features of society. Although a range of considerations have oriented the sociologist in his examination of science in society, there would seem to be four major problematic aspects under which most sociological inquiry can be subsumed: (1) science as an *institutional structure;* (2) the *organization* of science; (3) the relation of *science and politics;* and (4) science as an influential and pervasive social perspective, a *world-view* and *ideology*.

Science as an Institutional Structure   A slow, historical development since the Middle Ages has made of science a major social institution; it has become one significant structure distinguishing modern from traditional society. Furthermore science is now essential to modern society, for its division of labor, its advanced technology, its standard of living, its capacity to provide material and physical well-being for its citizens, all depend upon science.

Throughout the several centuries of the development the values that mark the scientist's outlook and his definition of his proper behavior have become so widely accepted and so built into the very structure of science that we can conceive of them as having been institutionalized. Around these values, then, has developed a social structure of scientific activity, and the analysis of this structure is one of the chief concerns of the sociology of science.

The Organization of Science   The attention of sociologists in recent years has been focused on the internal organization of science, and particularly of scientific research. Research has increasingly come to be undertaken in large organizations, and in industrial and governmental research organizations, as well as universities. The productivity of research efforts in varying kinds of research milieus, under varying kinds of sponsorships, has provided a practical motive for studying the organization of research behavior.

With the fantastic growth in the number of scientists, the problem of scientific communication has become an issue of considerable practical and organizational urgency in science, as has the recruitment of scientists into the scientific community and profession. If scientific research is organized, so is the scientific community, and through its organization it promotes its own ends, rewards its most successful members, confers prestige and recognition on successful scientists, and makes effective the ethics and values of science. It also invokes sanctions and effects social control.

Science and Politics   As science has increasingly become a more integral part of modern society, and as government increasingly uses and supports science for space exploration, military weaponry, as well as for problems in food supply, pollution, and a host of others, scientists have moved closer to an involvement in the making of social policy. The scientist and the politician, two seemingly incompatible if not irreconcilable roles, have had to learn to live with and understand one another and to share to some extent in understanding the complexity of one another's problems. The result has been a new dimension of social concern and moral responsibility for the scientist that makes the scientific world of pre–World War II seem innocent and naïve.

Science as a World-View and Ideology   To speak of science as an institution and to talk of the organization of science is to be concerned with the functions that science performs for society and the organization necessary to carry out that function. But the involvement of science with national policy is a new development that has unforeseen consequences for science and for society. So is the development in this century of science as a powerful ideological outlook for assessing change in society and for offering science as the major salvation for the ills of this world. Science has become a world-view that competes (as it has in the past) with religion for interpreting the natural order of things and for explaining and rationalizing what goes on. Its matter-of-fact and rigorously logical mode of inquiry is a model of thinking and explaining in the secular society. This impressive power of science has developed among scientists a fundamental confidence in their ability to provide solutions to human problems and to create a better world by creating new knowledge and making possible an even more productive technology. Many others, of course, share this perspective. An alternative perspective, however, one held by many humanists, not only rejects this confidence in the positive good of science but instead views science (with bureaucracy and technology) as the source of a technically efficient but humanly oppressive society that is destructive of individuality and freedom. These contrasting perspectives are the *two cultures* that C. P. Snow made reference to in his now famous and somewhat controversial discussion. The issues Snow raised in his little book are fundamental to the problem of the significance of science for society, even though sociologists have given little attention to them.

THE INSTITUTIONALIZATION OF SCIENCE

Science as we know it in our time warrants consideration as one of the major social structures of modern society. It is the historic outcome of several centuries of significant social development in the Western world and is inextricably interwoven with Western culture and history.

The Growth of Science   In a rudimentary manner, science is found in all cultures, even primitive ones. All men have made empirical observations about nature, generally related to practical considerations, and have developed arts and skills from these. There is thus some continuity from the most primitive of human origins in the development of science. Yet science has taken major developmental steps forward at particular times and in particular cultures. Over a thousand year span, for example, the Greeks developed an impressive science with a large number of significant achievements to their credit.

Even the Middle Ages, so often viewed as theologically dominated, made a notable contribution to the rise of modern science. Alfred N. Whitehead, in his influential *Science and the Modern World,* has argued cogently that scholastic logic and scholastic divinity contributed strongly to science by its "habit of definite exact thought."[1] The medieval scholar had a superbly rational mind, and this rational thought became a cornerstone of science. It needed but to be divorced from a primary concern with theological issues to make the necessary coupling of the rational and the empirical that is science. There were other ways, too, in which medieval thought contributed to science. For instance, as Whitehead noted, medieval thinkers had the idea that there was a secret to be unveiled. The rational mind of man was to be the discoverer, for God was a rational God and his rationality was manifest in nature. Like modern scientists, medieval theologians believed in the existence of discoverable general principles.

It was during the sixteenth and seventeenth centuries that there occurred a major breakthrough in scientific discovery and achievement that is usually defined as the period of the rise of modern science. A complex set of processes produced the social milieu that was congenial to scientific creativity, and thus developed one of the truly great periods in the history of science.[2] Perhaps the significant development *within* science was the creation of the Cartesian philosophy. René Descartes provided a new rational philosophy for science that was a sharp break with scholasticism. He stressed the need to make precise observations and rigorous logical and mathematical calculations in order to establish necessary relations among events. In addition there was a refinement of experimental techniques, enhanced by the invention of new instruments of observation and measurement: the telescope, the microscope, the thermometer, the barometer, the pendulum clock, and the air pump. A new mathematical rationality combined with a new emphasis on empirical observation to create a powerful modern science.

There were also external developments that created a social milieu favorable to the development of science. In fact, a whole series of important social, economic, and religious changes facilitated the development of modern science. One of these came from the Renaissance, which revived interest in ancient knowledge and thought and brought such significant works as that of Archimedes back into the mainstream of scientific effort. The concern for practical inventions useful in mining and other industries led to technological innovations that in turn made possible new scientific tools of observation and experimentation. In the background were the Western explorations of the newly mapped world and a mercantile capitalism that sought wider markets.

[1] Alfred North Whitehead, *Science and the Modern World* (New York: Macmillan, 1925; Mentor Edition, New American Library, 1948), Mentor Edition, p. 13.

[2] The following discussion is drawn from Bernard Barber, *Science and the Social Order,* Chapter 2 (New York: Free Press, 1942; Collier Books edition, 1962).

This period of scientific development, however, was also a period of religious change and development; the emergence of Calvinism provided a new, strong impetus to science. Max Weber demonstrated that the religious views of men had great significance for their everyday activities, particularly economic ones. His comparative studies of the world's great religions had convinced him that Western society was more congenial to the development of science than any other, in particular because its religious view presumed a rational God revealed in nature and discoverable by the rationality of man. Weber's work on Confucian China, in contrast, described a magical image of the world that hindered the development of science.

The contemporary sociologist Robert Merton carried out a now famous study that put Weber's ideas to careful, empirical test. Merton demonstrated that Puritans were proportionately greater in number than any other religious group in being active in science as well as in the extent of their scientific contributions.[3] The Puritan beliefs and their orientation to the world—what Weber had called the Protestant Ethic—contained, among other things, a positive and approving view of science. Science was not inimical to religion, for man, by a rational understanding of nature, could understand God. Furthermore, science enabled men to do good works, and good works were a sign of election to salvation. Also, they viewed man alone as possessing reason given him by God, and they placed high value on reason. What is necessary to understand here is that Merton is not asserting that religion positively influences science, or even that Protestantism does so. Rather, he is saying that a particular religious system—Calvinism—at a particular stage of its development had a determinable effect upon science. Such a religious support for science was not necessarily intended, and in time the importance given to rationality in Western thought came to depend less on specific religious orientations and became secularized.

These several factors, then, coming together at a particular time in history, brought into existence a social milieu in which science flourished and grew, and a great panorama of giants of science came upon the scene in a relatively short period—men such as Newton, Leibnitz, Copernicus, Kepler, Galileo, and Boyle. Significant to that social milieu was a *utilitarian* interest that frequently found a partner in science. However, the major value that towered over all was a belief in *rationality* that did not require practical results as justification. From this milieu and particularly from the religious support of Calvinism evolved a set of values that came to define "science as a moral enterprise," as Bernard Barber has called it, rather than science as a technical enterprise.

[3] Robert K. Merton, *Science, Technology and Society in Seventeenth Century England*, OSIRIS, IV, Part 2 (Belgium, 1938).

Science and Values   The moral enterprise of science constitutes a set of social values that govern and control scientific activities. Beyond its technical functioning science has developed a social organization that governs the individual scientific performance of individual scientists and mediates science's relation to society. But science is not a completely separate and autonomous system; rather, it functions best when it finds generous support and acceptance within society. That is most likely to occur when there is a general congruence between the values of science and the values of society. Such a congruence has occurred in modern Western societies, where a specific set of major values that have found general acceptance are then shared with the scientific community.

Again we turn to Barber for enlightenment.[4] Barber argues quite cogently that these values are *rationality, utilitarianism, universalism, individualism,* and *progress and meliorism.* The value of rationality has already been noted. Utilitarianism refers to modern man's singular interest in the affairs of *this* world rather than in other worlds, and in practical, empirical affairs, rather than in supernatural matters. Universalism, "derived from and still expressed most fundamentally in the Christian ideal of the brotherhood of man in God," has been secularized to mean that "all men are free to find that calling in life to which their merits entitle them."[5] Men are to be judged by their abilities and achievements, not by the particularities of race or religion. Individualism means the moral dictum that a man is to be guided by his own conscience, not by social authority. Thus, individualism is significantly anti-authoritarian. Lastly, progress and meliorism means a belief in the capacity of rational activity to improve the lot of man in this world.

Not only are these values congruent with science, they also express the outlook shared by most scientists. Utilitarianism, for example, is congruent with a this-worldly emphasis on the mundanely *empirical* that characterizes science, whereas individualism expresses the scientist's rejection of any effort to impose truth from an authoritarian source. Science, it is evident, possesses a set of values that are congruent with the values of the modern West, but particularly, as Barber notes, of the liberal democratic societies of the West.

The Values of Science   What are the values of science? Robert Merton has offered a now widely quoted set of four: *universalism, communism, disinterestedness,* and *organized skepticism.*[6] But these are not merely values; rather, they constitute what Merton called "institutional imperatives," the basis for an *ethos,* which he defined as "that affectively toned complex of values and norms

[4] Compare Barber, *Science and the Social Order,* Chapter 3.
[5] Barber, p. 98.
[6] Robert K. Merton, "Science and Democratic Social Structure," in *Social Theory and Social Structure* (New York: Free Press, 1957).

which is held to be binding on the man of science."[7] Here are the widely shared and deeply compelling values that organize the scientific life and control and sanction behavior.

In this context, *universalism* comes to have a specific meaning relevant to science, namely, that claims to truth are subject to *impersonal criteria* that are independent of such things as class, race, and nationality. A scientist's theory cannot be dismissed, for example, because he is a Jew, as the Nazis tried to do with Einstein's work. By the same token, there is not a bourgeois science and a communist science—there is only science.

Merton used the term, *communism,* (Barber suggests *communality,* instead, to avoid ideological misunderstanding) to make clear that science allows no personal monopoly of the knowledge gained by scientific research; instead, all knowledge is the communal property of the scientific community. There are no patents for scientific knowledge. What this makes imperative for the scientific community, then, is an adequate system of communication that makes all scientific discovery available to all scientists. Secrecy even in the national interest runs counter to this value.

The value of *disinterestedness* serves as a powerful imperative to control the varying motives of men who become scientists to see that they act to serve the interest of the scientific community, rather than self-interest, by the manner in which they conduct themselves. The demand for public scrutiny of their work means that scientists are subject to a policing that has little equivalent in any other field. The firm support for disinterestedness gives science a strong control over the varying motives and interests that scientists as human beings undoubtedly have, and exacts a high level of individual integrity that has kept science remarkably free of scandal and fraud.

That openness of mind and readiness to examine new evidence that presumably characterizes the scientist in his work is institutionalized in *organized skepticism,* an insistence on subjecting all issues to a suspended judgment until "the facts are in," and a refusal to exempt any aspect of nature or society as too sacred to be subjected to rational inquiry. There are to be no secrets or taboos from man's most powerful tool of inquiry, his rational mind.

The social institution that becomes organized around such an ethos invites numerous tensions in its relations to society. A society at best but tolerates an institution that operates in such a manner. But liberal, democratic society, as Barber has made so clear, possesses values that are highly congruent with the scientific ethos and thus provides probably the most compatible environment for science. Yet even in such a society there are obvious strains and tensions between science and various other segments of the society. The universalistic criterion runs counter to all the particularistic loyalties and prejudices that

[7] Merton, p. 551.

characterize social life. In time of war, for example, the international scope of science may be subject to attack, and science may be sternly harnassed to national interest. In recent years American and Soviet scientists in many fields have had difficulty in arranging mutual conferences because of political ideology. Yet this very universalism is a value that contributes to the institutional autonomy of science; to allow this universalism to be seriously infringed upon too many times would be injurious to science as a rational activity.

No less readily evident is that the scientist's objectivity, his emotional neutrality, and his organized skepticism is difficult for many others to accept. Some have, indeed, from time to time suggested a moratorium on scientific research, and there are numerous instances of opposition to scientific research into spheres of life that many people took to be too sacred or possibly to be morally injured by scientific inquiry. The pioneering efforts of Alfred Kinsey and his associates to study human sexual behavior met just such opposition.

The Autonomy of Science   What, then, has enabled science to remain a relatively autonomous process, its institutional imperatives functioning effectively to define the scientific life? First of all, there can be no question that science has been useful, and that modern, industrial society has had a major payoff for its investment in and its tolerant acceptance of science. Modern technology rests upon science. Indeed, science has become indispensable to any modern society, so that even the totalitarian societies have had to concede some autonomy to science, though they have done this more for physical science than for biological science, and least of all for social science.

Science has also benefited by its own success. The enormous fruits of natural science have given to it an unchallenged prestige, superior to that of any other kind of scholarship. This has worked to keep science both well supported and, more importantly, relatively free from interference by others on the basis of very different kinds of values or interests. The scientist has become a major authority figure in the modern world, and scientific method has become a major criterion for determining what to believe.

Over the centuries, scientific autonomy has also benefited by the fact that science was primarily housed within the university with which it shared many values. If the university has, at least in part, been an "ivory tower," somewhat detached from the rest of society, this has served well the scientific and scholarly communities. It enabled them to pursue rational inquiry and the intellectual life somewhat away from the impassioned scrutiny of partisan interests and from prejudiced and ideological (and anti-intellectual) perspectives. The university, in short, has brought the scientist together with those others who share much the same value perspective, for the values of science are also largely the values of the Western scholarly tradition. But science is no longer housed entirely within the university, though this still remains its primary home. Industry has created numerous large scientific laboratories, though, admittedly, largely devoted to applied rather than pure research. More importantly, government in any modern society has now become the primary support for basic scientific research, and to some extent, as in atomic laboratories and installations, has removed the scientist from the university.

Whether or not these long-established values of science can remain effective and intact in such new situations remains to be discovered. Norman Kaplan, a sociologist of science, has suggested that Merton's assumption that these values have remained unchanged for two centuries needs to be reexamined, and he cites one study that found substantial deviation from these values among some academic scientists.[8] But such a reexamination of the values of science at this point in history is just one of the major tasks of the sociologist of science. Kaplan's recognition that these values had a definite social origin and that they flourished to institutionalize science in relatively liberal societies implies that there is no imperative for them to endure forever. Science cannot operate in a vacuum; rather, as a social process it thrives in the right kind of social environment, and it changes with the moral climate that is its milieu.

The Scientist and His Institution   To interpret science as a social institution is the analytic perspective of the social scientist but not of the physical scientist. Natural scientists view science in terms of method and as an accumulated body of verified knowledge, but they have never developed a conception of it as an historically developed institution. The scientist's view of his own activity is remarkably *a*historical; his own disciplinary training serves to limit his capacity to understand the development of science in the Western world. It seems to impose one dominant view of the growth of science on scientists, an orthodox perspective that speaks of the *progressively cumulative* development of a scientific field as each stage of development is gradually succeeded by another. But this orthodox perspective is clearly deficient on at least one count, and possibly two. It is deficient in failing to see science in its relation to the social environment that influences to some extent the direction and magnitude of its growth. The external environment either supports science or hinders it, and science has flourished in the West because the historical conditions were supportive. Its history cannot be written, then, except as a dimension of the social and intellectual history of Western life.

But this viewpoint of scientists may also be deficient in viewing science as a gradual and cumulative growth in a single direction. Thomas Kuhn, in an important work, *The Structure of Scientific Revolutions,* has, with impressive his-

---

[8] Norman Kaplan, "Sociology of Science," in *Handbook of Modern Sociology* (Chicago: Rand McNally, 1964), p. 855.

torical scholarship, disputed this idea.[9] He distinguishes between "normal" science and revolutions in science, the latter of which are not merely the cumulative product of what went on before. Kuhn's work, indeed, is the first specific effort to challenge the adequacy of the ahistorical view of science that scientists hold. His work has enormous implications for a sociology of science, but sociologists have not yet begun to explore them. One humanistic student of science, Eric Larrabee, has put the scientists' view this way:

> The only thing wrong with scientists is that they don't understand science. They don't know where their own institution came from, what forces shaped and are still shaping it, and they have wedded themselves to an anti-historical way of thinking which threatens to deter them from ever finding out.[10]

THE ORGANIZATION OF SCIENCE

Although men of great creative innovation and individual talent are always a part of the scientific process, science is a communal effort; it demands that scientists interact to provide confirmation of one another's findings. More than that, most scientific research is now the work of a group rather than of a single scientist. The sociologist is particularly equipped by his own disciplinary interests and training to be sensitively observant of the organizational matrix within which science functions. There are several dimensions to this. One is the organizational structure within which research is carried on. Another is the social organization of scientists as a community and the function of such organization in sustaining the scientific enterprise. Yet another is the procedures by which science maintains its continuity over generations by constantly recruiting new members and socializing them in both the technical skills and moral outlook of the scientist. It is to these issues, so central to sociological analysis, that we turn now.

The Organization of Research   It is probably the laboratory that stands as the symbol of the organized unit within which scientists carry on research. In point of fact not all research in the natural sciences is carried on in laboratories; in some cases, it is because the phenomena studied cannot be removed from their natural context. The astronomer, for example, has no choice but to leave the stars in the heavens. In yet other cases the natural context, as

---

[9] Thomas Kuhn, *The Structure of Scientific Revolutions* (Chicago: University of Chicago Press, 1962).

[10] Eric Larrabee, "Science and the Common Reader," *Commentary*, 41, No. 6 (June, 1966), 48.

in ecological studies, is very much a part of the study, so the scientist must go to the field. Similarly, the geologist must go to mountains, glaciers, and ice caps. Nevertheless, the study of the organization of scientific research has focused upon the laboratory. In part this is because much of this study has been concerned with applied science and pragmatic concerns about productivity. In part also because the laboratory as a unit more easily allows study than does the field situation.

Despite a recent large accumulation of studies on the organization of research, few of them constitute adequate sociological analysis, and few are concerned with theoretical issues. Instead, they are primarily oriented to the practical problems of investing in and supervising applied research that will have a payoff in productivity. Perhaps the one major problem that can be gleaned from these researches is a concern with the way in which the organization of research creates an environment conducive to research. Administrators, of course, have simply wanted the most efficacious form of organization. But many scientists have been concerned about the effect of bureaucratization upon the scientist and his research.

Two recent sociological studies have been Simon Marcson's and William Kornhauser's analysis of scientists in industry.[11] Marcson took the familiar sociological distinction between formal and informal organization and perceptively applied it to an industrial laboratory. He found that the work groups within which scientists carried on their research became an informal network of primary relations and attachments that aided research, as well as providing rewards for the scientist in terms of colleague relationships and recognition from significant others for excellence of performance. Kornhauser, in turn, focused on the strains and tensions he saw as inherent in the relation between professions and organizations. He argued that there was no value in trying to restore the older image of the independent professional, for more and more scientists work in large organizations. His research, however, ended with the somewhat diffuse generalization that organizations will accommodate to the professional, and the professionals will learn to live with organization. It remains for future research to discover just how.

The involvement of scientists in bureaucratic organization has been a teasing problem that has yet to be handled significantly. Besides a concern about what happens to scientists in such circumstances, some have wondered how such an involvement affects organization, particularly since it has been felt that scientists are different from other people and cannot be "handled" in the same

---

[11] Simon Marcson, *The Scientist in American Industry: Some Organization Determinants in Manpower Utilization* (New York: Harper & Row, 1960); William Kornhauser, *Scientists in Industry: Conflict and Accommodation* (Berkeley, Calif.: University of California Press, 1962).

way. As a result there have been imaginative efforts to alter the conventional hierarchical pattern of bureaucracy so as not to alienate scientists. The productivity of the large industrial laboratories testifies to the fact that it is not impossible for scientists to work effectively in somewhat bureaucratized structures and to pursue their careers outside their traditional home, the university. But again it must be noted that the industrial laboratory is devoted to applied research, not basic research. With few exceptions, basic scientific research is still carried on within the university.

Communication among Scientists   A more significant issue that bears upon the effectiveness of modern science is that of *communication.* The need of a scientist to reveal his findings to the public scrutiny of his colleagues, and the need of scientists to know what others are doing, has always made imperative effective communication among scientists. Scientific societies, conferences, and scientific books and journals all serve in various ways to provide this necessary communication. Yet as scientists grow considerably in numbers across the world, and as publication in most established fields of research increases sharply, the problem of communication becomes very real.

Although computers have been utilized in order to create technical facilities for efficient storage and retrieval of information, there are still significant problems that can best be studied by those social scientists who have pioneered in communication as a social process. Scientists have periodically innovated new forms of communication as the structure of science itself changed. Scientific journals came into being in the middle of the seventeenth century as a way of allowing both scientists and laymen to know what was going on. Not until much later did they become the medium for the publication of the short paper by the individual scientist, a development that is hardly more than a hundred years old.

Some of the most systematic effort to delineate the social process of communication in science has been carried out by the Bureau of Applied Social Research at Columbia University, particularly the work of Herbert Menzel.[12] Menzel has pointed out that face-to-face and interpersonal communication has become increasingly important in science, despite all the technological innovations for storage and retrieval. The intensity of specialization and the time lag in publication has encouraged many scientists to utilize interpersonal communication: to engage in face-to-face discussion with relevant colleagues, for which scientific conventions and conferences provide a useful setting. There has also been well developed in some specialties the "preprint," the privately circulated mimeographed paper. This would be, notes Kaplan, a reversion to

[12] Compare, for example, Herbert Menzel, "Flow of Information on Current Developments in Three Scientific Disciplines," *Federation Proceedings,* 16 (1957), 706–711.

the privacy of the seventeenth century; yet, he says, some biologists believe that this is just what has already happened in molecular biology.[13]

The Recruitment of Scientists   Science cannot continue unless it is able to recruit new members into its ranks, and the rapid expansion of science has made necessary a new emphasis on recruitment. How science recruits is also, then, a significant social process, and the selectivity of that recruitment then establishes the pattern of who becomes a scientist and what they are like.

We know almost nothing about the social origins of those being recruited into science now; what information we do have is about an older generation. At least until recently scientists came disproportionately from selected segments of American society. Neither the lowest nor the highest of social class levels contributed their proportion; rather, most scientists came from middle-class and particularly professional backgrounds. More specifically, a large proportion came from small towns and went to small, liberal arts colleges. Indeed, middle western and far western colleges have produced more scientists than have prestigeful Ivy League colleges. Similarly, large universities have produced less than small, church-related colleges. The church relation, however, has been specifically Protestant; Catholics have as yet produced far less than their proportionate share of scientists in the United States.

This pattern of educational and class recruitment to science has probably prevailed in American society from the nineteenth century until recently. But we know little about how it has changed. The intensified recruitment of scientists, particularly through government support of science education, may very well broaden the selection process. The religious differential may lessen as Catholic education changes to provide better science instruction and to look more positively on the scientific career—and as more Catholics reach a middle-class level of education and aspiration.

If the enlargement of the scientific profession necessarily alters its recruitment process, and if a scientific career is increasingly rewarding in such conventional terms as income and class status (though also increasingly bureaucratized), we can anticipate changes, not only in who chooses to be a scientist but perhaps in the very ethos of science, particularly as these changes are exemplified in the conduct of the individual scientist. To understand the social nature of science now clearly requires new data on the origins of a new generation of scientists. Such data are yet lacking in any sufficiently large and representative sample that would permit us to make any generalizations. Nonetheless, our anticipation of significant change is upheld by several recent doctoral dissertations, which though based upon rather small and local samples, nonetheless give support to the hypothesis that there have been significant changes

[13] Kaplan, "Sociology of Science," p. 859.

in the values and attitudes of the newer generation of recruits to the scientific life.[14]

Basic and Applied Science   No analysis of the organization of science can ignore the distinction between basic and applied scientific research, not merely because it is a fundamental aspect of organization in science, but because it is also something of a problem, particularly for American science. Logically and historically, the distinction is one between "pure" research concerned with advancing fundamental, theoretical knowledge, and "practical" research that is intended to apply already existing basic scientific knowledge to the solution of practical problems.

Within science itself there is an important status distinction on this issue. Basic research is more prestigeful than applied, and some basic scientists are quite disdainful of applied scientists and engineers. Their assumption is that applied scientists depend completely upon basic science, and thus that technology rests exclusively upon science, so that advances in technology are only possible after advances in science. But this is an incomplete and inaccurate reading of the historical and contemporary record. The relationship between technology and science is one of mutual interaction and influence, rather than of one being wholly dependent on the other. Although technology does in fact advance by applying scientific principles to practical problems, its own successes often contribute in unanticipated ways to the advance of basic science.

This is unmistakably clear from the earlier historical record, where many times scientific advance was aided by technological development. Inventors of an earlier period rarely were applying any science at all; they tinkered until they made something work, though they rarely understood the scientific basis of it. Although many scientists would acknowledge that the scientifically untutored inventor contributed immeasurably to science in the past, they would claim that this is unlikely to be the case now. But it is still true that the inventor sometimes precedes the scientist. The distinguished scientist, Jerome B. Weisner, in *Where Science and Politics Meet*, attributed such a recent invention as the vacuum tube to inventors "who have an understanding of a scientific field."[15] But Eric Larrabee points out that this is not true; it was not Lee de Forest, the inventor, but the late Edwin H. Armstrong, who, in a series of subsequent papers, made clear what were the scientific principles involved, thus opening up for development the vast field of electronics.

This lesser status that scientists accord applied research has significant consequences for the organization of science. One is that the most creative

---

[14] Kaplan, p. 863.

[15] Larrabee, "Science and the Common Reader," p. 47.

minds in science tend to avoid the industrial laboratories and the applied career. Thus, the basic scientists tend to congregate in the universities, where almost all basic research is carried on.

The Allocation of Resources   The scientific community struggles constantly against the undoubted preference for applied research of the business community and sometimes government as well. Unless basic scientists can successfully make the case for the prior importance of basic research, an imbalance of support, even within the university, is likely to occur. There is thus a strain within science about the allocation of funds for basic and applied research, and a strain between science and those groups in business and government that allocate such resources. Despite the vastly increased support for science in the postwar world, the large part of such funds goes for applied work. Basic research in universities still receives but a small part of the total budget for science: it has always had less than 10 percent of all money spent for scientific research. Industry allocates as much as 97 percent of its research funds for applied research. As a consequence, the claim that basic research is undersupported is heard frequently, and some of the leadership in science claim that the share of funds for basic research has proportionately declined, and that good men go inadequately supported. The new importance of science has not appreciably lessened the tension over the relative support for basic and applied science.

The Scientific Community   The existence of a major ethos in science and the serious and dedicated commitment of individual scientists to it suggests that each generation of scientists receives more than a technical training. Rather, they are effectively *socialized* by older scientists into a moral and intellectual community of scientists. The socialization of the scientist in graduate training has not been studied, though the socialization of the physician is possibly comparable and undoubtedly provides suggestive insights. Graduate work is organized around the ongoing research of scientists, and this permits the individual scientist to be both researcher and teacher, senior colleague and mentor. By such an intimate process of close and congenial interaction, the student grows into the role of scientist, imbued with its values and sharing in its moral outlook, usually with little if any explicit instruction on such matters.

The existence of a scientific community that reaches across national boundaries reveals no bureaucratic structure, nor is there any easily defined hierarchy of organization. Rather, there is a loose and somewhat diffuse organizational pattern of scientific societies and associations, journals and conferences, and academically located honor societies, such as the prestigeful Sigma Xi. The vast majority of scientific organizations are the disciplinary ones that represent the particular scientific specialty. Given the increased rate of specialization, these organizations have proliferated in recent decades. The creation of such an organization gives some pattern of formal structure and some visible organization to the particular scientific specialty, and it readily enhances identification of specialists and their interaction and communication by means of journals and conferences sponsored by such societies.

In contrast to disciplinary societies an organization such as the American Association for the Advancement of Science functions to link together all these specialized groups into a general confederation of science and thus, by its very activity, protect and promote the healthy development of all science. The state academies of science perform a similar function at the state level, though much less effectively.

At the same time any sociological analysis of science must recognize the limitation of formal organizational structure: it does not make visible the informal hierarchy of scientific reputation and the inner circle or identifiable elite who are recognized by their peers as doing the important scientific work. Nor does it give recognition to a real if informal ranking of departments in terms of their reputation, within their own scientific community, for excellence in training scientists.

SCIENCE AND THE POLITY

For long periods of time in the history of science in the Western world, the scientist was relatively removed from the practical political affairs of his society. The roles of scientist and politician rarely led to any direct interaction. The more cloistered environment of the university served effectively to shield each from the other; the scientist, living in an academic world, has probably been less concerned with the larger world than any other academic. The politician, in turn, found little reason to stray upon the university campus, and if he did, he was unlikely to have any reason to be concerned with scientists.

The effort to determine the psychological make-up—the personality structure —of the most gifted of creative physical scientists supports this idea that scientists have been relatively isolated from the political world. Creative scientists have often been so obsessively absorbed in their work that other aspects of their life, even their family, tend to be neglected. By ordinary standards, then, they are relatively asocial. Ann Roe, one of the foremost students of the psychology of scientists, says these creative scientists are un-gregarious and "their interpersonal relations are generally of low intensity."[16]

[16] Ann Roe, "The Psychology of the Scientist," in Paul Obler and Herman A. Estrin, ed., *The New Scientist: Essays on the Method and Values of Modern Science* (New York: Doubleday, 1962), p. 91.

She adds that scientists "dislike interpersonal controversy in any form and are especially sensitive to interpersonal aggression."[17] David McClelland's careful effort to delineate the psychological characteristics of physical scientists from an analysis of varying studies supports these particular generalizations.[18]

The case of Robert Oppenheimer during the McCarthy period seemed to provide an individual confirmation of much of this. This highly gifted and exceptionally articulate scientist had been one of the leaders in the war-time atomic researches (he had been director of the Los Alamos Laboratory), but in 1953 his security clearance was lifted, not because he was personally disloyal, but because he had associated with and even been friends with others accused of being Communists. In a long letter answering the charges, Oppenheimer, speaking of his life in the 1930s, acknowledged that during that decade he did not read about economics or politics, nor did he even read a newspaper or a magazine like *Time* or *Harper's*. He had neither a telephone nor a radio, and he did not vote in a presidential election until he was thirty-two. He was, he acknowledged, "almost wholly divorced from the contemporary scene."

The seeming political innocence of the physical scientists, and perhaps particularly for the most creative of them, is much harder to sustain now, and Francis Bello's study of the new generation of scientists suggests that this is no longer the case.[19] It could hardly be; the political world impinges unceasingly and pervasively upon the world of science. Major political and military decisions now have significant scientific aspects, and major decisions about the funding of scientific research have serious political and military repercussions.

Science is now so interwoven with other major institutional structures of modern society that its very autonomy is subject to redefinition. Modern society is now heavily dependent upon science, and indeed could not dispense with science. It is in fact a society that science has helped to shape; a modern technology that has touched the lives of all and profoundly disturbed and rearranged the social structure is a direct consequence of scientific exploration. But it is equally true that the high evaluation of science by society has profoundly altered the place of science. It has moved from the university campus into industrial and governmental laboratories, and scientists are increasingly participating in decisions that are only partly scientific.

There are two significant aspects that clearly alter the older pattern of a highly autonomous and politically remote science. One is that a modern society now sees in science a major instrumentality for solving problems of military power, food production, physical disease, and the like, and thus has

[17] Roe, p. 91.

[18] David McClelland, "On the Psychodynamics of Creative Physical Scientists," in H. E. Gruber, G. Terrall, and M. Wertheimer, eds., *Contemporary Approaches to Creative Thinking* (New York: Atherton Press, 1962), pp. 141–174.

[19] Francis Bello, "The Young Scientists," in Obler and Estrin, *The New Scientist*, pp. 62–81.

attempted to harness science more closely than ever before to national policy. The other is that scientific knowledge and technology are so closely involved in military and political decisions that scientists now assume new roles of administrators and advisors that require judgments that are not only technical but also political and moral.

Science and National Policy No modern society today can be without a policy on science, for science is too important to be left to its own autonomous processes or to a haphazard development. In addition modern societies now invest heavily both in scientific research and in scientific education. The encouragement of young talent to develop into scientists has been paramount in American society for almost two decades. Congress established the National Science Foundation, which is an agency for supporting various kinds of scientific education and also for providing funds for scientific research. But governmental support of research comes from a whole variety of governmental agencies, including the military establishment.

This governmental support for scientific education has been intended to increase the supply of scientists. There is abundant evidence that the occupation of scientists undergoes immense expansion in modern society, and new ways must be devised to increase the supply and improve the training. Government becomes a partner in this process. But this has had as yet unmeasured repercussions on science. New patterns of recruitment and a vastly enlarged scientific profession now mean that the scientist is likely to be quite different in social origins and psychological characteristics than he was in previous generations. Bello's small study gives us some significant clues that such is the case.

But perhaps a more important social consequence of governmental involvement is that governmental subsidization of science means that others besides scientists have an impact upon the direction of scientific research. When a government amply funds one kind of scientific problem and not another, it affects the disposition of scientific talent and thus the development of science. Kaplan put it this way: ". . . the 'market place of ideas' determining choice of scientific problems is rapidly being replaced by a deliberate attempt to link the goals of society with the research goals of science."[20] Scientists are not compelled to study what the government thinks important, but they find it easier to gain financial support—and remember that research in the physical sciences is highly expensive—if they choose to work in those areas of scientific endeavor that are consonant with national policy. The one significant generalization warranted here is that the progress of science now depends quite heavily on convincing political and military elites about where to put funds

[20] Kaplan, "Sociology of Science," p. 871.

for scientific effort. These decisions are then not scientific and technical ones; they are political and moral judgments about the relevance of science for urgent human affairs. And the major difficulty, from the point of view of science, is that nonscientists frequently want scientific research that has direct applicability to practical affairs, failing to appreciate the importance of basic research designed only to advance scientific theory without regard for any immediate application.

The Scientist's Political Roles   Another major consequence of the new place of science in modern society has been to impose upon many scientists, and particularly the leadership of science, new roles that are essentially political. A government increasingly needing scientific advice as one aspect of crucial decisions about military and diplomatic action has turned to scientists for that advice. Indeed, there has been some institutionalization of this advisory role in the creation of numerous advisory boards and committees to governmental agencies and offices, and an official provision for consultative roles for scientists. During the 1950s a Special Assistant to the President for Science and Technology was appointed, and this was followed by the President's Science Advisory Committee.

Ideally, scientists are presumed to advise on matters that are within their technical competence, but experience with the hydrogen bomb, atomic power, and the radiation fallout and testing controversy in the 1950s suggests that these technical matters are often inseparable from political and moral issues. In addition, some scientists have not hesitated to speak out in moral terms, with the result that they have often been in the position of publicizing quite contradictory advice.

However, there is another kind of role that may very well have as much influence on science as the one above: the role of the scientific advisor on those decisions about how government can advance science. A modern government that wants to use science extensively knows that it also has to support science. It is here that the scientific advisor becomes a political emissary from the scientific community to the government, bringing the position of scientists about what should be done and what is needed in strengthening science: science education; recruitment of scientists; participation in international conferences; and investment in various new areas of scientific exploration.

The organization of science is influenced by this development. For one thing, its political emissaries develop an "inside" relationship to government with implications of political power, and a new establishment begins to emerge that has as one dimension of its structure a close relationship to government. A leadership role in science now is open as much on the basis of this political role as on the basis of prestige based on scientific achievement. When scientists are actually co-opted to become administrators of federal programs, or to constitute boards that allocate federal funds, new structures of a more centralized power develop within science.

All these postwar developments suggest that the institution of science is no longer remote from the political institutions of modern society. Its highly prized autonomy has been reduced, though this degree of loss has been paid for by allowing science to share in power and prestige and to obtain a vastly increased quota of material resources for its own use.

What we know about the complex problems involved in the new and closer relations between science and government has as yet come largely from some few perceptive scientists who have had some of these experiences, or from the work of political scientists, such as Don Price and R. Gilpin, rather than from the analyses of sociologists interested in a sociology of science. This dimension —the relation of science and polity—remains a vast frontier for sociological exploration. What is most significant is that the experiences since World War II have gone far to reshape the institution of science and to draw science close to the major power structures of modern society. Not only science but also modern society is affected by this change; just how is what yet needs to be spelled out.

This increasing involvement of scientists in the political processes of the society has rarely seen scientists in the role of social and political critic of society; in most cases they have participated on ideological terms congenial to the military and political leaders. In recent years this uncritical ideological orientation of scientists has been subject to considerable criticism, particularly since the onset of the war in Vietnam. One development that reflects a significant change in the relation of science to society is the emergence of such an organization as the Federation of Atomic Scientists. Its origin was in the moral concerns of atomic scientists engaged in research at atomic energy research laboratories during World War II. The terribly destructive potential of atomic energy, when harnessed to war uses, disturbed them, more so when the first atom bomb fell on Hiroshima. What activated the organization, specifically, was the unfamiliar (for scientists) task of organizing a scientists' lobby in Washington in 1945 to oppose the May-Johnson bill, which would have put control of atomic energy into the hands of the military. Since then the Federation has published the influential *Bulletin of the Atomic Scientists,* a monthly periodical that provides an intellectual forum for a wide range of issues having to do with the freedom of science and the responsible and humane uses of scientific knowledge. The *Bulletin* constitutes an intellectual bridge between scientists and other scholars concerned about the control and use of science in the modern world and such problems as radiation, disarmament, pollution, and the relationship of science to government and the military.

The common culture of values and world view that scientists manifest seems to be a knowledge of the natural world and a perspective on life that few other intellectuals share, or for that matter, even understand. This is the theme pursued by C. P. Snow, a British scientist and novelist, whose *The Two Cultures and the Scientific Revolution* stirred a world-wide intellectual debate when it was first published in 1959.[21] By two cultures Snow meant the culture of science, on the one hand, and the culture of literary intellectuals, on the other. These he saw as being the polar opposite of one another. This was why he spoke of two cultures, not because he did not recognize that there were still other cultures, as some critics have suggested.

Snow has been neither the first nor the only one to point to a gap between these two major intellectual groups in modern society. But as that singular rarity, a man both scientist *and* novelist, Snow felt he possessed an understanding of both cultures from within. He felt that "the intellectual life of the whole of western society is increasingly being split into two polar groups."[22]

Snow describes these two groups as encapsulated in their own culture worlds and amazingly ignorant of each other's. Scientist's, he argues, do not know the world of literary culture, and literary intellectuals do not have even a glimmer of understanding of the world of science. From his own experience and knowledge he documents this ignorance on both sides. A careful reading of his book—which was originally a lecture—suggests strongly that Snow, on this matter, sided somewhat more with the scientists than he did with the others. He makes it clear that an ignorance of science is more than deplorable, it is dangerous for the future of mankind. The sin of the scientists, in turn, that of being too ignorant of the great traditional culture of the West, seems to hold no such dire consequences.

Snow stresses one reason for the literary antipathy to science: the idea that the nonscientific intellectuals have never understood nor accepted the Industrial Revolution. "Intellectuals, in particular literary intellectuals, are natural Luddites."[23] Snow sketches the history of European intellectual opposition to and dislike of the Industrial Revolution. These intellectuals did not understand it to be one of the two great revolutions that had transformed the world—the other being the agricultural revolution, when men first learned to domesticate animals and raise crops.

[21] C. P. Snow, *The Two Cultures and the Scientific Revolution* (New York: Cambridge, 1961).

[22] Snow, p. 4.

[23] Snow, p. 23.

It is here that Snow clearly takes his stand, for he believes that "industrial-ization is the only hope of the poor."[24] Thus, he opts for industrialization and technology and the science that makes this possible. More than that, he sees in the scientific revolution of modern, electronic technology, a potential force for eliminating the great gap between rich and poor that now plagues the world. By seeing a primarily positive contribution coming from the techno-logical development that science makes possible, and in opting for an improved education that produces more scientists and makes everyone scientifically lit-erate, Snow is pressing for a solution that is the scientist's answer to the problem.

The Scientist's Commitment   For at least a century now the scientific com-munity in the Western world has shared with many others a view of the world that is rational and critical yet does not reject that world. As Barber's earlier discussion made clear (and as Snow's argument strongly supports), the scientific community has been reformist and has believed in progress. Scien-tists have strongly supported the effort to devote rationality and scientific knowledge to the task of solving human problems. But it is equally clear that, as a community, they have not been radical. They have had no basic and unresolvable quarrel with the society that has supported them. Science's col-lective posture has always been moderate, not militant, liberal, not radical, and reforming, not revolutionary. Until recently, at least, it has been strongly apolitical—though equally remote from the business and religious institutions of society.

Thus, the scientific community has had no fundamental quarrel with a society that has been giving great scope to and greater support for science and that has been reshaped by that science. It has certainly not rejected the extensive public funding of scientific research. Its basic commitment, then, has been to the use of scientific rationality to solve particular problems of material and physical well-being and thus to improve the lot of man within the pattern of an ever more rational and scientifically controlled society. It is most simply, *optimistic* in its basic outlook.

The Pessimism of Art   But the world view of art over the past century has not been an optimistic assessment of the condition of man; rather, it has been pessimistic to the point of despair. Its failure to understand science is a serious deficiency in a scientific world, but this is a symptom of its position, not the cause. The recognition that the world is becoming increasingly rationalized—more and more calculable, planned, and unspontaneous, and in that sense, less free—appears in nineteenth century literature at least by the middle

[24] Snow, p. 27.

decades, just as it appeared in some philosophical discourses. Literary intellectuals were repelled, not so much by the ugliness of industrialism, as by its relentless intent toward uniformity, manipulation, and rationalized bureaucratic control, producing a diminished spirit they felt could not survive successive onslaughts that came from every quarter of society. Science, from this perspective, was the servant of the bureaucrat and the new modern politician. The scientist was not only partner to the crime, he was its intellectual godfather.

It is not a question of whether there is truth in the literary case against science, or whether this is an irrational and misguided romanticism. What is important, *sociologically,* is that generations of men of literary talent for over a century now have built an established rage against this ever more scientific and rational society; it has engendered in them a deepened sense of disenchantment with the world and a mood of despair rather than hope. They are one with Max Weber in despairing about the future of man in a thoroughly rationalized world, yet seeing no reason to believe that the course of history could be altered, not even by the unremitting rage of their unceasing and denunciatory protest.

What is at issue here for the sociologist of science, and for other sociologists, too, is a sociological problem of immense scope. How can we state it? At the outset it must be recognized that the intellectual gap between science and the literary mind is not a matter of ignorance (though ignorance on both sides may complicate the matter), but rather of two radically opposed ways of viewing the world. The viewpoint of science is abstract, analytical, and piecemeal, and it is *value-free,* approaching all phenomena with the single intention of viewing them objectively and with no value-preference about them. But the artist and the humanistic intellectual is more likely to view the world in holistic, concrete, and situational terms, and with no intention to be value-free but instead with an approach freighted with emotion and with an intensity of emotional response and organized by a distinctly moral outlook. The world-view of science is congruent with much of a technologically and bureaucratically organized world, which looks to science, not literature, for its standards and norms. The literary mind rejects that same world and rebels against it.

Nor does the problem remain only within these dimensions. There is a further implication of enormous significance: that the intellectual community is fragmented and disunited. The modern world does not possess an intellectual *community,* but instead a number of discordant camps, where competing *Weltanschauungs* offer irreconcilable interpretations of modern life. The alienated and despairing view which today often expresses itself in an existentialist vocabulary springs from the literary world; but the scientific community offers no sense of kindred appreciation. It is not alienated, and no longer is it even as detached as it once was. Its rationality and sense of order and its universalism make it highly critical of specific actions and established interests, but it sees no reason to lose hope for modern society. It remains critical yet optimistic.

Perhaps, then, it is the task of the sociologist of knowledge, rather than the sociologist of science to seek to understand how there could be two such opposed cultural mentalities that look at the same world and see it from such irreconcilable perspectives. The problem is immense and urgent, yet its outlines have only begun to be grasped; it still awaits a precise and encompassing sociological definition.

Like other scientists, C. P. Snow did not understand the sense of oppression that modern society engendered in humanist intellectuals. Cesar Grana, in the last words of his book, stated the issue as well as we now can:

> The problem of a scientific versus a literary culture reaches, therefore, into much more intractable areas than those suggested by Sir Charles P. Snow. It is not merely a question of a vain and superstitious disregard for science or the provincialism of humanists who refuse to accept the enormous managerial problems of the modern world, or of the willful social obscurantism of the romantic mind. It is a question of the essential impact of an ever more rationalized mode of existence upon the life-space available to some of the oldest forms of human imagination. If a scientifically intended society means putting human experience on a flat, well-lit plane which leads in a straight line toward a perennially deliberate future, the literary mind may be said to represent in its most rebellious form a case of intellectual fatigue before the secular version of infinity.[25]

---

[25] Cesar Grana, *Bohemian Versus Bourgeois: French Society and the French Man of Letters in the Nineteenth Century* (New York: Basic Books, 1964), pp. 208–209.

1. Priest with slum children.
2. A sign in a New York slum area.
3. Pope Paul VI appealing for peace at the United Nations.
4. A Jewish family lights Chanukah candles.
5. The entire congregation of a Quaker church (1939).
6. Martin Luther King at the Los Angeles World Affairs Council.

4

5

6

RELIGION
AND SOCIETY

18

From the beginning of time, men have stood in awe and wonder before the majesty of nature. They have pondered over birth and felt dread at the prospect of death. Unlike the animals that populate nature, men are always aware that life went on before them and will go on after them. They are the only living creatures to recognize their own mortality and anticipate death. Consequently, in all human societies men have collectively shared a sense of awe and reverence before something that seems to transcend the ordinary and mundane, an ultimate that is beyond human ken. A sense of the *sacred* seems to emerge from this collective experience of men, one consequence of their effort to understand what cannot be explained by categories of thought that apply to the ordinary and profane aspects of life.

This inchoate sense of sacredness takes concrete form in objects and images that become sacred, whether these are persons, animals or natural objects, human artifacts, or symbolic expressions. The sacred also becomes conveyed and expressed for the living in *ritual,* where behavior gives objective form to mood and feeling. A division between the sacred and the profane, then, characterizes a universal human response, and the collectively shared symbolic form that this sacred aspect takes is religion.

Emile Durkheim defined religion as "a unified system of beliefs and practices relative to sacred things, that is to say, to things set apart and forbidden . . .,"—which beliefs and practices, he notes, unite those who share in them into a "single moral community."[1] But a comparison of religions in all known societies soon reveals that systematic belief, or theology, is not a universal component and thus not a basis for defining religion. This lack of doctrine or dogma does not imply a lack of meaning; it is, rather, a question of how that meaning is expressed. Not even a belief in a supernatural God, as in Christianity, is universal. In contrast to the Christian concern for belief and dogma, many other religions are characterized by an emphasis upon ritual, with the meaning of that ritual often being quite imprecise and varied. Ritual, then, seems to be the most universal aspect of religion.

Ritual is not to be regarded as simply formal and prescribed behavior. However formalized it may become, ritual stands apart from mundane behavior by its capacity to convey attitudes and emotions of sacredness. It has meaning and thus there is belief, even though this belief may not always be systematized into an orthodox doctrine. The sharing of ritual provides a common experience that is an affirmation of shared meanings and thus shared values; it affirms one's belonging to a community of others whose lives encounter the same hazards and problems.

As the most universal element of religion, ritual is a set of acts of symbolic expression concerned with the "ultimate" and the "transcendental" as these

---

[1] Emile Durkheim, *The Elementary Forms of the Religious Life,* trans. Joseph Ward Swain (New York: Free Press, 1947), p. 47.

manifest themselves in human experience. Therefore, interpreting ritual as symbolic suggests that what is universal is not ritual but the symbolism of the sacred, though ritual is probably the most common form of this symbolic process. Religion, then, can be defined as ". . . a set of symbolic forms and acts which relate man to the ultimate conditions of his existence."[2]

The lack of any systematic belief is typically characteristic of the religions of primitive people. Where the major religions of modern societies are concerned, however, a systematically articulated belief that becomes an orthodoxy is a significant dimension of religion; and being a conscious believer in a community of believers is an important aspect of the religious experience. It is notable that those who withdraw and cease to be members of the religious group are defined as nonbelievers who have "lost their faith." Modern man clearly sees religion in terms of a primary emphasis upon belief.

The Sociology of Religion   From the outset of the discipline sociologists insisted upon the importance of religion as a significant feature of society. Religion was studied in its social context to understand the significance of religious belief for the solidarity of human society and the ethical patterning of economic behavior. The sociological study of religion is not the study of religion, per se, but the study of the relation of religion to society. Like society, religion is a human enterprise, religion as *belief* is a major dimension of human culture, whereas religion as *social institution* has reference to the organized pattern of religious behavior that is often viewed as functioning to sustain society. Religion as *social structure* emphasizes that religion is invariably *organized* religion, appearing as churches and sects, revival meetings and worship services. Furthermore, all societies recognize religious *roles:* priests and ministers, missionaries, monks, bishops, prophets, and evangelists.

Whatever its orientation, religion is always in society, and its members are also members of other groups and institutions. There are myriad ways in which religion reflects the society of which it is a part, and there are significant ways in which religion influences that same society. The concern for that reciprocal process—the influence of religion on society and society on religion—is what the sociology of religion is all about.

THE PROBLEM OF RELIGION IN SOCIETY

An inquiry into the meaning of religion for society, we suggested, has been central to sociology since its beginning, and such major figures as Weber and Durkheim gave a great deal of attention to the importance of religion for

[2] Robert Bellah, "Religious Evolution," *American Sociological Review,* 29 (June, 1964), 359.

human affairs. Despite this central place of religion in the sociological tradition, however, American sociologists have somewhat neglected the sociology of religion, and only a very small body of empirical studies have accumulated over the years. Although there has recently been a renewed interest in religion among sociologists, it still stands as one of the lesser concerns of sociologists.

Undoubtedly, the first great concern about religion by sociologists started less with a *problem* and more with an *assumption:* that religion was necessary for society, for it welded people together by their sharing of a common conception of the sacred—religion, in short, was socially unifying. This approach to religion was basic to defining religion as a *social institution* and emerged rather naturally from the extensive studies of primitive and ancient religion in the nineteenth century, studies not primarily by sociologists, but by anthropologists, classicists, and other scholars. What is involved here is the famous *functional* issue: that religion is functional for society because it provides a source of moral unity in creating a common religious experience that binds people to their society. As long as this was assumed, and as long as studies were primarily of primitive and ancient religion, most studies merely sought to describe a particular religion in a particular society and to show how it created social unity. The issue became sociologically problematic, however, when the attention of sociologists turned to religion in modern society. There it was not at all self-evident that religion promoted social cohesion, or indeed that it was functionally relevant for modern society.

Whatever the content of religious belief or the pattern of religious ritual, *a* religion (in contrast to religion in general) is carried on by its members within some pattern of social organization. The common and enduring relations of its members evolve into a structure. Sociologists have been interested in this structure. The major work has been that concerned with delineating types of religious structures: church, sect, denomination, and the like, and the specific relation of each type to society.

The structure of society, in turn, has considerable relevance for religious belief and organization. Specifically, the stratification system of a society, at least modern society, seems to have major bearing upon religion. A pattern of belief and organization that attracts the middle class often repels the lower class; the loss of the working classes by organized religion, particularly in Western Europe and Latin America, is central to one of the crises of contemporary Christianity: its lack of relevance for those lowest in the class structure of modern society. More prosaically, the stratification system affects religion in that churches seem to draw disproportionately from specific social classes, and as a result, religion is influenced in subtle ways by the social class of its communicants.

Max Weber's sociological interest in religion focused on a problem basic to all sociology: the relation of ideas to behavior. Weber centered on religious ideas and sought to demonstrate their effect upon economic behavior. In this way he examined religion as a *cultural* phenomenon—a system of beliefs and values—that influenced behavior. Other work in this vein has sought to explore the way in which religion provides cultural meanings that are significant for nonreligious spheres of life.

But the decline in the modern world in the capacity of religion to provide an overarching symbolic structure of integrating meanings has turned sociological attention to the process of *secularization,* that social process most significant to what religion now is and can become in the future.

These, then, are the major problematic issues around which sociological inquiry has been pursued: (1) the functions of religion; (2) the organization of religion; (3) religion and stratification; (4) religion as culture; and (5) secularization. These several concerns have contained, as yet, the major work that the sociologists of religion have done in the past and are doing now.

THE FUNCTIONAL INTERPRETATION

Of all possible ways to understand the connection between religion and society the *functional* interpretation has been the dominant one. It emerged from a nineteenth century dissatisfaction with the effort to explain (and largely debunk) religion in rational terms; the question was changed from whether a religion was true to what was its function for an ongoing society. In *The Elementary Forms of Religious Life* Emile Durkheim gave the fullest exposition of this, though his work along this line was preceded by the brilliant student of Semitic society, William Robertson Smith, and followed by the work of such anthropologists as A. R. Radcliffe-Brown and Bronislaw Malinowski.

The functional interpretation asserts that every society has a number of necessary conditions that it must successfully meet in order to survive, and one of these is the cohesion or solidarity of its members. Religion is perceived as a universal aspect of human society by providing moral cohesion; it is the *integrative* and *legitimating* institution. This theory of the integration of human society by religion rests largely on the observation of primitive and other traditional societies, where the sharing in a common religion by all the members of that society served to bring the symbolism of the sacred into support of the more mundane aspects of social life. The sharing of the same relation to the supernatural and of the same religious interpretation of the meaning of life, united a people in a cohesive and binding moral order. But these people were also members of the same society; the religious order and the social order had the same members. The integration of society is clearly easier to sustain when a society is underpinned by a moral order, the ultimate values of which are ritualistically expressed in a religion shared in common by the members of that society. From this perspective, religion is the *legitimating* institution in a society; it provides a sacred sanction for the institutionalized order and for the values and meanings given objective form in those institutions.

Such an interpretation of religion fits the traditional, undifferentiated societies in which, in fact, all members of the society share the same religious belief and are largely involved in the same pattern of life. In these societies, the religious and the nonreligious spheres of life are not sharply differentiated; religious rites, for example, may be within the family or kinship group, or they may be public rites closely related to daily activities of the community. But in complex, highly differentiated societies religion and society are not synonymous. The emergence of different modes of life-experience leads to different meanings about life, producing a religious differentiation to accompany social differentiation. The all-encompassing church gives way to competing religious groups, when there is the freedom for this, or to sullen withdrawal from the church when this is not possible.

The history of Europe and of Asia, of Christianity and of the several Asiatic religions, testifies to the capacity of religions to be in strife among themselves; religious wars are invariably brutal and bloody contests, for the commitment of religion can lead men to struggle to the death, as well as to put the "infidels" to death. Although generally accompanied by less violence, religion has also come into conflict with civil authority, and learned to use quite secular power in such a struggle. In such circumstances as these, religion is not integrative; instead, it is an index of a social disintegration, of a break in existing social solidarity, or even, in a modern society, the lack of an inclusive social cohesion.

Religion as Social Control   A somewhat different though nonetheless comparable function for religion is that of social control. This is the now ancient observation that religious belief can work to keep people within the bounds of the social order. Whether it be the fear of hell and brimstone, as prevailed for so long in Christianity, or the injunction to do good works, religious belief can clearly influence the daily behavior of its believers. The recognition that religion can thus control human behavior and keep people "in line" makes it a useful instrument for ruling classes, and throughout history these classes have appreciated religion's utility, its instrumental value, regardless of their evaluation of religion in any other terms. Louis Schneider quotes F. E. Manuel that even skeptics and atheists in the eighteenth century recognized that "religion was a mechanism which inspired terror, but terror useful for the preservation of society. . . ."[3] In short, religion was regarded as a useful discipline of the masses and an effective control of the working classes.

---

[3] Louis Schneider, "Problems in the Sociology of Religion," in Robert E. L. Faris, ed., *Handbook of Modern Sociology* (Chicago: Rand McNally), p. 783.

That religion could serve the vested interests of dominant classes has been recognized by religious and nonreligious alike, but, more to the point, by both conservatives and radicals. Conservatives, of course, have valued religion positively for this protective function, but radicals have found in this a strong reason for seeing in religion a bulwark of the established order. Friedrich Engels once noted that the bourgeoisie in England shared with the ruling classes an interest in "keeping in subjection the great working mass of the nation."[4] This makes evident what Lenin meant when he said that religion was the opiate of the masses. He recognized that religious belief could keep the exploited classes from rebelling against their exploiters.

Religion as Psychotherapy   The use of religion to control the masses is an ancient function, but in twentieth century America there is another way in which religion is viewed instrumentally and is seen as possessing utilitarian value. That is the use of religion as a supporting psychology, a form of psychotherapy. Religion is viewed in upbeat terms, and God is conceived of as a humane and considerate God; such a hopeful perspective turns away from the older Christian conception of a stern and demanding God.

This "psychologizing" of religion has created an Americanized religion (as Louis Schneider and Sanford M. Dornbusch have called it) for which someone like Norman Vincent Peale with his "power of positive thinking" serves as a typical example. Such religion means a positive outlook and never negative thinking. It provides a source of peace of mind and peace of soul, promises prosperity and success in life, as well as effective and happy human relations. It is thus a source of security and confidence, of happiness and success *in this world.* Schneider and Dornbusch have undertaken a study of such "inspirational religion" through a content analysis of forty-six books that covered a period from 1875 to 1955.[5] The very time period revealed that the pattern has been a persistent one in American life, and that there has long been a market for such inspirational literature. Such recent best-selling authors as Peter Marshall, Norman Vincent Peale, and Fulton J. Sheen carry on the work of a preceding generation marked by such well-known names as Emmet Fox, Elton Trueblood, and Bruce Barton, on back to Hannah W. Smith, whose *The Christian Secret of a Happy Life* was first published in 1875.

The Limitations of Functional Religion   The functional interpretation of religion has contributed a great deal to understanding religion as a *social* phenomenon and as an *institution* of human society. But it makes its best case in the study of primitive religion, or at least religion in traditional societies. Its emphasis

[4] Karl Marx and Friedrich Engels, *On Religion* (Moscow: Foreign Language Publishing House, 1955), p. 303.
[5] Louis Schneider and Sanford M. Dornbusch, *Popular Religion* (Chicago: University of Chicago Press, 1958).

upon the presumed *integrative* function of religion leads to the question of what religion does for society, implying that it matters not what people believe as long as they believe the same thing, for religion integrates when there is common belief. Thus, however unintentionally, religion becomes trivialized, and the agonized concern of religious intellectuals over significant issues in meaning and faith then become opaque to the functional view. Louis Schneider cogently notes (in speaking of the instrumental view of religion in contrast to a view of an uncompromisingly stern and demanding God who could not be used for human ends) that "this is one of the many fields in which a sociology of religion willing to pose significant questions must take some account of theological positions."[6]

But contemporary stress on the instrumental value of religion may heighten our consciousness about religion as useful; it is no longer simply that it works that way without intent, but that the rational mind recognizes its function. What was latent (unintended) now becomes manifest (intended). Religion is deliberately utilized to serve us in this life for our earthly aspirations and goals. But, one can ask whether "it is possible to hold an instrumental view and yet adhere to authentic 'faith'" thus, "instrumentalization may be self-defeating."[7] Schneider quotes the penetrating remark by H. R. Niebuhr that "the instrumental value of faith for society is dependent upon faith's conviction that it has more than instrumental value."[8]

THE ORGANIZATION OF RELIGION

To the Western mind, religion is always socially organized, and thus faith and creed become institutionalized in social structures. The organization of religion makes possible social roles, such as priest and minister, that introduce a division of labor into the religious community, and thus create religious functionaries who assume specialized tasks both within the religious group and in relating the religious group to the society. Organization also creates hierarchy and authority within the group and makes possible the building of social power for the religious group within the society. Religious organization is also intermediate between the individual and his faith, and, indeed, may assume the task of mediating between God and the individual.

Church and Sect Sociologists of religion have long made use of a typology of religious organization developed by the German scholar Ernst Troeltsch,

[6] Louis Schneider, "Problems in the Sociology of Religion," pp. 786–787.
[7] Schneider, p. 786.
[8] Schneider, p. 787.

who distinguishes between *church* and *sect*.[9] (Since by *church*, Troeltsch meant something more limited than the general meaning usually conveyed by that term, we will follow the lead of other sociologists and substitute for it the Latin word, *ecclesia*.) For Troeltsch, the *ecclesia* is a form of religious organization characteristic of a religious movement in a late, mature state of development, whereas the sect, in turn, is a form that marks an early and more dynamic phase of its development. As a student of Christianity, Troeltsch viewed these in relation to Western society and was particularly interested in an interpretation that stressed Christianity as a religious *movement*, sometimes mature and settled and having come to terms with society, at other times in new dynamic phases that break with the established world.

The Ecclesia   This is a type of religious organization defined, fundamentally, by its acceptance of society in all its imperfections. The ecclesia does not fight society, nor does it withdraw. It is both *in* and *of* the world. Rather, the ecclesia seeks to control the world in behalf of its organization; thus, it seeks to be a power within the world. This leads it to engage in a close set of relationships with the secular institutions of the society, particularly the governmental.

A stress on its universality and inclusiveness helps us to understand why the ecclesia is oriented to the world and not away from it or against it. As a universal church, it defines as members all those born within a given territory; thus, it includes all members of society of all strata. This, in turn, leads to an emphasis upon a formal and hierarchical organization, a religious bureaucracy, with a chain of command from top to bottom, for the very inclusiveness of a large and diverse religious community requires large-scale organization. A variety of offices and leaders are developed in an ecclesia, for its complex set of relations to the secular world produces a divergent set of functions, only some of which are strictly religious. The priestly office is the central role of the ecclesia, the priest possesses authority sanctioned by the hierarchy and monopolizes the crucial function of administering the sacramental means of grace to the members of the faith.

By definition the ecclesia is a universal world church. But this is an ideal type which, as a pure case, is only approximated by actual existing churches. The Roman Catholic Church in the Middle Ages is perhaps the nearest historical approximation to the type, at least in the Western world. But since the Reformation the Catholic Church has less closely fitted the type. Nonetheless, it still approximates it closely enough to be called an ecclesia. The Anglican and Lutheran Churches, in turn, are examples of national ecclesia, in contrast to the international scope of the Roman Catholic Church.

[9] Ernst Troeltsch, *The Social Teachings of the Christian Churches* (New York: Macmillan, 1950).

The Sect   In striking contrast to the ecclesia the sect is typically a small and exclusive religious group whose members are not born into it but voluntarily join it. Its orientation to society is one of opposition, for sects are religious movements that reject the worldly society. Typically, they are *in* but not *of* the society. Sectarians are often hostile to the more established churches, rejecting and severely criticizing them for their worldly compromise. And they are sometimes also radical in their stance toward secular government; they may refuse to pay taxes, to bear arms, to serve in any civil or political capacity, or even to take oaths. Members of sects voluntarily choose to belong, and many sects may therefore count only adults as members. But those who choose to belong must be accepted on the rigorous terms set by the sect. Its discipline extends into the personal lives of members. What it lacks in controlling organization (and the sect develops only a rudimentary formal structure), it more than makes up in fervent commitment to a belief. Sectarians often set themselves apart from others by their acceptance of modes of behavior and a life-style that gives expressive manifestation of their beliefs.

Some sects take a militant posture toward the world, actively seeking to change it; the Anabaptists of the seventeenth century are an outstanding example of this. In its early years in England, in the decades just before and after the turn of the century, the Salvation Army was a notably militant sect. Other sects may be passive and withdrawing, seeking to remain as removed from society as possible. Such groups as the Old Order Amish in Pennsylvania and the Hutterites in the midwestern states and Canada are contemporary examples of such rejection of and withdrawal from the world.

Denomination and Cult   Sociologists concerned with the organization of religious groups have found it useful to elaborate the basic typology of Troeltsch by adding two other types: *denomination* and *cult.* The denomination is in between ecclesia and sect, it is a stable church that does not fight or withdraw from the world but unlike the ecclesia does not seek to control it, either. It is often large in number, complex in organization, and it recruits by birth. It lacks the fervid zeal of the sect and is no longer characterized, if it ever was, by a religious rejection of society. Denominations, in fact, are often sects that have made peace with the world. Frequently, this is because its members have moved from a disadvantaged or a marginal status to a respectable and conventional one. Now they are less critical of the world, and the sermons of their clergy lack the evangelical fire and zeal of old. They cooperate with the secular institutions and with civil authorities.

Denominations are not only former sects that have come to terms with a world they may have helped to change, and which in turn has changed them. Some denominations are former ecclesia that no longer have a monopoly status in the society. They may have no choice but to accept the status of denomination as a condition of their existence in the society. The ecclesia of Europe—such as the Roman Catholic Church, the Episcopal Church of England, and the Lutheran Church of Sweden—cannot have the same dominating status in the United States and must accept a status equivalent with other churches. They cannot possess the privileged status of being an established church.

The *cult*, in turn, is a small and almost formless religious organization, somewhat like the sect in that membership is voluntary. But the cult does not require the disciplined adherence to the group's religious values that a sect does. Cults appear most frequently in urban centers, where their appeal is often to those who feel lost and without a sense of belonging in the impersonality and anonymity of urban life. As a consequence the tie of the individual to the cult is weak and transitory, and there is often a high turnover in membership. There is no formal organization; rather, cults are usually organized around charismatic leaders.

Cults flourish in conditions of change and mobility, and are often to be found just where varied migrant populations have moved into cities. Cults flourished in Rome during the first centuries of the Roman Empire, when there were vast tenement sections of the city inhabited by varied foreign populations. So also in large American cities migrants who find themselves lonely and unattached in the strange and seemingly unfriendly city are excellent recruits for cults. Thus, cults flourish in slums and among minorities and can be found in abundance, for example, among the "store-front" churches in Negro areas. There they may preach a combination of Christianity mixed with varied exotic and mysterious ideas, perhaps drawn from other religions. The Black Muslims began in this way in Detroit in the 1930s.

But cults also appeal to middle-class groups in cities, who no less experience the pangs of loneliness and frustration. In this case a frequently more spiritualist appeal is made, one that offers an answer that asserts the existence of powers and forces science often denies. Some of these cults—such as Bahai, Psychiana, the "I Am" movement, Rosicrucianism, and Theosophy—have been successful in establishing themselves as spiritualist churches appealing to the urban middle class.

The Transition in Organization   The original distinction between church and sect that Troeltsch made was intended to conceptualize the idea that the form of religious organization is directly related to the position of the religious group in the society. Troeltsch fully appreciated the inherent tension between the sacred concerns of religion and the secular interests of society, and the fact that each informed and influenced the other. Religion constantly drew closer to society and then drew away. It accepted society, ignored it, or rejected it. Sects invariably drew their members from the less attached and more disadvantaged in society, so that religion always gives expression to the social experiences of groups and strata within society. Sects grow into denominations when there is change in the social status of their members; thus, the dissident religious groups are always gradually coming to terms with society, and tensions lessen as social status improves. But new sects and cults, too, constantly appear among those whom society materially and socially disadvantages, or among those who find life without a rewarding sense of meaning. There is thus constant religious movement, an increasing or lessening of tension between the sacred and the secular, between religion and society. Religion never completely embraces society, nor does it completely reject it. The several social types—ecclesia, denomination, sect, and cult—capture a sense of the structure that emerges in religious groups at different phases of their movement in relation to the secular world.

Whether sects, then, will become denominations depends both on the external social order and upon their religious definition of the world. The less rigidly stratified United States is a society in which the transition from sect to denomination occurs more easily and thus with greater frequency than in, say, the more rigidly stratified Britain. Sects interested in converting others are more likely—particularly if relatively successful—to change in the direction of a denomination than are sects that deny the secular world, practice separation from it, and do not permit conversion. When such separation leads to a highly distinctive life-style, marked by differences of speech, dress, and behavior, as among the Hutterites or Amish, there is even less probability of such a change.

Laity and Clergy   In any church there are varied ways in which the clergy and the congregation interact, but the very internal structure of the church greatly affects that interaction. In cults and sects the lack of a highly developed formal structure means that leadership is effective when it is charismatic. But denominations and ecclesia rely on well-organized church structures, with the careful placement of authority, which then tends to pattern the interaction of laity and clergy as well as create an internal power structure.

There are three major forms of internal government in Christian churches: *episcopal, presbyterian,* and *congregational.* In the episcopal structure authority is vested in a church hierarchy, with final and complete power vested in the person who holds the office at the top of the hierarchy. The position of the Pope and the hierarchy of the Roman Catholic Church is the best example of this, though the Anglican Church of England is also organized this way, as are some Protestant denominations. The priest in the episcopal system is appointed by and is responsible to only one superior officer, his bishop, and thus his power relative to his congregation is a strong one. He possesses locally the authority of the church, and he is in a position to resist local pressures. In the episcopal churches the lack of lay authority means that the congregation is expected to obey and accept the religious authority of the hierarchy.

The *presbyterian* structure, in turn, vests the governing power in a presbytery, or council of elders, which is made up almost entirely of ministers. There are no bishops or offices of supreme authority in such a governing structure, though there is some power in the local congregation. It can, for example, request the appointment of a preacher and can choose from among available candidates. The congregation, in turn, is subject to control by its own elders. Such a system balances power between laity and clergy, and places the individual clergyman in a sometimes difficult position between the presbytery and the congregation. It is a structure that often produces strong ministerial leaders.

The *congregational,* in turn, locates authority in the hands of the local congregation; whatever central organization it has is weak. The local congregation can conduct its own affairs without outside or superior interference. It also has complete control over its choice of minister, having the right to hire and fire as it chooses. This system requires that the minister be a democratic and conciliatory leader, who can work effectively with the several subgroups that make up the congregation. The loss of their pulpit by ministers in the South who displeased their white segregationist congregations is one of the more recent examples of what can happen in such a religious power structure.

These formal structures that locate authority in either a bishop or a council or a congregation, however, hardly designate all that is relevant in the interaction between laity and clergy. The sanction of ministerial function gives an influence to the clergy that may very well exceed any formal authority. At the same time there are frequently influential parishioners whom clergymen dare offend only at the risk of alienating much of their congregation. The building of a church, like any organization, requires mutual understanding and consensus, a reaching of agreements that permit people to interact to sustain a structure and the values for which it was organized.

RELIGION AND STRATIFICATION

Of all the dimensions of modern society that bear significantly upon religion, stratification is possibly the most relevant. The churches cannot avoid the simple fact that stratification differentiates the population into higher and lower statuses, and religious organization undeniably mirrors the class structure of society. Whatever may be their doctrinal position, churches rarely avoid developing a membership that draws disproportionately from one social class or another. There is often in an urban community a local hierarchy of churches, in which some are more socially prestigeful than others by criteria that have nothing to do with religion, per se.

Their *parish* organization often brings churches into some rough consistency with the ecological structure of the community. Since the ecological patterning distributes varied kinds of status clusterings into social areas made up largely of a social class, an ethnic group, or a racial group, church membership then becomes predominantly one social class or group. In the larger cities, with their wider range of social differentiation and cultural heterogeneity, this process is most systematically developed. Here the same religious denomination has local churches that have fairly homogeneous congregations—working class, lower middle class, upper middle class—depending upon the neighborhood the church serves.

In the first half of the nineteenth century the Catholic Church in the United States was predominantly an immigrant, working-class church; its parishes often reflected the ethnic lines that were a significant part of the ecological structure of a large city. There were Polish, Italian, and Irish parishes, congruent with the outlines of such ethnic neighborhoods. The breakup of these ethnic neighborhoods has led the Catholic hierarchy to attempt to reduce the attachment of its members with the historically *ethnic* parish, and to view it as a genuine parish; that is, a neighborhood area surrounding the church which the latter serves.

This ecological differentiation of class and status has considerable consequences for the internal organization of the particular denomination. Perhaps most significantly, it means that parishes vary in the challenges and opportunities they offer the clerical career. Middle-class churches are easier to organize and to keep organized, for their members are of the same social class as the minister or priest. Their greater affluence and supply of skilled managerial persons among the laity means that building programs are more likely to be successful. Their members participate in a wide range of church activities and maintain the church as an active and successful social-service organization.

Churches with working-class congregations, in turn, offer much greater difficulty. They may have to offer the clergyman a smaller salary, members are harder to recruit, less revenue makes a building program harder to carry out, and the less educated congregation does not offer the intellectual audience for the clergyman that the better educated middle-class congregation does. As a consequence only clergymen with particular dedications are likely to remain in such churches when they are offered an opportunity to go elsewhere. In short, mobility for a clergyman may be measured in his being "called" to more affluent churches, where a more responsive and better educated congregation offers what he finds to be a more rewarding and stimulating environment for the clergyman's vocation.

But not all denominations have drawn consistently across the class structure. In those societies, such as the United States, where no one religious grouping dominates, the several organized churches have tended to draw selectively from the class structure. For reasons that have less to do with doctrine and more to do with their historical origins, such denominations as the Episcopalians have been high-status churches, the Presbyterians have been middle-class churches, and such large denominations as the Baptists have been lower-middle or working-class churches. But this correlation of religion and class must always be qualified. The fact that the Episcopal Church is a high-status church by no means denies that it enrolls middle- and working-class members. For example, a poll on class background reported by Glenn Vernon indicated that about 40 percent of the Episcopal membership was in the working class, despite its strong appeal to high-status people.[10]

The Church and the Working Class The largely unequivocal and uncritical acceptance by the Christian denominations of the existing class structure, and their apparent readiness to reflect class patterns in their own membership, undoubtedly stands behind what has long been for them their greatest moral issue: the tension between organized religion and the urban working class. The Christian churches in most societies of the Western world are predominantly middle-class; at least their congregations come most regularly from that class. In turn the greatest failure of the Christian mission has been its inability to hold the industrial working classes within the church. The estrangement of the working class from the Christian churches, which has been greater in Europe than in the United States, has become (in Europe) one of the great moral crises of these same churches. Religious data from Great Britain, France, Italy, Germany, Belgium, *and* Latin America provide detailed support of the idea that the working class has largely abandoned any significant attachment to or involvement in the church, Catholic or Protestant. The fact of this detachment from organized religion is clear enough to all observers, but the reason for it is not so self-evident.

There have been two basic reasons given for the inability of organized religion to attract the working classes in industrial societies. One of these has to do with the seeming cultural affinity between church atmosphere and middle-class style, an atmosphere in which people of lower social status feel strange and out of place and even unwanted. A second line of analysis emphasizes the relative lack of integration of the urban, industrial masses into an urban, modern culture, and their failure to go to church is seen as only one more index of their alienation from modern culture.

The Church and Middle-Class Culture It is the analyses of American sociologists, particularly, that have stressed the affinity between a middle-class culture and the milieu within the church. They have stressed how much the liturgy, the sermon, the pattern of Sunday school, women's guilds, youth groups, and the like, reflect the tastes and standards as well as the interests and concerns

[10] Glenn M. Vernon, *Sociology of Religion* (New York: McGraw-Hill, 1962), p. 391.

of the middle class. Although it may very well be unintentional, the atmosphere is often uncongenial to working-class people; they find themselves uncomfortable and out of their environment. But, in addition, they have often felt themselves unwelcome. Despite the avowal of the church that all are welcome, and perhaps even the genuineness of a ministerial invitation, the person of lower status finds that the middle-class parishioners either ignore them, seeming to be cold and unfriendly, or, in not-too-subtle ways, make it clear that they are not welcome. James West, among others, has documented this in some detail in his study of Plainville; similarly, W. Lloyd Warner has done so for Jonesville, and Havighurst and Morgan for their study of a war-boom community in World War II.[11]

The Unintegrated Urban Worker In some European countries, particularly France, sociologists have pushed the issue further, arguing that the basic factor is the lack of integration of the worker into modern, urban life. Such French sociologists as E. Pin and A. Dansette view the urban worker as lacking the capacity to integrate into urban society, lacking comprehension of the modern world.[12] Their own culture is inadequate to master the complex, rational, highly organized world that is modern, urban life. They suffer from a sense of an unjust world. The French worker, in particular, lives in a society still sharply divided between *bourgeois* and *proletariat,* and his political orientation is still the anti-capitalist orientation of the labor movements in the nineteenth century. Thus, French workers have voted Communist in large numbers and have stayed away from the Catholic Church in equally large numbers. Pin, whose extensive studies of French workers and their estrangement from their church are reviewed by Louis Schneider, has argued that the French worker is estranged from the church precisely because the church gives no promise of pursuing justice *in this world;* it is just this hope that attracts him to the Communist Party.

In France, the recognition by the Catholic Church of its loss of the working class has led to several efforts to return them to the faith. The most famous of these has been the "worker-priest" movement of the 1950s, in which a number of priests left the sanctuary of the church and assumed the role, occupation, and life-style of the worker. They worked in factories, lived with workers, and attempted to reach them by sharing their life. The fact that a number of them responded to the workers' conditions by espousing secular and radical

---

[11] James West, *Plainville, U.S.A.* (New York: Columbia University Press, 1945); W. Lloyd Warner and Associates, *Democracy in Jonesville* (New York: Harper & Row, 1949); and Robert J. Havighurst and H. Gerton Morgan, *The Social History of a War-Boom Community* (New York: Longmans, 1951).

[12] For a review of the ideas of these French sociologists, see Louis Schneider, "Problems in the Sociology of Religion," pp. 796–799.

beliefs led a conservative hierarchy to stop the movement. More recently, under a closer scrutiny by church superiors, it has been renewed.

In some other countries, the United States in particular, the estrangement of workers from religion is not so pronounced. Indeed, the Catholic Church in the United States has managed to hold its immigrant, working-class members very well. This may be because, for the European immigrant, a stranger in a strange land, the church was a haven and a source of both spiritual and material assistance when so little else was available. Nonetheless, though there is considerable variation from one society to another, the general pattern remains clear and is supported consistently by data: those of lower social status are least attracted to the Christian churches, Protestant and Catholic.

Class and Sect   Although it is by no means universal, sects have most often been established by those who are marginal or socially disadvantaged; thus, they have more often emerged among those of low social status. Indeed, the movement from sect to denomination marks not only the organizational success of the sect, but also the personal mobility of its members. Liston Pope's *Millhands and Preachers*[13] is perhaps the best known of the sociological studies that examine the formation of sects by working-class people who feel themselves cut off from and even unwelcome in the more staid churches of the middle class. Their fervent and emotionally expressive services, though often looked down upon and made fun of by others, provide a religious outlet for feelings of deprivation and frustration engendered in the common experiences of lower-class life.

What is significant here is that, in the United States, Great Britain, and some few other countries where Protestantism has been dominant, the response of the working class and all others of low social status to their life conditions and to their alienation from more established churches has been to break off and regroup in newly created, small churches of their own. Each time this occurs, another sect is born. In Catholic countries where independent sect formation is not possible within the general structure of Catholic faith and organization, and where secular power may be hostile to new religious formations outside the established church, this occurs much less frequently. Instead, there is a general withdrawal from participation in the church.

Suburbia and the Church   A newer approach to the relation of religion to stratification focuses on the response of churches to the middle-class movement to the suburbs. Such suburbanization of the middle class has led, naturally, to the development of new, local churches; the churches have followed their most consistent parishioners out to the suburbs. But the matter is not simply

---

[13] Liston Pope, *Millhands and Preachers* (New Haven, Conn.: Yale University Press, 1942).

that new churches are established in new suburban communities, a natural enough process. In many instances, these are congregations that have moved, lock, stock, and barrel, from the city to the suburb, selling their former church building to those left behind, these people very frequently being Negroes.

There are two issues that flow from this suburban movement: one is the readiness of the church to join the middle class in "escaping" to the suburb; the other is the manner in which this movement determines the nature of the congregation and the concerns around which the church organizes its activities. The movement to the suburbs has often been defined as a "flight" that takes the middle class away from the difficult problems of the city, particularly those of race and poverty. When the middle class moves away, they leave behind in the city a large but less well-educated population—the old, the minorities, the poor—without the same capacity for leadership and with less organizational skill. The middle class, in short, escapes any responsibility for some of the most compelling and difficult problems of modern society. So does the church that follows them.[14]

A consequence (the second issue in the suburban movement) of this is that the suburban church organizes itself around the central interests of its middle-class congregations: family and teen-agers, leisure, and the concerns of morality and value. But these are far removed from the much more harsh problems that beset those that remain within the city. As Schneider remarks, "Physical removal and social and psychological irrelevance to lower strata thus sustain or enhance the alienation of the latter."[15]

The Church and the Negro   That all men are children of God, without exception, would seem to require that Christian churches reach out and bring the Negro, too, within the fold. And the historical record bears out their acceptance of such teachings: the missionary has sought out the heathen in distant lands and converted him to the faith. So, too, the Christian churches converted the African slave in the American South. Yet by and large the churches did not dispute the morality of slavery, though English Christians had strongly disputed the morality of the slave trade. After the Civil War the new patterns of racial segregation that became the Southern "way of life" included segregation in church. Even in the North, the Negro worshipped in his own church. Perhaps there was never a greater instance of the separation of the races than on Sunday morning.

But the significance of the relation of religion to the pattern of racial differentiation is not simply that there have been, and still largely are, white churches and Negro churches. In the first place, the Christianizing of the

---

[14] Such is the theme, for example, of G. Winter's provocative study, *The Suburban Captivity of the Churches* (New York: Doubleday, 1961).
[15] Schneider, "Problems in the Sociology of Religion," p. 796.

Negro when still a slave was a major factor in linking him with American culture, with the white man's culture, and in providing him with what often was to be his most sustaining source of belief in the face of a harsh and unrewarding life. The Negro poured into his version of Christianity his sense of grievance and suffering and created a wonderfully expressive mode of worship, exemplified in the deeply moving spirituals.

The separate Negro church has played a major part in the life of the American Negro. In the first place, given (in the past) so few other opportunities for middle-class roles, the church has attracted much of the potential leadership among Negroes, so that Negro clergymen have exercised leadership roles among Negroes in a way that white clergymen could not do in their own sphere. The Negro church, in short, has been a more influential institution than has its white counterpart. Also, the Negro church has been a major mechanism for integrating the disadvantaged Negro into the dominant white culture. Many Negro churches have been severely restrictive in their demands about behavior. They have, in short, sought to bring a stern control over the lower-class pattern of behavior, demanding close conformity to middle-class respectability in sexual behavior, for example. This has produced Black Puritans, whose rigorous espousal of the puritanic virtues of abstention may very well be a response to the apparent sexual laxity (by middle-class standards) of lower-class life. At the same time the Negro church has been a mainstay of those Negroes who have managed to attain a middle-class way of life. The church has been a central organization in the construction of middle-class life-styles for Negroes.

The manner in which religion can motivate Negroes to a life of sobriety and industriousness is apparent from the meaning of religious conversion, as these are earnestly sought by Negro Christian churches. But the conversion efforts of the Black Muslims has also enforced habits that we associate with middle-class life. Although the Black Muslims reject Christianity as the white man's religion, their conversion of lower-class Negroes to the Black Muslim faith produces a moral pattern of puritanic abstention of sexual behavior outside of marriage, a commitment to parental responsibility for wife and children, not functionally different in its effects than the Black Puritan pattern of Negro Christianity.

But lest it be thought that the one significant effect of religion on the Negro has been that of "middle-classisizing" him, and thus rendering a disprivileged group more amenable and conforming to the dominant culture, let us point out the several social consequences of religion for the Negro. The American Negro serves as an excellent case study of a severely disprivileged group whose very status as equivalently human was often simply not accepted by the dominant group. That the dominant group in this case once were their masters and they were slaves, and that this slave system was one of the most harsh systems of slavery ever known, suggests to us that the lot of the

Negro, even when legally freed from this slavery, remained a harsh and un-rewarding social existence.

In the light of this a strong commitment to religion gave the Negro a strength of belief and faith that made possible the sustaining of a sense of personal dignity and worth. And it gave him a capacity to endure the in-dignities and hardships of his life by taking seriously the Christian belief that "the meek shall inherit the earth." A reward in an afterlife sustained a people that otherwise could have found no legitimacy or even sense in the conditions of their existence, for certainly there was no reward in this life.

It is to be remembered here that the Negro existed for a long time in a white culture which insisted that he was inferior and insisted furthermore that he know it and acknowledge it. More than anything else, it was his religious faith that gave him a sense of dignity and a basis for not being fully "brain-washed" by dominant whites. The capacity of Negroes to endure and to resist very negative and demeaning versions of themselves was historically sustained, until now, largely by religion.

Nor, in a more active sense, has organized religion, the church, been only conservative and conforming. The Negro church has been the central insti-tution in much of the Negro revolt going on since 1960. It is the Negro church that has been the meeting place for protest, and Negro ministers have been a major part of the Negro civil rights leadership, particularly in the South. Furthermore, many of the protest songs, such as "We Shall Overcome," are secularized versions of Negro hymns, and their very mood and style is that of the spiritual.

If religion can then be judged as being a force to support middle-class behavior, and thus seeming to be conforming and nonrevolutionary in its effect, it has also sustained the spirit that made protest possible and has provided the one unique Negro organization usually safe from invasion by whites, the nearest thing to an untouchable sanctity. And although many Negro ministers have certainly preached a "pie in the sky" faith that encouraged their flock to endure this life for a reward in an afterlife, they have also been some of the most effective organizers of Negro protest and militant action, both North and South. It is no accident that such a major figure of Negro protest and revolt as Martin Luther King was a minister.

RELIGION AS CULTURE

Because they are interested in the relation of religion to society, most sociologists focus on the organization of religion and on such specific issues as the significance of stratification for religion. But such a sociologist of religion as Max Weber always understood religion to be a set of meanings by which men interpreted their social life and their society and sought to alter it or adjust to it or even reject it. Religion not only interpreted the world, it provided an orientation of ethical conduct; it helped shape the world, even as it, too, was fashioned by men's encounter with the world. Whatever may be its organizational features, religion is primarily belief and perspective and value. From the sociological perspective the problem of religion, when viewed primarily as culture rather than as social organization, leads to the questions: What is the significance of religious belief for human conduct? How do religious ideas affect social structure? How are meanings infused into social structure?

The basic conception of the problem owes its clearest articulation to Max Weber. He engaged in a major intellectual assessment of religion and society by carrying out a vast historical-comparative study of religion and its significance for social structure. His beginning point was in a problem posed by Karl Marx, whose distinction between structure and superstructure posited the idea that the economic, productive forces (the structure) were the fundamental determining forces in shaping society, and all else was superstructure, derived from and dependent upon the structure. In terms of social change Marx meant that change began with the economic organization, and change here led in time to changes in other spheres, including religion. Such phenomena as religion, philosophy, art, and ideology—or in general, the sphere of thought and ideas—had no determinative function of their own, no independent potentiality for acting upon other factors.

Although this Marxian position was later modified by Engels, it was the original idea that stimulated in Weber a monumental effort to demonstrate that ideas were not merely a reflection of human behavior and organization, but that ideas *interacted* with what Marx called the "material forces" to be *a* (but never the only) determinative force in shaping human society. For the realm of ideas Weber chose religion; for the realm of action he chose the economic, which was natural enough, given the fact that he was responding to Marx's assertion as to the determinative primacy of economic factors.

Weber's *The Protestant Ethic and the Spirit of Capitalism* is but one of several works that he wrote as he undertook his sweeping comparative analysis.[16] Weber built his study around a specific problem, the emergence of rational capitalism; his study of religion in Europe, in China, and in India explored the reasons why capitalism emerged or was blocked from development. In each case he

---

[16] Max Weber, *The Protestant Ethic and the Spirit of Capitalism* (London: G. Allen, 1930). Other works are *The Religion of China* (New York: Free Press, 1951); *Ancient Judaism* (New York: Free Press, 1952); *The Religion of India* (New York: Free Press, 1958); and *The Sociology of Religion* (Boston: Beacon, 1963).

found reasons in the character of religion as a set of fundamental meanings that led men to favor or disfavor certain modes of action, such as the type of economic conduct that produced capitalism. In each society the religious outlook on life produced an economic ethic, a religiously sanctioned standard of economic conduct. The emergence of Protestantism in Christian Europe yielded an ethic that encouraged the kind of economic behavior that resulted in the emergence of rational capitalism. But in China and India religion discouraged the economic behavior necessary for the emergence of capitalism. Religious belief in India, for example, was simply not of the order to induce an economic ethic that would provide religious sanction for individually acquisitive behavior associated with an ascetic pattern of self-denial that produced savings utilizable as economic investment.

The Protestant Ethic   The religious revolt generally known as Protestantism ushered in a period of significant breaks from the hitherto secure unity of Christendom. Some of the new sects that broke away were both socially and religiously radical, and their new interpretations were most appealing to a new rising social class that found itself opposed to and highly critical of an old order, one that had strong ecclesiastical support. The rising urban bourgeoisie, engaged in new and risky commercial ventures, found themselves with a weak voice in political affairs and often hampered by ways of doing business that were geared to an old order of medieval artisans and merchants and the noncompetitive and monopolistic practices of guilds.

To these people the new and revolutionary preachings of such men as John Calvin and John Knox provided a new religious perspective that was congenial to the search for new intellectual directions and in turn then strongly shaped the content of a new *Weltanschauung* for a rising social class. Calvin's teachings were religiously radical in their central challenge to a basic tenet of Catholic teaching: that the church, as the valid Christian ecclesiastical system, was the duly authorized administrator of the sacramental system. Calvin argued that the granting of sacraments could not influence the assignment of the person to an eternal life in heaven. The Catholic faithfuls' reliance on Mary and on saints was not only disputed, it was criticized. Only God, said Calvin, knew who was saved and who was eternally damned, and the intervention of no others, mortal or immortal—priests and bishops. Mary, Jesus, or saints— would change it. This God of Calvinism was a stern and terrible God who had predestined men to either heaven or hell, and neither their individual good works nor sacramental grace would save them.

Belief in predestination created for the Calvinist an anxious concern about his own unchangeable fate. He possessed a terrible fear of hell and eternal damnation, and he was saddled with the frightening necessity of facing God alone, without the intervention of the church. In the face of this he understandably sought some evidence of his predestined fate; instead of being frozen with fear, Calvinists effected an active campaign against the external world, warning the powerful that they were in danger of eternal doom. But more significantly, their own intense anxiety was relieved by their imputing some sign of their own divine salvation, their predestined selection by God.

Calvinists did not draw the conclusion that, since men were predestined for their eternal fate and could not change it, it mattered not how one lived one's life. Quite to the contrary, they insisted that each man should act as if he were one of the elect and live his life for the greater glory of God. But more central than this was the emergence of a Protestant conception of a religious theory of signs. The Calvinists came to argue that one's earthly fate was a sign of one's eternal fate. Accordingly, prosperity in worldly efforts signified election or salvation, whereas poverty and worldly failure signified an eternal damnation. Thus, as Schnieder notes, for the Calvinists,

> worldly conditions like prosperity and poverty symbolize or prefigure transcendental conditions . . . the world is plainly given transcendental or symbolic meaning in certain directions and heavenly or earthly realms are in symbolic contact.

The consequences of such a belief were revolutionary. Calvinists practiced industry, self-denial, and thrift; they considered it as sinful to indulge themselves in worldly goods or to lust after worldly pleasures. They became what Weber called "inner-worldly ascetics" by exercising their virtues in their occupation as a calling. Their hard work and ascetically harnessed energy led to savings and surplus, and so to investment that made an expanding capitalism possible.

Over time the belief in predestination diminished and ceased to be significant in religious belief, but the economic ethic that developed out of Calvinism became autonomous, detached from any particular religious faith. What Weber had called the Protestant Ethic came to be the dominant ethical orientation to work for the middle classes of Western industrial societies. It culminated in secular versions that placed a central value on work and made of economic success a this-worldly goal that needed no relation to anything beyond this life. Thus, it has taken to the middle of the twentieth century to rediscover a positive value in leisure and an ethical significance to the meaning of leisure in man's life.

Max Weber's work on religion and economy has made a magnificent case for the significance of ideas as dynamic forces in human affairs, with consequences that may often be unintended and unforeseen but nonetheless profoundly important in altering the social structure. Revolutions occur when men not only want to change the established order, but when they develop some notion of what mode of new order they want. As a rising, urban bourgeoisie, the Calvinists wanted a new political and economic order, but it was a framework of religious meanings that gave them new goals and the justification for radically new patterns of economic behavior. Without ideas about a possible future state of affairs, men's discontents merely break out in rebellions that strike out aimlessly, perhaps only violently, but which do not provide the goals and the organizational discipline that makes a revolution.

Religion: Radical or Conservative Religion in the modern world has come to be regarded as conservative, as supportive of the social order. The secular residue of the Protestant ethic does not escape that same judgment, for now it fits the established order: thus, we forget that once it was radical and innovative. But the very success of such efforts changed the world more nearly to fit the very ideal posited by the innovating ethic; in time it became the ethical orientation of the successful, and they in turn shaped the economic order to fit the ethic. Thus, the ethic was no longer radical but instead was the ethical orientation of those who were the dominants, the successful ones, in the new capitalistic social order.

Religion, then, is not inherently either conservative or radical. Historically it has been both; the religious belief that began as radical and innovative, when successful, became conservative, in the sense of defining and rationalizing the established social order. So, too, of course have secular beliefs. Communism is radical and potentially revolutionary in a noncommunist society. But after the revolution it is the defender of the new order, and it undergoes a subtle change of emphasis as it shifts function from a radical, critical, and future-oriented outlook to a defensive, supportive, and present-oriented (and even past-oriented) perspective on society.

Religion and the Millennium Throughout the long history of Christianity in the Western world there are a number of cases in which religion has served to support extraordinarily radical innovations in human behavior and social organization. Since Christian belief has always placed a central value on Christ as the Son of God and on His Resurrection, the possibility of His coming again to bring an end to an unjust world has become the core idea for a religion of hope for a long suffering and deprived people. They have acted upon the belief in an imminent, second coming of Christ, and a millennium of earthly perfection that His rule would bring about. This belief in a messiah, or supernatural savior, is built into the Judaic-Christian tradition but is not unique to it. Messianic cults have appeared in native populations when the old culture has been broken by conquest and an enforced modernization.

The Middle Ages in Europe was a period of considerable rebellion among oppressed and suffering peasants. However radically they rejected the oppressive world, including the church, they nevertheless projected new beliefs within the framework of their known religion. A desperation about their worldly status led to *eschatological* beliefs—that the end of the world and a final Day of Judgment was near—and particularly to *chiliastic* beliefs, heralding the second coming of Christ. This final event was to bring about the millennium, the rule of Christ for a thousand years in a world purged of suffering and sin, cleansed of injustice and the power of evil men.

However irrational the fantasies of these impoverished and rebellious people, their convinced belief turned them from being passive, long-enduring peasants, subservient to both church and aristocracy, to become revolutionary millennarians, intent upon establishing a new social order now. A striking case in point was that of the Anabaptists, a name that covers a somewhat heterogeneous grouping of religious sects, each organized around a charismatic leader. In 1534 and 1535 the Anabaptists established a New Jerusalem in the town of Münster in Germany. In a short period of time there emerged a radically new experiment in social order—in marriage and family life, in property and commerce, in status and authority. Although it was brutally crushed, Münster symbolizes in history, as does the whole chapter of the rebellious Anabaptists, the immense power of ideas to motivate men to act to change history and to challenge the established pattern of their earthly fate, no matter what may be the rational assessment of the likelihood of success.[17]

RELIGION AND THE SECULAR SOCIETY

Over the past century, it has become increasingly difficult to regard organized religion as a central institution of modern society. It has not only lost a significant hold upon the working classes of industrial societies, as we saw, but it has also lost considerably from among the ranks of the intellectuals and those educated classes most influenced by intellectuals. Furthermore, despite persistent efforts to the contrary, many of those who have remained within the fold have insisted upon separating the concerns of religion from the concerns of everyday life, rendering the message from the pulpit largely irrelevant for problems of social action. Religion, in short, in the secular societies of the twentieth century, is no longer a faith that permeates every aspect of life.

The Attack Upon Religion Religion in general and historic Christianity in particular were subject to a devastating intellectual attack in the nineteenth

[17] An historic description and social analysis of millennarian movements, and of the Anabaptists at Münster, can be found in Norman Cohn, *The Pursuit of the Millennium* (New York: Harper & Row, 1961).

century, largely from the perspective of the new doctrine of biological evolution. The specific clash, of course, was over incompatible conceptions of human origins and thus over the belief in the Bible as a literal description of human development and history. But this was but a single instance of a larger development, namely, a replacement of religion by rational science as man's primary cognitive orientation to his external environment. In this transition much of the specific content of Christian belief was attacked as empirically unverifiable, as historically inaccurate, and, more than that, as ignorance and superstition. Religious belief was reduced to "faith," viewed as blind and as an irrational acceptance of unscientific dogma. In the twentieth century the sweeping penetration of positive science has produced the claim that only that knowledge gained by the scientific method is valid knowledge, and thus only empirically verifiable questions have meaning; all others, whether from philosophy, religion, or aesthetics, are meaningless. Although the high tide of this logical positivism has run its course, even among scientists, the intellectual dismissal of the relevance of religion has taken a severe toll.

The sustained attack upon religion as intellectually and rationally wanting used science as its weapon, and the conception of a "war" between science and religion, in which rational science finally triumphed over irrational religion, was a common intellectual justification for the attack. More to the point the standards and perspectives of rational science seem more relevant to modern society, also rational and secular, than did religion. Certainly, the culture of science, as we saw in the previous chapter, manifests values that are also those of modern society: individualism, universalism, empiricism, and so forth. Science, in short, has become a major organizing belief for modern society, whereas organized religion has become less relevant as a social institution.

Secularization of the Modern World   But what seems relevant today is not the nineteenth century hostility to religion generated from the scientiism of that century, and the old-fashioned atheism it produced, but the *secularization* that to many theologians and sociologists of religion is the significant development of the twentieth century. The word *secular* is an ancient term of historically changing meaning, it is derived from the Latin word *saeculum* that means "this present age." It is one of the Latin words for *world,* and for a long time secular meant "worldly" contrasted to "religious" or "sacred." Secularization is a broad and pervasive process that penetrates all phases of social life, and its source does not lie in animosity to religion; rather, as the theologian Harvey Cox says, "secularization simply bypasses and undercuts religion and goes on to other things."[18]

But what is it? Most fundamentally, it means the elimination of religion as the source of the symbols of cultural integration. It occurs concomitantly with

---

[18] Harvey Cox, *The Secular City,* revised edition (New York: Macmillan, 1966), p. 2.

the institutional differentiation of modern society, whereby the political and economic spheres become independent of religious direction and control. As a cultural process, secularization is a *desacralization* of the world, one in which there is no overarching religious symbolism for the integration of society, and in which man's understanding of himself and of his society are no longer primarily in religious terms. Furthermore, it is a turning away from other worlds and toward this one, a process evident in the Protestant Ethic, but in fact has deeper biblical roots than that. The magic of the world is lost in what Weber called a "disenchantment," and the world instead becomes a natural process, a matter-of-factness, not a magical process or a divine entity. Such a conception of nature is a precondition for the emergence of science.

The Sources of Secularization Secularization is a salient issue in the world of the twentieth century, but it is hardly a new or even a modern process. It began centuries ago, and it is one of the great ironies of man's long history that its very origins in the Western world lie in the Christian religion, even though the process is interpreted as a loss of the power and effectiveness of religion. The religion of ancient Israel divorced God from the "natural" processes of the world, and there were significant consequences from this: God was not manipulable by magic, He did not confer divinity upon humans, even kings, and His divinity was not expressed in nature worship—thus the Hebrew opposition to temple prostitution and religious orgies. Harvey Cox expresses this Biblical source of secularization as constituting three pivotal elements: "the *disenchantment of nature* begins with the Creation, the *desacralization of politics* with the Exodus, and the *deconsecration of values* with the Sinai Covenant, especially with its prohibition of idols."[19]

Max Weber also credited Calvinism and the emergence of the Protestant Ethic as constituting a major development in the rationalization of the world— and secularization is part and parcel of that rationalization—when its teachings turned men from other-worldly preoccupations to an inner-worldly asceticism that served to reshape radically the social structure and was one of the major sources of the powerful rationalization that produced both capitalism and industrialism. Furthermore, Protestantism divested the world of much of the magic and the miracles of medieval Catholocism. It reduced the sacraments in number and eliminated all the intermediaries between God and man: saints, The Virgin, angels, miracles, and the sacraments through which grace could be dispensed.

The Consequences for Religion This steady secularization of the world throughout Christian history clearly has consequences for religion itself, first among which is a major shift in the functions of religion. Perhaps the basic trans-

[19] Cox, *The Secular City,* p. 15.

formation is the loss of religion's capacity to serve as the unifying and integrating symbol-system for society. A world more secular and rational is also a world more institutionally differentiated. In particular, the economic and political institutions have become separated from religious direction and guidance and have developed their own autonomous symbolic systems. As a consequence of secularization, religion no longer functions to integrate a total society, but at best to integrate particular social groups. When this happens, religion recedes from the public stage and becomes socially and politically innocuous; it becomes *privatized*. "The gods of traditional religions live on as private fetishes or the patrons of congenial groups, but they play no significant role in the public life of the secular metropolis."[20]

To most religious minds, the increasing secularization of the world is something to be opposed and a process to be reversed, if possible. Much effort is expended in trying to make religions "more relevant" to life. In the Catholic Church Pope John XXIII coined the term *aggiornamento* ("bringing up to date" in Italian), which became a powerful symbol of the reform and modernizing movement within the church itself. More conservative efforts to restore religious influence continue, as the action of the Congress of the United States in inserting "under God" in the Pledge of Allegiance. Nonetheless, no particular religious view is forced upon the citizens of the United States, and there is a tolerance of religious viewpoints and a pluralism of religious practices.

Although the conventional religious view is one that opposes secularization, there is nonetheless a significant contemporary perspective in theology that welcomes secularization, a viewpoint most effectively expressed in Harvey Cox's *The Secular City*, an analysis of secularization in the context of urbanization that became a controversial best-seller when it was first published in 1965. Cox calls secularization "the *liberation* of man from religious and metaphysical tutelage, the turning of his attention away from other worlds and toward this one."[21] He also refers to it as an "*emancipation*." His forthright and sociologically informed work is a theologically radical effort to shed the religious perspectives of presecular eras and to find a new grounding for religion in the unmistakably secular world of the twentieth century.

Cox's work is that of a radical theological thinker who seeks to present in theological terms what religion can be like in a secular society. Few sociologists have attempted any such effort, nor would they be likely to regard that as a sociological task. Yet, in attempting to assess the consequences of secularization for religion now and in at least the near future, several of them have predicted something of the religious future. Both Peter Berger and Robert Bellah, for example, suggest that religion becomes more subjective; it be-

[20] Cox, p. 2.
[21] Cox, p. 15.

comes, as Bellah notes, less orthodox, and established belief gives way to personal interpretation.[22] He observes that "for many churchgoers, the obligation of doctrinal orthodoxy sits lightly indeed, and the idea that all creedal statements must receive a personal reinterpretation is widely accepted."[23] Thomas Luckmann, too, suggests that in the modern world different social institutions are each autonomous within their own sphere; this then leaves a private sphere for the individual, in which he may develop a privatized worldview that may or may not be congruent with an official model of religion. Thus, there emerges the basis for a noninstitutionalized, privatized model of religion.[24]

Basic to this conception of what may not only be religion without orthodoxy but even without a church is the idea among these sociologists that no single world-view, religious or otherwise, organizes the thinking of the members of a society. Religion is no longer the overarching symbolic process of integration, for in the modern, differentiated society there is a *plurality* of social worlds and thus a plurality of world-views. Secular man apparently has a relativized view of the world and is conscious of the fact that his own point of view is relative and conditioned, rooted in his own historic experiences. Secular man is unlikely to claim absolute and eternal truths, for secularization is deliverance, as Cox claims, from tutelage to religious control and closed metaphysical world-views.

Religion in the Western world, then, may be entering what many Christian theologians and others have called a "post-Christian" era. What is occurring is a redefining of the social world for which religion, in its historic functions, provides a structure of legitimated meanings in sacred form. Christianity's capacity to provide this legitimation has waned considerably over the past century. Today's crisis of religion is a major moral and intellectual effort to make religious belief once more a relevant symbolic process which infuses livable human meaning into the secular order that is the new context for the human condition.

[22] Peter L. Berger, "A Sociological View of the Secularization of Theology," *Journal for the Scientific Study of Religion,* 5 (Fall, 1966), 3–16; and Bellah, "Religious Evolution."

[23] Bellah, p. 372.

[24] Thomas Luckmann, *The Invisible Religion* (New York: Macmillan, 1967).

"Sooner or later, Larry, you're going to have to take a stand on *something*."

Brian Savage from LOOK 8–20–68

Mort Gerberg from LOOK 6–11–68

PART 5 COLLECTIVE BEHAVIOR AND POPULATION

1. President Johnson visits Seattle.
2. London: demonstrators protesting the Vietnam war at the American Embassy.
3. Senior Citizen's Day in New York's Central Park.
4. Paris (1968): students and workers stage a protest march.
5. White crowd angered by the presence of a Negro on a beach.
6. The Beatles!

3 5

4 6

CROWDS
AND PUBLICS

19

Men move within the patterns set by social structure, within the limits set by role expectations, within the routines that give form and stability to social life—mostly, but not always. Social behavior is institutionalized and controlled by social norms—but not completely. The clash of whites and Negroes in a destructive race riot or the conflict between striking workers and police that results in upset automobiles, tear gas, and injured people, are both violent instances of human behavior, behavior which is neither routinized nor governed by the social norms that control more institutionalized behavior. There are other less dramatic examples of the same phenomenon: the artful manipulation of public opinion by the skilled propagandist; the rapid turnover in fads among teen-agers; the movements of workers or minorities for more rights or more equal status. Social scientists label such phenomena *collective behavior*. Collective behavior includes three major areas:

Crowd action: the fighting, violent mobs, the great masses of spectators, the ceremonial crowds either gay or solemn as the occasion requires; *Publics:* the physically dispersed aggregates of people who share an interest in some event or issue, political or cultural; and *Social movements:* the collective action of social groups or classes seeking either to change or resist change in social structure— a phenomenon of social protest, of reform and revolution. There are other phenomena, too, that fall under the loose rubric of collective behavior, such as fads and fashions and the rumor process, though the latter is often subsumed under a consideration of crowds and publics.

American sociologists have only recently returned to a major interest in the phenomena called collective behavior. After World War II there was a sharp decline in sociological interest in these phenomena, as evidenced by the fact that there was not a new textbook in the field from 1938, the publication date of Richard LaPiere's *Collective Behavior,* until 1957, when Ralph Turner and Lewis Killian published their *Collective Behavior.*[1] An explanation for this as an exercise in the sociology of sociology would undoubtedly stress the dominant interest of sociologists during this period in formal organization and small groups and a structural-functional perspective in theory; associated with this was a political and cultural environment in which the continuing bureaucratization of middle-class life and a "silent generation" of students seemed far removed from the turbulent period of the 1930s. But civil rights and student protests, race riots and demonstrations against war have radically changed the cultural milieu, and collective behavior becomes significant again to sociologists.

[1] Richard LaPiere, *Collective Behavior* (New York: McGraw-Hill, 1938); Ralph Turner and Lewis Killian, *Collective Behavior* (Englewood Cliffs, N.J.: Prentice-Hall, 1957). Since then two other textbooks have appeared: Kurt and Gladys Lang, *Collective Dynamics* (New York: Crowell, 1961); and Neil J. Smelser, *Theory of Collective Behavior* (New York: Free Press, 1963).

COLLECTIVE BEHAVIOR AS A SOCIOLOGICAL PROBLEM

It is difficult to organize the phenomena of collective behavior under a single set of sociological concepts or under a single theory. As the reader can see at a glance, collective behavior includes crowd behavior, publics, social movements, as well as fads and fashions. It is not immediately obvious why this wide range of social phenomena belongs under a common heading. What, then, do they have in common that allows them all to be treated as collective behavior? The literature on collective behavior gives persistent expression to three ideas: collective behavior as *less structured* or *unstructured behavior,* as *social disorganization,* and as *change.* What each of these three ideas has in common is the notion that collective behavior evidences less stability than we associate with social structure, that it is behavior which does not fall into a pattern of social routines. The concepts of social disorganization and change also rather explicitly suggest the idea of a *breakdown of social controls,* a decline of the normative controls that ordinarily constrain and limit behavior, keeping it within the established social patterns and relationships.

When the sociologist tries to explain collective behavior in terms of social disorganization and change, he is assuming that social life usually possesses a high degree of social order and is a well-organized pattern of groups and relationships, both functionally and normatively integrated. Then the emergence of the forms of collective behavior occurs only because some disorganization of this formerly high level of organization sets in. Thus collective behavior is taken to be an *index of social disorganization.* The concept of social disorganization also conveys the idea of *change;* specifically, it implies change from highly integrated to poorly integrated structures. Some sociologists see this disorganization as the first phase of a process of change from one social structure to another—disorganization is followed by reorganization, and a new structure of stable relationships and social routines emerges. Collective behavior occurs in the transition between the old and new social orders.

This way of conceptualizing collective behavior, however, does not manage to explain all of the phenomena. It best directs attention to revolutionary street crowds, acting dramatically against the established order, historically symbolized in the Parisian mob storming the Bastille. But not all crowd behavior is of this kind. This approach also is directed to an analysis of social movements, which are collective efforts to change the social order from an old to a new pattern or else to resist such a change. But it does not adequately explain publics and the formation of public opinion, which can be a legitimate and relatively orderly process in a democratic society.

The forming of public opinion may be conceived of as a process of social change, but it cannot adequately be thought of as disorganization or as a break in social routine, a decline of social stability, a loss of traditional norms and values. This suggests that some change, at least, must be viewed as a normal aspect of social life and is not necessarily treated satisfactorily as a disruption of routines. If change can be regarded as normal, then social life is not necessarily as highly integrated nor as well structured as some of the sociological literature seems to assume. Some situations of social interaction are not defined in terms of as specific a set of norms as define and limit behavior in other situations. Some population aggregates have no clear definition of group membership, little division of labor, no clearly situated role expectancies, no established authority, and an absence of stable leadership. Compared to bureaucracies or the highly integrated folk society, these are "loosely" structured.

There are several forms of social structure in modern social life that do not exhibit the high degree of organization that folk societies did, or bureaucracies do, and it would be an error to impute anything but "loose" structure to them. This rather imprecise term implies a more ambiguous normative control, a lack of specific role definition and of the other characteristics mentioned above. The modern urban community frequently is loosely structured, or less structured, as are class and status groups, and as are the forms of collective behavior: publics, crowds, and social movements.

When sociologists concentrate their efforts upon the study of social structure as the proper subject matter of sociology, the consequence is to give less attention to collective behavior. Because it does not fall clearly into the category of structured phenomena, some sociologists have conceived of collective behavior as primarily social psychology, rather than sociology. The manner in which the individual is caught up on the emotional contagion of the crowd, the measuring of the individual's attitudes and opinions, and their relation to his group memberships—these concerns of the social psychologist have often produced a greater interest in the phenomena of collective behavior for him than for the sociologist.

However, collective behavior does constitute social interaction and social communication among a socially defined population. There is pattern and regularity to the action. Furthermore, there is the sharing of a cultural perspective among the interacting persons—values, interests, past experiences, and the like. In this sense, however loosely structured the forms of collective behavior, they do constitute patterns of social interaction that fall legitimately within the concern of the sociologist.

Collective behavior has been sociologically problematic, then, because of some uncertainty about its relationship to social structure: whether to conceive of it as phenomena indicative of the disorganization and change of established social structure, or to conceive of it as social interaction that exhibits less structure than we observe for social groups. There would seem then to have been four related problems about collective behavior: (1) the long concern for the meaning of the phenomenon *collective behavior* and for the effort to develop a theoretical perspective; (2) an interest in the most dramatic and often frightening aspect of collective behavior, the *crowd,* the form of collective behavior probably most central to its conceptualization; (3) the *public,* a process of collective behavior of greater interest to contemporary social scientists, particularly since opinion polling has become systematically developed; and (4) *social movements,* those organized efforts at social change that reveal both collective behavior and organizational features and frequently overlap with crowds and publics.

THE CONCEPTION OF COLLECTIVE BEHAVIOR

The public is a social form particularly related to modern society, but crowd behavior and social movements have a long history within Western culture. The history of medieval life, for example, is replete with examples of peasant movements, of religious movements, such as the Crusades, and of crowd hysteria and mob action. In ancient Rome crowd spectacles were significant political operations, and the capacity to appeal to the crowd for political support was a politically significant skill in Rome's more turbulent periods. However, a more systematic concern for the significance of crowd behavior and social movements, as well as for the formation of public opinion, developed in the nineteenth century in response to the revolutionary changes that so thoroughly altered the social face of Europe. In particular there was a conservative concern about the loss of traditional controls over the common people, the "fear of the masses" now that the Industrial Revolution had brought in a new social order. In France, those who had experienced the revolution and the Reign of Terror, developed a fear of street crowds intent upon political attack.[2] Political action by violent crowds became a modern weapon in the internal political struggle, easily available to those who championed the rights of the common man against the old order.

Also in the nineteenth century in France and throughout Europe, great social movements emerged representing the working classes and advocating a socialist society. The fear of revolution against capitalism and against the propertied classes became a dominant concern of the European middle classes. It served to undercut enthusiasm for democracy and for the enfranchisement of the common people, and to provoke a concern over the more dramatic and expressive forms of political behavior, especially crowds and social movements.

[2] See G. Rudé, *The Crowd in the French Revolution* (London: Oxford, 1959).

This fear also led to a concern for publics and public opinion, a process which from a conservative perspective seemed to challenge traditional authority too readily and to allow public policy to be shaped by mass emotions too easily. Such conservative fears about the political consequences of mass participation in the political process, as well as doubts about the social stability of modern, democratic society, prompted considerable scholarly attention in the nineteenth century to the various processes of collective behavior. This historic concern gave rise to the study of collective behavior from a particular perspective, viewing it largely as social behavior that "breaks" with the more conventional and traditional organization of social life and thus signifies a decline in the stability of conventional social structure.

The salient work in creating a sociological image of collective behavior was *The Crowd*, by Gustave LeBon.[3] Its analysis of the crowd not only set forth a conception that dominated the thought of social science for years to come, but it also was significant in developing an image of the crowd as a threat to stable, rational social structure. LeBon viewed the crowd, not as a mere collection of individuals, but as an organized aggregation with a collective mind, in which the person loses his individual mentality. The crowd mind gives freer play to the subconscious, in which highly emotional qualities and instincts are dominant; thus the crowd mind is not capable of highly rational or intellectual effort but instead reflects the common mediocrity of its members. LeBon asserted that the modern age was an age of crowds, instead of one of a competent elite, and that the rule of crowds typically characterized periods of disintegration and decay of civilization. Statements such as these, as the framework within which the crowd was analyzed, as well as the nature of LeBon's analysis of crowd leaders and his interpretation of parliament as a form of crowd behavior, contributed considerably to the idea of collective behavior as a threat to social order.

The particular social and intellectual circumstances under which the study of collective behavior emerged (in modern social science) partly accounts for that one major stand of sociological thought that has viewed it as social disorganization and change, disruption of routine, and breaks in the normal social stability of a society. Here is felt the influence of conservative thinkers whose intellectual perspective assumes society normally to be a highly integrated organism.

Not only did LeBon create an image of collective behavior as a threat to normal social order, but he and others also helped to develop what has been the dominant theoretical perspective on collective behavior in sociology. The basic interpretative framework has been based upon two fundamental assump-

---

[3] Gustave LeBon, *The Crowd: A Study of the Popular Mind* (London: Benn, 1896); paperback edition (New York: Viking, 1960).

tions: (1) that collective behavior was radically different from the "normal" actions of the individual; and (2) that the basic explanation for such "abnormal" behavior lies in *contagion* induced by a crowd situation, whereby the usual predispositions of the individual are overcome by unanimous, intense feelings that permit action otherwise prevented by the normative controls of social structure. Besides LeBon, Walter Bagehot and Gabriel Tarde in the late nineteenth century argued along these same theoretical lines,[4] as did the American sociologist E. A. Ross in the first decades of this century;[5] then, Park and Burgess discussed the idea of collective behavior in such terms in their pioneering work[6] and Herbert Blumer, in a noted essay, restated it for a more recent period.[7] Kurt and Gladys Lang have made the most current statement.[8]

LeBon stated the basic premise of this perspective on collective behavior when he said:

> Under certain given circumstances, and only under those circumstances, an agglomeration of men presents new characteristics very different from those of the individuals composing it. The sentiments and ideas of all the persons in the gathering take one and the same direction, and their conscious personality vanishes.[9]

Efforts to explain such a process have invoked various psychological mechanisms such as *emotional contagion, imitation,* and *suggestion,* as well as the *anonymity* of the crowd and its restricted attention.[10] Perhaps the idea of suggestibility due to contagious excitement and a sense of power in the crowd has been the most frequent explanation. The process of *identification* with a leader has been another postulated mechanism.

To contemporary sociologists, however, there are some difficulties with this mode of explanation. For one thing, the development of the theory seems to have relied heavily upon historical accounts of often particularly horrible instances of crowd fury, not consistent with the kinds of observations that sociologists have been able to make. Secondly, this kind of explanation perpetuates what Ralph Turner properly calls a "dubious conception of the hu-

---

[4] Walter Bagehot, *Physics and Politics* (New York: Knopf, 1948), first published in 1869; Gabriel Tarde, *L'opinion et la Foule* (Paris: Librairie Felix Alcan, 1901).

[5] E. A. Ross, *Social Psychology* (New York: Macmillan, 1921).

[6] Robert E. Park and Ernest W. Burgess, *Introduction to the Science of Sociology* (Chicago: University of Chicago Press, 1921).

[7] Herbert Blumer, "Collective Behavior," in A. M. Lee, ed., *New Outline of the Principles of Sociology* (New York: Barnes & Noble, 1946), pp. 165–220.

[8] Lang and Lang, *Collective Dynamics.*

[9] LeBon, *The Crowd,* pp. 23–24 (same pages in both cited editions).

[10] The following review of the effort to explain collective behavior draws upon Ralph Turner, "Collective Behavior," in Robert E. L. Faris, ed., *Handbook of Modern Sociology* (Chicago: Rand McNally, 1964), pp. 382–425. See especially pp. 384–392.

man being as an animal with a removable veneer of socialization."[11] It is this that seems to require a separate level of psychological explanation different from that used to explain the organization of groups. In addition, for the empirical scientist, there is a problem in providing empirical verification of the psychological mechanisms. Although *suggestion* is probably the best verified mechanism, according to Turner "psychological research has led to narrower and narrower circumstances of the conditions under which suggestion takes place."[12] Then, too, contagion theory does not provide a basis for predicting the shifts that so often occur in crowd behavior, nor for understanding any differentiation of functions that provides some minimum organization to collective behavior.

The contagion theory has relied upon psychological mechanisms for its explanation. However, some psychologists have directly attacked the theory by presenting instead a *convergence* theory that accounts for collective behavior as the convergence of persons who share the same predispositions, which predispositions are then activated by the event or object that commands the attention of the crowd. Floyd Allport argued that the action of the crowd was the action of the individual, who had hated or dreamed of vengeance, so that nothing new had been added but an intensification of feeling and the opportunity to act.[13] Some theorists have then sought to define a *crowd-prone* category of persons, persons not fully committed to the community and its normative order. Thus, lower-class whites, whose insecure status was easily threatened by Negroes, have often been cited by researchers as having made up the active part of lynch mobs in the South in the 1920s and 1930s.

But the convergence theory also has its difficulties, two of which are crucial. One is that, although it was important to recognize that a crowd situation released latent tendencies not ordinarily recognized, the theory does not specify which of several latent tendencies are so released, perhaps because it had assumed there was only one relevant to the crowd situation. Furthermore, the theory focuses upon the *intensity* of response, not upon the *direction* of response. Direction of crowd action seems to be taken for granted as an automatic response of the individual to the self-evident situation. But Turner notes that

the "collective" definition of the situation may be the crucial part of crowd development, during which a situation which is ambiguous to individual perceptions is defined as dangerous, as reprehensible, as defenseless, or whatever other characterization serves to indicate the appropriate behavior.[14]

That just such a collective defining process goes on even in the most violent

[11] Turner, p. 386.

[12] Turner, p. 387.

[13] Floyd H. Allport, *Social Psychology* (Boston: Houghton Mifflin, 1924).

[14] Turner, "Collective Behavior," p. 389.

and dangerous crowds is the central point of yet another approach to crowd behavior, what Turner calls the *emergent norm* theory.[15] Central to this perspective is a conscious effort to minimize the seeming disparity between crowd behavior and normal behavior by viewing crowds no less than groups as governed by norms. Instead of seeing the crowd as a situation of released impulses and the removal of normative sanctions, there is postulated the emergence of norms appropriate to the situation. *Collective behavior is also interaction in which a situation is defined, norms for sanctioning behavior emerge, and lines of action are thus justified and agreed upon.*

The emergent norm perspective has particularly challenged the empirical description of crowd situations so often produced in the past, descriptions which seem to overemphasize the unanimity of the crowd and the contagion which captures the emotions of all. Rather, careful observers of crowds note that many people stand around but are not involved actively or even emotionally, and some are even opposed to the dominant orientation of the crowd. A crowd is rarely, then, unanimous or undifferentiated. But often the crowd suppresses opposing moods, and a fear of the crowd silences those who are not in agreement. Furthermore, there is a *developmental* process in crowds in which there is much preparation for action by a *symbolic exchange* that provides justification, selectively choosing from among "facts" supplied by rumor. Nor are the norms that emerge from such an exchange strikingly different from the norms which are usually operative; rather, as Turner notes, the crowd supplies "an atypical resolution of a long-standing normative conflict, defining a situation in which 'emergency norms' can be invoked, or providing sanction for the conviction that the usual normative order has ceased to operate."[16] Furthermore, the emergent norm perspective strongly suggests that there are limits to the development of crowd emotion and action; that is, there is a normative control that places limits upon the crowd, an observable fact about many historic events that the contagion theory has seriously neglected.

The search for a theory of collective behavior, then, has moved away from that initial position that viewed the individual as coming under the sway of the crowd and losing his capacity for rational judgment before the onsweep of an overpowering emotional contagion. Instead, the present effort is to encompass collective behavior under the same kind of theoretical framework that is used to explain the organization of social groups, and such concepts as norms and values are equally relevant here. Collective behavior refers to a developing collectivity in which normatively oriented interaction leads to defining justifiable action, even when this is a departure from other established ways.

[15] Turner, pp. 389–392.
[16] Turner, p. 392.

THE CROWD: TYPES AND FUNCTIONS

The term *crowd*, like the term *group*, is often used to indicate aggregates of people who are present in one place at one point in time. The presence of large numbers of people at a shopping center on Friday night might be referred to as a crowd, as might the large number of people in a downtown area pouring out of office buildings at noon or at the end of the workday. So might the large aggregate of people on a beach on a hot summer day or the large numbers at a football game on Saturday afternoon. But the football rally before the game, with bonfires and brass band, is also a crowd. So is the political rally alternately cheering its heroes and booing the opposition. There is also the mob bent on violent attacks on others or the destruction of property.

These varied situations have in common only the fact of the physical presence of an aggregate of people. Although common sense terminology may refer to all as crowds, the sociologist needs to make some further distinctions if he is to analyze crowd behavior. Although people may be physically present in one place, they may have no common concern, no particular awareness of one another. Busy shoppers and people hurrying home from work are involved in their own private objectives—making a purchase or catching the next bus. There is only a minimal social interaction; the individual is not involved with others in a matter of common concern. In the sociological sense, a crowd emerges when an aggregate of people share a common object of attention. They are no longer merely individuals; their attention is focused on a matter of common interest or concern, and there is interaction and communication. But there is no or little division of labor and no specified role behavior—there is, in short, a minimum of structure.

A crowd on the street watching the police handle an accident, or watching a building going up, or listening to a pitchman trying to sell his wares, are *casual* crowds, whose interest is moderate and whose emotional involvement is low. The individual has little difficulty detaching himself from the crowd, and there is no heightened emotional contagion in which he might be caught up. Nor do the norms of conventional behavior lose their force. The *casual* crowd occurs without being deliberately brought together; indeed, its presence in some situations hampers police work, as when a crowd gathers to watch a fire. But the deliberate planning of a crowd situation does occur, and any culture legitimizes certain crowd situations and the accompanying crowd behavior. These are *conventional* crowds, not only because cultural values sanction the crowd situation, but because such reoccurring, culturally defined situations are not lacking in normative controls; rather, behavior is organized and controlled by certain cultural conventions. These crowd situations are not, therefore, completely unstructured; some definite patterning of action occurs. In a football or basketball crowd there are conventions governing behavior, including some notion of "good sportsmanship" in the behavior of the crowd toward the players. There are conventional ways of expressing approval and appreciation, and the unity of support for the home team gives a particular focus to specific objects of concern to the crowd. If decisions by game officials are unfavorable to the home team, these officials become "villains" on whom the crowd vents expressions of disapproval. Lastly, a close score may produce tremendous excitement and the opportunity for the expression of relatively uninhibited emotions, for which few other situations would be a legitimate outlet. People can scream, cheer, yell, boo, wave their arms, stamp their feet, and shout at the top of their lungs. When the game is over, they may be both physically and emotionally exhausted.

Not all conventional crowd situations allow for such a high pitch of emotional involvement and unity. *Audiences* are generally more restrained in their behavior, and most audience situations are governed by norms of audience behavior. An audience at a concert or lecture may be more passive, and individuals, intent upon the speaker or performer, may be less conscious of others in the audience. There are, nonetheless, appropriate opportunities for emotional expression in the audience situation. The audience for lectures, concerts, plays, and other artistic performances are generally governed by definite customs and cultural expectations and also by norms of good audience behavior. Thus, Broadway actors dislike the "bad manners" frequently displayed by theater party audiences. On these occasions the house has been taken over by an organization that has sold the tickets as a way of raising money. But the audience contains many people who are not theater-goers and are unfamiliar with the cultural expectations of theater audience behavior; in addition, they may have little interest in the particular play. Their indifferent attention, loud rustling, and whispered conversations during the performance anger the cast. Theater, concert, and lecture situations are normatively oriented to cultural standards setting definite expectations for audience behavior. The same applies to a religious crowd, where the solemnity of the occasion and its symbolic meaning for the worshippers organizes behavior in well-structured ways. Yet the mood of reverence and awe is not only an individual response to the religious symbols of the ceremony, it is also communicated among the worshippers; the appropriate feelings are normatively dominant in the proper symbolic setting and define the mood people should have, even if all present do not.

The conventional crowd constitutes a situation that is a recognizable and legitimate part of social structure. Audiences are essential for artistic and dramatic performances, as are crowds for athletic events. No less a legitimate and functioning part of modern social structure are the political crowds that gather during an election year to listen to political candidates. Also, state and national political conventions constitute a specific form of crowd situation well-governed by cultural norms. These are all instances in which crowd behavior as a form of collective behavior is not an index of social disorganization and not necessarily one of social change. Audiences for lectures, concerts, plays, and political discussions are legitimate, organized forms utilized within institutional structures. Audiences for athletic events may find in the greater emotional contagion of the event an outlet or release for emotions in ways that are harmless to the social structure, and indeed which, by providing channels for expressing loyalty and support, may strengthen identity of the individual with the social structure.

Crowd situations that provide release of emotions in less inhibited ways without being socially threatening are *expressive crowds*. Many conventional crowds, as the football crowds, are expressive. Dances and parties give people an opportunity to express themselves freely and to release emotions and tensions without fear of violating norms. Political rallies also have this function, as do religious revivals. A mass meeting called in protest of something or other can also serve as an outlet for emotional expression. Although viewed as a threat by some, it may in fact provide a convenient release of feelings and actually reduce the likelihood of violent action in the community.

Contemporary thought in social science, concerned with the socialization of the individual and the integration of the social structure, seems to have given little attention to the problem of social opportunities provided within the social structure for permitting people to escape temporarily the demands and constraints of the social order. It requires no particular emphasis upon Freudian psychology to recognize that society restrains, limits, and inhibits the individual, and his mental health is sustained by occasional release from his own routines. This is one important function of the vacation, as it is of the holiday. Primitive societies often exhibit such institutionalized occasions when the social routines are temporarily interrupted, and the conventional social restraints are lifted. The community's moral standards may be set aside, only to be resumed again when the interlude is over. In many peasant societies the completion of the harvest allows an interruption in the routine of hard work, and this is a time for weddings and ceremonial occasions. Again, the situation sanctions uninhibited behavior, much drinking and eating, sexual license, and the outlet for pent-up emotions and tensions.

Modern society has not consciously built such expressive situations into its social structure, but they have appeared in two ways. First and most important is the holiday. Many critics of modern holiday behavior protest that these are intended as religious or patriotic occasions, and they are degraded by office parties or beach outings. Whatever the moral validity of such criticism, it is a sociological fact that patriotic and religious holy days have become secular holidays, and their original symbolic rationale now provides occasions for individual and group release from the highly demanding and constrained roles of modern social structure. The holiday thus functions as a safety valve, useful at both the individual and social levels. A second, though lesser, opportunity for emotional release is the convention. American society in particular is given to the holding of conventions. Business groups, veterans, professional associations, and others may conduct serious business at a convention. But for many a respectable, middle-class American the convention situation, away from the controls of family and neighbors, with his reputation not at stake, is an opportunity to indulge in behavior that would be unacceptable at any other time.

The expressive crowd may serve another function, too. By reasserting values and invoking common symbols, as in great political rallies, the crowd situation may serve to reinforce these values and strengthen the attachment of the individual to the group. The Nazis consciously utilized gigantic rallies, with Hitler's presence as the climax, as a means of reaffirming values and the loyalty of the individual to the cause. Under the emotional contagion of the situation the individual is drawn closer to the group, and the symbols evoked come to have greater meaning for him. Such crowd action integrates the participants and enhances group solidarity. The capacity of organizations and leaders to utilize the crowd situation to provide further socialization and strengthen group solidarity then gives another significance to the expressive crowd: it serves to demonstrate the strength of the group, as measured by the size and enthusiasm of the crowd. In conflict situations political leaders, labor leaders, and even religious leaders have sought to impress upon others their strength by means of great rallies and emotionally demonstrative crowds.

Types and Functions of Crowds: A Summary   Crowds, according to our analysis, can be considered as *casual, conventional,* and *expressive.* These last two categories are not mutually exclusive, for some conventional crowds are also expressive. In distinguishing conventional crowds from others we are pointing to the circumstances under which a crowd forms: conventional crowds are specifically provided for in the social structure and are relatively controlled and organized by norms of audience or crowd behavior. Furthermore, such conventional crowds are not a threat to the social structure or an index of social disorganization. Conventional crowds, and particularly the expressive ones, may also perform some significant functions for the social structure. Perhaps their most significant function is to provide a release of emotions and tensions for the constrained individual in the highly organized society and thus to constitute a safety valve for pent-up feelings, draining off emotions that might otherwise break out in harmful ways. Also, they serve to integrate the individual into the group, to socialize him, and thus to reaffirm and strengthen the group's values. The integration of political and religious institutions can be strengthened by this, but so can social movements, which represent challenges to the established institutions. Lastly, conventional and expressive crowds have a political function in conflict situations. By demonstrating group solidarity and support behind a leadership or an ideology, they may influence the distribution of power in a society and the resultant process of decision making.

Crowd Behavior and Manipulation Many images of crowd behavior have conceived of it as spontaneous, as emerging without intent or direction from the dynamics of the situation. But conventional crowds, though perhaps highly expressive, are not spontaneous in origin. Rather, they are organized and controlled for specific purposes, and the situation itself may be under the control of leaders who create and use the crowd situation for specific purposes.

Effective manipulation requires great skill. The feelings of the crowd may be aroused by frequent, skilled invoking of symbols significant to the crowd and to the occasion for its gathering together. Whether by speeches, by songs, by the use of flags and other material symbols, or some combination of these, the leaders arouse a strong response in the crowd and promote unity and solidarity by an emotionally arousing event.

In modern as well as in earlier times, such appeals to the crowd have usually been the actions of revolutionaries. In the twentieth century, they have often been utilized effectively by totalitarian and other nondemocratic leaders, who can nevertheless make effective appeal to masses of people in crowd situations, particularly the poor. Witness the appeals made by Juan Perón in Argentina to the poor, called the "shirtless ones," and more recently those of Fidel Castro in Cuba, with his mass rallies of workers and peasants. The manipulation of crowds by skilled leaders is a common feature of revolution, but the events of the twentieth century have taught us that such revolutions are not necessarily democratic in aspirations or outcome.

That quite legal demonstrations in democratic societies can lead to crowd action even when not intended is evident enough from recent experience with civil rights, student protest, and anti-Vietnam actions in cities and on campuses. But sometimes such an outcome can in fact be intended. Deliberately violating an ordinance or disobeying a police order and then resisting arrest, even if nonviolently, can often work to involve sympathetic bystanders into supporting action. In the political vocabulary of the 1960s this is "politicizing" people, and it can even be "radicalizing" them if they are induced to take action in behalf of the demonstrators. In short, the use of crowd action against unpopular authority can be an element of political strategy, a fact often overlooked when crowd action is described entirely as an unplanned, spontaneous outburst.

The Acting Crowd: Mobs and Riots   The fears aroused by the thought of crowd behavior is fear of the crowd in action, the mob. Most of the literature on crowd behavior has been concerned with this *acting crowd;* for this reason, we first explored other forms of crowd behavior. In class conflict and political struggle, in labor disputes and in race conflicts among others, we find the situations out of which an acting crowd emerges. Any time a large number of people are gathered together in one place, for some particular purpose, there is some potentiality that the crowd, whether originally casual, conventional, or expressive, will become an acting crowd, and a crowd in action is usually violent and destructive.

It is in situations of conflict and tension that the likelihood of crowd action emerges. Yet even here there must be the proper combination of elements. To become active, a crowd must be caught up in an emotional atmosphere of hostility directed against a definitely focused object; there has to be something to act *against.* The situation preceding action must build up an unambiguous imagery of friend and foe, *we* and *they;* and this in a cultural context, such as race or class loyalty, in which symbols unambiguously define the object of hostility, simplifies the character of the threat or problem, and creates the situation in which it becomes possible to define an immoderate, extreme course of action as legitimate. The acting crowd takes the law into its own hands and defies established authority in the process. In this situation, increasing hostility is directed to a focused object, either a person, viewed as an alleged offender against the group's values, or a category of people who might be attacked, precipitating a race riot. As emotional intensity increases, the original, more moderate leaders may lose control to more violence-demanding leaders, who emerge from the ranks of the crowd.

In the confusing situation in which a crowd gathers, *rumor* plays an important part in defining the situation for the crowd in such a way as to encourage direct action. In race riots, for example, rumors have swept through crowds, presenting some actual event in such a way as to arouse either whites or Negroes to violent action. The foremost sociological student of rumor as process, Tamotsu Shibutani, interprets rumor as the act of dealing with ambiguous situations when institutionalized forms of communication do not provide sufficient information; the resulting improvised definitions of what is happening is then a form of news, not necessarily false.[17]

Even when a crowd acts violently, not every one present in the crowd does so. Sometimes only a small active core commits any action, while the larger part of the crowd watches. But they do give moral support and serve both to

[17] Tamotsu Shibutani, *Improvised News: A Sociological Study of Rumor* (Indianapolis, Ind.: Bobbs-Merril, 1967).

encourage and protect the active core. Usually young males will make up the active core, with females, older people, and even children constituting the larger supporting crowd.

That many potential situations do not produce an acting crowd is evidence that one or more of the necessary elements is not present. Perhaps the moderate leadership can maintain dominance, or the crowd cannot focus upon a common object of hostility, or the symbols are too ambiguous to provide a clear definition of the situation encouraging action. Nevertheless, the gathering of crowds in tense situations always presents the possibility of crowd action, of mobs and riots.

Acting Crowds and Cultural Patterns Although mob behavior may seem spontaneous and the least predictable of human action, it is possible to find some rough relationship between acting crowds and the traditions and values of a culture. One might expect to find mobs and riots occurring around those issues and situations that constitute the deepest cleavage of values and interests within the society, where it is therefore most difficult to exert the controlling force of social norms. In the United States, at the present time, the race riot comes most readily to mind, for it is the racial problem of American society that can and does most easily induce mob behavior. For a long time in the South, the lynch crowd was a white weapon used to punish alleged Negro offenders against white women and to terrorize the entire Negro community. Since World War I, the large and destructive riots in America have been race riots (Chicago, 1919; Detroit, 1943; Rochester and Harlem, 1964; Watts in Los Angeles, 1965; Detroit and Newark, 1967), as have the numerous smaller disturbances that have beset communities large and small, North and South.

Labor In the nineteenth and early twentieth century, mob action in the United States was less frequently a racial matter, except in the South. From the Civil War until the 1930s, labor strife periodically broke out, and had as one of its consequences crowd behavior that sometimes resulted in rioting. Labor unions during this period were much smaller and weaker organizations than at present, and there was no labor legislation to protect the workers' right to organize and to be represented in collective bargaining. Furthermore, law enforcement in the form of police and courts was usually on the side of the employer. A strike, therefore, pitted the superior number of the workers against the superior armed force and legal power of the employer. The labor history of this period records numerous instances where such a combination of numbers against arms led to violent action, usually resulting in bloodshed, injuries, and death, largely of the strikers, and to jail and imprisonment for the strike leaders.

The sharp reduction in the acting crowd associated with labor disputes in the United States comes as a result of the labor legislation of the New Deal period, particularly the Wagner Act (1935), which brought labor-management conflict under law, gave labor the legal right to organize, and required management to participate "in good faith" in collective bargaining. The picket line was largely replaced by the bargaining table, and crowd action was reduced considerably in frequency.

In Europe labor strife has also been a source of crowd action, but there it takes on more of a political complexion. European labor unions are mostly associated with political parties of the left; traditionally, socialism was the politics of labor and of the large majority of the working class. The politics of Europe has been the politics of class: working class against middle class; the unpropertied versus the propertied; the poor against the rich. Ideologically, the cleavage between the classes has been the most articulated social difference in European societies, and the struggle over what has been interpreted as class interests has dominated European politics. In this context the political crowd, demonstrating its class solidarity and threatening action against its enemies, has been a standard feature of European urban politics since the French Revolution.

Youth   It is not only in Europe, however, that political street crowds are significant. In Asia, in the Middle East, and in Latin America, street crowds marching and shouting slogans and sometimes engaging in acts of violence have been a major factor in the revolutionary movements that have threatened established social structures. In all of these places, the youth, particularly the university youth, have been an important part of these demonstrating crowds. Here again we have a cultural phenomenon little understood in the United States: the widespread participation of university youth in political street crowds, in particular those demonstrating against the established order. Anti-American demonstrations by university students in Japan forced the cancellation of former President Eisenhower's planned visit to Japan, testifying to the still effective force of political crowds in modern society and to the significant role of youth in this form of political action.

The youth of the United States have only on occasion been involved in significant political or social action that parallels this political behavior by the youth of Latin America and Japan. There was such serious involvement during the depression of the 1930s, and there has been a renewal of youth involvement in and commitment to serious political action in the 1960s. Youth have made up a very large part of civil rights demonstrations in both North and South since 1960, and college students have undertaken active protest demonstrations on civil rights, on the war in Vietnam, and on behalf of their rights as students in the university.[18] The several days of demonstrations and related events on the campus of the University of California at Berkeley in the fall of 1964 gave significant impetus to the concept of direct student action, on campus and off; it also provided models of effective student protest action and helped to create a cultural milieu and shared perspective that encouraged further such action on large campuses across the country. Acting crowds of politically-oriented youth are often a consequence of utilizing large numbers to protest some action or policy and, as part of that protest, to picket or hold a rally, or to engage in some kind of sit-in. Thus, there may not be any intent to develop an acting crowd, but it can easily emerge as a natural consequence of the political strategy employed.

Race   Since at least 1965 the phenomenon of the "long hot summer" in the United States has centered upon racial violence in which, unlike previous decades, the initiative is with the urban black, acting violently against property and against (usually white) police authority. Unlike the great race riots of the past, such as Chicago in 1919 or Detroit in 1943, there is less of a direct confrontation between racial crowds, nor is there the invasion of one group's area by another, as so often happened in the past, when whites invaded Negro areas to attack people. Recent riots have been directed more against property, so that looting has become a prominent feature. That most of such property in Negro areas is white-owned is a relevant factor.

In an effort to understand the race riots of the 1960s the National Advisory Commission on Civil Disorders undertook a vast study, and its comprehensive *Report*,[19] issued in the spring of 1968, analyzed events in twenty-three cities, ten of which had had serious disorders during 1967. In describing the pattern of disorder the *Report* notes that there was no "typical" riot. Riots did not always spring from a single precipitating incident, and the rioters were not "hoodlums," criminals, or the least educated; instead, they were a more knowledgeable group than the average, even though they were also largely young high-school dropouts. But they were race-conscious, race-prideful young men, hostile to both whites and middle-class Negroes.[20] There were in most riots efforts by Negro counterrioters, made up usually of better-educated

---

[18] For a review of recent American student involvement in various forms of political action, see Seymour M. Lipset and Philip G. Altbach, "Student Politics and Higher Education in the United States," *Comparative Education Review* (June, 1966). The entire issue reviews student involvement in political action in international perspective. For a similar comparison, see the whole issue of *Daedalus*, 97 (Winter, 1968), entitled "Students and Politics."

[19] The National Advisory Commission on Civil Disorders, *Report* (New York: Bantam, 1968). The Bantam edition is a paperback, there is also a hard-cover edition published by Dutton. The official *Report* has also been published by the Government Printing Office.

[20] *Report*, p. 111.

Negroes, to prevent the riot or to "cool" the action. Negotiations between militant Negroes and civic authorities occurred in almost all the riots, both the issue of ending the riot and the underlying grievances were discussed.[21]

Although denying that the riots fitted any preconceived popular or even social-scientific pattern, in its persistent probing into a very large body of data the Commission felt that it had identified a "chain" made up of

> discrimination, prejudice, disadvantaged conditions, intense and pervasive grievances, a series of tension-heightening incidents, all culminating in the eruption of disorder at the hands of youthful, politically-aware activists.[22]

In reciting the series of incidents that led to an outbreak of violence, the *Report* asserted that often the final incident was too trivial to create a riot, but that it must be understood as the last in a series of exacerbating incidents. In Newark in 1967, for example, these incidents included the arrest of fifteen Negroes for picketing a grocery store, an unsuccessful effort by Negroes to oppose the use of 150 acres in the Negro area for a medical-dental center, an unsuccessful effort to get a Negro appointed secretary of the Board of Education, and the resentment at the participation of Newark policemen in a racial incident in East Orange. When on July 12 a Negro cab driver was injured in a traffic incident, a crowd gathered before the precinct police station, and later in the evening, as the crowd grew in size, Molotov cocktails were thrown, the police dispersed the crowd, and window breaking and looting began. One of America's most destructive riots had begun.[23]

But one major emphasis in the *Report* is upon the social conditions of deprivation and discrimination that are the long-run sources of riot behavior. Sociologists have often related the incidence of crowd violence to various social factors—runaway inflation, a decline in prices and resultant economic hardship, and the like. These however are often precipitous events, whereas the *Report* emphasizes instead the long developing condition of the Negro in America.[24] The important point in the *Report* is its effort to deal with riots at two distinct levels of analysis: the long-run factors that are the "basic causes," and the "more immediate factors" that may generate widespread rioting.[25] It identifies the former as basically three: *pervasive discrimination and segregation; black migration and white exodus;* and *black ghettoes.* But these factors are not sufficient to cause riots, except as there are also present more "immediate factors" that have "begun to catalyze the mixture." These the *Report* identifies as the *frustrated hopes* that surfaced when the judicial and legislative victories

[21] *Report*, pp. 111–112.
[22] *Report*, p. 112.
[23] *Report*, pp. 118–119.
[24] *Report*, Part II, "Why Did It Happen?"
[25] *Report*, Chapter 4, "The Basic Causes," pp. 203–206.

and the civil rights movement produced great expectations that were not realized; a *legitimation of violence,* when white terrorism against black demonstrators, and open defiance of law by state and local officials resisting desegregation, encouraged a climate that legitimized the use of violence. The open preaching of the use of violence by black militants have added to this. Also, a sense of *powerlessness,* of being used and exploited by the white "power structure" has contributed to the idea that there is no way to move the system except through violence.

Crowd Behavior and Law Enforcement   The maintenance of social control in crowd situations is a responsibility of law enforcement agencies; most frequently, this becomes the task of urban police departments. The actions of police can and often do contribute to crowd action in several ways: (1) by demonstrating hostility to the crowd, as police once did to strikers and sometimes yet do to minorities, thus making the police themselves a target of hostility and focus of action; (2) by not being present in time to provide police protection, or by doing little when there. Many a southern lynching occurred because the sheriff arrived too late (usually intentionally) to protect one or several Negroes from attack.

But race riots are destructive events, socially and psychologically, as well as physically, and communities south or north expect the police department to enforce order and prevent a riot. The avoidance of mob action is not easy to accomplish by even the most professional of police, and there is no guaranteed set of procedures for police to follow. In seeking to control outbreaks in recent ghetto-based riots, police have tried to walk a delicate path between enforcing law against looters and others, while not attacking crowds and further inflaming them to violent action; to act quickly but not to overreact. What works in stemming one possible outbreak fails in another—a show of force in one case may intimidate possible rioters, may only anger and rouse them in another.

The work of the Commission and of many social scientists in seeking to understand the causes of riots is not value-neutral. It is based upon the assumption that riots are undesirable in a democratic society. In the United States it is the racial situation that is most conducive to riots, for this is the issue that reveals the deepest internal social cleavage in American society. Once riots were instruments by which whites controlled racial minorities by fear and violence; now they are the means by which ghetto-bound black people express deep resentment against the conditions of their life. The value position against mob action is a preference for more rational and humane behavior, for whether oppressed or oppressor, the acting crowd is violent and unfeeling in its direct action against its target. But this preference also rests upon the assumption that democratic society offers effective alternatives: the courts, legislative action, public opinion, and the like. Where such alternatives do not prove to be effective, the moral argument against direct action becomes less convincing to many people. However uncertain as to the outcome of crowd action, revolutionary leaders may instigate it, or at least not seek to prevent it, when, in objective calculations of political power, the aroused crowd may do what reasoned behavior cannot seem to accomplish.

PUBLICS AND PUBLIC OPINION

The concern for publics and public opinion emerged with the democratic revolutions that overthrew aristocratic rule. Liberal thought gave rise to the idea of the significance of the public in the democratic process and to the preeminence of public opinion in the decision-making process. Conservative thought, in turn, expressed concern about the influence of public opinion on society, which emanated from a lack of confidence in the capacity of the people to make wise decisions.

In time the idea of public opinion came to develop a certain sanctity within the framework of democracy. Public opinion was the voice of the people— *vox populi*—and a means of majority rule. On the other hand the existence of pressure groups and lobbying points up sharply the simple fact that public opinion alone does not shape public decisions. In the twentieth century the analysis of propaganda suggests that the formation of public opinion is rarely today a chance or spontaneous process, but is influenced by groups that stand to gain something from a public decision.

The Public The concepts of *public* and of *public opinion* have never been defined to the satisfaction of all. The public lacks the structure that one associates with well-organized groups; it has no officials, though there may be opinion leaders; there is interaction and communication, though there is no definition of membership; and the public has no process of physically coming together —its interaction is not face-to-face.

The idea of public involves these several elements: (1) some (but not all) members of a society who have some concern or interest in a public matter; (2) an issue that requires resolution or decision within that society; (3) a process of discussion among these interested individuals, carried on through available means of communication; and (4) the emergence of public opinion from this discussion. From this it would seem that the concept of public denotes, not so much a group of people, as a social process—a process of public discussion leading to the formation of one or more widely shared opinions as to the advisability or desirability of a public policy or a mode of action by government.

This conceptualization of public may eliminate some common misconceptions about the nature of public. One misconception is to speak of *the* public as if it included everyone in the society. Potentially it does, but in practice it is more restricted. If the public includes those who are interested in an issue and participate in public discussion of the merits of that issue, this excludes those who are not interested and have not participated in the public discussion. Publics are smaller than the total adult population of a society. Furthermore, there is not *the* public in the sense of only one public—there are *publics*. Different public issues are of concern to different segments of the populations; labor-management relations, tariffs, taxes, national defense, conservation, and obscene literature are issues that do not interest the same or the same numbers of people. The public concerned with national defense will be larger than that concerned with conservation, as the public concerned with tariffs will be smaller than that concerned with taxes.

If public refers to the discussion of public issues that require resolution, then public as a social process is *political*. The formation of public opinion in a democratic society is one factor influencing the decision-making process. This political meaning of the concept of public limits the use of the term sociologically by restricting it to the process of forming public opinion about public issues. The term is also used commonly to refer to the fans of movie stars and the more devoted followers of public figures. It is also used to refer to the idea of everyone without restriction, as "the public is invited." Another use is to denote the customers and clientele of the mass producers of entertainment and material goods: the movie public, the auto-buying public, and so on. In these cases what might be called public opinion is usually *mass customer reaction* to products offered for consumption. Although this mass reaction may certainly influence production policies, this is not public opinion in a sociological sense of the term.

The public is not only a political process, it is a *democratic* one. The significant place of publics and public opinion in society arose from liberal political theory, concerned with designing the structure of parliamentary democracy. The concept of the public rests on the notion of the right of the citizenry to participate in decision making by voting for their representative in parliament and by openly and freely discussing public issues and coming to a common public agreement. The public and the making of public opinion in liberal theory assumes several significant liberal values. Perhaps the foremost is the basic enlightenment value of *rationality:* the public in a democratic society assumes the capacity of its citizens to think and discuss serious issues in a rational, dispassionate manner, minimizing personal prejudice and maximizing respect for demonstrated facts and for accurate reasoning. *Freedom* is another democratic value underlying the assumptions in liberal theory about the public process. Clearly, if there is to be a rational discussion of social issues, this requires not only the freedom to discuss all aspects, but the freedom of speech and press that will allow free and untrammeled communication of facts and ideas.

Ideally, then, the public process is conceived in liberal theory as a process of the political citizen—rational, intelligent, informed—discussing fully and seriously the important social issues facing the society, with free access to all relevant facts through the media of communication. Rational men in a free society—this is the liberal image of the public. Only a democratic society could fill the requirements set forth from this perspective. In totalitarian societies there is a great concern with the character of public opinion; however, free discussion of issues does not take place. There is no public in the liberal western conception of the term. Totalitarian elites are concerned with mass response and mass opinion, particularly as its affects morale and work performance. Also, they are concerned with inculcating mass opinions favorable to the state and use all media of communication for that purpose.

The Character of the Public   Even in Western democratic societies the public is an ideal that is only imperfectly attained, and sometimes the gap between the ideal and real seems to be considerable, as measured by social research. For over forty years now, beginning with an influential work by Walter Lippman,[26] social scientists, marketing researchers, journalists, and professional pollsters have been measuring public opinion in the United States, and, more recently, throughout the literate world. The result is not only a mass of data on the state of public opinion on a vast array of issues, but also an image of how far the public falls short of measuring up to the liberal ideal of rational, informed men involved in free discussion. The public seems neither well-informed nor deeply concerned about many of the serious public issues; nor does public opinion seem to be the product of informed and serious discussion.[27] Furthermore, the presence of interest groups whose propaganda obscures and beclouds basic issues, rather than clarifies them, adds to the inadequacies of public opinion and to the ineffectiveness of the public process in rationally developing public opinion.

The *knowledge* of the public about public issues is one criterion in measuring the adequacy of the public and its opinion. A recent polling technique has been to separate out the *more knowledgeable* from the *less knowledgeable* among

[26] Walter Lippmann, *Public Opinion* (New York: Harcourt, Brace, 1922).

[27] For a review of the status of public opinion as measured by polls, see Herbert H. Hyman and Paul B. Sheatsley, "The Current Status of American Public Opinion," in J. C. Payne, ed., *Twenty-First Yearbook* (National Council for the Social Studies, 1950), pp. 11–34.

the people whose opinions are being surveyed. This is done by asking background questions before asking for opinions. If the poll is about pending legislation, people may be asked about the issue itself or about some details of the legislation. Frequently the responses indicate that large numbers of people are unable to identify correctly the details of the proposed legislation or to define correctly words denoting significant concepts, ideas, proposals, or institutionalized procedures. For example, a national poll asked people what a reciprocal trade treaty was: 52 percent admitted they did not know; 31 percent gave incorrect definitions; 9 percent doubtful ones; and only 8 percent a correct one. Such a response gives an image of the public as ignorant, but only if everyone in the adult population is considered a part of the public. But if we define the public as those with an interest in an issue, then most of those who do not know what a reciprocal trade treaty is are not part of the public of this particular issue, which, indeed, may be a small public.

People who know little of an issue are not likely to have an opinion, either. Nevertheless, sometimes those who are characterized as less knowledgeable on some issue respond with an opinion. Is this ignorant and unenlightened public opinion? Perhaps. But it may also merely be a function of the interview situation: asked an opinion, they offered one, even though they have not thought about the matter before. Social scientists are aware that such "opinions" as these come from people who do not in fact have an opinion. This in turn has led to an interest in the *intensity* with which people hold opinions, an interest in identifying those with serious convictions about an issue that lead to stable opinions, not superficial and transitory ones. Again, pollsters have devised questions aimed at distinguishing those who hold opinions with some conviction and some depth of feeling, as well as with some knowledge of the issue.

However, there are times when people do have strong opinions, even though they may not appear to be knowledgeable about the details of an issue. Many workers, particularly union members, expressed strong and definite opposition to the Taft-Hartley Act, yet often they were not well-informed about the details of the act, or they even explicitly approved of some of its specific measures. On issues such as these, people respond to symbols which can be attached to specific issues. In this instance the Taft-Hartley Act was a Republican-sponsored, business-supported measure to modify the Wagner Act and was strongly opposed by labor leaders and liberal Democrats. Both workers and businessmen took their cues from this situation and held strong opinions of approval or disapproval of the act, even when relatively uninformed of its details. Knowledgeability, then, is only one factor in leading to clear and definite convictions. People respond, not only to the merits of an issue but also to the situation in which the issue arises. Like all social action, public opinion emerges from the interpretations people make in ongoing social situations. Who supports and who opposes an issue are important clues for people who seek to interpret the issue in terms of who wants something or who will have an advantage.

What organized groups support and oppose an issue is not the only significant part of the situation that shapes opinion. So also is the larger context of events when the issue is raised. Opinion favoring compulsory arbitration of labor disputes is likely to increase during and just after a serious national strike, such as in steel or the railroads. Gun control legislation had strong public support just after President John Kennedy's assassination and again after the assassinations of Senator Robert Kennedy and Martin Luther King. Those seeking such measures, of course, will find it strategic to advance their proposals when events in the society make it easier to mobilize a supporting public opinion.

If public opinion is in part shaped by people's symbolic response to the contestants in an issue, and to the particular sequence of events occurring when the issue is raised, it is also in part formed from *presituational* factors: prejudices, values, group loyalties, and the like, which people carry into a situation. Most studies of public opinion have found it useful to break down responses to an opinion poll into such categories as: urban and rural; Catholic, Protestant, and Jewish; old, middle-aged, and young; Republican and Democrat. Opinion varies in a predictable way in relation to these categories. It does also with education and with income, and with such broad class and occupational categories as workers, farmers, businessmen, and professionals. People interpret events and develop opinions in terms of how they think it will affect their *interests* as workers or as high income people. They also interpret events and develop opinions on the basis of their *values* as Catholics or rural people or Democrats. And they also interpret events and develop opinions from a perspective shaped by *past experience.* Older workers who have been through the depression, or even young ones who have experienced unemployment, strongly favor social security measures and develop opinions more favorable to governmental action.

The social positions and group affiliations of people, then, give them interests, values, and experiences that influence the way they respond to issues and the kinds of opinion they develop. It provides them with attitudes and prejudices that they carry into the public process and that function to interpret and assess the relative merits of the issue up for public discussion. The development of public opinion is not a process that starts with a blank slate; people are already predisposed by situational and presituational factors to form predictable opinions about public issues.

It is not entirely a rational process, either, though the public capacity for rational discussion is not necessarily as low as many social scientists have seemingly made it appear by their analysis of the modern public. The image of the public that emerges from this analysis of public opinion is a poor one, hardly seeming to sustain the liberal hope for an enlightened public as a significant element in the democratic process. Indeed, the unenlightened character of the public has been used as an argument supporting a conservative case against a universal electorate. Even democratic liberals have been chastened by the image of the modern public. However, the late V. O. Key, a distinguished political scientist and foremost student of the American political process, wrote a sober defense of the rational capacity of the voting public, challenging seriously the unflattering image of the public so widespread among, not only social scientists, but educated people.[28]

An analysis of how public opinion is ascertained, however, leads to the conclusion that the very opinion-measuring process itself contributes heavily to the widespread negative image of the public. For one thing, polls do not measure *public* opinion, they measure *mass opinion:* they ask a sample of all adults their opinion of a matter. But a public is not defined as all adults; it consists of those who have an interest in an issue. Although a large part of the total population may then evidence considerable ignorance and disinterest on an issue, this only signifies that the opinion-forming public is but a portion, and sometimes a small portion, of that total population. To be sure, opinion pollsters have introduced questions which sift out those who have more interest, are more knowledgeable, and have more definite convictions on an issue. But this has rarely been correlated with other social characteristics, such as region, age, class or occupation, income level, or group attachment, to provide a means of more precisely defining the relevant publics for specific public issues. In this manner, however, public opinion and not mass opinion does appear to be more informed and possessed of more definite opinions shaped by intelligent discussion than mass polling would show. As one might expect, the better educated are most likely to be better informed on a range of issues, and the poor and uneducated to be least informed.

The concern for the seemingly low level of public opinion is based upon the liberal democratic expectation that (1) all issues are within the intellectual grasp of the public, and (2) all adult citizens ought to be rational participants in public discussion. The first assumption undoubtedly provides one of the great challenges to democratic theory. Many of the issues requiring action are so complex in nature that an informed public is hard to obtain. Even political leaders who must make decisions, such as legislators, governors, and presidents, cannot be expertly informed on many matters. As a consequence, they are guided by the advice of experts as well as by the positions taken by the spokes-

---

[28] V. O. Key, Jr., *The Responsible Electorate: Rationality in Presidential Voting, 1936–60* (Cambridge, Mass.: Harvard University Press, 1966).

men for groups with definite interests in the issue. Interest groups, in turn, employ experts to advance their cause. Lobbyists, particularly in state legislatures, often function as experts for the legislators, a relationship little understood by a public with a negative image of lobbyists.

Few citizens expect that major decisions over national defense, such as the problem of choosing among alternate weapons systems, are matters to be decided by public opinion, and not because so much relevant information is necessarily a military secret. Even if the information were not, the technical complexity of the matter would far exceed the capacity of all but the technically trained. Even where issues are not as technical as military weapons systems, the issues are still complex, involving economic, political, administrative, financial, and tax factors understood only by those trained in these specialties. As a consequence, any concern for the function of public opinion in a democracy must recognize that the average citizen does not expect to have informed opinion on such matters. He does expect the nation's political leadership to be able to make informed judgments, with the assistance of disinterested experts, and to be held responsible for the decisions it makes.

Any sociological theory of public opinion in a democratic society that is also a highly complex, technological society, then, needs to include some assessment of the complexity of issues and of the expectations of large numbers of individuals in that society that the responsible political leadership will have to make decisions on their own. The public, as a *voting public,* will then formulate opinions as to the adequacy with which this leadership carried out its responsibilities; this opinion will be shaped largely by its assessment of the *consequences* of such decisions, a matter in itself requiring high levels of information for rational judgment.

Social scientists have long pointed out that those without opinions on many issues are drawn disproportionately from those of little education and low income. These same people are less involved in the numerous voluntary associations, membership in which serves to develop interest in issues, and opinions as well. The lower income masses, particularly in the cities, including such minorities as Negroes, are not drawn extensively into public life and share very little in the shaping of public opinion. It is not sufficient to say they are *apathetic* and *ignorant.* Ignorance of public issues is not caused, though it is aided, by a lack of education. And apathy, as a term, merely says they lack interest in public issues. The sociological problem is why.

The press of poverty makes it difficult for the poor to have the psychic energy, as well as the time, to devote to an interest in public issues. A lack of formal education hinders their capacity to become informed. But more importantly, the poor often lack confidence that their participation will lead to any significant change in their lot in life. They doubt the value of active participation in the democratic process for their own interests. They are not convinced that the choice between parties, candidates, and issues will make any difference for them.

To the politically active middle class, such a perspective may seem to be unduly cynical and pessimistic, but there is a basis in reality for it. The poor reason from their own experience, and the element of hopelessness, disbelief, and distrust that characterizes their social perspective is grounded in the nature of their social life. The failure of democratic society to incorporate voluntarily the urban poor and the minorities in the processes of public life is probably the most serious gap between its ideals and its reality. It is here that the measurement of mass opinion and the identification of the least informed and least interested provides a significant sociological assessment of the democratic character of modern society.

Propaganda: The Manipulation of Public Opinion In modern society the formation of public opinion is never left to chance; instead it is always the concern of interest groups seeking to shape it in support of their particular objectives and interests. As a consequence, it is never merely the *spontaneous* development from public discussion; rather, *manipulation by propaganda* is a major factor.

Propaganda is the deliberate dissemination of partisan communication in order to influence the formation of public opinion. It may be but it does not have to be untruthful, what distinguishes propaganda is its intent: to focus attention on an issue in such a way as deliberately to create a choice in public opinion and reduce the probability of alternative choices of opinion being made by the public. Unlike academic scholarship and science, its concern is not intellectual exploration for the pursuit of truth. Its objective is not to achieve truth but to convince people of a point of view. This does not mean that propagandists are intentionally dishonest, only that they are highly partisan about the issue.

There is no profession of people called *propagandists;* they are writers, editors, journalists, broadcasters, advertising copy-writers, and public relations practitioners. Propaganda, of course, can be the product of any group intent on shaping public opinion to its interests, and its production can be the effort of individuals from any profession. But systematic, professional work in propaganda does come from those professionally skilled in mass communication and from the communication professions. It is characteristic of modern society that propaganda is a major factor in public life, diffused extensively through the mass media; yet the term does have negative connotations, and none of its practitioners would willingly call themselves propagandists.

Advertising and public relations provide a professional source of skilled propagandists. Public relations firms in the United States have become major businesses manufacturing propaganda for clients. For example, when President Truman advanced his program for national medical insurance, the American Medical Association employed a California public relations firm, Whittaker and Baxter, specialists in political campaigns, to carry out a national program of opposition. Increasingly, political campaigns are carried on with the aid of professional propagandists, who do more than write speeches. They plan a campaign in detail in order to create images favorable to their party or candidate.

In contemporary America, terms like "hucksters" and "Madison Avenue" have become popular symbols of public awareness of sustained efforts to manipulate the opinion of masses of people about products, personalities, politicians, issues, and ideas. A popular book, Vance Packard's *The Hidden Persuaders,* became a national best seller by exposing the techniques by which advertisers and public relations practitioners sought to influence opinion.[29] The very title implies a sinister process; its major theme was that people did not know that so much of the material in mass communication to which they were exposed was deliberately contrived, without their knowledge, to shape their opinion. The fact that the book was a best seller, in turn, testifies to the deep suspicion of Americans that they are manipulated by "hidden persuaders."

The attempt to influence public opinion by propaganda is hardly a science, but it does put to use knowledge obtained by the social sciences. A propaganda message is built by appealing to existing *values* and *attitudes* in order to influence opinions. A knowledge of the values and attitudes of the target group is one essential in effective propaganda. The propagandist invokes *symbols* of these underlying values and attitudes to link his particular objective to these values and, as a consequence, mold opinion in the desired direction. Freedom, equality, socialism, private enterprise, individualism, big government, bureaucracy; these are some of the major symbols, both negative and positive, in American society that signify underlying values and attitudes. For example, when Whittaker and Baxter undertook to direct the AMA's campaign against President Truman's program for national medical insurance, they labeled it "socialized medicine" so effectively that the label remained attached to the program until the mid-sixties. The opinions of millions of Americans were influenced by this designation, given their attitudinal opposition to socialism.

The labeling of President Truman's program as "socialized medicine" is an example of *name-calling,* one of seven major "tricks of the trade" employed by propagandists. These were enumerated in an enlightening little book, *The Fine Art of Propaganda,* by two sociologists, Alfred McClung Lee and Elizabeth

[29] Vance Packard, *The Hidden Persuaders* (New York: McKay, 1957).

Briant Lee.[30] If *name-calling* means to place a bad label on something, *glittering generality* means to place a good label on it, using such "virtue words" as *American, democratic, individual,* and the like. Two other tricks, *transfer* and *testimonial,* refer to the process of transferring the prestige or esteem of respected symbols, or of obtaining statements from respected persons to support or oppose an issue. *Plain folks* is a process of identifying the propagandist's ideas with the people. *Card stacking* refers to the development of an argument that so arranges facts and falsehoods as to lead people to a particular conclusion, while *band wagon* seeks to build support by leading people to believe that everyone is for the idea, and therefore they had better "get with it."

There is no accurate measurement of the influence of propaganda. The resolution of any public issue is always both a victory and a defeat for propagandists, for they are employed by both sides. The definition of the issues at stake, the key terms applied, the kind of facts cited, and the direction of the conflict carried on by interested groups, will largely be the work of professional "mass persuaders."

What allows for such an influential role? The uncertain character of public opinion in a free society is bound to bring efforts to increase skills in influencing it, for interest groups of one kind or another develop vast stakes in programs and are not going to allow public opinion to develop spontaneously if that opinion has some bearing on its interests. Furthermore, the complexity of many public issues allows the propagandist to present simplified answers in acceptable symbolic terms. Nor does the mass media itself always present rational, objective discussions, free of propaganda. In America the fears and anxieties of masses of people about world trends, about the advances of world Communism, their insecurities about a changing, uncertain future, individual and collective, their unspoken concerns about shifts and transitions in power, their fear of hidden forces unduly influencing others or manipulating them— all these concerns give the propagandist an opportunity to influence the shaping of public opinion.

The existence of publics in a democratic society, capable of rational and informed discussion of public issues and capable of resisting the interpretations of propagandists, requires a level of political sophistication, of knowledge and understanding, and of commitment to rationality and objective facts, not to be found at the present time in other than smaller circles of informed citizens. Such a situation not only sets the stage for the manipulation of mass opinions, it damages belief in an informed and intelligent public opinion as a function of democracy.

Social science has contributed considerably to this damaged image of dem-

---

[30] Alfred McClung Lee and Elizabeth Briant Lee, *The Fine Art of Propaganda* (New York: Harcourt, Brace, 1939).

ocracy by its analysis of the state of public opinion and the manipulation of
it by propagandists. But the students of social science in particular need to
keep clear the distinction between the present state of affairs, *what is,* as
objectively described by social science, and an image of a future, more ideal
state of affairs, *what might be.* The present state of public opinion is not in
itself sufficient reason for abandoning a belief in the possibility of a more
rational process of forming public opinion, but it is a basis for understanding
the present gap between the reality and the ideal and also for understanding
what characteristics of modern society prevent the ideal from being more
nearly approximated.

Crowds and publics by no means exhaust the major forms of collective behavior significant for sociological analysis. Another is that of the social movement. The struggle for civil rights in the United States has recently restored
the social movement to a prominent place of intellectual concern and has
once more made it a salient object for sociological attention. In the following
chapter, we conclude our concern for collective behavior by exploring what
we know sociologically about the phenomenon of the social movement.

1 2

3

1. Shanghai: traditional Chinese gymnastics in front of a Red Guard poster.
2. San Francisco "hippie" bus.
3. Spectators at a Loyalty Day Parade, New York City.
4. Freedom March in New York.
5. A flower child in San Francisco.

4 5

SOCIAL MOVEMENTS AND IDEOLOGIES

20

Much of the social change that occurs in modern society is the consequence of technological, demographic, economic, and political developments, a consequence neither understood nor intended by those whose behavior is so drastically affected. When social change is viewed in this way, men are visualized as mere puppets who respond in predictable, determined ways to great historical forces without any rational awareness of what they are doing. Whatever the limitations on their rational understanding of human events, however, men rarely accept the processes of change without some effort on their part to give it direction in terms of their own values and goals. *Social movements* are the conscious attempts of masses of people to bring about change deliberately in the social structure by collective action. They are engaged in social protest, in processes of reform and revolution.

Out of the bewildering array of social movements observable even in modern society, types can be sorted out by several criteria. For example, one can distinguish social movements by the institution to which they are related by goals and values: there are *political* and *religious* movements, for example. Or, one can identify movements in terms of the classes or categories of people attracted to them and whose cause they serve: there are *working-class* movements, *farmers'* movements, *peasants'* movements, and *middle-class* movements. In even more limited categories, one finds *youth* movements, *women's rights* movements, *old age* movements, and *minority* group movements.

Movements can also be classified in terms of the extensiveness of their social goals. There are *reform* movements, which accept the basic values and institutional structure of society but seek to reform what the movement defines as abuses, defects, or inadequacies. The labor movement, for example, is a reform movement when it seeks changes benefitting the worker without altering the basic structure of capitalism. *Revolutionary* movements, in turn, seek to effect a fundamental change in the social structure, as in replacing capitalism with socialism or in democratizing an authoritarian society. Other movements, including some of those listed above, may seek a single limited goal. The Townsend movement in the 1930s sought old age pensions, and the women's suffrage movement sought the vote for women. Just because these specific objectives do not project any more extensive change, such movements may gain the support of a wider range of people. Nevertheless, the success of such movements may in turn have more ramifying consequences for change than intended or foreseen by their supporters.

SOCIAL MOVEMENTS AS A SOCIOLOGICAL PROBLEM

Like other forms of collective behavior, social movements have proven to be particularly problematic for sociologists. Since they are large and involved complexes of various social processes, they are difficult to observe. They occur over a period of time and generally go through a life-cycle; thus, a study at one point in time does not encompass everything we need to know about a social movement. Furthermore, social movements are not highly organized phenomena, yet are not simply the fluid, unstructured processes that crowds are; they do display some core of organization and develop some stability of leadership.

There is no question that the social movement, like all of collective behavior, has been a neglected aspect of sociology. Lewis Killian suggests that this is so because "men and groups have so often been regarded by sociologists as the creatures rather than the creators of social change."[1] He points out that many sociologists have viewed social movements, for all their drama and conflict, as being merely epiphenomena, whereas other processes are the "real" causal forces in human affairs. A deterministic emphasis in sociological theory over the past century has encouraged this viewpoint; such an emphasis had been uncongenial to the view that sees men as acting to alter the circumstances of their life and as creating the social patterns within which they will live.

No student of the discipline can also fail to note that the emphasis of sociological inquiry has been much more on social structure than on social process. Sociologists have studied bureaucracies extensively, social movements but little. The very nature of the social movement does not lend itself to study by the conventional techniques and modes of research current in the discipline. Whatever the several reasons, therefore, the study of social movements has never been high on the agenda of sociologists. In recent years, however, there has been a renewed interest in the study of social movements and a modest increase in the sociological literature. The rise of a militant social movement among Negroes over civil rights is the event in society that has sparked this renewed interest. Social movements have once again become socially relevant processes in American society, and their return to a central place in American intellectual interest has made them once more a matter of concern for social scientists.

The problem of social movements for sociology is to conceptualize it as an ongoing social process that is a mode of social change in society, one in which men are consciously assessing and evaluating their society and are initiating efforts to alter its structure in ways that more nearly fit their values. This leads to four problematic issues in the effort to study scientifically the process of a social movement: the nature of a social movement; its organization and leadership; its ideology; and its career.

The first concern about social movements is the still continuing effort to determine just what a social movement is, that is, what is a scientifically

---

[1] Lewis Killian, "Social Movements," in Robert E. L. Faris, ed., *Handbook of Modern Sociology* (Chicago: Rand McNally, 1964), pp. 426–455. Quotations from p. 426.

viable sociological conception. This concern focuses on the analytic elements that are taken to be common to social movements: the *genesis* of a movement; its *ideology;* its *social base;* and its *organization* and *leadership.*

All social movements possess an organized core of groups and leaders; there is a basic structure at the center, though this does not constitute the entirety of the movement. Nonetheless, a structure, including a leadership, is essential to give direction and focus to a movement. Nor can social movements be studied without a serious concern for ideology. In their conscious efforts to change society, movements generate ideologies that justify such efforts; in response, counter-ideologies emerge to defend the social order against such concerted efforts to change it.

One of the difficulties in studying social movements is that they occur over time and are not likely to be the same at two different points in time. Social movements emerge, develop, then usually end; either they become successful and institutionalized, or else they fail and perhaps gradually wither away or are transformed into some other kind of movement. A major aspect in the study of social movements, then, is a concern for its *career,* that development from beginning to end that characterizes the history of all social movements.

THE NATURE OF A SOCIAL MOVEMENT

A social movement, we saw above, has a history; it arises at some point in time, it flourishes, and then it recedes. In this process it manifests the various characteristics of a movement, including the fact of having a career or life-cycle. But however different in the content of their values and objectives, and however different in their careers and the consequences of their efforts, social movements reveal some common set of processes that enable us to place the label "social movement" on them. Certainly, social movements are more lasting than crowds, whose existence is usually a matter of hours and consists of those persons who are physically present at the same place at the same time. Also, a crowd has a narrow and immediate objective, whereas a social movement has a more rationally considered and broader objective, or even a set of objectives. Social movements also develop some structure—a core of organization, however diffuse and inconsistently integrated, and a leadership. In this way they differ from both crowds and publics. Yet the study of social movements "is not the study of stable groups and established institutions, but of groups and institutions in the process of becoming."[2]

A review of the scholarly efforts to define social movement reveals a fairly consistent reference to the idea of the attempt to change the social order by

---

[2] Killian, p. 427.

collective action. Turner and Killian's well-known definition will serve our purpose: "A collectivity acting with some continuity to promote or resist a change in the society or group of which it is a part."[3] This definition was intentionally phrased to convey the idea of collective rather than individual action and also to express the idea that men deliberately and consciously assert themselves in the processes of social change. Thus a social movement is not only social change, but specifically it is the change that comes about as a consequence of human efforts to realize specific goals, even though the social change that occurs is not what was intended.

Like all forms of collective behavior, a social movement is not particularly neat and well-organized. Its membership is never formally defined and usually remains somewhat unspecified. Some people may belong to formal organizations, such as labor unions and parties, but this is not an accurate measurement of the support for a movement.

The Genesis of a Social Movement   Although it would be safe to say that social movements arise because men want to change the order of things, this is hardly an adequate statement of why social movements come to be. To some extent men probably always and everywhere would like to change things, for the social worlds in which they live are always imperfect. But such a general wish does not bring social movements into being. Indeed, one long and persistently puzzling question about human life is why more people do not rebel against the circumstances of their life, why they so patiently endure oppressive and burdensome circumstances. The conditions for social movements, then, are endemic in the nature of social order. But they do not occur that frequently. All human societies are imperfect social orders, whose particular social institutions meet the needs and wants of its members in an imperfect manner. A dissatisfaction with the state of the social order is pervasive, therefore, and generates ideas about more ideal conditions that might be. Yet, if life is not perfect, neither do people expect it to be. They endure minor dissatisfactions and irritations as simply part of life. Also, many people see their life-circumstances as a peculiar and individual fate of their own, unrelated to the life-circumstances of others.

Some more enduring and fundamental dissatisfactions are a product of the way the unplanned social order develops and changes. The values held in a society become inconsistent with new patterns of behavior, and conflict is pervasive throughout the subgroupings that are produced by the division of labor. A social order thus normally displays value conflict as one consequence of having values, role and status conflict as one aspect of stratification, and group hostility as well as group consensus. Furthermore, any society has strata

---

[3] Ralph H. Turner and Lewis M. Killian, *Collective Behavior* (Englewood Cliffs, N.J.: Prentice-Hall, 1957), p. 308.

and groups who are more amply rewarded and more advantaged than others, and other strata and groups who get less reward for their contribution to society and are disadvantaged in the distribution of life-chances.

The emergence of a social movement, however, is not an automatic process from such general conditions of dissatisfaction. For one thing, individuals must communicate their dissatisfactions and share with others a *collective* sense of a shared lot in life. They must identify with others who share their same fate. Spontaneous acts of rebellion and protest, silent acts of sabotage and vandalism—these may reflect an underlying sense of grievance. So may an act of voting "communist" (or whatever is most heretical), or a withdrawal and refusal to be involved. There are many ways in which there is made manifest a sense of grievance shared by a segment of a society, but none of these may constitute a social movement. The emergence of a social movement from the appropriate underlying conditions requires the development, not only of a sense of collective fate, but of a belief in the chance to act collectively toward new goals that will bring a new life.

There is a problem of timing here that has yet to be adequately assessed. Why does a movement arise when it does and not before? Certainly, the Negro revolt in the 1960s in the United States stems from conditions of discrimination that have prevailed since slavery. Indeed, the situation now is not any worse than before and objectively is better than at most times in the past.

Social scientists have observed more than once that a social movement is likely to occur when by any objective measurement the life of an oppressed people has improved. It would seem that some change for the better is likely to generate a sense of hope and a dissatisfaction, not merely with things as they are, but even more to the point, with the slow pace of improvement. Whatever the objective conditions of life, a people without hope do not rebel. Yet we do not yet know enough to state any firm generalization about when and why people in disadvantaged situations will act collectively on a hope for a better life.

But what are the "objective" conditions that social scientists speak of? Most frequently they refer to *economic* conditions, as well as to educational and political ones. These, and particularly the former, can be objectively measured. Thus, some social scientists have sought to demonstrate that the lot of American Negroes, objectively, is better now than ever before. But others have argued that this obscures the *increased* economic impoverishment of the urban lower-class Negroes, the young among whom are the *activists* in the riots that burn and loot cities, a point the *Report* of the National Advisory Commission on Civil Disorders has seen fit to emphasize.[4] Whatever the facts about objec-

---

[4] National Advisory Commission on Civil Disorders, *Report* (New York: Bantam, 1968), pp. 128–129.

tive conditions, however, there is no doubt that the civil rights movement in the 1960s emerged out of a series of events, such as the Supreme Court decision in 1954. This gave Negroes reason to hope for better things, but soon after this effective white resistance produced disenchantment and disillusionment.

Such a point as this, however, does not necessarily explain the onset of social movements among those whose lot in life has been relatively advantaged but is now threatened. When people sense a threat to their established values, or when they see themselves as having suffered deprivations and a loss of status, social movements also emerge. But not all declining classes revolt; again, whatever their collective frustrations, there must develop some shared hope of altering the social order in a direction that meets their values.

Most social movements develop only after long experience, not only with the social conditions against which they will act, but also with a patient reliance on other alternatives. Movements are bred out of human experience about what action will *not* alter their circumstances; thus, it comes about as a conscious cognitive assessment of much that has already occurred in the collective life of those who constitute a social movement.

Although sociologists may as yet be unable to state in any rigorous fashion how social movements generate, it seems evident that several factors need to be present besides the objective social conditions that breed dissatisfaction and resentment. There needs to be a social consciousness that is not a philosophical acceptance of or resignation to the situation, but instead creates a social perspective that defines the possibilities of action. This is the crux of a social movement: not merely that people are in situations that lead to a strong sense of grievance, dissatisfaction, or resentment, but that there is developed a social perspective that generates a capacity for concerted, collective action.

THE IDEOLOGY OF A SOCIAL MOVEMENT

An ideology constitutes a set of ideas that expresses the sense of grievance and injustice about society, provides a specific criticism of the existing social structure, and projects goals which are to be sought by collective action. An examination of a social movement's ideology lays bare the source of social dissent from which the movement arises and identifies the social cleavage (class, race) in the society around which political struggle occurs. An ideology interprets an historical situation from the value perspective of a group or stratum in the society. Indeed, an ideology utilizes these values to find an intellectual standpoint from which to criticize and to project desirable change.

An ideology serves to unify masses of people into social movements by translating their experiences of grievance and wrong, their frustrations and aspirations, into specific arguments of criticism and into stated goals. It serves to concentrate the energies of people into specific projects and unites them around symbols and slogans that give specific content to their hitherto vague feelings of discontent. It gives hope to people by holding out objectives of reform or revolution as being within the realm of the possible.

This latter function is a significant aspect of the ideology of a social movement. What it may proclaim as within the realm of the possible may seem utterly impossible to other people, but movements generate a *utopian* mentality that fastens firmly upon a belief in a future state of affairs. One function of an ideology is to project such utopian *myths;* George Sorel speaks of the myth as the successful "framing of a future . . . when the anticipation of the future takes the form of those myths, which inclose with them, all the strong inclinations of a people. . . ."[5] The utopian mentality may seem to reach for impossible goals, but its very effort often has radical consequences for society. Karl Mannheim (1893–1947), whose *Ideology and Utopia*[6] is a brilliant exposition of the political meaning for the modern world of utopian myths, believed that modern politics began in the Middle ages from utopian movements.

> It is at this point that politics in the modern sense of the term begins, if we here understand by politics a more or less conscious participation of all strata of society in the achievement of some mundane purpose, as contrasted with a fatalistic acceptance of events as they are, or control from 'above.'[7]

And surely it is here that we can understand as viable myth the cry of *black power,* for it symbolizes the newly achieved conscious determination of black Americans to determine their own destiny and fate in American society in some politically viable manner; neither to accept fatalistically what has been nor to accept white actions and white power, no matter how well-intentioned. The historic record makes it clear that utopian myths have not produced utopias, but that is no measure of their significance. As Mannheim said: "The impossible gives birth to the possible, and the absolute interferes with the world and conditions actual events."[8]

Ideology often simplifies an interpretation for masses of people, for the real world is complex and baffling. It simplifies and thus distorts reality by defining "they" and "us," our side and their side, in relatively simple black and

---

[5] George Sorel, *Reflections on Violence,* trans. by T. E. Hulme and J. Roth (New York: Free Press, 1950).

[6] Karl Mannheim, *Ideology and Utopia,* trans. by Louis Wirth and Edward A. Shils (New York: Harcourt, Brace, 1946).

[7] Mannheim, p. 191.

[8] Mannheim, p. 192.

white terms. It may moralize great human events and designate the evil ones who can be held personally responsible, in short, scapegoats. "Vulgar" Marxism projected an image of the greedy, exploitative capitalist, though intellectual Marxism is concerned not with evil men but with an institutional process.

An ideology, then, may function at several intellectual levels. There is a "vulgar" level of slogans and catch-phrases and emotionally arousing stereotypes, as well as scapegoats that may be used for masses of uneducated and oppressed. There can be a popularized, middlebrow level, for the formally educated, who would read, for example, interpretations of Marx, though never read the original material. And there is a highbrow, intellectual ideology, for those with the interest and intellectual perspective to engage in the most erudite intellectual interpretations and analyses.

When we speak of levels of ideology, we refer in particular to ideology in the Western world, where intellectuals have functioned in the role of revolutionary and reformist critics of society and have given intellectual form to hitherto poorly expressed resentments and frustrations. But there is also an indigenous ideology, one which emerges from a people without benefit of intellectuals and intellectual expression. Such indigenous ideologies can also be found among rebelling natives, among peasants, and among workers, though in modern society the more a movement grows, the more likely it is to attract intellectuals who give coherent expression to its ideas.

The Social Base   If an ideology expresses the deeply felt sense of injustice and the resulting political goals of a segment of the population, it also helps us to identify the *social base* of a movement, that particular group or stratum in whose interest the movement speaks and who provides most, if not all, of the support for the movement. Thus, workers are the social base of the labor movement and of the socialist movement. But note that, while the entirety of the labor movement will be workers, the socialist movement will have considerable middle-class and intellectual support.

In some cases, the social base of a movement is fairly obvious, as in farmers or peasants constituting an agrarian movement. But in other instances it is not so obvious. Fascism, as a social movement in Europe, has frequently been characterized as middle class. Such a statement is correct in suggesting the widespread appeal that fascism had for the middle class, yet it obscures how much opposition to fascism also came from the middle class and how well it drew from other social strata. Fascism does not obviously identify itself as middle class in the same way that socialism identifies itself as working class. The political sociologist, Seymour Lipset, identifies fascism as an extremist movement of the middle class, the appeal of which finds broader support when critical events threaten middle-class interests and the resulting "status panic" induces it to choose extremist programs in preference to more moderate alternatives.[9]

This suggests that the social base of a movement is only partially identified for us by the ideology, and that the sociologist needs to examine in detail the nature of the support which a movement receives. The selectivity of its appeal may not enable it to get support from all those in whose name it purports to speak. For example, the Black Muslims as a movement among Negroes has an anti-white, anti-Christian ideology, which has found strongest appeal among the less educated, economically poorer Negroes; but even among them, many resist an anti-Christian orientation. In turn, people from other groups and strata may find in a movement a viable alternative, even though they do not belong to the group or class for which the movement presumes to speak. Middle-class people, for example, have long been an important part of the socialist movement, despite the working-class symbolism of its ideology. The influx of people into a movement includes many who are idealistically or ideologically sympathetic to the cause the movement manifests, whatever their own social origins.

True Believers   Mass movements apparently attract large numbers of alienated and disaffected persons, who find a meaning for their life in a complete dedication to the movement; in doing so they may find a solution to their own personal problems or at least some therapy for them. Eric Hoffer called these the *true believers* and suggested that the "frustrated," the "rejected," and the "disaffected" who flock to a social movement give to it some of their unreasoned zeal and enthusiasm, regardless of what that movement is all about.[10] But care must be taken not to confuse the true believers with others who are strong and devoted adherents of a movement but not in any way psychopathic and quite capable of rational judgment. There are such followers of a movement, just as there are others who are not so thoroughly committed, but who generally support and sympathize and can, on at least more critical and dramatic occasions, be mobilized in support of action.

ORGANIZATION AND LEADERSHIP OF A SOCIAL MOVEMENT

A social movement is not the same thing as an organization, yet it needs some degree of organization if it is to mobilize people for collective action. A political party, for example, usually provides the organized core for politi-

[9] Seymour M. Lipset, " 'Fascism'—Left, Right, and Center," in his *Political Man* (New York: Doubleday, 1960), pp. 131–176.

[10] Eric Hoffer, *The True Believer* (New York: New American Library, 1951).

cal movements, but so can civic organizations and labor unions. Organizational membership provides the most stable source of support for the social movement, but sympathetic supporters of social movements may not all be organization members. Organization gives coherence and structure to the movement and provides the mechanism and materials for its activities. It is the organization that plans rallies, publishes newspapers and pamphlets, holds meetings, and determines the strategy of the campaign. Also it is organization that provides a leadership with the resources with which to function.

When, however, organization becomes a major concern and becomes well-institutionalized, the movement may be on the way to becoming a pressure group, rather than a movement. This likelihood is enhanced if the movement is successful in achieving at least some of its goals. If the organization is accepted as the legitimate spokesman for the social group or stratum represented by the movement, the transition of the movement into a pressure group, such as a political party or a labor union, is further enhanced.

Leadership The leadership of a social movement is not necessarily drawn entirely from its social base; many leaders of movements of oppressed strata are themselves of more advantaged status. Middle-class people have long been drawn to leadership positions in workers' movements, Karl Marx being the most notable example. Whatever their own social origins, leaders of social movements are *charismatic;* they can rally masses of people in opposition to the established social order and require no institutionalized positions in bureaucracies or traditional social structures to legitimize their leadership. *Charisma,* according to Max Weber, contrasts with the *legal-rational* and *traditional* as a legitimate basis for exercising authority in a society.[11] Charismatic leaders have power because of the personal devotion by the followers of the movement, who impute to them great qualities; their behavior must always exemplify the sense of grievance of the movement and the fact that it is a "cause," not a business.

But this does not exhaust the leadership needs of a social movement; it also needs those more pragmatic, less flamboyant leaders who are organizational experts and administratively proficient, as well as those who can devise strategy and tactics. There is nothing to prevent one man from filling these several leadership roles, but it is rare that the necessary qualities and skills are to be found in one person. Although the name of one person may be charismatically identified with a social movement, there is in fact a group of leaders in whom are combined the several functions and skills necessary to carry out the collective action of a movement. One of the other functions of leadership in a movement is to provide *intellectual* direction and focus; thus, there is an

---

[11] Compare Hans Gerth and C. Wright Mills, *From Max Weber: Essays in Sociology* (New York: Oxford, 1946).

intellectual segment of the leadership. Intellectuals may create ideologies, adapt and alter them to fit changing circumstances, translate great ideologies like Marxism to the specifics of time and circumstance, and in a number of other ways provide a coherent rationale for the actions of the movement.

Legitimation and Leadership   Just who the leaders of a social movement are is a matter of consensus, not of constitutional validation or even necessarily a matter of organizational office. A charismatic leader, as Weber pointed out, is a leader because of his following and for no other reason. This consensus about the leadership of a social movement may frequently be quite imperfect, and competing claims to leadership status may exist. In part this may be a struggle for leadership as a coveted prize; the most dedicated of men are not without personal ambition. But often it also represents different intellectual interpretations of the goals and intentions of the movement, and a struggle over leadership may be the first visible evidence of internal tensions and potential splits within a movement.

If there are competing leaders in a social movement, there are often also competing organizations; the claims of any one organization to be the focus of the movement can be and often are disputed by other organizations with other leaders. The civil rights movements in the South, for example, never focused around one organization; there was Martin Luther King's Southern Christian Leadership Conference, but there was also the National Association for the Advancement of Colored People (NAACP), the Student Non-Violent Coordinating Committee (SNCC, called "Snick"), the Congress on Racial Equality (CORE), and other, more local groups, as well.

In the case of civil rights, the several organizations, sometimes competing but often cooperating, were in existence at the outset of the movement. In other cases new organizations came into being as part of the history of the movement, usually over differences of ideology and tactics. When success may lead to a muting of the protest voice of an organization and to some compromise with its society, a "pure" and uncompromising organization may be created by those who refuse to come to terms with society. In other cases, a failure of strategy may lead to new groups that invent new strategic approaches. In civil rights, old organizations such as CORE and SNCC have radically altered their goals, strategies, and their ideology, and many new groups dedicated to some interpretation of black power have emerged in the large cities.

Social movements, then, are not neat and tidy phenomena; they are never completely coherent and systematic and are usually a battleground of people who fight each other over the meaning of the movement just as strongly as they fight the common enemy. Claims and counterclaims as to who "legitimately" speaks for the movement and can act in its name and in terms of its values may not only be an unsettled issue at the outset, it may remain unsettled for much of the history of the movement.

The Problem of Unity and Cohesion The factors that make for division and disagreement are endemic to any social movement, yet the very effectiveness of a movement depends on the unity and cohesion of its members. Social movements are strong to the extent that a leadership can mobilize its members for concerted action. Disagreement and division weaken its efforts. Unity is thus a major value for a movement's leaders and its most committed members. The labor movement long sang "solidarity forever" as its recognition of and promotion of the idea that there was power in unity and weakness in division. Herbert Blumer has suggested that a movement has to develop an *esprit de corps,* an identification of its members with one another, a sense of being an ingroup.[12] An ideology functions to provide a rationale for this, and rallying behind a dynamic and appealing charismatic leader does also. The creation of informal patterns of interaction, particularly those that give followers an opportunity to interact with leaders, is significant in maintaining identification with the movement. So also are more formal and often solemn ceremonies that give ritualistic expression to the basic values and sentiments of the movement.

Thus, social movements thrive on an *enthusiasm* which is less essential for more mundane institutions and groups. But such enthusiasm is hard to maintain day in and day out, and particularly so in the face of adversity—and no social movement escapes some defeats and disappointments. A deeper conviction and commitment is necessary to maintain *morale.*[13] Again, it is probably the charismatic leader who is significant for the maintenance of morale during struggle and conflict. His own behavior must sustain unshakeable convictions about the unchallenged rightness of the cause, faith in the ultimate success, and a sense of a "sacred mission."

THE CAREER OF A MOVEMENT

Social movements begin at some point in history, at a time of crisis and dissent, but eventually there comes a time when they cease to exist. They grow and develop, and then they die away or become legitimate institutions. Herbert Blumer has asserted that social movements have a "career." What he means is that there is no one cycle through which all movements go, no one pattern that they all follow, other than the obvious one that they emerge, grow, and in some manner disappear. But the manner in which they do disappear varies considerably; along the way many different things happen to social movements.

[12] Herbert H. Blumer, "Collective Behavior," in Alfred M. Lee, ed., *Principles of Sociology* (New York: Barnes and Noble, 1951), pp. 167–222.
[13] Blumer, p. 208.

There is an early period in the career of all social movements when some tentative, somewhat unstable yet definite core structure emerges, and a first identification of followers and leaders takes place. It occurs only after some usually abortive efforts of one kind or another. Eventually a more definite interaction between leaders and followers, and between the movement and the society it seeks to change, serves to clarify issues, to provide a more specific conception of goals and values, and to test the potentiality for membership and the possibilities of action. An emerging leadership provides a more articulate clarification of values and goals, and an ideological rationale appears. The vagueness of mere discontent gives way to the pursuit of specific goals; strategies are formulated and tactics determined. In general strategy is a matter of choosing two approaches: to pursue and accumulate power; or to engage in the effort to convert ever larger numbers of people to the values and perspective of the movement. Such *conversion* strategies are likely to appeal to religious and ethical movements, whereas the *pursuit of power* finds its appeal in movements that, whatever their specific concerns, take a political form.[14] A young and relatively untried social movement may engage at first more in appeals, in efforts to articulate its aims and values and thus be concerned with clarification, both to itself and to society, as to what are its grievances and what are its objectives. But eventually it engages in some concerted action and puts to the test its claims that changes need to be made.

The response within the society to the collective action of a developing social movement is crucial for its further development and for the nature of its career. There may be a *tolerant* response because its moral stance is respected, and because it is not regarded as a serious threat. It may be defined as morally right but impractical, or it may be defined as peculiar (a bunch of "kooks") but harmless. In these instances, a movement may find it possible to develop and carry out strategy without serious opposition, but also find that it is not taken seriously and thus have difficulty in exercising influence. Where it is defined as "odd," it is subject to ridicule, which may be an experience that engenders bitterness and isolation from the main body of the society. Toleration by society may provide an advantage that a movement comes to value, and so it acts not to seem to be too dangerous or to be engaged in strong efforts to attain power. Subtly, this may serve to moderate the very efforts of the movement at change and to give it a vested interest in its acceptable status. The result may be a misleading support for the movement by many who could never be counted on for support under more critical conditions, as well as a loss of drive and energy that may disenchant the more active and committed members.

Tolerance or even indifference allows a social movement relative freedom in

[14] For a discussion of this issue, see Killian, pp. 448–450.

its action, however, opposition can be a constraining experience. When a movement is defined as a threat, its activities may bring strong and possibly punitive responses. It more readily has martyrs, and its leaders may become quite embittered and more alienated from the society than they were initially. Its ideology then emphasizes the evils of the society and the need for a more radical or even revolutionary change.

A movement that meets strong opposition from established institutions and organizations, as well as a climate of public disapproval, tends increasingly to emphasize the necessity for goals of radical change and the pursuit of power as a major strategic orientation. It may even be driven underground, to become a secret and conspiratorial organization, engaging in efforts at subversion and practicing deceit and subterfuge. Such an experience of opposition changes the internal character of the movement. Its leadership is the more "militant" type, more ready to use violence. Its values and ideology congeal into an orthodoxy that defines *we* and *they,* and one is always a partisan: if you are not for the movement, you are defined as against it—they concede no middle ground.

Movements such as these generate strong pressures for discipline and conformity and, consequently, they may maintain quite undemocratic procedures within their own structure. One frequent consequence is to establish different levels or types of members. There are, first, those committed and disciplined ones who constitute an inner circle of trusted members and who are also the ones to decide strategy. Others constitute outer layers—and there may be several—of adherents who are not taken fully into confidence but are assigned those tasks that are commensurate with their lesser commitment to the organization. Communist parties are frequently organized in this way.

Between the tolerance of a society that is unworried about a movement and the intolerance of a society that feels threatened by one, are a range of other possibilities. Thus, some social classes may feel severely threatened, while others may be somewhat sympathetic, giving the movement some measure of support and perhaps some allies in crucial circumstances. Public opinion may be split on the merits of a movement along lines of class, region, religion, or race, and support for a movement may shift in response to its tactics or in response to sanctions against it. Thus, severe punishment of the movement's leaders may bring sympathetic support, but a violent act that victimized innocent people may turn a hitherto sympathetic or even an indifferent public against a movement. Thus, *white violence* against young, nonviolent Negro demonstrators in the South in the early 1960s won widespread white, middle-class support for civil rights, but *black violence* in Northern cities since 1965 has dissipated much of that same support.

The career of a movement is in one significant way like the career of a person: what happens is a function of experiences at a number of crucial points in the early and middle stages of its career. Certainly, a movement does not develop according to some inherent unfolding of its characteristics, for what a movement is, is not given in its earliest stages. Rather, the experiences of the members and the leaders in pursuing goals in an uphill struggle can shape a movement in a variant set of ways. It was, for example, the bitter and disillusioning experiences of young Negro activists (like Stokely Carmichael) in civil rights action in the South, all largely committed to nonviolence, that led to a rethinking and reassessing of the meaning of the movement from which came the concept of black power and a radical change in the philosophy, the goals, the strategies, and the ideological interpretations of the movement. What had been an *integrated* civil rights movement struggling for equal rights became a *black* movement struggling for black identification and community, though yet ambiguous as to what specific forms that should take.

The Consequence of Success A movement may succeed in achieving at least some of its goals or it may fail. If it succeeds, it is soon transformed into one or more legitimate organizations and even into institutionalized ones. This is what happened to the labor movement of the 1930s, which fought against very strong opposition by corporate management but which also had support from the administration of President Roosevelt. Victory for the labor movement came in terms of these quite specific objectives: (1) federal legislation requiring bargaining elections and bargaining "in good faith" by employers; and (2) the signing of contracts recognizing the new mass-industrial unions as the legitimate representatives of the workers. *Legitimation* and *recognition*, then, meant a significant new status for unions. They were no longer illegitimate organizations, they were no longer underdogs, and they were no longer carrying on something resembling a class struggle. Instead, unions were now legally designated organizations that represented workers in bargaining and negotiations conducted according to legally established procedures, and the agreement was sealed in a contract that had status in the courts of the land.

Unions were transformed by this very process. The labor movement became organized labor—no longer a social movement but one of the major power structures in American society, significant in its capacity to exercise power, but integrated into the society, not alienated from it. This transformation brought a change in leadership, as well. Old leaders who had excelled at the organization of workers and the leading of strikes now had to excel at negotiation around the bargaining table, and those who could not make the change lost out to newer leaders who could.

The attaining of recognition and a legitimate status was an immediate and pragmatic goal of unions, one on which all in the labor movement were agreed. But many in the movement held more abstract and longer-range goals. They saw the labor movement as the organization of workers to overthrow capitalism and create a new kind of society. Communists, Socialists, Trotskyites, and a range of other radical positions, were all actively represented in the labor movement. During the embattled days of the thirties, the need for unity in the face of powerful corporate opposition muted the struggle among those who held different ideological positions on the goals of the labor movement, though there was always much behind-the-scenes infighting. However, with the achievement of the pragmatic goals, those who wanted a socialist movement of some kind, and those who wanted separate political action by labor—perhaps a labor party—fought with others for whom the immediate goals were sufficient; a decade of internal factional struggle ensued that ended when the more ideologically radical groups lost out.

Labor unions ceased to be the dynamic, critical groups they had been in the thirties. They became strong, bureaucratized organizations that were part of the liberal political structure in American life. Their gradual loss of the verve and orientation of a movement is evident in the late fifties and the sixties, when the new consciousness about race, peace, and poverty found organized labor taking no significant part. It was no longer the representative of the poor, its position on race was compromised by practices of discrimination in many unions, and its top leadership (with some exceptions) was largely unsympathetic to the various peace groups and their demonstrations, particularly over the Vietnam conflict. Labor found itself no longer regarded as the underdog, no longer speaking for the underdogs of the new period, and indeed it was being defined by the new social movements as part of the "establishment," to use the current fashionable phrase. In the 1960s, the New Left effort to create a new movement has looked to students, to poor people, to black people, and to strongly anti-war segments of the middle class as the social base.

When Movements Fail   But success does not always come to a social movement. Sometimes it fails to achieve its objectives—it fails to attain power, and it fails to convert any significant number of people to its cause. Failure breeds frustration and bitterness and sometimes more desperate and radical action. More importantly, the sense of a frustrated incapacity to achieve any significant goal deprives the movement of that morale-sustaining idea that the future lies with it. It loses adherents, retaining perhaps only a core of the most dedicated. Even the true believers may seek answers in more promising movements. In time, an unsuccessful movement may wither to a small handful of loyal followers and a leadership increasingly remote from the salient issues of the society.

But whether a movement fails or not is not an obvious matter. Certainly, no one would assert that socialism succeeded in America. Yet Norman Thomas, the Socialist Party's candidate for president for six elections, has quite correctly pointed out that one of the factors in the "failure" of socialism in America has been that its pragmatic program has been taken over by the major parties. Indeed, this has largely been the fate of third parties in American society. The reforms they have championed on behalf of various disadvantaged groups have gradually won acceptance and have been politically adopted. The various social movements achieved acceptance of their *program* without gaining *members*. Legislation on behalf of working women and children, the eight-hour day, unemployment compensation and social security, union representation—these once "radical" measures have in time won wide acceptance and become social policy. Once the leaders of the major parties sensed the growth of public support, they incorporated these issues into party planks and saw them converted into legislation.

In this way presumably "unsuccessful" social movements may in fact perform a vital function for a democratic society: they champion significant reforms when these are outside the realm of the ideologically acceptable. They develop an issue into a significant social cause. In particular, they utilize specific and pragmatic issues—such as child labor and the eight-hour day—to attract people to the more abstract values of socialism and the longer range goal of a socialist society.

It is in just this last aspect, of course, that they are vulnerable. A popular pragmatic issue can be usurped by the "established" parties of power. Although the issue wins, the movement loses an issue and its cause is weakened. Nonetheless, its action in carrying the issue has been a significant social process in a democratic society. The "failure" of a social movement, then, does not always mean that all it fought for has been lost. A movement may disappear or at least fail to convert a majority or to seize power just because its pragmatic issues were accepted and adopted by other parties or groups. Such a failure of a movement has nonetheless helped to change a society.

The Problem of Ethical Choice In the course of the career of a movement, there comes a point at least once when its stance toward the society within which it acts becomes a matter of ethical decision. The leadership of a movement must decide whether they are *of* the society as well as merely *in* it, whether they reject it in its entirety or seek instead to operate within the major values of the society. This issue has long been recognized. Some scholars, indeed, have characterized some social movements as being *reforming* because they basically accept the values of a society, and others as *revolutionary* because they do not and seek instead to create an entirely new social structure. Some social movements are never clearly either, having members with both stances and having both moderate and pragmatic goals and more radical ones.

But the issue is not simply reform or revolution, more radical or less, more militant or less, more or less compromising, though all of these are involved. At the heart of the issue is a fundamental question of ethical stance. In one of his great essays, "Politics as a Vocation," Max Weber explored the ethical question inherent in the necessary moral choices a political leader must make.[15] He sketched out two possible ethical choices for the guidance of conduct: *the ethic of ultimate ends* and *the ethic of responsibility*, and called them "fundamentally differing and irreconcilably opposed maxims."[16]

The Ethic of Ultimate Commitment   The ethic of ultimate commitment is the moral stance that is likely to be found among charismatic leaders of social movements, though not always and not only among them. Basically, it is a commitment to the ultimate and overriding value of the end in view, which is to be pursued without compromise and without concern for the harm or suffering that its pursuit may bring. Great sacrifices may be asked for small gains, and compromises may be spurned even though an ensuing conflict may wreak havoc on many innocent people. It is not that those committed to an ethic of ultimate ends are irresponsible; it is that their ethical view is such that the evil of the world is so great as to justify even further suffering for the attainment of a revolutionary end. Weber noted: "If an action of good intent leads to bad results, then, in the actor's eyes, not he but the world, or the stupidity of other men, or God's will who made them thus, is responsible for the evil."[17]

The Ethic of Responsibility   What marks the other ethical stance, however, is just this assumption of responsibility for the consequences of one's own action. One accepts the fact that the world and its people are imperfect, and that good intentions do not necessarily lead to good results. Good intentions, then, are not taken as sufficient justification for behavior—in the case of a leader, for his choice of a tactic.

Each of these ethical stances has its own temptation. In the first instance, it is the temptation not to compromise or deal rationally with a real world, but to invoke any means as justifying the sacred goal and to carry this through, regardless of consequences to society or even to the movement. It is not a far step for a leader with an ethic of ultimate commitment to become a *chiliastic* prophet, who proclaims that the next event is the coming of the millennium and thus there is justified that "last violent deed, that would then lead to a state of affairs in which *all* violence is annihilated."[18] The ethic of responsibility, in turn, tempts a leader into compromise for its own sake and into modes of action too moderate to challenge effectively the very evils of the world the movement would change. If the ethic of ultimate ends tends to breed men with whom the world cannot reason, the ethic of responsibility tends to breed

[15] Gerth and Mills, *From Max Weber,* pp. 77–128.
[16] Gerth and Mills, p. 120.
[17] Gerth and Mills, p. 121.
[18] Gerth and Mills, p. 122.

men whom the world can too easily buy off. Although Weber was here concerned with politics in general, his contrasting modes of ethical orientation has particular relevance to the leadership of social movements, for the choice between an ethic of responsibility and one of ultimate ends is one they can never avoid.

THE MAJOR SOCIAL MOVEMENTS AND IDEOLOGIES

The social scientist must examine a number of major social movements if he is to understand fully the emergence and development of modern society.[19] The transition in the Western world from feudal to modern society was a major transformation in social structure, and such movements as *liberalism* and *nationalism* were significant features of that historic transition. In the nineteenth century, the major social movements were generated by protest against the industrialization of modern society, as in the case of peasants and farmers, or against the conditions imposed by industrial capitalism, as in the case of workers. The *labor* movement and *socialism* were the outstanding social movements of the past century.[20]

Labor The labor movement did not represent any specific ideology, and, therefore, did not always have any specific goals. Social protest against the harsh condition of life by the working class was sometimes diffuse and unfocused, having no specific remedy. A major effort went into the organization of labor unions and into the struggle for their legitimation. Often, specific reform goals were advanced without a long-range ideology existing. The remedies that labor advanced were varied and diverse, but they can be defined as an effort to reduce the insecurities and poverty of working-class life by gaining some control over the job and by modifying industrial capitalism's subjection of the worker to the vagaries of the market. The labor movement in the nineteenth century was a constant challenge to the supremacy in society of the institutions of capitalism and of the property-owning middle class. Sometimes, particularly in Europe, the labor movement accepted socialism as

---

[19] For a penetrating review of social movements in Europe during the Middle Ages and the Reformation, with implications for modern totalitarian movements, see Norman Cohn, *The Pursuit of the Millennium* (New York: Essential Books, 1957). Harper Torchbook edition, 1961.
[20] For a cogent sociological analysis of these historic social movements, see Rudolph Heberle, *Social Movements* (New York: Appleton-Century, 1951). There is a vast amount of material on Marxism; for a short but penetrating treatment see Alfred G. Meyer, *Marxism: The Unity of Theory and Practice* (Ann Arbor, Mich.: University of Michigan Press, 1963).

an ideology and became the social base for that movement. Socialism did have a clearly defined ideology and a well-defined set of objectives; unlike the labor movement, however, it was revolutionary, not merely reforming, in its aims.

Socialism   As the dominant social movement of the nineteenth and early twentieth century, socialism signified the failure of the ideology of capitalism to find support in all segments of society. Although this was particularly true of the workers, the poor, and the propertyless, socialism also won converts from the middle class, particularly from the professional and intellectual spheres of that class. Indeed, much of the leadership of socialism was middle class in origin. Its challenge to the political and economic institutions of modern times gives us a rough measure of the lack of social integration within capitalist societies. Socialism succeeded in mobilizing millions of workers and middle-class persons against capitalism and sometimes also against parliamentary democracy. This is not a measure of social disorganization, but rather of the failure of capitalist institutions to achieve a complete integration of society around the symbols of the free market.

Agrarian Movements   These movements, in turn, emerged both from the protests of farmers against the transition from small-scale to large-scale capitalism and the impact that the rise of corporate capitalism had upon a market economy in which agriculture was a continually shrinking factor. In the United States, the agrarian movements of the nineteenth and early twentieth century were not anti-capitalist, for farmers were small, property-owning entrepreneurs, but the movements were anti-big business. They sought and to some extent succeeded in achieving reforms intended to bring the political process closer and more responsive to the people, such as the direct election of senators, the referendum, recall, and the like. The agrarian movements were the social base for such movements as Populism, with its ideological symbols of "the trusts," and "Wall Street," signifying monopoly capitalism and financial control within small but powerful circles.

Agrarian and workers' movements, including socialism, did not succeed in revolutionizing the United States or western Europe, but they did succeed in making workers and farmers an important factor in the political life of society. They also succeeded in instituting a number of major reforms. By the middle of the twentieth century, capitalism was no longer the unregulated institution it had been a hundred years prior, and power based upon such economic resources as property and wealth was no longer the only decisive power in modern society.

Social Movements in Africa and Asia   Socialism is no longer the vital challenge to capitalism that it was even thirty years ago in Europe. But it has become a significant ideology in the great social movements that are sweeping the non-Western world, the ancient tribal and feudal worlds of Asia and Africa. As these old societies disintegrate under the impact of industrializing and urbanizing forces, social movements emerge to provide direction and content to the change and to define the character of the new society. Two major changes are occurring in this transition to modern society. First, there are great changes occurring in the internal organization of old societies: changes in economic organization; in tribal structure; in family life; in class structure; in political organization; and the like. Secondly, accompanying these changes is the removal of control by European nations, the end to European colonialism.

The new social movements in Africa and Asia possess several major aims. One of them is *nationalism,* the development of a modern nation and a modern, effective government. The change in status from colony to nation gives meaning to an ideology of *anti-imperialism.* A second major aim is *racial equality* of non-whites with whites in the world. The emerging new nations of Asia and Africa proclaim the racial equality of man and are still sensitive to the inferior racial position they experienced as colonies. Many of these new nations are to some degree or other *socialist,* and they have leaders who see more hope in socialism than they do in capitalism. In part this stems from an ideological resistance to following the patterns of those very nations whose rule they have brought to an end. In addition, a socialist government seems to some to be a means to rapid modernization in a hitherto backward society. The new nations intend to do in a human lifetime what it took three centuries to achieve in the Western world.

Nationalism, anti-colonialism, racial equality, and socialism are a complex set of symbols. Their mixture into particular ideologies of new nations in Asia and Africa often produces some quite unanticipated policies and programs. But what is significant is that the ideas in these ideologies are from the Western intellectual tradition. Historically, modern society began with the Industrial Revolution in Western Europe, and the modernization of ancient societies in Asia and Africa is carried on by social movements organized and led by Western-educated elites.

The End of Ideology?   The nineteenth century has frequently been called an "age of ideology,"[21] a term intended to suggest that its social thought was predominantly ideological, and that it was a century in which such great ideologies as Marxian socialism and Social Darwinism dominated the social perspectives of intellectuals and nonintellectuals alike. Does the twentieth century offer primarily a continuity of this intellectual tradition of competing and conflicting ideologies? The symbolic phrase, *the end of ideology,* has

---

[21] For an exposition, see Henry D. Aiken, *The Age of Ideology: The 19th Century Philosophers* (New York: New American Library, 1956).

been invoked to express the idea that indeed there has been an end to the century of ideology, and that the great ideologies of the recent past no longer govern the actions of men today in the Western world. The sociologist, Daniel Bell, is the author of a remarkably cogent essay "The End of Ideology in the West: An Epilogue," which states the case for the position that in the twentieth century ". . . ideology, which once was a road to action, has come to be a dead end."[22]

The power of an ideology to convert people into a passionately acting collectivity relates ideas to social movements and, in Bell's words, "ideology is the conversion of ideas into social levers."[23] In passion derived from action, not abstract philosophical inquiry, lies the force of an ideology. Bell observed that a "social movement can arouse people when it can do three things: simplify ideas, establish a claim to truth, and, in the union of the two, demand a commitment to action."[24] In doing so, Bell adds, ideology not only transforms ideas, it also transforms people.

Why, then, can ideology not do this in the twentieth century? Too much has happened, Bell and others have noted, to give ideology the grip on human commitment and the capacity to arouse passion that it once had. Certainly, the radical intellectuals of the West have suffered disillusionment and a collapse of apocalyptic hopes by the Moscow trials of the 1930s, and the sad realization that a Marxist dream had become a totalitarian society. The rise of nazism in what was taken to be one of the more advanced human cultures, the use of gas chambers and concentration camps, and the Nazi-Soviet pacts—few ideologically utopian perspectives could survive this onslaught. On the other hand, the modification of unregulated capitalism, the emergence of the welfare state, and the new legitimate status of unions was a more positive set of developments that undercut the passionate ideological case against capitalism and its control of the political apparatus. The world, in short, is not the world that the great ideologies of the nineteenth century were talking about. They no longer possess the analytic relevance they once did, and their utopian answers to the problems of man no longer seem intellectually adequate, indeed, often naïve and simplified. Thus, they can no longer persuade, for they have lost the claim to "truth"; the age of ideology has come to an end.

Yet this interpretation of the modern world has by no means been accepted by everyone as sociologically accurate. A large number of scholars, intellectuals, and activists have not only disputed the idea, but have treated it as obviously wrong on the face of it. Although they readily acknowledge that the ideological character of the nineteenth century has not been carried over intact, they insist that the old ideologies still have their driving force in the world, pointing

[22] Daniel Bell, *The End of Ideology* (New York: Free Press, 1960), pp. 369–375. Quotation is from p. 370.
[23] Bell, p. 370.
[24] Bell, p. 372.

to such things as the still large working-class vote for communism in France and Italy and the new ideologies of the emerging nations. Perhaps more basically, they regard man as fundamentally a political and ideological animal, thus, there can never be an end to the function of ideology in human affairs.

But the thesis of the end of ideology is not to argue that no ideology has any place any longer, but rather that the great ideologies of the past century no longer define and interpret issues and no longer commit the intellectuals of the West to a belief in a cataclysmic showdown between irreconcilable forces that will produce revolution and the utopian world of the future. There has, instead, been widespread commitment to the welfare state, the decentralization of power, a mixed economy, and social and political pluralism. The rise of new ideologies in the emerging nations of Africa and Asia does not refute this thesis, which is concerned with the fate of ideology *in the West*. Perhaps Daniel Bell has stated the matter best:

> And yet, the extraordinary fact is that while the old nineteenth-century ideologies and intellectual debates have become exhausted, the rising states of Asia and Africa are fashioning new ideologies with a different appeal for their own people. These are the ideologies of industrialization, modernization, Pan-Arabism, color, and nationalism. In the distinctive difference between the two kinds of ideologies lies the great political and social problems of the second half of the twentieth century. The ideologies of the nineteenth century were universalistic, humanistic, and fashioned by intellectuals. The mass ideologies of Asia and Africa are parochial, instrumental, and created by political leaders. The driving force of the old ideologies were social equality, and, in the largest sense, freedom. The impulsions of the new ideologies are economic development and national power.[25]

Yet Bell, no less than do his critics, recognizes that the younger generation finds no satisfaction in such a decline of ideologies, and no enthusiasm for a "middle" situation of moderate reform. There has been a poignant search for a new, meaningful radicalism. What has come to be called the *New Left* is some renewal of passion and commitment, specifically characterized by a highly moral rejection of an affluent and bureaucratized society. Such issues as peace (particularly in Vietnam), civil rights, and poverty have provided sources for moral indignation and outlets for fervent expression. Yet, even its most sympathetic supporters recognize that there is as yet no emergence of a new definitive ideology, no utopian scheme for revolutionizing the world, and no apparent readiness to return to the older ideologies. The sight of radical students carrying both the black flag of anarchism and the red flag of communism seems ideologically inconsistent and politically incompatible to an older generation. That the students care little about that only says that neither position is for them a serious intellectual commitment.

[25] Bell, p. 373.

THE SIGNIFICANCE OF SOCIAL MOVEMENTS

Social movements, we suggested at the outset of this chapter, have been viewed by many social scientists as epiphenomena. They have looked upon them as much shouting and shoving by people who feel more keenly the consequences of changes in culture and social structure that have been long developing and are perhaps not as visible to the untrained eye. Are social movements, then, interesting, even exciting, because of their drama and conflict, but in fact of little importance in understanding society and its changes? No definitive answer for this rather large question can be found in the extant sociological literature—so no authoritative answer can be made here. Yet if social movements are worthy of study by sociologists, there must be some significance to them, some payoff for the sociologist for his effort. We suggest that a tentative answer can be found in three points: social movements as social change; the place of values and ideas in social life; and what social movements reveal about the nature of society.

Social Movements as Social Change   The constant emergence of new social movements in human societies not only testifies to the fact that social change is always occurring, but even more to the fact that men are conscious of that fact and respond, often quite passionately, to the changing circumstances of their lives. As Lewis Killian aptly put it: "The study of social movements reminds us of the irrepressible conviction of sentient men that they can collectively, if not individually, change their culture by their own endeavors."[26] Thus, at the outset, social movements are clear evidence of the fact that men act in circumstances of change and conflict to give direction and focus to the general trend of change, including the possibility of restoring or maintaining some aspects of the older social order. But the real question is, does it make any difference? Would society drift into the same pattern anyway, even if there were no shouting and shoving? In short, is the outcome of great social transformations, such as the Industrial Revolution, inevitable?

Whoever would answer this question authoritatively, one way or the other, must do so from the perspective of the philosophy of history. Sociology certainly is not prepared to provide an answer. Yet, those sociologists, and other social scientists, too, who assume social movements to be epiphenomena are in fact implying the philosophical position that social change is a determined consequence of definable factors; thus they imply that men can do no more than adjust to inevitable social change. Such is the underlying assumption of the famous *culture-lag* theory by the distinguished pioneering sociologist, William

[26] Killian, p. 454.

Ogburn.[27] Ogburn analyzed change in terms of technological and scientific innovations, whose adequate use was incompatible with older cultural ways. Social disorganization, thus, was an index of the "lag" of cultural and social processes in keeping abreast of technological change. Social organization then must (a moral imperative) adapt to technology, rather than the other way around.

Only a true believer in free will would postulate a reverse position—that men can change their society in any manner they choose. Perhaps all social scientists will agree that men are historical creatures, bound within the framework of the social institutions by which they are socialized and from which they get a perspective on the world. The area of disagreement lies in the question of whether or not there is some maneuverable room by which the conscious actions of men can choose qualitative differences even within the pattern of historical change. When men commit themselves to social movements, they assume that their action can make a difference.

If industrialization and technology make social change inevitable, in that they render obsolete old social groups and institutions and require new ones, do such changes in technology necessarily require any one specific form of social organization? Does not the record of Western experience with industrialization offer both liberal and communist structures, and an infinite variation within these, as possible institutional arrangements compatible with advanced technology? The social processes now going on within the newly emergent industrializing countries suggest strongly that no one specific social structure is necessary for industrialization, and that the industrialization of non-Western cultures may reveal much more of the qualitatively distinct social variation possible within the larger pattern of "inevitable" social change that is modernization.

These few comments can hardly be regarded as a resolution of a complex and significant issue. But they do suggest to us why social movements are worthy of study by sociologists. To treat social movements as epiphenomena may be assuming a technological determination of the specifics of social life that is simply unwarranted from any scientific and empirical outlook. Social movements need to be studied just because they are relevant data about the conscious efforts of men to determine within limits their own destiny and to direct the processes of change in terms of their own values and goals. As Lewis Killian says: "The study of social movements reminds us of the irrepressible conviction of sentient men that they can collectively, if not individually, change the culture by their own endeavors."

[27] William F. Ogburn, *Social Change* (New York: Viking, 1922).

Values and Ideas There is nothing more difficult to handle as objective social data than ideas and values. Yet social movements are inexplicable to us except as we give full measure to the place of values and ideas in them. Sociologists have long learned to handle values as relevant data in the study of human action and as relevant in the analysis of social structure. The normative character of human society demands that full attention be given to values.

However, the sociological analysis of values in the context of stable social structure and enduring social groups often treats them as stable and enduring also, and usually as taken-for-granted by the social actors. But when social movements emerge, men become critically conscious of what values they and others hold and also of the significance of values in shaping social life. Furthermore, they become conscious analyzers of social ideas. More than merely being conscious of values and ideas, men in social movements make passionate commitments to ideas about human society, whether these ideas are political, religious, or whatever, in their origin. Here is a realm of ideas somewhat different from the detached and objective scholarly treatment, where rationalized ideas are ideally bereft of passion and commitment. But passion and ideas mean power, for it is when men believe passionately in ideas that they act to bring about a new state of affairs. It is then that ideas truly have consequences. When we study social movements, we have an opportunity to see the consequences that ideas have when they catch the imagination of men.

A Perspective on Society When we study social movements emerging in the context of changing societies, we are in a position to gain a useful perspective on society. Social movements provide an excellent source of some important data about a society that may not be otherwise easily available even from the most careful sociological scrutiny. Not only do they point up social change, they also reveal the sources of that change in the cleavages that exist in the society and the conflict that exists among groups and classes. Thus, social movements are a useful antidote to that structural analysis that emphasizes society as an integrated phenomenon. Instead, social movements reveal (1) latent conflict that has long existed but may have been overlooked; (2) the depth of passion and intensity of group hostility that was not evident until a social movement provided an outlet for its expression; and (3) the manner in which seemingly stable social institutions and dominant values concealed the extent of force and coercion in making viable a particular society. Change and conflict as perspectives on society, then, find useful data and analysis in the study of social movements. They suggest how much any society is less an integrated social system and more an historical product of group conflict and domination, in which some segments of that society may have never accepted as fully legitimate its institutions and values.

Social movements give us, also, a salient perspective on social order. A conscious sense of the inadequacy or the moral unacceptability of the established social order leads men to undertake efforts to change it and to construct a new social order that more nearly fits their values. Whether the outcome is what they intended or not, and often it is not, men do share ideas about ideal social orders, and they do act with passionate commitment, often, to bring them about. A study of social movements, then, provides a perspective on human society without which our study of social order would be one-sided and incomplete.

COLLECTIVE BEHAVIOR IN MODERN SOCIETY

In these last two chapters we have examined the phenomenon of collective behavior in its varied forms: crowd behavior, public opinion, and social movements. The term obviously covers an array of human behavior that has little else in common, other than a lack of the tighter structuring that the sociologist normally attributes and expects to find in examining the organization of social life. If we proceed with the sociological assumption that society is normally well-integrated, then any form of collective behavior suggests that the otherwise well-structured organization of social life has experienced some disintegration—*disorganization* has occurred. It can then be expected that such a rupture in established routines will in time be repaired, and a new, albeit somewhat different, social stability created. Disorganization, then, is one aspect of change from one form of social structure to another. Social movements in particular, and some aspects of crowd behavior, can be explained in these terms of disorganization and change. The breakup of an historic social order dissolves the norms which once effectively controlled men's actions and leads to new expectations and hitherto undreamed of aspirations. Modern society emerged from the decline and fall of feudalism in Europe, and the Industrial Revolution, with its technological reorganization of man's ways of earning a living, provided the solvent that broke masses of human beings loose from the formerly solid structuring of feudal institutions.

Yet, collective behavior, viewed as disorganization and change occurring in the transition from one form of social order to another, is deficient as an explanation in two ways. First, it assumes that change only occurs spasmodically and is not evident in a well-structured society. But from the outset in this book we pointed out the ubiquitous nature of change; it is ever-present in society, and the stability of social structure is always a relative concept.

We cannot intelligently equate change with disorganization only; it is present even when we speak of social organization. Secondly, collective behavior viewed as change and disorganization does not explain certain things. Specifically, it does not adequately account for publics and public opinion, which are not indexes of disorganization but are one aspect of the organization of a democratic society. The public and its opinion is a process for influencing the change of social policy in society. In this context social change is not taken as disruption and disorder but as the orderly transition in the social structure and the systematic handling of public issues and problems. Change is conceived as a normal part of social order. Nor does all of crowd behavior exemplify disorganization; our analysis pointed out that ceremonial and ritualistic functions utilize crowd behavior, and that participation in crowd events can function to promote group solidarity and to socialize the person into a social group. Crowd behavior is not always mob behavior, and, therefore, not always a threat to established social order.

If the evidence of collective behavior is to be taken seriously, modern society is neither as highly integrated nor as well-structured as is bureaucracy or as traditional society. The rational ordering of human relationships and the effective controls over individual behavior that give to bureaucracy its tightly structured nature cannot easily be built into the larger society. In many spheres of social life modern society has less well-defined roles, ambiguous normative arrangements, and less stability in social relations. It is simply less structured, or more loosely structured, and it is a sociological error to impute more structure than in fact exists. Similarly, modern society lacks the cohesion to be derived from a set of legitimizing traditions, where stable and unquestioned beliefs can clearly and authoritatively order social relationships in stable patterns of long endurance. The Industrial Revolution dissolved the authority of tradition, and it has never since played as significant a role in organizing human society.

Lastly, collective behavior is mass behavior, and the study of these phenomena is significant to sociology in pointing up one major historical development: the emergence of masses of people to a permanent role in the social and historical processes of modern life. Unlike bureaucracy and traditional society, modern society is a loosely structured process within which great masses of people are involved in the great decisions of modern times. Even if they are manipulated, and their anxieties and aspirations exploited, even when elites cheat them and mislead them, their demands nevertheless count and cannot be ignored. The masses are never so completely integrated into any social structure but that they cannot be mobilized by charismatic leaders into challenging the legitimacy of the established social order. The masses may not rule, but no elite can rule without the masses.

1. Mexican children getting a medical checkup.
2. Italian family on Ellis Island (1905).
3. Slums in Rio de Janiero, Brazil.
4. Parking lot at Aqueduct Racetrack, N.Y.
5. Housing development near Cape Kennedy, Fla.
6. Houseboats in Hong Kong: an attempt to solve the housing shortage.

4

5 6

POPULATION
AND SOCIETY

21

A human society exists through the social relationships to be found among its members, who, as people in the aggregate, are a human population. There is a subtle but profound relationship between the social *organization* of a society and the *characteristics* of a population, and a mutual interaction. Significant changes in the structure of society invariably produce changes in the composition or characteristics of population, and these changes, in turn, have their consequences for the organization of society. Since population dynamics are so complexly interwoven with social factors, it may be useful to take a look at the demographic processes before completing our examination of human society.

The study of human population is called *demography*. In understanding any human population, the demographer studies the changes in and relationships among three variables: births, deaths, and migration. In quantitative form he measures these variables and expresses the results in *fertility* rates, *mortality* rates, and rates of *migration*. Taken together, these three variables account for the growth and decline of a human population, or its failure to do either. In most cases it is the ratio of births to deaths that accounts for growth and decline. Migration, in turn, may add or subtract somewhat from this.

Demography draws upon several sciences to explain population dynamics. Geography, biology, and chemistry, for example, all contribute to an understanding of factors affecting birth and death rates. The fertility of the soil, the abundance or scarcity of natural resources, the availability of water, and climate—all these natural factors are relevant for population change. So also is the practical knowledge obtained from these sciences, such as medicine and knowledge about nutrition. But the demographic processes are also affected by human culture. The organization of family life, customs about mate selection, religious and moral beliefs about conception and birth, dietary habits and the standard of living, sanitation and health practices—these and other cultural factors underscore the fact that social variables as well as natural ones are closely related to the demographic pattern. For this reason demography has always been closely related to the social sciences, and is frequently regarded as a subdivision of sociology. But the complete task of understanding the demographic processes is an interdisciplinary one.

The Origins of Population Study   The scientific study of the human population began with the work of Thomas Malthus (1766–1834), an English clergyman, whose short work, *An Essay on the Principles of Population*, was first published in 1798. Malthus posed a population problem and tried to indicate the factors that he thought were basic to that problem. He raised the specter of population outgrowing food supply, with resulting death and starvation, until population was once more reduced to the level of the available resources.

Although Malthus was not the first to have written a scholarly treatise on population, he was the first to attract any genuine public attention to the problem. The intellectual climate of Europe, and especially of England, was ready for a serious discussion of population, and particularly in the pessimistic vein in which Malthus wrote. There was a growing awareness that industrialization had increased population, and there was also a movement away from the social ideas of the Enlightenment. Indeed, Malthus' essay was particularly an attack upon the optimistic social thought of William Godwin and other liberal proponents of social progress.

The Malthusian argument that population could outstrip food supply served to stimulate the study of population and also to put that study in the context of a specific problem. Perhaps for the first time in history, men thought about the possibility of too many people and too little food. But the study of population was also stimulated by a more practical but nonetheless significant interest in population growth. An increase in the population had serious and practical consequences, and knowledge of that increase was useful for quite practical reasons. The growth of an economy was related to population growth, and national pride was often also involved. To learn just what the population was and how it was growing, many nations instituted a census in the nineteenth century. The United States began its census in 1790, so that from the very beginning of this nation there has been a record of its population growth and change.

Industrialization in the Western world brought a rising standard of living, which increased life expectancy; but it also brought changes in family patterns that lowered the birth rate. In addition, millions of people were on the move in great migratory shifts of population. The study of population not only had a practical impulse, it also seemed to provide some insight into the meaning of change in human society. Modern industrial society seemed to operate on different demographic principles than did agrarian society. The intellectual concern for understanding modern society extended logically to a growing interest in factors significant to population growth and decline.

POPULATION AS A SOCIOLOGICAL PROBLEM

In his effort at a scientific study of the human population, the demographer provides sociologists with rigorous statistical measurements of the basic variables of fertility, mortality, and migration. For this purpose, he frequently devises refined and specific measurements of these variables, enabling him to make precise comparisons of human populations, or comparisons among major groupings within a population.

But fertility and mortality are not merely biological processes that operate on laws of their own. They are intricately involved with the organization of human society, so that they change with changes in society, and their changes, from whatever diverse causes, have in turn an effect on the organization of society. It is this basic fact that makes the growth of population a relevant issue for sociology. The sociological interest in the demographic processes, then, is concerned with this mutual interaction between these processes and the social processes.

From the sociological perspective there would seem to be four major problems about the relation of population and society. The first and major one is the relation of *population growth and social structure,* in that premodern and modern constitute two apparently different types of social orders that maintain two different patterns of the relationship between fertility and mortality. The transition from premodern to modern in the Western experience has been accompanied by a demographic transition in which there is for an extended period a more rapid decline in mortality than in fertility, with a consequent rapid gain in population. Secondly, once that transition has been made, the sensitive changes in as well as differentials in *fertility and mortality in modern societies* is a major issue for understanding significant changes in such societies, as well as for the making of public policy. Thirdly, *migration* historically has been a significant means for shifting populations; though there has been a rapid decline in the opportunity for voluntary migration in the twentieth century, it cannot be said that such opportunity will not occur again. Then, lastly, there is the issue that Thomas Malthus raised: *the Malthusian problem* of too many people for available resources. At the present time, the concern is global, for in the world viewed as a single population unit there is a rapid growth that cannot continue unaltered without threatening human survival.

POPULATION GROWTH AND SOCIAL STRUCTURE

For a long time now social scientists have been pointing out that the reproductive process in the human species is not only biologically determined, important as that is, but that human culture and social institutions also have a lot to do with the process. Sex is always regulated in some fashion in all human societies, and the result is always some consequence, even if usually unintended, on human fertility. Whether population grows or not, in short, is not only a matter of man's sexual urge, and the availability of food; it is also a consequence of the social structure that organizes his life.

Fertility and Mortality In recent years a popular emphasis upon the "population explosion" has emphasized the increasing birth rate and has seemingly attributed to this the growth of the population. But population growth is not alone a function of the birth rate, for potentially a high birth rate could be offset by a high death rate. The growth of a population is determined by the *relationship* between the birth rate and the death rate, between fertility and mortality. Migration, of course, can add to or subtract from this.

If we start with the idea that the birth rate can be either high or low, and the death rate can also be high or low, this allows for four logically possible combinations: (1) high birth rates and high death rates; (2) low birth rates and low death rates; (3) high birth rates and low death rates; and (4) low birth rates and high death rates. The first three of these occur frequently enough to be useful for analysis.

The combination of high birth rates and high death rates is found in the agrarian, nonindustrialized sections of the world, even as it was found in the Western world prior to the Industrial Revolution. In tribal and peasant societies the large extended family is the basic organizing unit of social life, the work group of an agrarian economy. Such societies have a high value on fertility built into their very way of life. But the death rate is also high. A low standard of living, hard physical toil, exposure to disease, poor diet, a lack of sanitation, and little if any scientific knowledge produces a high death rate and a relatively short life expectancy, perhaps between twenty-five and thirty-five years. This means that the number of people over forty, for example, is a very small part of the population. Thus, almost all adults are in the child-bearing years, a fact that sustains a high birth rate. It is also a "young" population, as measured by the average age of persons in the population.

According to Irene B. Taueber, in such premodern societies life expectancy fluctuates around 25 years, and the death rate averages around 40 per 1000 total population.[1] The birth rate fluctuates with circumstances but also averages 40 per 1000 population. Although population changes both up-ward and downward in the short run, there is no persistent trend in either direction.

In these societies the birth rate is relatively stable and is supported by family and religious values. The death rate is more of a variable, for it is not high by choice and is likely to be lower if the harvest is good, or higher if there is pestilence or famine in a particular year. Nevertheless, it averages high. But it is the death rate that is most easily subject to change by deliberate human effort. Let there be any improvement in the food supply, or in dietary measures, or the elimination of some source of disease, and the death rate can drop considerably. Given the stability of a high birth rate in such societies, the consequence is a rapid gain in population.

---

[1] Irene B. Taueber, "Population and Society," in Robert E. L. Faris, ed., *Handbook of Modern Sociology* (Chicago: Rand McNally, 1964), pp. 87–88.

The Western Demographic Transition   Historically, the Western world experienced a major change in the relation of births to deaths that led to an enormous gain in population. Economic and social progress in the seventeenth and eighteenth centuries, followed by increased industrialization in the nineteenth, reduced the death rate, although the birth rate at first remained relatively stable. It gave Europe a tremendous growth in population, from 103 million in 1650 to 274 million in 1850, while millions more migrated to the Western hemisphere.[2] The development that brought down the death rate signified a transition to modern society, and in due time the birth rate began to fall as well. The great surplus of births over deaths, which had increased the European population so much and had produced a doubling of population once every 23.5 years in the United States between 1790 and 1860, was only a transitional phase. Nevertheless, even falling birth rates still yielded an excess of births over deaths until the twentieth century, for the death rate continued to decline.

The modernization of society in the Western world produced a growing middle class that voluntarily reduced its birth rate and placed high positive value upon the small family. Although this was more true of predominantly Protestant countries than Catholic ones, the middle class in all modern, industrial societies has generally been characterized by a *relatively* low birth rate. The gap between births and deaths that produced such leaps in population growth, then, occurs in a demographic transition from a high birth rate—high death rate society to a low birth rate—low death rate society. In this transition the mortality of the population declines before and faster than the fertility of the population, and the result is a temporary burst in the size of the population.

If this transition in the relationships of birth and death rates, with great population growth, was a revolutionary development, the pattern of low birth rates and low death rates that emerged in the twentieth century in Europe and the United States was also an historic new experience for mankind. The period of tremendous population growth was over, and the composition of the population changed. With a lower birth rate and a longer life expectancy due to a low mortality, the average age of the population was older. There was a higher proportion of people over forty, and increasingly a higher proportion over sixty-five.

When the falling birth rate and the age composition of the population were apparent in the 1930s there was much speculation that actual population decline would occur in the countries of western Europe. Only in France, however, was there an actual decline for a period of time, and an increase there in the

---

[2] Taueber, p. 85.

birth rate has checked that. Of greater interest today, however, is the situation in other parts of the world, where many nations are now in or at the threshold of the transitional phase where births exceed deaths in the face of a falling mortality. Improvements in medicine and sanitation, for example, in still non-industrialized parts of the world reduce the death rate while the birth rate remains high. The resulting gain in population threatens the capacity of such countries—India is an example—to feed an already huge population. As a consequence India has begun to look upon birth control as a matter of national policy.

That still largely agrarian societies may borrow from the more technologically advanced means by which they can lower their death rate, while their birth rate yet defies control, suggests that the model of demographic transition based upon the Western experience may not at all be universal. In recent years demographers have been critical of the adequacy of the model as applied to non-Western societies and have even taken a second look at its full applicability to the Western experience.[3] At best, apparently, it is a crude model that overlooks both temporal and localized variations and fluctuations. Although asserting a "high" birth rate for Europe prior to industrialization, the model fails to note that the European birth rate then was considerably lower than that found in Asian and African societies today. Nonetheless, it was high relative to contemporary levels in industrial Europe. However, there seem to have been some countries which did not conform to the transition described in the model.

It would be a mistake to assume that the demographic transition now under way will necessarily conform to this very general model of what occurred in population change in western Europe. For one thing there is a much greater density of population in some of the Asiatic countries, hence a gain in numbers threatens levels of living and a precarious control over mortality. There is also a vastly different political situation. The demographic transition in the Western world was spread out over almost three centuries, in part because the social revolution took that long. But that same social revolution is now being exported elsewhere and at a much faster pace. New nations undergoing modernization do not repeat the three centuries of development, but instead proceed immediately to the latest phase of scientific and technological development. They bypass the earlier technological stages; in short, they leap from a primitive technology to an advanced technology in a few years. Under these circumstances, demographers hesitate to predict what in the short run will be the demographic adjustment to such a radical social change.

[3] For a brief discussion of this issue, see Dennis H. Wrong, *Population and Society,* revised edition (New York: Random House, 1962), pp. 17–23.

The revolutionary transition in population which produced a pattern of low fertility and low mortality was a consequence of the modernizing revolution that altered human society. In turn this demographic change had significant effects upon society. Low mortality, for example, increased life expectancy and altered the age distribution of society. It also changed the major causes of death. The generally low fertility was somewhat differentially distributed, with some strata contributing more to the low birth rate than others.

Mortality   Unlike fertility, death is not a major positive value in any society. The mortality of man is accepted from one or another religious orientation, but any society will reduce the death toll by whatever means is available to it, except where such means would violate sacred values. Prior to the modernizing of society, few societies had any effective means for warding off an early death, and life for the vast majority of men was short, harsh, and brutal. Poorly fed populations were ravaged by diseases that they little understood and over which they had no control.

Life is a risk at any age, for the possibilities of death are always present. However, at given ages, there are greater or lesser probabilities of escaping death. Once past infancy, the probability of death will be lower, then gradually increase with advancing age. How rapidly the probability will increase varies from one society to another, of course, and in modern societies, the death rate remains very low for the first three decades of life.

Perhaps the single factor most significant in reducing the death rate has been the spectacular reduction in infant mortality in the twentieth century. Historically, the first year of life has always brought the greatest danger of death; it is death within this first year that is called *infant mortality*. In impoverished, agrarian populations, the infant death rate is always high. In the United States, infant mortality remained fairly high as long as we were an agrarian nation, and in fact has dropped most rapidly only in the last sixty years. The infant death rate in 1900 was 162.4 (meaning 162.4 deaths out of one thousand live births), while in 1930 it was 64.6. Since then it has dropped below 30, reaching 26.9 by 1958 and down further to 24.2 by 1964.[4]

The reduction in the death rate has increased life expectancy in modern society; in the United States, by 1962, life expectancy for females was 73.4 years, and for males, 66.8. (It was slightly higher for white Americans than

[4] Source: United Nations, *Demographic Yearbook, 1959* and Population Reference Bureau, *World Population Data Sheet*, December, 1965.

for black Americans.) This compares, for example, with only 45.2 years for males in India in 1957–1958, and 54.7 for males in Costa Rica in 1949–1951.[5]

When the decline in mortality increases life expectancy, significant changes occur in the population. Since people live longer, there is a higher proportion of the population in the older age brackets. In the United States those over sixty-five years of age have increased, not only in absolute numbers but as a proportion of the population. As a consequence, a concern for the problems of the aging becomes of increasing importance. In the United States, there has been an accelerated interest in the field of gerontology in the last decade; the physical, mental, and social needs of elderly people have become a major social problem in the United States now, even as the financial and economic needs of the elderly induced social movements and national action for old age pensions in the 1930s. The new Medicare program is the most recent attempt to act upon these needs.

Mortality Differentials   Although the mortality rate in the United States and other modern societies has been appreciably reduced, there are still significant differences in rates of mortality within the population of such societies. Some of these, such as the traditional lower death rates in rural areas, are less significant as urban death rates approach the rural ones. Two differentials in the United States that are still significant are *sex* and *race.*

Women have a lower death rate and a longer life expectancy than men. Recent figures indicate that the life expectancy of women has now exceeded seventy-three years, bettering that of men by six years. This higher life expectancy among females is true of modern society, but it was not so in agrarian or even earlier industrial society. There, the hard toil of daily existence, coupled with the burden of frequent childbearing, produced a higher death rate for females. Over the last century, the reduction of the maternal death rate has been spectacular; very few women now die in childbirth. In addition the lowering of the birth rate has meant that the average woman bears fewer children, and she also spaces them. In short, great advances in medicine, in health standards, as well as the decline of the birth rate, have enabled women to escape one major factor in their previously high death rate; now, they have surpassed men in life expectancy.

This uncomfortable (for men) fact has often been explained by pointing out that men are the gainfully employed, assume responsibility for supporting the family by going out each day into the "jungle" of economic struggle, fight the wars, and so pay a price of wear and tear on the physical organism.

[5] Source: United Nations, *Demographic Yearbook, 1963.*

Such an argument defends the notion that males are the stronger sex. But some evidence from nature contests this. For example, there are about 105.5 boys born to every 100 girls; thus, the male sex has a head start in the sex ratio. It needs it, it seems, for its death rate is higher at every age, and by the beginning of adulthood the two sexes are even in numbers; after that, women outnumber men. Occupational hazard, then, is not a sufficient explanation, for males die at a faster rate than do females at every age from birth.

In the United States, the other great differential is *race*. Whites have a significantly longer life expectancy than do nonwhites. Like the differential between the rural and the urban, this one is not as great as it once was. Some 30 years ago there was a differential of almost 12 years; by 1954 it was only a little more than 6 years, with white males at 67.4 and nonwhite males at 61.0. This differential is one too closely bound up with economic differences to escape our notice. Most Negroes experience low living standards, low and irregular income, and discrimination in their access to adequate medical care. But as the education of Negroes improves, as their income and living standards improve, and as discrimination in medical and health services decline, the Negro's life expectancy improves, and the differential between Negro and white is appreciably lessened.

Fertility   Even in societies in which fertility is high, there are still socially induced limits on the birth rate. *Fecundity* is the term that designates the full potential of reproduction in the population—the birth rate that would result if every woman had as many children as she was biologically capable of bearing during her entire span of childbearing years. *Fertility* refers to the actual rate of reproduction. Even when it is high, it is well short of fecundity, for no society achieves the full potential of fecundity, in part for biological and physical reasons, but in part also for social and cultural reasons. The regulation of sexual behavior in some manner or other occurs in all societies, and most societies, as an unintended consequence of such regulation, limit fertility. Most societies discourage childbirth in females not yet married, even though all do not limit sexual intercourse to the married. Since in most societies females do not marry until some years after puberty, some fecundity is thereby lost. Religious restrictions on frequency of intercourse, the ban on the remarriage of women in some societies, these and other factors all serve to make fertility considerably less than fecundity.

Differential Fertility   Although modern societies may have relatively low birth rates, there is considerable variation within each society. Some groups and strata have consistently higher than average birth rates within that society, others, consistently lower than average. This is the problem of *differentials* in the birth rate. In modern society, there are a number of differentials in fertility, but the most significant are *class* and *rural-urban,* with *religion* as an additional differential of some importance.

The agrarian pattern of life has been characterized by a high birth rate, and even in societies that have become industrialized, the agrarian segment of the population still retains a relatively high birth rate. The decline that produces the low birth rate in such societies occurs most markedly among urban-dwellers. There is some historical evidence that the rural-urban differential is an old one, for writings of past civilizations have noted the large families of peasant and farm people, and the smaller families of townspeople. However, this differential spread rapidly with the urbanization that accompanied industrialization. Family limitation by means of contraception originated in the cities and occurred first among the urban middle classes. When in the late nineteenth century it spread somewhat among the working class as well, the gap between the rural and urban widened rapidly.

In more recent decades, rural birth rates have been moving downward. This is particularly true where farm mechanization alters the relationship of the family to farming, and where the agrarian standard of living is higher. In the United States there has been a steady decrease in the rural birth rate, though it remains higher than the urban. But the gap between the two is much less than it once was.

The *class differential* in the birth rate has been observed for a long time, and seems to be one of the more stable differentials in fertility. Consistently, from one nation to another, the working class has a higher birth rate than do the middle and upper classes. The working class also has a higher death rate, but despite this, it has a greater rate of reproduction than do other classes; it contributes more to the total population of the next generation.

Low fertility in the urban areas and in the middle classes converged to produce the lowest rate of fertility in the urban middle classes, and lowest of all among the better educated ones—the professional classes. Indeed, over the past century or more, these people failed to reproduce themselves, so low has been their fertility.

During the last fifty years, this class differential has been a particular matter of public discussion. In particular, the failure of the educated middle classes to reproduce themselves has frequently been heralded as courting disaster for mankind, for it seemed to many that the least fit were adding an ever increasing proportion to the population, whereas the most fit were declining in number. The fear of the consequences to society from such class differentials has been based upon confused conceptions of what constitutes "fitness" in the human species. Specifically, the social and biological measures of fitness are confused. The higher scores on IQ tests characteristic of the better educated are not scientific evidence of an inherent, biological superiority. Nor are the low IQ scores evidence of an inherent inferiority of the lower classes.

Whatever the character of the concerns, the formerly wide differential between higher and lower classes is now much less pronounced. This has come about as a result of a decline in working-class fertility, on the one hand, and of an increase in middle-class fertility, on the other. In the period between the two world wars, the working-class birth rate was declining more rapidly than that of other classes, and the differences in fertility among the classes was less marked than previously. In the years since World War II, the middle classes have contributed significantly more to the recent increases in fertility, thus further narrowing the class differential. Nevertheless, the differential is still there. It seems, however, less of a fixed social pattern than it did a decade or more ago.

In societies in which there are large Catholic and Protestant populations, as in the United States, religion also contributes to the differential fertility; Catholics have a substantially higher birth rate than do either Protestants or Jews. This is not a universal feature of Catholic populations, however, despite the consistent official Catholic position on birth control—witness the low birth rate that has prevailed in France. The nature of the religious differential was long obscured because comparative studies did not take into account class and rural-urban factors. The differential could only be uncovered by comparing Catholics and Protestants who were both urban or rural and who came from the same social class. Although it has long been known that Catholics in the United States had a high birth rate, it was also true that most American Catholics, until World War II at least, were working class. Since the working class is also characterized by a higher birth rate, it was possible to attribute the Catholic birth rate to their working-class status or to attribute the high birth rate of the working class to the high proportion of Catholics in the working class.

Comparative studies have demonstrated that there is in fact a class differential, but that there is also a religious differential. Catholics at both the working-class and middle-class levels have a higher birth rate than do Protestants at the same class level. Social class, however, does have some effect upon religious differentials. The Catholic birth rate declines with mobility in class position, so that middle-class Catholics have a lower birth rate than do working-class Catholics, and working-class Protestants, in turn, have a higher birth rate than do middle-class Protestants.

When Catholics are working class, both their religion and their class position support one another in encouraging a high birth rate. When Protestants are middle class, the same thing occurs: their religion and their class position support one another in encouraging a low birth rate. But when Catholics are middle class and when Protestants are working class, religion and class act as cross-pressures. These cross-pressures produce birth rates that fall between those whose birth rates are mutually supported by both class and religion. Middle-class Catholics, for example, have a lower birth rate than do working-class Catholics, but a higher birth rate than do other middle-class people. Working-class Protestants, in turn, have a higher birth rate than do middle-class Protestants, but a lower birth rate than do working-class Catholics. Another way to say this is that working-class Catholics have the highest birth rate and middle-class Protestants the lowest, with the other two categories falling somewhere between them.

Until very recently, the higher Catholic birth rate in the United States seemed to be a secure demographic fact, for Catholic belief on the matter appeared to be a firm article of faith. But the revolutionary change in Catholicism instituted by Pope John XXIII has opened up for discussion many previously fixed matters of dogma, and the Church's position on birth control is one of them. There is every possibility that a significant change here may eventually come about, and that the religious differential in fertility may therefore decline. There is already substantial evidence of an increasing practice of birth control by American Catholics.

Changes in American Fertility   The general pattern of fertility, including the differential fertility discussed above, has been characteristic of the United States and other Western countries for a century or more. Basic to this pattern has been a long run decline in the rate of fertility. But since the late thirties, in the United States as well as the nations of western Europe, the decline in fertility has stopped, and an increase in birth rates has occurred.

In the United States the more than a century old decline in the birth rate reached an historic low in 1935. Most demographers expected it to go even lower, and in the thirties they were predicting a future population based upon a continued lowering of the birth rate; they even anticipated it falling below the death rate and producing a decrease in population before the end of the century. By extending the trends in the birth and death rates into the future, they confidently predicted what the American population was to be.

Never were experts so wrong in so short a period of time. Instead of continuing downward, the birth rate moved up slightly in the late thirties, a fact credited to the return of prosperity. However, contrary to expectations, it continued to increase both during and after World War II. Indeed, it continued at a high level well into the fifties and only showed a tendency to drop off, and then but slightly, in the late fifties. This new pattern, which violated all previous predictions, was all the more inexplicable because it was, in part, based upon a change in the historic pattern of class differentials in fertility. A greater contribution to the increased fertility came from the middle class, and particularly from those segments which had had the lowest fertility.

Whatever the long-time trend, there were also short run factors influencing the birth rate, such as the economic cycle of depression and prosperity, as well as war. The depression, by forcing postponement of marriage for many, undoubtedly depressed the birth rate even further than would have otherwise occurred. The end of the depression and the war-induced prosperity of the early forties encouraged more marriages, with a resultant increase in the birth rate. The war itself encouraged more marriages. In modern societies, where wars are fought by conscript armies, deferment of fathers and married men always produces a temporary increase in the birth rate. After World War II the demobilization of millions of American soldiers in a matter of months brought a rush of marriages, and millions of married men resumed family life, in many cases having those children that military service had postponed.

These economic and military factors induced an increase in the birth rate and halted the long-time downward trend. In most cases the births were for first and second children; the increase in the birth rate did not signify a change to large families. It did indicate a birth rate that reflected economic prosperity, and because of that, an opportunity to make up for postponements in marriage and childbearing induced by depression and military service.

Once the war ended, birth rates were expected to drop again, but this did not happen. Economic prosperity was, of course, still encouraging a higher birth rate, but it was questionable whether that was a sufficient reason. Undoubtedly it did encourage people to marry earlier than they might otherwise have done and also to have their children earlier than they might otherwise have.

One thing was evident: in the late 1940s and during the 1950s, young people were marrying at an earlier age, and their first child was born sooner after marriage than had been the case in the United States earlier in this century. This fact contributed considerably to the postwar baby boom. It was evident, also, that marriage was never more popular: there were fewer unmarried people than before, and among the married there were fewer childless couples.

All of these factors could sustain an increase in the birth rate without resulting in larger families. It was possible that women might be having their children while they were in their twenties, rather than their thirties. By the mid-fifties there was some evidence that many women in the United States were having their third and fourth child. This suggested an increase in the average size of the American family, though still far from the large family of our agrarian past.

Economic prosperity alone did not sustain this baby boom, but it undoubtedly created the social climate within which it was possible. The earlier marriages and earlier birth of a child after marriage are objective facts, but an explanation requires us to examine values about marriage, family, and careers in the postwar generation of youth. It is evident that young middle-class women were more satisfied with the conventional role of mother and housewife and were less concerned with it as a competitive threat to a career than were young women in the 1920s and 1930s. (In Chapter 13, we examined the postwar familism which produced the new upsurge in the birth rate and the baby boom.) If the postwar generation defined marriage and family differently than was done before the war, and if as a result they married sooner and had their children sooner, and had three or four rather than one or two, the resulting higher birth rate could be expected to be sustained for as long as these values about family life were held. Yet already this postwar pattern has peaked, as is evident in Table 1. There has been a steady decline in the birth rate since 1957. By 1965 the birth rate had fallen to where it was in 1940, only slightly above its historic low in 1935.

One significant consequence of the postwar increase in the birth rate, concomitant with an historic low in mortality, is a significant change in the age pyramid of American society. Specifically, there has been a greater increase in the proportion of those over sixty-five years of age and those under nine

TABLE 1   CRUDE BIRTH RATES IN THE UNITED STATES, 1920–1964

Year	Number of Crude Births Per 1000 Population
1920	27.7
1925	25.1
1930	21.3
1935	18.7
1940	19.4
1942	22.2
1945	20.4
1947	26.6
1950	24.1
1952	25.1
1955	25.0
1957	25.3
1960	23.7
1962	22.4
1963	21.7
1964	21.0

SOURCE   U.S. Department of Health, Education and Welfare, *Vital Statistics of the United States, 1964*, vol. I (Washington, D.C.: U.S. Government Printing Office, 1966), Table 1–2, pp. 1–4.

TABLE 2 **POPULATION BY AGE GROUPS IN THE UNITED STATES,**
1940 and 1960

	1940 (in millions)	1960 (in millions)	Percent Increase
65 years and over	9.0	16.5	83.3
55–64 years	10.6	15.6	47.1
45–54 years	15.5	20.5	32.2
35–44 years	18.3	24.1	31.6
20–34 years	33.0	33.6	1.8
10–19 years	24.1	30.0	24.5
0–9 years	21.2	39.0	83.9
Total population	131.7	179.3	36.1

SOURCE U.S. Bureau of the Census, *U.S. Census of Population, 1960*, vol. I, chap. B.

years of age. The older and the younger end of the population pyramid grow at the expense of the middle years. Table 2 reveals how the population by age groups changed from 1940 to 1960. As time goes on, there will be further changes in the proportion of age groups in the population, given the simple fact that there is now a declining birth rate, and also that the 39 million under nine years of age was the single largest group in the total American population. By now they are becoming the largest group of Americans ever to be educated, with a tremendous pressure on educational and other resources. This also accounts for the fact that the average age of the American population has become younger. Although this group may not reproduce at the same high rate, their sheer numbers suggest that there will continue to be an *absolute* addition to the American population of a considerable magnitude; the American population is not going to slow up in its growth very rapidly, for its absolute base has grown so considerably.

To predict what will happen in the population is a risky proposition. In the 1930s demographers were confident that they could accurately predict population trends for decades to come. But their confidence was seriously dented by the unpredicted change to a higher birth rate, and particularly by its staying high after the wartime situation had ceased to be a significant factor. What, then, might have been defined as an objective process to be measured in population statistics is only too evidently a cultural process subject to the changing definitions of the situation, as well as to the shifting values and altered perspectives that each new generation brings to the age-old process of mating and reproduction. The cultural framework of values and personal goals, as well as the social organization of life, provides the complex and changing context within which millions of people individually make personal decisions about marriage and family that add up to great trends in fertility and gains or losses in human population.

Besides fertility and mortality, migration is a third major factor in the demographic process. It is a much less predictable factor than fertility and mortality, for it is highly responsive to political controls as well as political events. When we speak of immigration, we refer to migration *into* a country; similarly, emigration is migration *out* of a country. *In-migration* and *out-migration* refer to the same processes when they occur among the regions of a country.

Men have continually moved from one part of the earth to another, but the reasons have been varied.[6] People have moved to pursue a better living, to escape persecution, to seek new food sources, or they have been compelled to move by virtue of conquest or natural disaster. Thus, some migration is voluntary or *free* and some is *forced*. In the early history of man, most migrations were by groups of men, by whole tribes or clans, rather than by individuals. Sometimes this was because of conquest, sometimes by the pressure for food and resources. Whatever the reason, human migration was a group process until relatively recent history.

The nineteenth century was the great period of free individual movement, when millions of individuals chose to migrate, the majority of them crossing the Atlantic from Europe to the Western Hemisphere, particularly the United States. The lure of greater economic opportunity was probably the one dominant motive in the decisions of millions of Europeans to emigrate to the United States. In a smaller number of cases, as for East European Jews, migration to America was an opportunity to escape centuries-old anti-Semitic persecution.

During the 1800s changes occurred in the source of European immigrants.[7] For most of the century they came from western and northern Europe. The British Isles—the English, Scottish, and Welsh—supplied most of the early settlers. Although the French sent many to the New World in the eighteenth century, most of them located in what was to become Canada. Only around New Orleans did the French constitute a sizable ethnic colony. From the

---

[6] For a succinct review of migration, see Wrong, *Population and Society*, Chapter 6.

[7] For a review of the American experience with immigration, see Marcus Lee Hansen, *The Immigrant in American History* (Cambridge, Mass.: Harvard University Press, 1940).

1840s on, new immigrants came from Germany, Ireland, and the Scandinavian countries, particularly Sweden and Norway. This was still the same part of Europe, however, and except for the Irish, these people were still largely Protestant. The coming of the Irish in the 1840s, whose immigration was first induced by famine in Ireland, brought the first sizable Catholic population to the United States. It created the pattern of Protestant-Catholic tensions that were to be so much a part of the political and social life of the United States after that.

After 1880, a last great wave of immigration brought to the United States millions of people from eastern and southern Europe: Poles and Italians, particularly, but also Austrians, Russians, Greeks, Hungarians, and Slovaks. They came in great numbers; over five million immigrants arrived between 1881 and 1890, to be surpassed by the almost nine million immigrants from 1901 to 1910. Coming out of a peasant milieu, these immigrants nonetheless converged on the large cities of the industrial North, for it was there that jobs awaited them. After all it was the industrial expansion of the United States that made an "open door" policy on immigration acceptable, even desired, by politically powerful industrial employers. This concentration of immigrants in northern cities gave to these dominant urban complexes an ethnically and religiously heterogeneous character. America was no longer so overwhelmingly Anglo-Saxon and Protestant, though its dominant majority was still so, and its middle class was to remain predominantly so until the 1930s. But if America became more heterogeneous, it also was beset with all the tensions involved in absorbing culturally different peoples into the nation's social structure.

From then on, the United States became a society whose very social character was strongly influenced by its cultural diversity. Ethnic diversity was one significant basis for political life, and ethnic attachments to one or another of the major political parties still remain important in our political life. Ethnic rivalry and contest was a prime source of group tension and conflict, particularly in northern cities. In addition, religious identification became a significant element in urban politics. Nevertheless, the idea of America as a "melting pot" pointed up the value that most middle-class Americans placed upon the assimilation of diverse groups into a single way of life. In the first part of this century, the public schools probably did more than any other institution to "Americanize" immigrants, particularly their children. But there has also been a contrasting emphasis upon a pluralist America, the United States as a nation of many nations, where people of diverse national origins and varied cultures can live side by side.[8] This image, expressed more frequently in recent

[8] For a discussion of assimilation and pluralism, see Nathan Glazer, "Ethnic Groups in America: From National Culture to Ideology," in Morroe Berger, Theodore Abel, and Charles H. Page, eds., *Freedom and Control in Modern Society* (New York: Van Nostrand, 1954), pp. 158–173.

years, suggests a greater appreciation of differences, a willingness to see them persist longer, and a more tolerant view of the cultural and religious diversity in American life. Whatever the contrasting meanings that European immigration has had for Americans, it has had an immeasurable impact on American society and upon the cultural experiences of Americans. Probably only the race problem has more seriously challenged the capacity of Americans to build a society from people of diverse social origin.

The Closing of Immigration   The nine million immigrants who reached American shores between 1901 and 1910 were the last of the great waves of migrants to the United States. The opposition to unrestricted immigration, which had always had a place in American opinion, began to be heard more loudly and more often in the land, and the first attempts were made to establish some limits on immigration. However, it was the outbreak of war in Europe in 1914 that effectively cut off migration to America, and it was never resumed in any substantial numbers after that.

In 1922 the United States Congress passed legislation ending free immigration and establishing instead *controlled immigration.* This was done by establishing annual quotas for each nation, based upon their proportion of the American population according to the census of 1890. To go back to the year 1890 meant to pick a time when eastern and southern Europeans had not yet become a sizable segment of the American population. As a result these areas of Europe received smaller quotas compared to the quotas for western and northern European countries. This quota system also restricted immigration from the Catholic and Eastern Orthodox countries, giving a definite preference to Protestants. Jews also were more severely restricted, for although Jews lived in all European countries, a large proportion of European Jewry lived in Poland and Russia, and the increase in Jewish immigration after 1890 had come from these countries.

The American quota system for immigration has been a source of controversy since the legislation was created in 1922. Critics have charged that the law deliberately discriminated against Catholics, as well as the Greek Orthodox and the Jews. From an ethnic perspective, it seemed to its critics to discriminate against eastern and southern Europeans. As a consequence of such criticism, and also because of a concern for displaced persons after World War II, Congress reopened the immigration problem. This resulted in the Walters-McCarran Act of 1952, however this did not appreciably change the quota system established thirty years before.

If quota restrictions had been lifted by Congress in 1952, it does not necessarily mean that immigration to the United States would have resumed at the high level of the period from 1890 to 1910. Even if quotas had been abolished, the total number permitted in was kept low. But there is no evidence that the demand for immigration to the United States is any longer of that magnitude. For one thing European countries are now more industrialized and consequently more able to absorb the peasantry into their own industrial cities. In addition the political control of the Soviet Union over much of eastern Europe would also make unlikely the resumption of free immigration at a high level.

Migration in the Twentieth Century Immigration to the United States in the nineteenth century was the free individual immigration widely possible in that century. But such uncontrolled immigration has become less common in the twentieth century, as various nations, including the United States, have taken steps to control the flow of immigrants in what is conceived to be the national interest. There has reemerged in this century the forced immigration of a type and at a magnitude unknown in human experience for a long time. Totalitarian nations have not hesitated to ship whole groups of people from one place to another and to dispossess them from what had been their homeland for centuries. War, too, has often disrupted a settled population and forced entire groups of people to move. The Nazis shipped Jews to concentration camps and to death chambers and, during the war, moved slave laborers from occupied countries into German industrial cities. The Soviets, in turn, practiced the mass expulsion of ideologically resistant groups, such as the *kulaks* (land-owning peasants), and removed whole ethnic colonies, such as Tartars and Volga Germans, to labor camps operated during World War II. Soviet economic development of Siberia and Soviet Asia has been carried out partly by a forced colonization.

Displaced people abounded in Europe after World War II ended, and many either could not or for political reasons did not want to return to their native land. Postwar immigration was a necessity, and such sparsely populated countries as Canada, Australia, and New Zealand accepted substantial numbers of European "displaced persons," as they were commonly labeled in the postwar years. Based on existing population, the United States took very few, and it required some special legislation in 1952 to enable President Eisenhower to develop a program for American acceptance of displaced persons.

Asiatic Immigration One of the sources of greatest immigration potential is Asia, where large populations live with low living standards. The Western world, however, has long practiced immigration restrictions on Asiatics. The United States, for example, passed the Chinese Exclusion Act in 1880 at the very time that unrestricted immigration into America was national policy. The countries of Latin America, long anxious to receive immigrants, have nevertheless strictly limited migrants from China and other Asiatic countries. The Chinese have been vigorous emigrants, and long ago established large

Chinese colonies in southern and southeastern Asia, where they often became influential in commercial organization of these little industrialized societies.

Advocates of unlimited immigration see Asiatic emigration as a means for relieving population pressures in those parts of the world. Migration, however, is not a permanent solution to the problem of population pressure. Over the long run it probably only postpones the severity of the pressure and perhaps increases the problem elsewhere. However, the communization of China sharply reduces, if it does not eliminate, the possibility of migration to the west. Military conquest by Communist China, however, could open up areas for active colonization.

Internal Migration   Migration is not entirely an international or intercountry issue. Substantial migration occurs within societies, particularly large ones, and especially when they are undergoing industrialization. The most significant form of internal migration is rural to urban, an outcome of the industrializing process. With the decline in agricultural employment induced by this industrialization, large numbers of rural migrants have of necessity been absorbed into the cities and into industrial employment. In the United States, the rural-urban migration has also produced a regional migration. Southerners, both white and Negro, have migrated from the South, the least industrial region of the United States, to the North, and in more recent years to the west coast.

Such an internal population shift has produced some problems, of which the most significant is the lack of educational and industrial skills among rural southerners, who now make up a large part of the unskilled and most frequently unemployed segment of the industrial North. As technological skills necessary to modern industry increase, migrants from rural areas, and particularly the South, become more and more the group hardest to absorb into the labor market. They not only are frequently unemployed, they are often unemployable.

Migration and Population Growth   When migration occurs in substantial numbers, it has an impact upon the population growth of the society. This point has often been debated among demographers, for many have argued that immigration induces the native population to reduce its birth rate, thus offsetting any apparent gain from immigration. As the history of immigration to the United States reveals so clearly, the immigrants come in at the lowest economic level and take the least rewarded jobs, this then enables the native population more rapidly to improve its social status. Since a lowered birth rate goes with higher social status, it is argued that immigration, by increasing status opportunities for the native population, induces a more rapid decline in the latter's birth rate. However, American demographers are convinced, nonetheless, that the United States gained in population from immigration.

There has been a similar discussion about the effect of substantial emigration from a society. Some have insisted that the resulting lowering of the population in such a country is only temporary, for the relieving of population pressure may then permit a greater natural increase in the remaining population. Emigration only reduces population when it is associated with fertility control. This is what happened in Ireland, where after the 1840s the population was reduced from eight to four million by mass emigration combined with fertility control in the form of delayed marriage. Unless a society does put some form of fertility control into practice, emigration is unlikely to be anything more than a temporary reduction in population pressure.

It is this fact that supports the argument that migration is not the answer to Asia's population problem. Asiatic societies seem as yet unready to bring about a lowering of the birth rate. Under the circumstances, a mass emigration to other parts of the world, by temporarily relieving the pressure on a limited food supply, coupled with a high birth rate, would likely soon replace those who emigrated. Fertility control rather than emigration is the key element in the population problems that beset the modern world.

MALTHUS: THE PROBLEM OF HUMAN SURVIVAL

Thomas Malthus advanced the proposition that population growth exceeds the food supply, with resulting vice and misery for the human race. Such a proposition was not only advanced to say something about population; it was also a contribution to an ongoing intellectual controversy between those eighteenth century rational optimists and social reformers who believed in the possibility of unlimited human progress, and a newly developing intellectual circle of English social thinkers who denied that progress was to be attained by social reforms, and in general argued against human interference in "natural" processes.

Malthus was intellectual kin with Adam Smith, David Ricardo, James Mill, and other English economic liberals, who attempted to provide logical and scientific support for an unfettered, laissez-faire capitalism, and who in particular argued against any attempts at reform through social legislation. Ricardo, for example, had postulated an "iron law of wages," a thesis that wages tended to attain a subsistence level which enabled laborers to exist without increase or decrease in their numbers. Any legislation, he argued, would merely increase the population, not diminish poverty. Furthermore, it would have other harmful effects, such as lowering profits, increasing unemployment, and so on. Malthus also opposed remedial legislation to improve the lot of the very poor. He argued that such legislation could not improve the living conditions of the worker and would only have harmful consequences. He blamed the poor for creating their own misery by an excessive birth rate and argued that they had to learn "moral restraint" to improve their position. Malthus, in short, was one of a group of thinkers whose ideas stemmed from Adam Smith, and who were erecting the intellectual defenses for an unregulated capitalism in nineteenth century industrial England. Their scholarly ideas lent themselves easily to a public ideology which opposed any and all forms of legislation of a reforming or humanitarian kind in behalf of the working class. The resulting brand of economics, so pessimistic in its hopes for human progress, was frequently called "the dismal science."

Malthus' Social Theory Malthus' essay on population was obviously more than a discussion of that problem. It was part of a scholarly argument about the nature of human society, which provided reasons for opposing the impulse to reform, and for doubting belief in human progress through rational thought and remedial legislation. Malthus' principles of population, then, rested upon a theory of social structure. Malthus began with a rather somber view of man— he believed him indolent by nature and therefore in need of motivation to work. He also believed that the sex drive is a constant element in human affairs, and that sexual passion leads to marriage for satisfaction. As a consequence, support of the family acquired by marriage forces men to work, and the institution of marriage impels the activity to which is due human progress. Marriage is then a necessary institution, for without it man's indolent nature would not be motivated to work.

In keeping with this, Malthus argued that parents must be responsible for their progeny. Accordingly, there should be no poor relief, family aid, or other measures of relief by which the community assumes some responsibility for the care of children. Such measures, Malthus argued, would remove the stimulus to work. From his assumptions about the nature of man and about the necessary organization of human society, Malthus was able to derive some convenient arguments that fitted the dominant economic ideology of his day and satisfied broad sections of the British middle classes by giving them seemingly scientific arguments for opposing poor relief, wage increases, or other humanitarian measures.

Having established the motivation for work in the necessity for caring for family, Malthus then went on to discuss the relation of food and population. Man must have food, and this fact, Malthus observed, necessarily limits the population. Specifically, he postulated that population grows at a geometric ratio of 1:2:4:8:16, whereas the food supply grows only at an arithmetic ratio of 1:2:3:4:5. Accordingly, human misery increases until population is checked. This, says Malthus, is an "iron law" of nature, which prevents any utopias on earth. But the motivation to work in order to eat is also man's means of progress.

There are two kinds of checks on population growth, according to Malthus, the *positive* and the *preventive*. The positive checks occur when men do nothing to prevent population exceeding food supply; in such cases what Malthus called misery and vice sets in—war, plagues, famine, and infanticide. As Malthus saw it, the only alternative to the positive checks is the preventive one of moral restraint. By this Malthus meant the abstention from sexual relations outside of marriage, and the postponement of marriage until such time as the individual is able to support a family. Malthus did not preach abstention from sexual relations between husband and wife after marriage, and he did not view birth control as a morally acceptable alternative; he felt it lowered "the dignity of human nature." Although Malthus believed that moral restraint is the only possible alternative, his pessimistic outlook was that most of mankind, and particularly the lower classes, are incapable of this; thus he foresaw only misery and vice in man's future.

The Criticisms of Malthus Demographers have long since abandoned the details of Malthus' theory, although his basic thesis—that population exceeds food supply—has become one of the great controversial issues of our time. Yet the proposition which Malthus advanced has provided no empirical description of the Western world. Here, at least, food has increased in abundance, even as population has grown. Also in the Western world, as apparently in time in all industrial societies, the birth rate dropped rather than increased with improvement in the standard of living. The practice of birth control and the deliberate spacing of children by the middle classes in industrial societies was the major factor involved.

The rapid spread of industrialization in the nineteenth century and the opening up of the grassy plains of North America to cultivation seemed to make a mockery of Malthus' dire warnings of vice and misery. Rather than these, a constantly improved standard of living and an abundance of food has characterized Western life in the more than a century and a half since Malthus wrote his essay. Even Malthus was moved to admit that he did not anticipate the great increase in cultivable land, nor the improvement in agricultural techniques that increased food production several times over.

These developments did disprove one part of Malthus' theory decisively—his notion that population was a *constant* pressure on the food supply. Clearly, for generations at least, men could have more than enough to eat. Nature was not necessarily niggardly. Yet this may also mean only a postponement of the problem that Malthus postulated. In time, perhaps, the population of the entire world will exceed the available food supply.

The overcrowded and underdeveloped countries are sometimes taken as evidence of the contemporary relevance of Malthus' theory. Here, population *is* a constant pressure on an inadequate food supply. The standard of living is low, the birth rate is high. But so is the death rate, and misery is rampant. What is true of some parts of the world might at some future date be true for the entire world—or so some have argued who accept Malthus' basic thesis that population cannot grow beyond the limits of subsistence, and thus it cannot increase indefinitely, if we assume that the food supply also has some limit even if not yet attained. There is a danger, argue the neo-Malthusians, and it is not in some remote time but in a foreseeable future.

The Growth of World Population The measurement of world population is at best a somewhat hazardous process, and even now large areas of the world possess no accurate census. Careful estimates of population and of rate of growth is necessary. Thus, the following is a demographic assessment from the best available evidence of world population since 1650:[9]

year	population (in millions)
1650	545
1750	728
1800	906
1850	1171
1900	1608
1950	2406

What the above figures say is that world population is increasing rapidly, and that it has increased fivefold since 1650. But prior to that, demographers are convinced, it increased only slowly, with the gains of high birth rates offset by pestilence and famine and serious social dislocations. But after 1650 the *rate* of population growth increased steadily: from an average of three per one thousand total population from 1650 to 1750; four from 1750 to 1800; five from 1800 to 1850; six from 1850 to 1900; and eight from 1900 to 1950.[10] Although these are slow rates of growth, they nonetheless generated large absolute increases: 200 million from 1650 to 1750; 400 million from 1750 to 1850; and 1.4 billion from 1850 to 1950.[11]

But now the generally agreed upon figure of rate of growth is 18 per 1000, though Irene Taueber points out that this figure is regarded as being too low.[12] "Given at least 3 billion people increasing at rates of growth four or five

---

[9] United Nations Department of Social Affairs, Population Division, *The Determinants and Consequences of Population Trends* (New York, 1953), Table 2, p. 11.

[10] Taueber, "Population and Society," p. 85.

[11] Taueber, p. 85.

[12] Taueber, p. 85.

times those of recent centuries, simple forward projections for a few more centuries yield numbers that are not possible on a finite earth."[13]

The great continent of Asia has apparently always had more than half of the world's population. Demographic estimates are that almost three of five persons in the world were Asiatics in 1650, but this margin declined steadily as Europe and North and South America underwent great population gains. Yet it was not until 1930 that the Asiatic population was only slightly more than 50 percent of the world's population—1072 millions out of 2015 millions in the world. Since then its rate of growth has been slightly above that of the world increase as a whole and well above that of Europe. By 1960 Asiatics were 1679 million in a world population of 2995 million. Their births per 1000 population exceeded deaths by a margin of 41 to 22, almost two to one.[14]

Asia is still one of the great undeveloped continents of the world, with Japan as perhaps its only completely modern and developed nation. Yet, given declining mortality and a continuing high fertility, it is the undeveloped areas of the world—Asia, Africa, and Latin America—that are contributing more to the vast increase in the world population. Their premodern social order maintains a high birth rate, and there is no immediate prospect of any radical change. Meanwhile the modern social orders are increasingly characterized by *voluntary* birth controls and the preference for a small family, as well as a positive value placed upon birth control by modern governments and thus reflected to some extent in social policy. But in Asia there has as yet been no successful innovation of birth control policies to check the high fertility associated with an agrarian economy, village occupations, a subsistence level, poverty, ignorance, and malnutrition. Thus, the curious and possibly dangerous paradox is that in Asia and other underdeveloped areas of the world, modern science and technology have had spectacular success in lowering the death rate, sometimes by such a simple process as introducing DDT—in Ceylon in 1946 and 1947 the spraying of houses with DDT reduced the death rate by 40 percent in a single year.

What the present trend suggests, then, and as Table 3 makes evident, is that the population of the developed nations will increase steadily in numbers but will decline quite rapidly as a proportion of the world's total, from one-third in 1950 to about one-fifth in the year 2000. Furthermore, this will be accompanied by a shift in the age proportions. Thus 74 percent of those age 15 and under lived in underdeveloped areas of the world in 1950; this will be 79 percent by 1975. But, while 44 percent of those aged 60 and over lived in underdeveloped areas in 1950, this will increase to only 45 percent by 1975. In short, the underdeveloped world, with a declining but still higher mortality

---

[13] Taueber, pp. 85–86.

[14] The source for these figures is the United Nations, *Demographic Yearbook, 1961.*

TABLE 3 ESTIMATED AND PROJECTED POPULATIONS IN DEVELOPED
AND DEVELOPING AREAS, 1900–2000

Year	DEVELOPED[a] Population (in millions)	Percent Increase	Percent of World Total
1900	554		35.7
1925	700	26.4	36.7
1950	838	19.7	33.6
1975	1,115	33.0	28.9
2000	1,448	29.9	21.0
	DEVELOPING[b]		
1900	996	21.2	64.3
1925	1,207	21.2	63.3
1950	1,659	37.4	66.4
1975	2,741	65.2	71.1
2000	5,459	99.2	79.0

[a] Europe, U.S.S.R., Australia, Japan, New Zealand, and Northern America
[b] Africa, Latin America, and Asia, excluding the Asian portion of Japan and U.S.S.R.
SOURCE United Nations, Department of Economic and Social Affairs, *The Future Growth of World Population* (New York: The United Nations, 1958), Table 5.

rate, will possess an ever large segment of the youthful population of the world. A further declining mortality rate suggests that by the end of the century the economically advanced areas of the world will include even smaller proportions of the world's people. Its claim upon most of the world's wealth may not go unchallenged in these developing nations of increasing populations, as they struggle to modernize, to control population, and also to find a somewhat larger share of the world's resources for themselves.

As Irene Taueber notes, "It has always been obvious that growth must slow down sometime. It is now evident that the timing of such slowing may be a critical factor in determining man's future on earth."[15] The issue of population growth in the world as a whole is an issue that cannot be avoided, but as yet policy to control population growth is still a matter of *national* policy, for there is not a world organization capable of imposing such a policy upon the world as a whole. The rapid growth of Asiatic population, marked by a

[15] Taueber, "Population and Society," p. 86.

"coexistence of very high birth rates and declining death rates, and hence in rates of population increase that, continued, jeopardize not alone economic development and social advance, but human survival itself."[16] There is not much time, and what science and technology can do is limited. It would seem that the hope for control of population growth lies in the effective economic and social development of the as yet underdeveloped areas of the world, and a transition on their part to the kind of social organization which sustains the values and sanctions for a voluntarily controlled fertility that more nearly matches the remarkable low mortality that modern science and medicine make possible.

Neo-Malthusianism: Pro and Con   The neo-Malthusian argument grants that Malthus was in error in failing to recognize the agricultural revolution that would provide an abundance of food. But this, they maintain, merely postponed the operation of Malthus' principle for a century and a half, and now the danger is real and present. The considerable gain in the birth rate in some parts of the Western world, including the United States, the maintenance of high birth rates in other areas of the world while death rates fall, the destructive use of arable land, and the diminishing supply of new arable land—all these have been cited as evidence of a population crisis in the world. The basic argument is that there is a rapid increase in the world's population to be sustained by an agricultural yield that is now close to the limit of potential production, and indeed a yield that is likely to decline as men exploit the soil in such a way as to deplete it.

Such alarming arguments as these have not gone unanswered. The critics of the neo-Malthusians have charged them with underestimating the capacity of science to increase the food supply. They speak of bringing tropical land under cultivation, of getting food from the sea, and other scientific marvels. The earth, they maintain, can support a much larger population.

The argument about the limits of food supply on earth is a technical issue beyond the competence of the sociologist, and the demographer, too. But whatever the merits of the argument for asserting that science can produce much greater yields of food to support much larger populations than the world has yet seen, and however much the neo-Malthusians may have advanced unrealistically alarming arguments, demographers tend to take seriously the issue of population pressure on the earth's resources. Some of science's solutions may be in a too distant future to resolve problems of the next fifty years, or even the next century. In the long run, demographers believe, mankind must reduce its birth rate, or experience a serious threat to its standard of living, as well as a threat to available living space on this planet. High birth rates

---

[16] Taueber, p. 103.

and low death rates promise a continued growth of the world's population. The resulting problem cannot be dismissed as inconsequential.

In Conclusion   Demography can evidently contribute much that the sociologist finds useful in understanding society. The complex demographic processes of fertility, mortality, and migration are not merely dull statistical compilations, fitted into tables; instead, they are the results of rigorous efforts at generalizing the processes, and the consequences of these processes, viewed in the aggregate, that emerge from the millions of births, deaths, and movements that go on every day. It is a means of seeing in large-scale and societal terms the significance of what are the individual decisions and actions of millions of people. What are individual decisions somehow add up to complex processes that have a dynamic patter of their own, and these can be measured and their consequences assessed.

These demographic processes, then, are three things. First, they are the result, the unintended consequences of actions by millions of individuals, taken separately and individually, that add up to a describable social pattern. Secondly, these processes have consequences for society and particularly for changes in society. Thirdly, the shape or profile of the population constitutes a set of *conditions* that press upon social organization. Although they are not determinative of any particular form of social life, they do provide a context of demographic factors that set limits upon social organization and make strong demands upon it. For example, an increase in life expectancy adds further differentiation to the age grading of society and also adds further to the generational differences and possible generational conflicts that beset modern societies, as when social movements emerge to improve the economic status of the less affluent elderly. Also when a rising birth rate adds considerably to a population in a short time, as in the United States during recent decades, there is a strong pressure to divert more social resources into meeting the needs of the younger members of the society, particularly for the purpose of education. These examples suggest clearly enough why the sociologist has always given respectful attention to the demographic factor in the analysis of social life.

PART 6 THE STUDY OF SOCIETY

1

2

3

1. A young looter during the 1968 Detroit riots.
2. Puerto Ricans in New York.
3. Sunning in front of a New York tenement.
4. A "hippie" serenade to a drunkard.
5. Ku Klux Klan members parading in Florida.
6. Elderly shuffleboard players in St. Petersburg, Fla.
7. A couple at a love-in.

4

6

5

7

SOCIAL
PROBLEMS

22

The study of social problems has long been one of the central concerns of American sociology. Not even the commitment to develop a science of society has seriously weakened this involvement of sociologists with research on a wide variety of social problems. To be sure, sociologists do not define their discipline as the study of social problems, even though such a conception of the discipline is probably widely diffused throughout the general public. Research on crime and delinquency, on race and ethnic tensions, on divorce and family breakdown, on "deviant" rather than "normal" behavior, on mental illness, and on the problems that beset education and the urban community—these have been the concerns of sociologists for a long time. Furthermore, they have occupied the efforts of a considerable number of competent sociologists during the recent decade, when a national concern with poverty, race, urban renewal, and education focused on a complex set of highly interrelated issues that have been the object of social policy at community, state, and national levels.

Nonetheless the study of social problems has been a source of concern and disagreement among sociologists. There has always been some tension between the desire to be socially relevant, with its implications for supporting reform and change in society, and the desire to build a scientific sociology. The latter interest, emerging strongly in the 1930s and 1940s, developed in sociologists a dominating interest in scientific research free from bias and the contamination of value-judgments. This was obviously most difficult to attain when the research interest was focused on social problems that generated controversy and were clearly fraught with significant value-judgments about what should and should not exist in the real world.

Such a development did somewhat reduce the degree of concern for social problems in sociology, but only for a time. During the 1950s a renewed interest in the study of social problems returned to American sociology under the banner of the Society for the Study of Social Problems. This new organization frankly rallied those sociologists who felt that the discipline was neglecting what had historically been one of its primary intellectual pursuits and one of its important ways of relating itself to society—namely, the study of social problems. By now the position it sought to reestablish in sociology has become widely accepted among sociologists.

But there has remained a set of other problems generic to the issue itself. One of these has been the place of social values in the work of sociologists, for social problems inevitably involve serious value considerations. Another has been the issue of just what social problems are—whether there is a *sociological* as against a *social* definition of problems. At issue is a sociological stance toward society's conception of its problems.

Sociology began as an American discipline focused around the problems of a rapidly industrializing and urbanizing society. In the first days of American sociology, just before and after the turn of the century, there was not yet a concept of social problems: rather, the organizing concept under which the problems of that day were subsumed was *social pathology*. That was to be followed by *social disorganization* before *social problems* became firmly established in the vocabulary of sociologists.

Social Pathology The term social pathology entered sociology as part of a larger sociological perspective. As a concept it assumed the social evolutionary approach that was generally widely shared among that first sociological generation. It was a perspective that invoked Darwinian biology to make an anology between the organism and society. If society could be viewed for purposes of analysis as an organism, then it would follow logically that it could, like an organism, have a natural state of health and have a "normal" condition. Any deviation from this was *pathological*, an abnormal state of the organism. Thus, social pathology signified an unhealthy state of the social organism, a sickness of society by virtue of some departure from what was normal and natural to society.

As evidence of social pathology, sociologists examined the lives of the immigrant poor in rapidly growing cities, the manner in which urbanization, immigration, and social mobility detached people from traditional social groups, such as family and village. They looked at slums and poverty, crime and delinquency, desertion, divorce and the broken family, and ethnic conflict. It was these phenomena in America's rapidly developing urban society that they labeled "social pathology."

In one of his most brilliant essays, the late C. Wright Mills examined the social origins and values of the social pathologists.[1] He noted that they usually were not themselves urban in origin but instead had grown up in rural communities, as indeed had probably most adult Americans at that time. More than that, they were middle-class and Protestant, yet their focus of attention was on lower class, urban people of European immigrant origin, many of whom were not Protestant. From such a particular value perspective, they interpreted this new and disturbing phenomenon of urban growth and transition as *pathological*. Their obvious value preference for an older, rural

[1] C. Wright Mills, "The Professional Ideology of Social Pathologists," *American Journal of Sociology*, 49 (September, 1943), 165–180.

way of life, characterized by social unity, a cohesive value system, and effective social control by family and small community, was expressed as a seemingly scientific analysis.

But the concept of social pathology gave way in time to a concept of *social disorganization.* The collapse in American sociology—indeed, in all American social science—of social evolution as the accepted scientific outlook necessarily brought into question the intellectual status of the concept of pathology. Clearly, another term was needed.

Social Disorganization The change from pathology to disorganization did not represent any substantial change in the social problems that were analyzed. What before had been looked upon as evidence of social pathology was now taken to be indexes of social disorganization. Thus, divorce and desertion served as indexes of the disorganization of the family. By implication, then, a presumed (rather than proved) older stable pattern of family life was taken as the *organization* of the family, departure from which meant a *disorganizing* process in the normal pattern of family life. In other problems the same assumption held: what had prevailed before but was undergoing change was labeled organization, and the departure from it was disorganization. A sociological concept that overtly pretended to scientific analysis concealed a covert value judgment about social life.

There were other difficulties with the concept of social disorganization. For one thing the assumption of a previous state of organization—much like the pathologist's assumption about a normal state of the social organism—then implied that the indexes of disorganization had only been observable in society when social disorganization occurred. And this process, it must be remembered, was linked to the rapid industrializing and urbanizing of America, thus it was a historically recent event. But prostitution and crime, for example, were hardly new phenomena; rather, there was good historical evidence of their having existed for as long as we have any adequate records. No sociologist was so naïve as to argue that recent social disorganization had *created* such social phenomena as crime, prostitution, and divorce, but he was prone to argue that it had produced *a sharp increase.* What had before been perceived as an occasional and individual problem now was perceived as frequent and common and thus a concern of the community.

Such an approach made it necessary to assume that it was possible to measure any increase in the rates of the various indexes of disorganization. But there was in fact great difficulty in obtaining any accurate data on what rates prevailed, and there was almost a complete absence of any historical measures of disorganization against which contemporary rates could be measured. Thus, for a long time it was assumed that rates of mental illness had increased sharply in America in this century. But the absence of any measures of mental illness in the nineteenth and even early twentieth century made this impossible to prove. It also made it impossible to disprove, a convenience for those who believed it and wished to assert it and who did so from a value position about the nature of American society and the changes it was undergoing. Social disorganization, then, did not escape the difficult value problem that had also beset social pathology. What the values of an earlier generation of sociologists did not approve, they labeled pathology; the next generation labeled them disorganization.

Yet this is not to say that there was no conceptual or theoretical gain in changing from pathology to disorganization. For one thing a concern for social disorganization brought into sharp concern the process of social change, even though it too frequently viewed change as only disorganizing in its consequences. Furthermore, some sociologists were less concerned with social reform than they were with social change, and the concept of social disorganization provided them with a theoretical perspective. These sociologists tended to talk in terms of a process of social organization to social disorganization to social reorganization. Nonetheless, social disorganization remained the dominant perspective for sociologists until the late 1930s, when two young sociologists at the University of Michigan, Richard Fuller and Richard Myers, wrote several papers advancing the concept of *social problems*.[2]

Social Problems   The conception of social problems offered by Fuller and Myers relieved the sociologist of making judgments—which turned out to be value-judgments—about whether there was disorganization or not. Instead it defined as social problems those conditions or situations which members of the society regarded as in some way a threat to their values. Most simply put: social problems are what people think they are.

To be a social problem, then, two things must be present. There must first be an *objective condition*—crime, poverty, racial tensions, and so forth—the presence and magnitude of which can be observed and measured by impartial social observers. It is not a figment of someone's imagination, but can be verified. Then, secondly, there must be a *subjective definition* by some members of the society that the objective condition is a "problem." Here is where values come into play, for when values are perceived as threatened by the existence of the objective condition, then that objective condition becomes a social problem.

Poverty and race relations provide excellent examples of this approach to social problems. Poverty can and does exist in many societies without being

[2] Richard C. Fuller and Richard R. Myers, "Some Aspects of a Theory of Social Problems," *American Sociological Review,* 6 (February, 1941), 24–32; and "The Natural History of a Social Problem," *American Sociological Review,* 6 (June, 1941), 320–329.

defined as a social problem, for people accept the objective condition of poverty as inevitable, even perhaps necessary; they are philosophically resigned to it as a normal condition of man. Discrimination in race, also, is not a problem for those who hold prejudicial attitudes on race, and indeed they may not even describe the objective condition of differential treatment as "discrimination." It requires the value of equality to define a problem of discrimination and to interpret the objective conditions of such differential treatment as a threat to such a value.

Two questions naturally come to mind at this point. Can there be objective conditions that are indeed threatening to the community or the society but are not social problems? Can there be social problems perceived on an illusory basis?

No matter how threatening an objective condition may be, it does not constitute a social problem unless and until at least someone so defines it. It is not defined as a social problem unless some people in the society become aware that such an objective condition poses a threat to their values. It will not be a matter of public discussion or be acted upon as a matter of social policy until there is perceived a relation between objective situation and social values.

It is also possible for people to perceive the existence of objective conditions that other people may very well believe to be entirely illusionary. Nonetheless, if they "perceive" some phenomenon to exist and define it as a threat to their values and thus act accordingly, *for them* a social problem exists. The sociologist Howard S. Becker has pointed out that the citizens of colonial Salem believed that witches existed, and that their own community had many of them.[3] The witch trials followed from a definition of such a condition existing and as being a social problem.

It is evident, then, that almost any condition can constitute a social problem for some people in the society, and also that there can be strong disagreement as to whether or not a given condition constitutes a social problem. The mere existence of a set of demonstrable facts does not make a social problem; instead, the facts must be interpreted in such a way as to be definable as a problem. Automobiles have polluted the air with their discharge and killed and maimed large numbers of people each year. Yet Americans accepted these as inevitable by-products of the utility and value of the automobile. Only when the concern for air pollution from many sources reached the consciousness of a larger public, and when control of air pollution became more technically feasible and less expensive, did the automobile's contribution to air pollution become one aspect of a larger social problem. Similarly, only with the invention of seat belts and other safety devices, and a number of law

---

[3] Howard S. Becker, *Social Problems: A Modern Approach* (New York: Wiley, 1966), p. 5.

suits involving injured people and the automobile manufactures, did auto safety emerge as a social problem that involved more than training in safe driving. Now the issue of whether the manufacturers sacrificed safety for speed or for salability features became a public argument and a concern for Senate hearings. The government was urged to require the manufacturers to build adequate safety features into automobiles. Only then did a long existing objective condition become a social problem.

Social problems, then, require a perception of an objective condition as in some way threatening before it actually becomes a social problem; but it also requires the belief that something can be done about the condition. If the situation is technologically or socially impossible to change, or at least perceived as such, then it will be endured. Automobile accidents were not a social problem as long as people believed that accidents were merely a consequence of human error and judgment. Instead the annually increased rate of deaths from accidents became a lamentable but accepted feature of the use of the automobile in the United States.

There are, of course, significant cultural differences in the readiness to accept objective conditions as inevitable or not. Some cultures manifest a greater readiness to bow to the inevitable, to be philosophically resigned in the face of the vicissitudes of nature and society. Western cultures, however, have generally been more activist in their orientation to human society. The outlook that characterized the Protestant ethic, the emergence of science, and the development of numerous technical inventions, is one of an activist mastery of the environment. Such an outlook is more likely to demand the alteration of objective conditions and thus to define them as social problems. In American life, this leads to the frequent mobilization of active voluntary groups to campaign for social change, and to the equally frequent position taken by Americans that "there ought to be a law."

The definition of a problem that captures the attention and concern of a wider public brings it to the center of political action within the society. But the prevailing ideology, or the strong social interests that define such a problem, may differ significantly from the position taken by professionals or social scientists. Although these people may conceive of themselves as more expert, their conception of the objective conditions that are a problem may be without any significant response from larger publics. Thus, some experts for decades defined population growth as a problem, but found little serious response in the citizenry and outright disagreement from religious groups that opposed any human effort to control the birth rate.

The Types of Social Problems   Although there are a vast number of social problems in modern American society, sociologists have been concerned with a recurring set of them. Crime and delinquency, poverty and dependency, race and ethnic tensions have always been to the forefront. So have the problems of the family in an urban society. Some problems, in turn, such as those stemming from immigration, have simply dropped out of sight as immigration ceases to be a significant dimension of American life.

A rough if not fully precise distinction can be made between those problems that are defined as arising from the difficulties of the individual adjusting to and meeting the demands of a changing society, and, in turn, those as arising from the mode of social organization and its apparent inadequacy to deal with the new and changing situations of modern society. Some problems, then, are seen more in terms of the relation of the individual to society and others in terms of the very way in which community or society is organized.

Some of the most familiar of social problems are defined in terms of individual adjustment. The problems of the *life cycle,* such as the problems of adolescents and old age, have to do with the relation of the individual to society.[4] There is tension between the demands and expectations of the society and the ability of people at given stages of the life cycle to act consistently with them. If adolescence, in turn, is a problem, it is because the adult generation finds a puzzling discrepancy between what it expects and wants and what it observes in the behavior of those called adolescents. Similarly, as people live longer, there emerge problems having to do with adequate economic support for aged people as well as the more difficult issue of any kind of meaningful role for them.

But problems of the life cycle are not the only problems having to do with the adjustment of the individual to society. A major interest of sociologists is in problems of *deviance* or *deviant behavior.* Here the concern is with people defined as deviating from established modes of action and thus from the social rules of society. Delinquency is a problem in deviancy, as in criminal behavior; drug addiction, particularly among young people, is another example of a problem of deviancy today. When homosexuality is defined as a social problem, it also falls into the category of deviancy. Mental illness, too, is such a problem.

But not all problems are best viewed as problems of individual adjustment to society, even though that aspect is undoubtedly present in many if not most social problems. Some problems have to do with the relations between groups, such as between whites and Negroes or between labor and management, and some with the organization of the community, such as housing, slums, and urban renewal. These are basically problems of *social organization,* in that the prevailing pattern of social organization is itself the problem. Thus, the established mode of Negro-white relations, replete with prejudice and discrimination, is defined as the problem, for it is this established pattern of

---

[4] For a discussion of *life cycle* problems, see Becker, *Social Problems,* pp. 28–29.

race relations that threatens the value of human equality and equality of opportunity and even the value of fair and decent respect for the rights and integrity of all persons.

To be sure, it requires a particular definition, and a very sociological definition at that, to see such problems as primarily though never exclusively problems of social organization rather than social adjustment. Obviously, many people would disagree. Some would do so because their individualistic outlook leads them to see all problems primarily in social adjustment terms.

A man who believes that Negroes suffer from inadequacies of their own making and not from social discrimination is likely to interpret the race issue as a problem requiring Negroes to "pull themselves up" as other groups have done. Similarly, a person who sees poverty as a consequence of individual laziness or moral failure is also likely to see this problem as one of inducing poor people to act like middle-class people do in order to enjoy the same chances for a comfortable life and adequate employment. Nonetheless, sociologists have, for a long time, separated out those several social problems that they believe to be largely problems of social organization rather than problems of social adjustment and deviancy.

DEVIANT BEHAVIOR

The study of deviant behavior by sociologists—and by psychologists and psychiatrists and others—has deep roots in the persistent concerns about problems of conformity and social control. In an effort to understand deviant behavior, the major effort of past social research for a half century, at least, has concentrated upon the *deviant person*. Criminals, juvenile delinquents, prostitutes and the like have been studied in detail, with an emphasis both upon their psychological characteristics and upon their environmental attributes. Criminals, for example, have been viewed as having a weak ego structure, a poorly developed moral sense, meaning, in short, a psychic inability to meet the demands and expectations of society. In turn, this distinctive psychological structure of the deviant was seen as the outcome of some types of environmental exposure: a broken home; poverty; association with other deviants; and so on.

This focus on the *individual* deviant sought to find the cause of deviancy in some attribute or characteristic of the person. Much of this research was an effort to counter an even older conception of deviant behavior as *inherent— born* criminals, for example—and thus as genetically caused. The shift to a *social* perspective instead of a *biological* one retained a focus on the individual, but now he was viewed as becoming a deviant because of psychological attributes emerging from deviant-producing environmental circumstances. Thus, deviant behavior was *learned* rather than innate. Deviancy was still a matter of deviant *persons,* but deviant persons were now viewed as somehow being socially rather than biologically produced. Put most simply, this approach concentrated on the deviant and asked: Who is he? How did he get to be a deviant? But a vast amount of research in the several areas of deviancy failed to provide any clear explanation. The various studies only partly supported one another, and many provided contradictory findings. The unsatisfactory guide to the handling of youth offenders that this delinquency research provided provoked Barbara Wooten, a British magistrate and teacher of social work, to undertake a careful, systematic critique of such research, reported in her book *Social Science and Social Pathology.*[5] What Miss Wooten did was select twelve factors most commonly reported in both the popular and professional literature as being causes of delinquency and then examine what twenty-one major empirical studies in three countries over a period of four decades had discovered.[6] Her results produced a bewildering array of findings, frequently noncomparable, and usually subject to over-generalization. All of this led Miss Wooten to say: "All in all, therefore, this collection of studies, although chosen for its comparative methodological merit, produces only the most meagre, and dubiously supported generalizations."[7] By the time *Social Science and Social Pathology* was published, it constituted but one strong voice among others in declaring that the study of the individual offender as a bundle of traits or deviant-producing factors had about exhausted its value. A new perspective was beginning to emerge.

A New Perspective on Deviancy   What was most common to the new effort to define deviancy was an insistence that a sociological analysis had to focus upon deviant *behavior,* rather than some conceptions of deviant personalities. One of the leading students of delinquency, Albert Cohen, insists that "much —probably most—deviant behavior is produced by clinically normal people."[8] His insistence on this perspective is evident in the following:

> In order to build a sociology of deviant behavior, we must always keep as our point of reference deviant behavior, not kinds of people. A major task before us

[5] Barbara Wooten, *Social Science and Social Pathology* (New York: Macmillan, 1959).

[6] For a brief summary and analysis of these twenty-one studies and the twelve hypothetical causative factors, see Louise G. Howton, "Evaluating Juvenile Delinquency Research," in Bernard Rosenberg, Israel Gerver, and F. William Howton, *Mass Society in Crisis* (New York: Macmillan, 1964), pp. 152–156.

[7] Wooten, p. 134.

[8] Albert K. Cohen, "The Study of Social Disorganization and Deviant Behavior," in Robert K. Merton, Leonard Broom, and Leonard S. Cottrell, Jr., *Sociology Today* (New York: Basic Books, 1959), p. 463.

is to get rid of the notion, so pervasive in sociological thinking, that the deviant, the abnormal, the pathological, and, in general, the deplorable always come wrapped in a single package.[9]

Well before any new perspective had emerged, an early and influential essay by Robert Merton maintained that the source of deviancy was in the social structure.[10] Social structures generated deviancy when there was, according to Merton, a disjunction between culturally prescribed goals and socially sanctioned means (modes of behavior) for achieving those goals. The culturally prescribed goal of "success," for example, is to be achieved by hard work, educational achievement; but such a means is not equally accessible to all, and it does not work well for those who, despite hard work and educational achievement, may be held back by racial discrimination.

The deviancy generated by such a disjunction between goals and means, says Merton, can take one of four possible forms: ritualism, retreatism, innovation, and rebellion. *Ritualism* is a giving up on the goals while still going through the motions of the means, conforming to the prescribed patterns of behavior even though no longer pursuing the goal. The lower middle-class citizen who no longer aspires for high office and is content with his small gains and limited mobility, who "plays it safe" and asks nothing, is Merton's model of ritualism.

The opposite mode is that of *innovation*, where the goal is kept in view, but new and very likely illegitimate means are utilized to attain success. This, Merton feels, is more likely to be characteristic of the lower class. Here are all the means of illegal activities such as rackets that produce the desired and widely admired ends of wealth and power. The lower-class boy who wants to "make it big" but lacks the institutionalized means for a rewarding career in business or the professions may find the rackets a route to wealth and power and even some fame. But innovation in this sense is no monopoly of the lower class. The sharp business practices that cheat customers and clients, as well as many other forms of "white-collar crime" among businessmen and professionals, are evidence of this.

But the "true aliens," says Merton, are those who are *in* the society but not *of* it by virtue of having given up on both goals and means: *retreatism*. When some individuals have strongly internalized both goals and means, but are effectively blocked from the means, their strong internalization prevents them from resorting to illegal means. They resolve their intense personal dilemma by withdrawing from the process altogether: they escape.

[9] Cohen, p. 463.
[10] Robert K. Merton, "Social Structure and Anomie," *American Sociological Review*, 3 (October, 1938), 677–682. Reprinted in Robert K. Merton, *Social Theory and Social Structure*, revised edition (New York: Free Press, 1957), pp. 131–160.

Lastly, some men who cannot succeed within the prescribed system withdraw their allegiance to the system, to both the goals and means, and instead project a new conception of society. *Rebellion* takes the form of renouncing the previous goals and the social structure which legitimized it and then of seeking to create a social structure in which a new set of cultural goals and institutionalized means are possible.

Perhaps the major value of Merton's essay was in the sociological discussion it created around the relation of deviancy and social structure, the idea that deviancy was rooted in the structure of society, not in the attributes of persons. Yet even this formulation was so organized as to provide explanations of the *motivations* of people to deviate from the prescribed patterns of behavior. The formulation accepted the major cultural definition of these people as deviants and simply incorporated that into a sociological analysis. It remained for a new, younger generation of sociologists to take off from this observation to redefine deviant behavior.

The Outsiders   Perhaps the most provocative work has been that of Howard S. Becker, whose book-length essay, *Outsiders: Studies in the Sociology of Deviance*, spelled out a new perspective for the students of deviant behavior.[11] Becker refuses to accept society's definition that people are deviant, but recognizes that in fact society does *label* people as deviants. And the majority do so when the others violate the rules that the majority have made and insist upon. Becker says:

> . . . *social groups create deviance by making the rules whose infraction constitutes deviance,* and by applying those rules to particular people and labeling them as outsiders. From this point of view, deviance is *not* a quality of the act the person commits, but rather the consequence of the application by others of rules and sanctions to an 'offender.'[12]

What this new approach does is shift the analysis from the presumed deviant to the interaction between the rule-applier and the rule-breaker. People are labeled deviants by others and thus become "outsiders," even though they may have violated a rule but once, while others have done so several times with impunity. Furthermore, the same behavior that violates a rule—say, gambling—may not be in violation where such a rule does not exist.

The Deviant Career   A permanent involvement in a deviant pattern does not come quickly, once the deviant act has been committed. There can be much experiment and withdrawal before there is that progressive involvement

---

[11] Howard S. Becker, *Outsiders: Studies in the Sociology of Deviance* (New York: Free Press, 1963).
[12] Becker, p. 9.

that defines a "deviant career," as Becker has called it.[13] The first nonconforming act may be accidental and unintended, undertaken as a lark, but without any clear intention to deviate. It may be a response to taking a "dare," or while "out on the town" and feeling less responsible and conventional than usual. Put this way, it is evident that deviant behavior is not peculiar merely to some people but in fact is experienced by all people. Most people, probably, do in fact commit one or more deviant acts in their lifetime, particularly when young. But most people do not follow a deviant career; instead, they become progressively "committed" to conventional rules and behavioral patterns of their own groups in society. Some others, however, become progressively drawn into some kind of deviant behavior.

To be pulled into a deviant pattern of behavior is to be drawn into closer association with others who deviate in the same manner, say, in taking drugs, and to reduce one's significant interaction with others who clearly disapprove of such behavior. Such association with fellow deviants provides support for the deviant behavior, as well as rationalizations and justifications for the rule-breaking behavior and protection from the enforcers of the rules. It further provides a milieu in which the deviant behavior can occur without detection or criticism, and indeed one in which it may be approved.

In such a thing as taking drugs, which Becker studied among jazz musicians, there may be a progressive involvement by the individual over a period of time, strongly encouraged by his association with other jazz musicians, who define themselves as different from "squares" in every way. But for many others, a major factor in becoming a career deviant may be simply the brutal fact of being caught in a deviant act and then labeled a deviant. This one act may lead to a public definition of the person as a delinquent, a criminal, a dope addict, or as insane—and the label may stick to him, regardless of any other act on his part. Thus, defined by others as a deviant, he may find it hardly possible to be anything else but a deviant, and perhaps his only viable role is to move toward a deviant career and closer association with other deviants.

Deviant Subcultures   The conception of deviant behavior which Becker and others have advanced recently is particularly concerned with the genesis of deviancy for the individual in a society in which the line between deviancy from and conformity to social rules is not a sharp one. The association with other deviants is usually seen as coming after that. But other analyses have been concerned with the genesis of deviant behavior in social groups whose marginal or disadvantaged status in society leads them to generate a cultural perspective that is deviant. Such a group rejects at least some of the rules and

[13] Becker, pp. 24–39.

norms of the larger society and develops norms of its own. It creates a *subculture* that is deviant and that provides a strong group basis for deviant behavior.

A concern about group-based deviancy goes back to the 1920s and 1930s, when the pioneering generation of sociologists at the University of Chicago were strongly impressed by the fact that certain social areas were characterized by high rates of delinquent acts committed by youths in association with others, rather than alone. From such research in Chicago came Edwin Thrasher's *The Gang*, a study of a large number of gangs that emerged from the changing immigrant, lower-class neighborhoods of Chicago.[14] Thrasher pointed out that boys learned to be delinquent by their participation in the gangs that were the normal part of life in their urban neighborhoods. They were not deviating from the conventional behavior of others; rather, they were conforming by being gang members and acting as other gang members did. Delinquency was the "natural history" of a juvenile under such circumstances, and involved no psychological problems of frustration or deprivation that might provide individual motivations to commit deviant acts.

The key idea in this approach to the study of delinquency is that individuals *learn* to be deviant through their association with others who are already delinquent. They are *socialized* to deviant norms in social circumstances in which these norms are the dominant ones, as in the gangs that inhabit the lower-class areas of large cities. This conception of how delinquency occurs then clearly takes for granted that delinquency *areas* and delinquent *gangs* already exist, and then focuses on the fact that those exposed to these groups in these areas quite naturally learn to be delinquent, also. The late distinguished criminologist, Edwin Sutherland, developed the theory of *differential association* as an explanation of delinquency and criminal behavior, asserting that youths become delinquent

> to the extent that they participate in settings where delinquent ideas or techniques are viewed favorably, and that the earlier, the more frequently, the more intensely, and the longer the durations of the associations in such settings, the greater the probability of their becoming delinquent.[15]

The gangs that Thrasher and others studied in the 1920s and 1930s were the informal, loosely-knit groups of youths that emerged in the delinquency-oriented milieu of urban, lower-class neighborhoods, many also distinctive ethnic areas. But in the 1950s, a number of sociologists began to give closer attention to gangs that seemed to be more formally organized than were those studied in prior decades. The key concept that emerged was that of

[14] Edwin Thrasher, *The Gang* (Chicago: University of Chicago Press, 1936).
[15] Quoted in Becker, *Social Problems*, p. 229.

delinquent subculture, which points to the existence of norms and values that place positive value upon delinquent behavior and that confer status on gang members for delinquent acts. Such a subculture also defines the attitudes to and behavior toward those outside the group. Albert Cohen's *Delinquent Boys: The Culture of the Gang* made an impressive case for viewing delinquency in terms of a delinquent subculture that functions in direct opposition to that of the conventional culture.[16] It is, thus, negative and malicious. The source of the subculture lies in the experiences of boys low in the social status, who suffer when judged by "middle-class measuring rods" (as Cohen called them). Their family and class origins leave them disadvantaged in the middle-class world of education, and they find themselves facing low social status in adult life. They have then the motivation to create a more rewarding status by developing social groups of boys like themselves in which their own skills and abilities are prized, and which then give them a basis of self-esteem and for being esteemed by others. This means fighting, aggressive behavior, and acts directed against the larger society and its social institutions, particularly the school.

If the groups that Cohen studied were gangs, they were not, nevertheless, highly organized and disciplined units organized to pursue single activities. But Richard Cloward and Lloyd Ohlin have described just such a kind of social group of delinquent youths in large urban areas.[17] Their study details three different types of delinquent subcultures: one organized to engage in violent activity with rival gangs; a second to engage in theft; and a third around such escapist activity as the taking of drugs. Cloward and Ohlin explain the differences among the three types of subcultures in terms of some distinctive conditions unique to each. The subculture of theft, for example, occurs when there are ties to the adult world that permit the youthful thieves to move into the adult world of organized crime and the rackets. When, in turn, there are few such ties to the adult world, the frustration that a lack of legitimate opportunity breeds then manifests itself in the conflict subculture with its constant fighting with other gangs. The escapist subculture, in turn, is made up of those who are "failures" in the other two.

It is not obvious just how extensive are such quite distinctive subcultures in any large urban area. Some have argued that perhaps only in very large cities like New York and Chicago can such specific differentiation of youthful gangs be evident. One investigation found that the delinquent groups tended not to be so specialized but to shift their activities from one form of delinquency to another.[18] The sociologist Lewis Yablonsky has argued that the formally

---

[16] Albert Cohen, *Delinquent Boys: The Culture of the Gang* (New York: Free Press, 1954).

[17] Richard Cloward and Lloyd E. Ohlin, *Delinquency and Opportunity: A Theory of Delinquent Gangs* (New York: Free Press, 1960).

[18] James F. Short, Jr. and Fred L. Strodtbeck, *Group Process and Gang Delinquency* (Chicago: University of Chicago Press, 1965).

organized group with a definite membership is less common, and that a shifting temporary membership and an irregular involvement in activities is more characteristic of what he calls "near-groups."[19]

In delineating the concept of delinquent subcultures, the essence of the argument is clear: the lack of opportunity for achieving conventional social goals creates problems of status in society for which delinquent subcultures are a solution. An earlier argument had stressed the problems of the individual in feeling deprived and rejected by others. Here the stress is on the collective sharing of problems and the development of collective, rather than individual solutions in the forms of organized group activities oriented around norms and values peculiar to the disadvantaged group and providing rewards of esteem and status from within their own ranks.

The Significance of Subcultures Many forms of deviant behavior besides delinquency lend themselves to the emergence of deviant subcultures when those who share the same deviant interests and motivations have opportunity to come together. Youthful delinquents provide one of the more obvious examples of such subcultures, but there are others: homosexuals, drug addicts, and adult criminals are three such cases. Drug addicts and adult criminals create subcultures that provide the basis for their collective action when individual action is insufficient. Drug addicts, for example, need a systematic organization for obtaining and distributing drugs. Such a subculture also provides a set of beliefs and attitudes that justify the deviant behavior, define prodeviant values as well as define both deviant status, conventional status, and the interaction between them. The deviant, in short, takes a stance toward the conventional world, and this is the very essence of a deviant culture.

Deviant subcultures, also, are forms of protection for the individual deviant. They define a world of friends and foes and they define the values that bind those who share them to aid one another against the pressures and threats of the conventional society. Codes of secrecy are often part of it. Homosexuals, for example, find in a homosexual community protection from a hostile society as well as psychic support for sexual interests condemned by most others. They also find opportunity for a homosexual life not otherwise possible.

Situational Delinquency When delinquency is viewed in subcultural terms it is regarded as deeply rooted in the life conditions of its participants; yet there has long been much evidence that delinquency declines sharply among these

[19] Lewis Yablonsky, "The Delinquent Gang as a Near-Group," *Social Problems*, 7 (Fall, 1959), 108–117. See also his *The Violent Gang* (New York: Macmillan, 1962). For a critical analysis of this conception of delinquency, see Harold Pfautz, "Near-Group Theory and Collective Behavior: A Critical Formulation," *Social Problems*, 9 (Fall, 1961), 167–174.

same youths as they enter adulthood. Not all of them, not even most of them, become adult criminals. This observation has suggested to sociologist David Matza that delinquency is not, for many at least, so deeply rooted.[20] It may be that delinquency occurs where there is less effective control by family and other primary groups, where socialization has failed to create strong inner controls that restrain deviant impulses, where there is poor control and surveillance by the community, and where there are those who have less to lose when caught in a delinquent act. This suggests that delinquency frequently is a taking advantage of opportunities presented in the immediate situation, rather than something as involved as creating alternative opportunities for a new status in life.

Sociologists, then, have found several different ways of looking at delinquency. The concept of the delinquent subculture has been a theoretically sophisticated analysis that has stressed how the very stratified and unequal organization of society creates cultural responses on the part of the most disadvantaged, which then confront the conventional culture with opposing values and norms and create alternate opportunities for finding a rewarding social status and sources of personal esteem. But how extensive this pattern is remains somewhat uncertain. There is apparently still much delinquency that is not explained adequately in these terms. One must remember that delinquency is a term that merely specifies youthful acts of law violation. It is reasonable to assume that there can be diverse sources and motivations for the wide variety of behaviors that qualify as delinquent. The subculture thesis, for example, particularly focuses on lower-class delinquency. Middle-class delinquency is thus left unexplained. It may be more *situational* than cultural, more sporadic and occasional than organized, more concerned with "kicks" than with solving the problem of status. And that rejection and frustration may function as a source for more individual and isolated acts of deviancy constitutes a still relevant psychological issue.

Mental Illness and Delinquent Behavior   Some forms of deviant behavior do not easily provide a basis for a deviant group or a deviant subculture. Mental illness is one such form of deviancy. Becoming mentally ill is something that happens to the individual in such a way as to isolate him from his usual groups, but not to provide him with deviant groups to which he might flee for support or protection.

Mental illness is one of the more widely recognized social problems in American society and also one of the more costly. The public provision of mental hospitals and clinics usually ranks among the larger commitments of

[20] David Matza, *Delinquency and Drift* (New York: Wiley, 1964).

the budget of a state. The federal government, also, has considerably increased its appropriations for mental health in recent decades, particularly in supporting extensive research efforts as well as clinical facilities.

The harsh and fearful treatment of the mentally ill has been one of those now well-told histories, and the long struggle for humane treatment of such people has reached a fairly wide level of acceptance in modern society. At the core of such a struggle has been the effort to win public acceptance of *mental illness* as just that, an illness, to be treated as any illness, not punitively but with therapy. An additional aspect of this struggle has been convincing the public that mental illness is not genetically based and thus no reflection upon a family or upon the individual. And much progress has been made.

One disturbing note in this has been the sociological finding that mental hospitals have not, in the past, been organized primarily for purposes of *therapy* but rather for *custody* of mentally disturbed people who are socially disruptive in their normal surroundings. Thus, hospitals have been organized to take the mental patient out of and away from society, to insure his being kept in, (emphasizing maximum security like a prison), and to organize and control patients so that there is a smooth and undisrupted flow of routine procedure.

Erving Goffman characterizes mental hospitals as one among the "total" social institutions of modern society that are organized to move whole blocks of people through routines of activity according to schedules, to keep a close surveillance upon them, and to enforce a close association with others, all so unlike ordinary life.[21]

During the 1950s the work of a number of sociologists explored the structure of mental hospitals and how their internal social organization affected the patients, particularly their chances of recovery.[22] Many features of the ordinary routines of the mental hospital, it seemed, detracted from his recovery, particularly the rather insensitive and impersonal "handling" of patients by nonprofessional attendants, by which dignity and respect were effectively denied. Disclosures such as these suggested the need for quite radical alteration of hospitals if they were to be genuinely therapeutic. It also suggested alternatives to mental hospitals, such as an out-patient program, the "half-way house" for those patients who were not quite ready to cope with society, and community mental health clinics for early detection and treatment of people with problems.

[21] See Erving Goffman, *Asylums: Essays on the Social Situations of Mental Patients and Other Inmates* (New York: Doubleday, 1961).

[22] See, for example, Alfred Stanton and Morris Schwartz, *The Mental Hospital* (New York: Basic Books, 1954); William A. Caudill, *The Psychiatric Hospital as a Small Society* (Cambridge, Mass.: Harvard University Press, 1958).

The Myth of Mental Illness   It is a paradox of our time that just as generations of effort to convince the public to think of the mentally distraught as *ill* in the same fashion that the physically suffering are ill was bearing fruit, there came from within the ranks of psychiatry a fundamental attack upon this very conception of mental illness. The psychiatrist Thomas Szasz has asserted persuasively that there is no such thing as mental illness, it is a myth.[23] What are regarded as mental ills, he said, are *problems of living.*

Szasz' principal point is that *mental illness* is the label placed upon certain deviant behavior, which is then made into the *cause.* Such behavior is taken as evidence of mental illness, and then this mental illness is cited as the cause of this behavior. This is logically fallacious but is only one of the fallacies inherent in the concept of mental health. Szasz challenged the use of the concept of illness derived from medicine, where a malfunctioning of the organism evidences itself in various symptoms that are then regarded as amenable to medical treatment. In mental problems, he says, what happens is that behavior, much of which may be the person's verbal communication about his problems, is covertly measured by the psychiatrist's reference to norms of what one expects from "normal" persons. The norms are not medical but *psycho-social, ethical* and *legal,* as, for example, the judgment that a chronic hostility signifies mental illness because it is a deviation from the ethical norm of the desirability of love and kindness. Yet medical remedies are sought. The disorder is defined by one set of terms and its remedy sought in others.

Note that Szasz is not arguing that there are not emotionally troubled people. Instead, he insists that the problems of living in modern society prove to be troublesome and disturbing for many people. But they are not "ill" in some medically objective sense; instead, they have problems of living that may be much more disturbing to them than they usually are to other people.

It should not be difficult to recognize that what Szasz is saying about mental illness as a myth is close to Howard Becker's definition of deviancy. Mental illness is assumed, according to Szasz, when people deviate in certain disturbing ways in their interactions with others; then, being mentally ill is the label that others place upon them. And like other cases of deviancy, the people so labeled may come to accept the label and thus believe that they are mentally ill.

The problem of mental illness, then, is only partly a problem of those so defined. It is also a problem of definition; that is, a problem of how definitions of normality and reality are made in society and used as judgments of what

---

[23] Thomas Szasz, "The Myth of Mental Illness," *American Psychologist,* 15 (February, 1960), 112–118; also, *The Myth of Mental Illness* (New York: Harper & Row, 1961).

is conventional and what is deviant behavior. Whether or not there is a social problem, and what kind of social problem, depends upon the definition of the behavior commonly used.

PROBLEMS OF SOCIAL ORGANIZATION

Although there has been a predominant interest in problems of deviant behavior in recent years, the problems of social organization nonetheless persist as compelling issues that demand attention. Problems such as race relations, poverty, slums, and urban renewal are obvious instances of such problems. But urban schools are also a social problem, and indeed, education can be viewed as a locus for a whole set of problems: teacher strikes; school dropouts; inner-city schools; segregated schools; schools and delinquency; motivating deprived children for academic achievement; changing curricula to meet social changes; and the like.

But each of these, also, is not simply a problem of education. The problems of inner-city schools, segregated schools, school dropouts, and motivating deprived children, are also aspects of the problems of poverty and race. In the same fashion the problem of urban housing and replacing slums by an urban renewal program involves considerations of housing the poor as well as the problem of the hitherto segregated housing of poor Negroes. A number of social problems, then, prove to be significantly interrelated, and it often becomes difficult to treat any one of them in an isolated fashion. Certainly, the sociologist engaged in the study of social problems soon recognizes that this interrelatedness makes it hard for him to study a single problem as if it existed without reference to others.

Race and poverty constitute social problems of our time, if for no other reason than that major social attention is given them. There is a consensus of some degree that gives prominence to some problems and thus makes them major ones. Race and poverty obviously qualify. So do some of the problems of deviancy, such as delinquency and crime, mental illness, and drug addiction. Problems of housing and urban renewal and the redevelopment of the city are others. Mass transportation in metropolitan areas is another one, as is air pollution. Birth control and the use of birth control pills are others.

Major problems receive a great deal of attention by the mass media, particularly in television documentaries, in newspapers and mass-circulation magazines. Thus, as debatable issues, they are kept before the public; the essential facts become well-known; the various and often conflicting interpretations and explanations are also publicized; the ideas of social scientists and various "experts" are given large audiences. But, in addition, these are major problems because they are the concern of policy-makers who seek to develop programs to eliminate or at least seriously alleviate the problems. And because of this, governmental agencies and private foundations often make substantial sums of money available as research grants to social scientists and others to study these problems. These research resources are often significant in providing the familiarity, the knowledge, and the experience that create professional "experts" whom the public looks to for guidance on these troublesome matters.

The major problems of American society are clearly subject to change over time. In the first half of this century there was a concern with immigration and with the settlement of immigrants. There was also a greater concern about the future of the family as a social institution, and divorce was regarded as a major social problem. There is no less divorce today than forty years ago, but it is much less of a social problem, simply because divorce is no longer viewed as widely as an index of family disorganization in American life and thus no longer the threat to family stability it once was.

The social problems that are problems of social organization in American society are many, and along the way this book has pointed to a number of them. The chapters devoted to the analysis of minority groups and to poverty and the lower class could be viewed, in fact, as a discussion of major social problems that emerge from the stratification of American society.

But note some others that were pointed out, however briefly: (1) the problems of metropolitan unity and urban renewal in the chapter on the community; (2) the problems of divorce, the status of women, and parent-child relations in the chapter on the family; and (3) the problems of school dropouts and the multiversity in the chapter on education. The chapter on the economy and society pointed out the problem of automation and the displacement of labor, and the ever present economic conflict. The chapter on the polity noted the problems of political apathy and political extremism, and the chapter on science focused on the problem of the relation of science to government and of "the two cultures."

In what way are each of these a problem of social organization? If there is any single concept that might orient us to the relations between social problems and social organization, it is *social change*. Social organization is never a fixed and static phenomenon, however much it may seem at times to be that, but it is always an evolving process. Social structure must always be seen as changing.

Social Problems and Social Change   There are at least two major ways in which social change produces social problems. One of these is when new, emergent behavior disrupts an established structure and challenges those social values closely related to the older patterns of behavior. One such process is the emergence of new skills and occupations as a consequence of technological development, of which automation is but the most recent example, which then disrupt older work systems and threaten established occupations.

A second major way in which social change produces a social problem is when, as a consequence of social change, there are new definitions of the social organization. Many older role definitions, for example, no longer seem appropriate; the status of women and the relation of parent to child are examples here. Another is that of school dropouts. Here the behavior is not new, for youths of low social status have long left school at the earliest possible legal age. But now the educational demands of a changing job market make these youths less and less employable. What was once a source of labor for the less demanding jobs of the society now is a social problem. Also, the new major interest of government in science, and its willingness to provide massive funding for research, alters older conceptions of the relation of each to the other and of the place of science in democratic society.

This rather simple distinction between social change producing new and disruptive patterns, roles, and values, and social change making necessary new definitions and reassessments of older structures, is not a sharp one. Clearly, both may be involved in some social problems. The "multiversity" as a symbolic term for the new problematic status of the university testifies to both disruptive changes within the university, such as the neglect of undergraduate teaching, and to new and highly critical reassessments of the appropriate obligations of the university and its place in modern society.

The long standing problem of the minority group can be understood as generated from the gap between the value of equality and the practices that deny such equality to some groups within the society. But that simple and quite true definition of the problem fails to make it clear to us why there can be the crises of civil rights in the 1960s. Those events are not adequately defined as simply a periodic outbreak of the tensions that exist between the races. Over several decades there had been an evolving definition of civil rights culminating in the 1954 Supreme Court decision. This one event, as we saw in Chapter 11, altered Negro expectations. Parallel with this is the rise of a new Africa, with consequent impact upon the conception that Negroes have of their own identity.

Some social problems are an effort to confront changing structures with policies and programs intended to control and direct the change. Urban renewal, for example, is an effort to fight the decay and deterioration that is inherent in the way that property is subject to ecological definition and use in American cities. An effort to restore the city has disturbing impact upon those whose homes and neighborhoods may be cleared away to make room for urban renewal. Negroes in particular find that such displacement may reduce the amount of housing available to them.

The changing organization of modern society generates an unending supply of social problems. Tensions long latent may erupt to the surface when the former constraining factors are no longer effective. Once inviolate interests may be stepped on as new technological changes alter relationships. New patterns of behavior are viewed as deviations from acceptable behavior or as threats to prevailing values. Also, there is a significant viewpoint in modern life that is alone productive of social problems. If it follows that problems exist because people define them as problems, one must remember that modern men, and particularly Western men, are not likely to be philosophically resigned to fate. Instead, they are likely to believe that "something must be done" and indeed that something can be done. This activist view toward life then defines a situation as a *social problem* to be acted upon, rather than as a *condition* one must accept with philosophical resignation.

Modern society, then, is so complex in its structure, so intricate in its internal organization, that one could not expect other than an inconsistent and loosely fitting structure within which tensions and strains are productive of social problems. The fact of change adds immensely to the likelihood that problems will be plentiful in such a society. And the activist orientation produces a tendency to define value conflicts and internal tensions as problems to be acted upon, not situations to be accepted as fate.

This tells us two things. First, there will continue to be a great number of social problems in our society, though specific problems will change in importance and detail over time; some will be forgotten as others rise. Secondly, the involvement of the sociologist in social problems constitutes one of his important linkages to the society, one in which his capacity to be of service is magnified. Although not the only tie of academic sociology to society, social problems provide one channel by which society and its processes are observed and analyzed by sociologists. They are a major preoccupation of sociologists that continually sensitizes them to the issues of values and objectivity in sociological analysis.

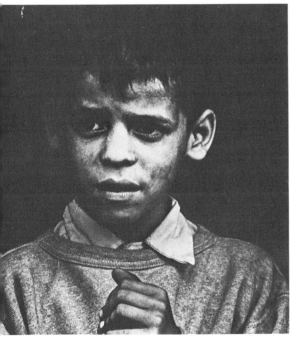

SOCIOLOGY
AND SOCIETY

Over the past quarter century or so the discipline of sociology has grown in richness of findings and sophistication of method. It has moved from America, where it flowered best, to much of the rest of the world. More than that it has become a household term in middle-class America, marking a degree of social acceptance that would have been unimagined by sociologists in the decades before World War II. Furthermore, research and the training of graduate students has now assumed central importance in the discipline, and a relative abundance of research resources has now become available. But with success, acceptance, and affluence come problems. One primary one is an expectation, even a demand, for answers to questions and for solutions to problems that no sociologist would presume to provide, given the present limited state of knowledge. His scientific modesty is then embarrassed by the heightened expectations of what knowledge he can provide; it is a temptation to anyone to let others confer on you a wisdom you know you do not possess. Fortunately, most sociologists have successfully resisted such lures.

Another set of problems emerges out of the new and valued status of sociology in modern society. Along with other social science disciplines, sociology has knowledge and research skills that are potentially applicable to the many problems of modern society, and this creates both opportunity and problem. Sociology has changed from a small, teaching discipline within colleges and universities to a large, research-oriented discipline located in many institutions besides universities. It is thus related to society in ways hitherto not experienced. The very usefulness of sociology, therefore, creates some new and difficult problems. The relation of sociology to the institutions and power structures of modern society poses new issues that affect the very values of sociologists.

At the same time sociology is a growing and expanding discipline, moving forward on several new frontiers, some of which are a return to old interests once abandoned and now rediscovered. The persistent desire of sociologists to develop a science of society maintains a constant pressure to develop a rigorous discipline and continues to be one significant line of development, particularly around methodology and theory. But new *substantive* interests also move the discipline in new and untried directions. It seems evident enough that the *application* of sociology to systematic efforts to resolve major social problems provides one distinct vitality to the field. So does the shedding of an American parochialism that now leads sociologists to study in developing countries and to turn more and more to cross-cultural and comparative analyses for the testing of generalizations. There is also a renewed interest in "the big picture," that is, the large society. A return to a macro-sociology, once the central concern of the discipline's founders, now engages the interests of an ever larger number of sociologists. There has also emerged in recent years a new, younger generation of fieldworkers, who carry on in new sociological problems and in new conceptual frameworks the tradition of the single, probing investigator.

A society that finds sociology useful will do two things: (1) it will request sociology's cooperation in providing skills and knowledge in solving problems and developing social programs, and (2) it will provide the resources by which sociology can in fact apply its knowledge and seek new knowledge. It will, in short, create a climate of opinion favorable to sociology, which will then become accepted by social elites and decision-makers. If this is not an exact description of what has happened to sociology in contemporary America, it is not badly off the mark. Sociology has come nearer to arriving at a status of being publicly accepted than at any time in the past, and promises to become even more so in decades ahead. It has proved to be moderately useful to institutional administrators and decision-makers, particularly in the complex problems that beset urban communities, large-scale organizations, and rapidly changing institutions, such as education. There is, then, a set of *applied* uses of sociology that has attracted various kinds of policy-makers. But there is a more general use of sociology in American society (and in European societies, too) that is quite independent of any specific application of sociological knowledge to particular issues. This is an *intellectual* use that informs and liberates and provides perspective, not merely for policy-makers, but for all who would be informed citizens and more self-conscious and critical persons.

The Applied Uses of Sociology An applied sociology is hardly new, for the pragmatic temper of American life could be expected to encourage efforts to make use of knowledge. What else is it for, if it is not useful? But many sociologists have, at the same time, insisted on the distinction between *applied* and *basic* that operates in the physical sciences, with basic research being fundamental. From such a perspective, applied research has less prestige and is usually discounted as being a potential contribution to new knowledge.

A new generation of American sociologists has returned with enthusiasm to the concerns of applied sociology, for there is now a renewed interest among sociologists in how sociology can function in the organizations and communities of American life. Two American sociologists long concerned with applied sociology put their position this way: "It is the historic mission of the social sciences to enable mankind to take possession of society."[1]

This resurgence of applied sociology in recent decades has produced among sociologists some reassessment of the significance and meaning of applied

[1] Alvin W. Gouldner and S. M. Miller, eds., *Applied Sociology: Opportunities and Problems* (New York: Free Press, 1965), p. vii.

research.[2] For one thing, the distinction between applied and basic research is evidently not a sharp one in sociology. Research intended to explore the problems and consequences of an integrated housing policy for public housing projects has obvious importance for application. But such research also contributes new knowledge to such substantive areas as race relations, the impact of housing arrangements on friendship and neighboring, the significance of neighboring proximity on interracial interaction, and the like. A study of the kind indicated above, and many others like it, have been carried out without necessarily being designated as applied research and without any agency intending to put such knowledge to use. Whether a study is a contribution to applied sociology, then, may be as much a matter of the intentions and concerns of the sociologist as whether it is formally sponsored as applied study.

The Levels of Analysis in Applied Sociology   The low regard in which applied research has often been held is a reflection of the rather low level of analysis often carried out in such research. But a low level of research, emphasizing fact gathering rather than analysis, is not an inherent or necessary quality of applied research. Nonetheless one basic characteristic of applied sociological research is always the careful discovery and identification of the relevant facts about a social problem. This is an important function in its own right, for so often there are myths and misconceptions about significant areas of human action that can only be dispelled by an accurate description of action in the context of a social situation. But if applied research does no more than gather facts, however accurately, the interpretation and use of these facts is then left to those who sponsored the research. Such interpretations can be shaped by the assumptions and goals of the sponsor, and their selective use reflects the sponsor's values more than anything else. Perhaps it is this factor that has given applied research a poor name.

Evaluating Performances   One of the newer dimensions of applied research has been that of *evaluation research*. Here there is a careful gathering of facts but done in such a way as to evaluate adequacy of performance, that is, to evaluate how effective action is in attaining goals. Many of the new programs intended to effect changes in poverty or in educational disadvantage have a built-in requirement for research to evaluate the program itself. This means that the

[2] Three recent books devoted primarily to this issue are the Gouldner and Miller work cited above; Paul Lazarsfeld, William Sewell, and Harold Wilensky, eds., *The Uses of Sociology* (New York: Basic Books, 1967); and Arthur B. Shostak, ed., *Sociology in Action: Case Studies in Social Problems and Directed Social Change* (Homewood, Ill.: The Dorsey Press, 1966). There is also a book of readings, Donald M. Valdes and Dwight G. Dean, *Sociology in Use: Selected Readings for the Introductory Course* (New York: Macmillan, 1965).

study is organized selectively to define both the subjects of the program—the poor or disadvantaged children in schools, for example—and the administrators of the program as subjects of the research.

Research of this kind moves to a higher level of analysis than just fact gathering. For one thing the sociologists doing the study must interpret the facts and make judgments, with the objectives of the program serving as the standard for making these judgments. Secondly, they must function in an entirely new kind of relationship with the administrators of the program, a delicate and sensitive relationship, since they must make evaluations of the success of the program, a matter of deep personal concern to administrators. Yet the researchers need the active cooperation of these same administrators in order to carry out their task effectively.

Reanalyzing Social Goals   Evaluation research seeks to evaluate the effectiveness of a program in terms of the goals of the program; that is, does a Headstart program in fact give to deprived children a start in school roughly equal to that of more advantaged children? The evaluation is one of the processes developed to accomplish this end, but the end itself, the goal of the program, is unchallenged. However, another level of analysis is that in which social goals or policies are themselves subject to scrutiny and critical analysis. When this occurs, applied research shifts from an *engineering* model to a *clinical* one, to use the terms of Alvin Gouldner:

> From an engineering standpoint the problems as formulated by the client are usually taken at face value; the engineer tends to assume that his client is willing to reveal the problems which actually beset him. The clinical sociologist, however, makes his own independent diagnosis of the client's problems. He assumes that the problems as formulated by the client may often have a defensive significance and may obscure, rather than reveal, the client's tensions. Not only does the clinician assume that the client may have some difficulty in formulating his own problems but he assumes, further, that such an inability may in some sense be motivated, and that the client is not entirely willing to have these problems explored or remedied. The clinician, therefore, does not take his client's formulations at their face value, any more than he does comments made by an ordinary interviewee; but he does use them as points of departure in locating the client's latent problems.[3]

When applied sociologists raise critical questions about the appropriateness or about the normative legitimacy of social goals, they are also questioning the assumptions on which social policy is based. These may be *empirical* assumptions, that is, assumptions about the social facts in the situation; but they are more likely to be normative assumptions, that is, assumptions about the norms of action that ought to prevail in acting upon social problems. Thus, Scott

---

[3] Alvin W. Gouldner, "Explorations in Applied Social Science," in Gouldner and Miller, *Applied Sociology*, pp. 5–22. Quotation from p. 19.

Greer's analysis of the metropolitan problem brought into question the assumptions that experts had made.[4] One of these major assumptions was empirical. Having revealed through survey research a wide range of public discontent, many experts incorrectly interpreted these as constituting a demand for social action. But no demand, according to Greer, was evident. Furthermore, having recorded public complaints, the experts used these as a basis for presuming a support of their own desired solution to the problems of metropolitan life, namely, metropolitan government. But no such support existed, as the failure of efforts to create metropolitan governments showed.

The range of applied social research, then, is considerable; it goes from basic fact gathering to the evaluation of institutional and programmatic performances to the clinical reassessment of social goals and questioning the assumptions of social policy. These various levels of analysis move applied research closer to the decisions about goals and policies and thus bring values and norms into active play in the work of the social scientist.

The Problems of Applied Research   Applied research inherits all the problems of social research, from that of objectivity and theoretical relevance to methodological issues of data gathering, sampling, and the like. But applied research also faces a set of problems that are particularly germane to its activity, though not always peculiar to it. These problems are largely ethical and political. When research is conducted about ideologically inoffensive matters, or about matters that have no political impact, then there is much less concern among the groups studied, or among other social scientists, about any ethical or political issues. But when the issues studied are close to the heart of controversial matters, when the groups studied are politically powerful, or even politically active, and when the results of research can be viewed as threatening or at least as politically consequential, then the researcher finds that the usual canons of scientific objectivity learned in graduate training do not suffice as a guide. Applied research is most susceptible to such problems, but much other social research is equally perplexed.[5]

What is the nature of these problems? A major one is the manner in which the social values and the political ideology of the researcher serve to define the kind of study to be done, choose the concepts, and shape the questions asked and thus the data to be elicited. Most frequently this is likely to be an implicit and even unconscious aspect of the thought processes of the researcher. In short, he is not necessarily aware of how his own values and ideological preferences influence his presumably scientific judgments. In some innocuous

[4] Scott Greer, "Where Is the Metropolitan Problem?" in Gouldner and Miller, pp. 237–247.
[5] See Gideon Sjoberg, ed., *Ethics, Politics, and Social Research* (Cambridge, Mass.: Schenkman Publishing Co., 1967) for a series of essays addressed to these and related problems.

research no one might ever care enough to raise the issue. But in research that matters to others, they do care. And their very criticism will point out how the ideology of the investigator influenced his conception of the problem being studied, the formulation of his research design, and even his interpretations of the data. It is uncomfortable to many social scientists to acknowledge the powerful role that values and ideology still play in social research, but most social scientists are now willing to recognize that they do; the earlier image of a value-free social science is no longer as widely held as it was a decade or more ago.[6]

When applied sociologists venture into controversial and problematic areas of research, other problems present themselves. Many times such research goes beyond the usual kind of objective and impersonal relationship of an interviewer and a subject. Rather, a complex set of intricate and sensitive relationships are often necessary in making studies within various types of social organizations, such as relationships with administrators and with various levels of authority and responsibility within an organization. Also, there are relationships with sponsors and funding agencies, as well as relationships with powerful social groups that have some stake in the outcome of the research and may intervene at any number of points in the development and conduct of the research. The sociologist Joan Moore, for example, has reported the way in which political considerations affected a large-scale study of Mexican-Americans by effecting a "modification of structure, techniques, and location of research in the course of nearly a year's communication with our subjects and their neighbors, and our fellow academics."[7]

The issue of sponsorship and autonomy then is another significant problem for applied sociologists. Social scientists subscribe to the value of academic freedom, but its practice in concrete research situations can be difficult. The presumed autonomy and independence of the social researcher can be threatened in various ways by those who feel threatened by publication of research results or by particular lines of research; for example, research into the lack of internal democracy in an efficient labor union. When research is organized and conducted by research centers and institutes that depend upon the good will of specialized publics, powerful social organizations, and perhaps influential leaders, then there is a potentiality for pressure upon research, either planned or undertaken. Jane Record, a sociologist, has described four cases in which established research institutes have yielded to pressures from their "constituency": (1) deleted a chapter from a book; (2) failed to publish a monograph; (3) left a social scientist of national reputation out of a study

[6] Perhaps the most influential statement in recent years has been that of Alvin Gouldner, who labeled the concept of value-free sociology a myth. See his "Anti-Minotaur: The Myth of a Value-Free Sociology," *Social Problems,* 9 (Winter, 1962), 199–213.

[7] Sjoberg, pp. 225–244.

within his field after he had demonstrated a highly critical approach to the strict controls over the research to be utilized by the sponsor, a federal agency; and (4) managed to get a scholar to return a contract he had signed to conduct a public administration study after it was discovered he was not acceptable to the mayor of one city to be studied because of what he had written in an earlier book.[8] In similar fashion, Thomas F. Pettigrew and Kurt W. Back have described the timidity of foundations and governmental agencies to support research on desegregation and the particular problems of two southern sociologists, Kenneth Morland and Lewis Killian, in studying desegregation.[9]

There are, of course, a conventional set of safeguards that most sociologists would invoke, such as the right to publish results and the denial of a censorship function to sponsors. But these would not necessarily protect the scholar in the several cases cited above, particularly in those in which a research institute stands between the sponsor and the researcher, or in which research is a team project, not that of a single investigator. These are the newer problems of an affluent period, in which research funds come generously and in larger amounts, but never fully detached from the values and interests of some institutional setting.

Useful to Whom?   One of the major issues of applied sociology, after all the other problems have been discussed and analyzed, is the simple question, useful to whom? In whose interest and for whose problems is applied research conducted? This may very well be the most fundamental question. The autonomy and freedom to pursue research and publish the results, which all social scientists claim as their right and the bench mark of their academic freedom, may in fact be met quite satisfactorily. But if this freedom to inquire and publish enters in *after* research problems have been selected and designed from the perspective of the interests and problems of sponsoring groups, then they may not have the consequences they are usually presumed to have. An applied sociology tied too closely to established clienteles and constituencies and to their intellectual perspectives and their own definitions of their problems can easily be a "servant of power."[10] But sociologists have recently become sensitive to such issues, and the volumes cited above by Gouldner and Miller and by Sjoberg have explored many of the issues raised in the relationship of

[8] Jane Cassels Record, "The Research Institute and the Pressure Group," in Sjoberg, pp. 25-49.

[9] See Thomas F. Pettigrew and Kurt W. Back, "Sociology in the Desegragation Process: Its Use and Disuse," in Lazarsfeld, Sewell, and Wilensky, *The Uses of Sociology,* pp. 692-722.

[10] A phrase taken from the title of a book concerned with the uses of social science in industry. See Loren Baritz, *The Servants of Power* (Middletown, Conn.: Wesleyan University Press, 1960).

applied research to establishments. So also does *The Uses of Sociology* (see footnote 2) in which forty-one sociologists discuss the "uses of sociology"; their varied conceptions of the term "uses" had no one meaning or focus. One section of the book contained a number of papers under the heading: "The Uses of Sociology in Establishments." The several papers make it evident that there has been an extensive use of sociology in established institutions and organizations.

The concern for the effect of the social acceptance of sociology by various establishments has been sounded loud and clear for some time now by a small number of sociologists. Alfred M. Lee, for one, feels that the new era of well-funded research threatens to involve the sociologist in that manipulation and "integration" of society that reduces human freedom and choice.

> Many a social scientist has turned from the rocky path of creative individualistic investigation and criticism to be embraced in the lush sympathy and support given those who deal 'constructively' (i.e., protectively) with the problems of constituted authority, and who do not irritate their clients with critical analysis.[11]

Useful to whom, then, remains one of the central value issues of applied research, and in fact of all sociological research.

The Intellectual Use of Sociology   The limited scientific value of sociological findings, to this date, has meant that the useful contribution of sociology to solving specific problems and to providing clear bases for social policy has been quite modest. Nonetheless the value of such contributions is growing, as a careful perusal of *The Uses of Sociology* makes evident. But such a frequent comment by sociologists about the usefulness of their discipline may in fact miss the central contribution of sociology to modern society. Its primary usefulness may be *intellectual* rather than practical. A strong case could be made for the idea that sociology has been, and indeed continues to be most useful to society in providing a sociological perspective by which a broad middle class can interpret the significance of values and behavior. Sociology provides meaningful clues to what is going on around us, to the outlines of a complex and changing social reality.

To the extent that sociology makes a significant contribution to shaping modern man's conception of himself and his social world, of his problems and his dilemmas, it attains a significance that is unmatched by its value to practical men of affairs. This is the reason that sociology is always found in popular versions, and that the vocabulary of sociology so quickly moves into the mainstream of contemporary discourse. Concepts such as *socialization, alienation,*

---

[11] Alfred M. Lee, "Items for the Agenda of Social Science," in Gouldner and Miller, *Applied Sociology,* pp. 421–428. Quotation from p. 422.

social status, peer group, identity, power structure, power elite, subculture, bureaucracy, and a host of others, have become part of the middle-class's intellectual tool kit. They have become means for constructing interpretations and explanations of the ongoing social processes of modern society, in short, for constructing reality. Through them sociology has become a major intellectual perspective for *the definition of the situation* in the contemporary world.

But many sociologists serve this function without consciously intending to do so or without being aware that in fact that is what they are doing. However, there have always been those sociologists who clearly advocated such an intellectual role for the discipline. C. Wright Mills symbolized for many sociologists the role of sociologist-critic-intellectual, and his *The Sociological Imagination* remains perhaps the most influential effort of a sociologist consciously to state the case for the sociologist as intellectual interpreter and social critic of contemporary society.

THE SEVERAL WORLDS OF CONTEMPORARY SOCIOLOGY

The discipline of sociology has become a multifaceted, empirical social science intent both upon being *scientific* and upon being *relevant* to modern society. These two intentions are not necessarily contradictory and indeed can be viewed as being complementary. Nonetheless, they produce a discipline that has several different dimensions about it, and that seems at times to be going in more than one direction. Sometimes sociologists try to distinguish the mainstream of the discipline from minor streams of interest and activity, but it never is clear that there is a single mainstream; instead, there would seem to be several dominant directions in the present development of the discipline.

Mathematical Sociology and Formal Theory   The commitment to scientific status has always been a part of sociology. Since the 1930s, there has been a strong emphasis upon a *quantitative* methodology, and an increasing use of *statistical* analysis. But in more recent years, the aim of a highly rigorous science has led to the development of an interest in a *mathematical* sociology that goes well beyond the average statistical skills that have become the working tools of most sociologists. Mathematical sociologists' conception of what the discipline should be is shaped by their reading of the contemporary philosophy of science, which in turn is shaped largely, though not exclusively, by the development of the natural sciences, particularly physics. There are, of course, large and difficult problems in developing any social science along these same lines, but a rigorous-minded group of sociologists is committed to just such an objective.

The demands for rigor and control so necessary to a mathematical sociology are hard to achieve with the data typically gathered by sociologists, so that mathematical sociologists are often attracted to the *experimental* approach, using subjects in laboratories much as do psychologists. The criticism they, in turn, receive from colleagues is that laboratory experimentation, while offering a more rigorous control of variables, severely limits the sociological problems that can be studied. Only those forms of social interaction that can be duplicated in a laboratory can be subject to analysis. But the experimenters, in turn, do not accept this as a serious limitation; they feel that they can create a test of sociological propositions, although admittedly not under the field conditions in which such interaction is normally observed. But in addition to the laboratory there is now a new dimension, that of using the computer to simulate human behavior.[12]

Mathematical sociologists speak of theory construction and of the formalization of theory. They are intent upon developing a parsimonious set of postulates from which can logically be deduced theorems, the empirical testing of which serve to corroborate the theory. Thus, much of the empirical work of mathematical sociologists is a process of *verification* of deduced postulates that are logically valid within the theoretical system but must be empirically verified as well. Within sociology the formalization of theory and contributions to mathematical sociology are found most in social psychology and in small group research, though it has also occurred in lesser degree in a wide range of other work in the discipline.

Comparative and Macro-Sociology   American sociology has been notoriously parochial, its observations of social life have been largely confined to the American scene. But in recent decades sociologists have taken their study to the far corners of the world and have sought to analyze societies and cultures other than the American one. Sociology has gone *cross-cultural* and comparative, thus considerably broadening the scope of sociological analysis and yielding a much wider range of relevant sociological data.[13] The generalizations of sociology are thus less likely to depend upon observation within only one society. In this sense comparative study has a methodological imperative in that it seeks *transcultural* and *transsocietal* generalizations. But there is another

[12] For a discussion of recent developments in mathematical sociology and computer simulation, see James S. Coleman, "Mathematical Models and Computer Simulation," in Robert E. L. Faris, ed., *Handbook of Modern Sociology* (Chicago: Rand McNally, 1964), pp. 1027–1062.

[13] For a review of recent work and current developments in comparative sociology, see Robert M. Marsh, *Comparative Sociology* (New York: Harcourt, Brace, 1967).

and perhaps even more important consequence of the growth of a comparative sociology: the return of sociology to one of the fundamental tasks so central to the intellectual perspectives of the founders of the discipline—the analysis of whole societies. Comparative sociology goes well beyond the methodological imperative to transcend the limits set by a culture or by the particular, historical structure of a society; it returns to a larger context of observation and analysis, the study of larger social structures.

This renewed interest by sociologists in the study of larger social units springs from a different source than that which produces a mathematical sociology. It is largely a product of the involvement of the Western world in the non-Western and of a Western concern for both aiding and abetting as well as understanding the complex processes of changes going on within societies. To contrast *developing* with *developed* societies requires, methodologically and theoretically, an effort to study society as an entity. Thus, one of the dominant intellectual concerns of the twentieth century—to know the direction in which the new nations of Africa and Asia will develop—serves as a major intellectual definer of what sociologists should be studying. It directs their research interests, and it defines new problems that challenge older sociological ideas about structure and change in human society.

Applied Sociology   We have already explored the reemergence of an applied sociology and some of its problems. What seems evident now is that applied, policy-oriented social research will become one of the larger activities of sociologists in the years that lie ahead. This, in turn, has the consequence of requiring sociologists to be more conscious of the impact of values upon research at every point in its development, from the very outset of selecting a research problem and defining it. Indeed, sociologists have become a great deal more sophisticated about the place of values in social research than they were a decade or so ago, and much of this is due to their involvement in applied or policy-oriented research. Also, such a renewed emphasis returns sociology to some of the interests and concerns that animated the founding fathers of the discipline. An applied sociology is an effort to be socially relevant in modern society.

The New Fieldworkers   Fieldwork in the urban community marked the efforts of earlier generations of sociologists to uncover important facts about social life and to make pertinent observations. To do this they went into the slums and ghettoes and indeed explored every facet of urban life to observe for themselves. They filled their notebooks with their observations about the color and confusion of urban life. At the University of Chicago a pioneering generation of sociologists produced a series of sociological monographs on hoboes, minorities, rural migrants to the city, Jews in the ghetto, rich and poor, taxi-dance halls, and such. But in time the fieldworker tradition in sociology declined. A new generation turned extensively to the sample survey, emphasizing the design of representative samples and the construction of questionnaires. The observation of behavior was left to the interviewers making house-to-house canvases in filling out questionnaires. The result was a sharp reduction in the direct contact of sociologists with people being studied.

Yet the older tradition never quite died out, and recently it has returned in strength. William F. Whyte's *Street Corner Society*, a classic piece of socio-logical fieldwork, links today's fieldwork with the pioneering work in Chicago in the 1920s and 1930s.[14] More recently, Herbert Gans' *The Urban Villagers*, based upon his own participant-observation of a Boston working-class ethnic neighborhood, stands out as a first-rate sociological study of the same kind.[15] Howard Becker's study of jazz musicians, cited in Chapter 22, is another example,[16] as is Ned Polsby's study of pool hall hustlers.[17]

These are all one-man studies, but the technique of participant-observation lends itself as well to a team approach; the study of medical students, *Boys in White*, is a fine example of such work.[18] Furthermore Herbert Gans has recently completed a participant-observation study of suburban life, *The Levit-towners*, in which his own participant-observation is integrated with a sample survey of the community, and he is able to utilize both sets of data.[19]

The development of such new research techniques, then, as sampling and surveying, as well as the utilization of the computer to process large quan-tities of data, has not eliminated the qualitatively rich and insightful work of the lone participant observer with his patient and close observation of human behavior. It is a still viable tradition of sociological research that remains fresh and vital among the younger generation.

The Substantive Concerns of Sociology　　A rich body of substantive research in-terests characterizes contemporary sociology: the study of bureaucracies and peer groups; of political and industrial structures; of communities large and small; of conflict and social control; of power and decision making; of class and status; of youth cultures and deviant behavior; and of family and kinship and education. Some of these are long established research interests of the

---

[14] William F. Whyte, *Street Corner Society* (Chicago: University of Chicago Press, 1942).

[15] Herbert Gans, *The Urban Villagers* (New York: Free Press, 1962).

[16] Howard Becker, *Outsiders: Studies in the Sociology of Deviance* (New York: Free Press, 1963), Chapters 5 and 6.

[17] Ned Polsby, *Hustlers, Beats, and Others* (Chicago: Aldine, 1967).

[18] Howard Becker, Blance Geer, Everett C. Hughes, and Anselm L. Strauss, *Boys in White: Student Culture in Medical School* (Chicago: University of Chicago Press, 1961).

[19] Herbert Gans, *The Levittowners: Ways of Life and Politics in a New Suburban Community* (New York: Pantheon, 1967).

discipline, whereas others, in turn, are newer and still developing. Political sociology, for example, remained poorly developed among sociologists until the 1950s (as noted in Chapter 16).

One of the older subfields of sociology that has roots deep in the origins of the discipline, but has suffered from studious neglect by American sociologists until recently is the sociology of religion. We took note of its resurgence as a field of sociological research in Chapter 18. The neglect of and then return to religion as a subject for sociological analysis is not to be explained by any internal pressures within the discipline, such as the pressure for scientific status. Instead, it can only be attributed to a renewed intellectual interest in a changing religion and its place in a changing society. Indeed, the changes in historic Christianity in the Western world constitute one of the basic testing grounds for propositions about the increasingly rationalized and secular character of modern society. And the renewed ferment for theological change and for moral and social relevance within the established churches, Catholic and Protestant, only adds to the sociological interest in this dimension of human action. The return to a sociology of religion once more renews the linkages back to the classical sociological studies, and it also rounds out the institutional analysis that marks contemporary sociological study.

The Multiple Worlds of Sociology Sociology is not a single and cohesive discipline marked by one theoretical perspective, a unity of method, and a narrow range of substantive research interests. Rather, it clearly stands forth today as a discipline that offers several different perspectives on human reality, a wide range of research interests, and a divergent set of research approaches. Sociology is undoubtedly a house of many rooms. This diverse and manifold nature of sociology can be viewed as both a weakness and a strength. For those who see it as weakness, it signifies a lack of that theoretical and methodological unity and cohesiveness so essential in developing sociology as a science and thus in creating a general sociological theory. But for those who see it as strength, sociology is a discipline of many related scientific and intellectual activities, each of which has its own place. It is livelier and more exciting for the diversity of practitioners within it.

Sociology has never been a single-minded and closely coordinated activity for one good reason: it has always lived in tension between two competing, sometimes contradictory, sometimes compatible imperatives. One is to become a science, the other is the ethical and moral imperative to be relevant to the problems and issues of society. Thus, one significant factor in changing and developing sociology has been its *internal* compulsion to be scientific. This has been the strongest factor in creating the methodological emphasis that is significant in the discipline today and also in creating more formalized conceptions of theory. But the imperative to be relevant has never allowed sociology to ignore for long the social problems and issues that beset society. The consciousness of social problems and the need to understand them and provide intellectual sources of action have taken sociologists out into society. As a consequence they have probed into delinquency and youth cultures, into problems of alienation, and into situations of conflict and dissensus.

These two imperatives remain strong within sociology. Now one, now the other, may seem to be dominant in shaping sociology as a discipline, but never for too long. Some within it find the commitment to building a science the compelling issue for their involvement, and they dedicate their efforts to that end. But others explore facets of the social order because of a desire to know substantively something about social reality, to know something that has meaning for man's contemporary existence and for the problems that frustrate his efforts to reconstruct social life. The first type of sociologist will insist upon the primacy of rigorous methodology, even at the possible sacrifice, for now at least, of substantive relevance. The other type of sociologist will insist upon holding in central focus the significant sociological issue, even at the possible cost of some methodological rigor.

For this reason there is no single orthodoxy for sociology. In a time when the great ideologies of the past have lost their hold and when religious orthodoxies no longer command the unquestioned faith of believers, sociology, as other social sciences, is a humanistic as well as a secular and scientific effort to provide perspective on the collective enterprise that is society. It seeks to offer some knowledge by which men can be more rational and more humane in the decisions they make about the collective organization of their lives, its quality and magnitude, and the direction of its conscious change. Such an enterprise, however modest in its skills, is surely a worthy one.

PHOTOGRAPH CREDITS

CHAPTER 1
1. Baron Wolman
2. Mike Levins
3. Ken Heyman
4. Ken Heyman
5. Charles Gatewood
6. Baron Wolman

CHAPTER 2
1. Brown Brothers
2. The Granger Collection
3. Courtesy, Nebraska State Historical Society
4. Courtesy, Chicago Historical Society
5. Brown Brothers

CHAPTER 3
Ken Heyman

CHAPTER 4
1. Ted Spiegel from Rapho Guillumette Pictures
2. Courtesy, Collection of the Whitney Museum of American Art, New York
3. Courtesy, Peace Corps; photo by Paul Conklin
4. Charles Biasiny
5. Clemens Kalischer
6. Bill Powers

CHAPTER 5
1. Ken Heyman
2. Ken Heyman
3. Ken Heyman
4. Marc and Evelyne Bernheim from Rapho Guillumette Pictures

CHAPTER 6
1. Baron Wolman
2. Baron Wolman
3. Ken Heyman
4. Courtesy, Collection of the Whitney Museum of American Art, New York
5. Baron Wolman
6. George Reimer

CHAPTER 7
1. Ken Heyman
2. Ken Heyman
3. Dick Durrance, Jr., from Photo Researchers
4. Depardon from Pix
5. Ken Heyman
6. Ken Heyman

CHAPTER 8
1. Ken Heyman
2. Ken Heyman
3. Ken Heyman
4. Courtesy, The Metropolitan Museum of Art, George A. Hearn Fund 1956
5. Clemens Kalischer

CHAPTER 9
1. Baron Wolman
2. Bob S. Smith from Rapho Guillumette Pictures
3. Baron Wolman
4. Ken Heyman
5. Courtesy, Salt Lake Area Chamber of Commerce

CHAPTER 10
1. Ken Heyman
2. Ken Heyman
3. Rue Faris Drew from Photo Researchers
4. Ken Heyman

CHAPTER 11
1. Mike Levins
2. Mike Levins
3. Mike Levins
4. Marc and Evelyne Bernheim from Rapho Guillumette
5. Bruce Roberts from Rapho Guillumette

CHAPTER 12
1. Hanns G. Kohl from Pix
2. Arnold Michaelis from Pix
3. Camera Press–Pix
4. Bradley Smith from Photo Researchers

CHAPTER 13
1. Marc and Evelyne Bernheim from Rapho Guillumette
2. Ken Heyman
3. Bob Adelman
4. Ken Heyman
5. Ken Heyman
6. Ken Heyman

CHAPTER 14
1. Molnar
2. David Plowden from Photo Researchers
3. Tom Hollyman from Photo Researchers
4. Ken Heyman
5. Clemens Kalischer
6. Marc and Evelyne Bernheim from Rapho Guillumette

CHAPTER 15
1. Billy E. Barnes from Pix
2. Gary Renaud from Pix
3. Enrico Natali
4. Enrico Natali
5. Enrico Natali

CHAPTER 16
1. Courtesy, Library of Congress
2. Depardon-Gamma from Pix
3. Cornell Capa from Magnum
4. Baron Wolman
5. D. Jordan Wilson from Pix
6. Mike Smith from Pix

CHAPTER 17
1. Courtesy, Bell Telephone Labs
2. Courtesy, NASA
3. Courtesy, Charles Pfizer and Company, Inc.
4. Charles Biasiny

CHAPTER 18
1. Ken Wittenberg
2. K. W. Gullers from Rapho Guillumette
3. Courtesy, United Nations
4. Hanna W. Schreiber from Rapho Guillumette
5. Courtesy, Library of Congress
6. Ernest Reshovsky from Pix

CHAPTER 19
1. Ted Spiegel from Rapho Guillumette
2. Camera Press–Pix
3. Hanna W. Schreiber from Rapho Guillumette
4. A.F.P. from Pictorial Parade
5. Ken Heyman
6. Van Bucher from Photo Researchers

CHAPTER 20
1. Paolo Kock from Photo Researchers
2. David Donoho from Photo Researchers
3. David Krasner from Photo Researchers
4. Hella Hammid from Rapho Guillumette
5. Baron Wolman

CHAPTER 21
1. Ken Heyman
2. Courtesy, George Eastman House Collection
3. Carl Frank from Photo Researchers
4. George Gerster from Rapho Guillumette
5. Courtesy, UNICEF; photo by Ling
6. Gerry Cranham from Rapho Guillumette

CHAPTER 22
1. Enrico Natali
2. Charles Gatewood
3. Rollie McKenna from Photo Researchers
4. Charles Gatewood
5. Enrico Natali
6. Ken Heyman
7. D. Jordan Wilson from Pix
8. Lynn Pelham from Rapho Guillumette

Index

Name Index

Subject Index

Abstraction, level of, 39
Academic Man, The (Wilson), 410
Academic subculture, 417
Accommodation, 69
Achievement, motivation for, 104–107
  talent and performance, 106–107
Achieving Society, The (McClelland), 104
Adolescents, peer groups and, 154–155
Adult socialization, 100–101
Affectional function of the family, 362–364
Affluent Society, The (Galbraith), 322
AFL-CIO, 204
Africa, social movements in, 599–600
Agents provocateurs, 327
Aggiornamento, 542
Agrarian movements, 599
Agrarian Socialism (Lipset), 187, 468
Aid to Dependent Children (ADC), 343
Aid to the Families of Dependent Children (AFDC), 373
Alienation, 117–118
  work and, 443–445
America, social mobility in, 280–281
  fact and belief, 281–283
American Association for the Advancement of Science, 504
American Farm Bureau, 188
American Journal of Sociology, 32
American Medical Association, 575
American Soldier, The (Stouffer *et al.*), 144, 151
American Town, An (Williams), 200
Amish, 524, 526
Anabaptists, 250, 539
Analysis, sociological, 37–46
  multivariate, 38
Anatomy of an Agricultural Community (Galpin), 200, 206–207
Anglican Church of England, 525, 526, 529
  structure of, 526–527
Animal symbolicum, 60

Anomie, 26, 70, 439
Anonymity, 553
Anthropology, 5, 21
Anti-city, suburbia as, 228–229
Anti-colonialism, 600
Anti-imperialism, 600
Anticipatory socialization, 100
Apartheid, policy of, 302, 306
Apathy, 466–467, 573
Applied sociology, 676
  analysis of, levels of, 668–670
    performances, evaluating, 668–669
    social goals, reanalyzing, 669–670
  research, problems of, 670–674
  use of, 672–673
Art, 76
  pessimism of, 510–512
Asia, social movements in, 599–600
Assimilation, 69
Association, 4
  differential, 654
  voluntary, 463–464
Assumption of educability, status and, 401–402
Audiences, 557, 558
Authoritarian personality, 113–114
Authoritarian Personality, The (Adorno *et al.*), 113, 115
Authority, 131, 455, 457, 458
  bureaucratic, 176
  rules of, in the family, 358–359
Automation, 330, 437
Autonomy of science, 496–497

Bandwagon, 576
Bank Wiring Room study, 149–150
Baptists, 527
Behavior, collective, *see* Collective behavior
  deviant, *see* Deviant behavior
  crowd, 560

691